RESOLVING SOCIAL DILEMMAS

RESOLVING SOCIAL DILEMMAS: DYNAMIC, STRUCTURAL, AND INTERGROUP ASPECTS

Edited by

Margaret Foddy, Ph.D.
School of Psychological Science, La Trobe University

Michael Smithson, Ph.D.
Department of Psychology, Australian National University

Sherry Schneider, Ph.D.
Department of Psychology, Monash University

Michael Hogg, Ph.D.
Department of Psychology, University of Queensland

USA	Publishing Office:	PSYCHOLOGY PRESS
		A member of the Taylor & Francis Group
		325 Chestnut Street
		Philadelphia, PA 19106
		Tel: (215) 625-8900
		Fax: (215) 625-2940
	Distribution Center:	PSYCHOLOGY PRESS
		A member of the Taylor & Francis Group
		47 Runway Road, Suite G
		Levittown, PA 19057-4700
		Tel: (215) 269-0400
		Fax: (215) 269-0363
UK		PSYCHOLOGY PRESS
		A member of the Taylor & Francis Group
		27 Church Road
		Hove
		E. Sussex, BN3 2FA
		Tel: +44 (0)1273 207411
		Fax: +44 (0)1273 205612

RESOLVING SOCIAL DILEMMAS: Dynamic, Structural, and Intergroup Aspects

1 2 3 4 5 6 7 8 9 0

Printed by Edwards Brothers, Ann Arbor, MI, 1999.
Cover design by Curtis Tow.

A CIP catalog record for this book is available from the British Library.
   The paper in this publication meets the requirements of the ANSI Standard Z39.48-1984 (Permanence of Paper).

Library of Congress Cataloging-in-Publication Data
Resolving social dilemmas : dynamics, structural, and intergroup
   aspects / edited by Margaret Foddy . . . [et al.].
      p.   cm.
   Includes bibliographical references and index.
   ISBN 0-86377-574-8 (case : alk. paper)
   1. Social conflict.   I. Foddy, Margaret.
HM1121.R47   1999
303.6—dc21
                                        99-12960
                                        CIP

ISBN: 0-86377-574-8 (case)

Contents

About the Editors

Margaret Foddy completed a B.A. in Sociology at the University of Saskatchewan, and a Ph.D. at the University of British Columbia, Canada. She is currently an Associate Professor in the School of Psychological Science at La Trobe University in Melbourne, Australia. In addition to experimental studies of social dilemmas, her research interests include status processes in small groups, the social psychology of ability evaluation, and the study of gender stereotypes. Her papers have appeared in books and journals, including *Social Psychology Quarterly, Journal of Conflict Resolution,* and *Personality and Social Psychology Bulletin.*

Michael Smithson received a B.Sc. in Mathematics from Harvey Mudd College, and a Ph.D. in Sociology from the University of Oregon. He taught at James Cook University, Australia, before moving to his current appointment in the Division of Psychology at the Australian National University. He has published widely in the area of uncertainty and ignorance. He is the author of *Fuzzy Set Analysis for Behavioral and Social Sciences* (Springer-Verlag, 1987), and *Ignorance and Uncertainty* (Springer-Verlag, 1989). A new statistics textbook, *Statistics with Confidence*, will be published by Sage in 1999.

Sherry Schneider received her Ph.D. in Social Psychology from the University of California, Los Angeles, and was then appointed to the University of Arizona Department of Management and Policy. She is currently a Senior Lecturer in the Organisational Psychology Masters Programme at Monash University, Melbourne, Australia. Her research interests are in the area of group and team dynamics, especially issues related to decision making, leadership, and technology. She has co-authored articles which have appeared in journals such as *The Academy of Management Journal* and *Human Relations.*

Michael Hogg is Professor of Psychology and Director of the Centre for Research on Group Processes at the University of Queensland. He obtained his B.Sc. from Birmingham University, his Ph.D. from Bristol University, UK, and has held faculty appointments at Bristol University, Macquarie University, and Melbourne University. He is foundation editor of the journal *Group Processes and Intergroup Relations* and has published widely in the areas of social identity, social cognition, group processes, and intergroup relations. His most recent books include *Social Identity and Social Cognition* (Blackwell, 1999) and *Attitudes, Behavior and Social Context* (Erlbaum, 1999).

Contributors

Wilfred Amaldoss
Krannert Graduate School of Management
Purdue University
United States of America

Wing Tung Au
Department of Psychology
The Chinese University of Hong Kong
People's Republic of China

Martin Beckenkamp
Department of Psychology
University of Saarland
Germany

Anders Biel
Department of Psychology
Goteborg University
Sweden

Marilynn B. Brewer
Department of Psychology
Ohio State University
United States of America

David V. Budescu
Department of Psychology
University of Illinois at Urbana-Champaign
United States of America

Xiao-Ping Chen
Kelley School of Business
Indiana University
United States of America

Ulf Dahlstrand
Department of Psychology
Goteborg University
Sweden

Axel Franzen
Institute for Sociology
University of Berne
Switzerland

Tommy Gärling
Department of Psychology
Goteborg University
Sweden

Jörgen Garvill
Department of Psychology
Umea University
Sweden

Mathias Gustafsson
Department of Psychology
Goteborg University
Sweden

Guido Hertel
Department of Psychology
University of Kiel
Germany

Chester A. Insko
Department of Psychology
University of North Carolina
United States of America

Norbert L. Kerr
Department of Psychology
Michigan State University
United States of America

David M. Messick
Department of Organizational Behavior
Northwestern University
United States of America

Brenda Morrison
Department of Psychology
Australian National University
Australia

Keren Or-Chen
Department of Psychology
University of Haifa
Israel

Axel Ostmann
Department of Psychology
University of Karlsruhe
Germany

Amnon Rapoport
Department of Management and Policy
University of Arizona
United States of America

John Schopler
Department of Psychology
University of North Carolina
United States of America

Ramzi Suleiman
Department of Psychology
University of Haifa
Israel

Jim Sundali
Department of Psychology
Kent State University
United States of America

Eiji Takagi
Faculty of Liberal Arts
Saitama University
Japan

Mark Van Vugt
Department of Psychology
University of Southampton
United Kingdom

Chris Von Borgstede
Department of Psychology
Goteborg University
Sweden

Yoriko Watanabe
Faculty of Letters
Hokkaido University
Japan

Janine Webb
School of Psychology
Deakin University
Australia

Toshio Yamagishi
Faculty of Letters
Hokkaido University
Japan

Preface

Typically, the Preface describes a book's contents. In this book that task is taken up by the introductory chapter. Here, we wish to provide a brief account of the book's origins and to acknowledge those who made it possible.

The study of social dilemmas brings together researchers from many disciplines, including social psychology, sociology, political science, economics, philosophy, and history. This diversity is reflected in the chapters of this volume and the introductory chapter surveys the common themes that link scholars from these different domains. Another feature of this volume is the multinationality of its contributors. The authors hail from all four hemispheres of the globe, which is salutary given the international nature of important social dilemmas and the need for diverse perspectives on how to solve them. We are particularly pleased that the book includes several chapters from Australian researchers, reflecting the growing interest among Australian social scientists in the study of social dilemmas.

A guiding influence has been the international conference on social dilemmas, the first of which was held in Haaren, the Netherlands, in 1984. This volume benefited greatly from the extensive discussions that formed part of the Seventh International Conference on Social Dilemmas held in Cairns, Australia, in 1997. That conference was generously supported by the following institutions:

The Australian Psychological Society
The Ian Potter Foundation
The School of Psychological Science, La Trobe University, Melbourne
The School of Psychology, University of New South Wales, Sydney
The Faculty of Science, Technology and Engineering, La Trobe University, Melbourne
The Department of Psychology and Sociology, James Cook University, Townsville

A number of people contributed to the "nuts and bolts" that went into producing this book. James Willis played a major role in organizing the conference and preparing the manuscript for publication. John Beale and Michelle Ryan provided painstaking and accurate editing. The staff at Psychology Press, particularly Alison Mudditt and Kelly Huegel, were a model of professional support and encouragement.

Finally, we would like to acknowledge the patience and support of Pat O'Malley, Susan Smithson, and Bridget Hogg, who hosted and tolerated several editorial meetings during which we hammered out the emerging themes in the contributions to this book as well as plotting our own research programs.

Chapter 1

Theories and Strategies for the Study of Social Dilemmas

Michael Smithson
Margaret Foddy

When individuals have access to a scarce common resource such as fisheries, parks, and water supplies, the nature of their interdependence can be characterized as a social dilemma. The dilemma arises because actions dictated by individual rationality (overfish, use as much water as you like) threaten the common resource in the short or long run. Since the individual's own self-interest derives from the existence of the common resource, a seemingly rational choice by all may produce just the opposite. Thus, while a person may prefer to take long showers in drought conditions, the aggregate effect of everyone choosing this alternative may be severe water shortage. The drastic decline of the cod fishing industry in the Atlantic in recent years (Kurlansky, 1997) illustrates the major economic and social consequences associated with social dilemmas in which participants were unable or unwilling to find a collective solution to overuse. There is a growing realization that much of human interdependence can be understood in terms of social dilemmas, making it important that we understand their nature and ways which humans have devised to resolve them.

More precisely, social dilemmas can be defined as situations in which the reward or payoff to each individual for a selfish choice is higher than that for a cooperative one, regardless of what other people do; yet all individuals in the group receive a lower payoff if all defect than if all cooperate (Dawes, 1980). This interdependence structure exists in *one-shot* social dilemmas (e.g., a power blackout caused by overuse), and longer-term commons dilemmas, in which a resource may deteriorate over time until it cannot be replenished (e.g., overfishing). Modern developments in technology reveal new examples of social dilemma structures—gridlock on freeways filled with cars driven by single occupants and long delays in accessing the Internet are two examples. The fascination of this area of study is that, while some dilemmas end in collective disaster, human beings have shown a remarkable capacity to generate a variety of mechanisms to manage, if not resolve the conflict between individual and collective interest.

The study of social dilemmas spans a few decades as well as several disciplines. This book presents a representative sample of cutting-edge theoretical and empirical work in this area. It is our intention to provide specialists and nonspecialists alike a sense of a field that encompasses a wide variety of approaches that are nevertheless connected by a core of common concerns, themes, and methods. It brings together critical new developments and directions in social dilemmas research that demonstrate that it is a burgeoning field with increasing relevance to social problems that are becoming more evident with increases in world population and greater globalization.

Almost all of the work on social dilemmas is predicated on the ideal of a cumulative science, even if researchers may differ on how close the field has (or may ever) come to achieving that ideal. Several thorough reviews have been published recently with such an assessment as their primary object (e.g., Komorita & Parks, 1994; Ostrom, Gardner, & Walker, 1994), so we will not repeat that exercise here. Instead, we will outline the relevance of the work presented in the book to the current trends in theoretical development and empirical research in this area. For our analysis, we will borrow a framework from Wagner and Berger (1985) concerning the relationships among theories and research programs that share a common field of interest (see also Berger & Zelditch, 1993a).

Wagner and Berger (1985) observe that anything regarded as a *field* in the social sciences usually contains a core of *orienting strategies* that incorporate widely agreed-upon concerns, goals, metatheoretical concepts and presuppositions, research standards, and methodological prescriptions. We will argue that the field of social dilemmas is no exception to this rule. In fact, Berger and Zelditch (1993b) mention rational choice theory as an example of an orienting strategy. However, the core of this field is somewhat more heterogeneous than the examples considered by Wagner and Berger. Since the study of social dilemmas is multidisciplinary, the core concerns, metatheoretical underpinnings, and methodological strategies are continually debated and reassessed. We will devote the first three sections of this chapter to those strategic issues and what this book contributes to the discourse about them.

Wagner and Berger (1985) claim that a field comprises a collection of interrelated theories and empirical research, through which the field's "theoretical research program" (Lakatos, 1970) is negotiated and modulated. They characterize the relationships among these theories in terms of *elaboration, proliferation, variation, competition,* and *integration.* Elaboration and proliferation refer to expansions in analytical power and theoretical scope, respectively. We will assess these together since they overlap considerably in the social dilemmas area because of the widespread use of game theory and simulations to accomplish both kinds of expansions simultaneously.

Variation, competition, and integration all refer mainly to relations among theories that are of similar scope. A theory is a variant of another if it employs similar concepts and addresses similar explanatory problems (e.g., game theory and decision theory are variants of rational-choice theory). Competitors, on the other hand, employ different (usually incompatible or conflicting) premises but address the same explanatory problems (e.g., social identity versus social cognitive approaches to stereotyping). An integrative theory combines two or more theories in such a way as to account for the relationships among those theories (see, for instance, Aronson's, 1992, call for incorporating several social psychological research programs under the umbrella of dissonance theory). In the area of social dilemmas, the nature of intertheoretical relations can change quite rapidly, so we will consider these three topics together in the final section.

WHAT ARE THE CORE CONCERNS OF THE FIELD?

The title of this section poses a question whose answer seems obvious, and indeed persuasive answers abound in most review articles, textbooks, and handbooks whose scope encompasses social dilemmas. Nonetheless, even a cursory comparison of those answers reveals important differences in why scholars think social dilemmas are worth studying and what the main focus of social dilemma research should be. These differences do not constitute unbridgeable abysses, and in fact there is considerable overlap among them; but they can make this area hard to pin down for nonspecialists. At the risk of oversimplifying, we identify four traditions in social dilemma research and theory.

In one tradition, social dilemmas are characterized in terms of a conflict between a motive to maximize personal interests and a motive to maximize collective interests (for a textbook version, see Komorita & Parks, 1994). This view goes back to Anatol Rapoport's (1960) notion of a "mixed-motive" game and before that, to Durkheim's theory about the relationship between the individual and society (Durkheim, 1893/1964). Social dilemmas are mixed-motive games in which the attempt by all to maximize their personal interests leaves everyone worse off than if everyone pursued the collective interest instead. The foremost parable here is Hardin's (1968) Tragedy of the Commons. In this tradition, the main object of inquiry is how this conflict between motives gets resolved and when the balance may be tipped in favor of collective interests. That focus has informed much of the earliest psychological research in this area. As Komorita and Parks (1994) put it, "What can be done to encourage people to be more cooperative?" (p. 3). The main orienting strategy here has been to think of people's behavior as determined by their preferences in the spirit, if not the letter, of subjective expected utility (SEU). That is, preferences are assessed in terms of the values placed on outcomes to self and to others, together with the perceived probabilities of alternative outcomes, the latter determined by the intersection of own and others' choices. Increases in cooperation are then seen to be due to variables that increase the SEU of cooperation relative to defection. Ensuing investigative strategies have included altering the gap in rewards for cooperation compared with rewards for non-cooperation, attaching material and social costs to noncooperation, and manipulating the rate of cooperation by others.

While the mixed-motive game tradition is not as dominant even in psychology as it once was, it still yields plenty of interesting problems and useful results, as well as starting points for other approaches. In this volume for example, Hertel's chapter reviews recent work on the influence of mood on cooperation, and the chapter by Au and Budescu takes as their point of departure a critique of the motivational interpretation of give-some and take-some games in terms of prospect theory (Kahneman & Tversky, 1979). It is noteworthy that field studies and applications are also influenced by this tradition. The chapter by Van Vugt is an example of this, as are two of the chapters on normative influences on

cooperation (Garvill; and Biel, von Borgstede, and Dahlstrand). Another fairly recent variation on this general theme is to link motivations with external influences. It is in this vein
that Chen explores the mediational impact of motives and expectations on reward structures. Likewise, Suleiman and Or-Chen explore the impact of the likelihood of external
supply on the willingness to contribute to a public good, and Smithson argues that exogenous influences on the state of a resource can affect the perceived payoffs of cooperation
or defection.

A second tradition takes its cue from Hobbes' (1651/1939) *Leviathan*, the famous
17th century treatise on governance, that stipulates that without a strong central authority,
society consists only of selfish ruthlessly competing individuals. The central questions for
researchers and theorists in this tradition spring from two concerns. One is simply whether
Hobbes might be wrong, and under which conditions it is possible for selfish agents to
develop or evolve into a cooperative society without a central authority. In the past 15
years or so, a large literature using simulations to address this question has emerged, some
of it inspired by Axelrod's early computer tournaments (Axelrod, 1984, 1997a; Danielson,
1992; Flache, 1996). The chapters by Takagi and by Watanabe and Yamagishi exemplify
this approach, and indeed the modern version of Adam Smith's "invisible hand" applied to
the problem of cooperative or collective action (Smith, 1970).

The other concern arises from the realization that Hobbes' solution contains an infi-
nite regress: What central authority will guarantee that the central authority is not selfish?
Mere provision of a central authority does not guarantee the solution of a social dilemma.
This concern motivates researchers to investigate the concomitants and underpinnings of
benevolent and/or cooperative leadership or authority, and the possibility of alternative
structural solutions (Yamagishi, 1986b). Webb's chapter provides a taxonomy with which
to describe a range of alternative structures. Again, the institutional-design view of social
order has a long history, dating back to the original social contract theorists of the Enlightenment. Social scientists and social philosophers alike may see institutions as the means
for resolving collective dilemmas (Bates, 1988), but not just any institution will do. Ostrom
and her colleagues (e.g., Ostrom et al.,1994) have pursued an empirical research program
motivated by this concern.

Foddy and Hogg's chapter takes on the central authority problem directly, assessing
the conditions under which leaders will effectively manage a common resource. Their
work is in the category of institutional-design approaches that are based on notions of the
State, but connect to social psychological theories of group relations. Another large category of structural solutions stems from the notion of a social contract. Among the most
popular contractarian versions of structural solutions are those incorporating public knowledge of behavior, monitoring, and sanctioning. These are addressed by Kerr, Van Vugt, and
Beckenkamp and Ostmann, respectively. A third and newer kind of structural solution
entails embedding the dilemma in a supergame. As an example of this alternative, Rapoport
and Almadoss investigate the effect of embedding subgroup dilemmas in an intergroup
competition.

A third tradition starts with the observation that despite the appeal of selfish behavior
such as free-riding, at least some cooperation does occur in the absence of any Hobbesian
central authority. Therefore any theory of exchange that rests on the *homo economicus*
model of a rationally self-interested agent is unable to explain the successful provision of
a public good or sustainable usage of a common resource pool, unless some additional
provisos are brought in. Taking matters one step further, the free-rider problem in particular has been cast by some theorists in the role of a crucial test case in debates over whether

human nature is innately selfish or sociable (see Caporael, Dawes, Orbell, & van de Kragt, 1989 and the accompanying commentary for a fairly wide ranging sample of views on this issue). Among the chapters in this book, Morrison's investigation of the connections between functional interdependence and social identity, and Foddy and Hogg's chapter on the effects of group identification on cooperation exemplify a recent turn in social psychology to considering group membership as a basis for cooperation. The concluding chapter by Schneider and Brewer addresses this ancient and fascinating issue from a more evolutionary standpoint.

Contrary to popular views, the debates over the *homo economicus* model pose a problem not only for economists but also for those sociologists pursuing what some (e.g., Coleman, 1986) have claimed is the central theoretical problem in sociology, namely the constitution of social structure. The free-rider conundrum figures centrally in debates over methodological holism versus individualism. In order to construct an individualistic theory of social structure, many theorists believe they must start with a hypothetical state of nature populated by individuals whose choices are socially unconstrained, and then demonstrate how social structure could arise as a solution to the pursuit of commonly held desires (c.f. Lomborg, 1996). The *first-order* free-rider problem, whereby rational agents opt out of any cooperation from the beginning, stands squarely in the way of this demonstration. And even an effective demonstration that institution formation will occur may not suffice to demonstrate their invulnerability to *second-order* free-riders. As Hechter (1991) expresses it— "The real trick in building an individualistic theory of social structure is to explain how agents who are themselves unconstrained by any structure nevertheless will produce institutions that can sanction potential free-riders" (p. 47).

There are two identifiable variants of research that have emerged from this debate, despite the fact that the social dilemma area has been dominated by methodological individualism for some time. The first comprises, predictably, attempts to demonstrate that institutions can arise from interactions among unconstrained agents. The idea that social order might arise from the unintended actions of individuals is, of course, an old one and has a long history in the social sciences (see Lichbach, 1996, pp. 16–18 for a recent survey). Takagi's chapter confronts this issue head on, by examining the conditions under which club-like institutions or welfare systems could develop. Watanabe and Yamagishi's simulation research program clearly has kindred goals. The conditions investigated in these studies refer mainly to characteristics of the agents' strategies, rather than social or environmental conditions.

The second variant includes those who bring social or environmental constraints into the consideration of what agents (rational or otherwise) might do. The impact of the distribution rule (usually equity versus equality) is a subject in four chapters (Takagi, Rapoport and Amaldoss, Chen, and Webb). Kerr's chapter on the effects of anonymity and Schopler and Insko's on whether groups are more competitive than individuals in social dilemmas are examples of research on how specific structural matters may influence cooperation, whether positively or negatively. Franzen, Au and Budescu, and Smithson's chapters each investigate the effects of nonsocial or quasi-social constraints. Franzen, and Au and Budescu, both focus on the consequences of sequential access to a resource and agents' positions in the queue. Additionally, Au and Budescu demonstrate that a reasonable level of consumption depends on one's position and how much has been consumed by earlier agents. Smithson shows that the very definition of *cooperation* may depend on exogenous influences, as in a resource dilemma where depletion of the resource can be caused not only by high consumption rates but also highly variable consumption.

Finally, a fourth tradition characterizes social dilemmas as a counterexample against a long-standing philosophical quest for an equation between rationality and morality. After all, if no such equation exists then morality of any kind (and thence ethics) must be construed as independent of or even contrary to rationality, and any rationalist must consider morality to be nonrational or outright irrational. Social dilemmas push matters to the latter extreme since rational choices yield suboptimal outcomes, and so they present philosophers with a "deep problem for the theory of rationality" (Danielson, 1992, p. 9), "the profoundest problem of ethics" (Parfit, 1984, p. 19), or a conundrum that "defies commonsense reasoning" (Poundstone 1992, p. 121). In fact, according to Poundstone's account, Flood and Dresher, the inventors of prisoner's dilemma, initially hoped that game theorists would somehow solve it, but eventually came to believe that the dilemma has no solution. Is it possible that the apparent insolubility of prisoner's dilemma arises because the version of commonsense reasoning Poundstone speaks of, and the theories of rational choice aligned with it, are faulty?

In this tradition, the object is to rehabilitate unconstrained selfish rationality in such a way as to bridge the gap between it and morality, usually by linking it with notions of constraint, conditionality, and possible future consequences. Gauthier (1986), for example, proposes a quasi-rational theory of cooperation that is similar to Takagi's "generalized exchange" and "ingroup altruist strategy," whereby moral constraint is conditional on others' cooperation. Outright antirationalist alternatives have proved unpopular in this literature, despite the long-standing contest between Romantic and Enlightenment strains in the human sciences. Whether rationality can be rehabilitated while preserving other hallmarks of rationality (such as coherence) is an open question. Several chapters in this volume address the problem of rationality in the sense of doing more than merely using game-theoretical equilibria as worst case benchmarks against which to compare what agents do. The chapters in which this concern is central are those by Takagi, Watanabe and Yamagishi, and Suleiman and Or-Chen. The chapters by Morrison, and Foddy and Hogg, point toward an alternative formulation of rationality in which individuals' utility functions could be extended to include regard for members of their ingroups.

It should be clear by now that while social dilemmas have stimulated research and theoretical developments in several disciplines, not all scholars have interpreted the importance of dilemmas in quite the same way. It is this plurality of interpretations that makes the area appear somewhat phenomenon-driven rather than theory-directed. In fact, much research on social dilemmas really is theory-directed, but researchers and theorists have adopted different strategies and goals depending on their intellectual and disciplinary backgrounds. One of the more salutary outcomes of this pluralism is that scholars from heretofore isolated disciplines have not only communicated with, but also borrowed from one another so that the previously sharp distinctions among them have blurred and blended over time. The upshot is a more or less shared "core" of theoretical concepts, terminology, models, strategies, and methods.

METATHEORETICAL CONCEPTS AND STRATEGIES

All theorizing and research must begin with some assumptions or presuppositions, metatheoretical concepts, and working strategies regardless of whether they spring from a foundationalist tradition or not. As Berger and Zelditch (1993a, pp. 12–13) observe, these metatheoretical constructs deal with "about what" and "how to" problems, with the former pertaining mainly to theoretical and the latter to methodological strategies. New empirical findings, theoretical developments, or external influences on research may change these working strategies. In this section we locate the work presented in this book within the past and current metatheoretical underpinnings of social dilemma research. Those under-pinnings range from the relatively unquestioned to the hotly debated, but the most crucial among them are as follows:

(a) interdependence structures,
(b) rational choice and self-interest versus constraint,
(c) one-shot (unique) versus repeated situations, and
(d) structural conditions leading to dilemmas.

Interdependence and Self-Interest

The structure of interdependence and the rational pursuit of self-interest are clearly the nub of the matter. As Ostrom et al. (1994) point out, not all public goods or common pool resource situations entail dilemmas. In order for such a situation to be a dilemma, it must be demonstrated that suboptimal outcomes can occur and that there is no feasible institutional or social alternative that will prevent those outcomes. Suboptimal outcomes can occur only if there is an interdependence structure such as prisoner's dilemma or chicken (see the Glossary for definitions of these structures), and people pursue self-interest in a fully informed rational way. There is a widely held consensus that the basic kinds of inter-dependence structures for certain classes of simple dilemmas are known, and the chapters in this book reflect that agreement. Most of the developments presented in this volume concerning interdependence structures refer to ways in which those structures might be altered, whether by design (as in imposed structural solutions) or unintentionally (e.g., via exogenous dynamics or through repeated interactions among agents).

The metatheoretical assumption that prisoner's dilemma and related games are effective models for important real world situations has stood up well under scrutiny. This should come as no surprise (Axelrod, 1997a). After all, many ethico-religious systems include principles that more or less directly address the need to consider what would happen if everyone pursued identical self-interests (e.g., the golden rule in its various forms, or Kant's categorical imperative). Prisoner's dilemma-like situations abound in literature and drama (a classical example being Puccini's opera *Tosca*).

On the other hand, the assumption that humans are self-interested has remained controversial. Its fundamental importance should not be underestimated, since nearly all attempts to solve social dilemmas must begin by taking a position on whether the basis for a solution is to be found in appeals to self-interest or to some form of altruism. In the last two decades, the self-interest camp has been given a boost by selfish-gene arguments from neo-Darwinians, although some of them may have overstated the extent to which evolution directly supports the notion that people are inherently selfish. In turn, the self-interest thesis has come under attack from social scientists on various grounds.

Constructivists such as Sahlins (1976) argue that *homo economicus* is not a fact of nature but a creation of modern Western culture. The implication is that human nature is protean and malleable under sociocultural influences, and that in other cultures one might find true collectivists (Markus & Kitayama, 1991). Calhoun (1991) presents an argument that, while avoiding radical cultural incommensurability, presses home the point that there is no "natural state" for humans that entails isolated individualism. However, even if we begin with a social structure in place, we still require explanations and predictions of when cooperation will decline or sustain itself, and the extent to which culture plays a determining role.

In the psychological camp, an exemplar of a strong claim against the egoistic incentive thesis is presented by Caporael et al. (1989), in which they argue that human cooperation is not explicable in terms of selfish incentives. Instead, they claim that group life has characterized the human species for a long enough time to have evolutionary impact on human nature, thereby imparting an adaptive edge to traits that enhance the ability to live effectively in groups. According to this viewpoint cooperative behavior is not deviant, as it seems in individualistic choice theories. Instead, as Brewer and Schneider point out in the concluding chapter to this book, the existence of stable societies implies successful cooperation among genetic competitors and therefore evolved mechanisms that enable resolutions of social dilemmas.

Most of the chapters in this book include the self-interest maximizer assumption among their premises. However, they also reflect an increasing tendency among researchers in this area to incorporate fully social interests and constraints in the things that are being maximized. Among these are the interests arising from ingroup identification and favoritism (Morrison, Foddy & Hogg, Suleiman & Or-Chen, Chen, and Takagi), the operation of social norms (Kerr, and Biel et al.), interpersonal processes such as turn-taking, identification and sanctioning (Au & Budescu, Kerr, Beckenkamp & Ostmann, and Van Vugt), and intergroup relations (Foddy & Hogg, Schopler & Insko, and Rapoport & Amaldoss). This trend may even reflect a rapprochement between the Romantic and Enlightenment strains in social dilemma theory development.

One-Shot Versus Repeated Dilemmas

Research on social dilemmas during the past two decades also has shifted from a focus on one-shot dilemmas to repeated dilemmas. There are at least two reasons for this. One is simply that many real world dilemmas are repeatable. The second, more telling reason, is that repeated dilemmas provide the best hope for voluntary cooperation through shadow-of-the-future and learning-from-the-past mechanisms (cf. Schopler & Insko's chapter). However, opinion is still divided on how significant the difference is between them, for much the same reasons as decision scientists argue about whether unique and repeated decision making requires different theories or even different notions of rationality (e.g., Lopes, 1981; Morris, Sim & Girotto, 1998; Taylor, 1990).

Danielson (1992) is an example of someone who is convinced that one-shot and iterated dilemmas present fundamentally different requirements in order for cooperation to be assured. In iterated dilemmas, he argues, it is sufficient for any agent to know just that the other agent is rational and not short sighted. In a one-shot dilemma, however, each agent must also know that the other is *constrained* in some relevant fashion (e.g., unable to lie effectively). One-shot dilemmas are definitely the tougher problem and may, in the end, turn out to be genuinely insoluble without appeal to some generalized notion of forward-looking or backward-looking constraint.

Several chapters provide further explorations of the primary interests in repeated dilemmas, namely the shadow-of-the-future and learning-from-the-past. It is no coincidence that these are also the chapters that advance our understanding of when (or whether) self-interest maximizing agents will cooperate. The chapters that are most applicable to one-shot dilemmas also tend to be those that explore structural solutions, particularly imposed solutions. So regardless of whether scholars such as Danielson are correct, most of the recent work in this area still proceeds as if there is some basic underlying difference between one-shot and repeated dilemmas. The main exceptions invoke an evolutionary source of *constraint* and the requisite capacity to distinguish a cooperator from a competitor.

Structural Conditions for Dilemmas

Finally, social dilemma theory and research have long been informed by economists concerning the structural conditions that lead to dilemmas. The key issues are difficulty in excluding noncontributors from benefits (whether these be free-riders on a public good or excessive consumers of a common resource), and the extent to which one agent's benefit subtracts from others'. These two issues go under the names of excludability and subtractability.

Inability to exclude potential beneficiaries is the hallmark of both public goods and common pool resources. Absence of *excludability* is widely considered to be necessary (but not sufficient) for a social dilemma to arise. Consequently, mechanisms for increasing excludability cover all structural solutions to social dilemmas that do not alter payoff related aspects of interdependence or mechanisms for harvesting/contributing. In Alaska, for example, access to fishing is controlled by government issue of licenses, which are not only expensive, but limited in number. Nor is the control of excludability limited to regulatory mechanisms imposed from the top down. Even so called *emergent* solutions as exemplified by Watanabe and Yamagishi or Takagi's simulation work are predicated on the idea that agents are free to choose with whom to interact and therefore who to exclude from further interactions.

Subtractability, on the other hand, distinguishes a common resource from a public good (cf. Ostrom et al.,1994). This distinction, while clear in the abstract, can prove difficult to apply in specific cases (Keohane & Ostrom, 1995). For example, the establishment of a public park may require contributions up to a threshold level (public good), but the management of the use of the park may be closer to a common pool resource problem. The theoretical importance of subtractability is associated with the distinction between give-some and take-some games, with public goods dilemmas being embedded in the former and resource dilemmas in the latter. In a give-some dilemma, the potential for free-riding often is enhanced if the good is nonsubtractable. In a take-some dilemma, on the other hand, overconsumption is not possible unless the resource is subtractable. Attempts to identify and explain differences in cooperation rates between give-some and take-some games have not been satisfactory to date (cf. Sell & Son, 1997; and Kerr's chapter). Au and Budescu's chapter addresses some of these concerns and they extend the analysis of give-some and take-some games into the realm of sequential provision and harvesting.

METHODOLOGICAL STRATEGIES: MODELING, SIMULATION, AND EXPERIMENTATION

Social dilemma research has relied heavily on three methodological strategies. One is the use of game theory to construct and evaluate social dilemmas and to guide empirical research. A variant of this strategy invests game theory analyses with descriptive capabilities; another treats it as a prescriptive or bench-marking framework. A second strategy is the use of experiments for testing theories and making claims about real world phenomena. The third, and most recent, strategy is the use of simulations for hypothesis and theory construction, and as a substitute for game-theoretical solutions in intractably complex systems.

These strategies raise issues that are not new but nevertheless remain hotly contested. Beckenkamp and Ostmann go right to the heart of the matter at the beginning of their chapter. First, they point to the perennial problem of deciding whether, and in what ways, a formal model or experimental study may be applicable to its real world counterparts. Second, they recognize that the use of models that are known not to describe real world behavior (such as *homo economicus*) requires some justification. We may add a third concern, namely the evidential status of computer simulations, as distinct from mathematical derivations. Since the study of social dilemmas has traded more heavily in experiments, formal models, and simulations than most fields in the human sciences, these concerns merit at least our brief but critical attention.

Using models that do not describe real behavior and experiments that do not slavishly imitate the real world are practices that characterize nearly all of the natural sciences, but they are controversial in the human sciences. To start with, formal models and experiments alike may provide ideal benchmarks against which to compare real world situations and behaviors. Beckenkamp and Ostmann's argument that the rational actor model is a "worst case scenario" regarding cooperation in social dilemmas is a case in point. Smithson's "null models" that estimate how long a resource pool will last with random consumers exemplifies another type of benchmark akin to statistical null-hypothesis testing.

As Beckenkamp and Ostmann observe, experiments and models that make simplifying assumptions are still our primary method of screening out real world "noise," which takes the form of arbitrary complexity or unwanted interference. Models and experiments used in this way are, again, providing researchers and theorists with ideal cases, the social scientific equivalent of massless pulleys, perfect vacuums, or pure reagents (Zelditch, 1969). For models and experiments employed strategically in this way, too much ecological validity (especially in the naïve particularistic sense of a resemblance to specific instantiations) is not only irrelevant but an outright handicap.

A third, often underutilized, strategy involves unrealistic models or experiments as counterexamples or demonstrations that something is possible, contrary to some generalized theoretical argument. Axelrod's (1984) first computer tournament is an example of this, since it demonstrated the possibility that a quasi-cooperative strategy (tit for tat) could outperform egoistic competitive strategies. A related use is hypothesis generation, as in Rapoport and Amaldoss' suggestive analysis in this book.

The increasing popularity of simulations has raised a number of concerns about their evidential status and what conclusiveness should be ascribed to them. It could be argued that they have been elevated to a status somewhere between a philosopher's thought experiment and a mathematical proof. At first glance, to a traditional mathematical modeler simulations seem like "impoverished" mathematics, the last resort in the face of mathematical or computational intractability. Likewise, to an empirical social scientist simulations may appear to function as impoverished experiments or pseudo-field studies with virtual agents and environments acting as pale substitutes for the real thing. The implication of both viewpoints is that simulations are to be used only when the real thing is not feasible. To be sure, simulations lack the conclusive proof status of mathematical derivations and likewise the ecological validity of empirical research.

Despite their shortcomings, simulations have a number of advantages that make them indispensable in this field. Their foremost strengths are the obvious ones. First, they may be used to explore very complex hypothetical worlds or models that are mathematically intractable, empirically unavailable, or both. Second, they may be employed for all of the strategic purposes mentioned earlier that benefit formal models and experiments. Simulations are at their best as ground breaking and hypothesis generating tools (Messick and Liebrand, 1995).

Third, and not quite so obviously, simulations afford greater control in several respects than experiments with people. As a result, while they cannot attain the conclusiveness of mathematical proofs, simulations can *cover* the range of relevant conditions exhaustively and repeatedly with a systematic thoroughness that is usually unattainable by experiments with human participants. Virtual agents may be *zeroed* back to their initial conditions for reruns of virtual experiments. This simply is not possible with humans or, indeed, most mammals (cf. Luce, 1997, for his remarks on the difficulties facing research on learning because of this problem). And fourth, while simulations may not have the ecological validity of empirical studies, they do enable the modeler to incorporate more of the real world's complexity and disorder than is usually possible with mathematically tractable models. So simulations, when carefully and thoroughly executed, may be somewhat more conclusive than experiments and more ecologically valid than mathematical models. In the words of Willer and Markovsky (1993), simulations "strike an attractive balance between theoretical rigor and empirical complexity" (p. 356).

To an outsider it may seem odd that social dilemma research starting as it does from real world phenomena, has tended to emphasize formal models, simulations, and experiments rather than naturalistic field studies. After all, field studies provide information about actors' beliefs and values systems, variables currently receiving increased attention from theories of collective action (e.g., Keohane & Ostrom, 1995). Further, field studies may reveal unsuspected political and institutional limits to structural or other solutions that may seem simple and straightforward in simulated environments. Nevertheless, in social dilemmas there is a tension between naturalistic research strategies and their formalistic or experimental counterparts. It is surprisingly difficult to conduct effective field studies of social dilemmas. Few pure dilemmas exist in the real world; instead they are likely to be mixed forms whose antecedents are difficult to disentangle and outcomes impossible to predict. Until we have frameworks that deal with heterogeneity in structure or agents more effectively, perhaps along the lines suggested in Webb's treatment, this difficulty will remain with us.

Difficulties notwithstanding, field studies are becoming more popular in this area. Ostrom and her colleagues' research programs have invested considerable time and effort in field studies in several countries (Ostrom et al., 1994). Van Vugt recently organized a conference devoted solely to field studies of dilemmas. Likewise, there is a growing recognition that real world interventions and other attempts to solve dilemmas provide opportunities for quasi-experimental field studies to supplement laboratory-based experiments and simulations.

ELABORATION AND PROLIFERATION

We begin this section with some remarks about the scope conditions in social dilemmas research. One of the principal strategies in this area has been to start with a rather restricted template, such as a one-shot two-person game with rational players possessing full information, symmetric payoffs, and a prisoner's dilemma payoff structure; and then to widen the scope by weakening one or more of these restrictions. Notable scope extensions during the past two decades or so include the following:

1   Incorporating repeatability or iteration, particularly with regard to strategy.
2   Extending the time horizon into the future and the past.
3   Investigating processes and dynamics.
4   Including different kinds of dilemmas (such as chicken and deadlock).
5   Expanding motivational accounts for choice behavior (e.g., fear and greed).
6   Including nonhuman agents, both natural and artificial.
7   Expanding the number of participants.
8   Complicating the relationships among participants and groups (including layering dilemmas, group relations, embedding dilemmas in supergames).
9   Moving from an exclusive focus on the individual to groups and institutions.

This book continues that expansive trend. Taken together, the chapters convey a shift in the field *outward* from the interstices of dilemmas themselves to externalities and exogenous dynamics, from the intrapersonal to the interpersonal, institutional, and even societal, and from the laboratory experiment to not only the real world but counterfactual ones besides.

A somewhat more systematic appreciation of the expansion in scope is available from Ledyard's (1995) survey of public goods research. As Au and Budescu point out at the beginning of their chapter, Ledyard identifies five components of social dilemmas studies:

1   Models of behavior of the participants.
2   The final outcomes for the participants.
3   The performance criteria for evaluating those outcomes.
4   Institutions and/or protocols for coordinating actions or information.
5   The environment in which the dilemma is embedded.

In the past, experimental studies, formal models, and simulations alike have emphasized models of behavior and outcomes while often neglecting the other three components. Many of the chapters in this book rectify that imbalance to some degree.

Performance criteria define a preference ranking over outcomes. In most social dilemma research, these preferences are assumed to be symmetric for all participants, whether by definition or by virtue of symmetric access to information. Franzen's chapter on the volunteer's dilemma investigates variants in which preferences and information access are not identical for all players. Likewise, in resource commons and public goods dilemmas, performance criteria are defined exclusively in terms of rates or mean levels of consumption and provision, respectively. Smithson's findings indicate that the criteria for evaluating resource consumption behavior should include variability in addition to mean level.

As for *institutions and protocols*, as indicated in the first section, these are the focus of several chapters. Au and Budescu model the effects of sequential protocols on behavior in both public goods and resource dilemmas. Schopler and Insko likewise find that sequential rather than simultaneous responding reduces intergroup competition. The chapters by Kerr, Van Vugt, and Beckenkamp and Ostmann trace the implications of using sanctioning and related measures as a structural solution for social dilemmas. The chapters by Biel and Garling provide real world examples of normative constraint. Messick observes that the distinction between legal and moral issues has implications for whether decisions in social dilemmas will be mainly outcome-based or rule-based. And finally, Foddy and Hogg address the benevolent leader problem.

These are all imposed structural solutions, of course, and the alternative possibility is an "invisible hand" institution. The invisible hand institution might be built in from the beginning or one that emerges from agents interacting over time. As an example of the built in kind, the Rapoport and Amaldoss chapter provides a formal analysis of the consequences of embedding within-group dilemmas in intergroup competitions. This chapter echoes earlier work by Rapoport (1967, well before Axelrod's tournaments) in which he proved that the defecting choice in a prisoner's dilemma game is no longer dominant if embedded in a metagame in which reciprocity can make cooperation nondominant on some occasions.

Five chapters extend the range of *environmental considerations*. Garling et al. review an already sizeable literature on the effect of uncertainty in resource provision on harvesting from a common pool. Likewise, Suleiman and Or-Chen investigate the impact that uncertain external supply has on willingness to contribute to a public good. Smithson's focus is on delineating the ways that exogenous dynamics can shape agents' perceptions of their own interest, outcomes, and thence performance criteria. This chapter thereby extends recent attempts in this field to model or at least simulate the interactive processes inherent in dilemmas, whereby agents and environments mutually shape each other. In the same vein, Watanabe and Yamagishi focus on the *social* environment as shaped by microinteractions among agents and agent mobility, and Takagi's work extends that to the institutional environment.

At a theoretical level, proliferation and elaboration both involve extending existing accounts to predict or explain new phenomena. Recent assessments of social dilemma solutions and associated theories differ on how successfully this task has been accomplished. Kerr (1990) and Komorita and Parks (1994) exemplify the pessimistic camp, while Ostrom et al. (1994) and Lichbach (1996) are more sanguine. Lichbach in particular claims that the best strategy for understanding social dilemmas is to study real ones, and several chapters in this volume present either studies of real world dilemmas or applications.

Van Vugt's chapter presents a field study of the impact of water consumption monitoring (via meters), and the extent to which that impact is mediated by social psychological factors such as concern for responsible usage, personal costs, efficacy, and trust. Likewise, Schneider and Sundali's field study focuses on recycling behavior. In the chapter by Biel et al. the norms and intentions of survey respondents are investigated for four everyday environmentally relevant situations: commuting by car or by public transport, reducing electricity consumption, recycling, and buying environmentally-friendly products such as organic food. In a similar vein, Garvill's chapter is a field study of choices among transportation modes, as influenced by perceived efficacy, expectations of others' cooperation, moral obligations, and beliefs about consequences. Morrison's study, although to some extent hypothetical, nevertheless involves people from a non-Western culture in a situation closely tied to relevant local issues.

THEORETICAL VARIATION, COMPETITION, AND INTEGRATION

Variations on and competition among theories are both profitable undertakings in any field, often catalyzing attempts at theoretical integration. This book provides examples of both kinds of theoretical development. The chapters by Rapoport and Amaldoss, Au and Budescu, Franzen, and Beckenkamp and Ostmann explore variants of social dilemma solutions as well as extending the scope of their coverage. It is still premature to speak much of theoretical integration, despite the proliferation of competing solutions and explanations for social dilemmas.

However, many theorists believe that competition is where the cutting-edge is, and at times disputation may crop up in unexpected places. Kerr, for example, dissents from a commonly held view of the effects of anonymity on cooperation, which in turn is linked to a debate about the impact of deindividuation on prosocial behavior. He wryly observes that apparent consensus in a field sometimes may have less to do with an "expanding and ever-more-conclusive data base than with the tendency of later reviewers to rely too strongly on early results and reviews" (Kerr, this volume, pp. 104).

Other contentious issues are better known, and receive their share of attention in this volume. The long-running debate in the field over whether cooperation can spontaneously emerge or whether it must be coaxed into existence through institutional arrangements is contributed to by several writers. There is still plenty of interest in how or whether cooperation can be produced *de novo*. This issue is one of the motivations for the recurring arguments over the primacy of interdependence versus group identity. Foddy and Hogg's and Morrison's chapters bring us up to date on the social psychological view of the debate.

The character of this debate has changed, however, from an all or nothing contest to one in which contingent and hybrid solutions are becoming the rule rather than the exception. Lichbach's (1995) thorough assessment of the field is that all one-factor solutions to social dilemmas have limitations. He contends that while any one-factor solution might be arguably necessary to solve a social dilemma, none are sufficient. He therefore recommends considering combinations of solutions and recognizing that each will have limited domains of validity. Several chapters reflect a similar assessment. For example, Takagi's adaptation of Olson's (1965) federal group notion combines tit for tat and ingroup favoritism, demonstrating that they may be jointly necessary for cooperation to emerge and stabilize.

The contrasts between chapters by Schopler and Insko and Rapoport and Amaldoss. indicate the need to think contingently about solutions to dilemmas. Schopler and Insko are concerned that repeated intergroup encounters may produce higher rates of competition than encounters between two individuals from the same groups. This effect occurs even though competition yields worse joint results than mutual cooperation. Yet Rapoport and Amaldoss present intergroup competition as a solution to intragroup dilemmas, provided that the competition is not a dilemma and the likelihood of winning the competition increases with cooperation rates within the groups. Theoretical integration also involves taking still other influences on behavior in social dilemmas into account besides the well studied ones. Hertel's chapter on mood influences makes the case that mood affects cooperation via its impact on how people construe information, but concludes that the connection between them still lacks theoretical integration. Likewise, the chapters by Suleiman and Or-Chen, Smithson, and Webb point to the need for social dilemma frameworks to incorporate exogenous effects.

From a Kuhnian (1962) viewpoint, social dilemmas constitute a class of anomalies preventing earlier attempts at theoretical integration in related disciplines, such as game theory, classical economics, and psychological versions of exchange theory. As desirable as it may be, the goal of theoretical integration has proven elusive and its prerequisites remain unclear. Among existing theories and perspectives, any one of several candidates may hold the keys to a future overarching framework. However, the theoretical diversity may reflect an ontological diversity. The final chapter by Brewer and Schneider provides important insights into quests for single solutions to social dilemmas. The dependence of humans on others may have produced multiple mechanisms for cooperation, none of which succeed under all conditions, but in the aggregate, are sufficient to guarantee a level of cooperation necessary to survival of the species.

Part One

Formal Models
and Dynamic
Systems Approaches

Chapter 2

Taking Exogenous Dynamics Seriously in Public Goods and Resource Dilemmas

Michael Smithson

WHY BOTHER WITH EXOGENOUS DYNAMICS?

Most studies of social dilemmas do not incorporate exogenous influences on the dynamics of the resource or public good (which will henceforth be referred to simply as exogenous dynamics). The renewal functions are usually just a constant renewal rate or a production function influenced solely by what the consumers do. While these kinds of renewal functions have a place in this kind of research, they invite researchers to ignore some important aspects of the interplay between human action and environmental reaction.

At least three arguments may be made to support the claim that exogenous dynamics are essential to understanding the nature of resource dilemmas and intertemporal choice. First, actors learn not only from each other's actions but also from the responses of the resource itself. Feedback from the latter influences actors' causal attributions, beliefs, and perceptions of resource criticality, which in turn informs their future choices. Second, exogenous dynamics influence time discounting (i.e., the tendency to perceive longer-term outcomes as less impactful than shorter-term ones), which in turn may influence actors' payoffs. Third, as will be demonstrated in this chapter, exogenous dynamics critically affect the influence of consumption rates and variability in consumption on the state of a resource. Identical consumption patterns may produce dramatically different results in one environment than in another. Therefore exogenous dynamics are an important determinant of the criticality of timing, cooperation level effects, or both in resource use.

Let us examine the first argument. Given experience and time, actors will learn from participating in social dilemmas. Two things they are most likely to learn about, if given the required information, are each other's behavior and the behavior of the resource. In this connection, Ostrom, Gardner and Walker (1994) present evidence (but somewhat underexplained) that experienced players show less variation in their harvests and get closer to a Nash equilibrium (collectively, not individually). Likewise, Axelrod's (1984) perspective on how cooperation may emerge even in relatively uncooperative environments hinges on actors being able to learn and remember who cooperates and who does not.

In the same vein, M. W. Macy (1990) takes up the earlier Rapoport and Chammah (1965) social learning thesis regarding prisoners' dilemmas (PD), which emphasizes that players are adaptive and backward-looking rather than preemptive and forward-looking. Their behaviors are shaped by repeated trials of the game. Macy strongly favors a stochastic learning model. Axelrod (1984) also argues strongly for the idea that the emergence of cooperation does not require foresight, merely the ability to remember and learn from the past.

Now let us turn to temporal discounting. Consider a single actor's perspective in a destructible resource dilemma. Suppose the actor is in a *take-some* game and must choose whether to overconsume on the present turn. The amount the actor will get is an immediate outcome, for all practical purposes. If feedback is provided, then comparing his or her own amount with the amounts others get also is an immediacy. These immediacies seem unlikely to change their utilities for the actor over time (unless satiation or starvation sets in).

In contrast, the resulting change in the resource pool may also be immediately observable, but for many kinds of destructible resources its meaning and therefore utility for the actor are likely to change over time. Various declines in the resource pool size will have only small disutilities and will differ little from each other if, in either event, on the next turn everyone still is able to consume up to their appetitive limits. However, once the actor foresees (even intuitively) that continued overconsumption by too many will restrict future harvests or even destroy the resource, then the utility of mutual overconsumption should fall (and the utility of mutual restraint should rise) as a function of how soon the actor thinks such an outcome is likely to occur. This argument leads to the conclusion that the structure of the payoffs in a dilemma may change over time. Ever since the economist Jevons (1871/1911) noted that people sharply discount future outcomes, economists have used various time discounting models of utility and calculated discount rates to describe human economic behavior. A large behavioral research literature confirms this phenomenon empirically for humans and other organisms (e.g., Ainslie 1975, and see Rachlin, 1989, for an overview of the analogous relationship between uncertainty and time discounting).

Three well known payoff structures are shown in Table 2.1: *deadlock, prisoner's dilemma,* and *chicken*. Here, we have simplified both players' choices to whether to consume *less* (L) or *more* (M). If the possibility that the resource might be depleted is remote, we should expect that the utility of (M,M) would be only mildly attenuated from worry about the future, and the utility of (L,L) would be only slightly increased by reassurance. The resultant rank order for the utilities of these outcomes for, say, player A, is (L,[M]) > (M,[M]) > (L,[L]) > (M,[L]), where A's choices are in the square brackets. The consequence of a distant-future, highly discounted resource depletion is deadlock, and there is little motivation for either player to consume less.

Table 2.1   Three payoff structures.

		Deadlock A			Prisoner's dil. A			Chicken A	
		Less	**More**		**Less**	**More**		**Less**	**More**
	Less	2,2	1,4	Less	3,3	1,4	Less	3,3	2,4
B									
	More	4,1	3,3	More	4,1	2,2	More	4,2	1,1

As the destruction of the resource looms nearer, however, the resulting worry may detract sufficiently from the utility of the (M,M) cell to make it rank below (L,L), whose utility is enhanced by reassurance. No other change need occur, but the result is a transition from deadlock to prisoner's dilemma. Should the destruction of the resource be perceived as imminent, it may detract from (M,M) so much that it becomes the least preferred outcome, dropping below even (L,M) for the player who consumes less. In that case, the game has transited from prisoner's dilemma to chicken.

This type of time discounting differs from the kind discussed in much of the literature on iterated prisoner's dilemma (e.g., Axelrod, 1984; Shubik, 1970). In the PD paradigm, payoffs are static immediacies insofar as pairs (or groups) of people receive payouts directly after they have made their choices. The entire payoff matrix is discounted by a temporal multiplier which, if large enough (i.e., if the long-term is important enough), guarantees that there is no best move independent of other players and enables a strategy such as tit for tat to be collectively stable.

The argument advanced here is that in dynamic resource and public goods dilemmas, there is another kind of time discounting that discounts some outcomes differently from others, rather than discounting all outcomes equally. So temporal discounting, although mainly a matter of graduated quantitative change, may produce qualitative structural changes in payoffs, thereby altering the nature of the dilemma—or even determining whether a dilemma exists at all. However, it is quite likely that we will not observe a simple monotonic increase in cooperation as ruin approaches.

Let us bring some additional strategic considerations to bear on the question of what happens as the prospect of total resource depletion looms very close. In times of extreme hardship or disaster, even casual observation reveals a preponderance of behavioral extremes: both great self-sacrifice and selfishness to the point of cruelty. One possible explanation for this is a critical-effect motivation involving two competing anticipations: (a) that the resource is critically endangered, and (b) that it can be saved. The likelihood of both must be perceived to be high for the rank order of (M,M) to decline and that of (L,L) to increase substantially. If (a) is low then greed is likely to dominate, and if (b) is low then fear is likely to dominate. In short, the actor must believe that her or his effort has a critical effect on the outcome.

While the question of when either fear or greed dominates reasons for noncooperation has been investigated by a number of researchers (e.g., Dawes, Orbell, Simmons, & Van de Kragt, 1986; Komorita, Sweeney & Kravitz, 1980; Poppe & Utens, 1986; Rapoport & Eshed-Levy, 1989; Yamagishi & Sato 1986), a consistent picture has yet to emerge. One possibility that has been suggested is that when the resource is viewed as plentiful greed dominates, whereas when the resource is viewed as nearly depleted, fear dominates.

An implication of all this is that if the resource is depleted below what the actor thinks is a salvageable level, then she or he will be motivated by fear to grab while it is still possible. In studies where a resource does plummet to the point of no return, instead of witnessing a monotonic increase in cooperation (or restraint) as time discounting alone would predict, we should see an increase followed, in the last stages, by a reversion to competition or overconsumption.

A schematic representation of the critical-effect heuristic is shown in Figure 2.1. The time at which ruination is achieved is given a value of 0 (since the game ends), and *the critical time* beyond which salvation of the resource is believed impossible is denoted by t_c. The time scale is in t_c units. The utilities graphed in Figure 2.1 are those of Actor A from Table 2.1, whose choices are square bracketed. Figure 2.1 depicts conditions in which the discounting effect is large enough for outcomes to change their rank order in the manner described above, so that in a region around t_c, the structure of the dilemma is prisoner's dilemma and outside of it the structure is deadlock.

The critical-effect motivation and the expectancies involved therein link the actor's time horizon (i.e., time discount) directly to her or his assessment of the *likelihood* that the game will continue beyond the next turn. While a few modelers such as Glance and Huberman (1993) have made this link formally, most social psychologists have not incorporated it into their research. Again, different exogenous dynamics may lead to quite different attributions by actors about criticality or even the impact of others' consumption patterns. Temporal discounting and the impact of expected level of cooperation both are likely to hinge on how actors believe these matters relate to the near-term state of the resource. A rational actor with sufficient time would calculate an expected cooperation rate on the basis of prior information, derive an expected consumption rate, and from that calculate the survival hazard function for the game *given the present state of the resource and what the actor knows of its production function*. She or he would then discount cooperation if the survival hazard function were sufficiently high, or enhance its utility if the

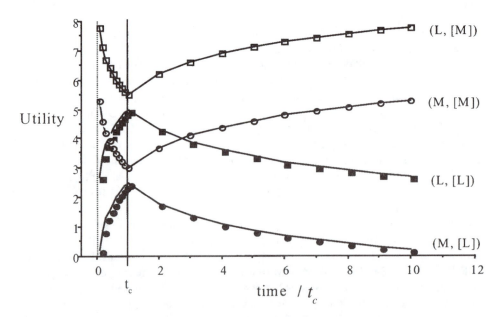

Figure 2.1   Changes in utilities of outcomes with time's proximity to t_c

survival hazard function were sufficiently low. Even a *satisficing* subrational actor's heuristics would be conditioned by the perceived state of the resource.

PERFORMANCE BENCHMARKS AND MARKOV MODELS

Performance Benchmarks

We need a framework for comparing the consequences of what actors do against performative benchmarks, such as a random player or a rational one. There are several ways we can compare two or more strategies of resource consumption or public goods provision in terms of performance indicators. In the classical modeling literature on stochastic processes, two frequently used benchmarks are probability of *ruin* or *absorption*, and the expected duration before absorption. Neither of these are very satisfactory for our purposes, because resource dilemmas almost always require that the resource be depletable. This requirement entails that the probability of ruin should be 1 for all starting values when consumption is above a certain level. An additional reasonable criterion to add is that the probability of ruin be 1 for some reasonable random consumer model that the researcher may wish to use to compare against human performance.

The primary drawbacks to using expected duration before ruin are twofold. First, in most experimental paradigms this benchmark would permit only comparisons with entire samples of participants rather than with individual performance. Second, the expected duration is greatly influenced by long distribution tails but at the same time gives little indication of the shape of the distribution itself.

Another alternative is to model the state of the resource at each turn. There are standard Markov model maximum likelihood estimation techniques for testing such models (cf. Agresti, 1990). However, they suffer a major disadvantage in the form of sparse matrices, especially where there are many possible levels for the resource. Other conventional benchmarks include the *survival function* (i.e., probability that ruin does not happen before the nth turn) and the *proportional hazard function* (probability of ruin on the nth turn given that it has not yet happened). In many consumption dilemmas, the exhaustion of the resource leads to irrecoverable ruin so ruin-based benchmarks are probably the most widely applicable.

I favor the survival function and proportional hazard function because they are not as vulnerable to the sparse matrix problem, can be used on individual participants as well as samples, and yield straightforward estimates under a wide variety of conditions. The proportional hazard function also helps with the right-censoring difficulty insofar as it takes the ratio of the probability of ruin on the nth turn to the probability that it has not yet happened. It may therefore solve the statistical power problem that arises from considering the survival function on its own.

Markov Models

In this section we develop the Markov models needed for benchmarking performance. Suppose we have a resource pool capable of having a finite number of integer-valued amounts of resource. It has a lower absorbing state (which we may set at 0) and an upper absorbing (limiting) state (a, say). We model consumers by stationary probabilities of consuming various amounts of the resource. These probabilities may be conditional on other events or they may be unconditional. In addition, the resource has a renewal (or production) function, which may be either deterministic or stochastic. Here, we will assume that both the consumer probabilities and renewal functions are conditional on only the most recent state of the resource, so that the resulting Markov process is first-order.

We now develop a two player system with the renewal function, consumption probability density function (PDF) for a random player, and a conditional PDF for a human player. Suppose we have a deterministic integer-valued renewal function $g(k)$, which depends solely on the state, k, of the resource. Next, we model the random player as an ensemble of c_1 unit consumption impulses, each of which has a probability, p, of consuming one unit of the resource. The consumption PDF for the random player is therefore just the binomial $f(p,c_1,b_1)$, which is the probability of consuming b_1 units for $0 < b_1 < c_1$. Finally, let $h(b_2|k)$ denote the probability of the participant consuming b_2 units given that the state of the resource is k. We assume that the player may consume anywhere from 0 to c_2 units, so that $0 < b_2 < c_2$.

Then the change from k to some other level, j, for the resource pool is completely defined by $j = k + g(k) - b_1 - b_2$. Of course, there may be more than one possible combination of b_1 and b_2 that could yield j as the next level. So for any transition from k to a specific value j, we have the transition probability p_{jk} defined by:

$$p_{jk} = \Sigma_{jk} f(p,c_1,b_1)h(b_2|k),\qquad(1)$$

where Σ_{jk} denotes the sum over all possible combinations of b_1 and b_2 where $b_1 + b_2 = k + g(k) - j$.

j falls below 0, we sum the p_{jk} for which $j < 0$ to generate a final transition probability p_{0k}.

Likewise, where j exceeds the maximum size of the resource pool (a, say), we sum the p_{jk} for which $j > a$ to generate a final transition probability p_{ak}.

Given transition probabilities, we may estimate the probability of ruin when starting from k before exceeding a, which is denoted here by u_k. They are solvable as a system of $a - 1$ linear equations in $a - 1$ unknowns:

$$u_k = \sum_{j=1}^{a-1} u_j p_{jk}\qquad(2)$$

For resources that can be depleted with nonzero probability, all u_k must equal 1. This is a necessary but not sufficient criterion for dilemmatic systems. Likewise, the expected duration of a game starting from k, e_k, is also solvable by such a system of equations:

$$e_k - \sum_{j=1}^{a-1} e_j p_{jk} = 1\qquad(3)$$

Solutions for expected resource gain follow immediately from this result.

We may also calculate the higher-level transition probabilities given a start in the kth row, denoted here by $p_{jk}^{(n)}$ and taken to mean the probability of moving from the kth to the jth state in exactly n turns. They are recursively solvable by the relation:

$$p_{jk}^{(n+1)} = \sum_{v=1}^{a} p_{jv} p_{vk}^{(n)}\qquad(4)$$

This result is the most important aspect of these models, because it provides the wherewithal for estimates of the probability of the game surviving longer than n turns.

For any number of turns (n, say) and a particular starting state k, we need only set $j = 0$ and apply the recursive formula above to get the probability of ruin on the nth turn starting from k. We then sum those probabilities for $m = 1$ to n, to obtain the probability of ruin on or before the nth turn. Denoting this probability by r_{kn}, then $q_{kn} = 1 - r_{kn}$ is the probability of surviving longer than n turns starting from the kth state, and it provides an approximate "significance test" of a model of consumer behavior in terms of the duration of the resource. That is, given our first-order Markov model as a benchmark against which to compare consumer performance regarding the maintenance of the resource, we may justifiably claim that a consumer maintained the resource significantly longer than the model if q_{kn} is sufficiently small. This approach also enables us to compare systems with quite different resource dynamics, since it imposes a relevant scale that is common to all.

It should be noted here that this framework is not a model fitting or model comparison exercise in the usual sense. As mentioned earlier, we are not testing whether consumer behavior fits the Markov model, since that exercise would require considerably more data points than are available per participant in this study. Instead, we are merely testing whether the hazard to the resource posed by the consumer differs reliably from the hazard that would result from a first-order Markov consumer with the real consumer's marginal probabilities of consumption.

Despite its simplicity, this framework is quite general. It may be extended to higher-order Markov models, which are influenced by a longer history than just the previous turn. It is capable of modeling a wide variety of deterministic and stochastic exogenous dynamics. It encompasses consumer models whose consumption probabilities are conditioned on the state of the resource on previous occasions. Those models may, in turn, be extended to more than one consumer (in this chapter we will limit discussion to one- and two-consumer models), each of whom conditions their probabilities on the basis of others' prior behaviors as well as the state of the resource.

MODELING AND SIMULATION STUDY

Does the type of resource renewal dynamic matter? That is, how do different kinds of renewal functions influence duration of survival when their expected gain and consumption rates are identical? In this section we consider modeling and simulation results from three common examples:

1   Constant gain with overflow loss at an upper limit (e.g., a finite storage reservoir fed by a constant source).
2   Decaying exponential gain with an upper limit (e.g., a growth and maturation law).
3   Parabolic/logistic (or at least nonmonotonic) growth with both gain and loss (e.g., a population whose breeding rate is limited by the carrying capacity of the environment).

We will compare three such dynamical regimes that are simple first-order stationary Markov processes. The resource pool for each regime has a maximum size of 12, and is integer-valued. Each of them contains an ensemble of 7 random consumers who consume 1 unit each with probability .43, so the expected consumption per turn is 3.01 units. Moreover, the gain functions are constructed so that expected gains from any of the 12 possible starting positions are quite similar for all three regimes and close to 3.01.

The Form of Resource Renewal Affects Expected Duration

Even though the expected consumption and gain are quite close, the probability of ruin for each regime is 1 from any starting position. Table 2.2 shows the expected gain from each of 12 possible starting positions, and the expected number of turns taken until ruin (i.e., expected duration). Despite all of the equivalences among the three regimes, and even though expected gain per turn is nearly identical for all of them, their expected times to ruin differ dramatically.

These examples suffice to demonstrate that the type of renewal function can dramatically influence the expected duration, since consumption behavior and expected resource gain are nearly identical in all of them. So average gain per turn for the consumer or for the resource has no necessary connection with proportional hazard or survival functions; instead, the relationship between them is modulated by the nature of the renewal function.

The Impact of Usage Rates Depends on the Renewal Dynamics

Consider the three regimes shown above and suppose that we increase the probability of consumption by the same amount for each of them. The expectations in each cell represent the average expected time to ruin (upper subtable in Table 2.3) or resource gain (lower table) over all starting positions, under the assumption that each starting position is equally likely.

The constant gain system is the most sensitive to this increase, as both tables show, but the most remarkable trend is that the parabolic regime increases its gain and expected duration as usage increases. The reason for the parabolic regime actually improving its performance with increasing usage rates is that its maximum renewal rate exceeds the number of consumers (7) which is also the maximum possible rate of consumption, and as the probability increases the variance in usage decreases, thereby tending towards equilibrium at the points where the gain is 7. The equilibrium is when the resource pool has 3 units left.

Several implications follow from these examples. Not only do the large differences in expected survival times indicate that usage rate is very influential, but they also highlight

Table 2.2   Expected gain and time to ruin.

Function:	Constant renewal		Decaying exp.		Parabolic/logistic	
Starting amount	Gain per turn	Time to ruin	Gain per turn	Time to ruin	Gain per turn	Time to ruin
1	3.00987	24546.4	3.00958	7099.70	3.00227	440.00
2	3.00985	28452.0	3.00944	7099.70	3.00497	863.15
3	3.00983	29982.7	3.00929	7099.70	3.00392	877.70
4	3.00980	30463.7	3.00916	7125.88	3.00277	876.67
5	3.00977	30611.0	3.00902	7129.46	3.00163	876.67
6	3.00973	30657.3	3.00888	7129.46	3.00049	876.67
7	3.00970	30671.2	3.00874	7129.46	2.99935	876.67
8	3.00967	30675.0	3.00860	7130.89	2.99821	876.67
9	3.00964	30675.0	3.00846	7131.65	2.99707	876.67
10	3.00960	30675.0	3.00832	7131.65	2.99594	877.81
11	3.00957	30675.0	3.00818	7131.65	2.99480	877.66
12	3.00954	30675.0	3.00804	7132.21	2.99223	806.71

Table 2.3   Expected ruin and gain with increase usage.

Expected time to ruin with increasing usage-rates

Prob.	Constant	Dec. exp.	Parabol.
.43	29896.6	7122.6	833.6
.5	600.1	793.4	754.5
.517	40.8	138.6	960.8
.6429	12.1	38.0	1612.9
.7143	7.0	15.5	3204.3

Expected resource gain per turn

Prob.	Usage	Constant	Dec. exp.	Parabol.
.43	3.01	3.010	3.010	3.000
.5	3.5	3.485	3.489	3.487
.517	4.0	3.757	3.929	3.985
.6429	4.5	3.610	4.240	4.489
.7143	5.0	3.390	4.336	4.987

some problems in obtaining the statistical power to compare human performance with chance models. Clearly, random systems with extremely long expected survival times will be more difficult to distinguish from human performance than ones with very short expected survival. This fact poses a special problem for anyone designing a dynamic resource environment, since they are likely to want to be able to reject a *dumb random agent* model.

A second implication is that some renewal functions (e.g., the parabolic one) can exhibit an inconsistent response to increased numbers of consumers. Table 2.4 compares $c = 8$ with $c = 9$, and shows that increasing average consumption rates has a dramatically opposite effect on the expected time to ruin (maximum expected time over all starting positions is shown here). Such systems may be locally unstable with respect to changes in number of consumers and changes in consumption rates. Experimenters should check the behavior of their systems across a range of consumption rates, number of people, and other potential independent variables to determine whether those systems suffer from any local instabilities. It is also possible that those very instabilities may suggest some productive experimental manipulations.

Table 2.4   Maximum expected time to ruin (parabolic function).

Average consum.	$c = 8$	$c = 9$
3.01	642	544.0
4.00	675	488.0
6.00	5142	215.0
7.80	1.9×10^8	7.8
8.00	∞	6.6
8.50		4.8

Increasing the Variance in Usage
Decreases the Expected Time to Ruin

If we hold the expected total usage rate (cp) constant and increase the number of users, the variance, $cp(1 - p)$, also increases, although not at a great rate. Nonetheless, that has a dramatic effect on the expected survival times of all three systems, as Table 2.5 shows.

The effect is not nearly as large for the parabolic regime as for the other two, but it is clear from both this example and the material in the previous section that variation in usage has a crucial impact on sustainability, independent of total consumption. Variability deserves a place on the research agenda for resource dilemmas and public goods alongside reduced consumption rates (or greater cooperation).

Most importantly, research comparing group consumption with individual consumers should examine not just resource consumption (or cooperation) rates but also the ability of the group to induce coordination among consumers so as to reduce variation in consumption rates over time. It seems likely that this is where groups (at least those with leaders or communication among members) will clearly outperform individuals in contributing to sustainable consumption.

Moreover, there is an implication for studies that vary the number of consumers (c). If cp is kept constant, then variance still increases and expected survival decreases. In order that the effect on the resource from actual changes in consumption rates be separated from that due simply to an increase in c, it is important to use at least two benchmarks: (a) where cp is constant, and (b) where p is constant but c increases.

Lastly, simply scaling up the size of the resource pool to compensate for increased numbers of consumers will not result in equivalent outcomes under random consumption. In a system where $c = 6$ and $p = .2508$, for the decaying exponential renewal function of $(1/2)(6 - x)$ for $0 < x \leq 6$, the expected survival durations average about 44 turns. In a system where $c = 24$ and $p = .2508$, for a renewal function of $(1/2)(24 - x)$ for $0 < x \leq 24$, the expected survival durations average about 114,850 turns.

Implications for Designing and Conducting Experiments

Thus far, the following claims have been established:

1   The type of renewal function can dramatically influence the expected survival duration, independent of consumption rate and expected resource gain.
2   Variation in usage also can influence survival duration, independent of consumption rate.
3   Some renewal functions exhibit an inconsistent response to increasing consumption rate.

Table 2.5   Expected time to ruin with increasing c.

c	Prob.	Var.	Constant	Dec. exp.	Parabol.
7	.4300	1.716	29896.6	7122.6	833.6
9	.3344	2.003	5469.2	1370.0	515.4
12	.2508	2.255	2030.9	571.3	362.3

These outcomes indicate certain problems in designing experiments and in comparing the results of studies. Perhaps the most obvious design problems are how long the experiment should run and what its stopping rule should be.

The renewal function should provide feasibly low expected game durations for the usage rate that yields the highest durations (often this will be the lowest usage rate). Otherwise, the experimenter may be unable to reliably distinguish human performance from chance outcomes. The renewal function should be designed so that ruin is highly likely to occur by chance within a feasibly small number of turns.

At the same time, there must be sufficient sensitivity in survival times to changes in consumption rates that the experiment has a reasonable level of statistical power to detect differences in consumption rates between experimental conditions. Pilot studies or existing data may help establish what the lowest and highest rates are likely to be. The renewal function can then be designed to suit that range of consumption rates.

Some authors have noted that strategic artifacts arise when a game has a preordained duration. The most common prescriptions against this are a randomly chosen or a secret duration. That prescription cannot always be applied here because ruin may occur beforehand and a randomly chosen duration leaves the experimenter unable to select even the probability of making a Type I error.

Instead, I propose the following stopping rule as an alternative to the conventional ones. First, select an α-level for Type I error. Before the next (nth) turn, compute the probability of surviving for n turns or longer using an appropriate random player model. If that probability falls below α and the system survives the nth turn, end the game. Otherwise, the game ends at ruin on the nth turn or continues on to $n + 1$.

Now let us turn to the problem of evaluating competing models or hypotheses, and comparisons across environments and studies. Clearly neither average consumption rate, average resource gain, nor survival duration are directly comparable across environments with different renewal dynamics, even though they may be crucial outcomes for making comparisons within the same experiment. Moreover, they cannot be used to assess the superiority of one model over another even within a single study, without at least some probabilistic machinery.

Suppose now that the game has ended on the nth turn. There are two cases: ruin or survival through the nth turn. In the case of ruin, for each alternative model, calculate the probability of surviving at least $n - 1$ turns if each alternative model were true. For a game that has ended in survival, we should calculate the probability of surviving at least n turns. These probabilities provide measures that may be compared across studies and environments with different renewal dynamics, because they enable researchers to assess how likely each study's outcomes are if a given model holds. They do not, of course, tell us how likely it is that a particular model describes what the consumer is doing. Nevertheless, they enable researchers to ascertain whether one model reliably outperforms another, or whether participants have reliably outperformed particular models.

Finally, there are at least three important research concerns, in addition to resource consumption rate, suggested by studies of dynamical systems. One is variability in consumption, which already has been discussed. Two related issues are (in)dependence among consumers on each turn, and (in)dependence between present consumption behavior and past consumption or resource states. First-order stationary Markov models assume independence on both counts, and alternative models may be constructed that revise one or both of those assumptions. A survey of such models is beyond the scope of the present discussion, however.

ILLUSTRATIVE EMPIRICAL STUDY

Aims

This study set out to investigate how actors' collective performances in maintaining a resource while attempting to maximize their harvests compare with random consumption models that mimic the actors' consumption probabilities. The aims were twofold: First, to ascertain whether the resource lasts longer under human management than under random harvesting; and second to investigate the extent to which different kinds of renewal dynamics affect performance.

What kinds of dynamics are learnable? It seems likely that a constant renewal rate is more easily learned than any kind of variable renewal function, but we may make somewhat bolder statements than this. Evidence thus far suggests that randomicity is learned only with a lot of training, but that short-term predictions of chaotic sequences may be achieved by naive participants with limited training (see Metzger, 1994; Neuringer & Voss, 1993). Smithson (1997) compared participants' short-range predictions of identically distributed chaotic and random sequences, and the results strongly indicated that untrained participants easily gained proficiency at short-range prediction of both persistent and antipersistent chaotic sequences. This is a relatively unexplored area, but we should expect that complicated regimes will be more difficult to learn than simple ones, and that people may have intuitions or heuristics about dynamical systems that predispose them to respond in particular ways.

Method

Participants were 94 volunteers, all either undergraduate or graduate students at James Cook University. They were divided into three groups, with 36 of them assigned to a version of the constant-gain condition, 36 to a version of the parabolic-gain condition, and 22 to a version of the decaying exponential-gain condition. The apparatus consisted of a Macintosh Quadra 640 AV computer located in a small laboratory room. The procedures were programmed in Extend 3.13, a graphically oriented simulation environment.

The three dynamical regimes are described below. They were calibrated to make their expected durations as nearly equal to one another as possible and sufficiently short under random consumption to enable skilled participants to demonstrate that they can make the pool last significantly longer than an equivalent random player would.

Constant (with overflow):
1   Renewal function: $g(j) = 6$, where j denotes the current level of the resource, if $0 < j < 6$; $g(j) = 12 - j$ if $6 \leq j \leq 12$.
2   Random player: Ensemble $c = 6$; expected consumption $= 6(.54) = 3.24$ per turn.
3   Maximum size of resource pool $= 12$; Starting state $j = 12$.
4   Real player may consume 0, 1, 2, 3, 4, 5, or 6 units on each turn.
5   Expected duration with two random players $= 10.855$ turns.

Decaying exponential:
1   Renewal function: $g(j) = \text{Int}[(s - j)/2]$ if $j > 0$; otherwise 0, where Int denotes the integer part of the expression.
2   Random player: Ensemble $c = 5$; expected consumption $= 5(.50) = 2.50$ per turn.
3   Maximum size of resource pool $= 12$; starting state $j = 12$.

    4   Real player may consume 0, 1, 2, 3, 4, or 5 units on each turn.
    5   Expected duration with two random players = 11.416 turns.

Parabolic (truncated):
    1   Renewal function: $g(j) = \text{Int}\{\min\{(3.9/12)j(12-j)] - j/2, 12-j\}\}$.
    2   Random player: Ensemble $c = 6$; expected consumption = 6(.54) = 3.24 per turn.
    3   Maximum size of resource pool = 12; starting state $j = 11$.
    4   Real player may consume 0, 1, 2, 3, 4, 5, or 6 units on each turn.
    5   Expected duration with two random players = 11.657 turns.

Participants were instructed beforehand that they would be playing a harvesting game for 300 turns with another harvester, during which they could restart their game if they crashed the resource. They were told that the object was to harvest as much of the resource as possible without depleting the resource pool. The 300-turn session began after a 50-turn practice run. At each turn the computer display showed participants the following six variables, which also were appended to a data file:

    1   Turn number in the current run.
    2   Amount of resource pool remaining on the current turn.
    3   Amount consumed by the participant on that turn.
    4   Amount consumed by the random player on that turn.
    5   Total amount consumed by the participant in the current run.
    6   Total amount consumed by the random player in the current run.

Participants made their choice on each turn by clicking a radio button next to the number of units they decided to consume.

Differences Among Dynamic Regimes

For each participant, only the data from their longest game was included in analyses. Six performance measures were analyzed:

    1 $\text{Ln}(n)$, where n is the number of turns in the longest game for each participant.
    2   The log-odds of surviving at least as long as n turns, given a random player with the participant's own consumption PDF.
    3   Average consumption per turn (standardized).
    4   Coefficient of variation (standardized).
    5   Correlation between consumption on each turn and state of the resource on the previous turn.
    6   Correlation between consumption on each turn and consumption of the other random player on the previous turn.

There were no differences among the three dynamic regimes (experimental conditions) in number of turns, correlation between consumption on each turn, and state of the resource, or correlation between consumption and random player consumption. However, there were differences between the decaying exponential condition and the other two conditions on the remaining three indicators.

A MANOVA test for these differences using the log-odds of survival, average consumption, and coefficient of variation as dependent variables yielded a multivariate $F(8, 176) = 12.152$, $p < .0005$. All three univariate F-tests were significant, and the effect sizes ranged from 11.7% to 39.2% of variance explained (see Table 2.6).

For each experimental condition, the mean log-odds of survival was generally quite low (e.g., a log-odds of -2.944 corresponds to a probability of surviving longer than n turns of .05, and a log-odds of -4.595 corresponds to a probability of .01), indicating that participants were lasting longer than random players with their PDFs could be expected to. There was a significant difference between the decaying exponential condition and the other two, however: Players in that condition tended to have less impressive log-odds of survival.

While 26 out of 36 participants in the constant condition and 28 out of 36 participants in the parabolic condition had a log-odds survival of lower than -3, only 11 out of 22 did so in the decaying exponential condition. Likewise, only 2 participants in the decaying exponential condition had a log-odds of lower than -5, whereas 21 in the constant and 22 in the parabolic conditions did so.

Participants generally consumed less than the random player ensemble, particularly in the decaying exponential condition. However, participants had higher coefficients of variation in the decaying exponential condition, which may have contributed to their poorer performance in terms of log-odds of survival.

Effective Strategies for Resource Consumption

The strategies used by participants for consuming resources while avoiding the collapse of the resource pool may be ascertained only indirectly. The main object here is determining

Table 2.6   Effect of dynamic regime on performance measures.

Log-Odds of Survival
$F(2, 91) = 6.032$, $p = .003$, $\eta^2 = .117$):

Condition	N	Mean	Std. Dev.	Std. Error
Constant	36	−6.68913	5.807225	.967871
Dec. exp.	22	−2.39913	2.217464	.472765
Parabol.	36	−5.20478	4.193754	.698959

Standardized Average Consumption
($F(2, 91) = 29.335$, $p < .0005$, $\eta^2 = .392$):

Condition	N	Mean	Std. Dev.	Std. Error
Constant	36	2.5625	0.4061	.06768
Dec. exp.	22	1.8866	0.4554	.09710
Parabol.	36	2.8843	0.5623	.09372

Coefficient of Variation
($F(2, 91) = 13.715$, $p < .0005$, $\eta^2 = .232$):

Condition	N	Mean	Std. Dev.	Std. Error
Constant	36	.430043	.102871	.0171451
Dec. exp.	22	.581502	.170006	.0362455
Parabol.	36	.412748	.116310	.0193850

which strategies seem to predict the greatest success, as measured by log-odds of survival. Essentially, there are three strategic components to participants' success in surviving the game—low consumption, low variability relative to consumption, and negatively covarying their consumption with the level of the resource.

A linear regression model incorporating the dynamic regime and average consumption, coefficient of variation, and correlation between consumption and resource level as predictors of log-odds of survival accounted for 64.1% of the variance and revealed significant independent contributions from each variable (but no reliable interaction effects). The largest independent contribution came from average consumption level, as indicated by the squared semipartial correlations in Table 2.7.

Finally, we may determine whether participants appeared to respond more to the state of the resource or to the consumption of the other (random) player. A t test indicated that participants' consumption levels correlated more highly with the resource level than with the amount consumed by the random player on the previous turn. The t test was performed on normalized semipartial correlations from a linear regression model predicting participants' consumptions from the resource level and the amount consumed by the random player on the previous turn. The $t(93) = 4.149$, $p < .0005$, mean difference between correlations = .083, and 95% confidence interval for the difference is [.044, .123].

CONCLUSIONS AND FUTURE DIRECTIONS

I began with three arguments for taking exogenous dynamics seriously in understanding human resource consumption behavior:

1   actors learn not only from each other's actions but also from the responses of the resource;
2   exogenous dynamics influence time discounting (i.e., the tendency to perceive longer-term outcomes as less impactful than shorter-term ones), which in turn may influence actors' payoffs; and
3   exogenous dynamics critically affect the influence of consumption rates and variability in consumption on the state of a resource.

Simple Markov models were then proposed as random player models, providing a common metric and framework within which to compare the performance of human agents in maintaining a resource with exogenous dynamics. Arguments (a) and (c) were supported by findings in both a simulation study and an experiment with human participants.

The simulation study demonstrated that the type of renewal function can dramatically influence the expected survival duration, independent of consumption rate and expected

Table 2.7   Predictors of log-odds survival.

Predictor	Semi-partial r^2
Dynamic regime	.092
Avg. consump.	.279
Coef. variation	.039
Corr. w/ resource	.049

resource gain. Moreover, it highlighted the potential influence of variability in usage (not just mean usage) on maintenance of the resource.

The experiment demonstrated that human participants can quickly learn to perform better than a random player under real time dynamical regimes, and that they seem to utilize the following heuristics in managing resources: low consumption, low variability relative to consumption, and negatively covarying their consumption with the level of the resource. The results also indicated that their strategies are influenced by the nature of the resource dynamics.

These preliminary findings, when coupled with the earlier theoretical arguments, herald a rich set of possibilities for future research. There is potential here to incorporate stochastic learning, criticality, discounting, and environmental uncertainty in a larger framework. Exogenous dynamics also provide a way to disambiguate uncertainty from criticality, which is extremely difficult to do if the state of the resource is entirely determined by people's choices (see Chen, Au, & Komorita, 1996, for an example of an attempt which fails because of exactly this problem). However, space limitations permit only a brief treatment of one topic area, by way of illustration.

Probably one of the most important characteristics of a resource production function is its persistence. Roughly speaking, a process is *persistent* if its state next time is similar to (or positively correlated with) its state this time; and it is *antipersistent* if its state next time is dissimilar to (or negatively correlated with) its present state. Random processes are precisely halfway in between (cf. Casti, 1994, for an accessible account of persistence).

Smithson (1997) links persistence and antipersistence to two well known heuristics that people use in their attempts to predict or control processes under uncertainty. Persistent processes probably reinforce *conservativism*, the tendency for people to anchor their predictions more firmly in the past than is reasonable under randomicity. Under persistence (even chaotic persistence), of course, such a heuristic is quite reasonable. Antipersistence, on the other hand, may reinforce *gambler's fallacy*, a belief that an oscillatory process will self-correct in the short term, i.e., "the cards will turn." Again, while under randomicity this heuristic misleads people into underestimating the likelihood of long runs or clustering in stochastic processes, under antipersistence it is not an unreasonable belief.

An interesting question for future research is whether persistence and antipersistence have different effects on greed and fear levels. One possibility is that persistent processes will induce more greed when the resource level is high and more fear when the level is low than antipersistent processes will, because people may attribute greater likelihood of continuing plentitude or scarcity to the persistent process. Antipersistent ones, on the other hand, may blunt extremes of greed and fear because of a belief that luck will turn and the current feast (famine) is unlikely to continue for long.

Chapter 3

Solving Social Dilemmas is Easy in a Communal Society: A Computer Simulation Analysis

Eiji Takagi

THE GENERALIZED EXCHANGE PERSPECTIVE ON A COMMUNAL SOCIETY

A Communal Society as a Generalized Exchange Club

The argument that follows is based on the supposition that a society has a dual structure. On the one hand, a society has a social system of division of labor, where each person's specialized activities are linked with those of others through mechanisms such as a market, and where each enjoys goods and services others provide to attain a higher level of benefits. I call such a social system an *organic* sector of a society, because *organic solidarity* (Durkheim, 1893) adequately represents the properties of such a system. In an organic sector, a person is well modeled as an egoist, motivated by direct returns from others. Cool calculation and opportunism are the dominant principles. Social exchange theory of a traditional type (Blau, 1964) will be most applicable for the relationships in such a sector. On the other hand, a society has a *communal* sector that is composed of many *communal societies*, such as families, peer groups, and residential or occupational communities. In a communal society, concern for other ingroup members' welfare will be stressed, and unilateral giving will be more common than exchange. Though people usually seek various kinds of benefits in an organic sector outside a communal society, they are still dependent on the benevolent environment of a communal society.

The dual structure notion of a society is, of course, an old and long-standing one. Classical sociological writings used to provide us with concepts such as *Gemeinschaft* (Tönnies, 1887), *basic society* (Takada, 1922) and *mechanical solidarity* (Durkheim, 1893), which roughly coincide with communal society or its structural property. Similarly, *Gesellschaft*, *derived society* and *organic solidarity* well describe the nature of an organic sector.

Given this distinction between communal sector and organic sector, the essential feature of a communal society is, in my view, that it is basically a world of altruism. From the generalized exchange perspective (Takagi, 1996), such altruism can be seen as generalized exchange or generalized reciprocity (Sahlins, 1965, 1972). Generalized exchange is a special kind of social situation where any party gives his or her own resource to other parties altruistically, that is, without expecting direct return. An individual who is involved in generalized exchange does favors for others, and receives help from someone later. There is no definite connection between giving and receiving.

The reason why generalized exchange, and therefore a communal society, is possible is not self-evident. Generalized exchange has a prisoner's dilemma (PD)-like property in the sense that by being nice to others an altruistic giver might be exploited. Thus, a strategy that tried to establish generalized exchange might die out in the course of strategic evolution within any human society.

Understanding how generalized exchange is possible requires an evolutionary perspective such as that applied by Axelrod (1984) in the analysis of the emergence of cooperation. Axelrod constructed a situation involving players with various strategies, each of whom played a 2-person PD game with every other player, and examined which kind of strategy could bring about stable cooperation. Through this examination, Axelrod arguably proved that the tit for tat strategy evolved and could be evolutionarily stable even among egoists, assuming a certain degree of future contact. If the same line of analysis shows that some strategies enable generalized exchange to emerge, one could infer that generalized exchange is also possible in human societies.

In accordance with the prospect above, I conducted computer simulation analyses based on the *evolutionary giving game* (Takagi, 1996). In these analyses, an artificial player, a strategy-carrier, is assumed to have a fixed amount of resource budget and can freely divide it to give any portion to any player. A player must get as much resource as possible from others in order to attain a high payoff. Altruist strategies with different attributes and the nonaltruist strategy were in competition. Superior strategies that earn high payoffs displace poor strategies, and strategic learning develops in a simulated society. The results showed that even the *conditional altruist strategy*, which stipulates that its carrier gives its resource only to altruists, was not strong enough to beat nonaltruism. It was the *ingroup altruist strategy* that evolved most robustly in an egoist dominant environment and finally established generalized exchange (altruism). The ingroup altruist strategy dictates its carrier to give its resource exclusively to those who are nice only to altruists. This strategy views not only nonaltruists but also altruists who do favors for nonaltruists as enemies, and discriminates against them. Without such a highly ingroup oriented strategy, it is difficult for generalized exchange or altruism to emerge victorious.

Why the ingroup altruist strategy establishes generalized exchange can be restated as follows. Generalized exchange as altruism is in a sense the public good of a given society. If generalized exchange is provided as a *pure* public good that is nonexcludable, even a free-rider (nonaltruist) can enjoy the fruits of it. Thus, generalized exchange will be accompanied by a free-rider problem and will eventually fail. The free-rider problem will be solved if generalized exchange is converted into a *club good* that is available only to the members of *a generalized exchange club*. The ingroup altruist strategy completes this conversion. The rule of this club, namely to follow the ingroup altruist strategy, prescribes that every member must be nice to other members, and that violators or those who support a violator will lose membership. Once members adopt such a rule, none will be better off by violating this rule, so that generalized exchange as a club good will be maintained. As a result, the rule will lead to discrimination against nonclub members, since given a limited budget, a member cannot be very nice to nonmembers while abiding by the club rule. In this sense altruism must be discriminating, as G. Hardin (1982) has argued.

This implies that a strategy such as ingroup altruism will survive and evolve through strategic interaction, and will bring about generalized exchange in human societies. If we can posit generalized exchange emerging spontaneously in this way, a communal society as a generalized exchange club will also emerge spontaneously in a self-generating fashion. I suspect this is the reason why we find many instances of communal societies. It can be said that the existence of altruism is not a product of unique cultural ideas but a matter of social dynamics.

Generalized Exchange as a Source of Social Order

The ultimate goal of the generalized exchange perspective (Takagi, 1996) is not to explain the emergence of generalized exchange but to explain, using this perspective, why the order of a society is as it is. Since generalized exchange or altruism is a crucial element of society, various forms of social order or "social facts" (Durkheim, 1950) should emerge, at least within a communal sector, as consequences of generalized exchange. Communal societies are a widespread phenomenon, and they seem to have more or less similar characteristics. It is therefore natural to suppose that these characteristics are just the consequences that generalized exchange has produced.

In order to explore the possibility that generalized exchange may be a source of social order, I have conducted computer simulations, or computer aided thought experiments. Though this line of research is still ongoing, at present I expect the following to be the consequences of generalized exchange:

(a) group centrism,
(b) stratification,
(c) a system of supporting incapable members,
(d) rules of justice such as *equity* and *equality*, and
(e) the ability to solve social dilemmas.

I will present the first four briefly here, and deal with the fifth consequence in detail later.

Group Centrism   Within a large society, we find many observable group markers, such as different religions, languages, hairstyles, and political beliefs. People are usually divided into different groups with different markers. Group centrism refers to the group level pattern that generalized exchange occurs only within a group, which is identified by its members' specific markers. In group centric situations, a group is benevolent to its ingroup members while it discriminates against nonmembers. Ethnocentrism is the most prominent example.

The individual level counterpart of group centrism is well known as ingroup favoritism (Brewer & Kramer, 1985; Messick & Mackie, 1989; Tajfel, 1982). Instances of ingroup favoritism are widespread. Even the well established linkage between attitude similarity and interpersonal attraction (Byrne, 1971) can be understood as a reflection of ingroup favoritism if we take similarity as group membership relatedness.

There are many theories explaining group centrism or ingroup favoritism (LeVine & Campbell, 1972), including group identification theory (Tajfel, 1982), cultural evolution theory (Allison, 1992), and genetic similarity theory (Rushton, 1995). The generalized exchange perspective presents another *social* explanation for group centrism.

The generalized exchange perspective on group centrism provides the following argument. The ingroup altruist strategy establishing generalized exchange does not take into account the group membership of potential recipients, though it discriminates against the enemies of the generalized exchange club. Thus, if a society's population selects the ingroup altruist strategy, *universal altruism* will occur and group membership will be disregarded. However, if this strategy happens to be redefined so as to identify the recipients' group memberships, it may turn into a *group centrism strategy*. A group centrism strategy will stipulate that its carrier gives resources only to the members of a specific group, say Group A, who are also nice only to A-centric members. The only difference between the ingroup altruistic strategy and a group centrism strategy is that the latter specifies the group membership of its recipients. Group centrism strategies will lead to social differentiation in line with group markers, as long as the markers are prominent and well recognized by all.

A simulation analysis was used to demonstrate the advantage of group centrism over universal altruism (Takagi, 1995b). This simulation is based on the following assumptions. Half the players have a marker for A and the other half for B, every player's marker being completely identifiable. Several strategies that take into account the A/B-group distinction as well as universal altruist strategies and the nonaltruist strategy are distributed among the players at the initial stage of simulation. What emerged through competition and strategic learning was a group centric order. That is, only A-centric strategy survived in A group and only B-centric strategy in B group. Universal altruism was easily defeated by group centrism.

Another simulation showed that *antidiscrimination* strategies also survived as well as group centric strategies. An antidiscrimination strategy insists that group membership must be disregarded. However, this strategy has the same structure as a group centric one. Such a strategy requires its carrier to give resources to the members of both groups, and the recipients must also be supporters of antidiscriminative givers. Thus, antidiscrimination functioned as a marker guiding the operation of this strategy.

In this simulation model, the expected payoff a player receives under group centrism is the same as that under universal altruism. Under group centrism, a player will find a smaller number of nice friends, but the number of friends it must support is also smaller. There are no intrinsic advantages or disadvantages in the group centric order. On the other hand, one can imagine a case where group centrism is a more efficient social arrangement than universal altruism. Suppose that a population is composed of many groups and that the members of each are living in a different place. Moving from one place to another entails some cost, while the cost of moving within a place is negligible. In this case helping the other groups' members entails *transfer losses*. In an analysis simulating such a situation, it was, as expected, after group centric strategies had been introduced that social efficiency was attained.

The above results imply that group centrism might emerge spontaneously. From the generalized exchange perspective, group centrism is provided as a form of altruism. Though it may have its dark side in the form of discrimination, group centrism can be a reasonable social arrangement in the case of transfer losses, as the contemporary family system actually is.

Stratification of Sociability   What is proposed here is a form of social differentiation such that, given stratification in terms of wealth or budget size in a society, generalized exchange is maintained within each wealth stratum. It is common knowledge that rich people tend to interact with rich people and poor with poor. Such is an inevitable fact of human societies. Since social interaction proceeds with generalized exchange, the generalized exchange perspective might explain why we find sociability stratified almost everywhere.

The stratification of sociability can be derived from a slightly modified logic of generalized exchange as used in my previous analyses (Takagi, 1996). In these analyses, an altruist strategy is expressed as $S(x,y)$, where x represents a giving level which the carrier player allocates to generalized exchange out of its budget, and y is a standard for another player identified as a friend by the carrier player. For example, in the case of the ingroup altruist strategy I_Alt(x,y), a friend (A) of I_Alt(x,y) carrier (B) must contribute more than or equal to y in generalized exchange, and the amount A gives to B's other friends must be at least y.

First, I considered a society composed of two strata, upper and lower. In the upper stratum, a player's budget size is 10 while in the lower stratum it is only 5. At the initial state of simulation the same strategies as in the previous study were introduced, under the constraint that a player's giving level x must be equal to or lower than its budget size. The result showed that in the upper stratum I_Alt$(10,10)$ dominated and generalized exchange was firmly established. However, in the lower stratum, it was the altruist strategies whose y is more than the carrier's budget size that gained carriers at first. Then, the nonaltruist strategy gradually became dominant, finally expelling other strategies completely.

The failure of the ingroup altruist strategy in the lower stratum comes from the fact that this version of ingroup altruism cannot expel the enemies of the poor. The ingroup altruist strategy was then modified. The new version of this strategy treats players who contribute more than y or support those who contribute more than y as enemies.

In addition to the previous version strategies, new version strategies were introduced into the same simulation model. This time, the result showed generalized exchange being established in both strata. In the lower stratum, the new version of I_Alt$(5,5)$ expelled other strategies, including old I_Alt(x,y).[1]

These simulation results lead to the conclusion that communal societies will take the form of a system stratified along a wealth dimension. It may be thought that such stratification is a special case of the social differentiation I have discussed as group centrism, for in the stratification simulations budget size is considered to work as a group marker. This stratification tendency, of course, will be counteracted by other considerations, as will be seen below.

Supporting the Incapable   My concept of altruism as generalized exchange may well be criticized on the grounds that generalized exchange is nothing more than reciprocity and is not genuine altruism. Genuine altruism requires sacrificing one's self-interest for others. In contrast with the case of *restricted exchange*, giving and receiving in generalized exchange are not directly balanced. Nevertheless, parties of generalized exchange will have an expectation of future rewards. In order to be called altruism, generalized exchange must have an element of self-sacrifice.

Generalized exchange can be called genuine altruism if it is equipped with a system for supporting the incapable or incapacitated. By the incapable, I mean players who have no resource to give and cannot contribute in generalized exchange. It can be supposed that most communal societies have such systems of support. In hunter-gatherer societies, where generalized exchange is sustained as a form of food sharing, it was observed that skilled hunters were always net givers and that the unskilled were net receivers (Kent, 1993; Pryor & Graburn, 1980). In terms of self-interest, skilled hunters should form a new generalized exchange club by excluding unskilled hunters. Yet generalized exchange was maintained by including the unskilled.

A system supporting the incapable can be derived from the logic of generalized exchange by applying the "insurance-mechanism model" of generalized exchange (Cashdan, 1980, 1985; Smith, 1988). Given income uncertainty, a player has a chance of being incapable temporarily. Generalized exchange will emerge in such a case because it works as an insurance mechanism by buffering fluctuation in resources (Takagi, 1996). The same logic can be extended to the case of permanently incapable players.

The following simulation model was constructed.[2] There are two classes of players, the inborn incapable and the inborn capable. An inborn incapable player is assumed to be incapacitated and to have no resource throughout its life. An inborn capable player turns into an acquired incapable player with a fixed probability. It is also assumed that there are two clubs,[3] the *support club* and the *discrimination club*, in the simulated society. A player's strategy is represented by its club membership. In the support club, a capable player gives its resource to others without discriminating against the incapable. In the discrimination club, a player gives only to those who contribute enough. Thus, in this club generalized exchange occurs only among the capable players and the incapable are not supported at all. At the start of its life, a player chooses club membership without knowing whether it will become incapable. A player's decision is based on its inborn status and the observation of the payoffs of the previous generation. The simulation result shows that the support club can win if the probability that an inborn capable player becomes incapable is not low, and if the proportion of the inborn incapable in the population is relatively small. Otherwise, the support club is unattractive and the incapable will be regarded as a social burden.

The simulation result just cited demonstrated the possibility that generalized exchange might be equipped with a system supporting the incapable. Admittedly the support club still contains a self-interest element. However, altruism completely free from self-interest would not survive as a social fact because altruistic behaviors would not be reinforced at all, though self-interest-free altruism might survive as an individual conviction.

Rules of Justice   Another social fact which generalized exchange might generate is the existence of rules of justice. Social psychologists and sociologists have proposed various forms of justice, which answer the situation sometimes differently (e.g., Meeker, 1971; Walster, Berscheid & Walster, 1973). Some argue that different justice rules will apply to different settings (e.g., Deutsch, 1975). However, justice research still requires considerable clarification. For example, why do justice rules emerge in a society? Why do alternative rules coexist within the same society? These questions are seldom addressed.[4] The generalized exchange perspective may provide answers to these questions.

I assume that generalized exchange establishes norms and notions of justice in the society. A strategy of generalized exchange must specify to whom and how much its carrier gives resource. Thus, an effective strategy is equipped with some justice rules linking the other players' attributes and their respective entitlements. Since players within a system will change in the long run and since every player's behavior can change in a short period, this rule should be generally defined rather than person specific. This rule will be a social norm accompanied by social pressures, since, like the ingroup altruist strategy, a viable altruist strategy discriminates in favor of conformers and against deviants.

The present argument is directed toward the most famous rules of justice, equity and equality. Consider again the case where a society is differentiated into two strata, rich and poor. In such a case, as argued earlier, each stratum will provide generalized exchange by itself. However, adopting considerations described previously regarding a system for supporting the incapable, there is still the possibility of generalized exchange being maintained by both rich and poor. Given that it is maintained by both, equity and equality will offer different solutions. The rich will contribute more and the poor will contribute less. In this case, equity states that a rich member should receive more from generalized exchange than a poor member. In opposition to this, equality replies that a rich member and a poor member should receive equally. It seems that the poor cling to equality while the rich advocate equity (Komorita & Chertkoff, 1973; Pruitt, 1972). In general, equity is a rule for the rich, while equality is a rule for the poor.

For the purpose of investigating the differential workings of equity and equality, I constructed the following simulation model.[5] I assumed that in the simulated society there were two clubs, the equity club and the equality club. Generalized exchange occurs within each club. In the equity club, the amount a member gives to another, A, is proportional to the size of A's contribution in generalized exchange. Thus, the equity club will attract the rich. In the equality club a member gives equally, so that this club favors the poor. A player's strategy is represented by its club membership. A player can be a nonaltruist by not joining either club.

The simulation result showed an interesting pattern of rise and decline in the equality club. In the earlier stage, as expected, rich players moved to the equity club while poor players moved to the equality club. However, when the equality club became dominated by the poor, they began to transfer from the equality club to the equity club. Finally the equity club won, and the equality club disappeared together with the nonaltruists. The rise and subsequent decline of the equality club can be understood as follows. The equality club favors the poor at the expense of the rich. In a sense, rich members are exploited by poor members under equality. After most of the rich have moved to another club, the poor can no longer find the rich to exploit. Now the equity club's members are almost all rich. Thus, it has come to be profitable for the poor to join the equity club, even though they will not be treated equally.

This simulation result demonstrates that equity rather than equality is likely to be selected with uneven resource distribution, given that a player's choice is free. However, this will not be the case when obtaining resource income is uncertain and other mechanisms such as storage are not available. Generalized exchange serves the function of buffering fluctuation in resources and of coping with risk (Cashdan, 1980, 1985). This function will be maximized if generalized exchange follows egalitarianism. Thus, under conditions of high uncertainty, equality will be selected. This expectation was confirmed in another computer simulation that assumes high uncertainty and players' risk aversive utility functions.

These simulation results suggest that selection of equity or equality is a matter of income uncertainty. In such a society as ours, where the degree of uncertainty varies with the situation, both equity and equality will be stressed depending on the situation. On the other hand, in societies such as foraging societies, where uncertainty is usual, egalitarianism will be dominant (e.g., Tanaka, 1980; Woodburn, 1982). I suspect that the present results are only a part of the justice story. What is important is that the generalized exchange perspective may be one of the efficient explanatory models for the emergence of justice rules.

Generalized Exchange May Solve Social Dilemmas

The last social fact I am considering as a product of generalized exchange is a communal society's ability to solve social dilemmas, which is addressed later in this chapter. Theories concerning social dilemmas tell us uniformly that they are difficult to solve. According to these theories, commons will collapse and public goods are unlikely to be provided. However, common sense states that this is not always the case. Within closely knit societies, usually of small size, people might be able to solve social dilemmas (e.g. Ostrom, 1987). Viewing these societies as communal societies, the common sense notion of solving social dilemmas will be restated as follows.

Let us suppose a small scale society where members interact with each other more or less directly. Suppose further that this society is confronted with a social dilemma. That is, members will be better off if some common resource is well managed or if a public good is amply provided. Some members will naturally come to think that cooperation in this situation should be treated as a requirement to be a member of this communal society, and thus of the generalized exchange club. These members will advocate a strategy linking cooperation with generalized exchange. As the number of members who have such a *linkage strategy* increases, members in general will cease to be defectors with regard to the social dilemma. In order to have the fruit of generalized exchange, members must forgo the temptation to defect. In other words, generalized exchange will "pull up" the cooperation level in a dilemma situation. Generalized exchange and cooperation will grow hand in hand.

Though the above common sense notion seems attractive, much remains to be clarified. Is this notion logically consistent? What kind of linkage strategy will achieve both generalized exchange and the solution of dilemmas? The aim of the rest of this chapter is to seek answers to these questions with the aid of computer simulations.

COMPUTER SIMULATION ANALYSES

Procedure

I describe below the structure of the computer simulations I used to test my ideas. I construct a small society of artificial players who act as their strategies dictate. Strategic learning or evolution takes place among these players, and poorer strategies are replaced with more benefit producing strategies. Observation of these simulation results enables us to infer which properties of strategy are needed to attain generalized exchange and the solution of social dilemmas.

Rules of Simulation   The simulation models described are based on the paradigm of the evolutionary giving game (Takagi, 1994). The rules of simulation are as follows:

1 The simulated society is composed of 100 players.

2 A player is a *strategy*-carrier and acts as its strategy dictates.

3 Interaction among players is assumed to be *noncooperative*, in the sense that they cannot coordinate mutual actions through communication with each other.

4 A simulation run is composed of iterated *rounds*. A round is composed of repeated trials. For every round, 200 trials are repeated.[6]

5 On every trial a player receives its *payoff*. A player's payoff on a round is a discounted sum of payoffs on the trials. Let x^i_m be the payoff which player i receives on the mth trial. The payoff player i receives throughout a round, X_i, is as follows.

$$X_i = \sum_{m=1}^{200} x^i_m \, w^{m-1},$$

where w is a discount factor ($0 < w < 1.0$). I assigned a value of .95 to w.

6 Players' strategies change as the round iteration proceeds. At the end of a round, learning of strategies occurs. The strategies of the n players whose payoffs belong to the lowest n are replaced with the strategies of the n players whose payoffs belong to the upper n. The other players' strategies remain the same. Thus with every round, the strategies of n players change. Below I assume n as 5.

7 A simulation run is terminated when the distribution of strategies has been fixed. The distribution of strategies is judged to be fixed if one of the following termination conditions is satisfied: (a) Only one strategy has survived; (b) though more than one strategy has survived, all the strategies work in the same way under the current distribution of strategies; and (c) the same distribution of strategies has continued for three consecutive rounds.

8 A player plays two games on every trial. One is the *generalized exchange game* (denoted as *GE game*), the other the *public good game (PG game)*. A player's payoff is the sum of the payoffs in both games.

Generalized Exchange Game The GE game is the same as the *giving game* I used in the simulations of generalized exchange (Takagi, 1996). The outline of GE game is as follows:

1 A player has its resource budget (endowment) for every trial. In the following analysis, the budget size is assumed as 10.0.

2 A player can freely divide its resource budget and give any portion of it to any player. When a player consumes some of the resource alone, that player can be said to give it to itself. The only requirement is that the player must dispose of its budget on the current trial.

3 The payoff that a player receives on a given trial, x, is the weighted sum of the amounts of resource given to the player on the trial. That is,

x = (the amount given by oneself) + r_v (the amount given by the other player).

r_v represents the ratio of the value of the other player's resource to that of the player's own resource. If r_v is more than 1.0, a player confronts a PD-like dilemma situation

(Takagi, 1996). Throughout the following analyses, r_v is assumed to be 2.0. Thus, the other's resource is assumed to be twice as valuable as the player's own resource.

4 It is assumed that every player can observe all the other players' behaviors. Thus every player knows the past exchange history of every other player, though the player cannot know what the other player's strategy is.

Under these assumptions, if all the players are *isolationists* and do not give at all, every player receives a payoff of 10 on a trial. When each player gives all of its resource to others and perfect generalized exchange is realized, the mean payoff a player receives is 20. The difference between the two values, 10, is a standard value which represent the benefit a player receives by engaging in generalized exchange.

Public Goods Game   The PG game is another device incorporated into the present simulation model. PG game is nothing but a classical N-person prisoner's dilemma (NPD) game. Using a take-some game instead of a give-some game makes no difference in the following simulations. Game specifications are as follows:

1   This game is a NPD game in a give-some format.
2   The public good is a pure public good, so that it is completely nonexcludable and nonrival.
3   A player has two alternatives, C and D. C is a cooperative response that means paying for the public good. D means not paying.
4   As each player becomes a cooperator, every player obtains a positive effect (reward).
5   C is accompanied by cost. The value of the cost is the same for all players.
6   This game has two parameters, reward and cost. The default value of reward is 2 and that of cost is 7.5. The *temptation* to defect, which is defined as cost *minus* reward, is 5.5.

Description of Strategies   I describe here the strategies that come into the simulation analysis. Since a player must engage in two different games, each of these strategies has two components or factors, the GE component and the PG component. Thus a strategy S should be expressed as follows:

$$S = S(GE \text{ component, PG component}).$$

The PG component has the following two levels:

C: cooperate in PG game
D: defect in PG game

Regarding the GE component, I considered the following four levels:
N: This means not engaging in generalized exchange. N players are isolationists.
A strategy with one of the three levels below requires its carrier to give a resource[7] only to *friends*. Those who are not friends are *enemies*. These strategies are never nice to enemies. However, the definition of a friend depends on the strategy.
G: This means to engage in generalized exchange. G strategists' friends *are generalized exchange members*—those who give their whole resource only to altruists, that is,

those who also give resources away to others. *G* strategies are equivalent to the ingroup altruist strategy and are strictly altruism facilitating.[8]

G+: This also means engaging in generalized exchange. However, friends of G+ strategists are required both to cooperate in the GE game and to be generalized exchange members.

G++: A strategy with G++ also dictates its carrier to engage in generalized exchange. Its friends are required to give their whole resource only to those who cooperate in the PG game and are generalized exchange members. G++ strategists are highly facilitating not only giving in the GE game but also cooperation in the PG game.

Table 3.1 shows the resulting eight types of strategy. A player with S(D,N), for example, will defect in the PG game and will not give any resource in the GE game. An S(C,G+) player will cooperate in the PG game, and will give its resource only to those who have cooperated and are altruists.

As was assumed above, a player observes other players' behaviors and judges who have cooperated and who have given away their resources. A player's action on a given trial is assumed to be based on such observation on the previous trial.

Simulation Results

In the following analyses, I increase strategies to be included in the simulation model in a *stepwise* fashion. First, I consider only four strategies: S(D,N), S(C,N), S(D,G) and S(C,G). Next, I add S(D,G+) and S(C,G+), in order to examine the effects of G+ strategies. Finally, G++ strategies are added. For every simulation analysis described below, I repeated ten simulation runs.

No Linkage Case   Here I consider only four strategies, S(D,N), S(C,N), S(D,G) and S(C,G). In this case there is no linkage between the GE and PG games. No strategy attempts to link response in the GE game with the PG game results. The GE game and PG game will proceed independently. It is then expected that generalized exchange will grow, as demonstrated in the analysis in Takagi(1996), and that a public good will quickly decline, since the PG game is a simple NPD game.

I conducted ten simulation runs.[9] The result confirmed the above expectation. Only S(D,G) survived. Figure 3.1 shows the change process of the frequency distribution of strategies of a simulation run. The other nine runs followed the same pattern.

Figure 3.2 displays the process when S(C,G) is replaced with S(C,G+). In this case the winner is S(C,G+). However, this simulation was not fairly conducted, because it excluded potential enemies of S(C,G+).

G+ Strategy is Not so Strong   Next, I introduced S(D,G+) and S(C,G+) into the simulation model.[10] In five of the ten runs conducted, strategies other than S(C,G) and

TABLE 3.1.   8 Strategies used in the simulation.

		GE component			
		N	**G**	**G+**	**G++**
PG component	D	S(D,N)	S(D,G)	S(D,G+)	S(D,G++)
	C	S(C,N)	S(C,G)	S(C,G+)	S(C,G++)

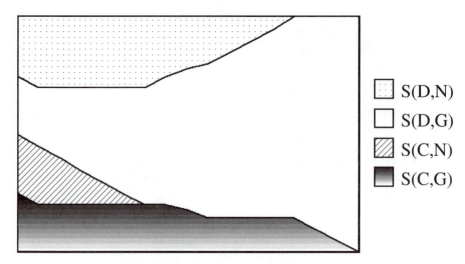

Round

Figure 3.1   A run with 4 strategies

S(C,G+) died out almost perfectly. Figure 3.3 shows the process of one of these simulation runs. S(C,G) and S(C,G+) work as the same strategy on the final round. Both the public good and generalized exchange were firmly established.

In the remaining five runs, however, generalized exchange was attained while the public good was only partially provided. There occurred a strange combination of S(C,G) and S(D,G+), as is shown in Figure 3.4. In the equilibrium state, dominant S(C,G) strategists not only participate in generalized exchange but also pay for the public good. On the other hand, S(D,G+) strategists continue to be free-riders while they give resource only to

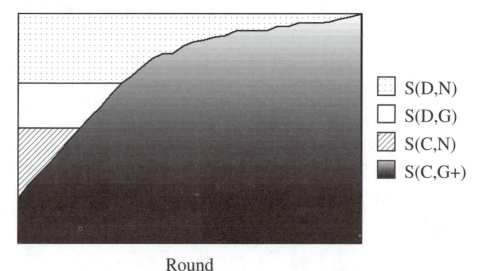

Round

Figure 3.2   Another run with 4 strategies

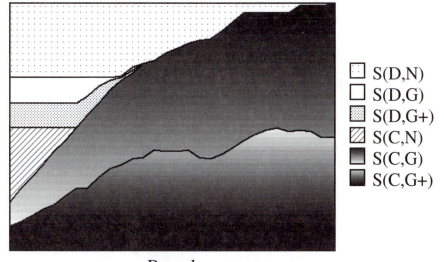

Round

Figure 3.3 A run with 6 strategies

S(C,G) players. In the GE game, S(C,G) players receive more than S(D,G+) players, but in the PG game S(D,G+) players receive more. In sum, both receive almost equally.

The additional simulation analysis revealed that the result of simulation runs with these six strategies depended on both the temptation level and the initial distribution of strategies. As may be expected, the public good and generalized exchange are likely to be established jointly when the value of the temptation to defect is low. Moreover, S(D,G) is likely to defeat G+ strategies if the simulation run starts from an initial distribution of strategies of specific patterns. Figure 3.5 gives an example of such a simulation run. In

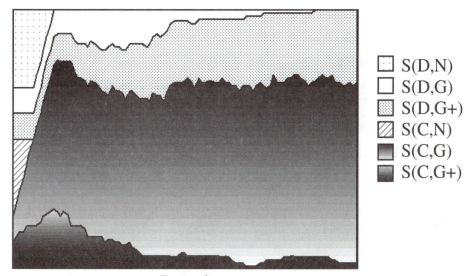

Round

Figure 3.4 Another run with 6 strategies

Figure 3.5, S(D,G+), which is favorable to S(C,G+), is missing from the start. S(C,G) players increase more than S(C,G+) players,[11] and S(C,G) players tend to be exploited by S(D,G) players. Thus S(D,G) finally defeats S(C,G) and S(C,G+).

In order to see how much the simulation outcome depends on the initial distribution of strategies, I conducted a further 200 runs by randomizing the initial frequencies of strategies. I considered the number of a player whose strategy on the final round is S(C,G) or S(C,G+) as an index of the joint establishment of generalized exchange and the public good. If the index of a run was more than or equal to 95, the run is said to have achieved joint establishment. The mean index among the 200 runs was 85.4. Fifty-seven percent of runs attained joint establishment, while 43% failed. I applied discriminant analysis whose dependent variable is whether or not joint establishment was attained and whose independent variables were the initial frequencies of strategies. The most discriminant and significant predictor was the frequency of S(C,G) relative to that of S(C,G+). In the successful runs, the ratio of S(C,G) frequency to S(C,G+) frequency was, on the average, 14 to 22, while in the unsuccessful runs, the mean of this ratio was about 22 to 8. It thus seems that S(D,G) or S(D,G+) can hold some share within a society when S(C,G) players increased in comparison with S(C,G+) players.

In sum, the above results suggest that S(C,G+) is not sufficiently strong. This occurs because S(C,G+) benefits a friend [S(C,G)] of its intrinsic enemy [S(D,G)].

G++Will Solve Social Dilemmas   Finally, I introduced G++ strategies, S(D,G++) and S(C,G++), to the simulation model, in order to examine the effects of their inclusion upon simulation processes. I expected these two strategies to facilitate coevolution of generalized exchange and cooperation in the PG game, because they do not benefit their enemies.

The simulation results followed this expectation. All of the ten runs conducted manifested the same process pattern.[12] An example is shown in Figure 3.6. S(C,G+) and S(C,G++)

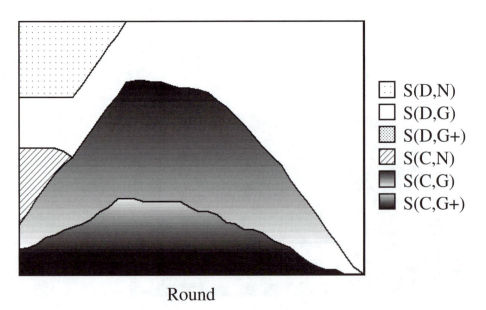

Round

Figure 3.5   PG breaks down

Legend:
S(D,N)
S(D,G)
S(D,G+)
S(C,N)
S(C,G)
S(C,G+)

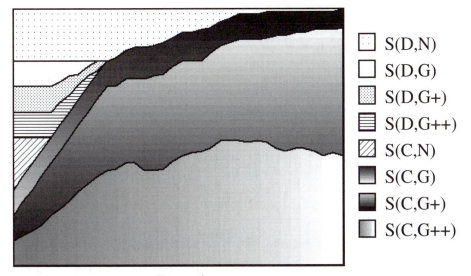

Round

Figure 3.6 A run with 8 strategies

gained carriers, and S(C,G) also survived. These three strategies worked in the same way in the frequency distribution of the final round. Thus, cooperation in the PG game and generalized exchange was fully realized.

It was expected that S(D,G+) and S(D,G++) would support S(C,G+) and S(C,G++) strategists. I then conducted another simulation analysis,[13] removing S(D,G+) and S(D,G++). Generalized exchange and the public good were again established, as shown in Figure 3.7.

I conducted a further 250 simulation runs by randomizing the initial frequencies of

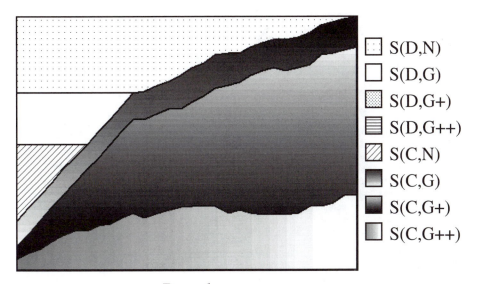

Round

Figure 3.7 GE and PG still grow

strategies to find out how the simulation processes depended on the initial strategy distribution. The number of a player whose strategy on the final round is S(C,G), S(C,G+) or S(C,G++) is defined as the index of the joint establishment of generalized exchange and the public good. Again, a run whose index value was more than or equal to 95 was considered to have attained joint establishment. The mean index value was 99.4, and 98% of the runs succeeded in joint establishment. The minimum of the index was 71. Thus it can be said that the simulated society almost always achieves joint establishment of generalized exchange and the public good if it includes G++ strategies.

These simulation results demonstrate that S(C,G++) can effectively link cooperation in the PG game with generalized exchange, and that it would attain the happy combination of generalized exchange and the provision of the public good. If we assume that a player can think of such a strategy as S(C,G++) during the course of players' strategic interactions, generalized exchange and the public good will emerge spontaneously.

Solving Social Dilemmas is Still Difficult but not Impossible

The above simulation results show that the linkage between cooperation in the PG game and generalized exchange will make a social dilemma easy to solve. However, it is also expected that this linkage is dangerous when the cost of cooperation in the PG game is so high that the temptation to defect exceeds the benefit of generalized exchange. In the case of such high temptation, the public good would decline, and because of the linkage, this declining public good would also pull down generalized exchange.

This expectation eventuated in my simulated society. Figure 3.8 depicts the strategy evolution process of one of the simulation runs.[14] The other runs followed the same pattern. As with the process shown in Figure 3.6, S(C,G+) and S(C,G++) grow at first, then go down, and finally both generalized exchange and the public good disappear.

Thus, it must be said that solving social dilemmas is still difficult. As long as the

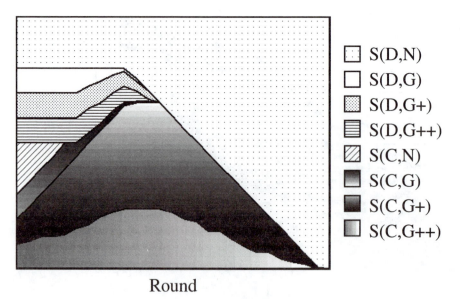

Round

Figure 3.8 A run under high temptation

public good is not a heavy burden, generalized exchange can pull it up utilizing the linkage with it. When the public good is heavy, however, it will pull down generalized exchange, and both will sink hand in hand.

The joint collapse of generalized exchange and the public good may be avoided when the following conditions hold:

Condition 1. There is more than one subgroup that is seeking a different level of public good.

Condition 2. The members of each subgroup regard those who support only this group's goal (public good level) as friends.

Given these two conditions, it is expected that only a reasonable level of the public good will be selected. A subgroup that seeks an expensive public good will destroy itself.

However, there will be yet another problem. Suppose that conditions 1 and 2 hold and that a subgroup that seeks a cheaper public good appears constantly. The lower level of the public good will always be selected. This means that the level of the public good becomes lower and lower, and finally the public good disappears. The question arises of how to avoid this problem.

The above problem will be avoided if we replace condition 2 with condition 3:

Condition 3. G+ strategy dictates its carrier, A, to see a player, B, as a friend, if and only if B pays more than or equal to A's standard of payment in the PG game and B is a generalized exchange member. However, if B pays more than A's standard so that B seeks a public good whose temptation to defect exceeds the benefit of generalized exchange, G+ strategy will regard B as an enemy. G++ strategy is redefined accordingly.

Under the assumptions of conditions 1 and 3, G+ and G++ players whose goal is to establish a cheaper public good will support those who are trying to establish an expensive public good, if the temptation value of the expensive good does not exceed the benefit of generalized exchange. On the other hand, when a subgroup appears seeking an expensive good whose temptation exceeds the generalized exchange benefit, these G+ and G++ players will reject this subgroup. In other words, these players regard not only noncooperators but also unrealistic dreamers as enemies. It is then to be expected that only a reasonable public good will be safely selected.

In order to test this idea, I rewrote the program of the simulation model as follows. First, the new model supposes a society where two levels of public good, high and low, are being proposed. A player then has three alternatives in the PG game: defect (D), low cooperation (CL) and high cooperation (CH). Both reward produced by a player's choice of CH and cost accompanied by choosing CH are higher than those by CL. Thus CH is a nice but expensive purchase.

Secondly, levels of the GE component are also redefined as N, G, GL, GLL, GH and GHH. N and G remain as previously defined. Though both GL and GH correspond to G+, GL's friend must be at least a low cooperator, and GH's friend must be a high cooperator. In the same way, GLL and GHH correspond to G++. GLL's friend must be at least a supporter of lower PG, and GHH's friend must be a high PG supporter. As identification of friends is assumed to follow condition 3, GL and GLL strategies may reject high PG cooperators and high PG supporters respectively if the temptation value of high PG exceeds the benefit of generalized exchange.

Eighteen strategies (3 × 6) are possible in this simulation model. Using it, 10 runs were repeated under each of the two conditions, the low cost condition and the high cost condition.[15] Under the low cost condition, the parameters of the PG game were defined as follows:

1 reward = 2, cost = 7.5 for CH choice.
2 reward = 1, cost = 7.5/2 for CL choice.

Thus the temptation value is lower than the expected benefit of generalized exchange for both levels of the public good.

Figure 3.9 shows the change process of the distribution of strategies of one of the ten runs conducted. The 18 strategies were classified into S(D,*), S(CL,*) and S(CH,*), where * can be any value. As is seen, S(CH,*) expelled other strategies and dominated the society. Figure 3.10 depicts the frequencies of six strategies which belong to S(CH,*), indicating that S(CH,GH) and S(CH,GHH) finally dominated the society. The other runs followed the same pattern.

Under the high cost condition, the parameters of the PG game were as follows:

1 reward = 2, cost = 15 for CH choice.
2 reward = 1, cost = 15/2 for CL choice.

Thus the temptation value is lower than the benefit of generalized exchange for the lower public good, but higher for the expensive public good.

I repeated ten simulation runs and found the same result among all of these runs. Figure 3.11 shows an example. This time the winner is S(CL,*). S(CH,*), which is seeking an expensive purchase, disappears. Figure 3.12 depicts the details within S(CL,*) group, showing that S(CL,GL) and S(CL,GLL) expelled the others.

Thus, the simulation model worked according to the reasoning I outlined above. If we assume conditions 1 and 3, a joint collapse of generalized exchange and the public good will be avoided, and only a reasonable public good will be selected, as long as a subgroup appears which proposes such a public good. It can be safely argued that a public good will be provided through its linkage with generalized exchange.

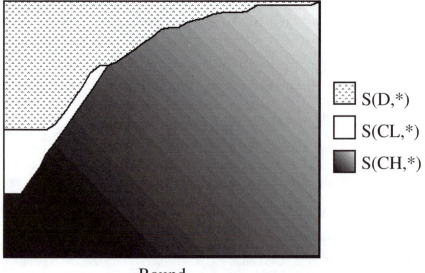

Round

Figure 3.9 A run under low cost

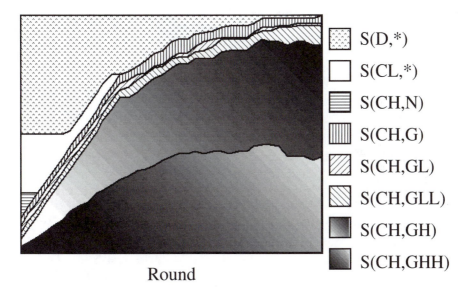

Figure 3.10   A run under low cost

DISCUSSION

A straightforward implication of the simulation results I have just described is that social dilemmas are likely to be solved in a communal society. This is because generalized exchange characterizes a communal society and promotes the cooperation level in it. For example, Watabe, Jin, Hayashi, Takahashi, and Yamagishi (1992) empirically showed lower cooperation in unorganized residential districts. Such results are in accordance with the

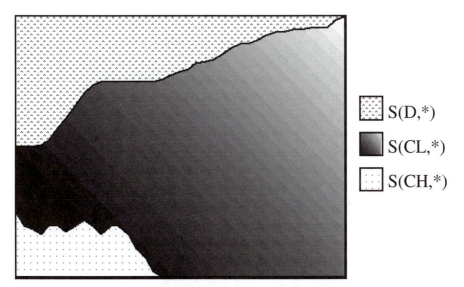

Round

Figure 3.11   A run under high cost

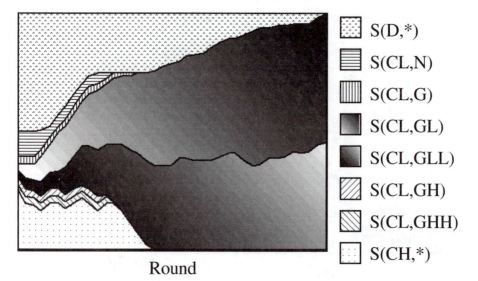

Figure 3.12   A run under high cost

perspective presented so far. Below I add some related remarks on solving social dilemmas and the generalized exchange perspective.

Solving Social Dilemmas

A General Principle and Meta-Norm Simulation   The computer simulation analysis of generalized exchange (Takagi, 1996) revealed that there must be highly ingroup oriented strategies such as the ingroup-altruist strategy for generalized exchange to emerge robustly within a society. The ingroup-altruist strategy requires its carrier player to support only those who support only altruists. The analysis of this chapter has produced a similar result, namely that the stable establishment of a public good will be attained if the society includes G++ strategists. S(C,G++) strategy dictates a player to support only the supporters of the *public good supporting altruists*.

These results in sum lead me to the tentative conclusion that there may be at least one general principle that enables people to establish a beneficial system within a society. This general principle might be stated as follows:

1   Differentiate friends from enemies.
2   Regard a friend who is a friend of an enemy as an enemy.
3   Treat friends and enemies differently.

Consideration of this general principle reminds me of Axelrod's (1986) meta-norm-game simulation. The essence of Axelrod's analysis can be restated as follows. Social order is attained if one punishes deviants as well as conformers who do not punish deviants. The results of my analyses are in line with Axelrod's, and I suspect that all these results are different expressions of the general principle stated above.

The Limitation of Generalized Exchange   The simulation analysis presented in this chapter has indicated that the temptation to defect in the PG game must be lower than the benefit of generalized exchange. Otherwise, the public good is not provided. However, one may well ask why the temptation must be lower. Let us suppose a case where the cost of cooperation in the PG game is 20 and the reward is 2. With these parameter values, the simulation model predicts that the public good will collapse. Nevertheless, in this case, if all the 100 players cooperated, the public good would bring to every player a payoff of 200, which is far higher than the cost of 20. Why, then, is generalized exchange unable to solve the social dilemma?

The reason is simple. The incomplete ability of generalized exchange to solve social dilemmas comes from the assumption of noncooperative nature stated as rule 3 under *rules of simulation* above. From the game theoretical point of view, noncooperativeness is the essential cause of social dilemmas. A strategy such as S(C,G++) may link a dilemma with generalized exchange, but the noncooperative nature of the game remains intact. A full-fledged ability to overcome social dilemmas will be attained only when some factors, including generalized exchange, can remove this noncooperativeness from the situation.

The Generalized Exchange Perspective Reconsidered

Congruent Psychological Tendencies   Artificial players in the simulation models described do not have any psychological dispositions such as ingroup favoritism and need for approval. They simply observe the results of other players, adopt the strategies of successful players, and act as their strategies dictate. However, I do not suppose that real people act in this way. Rather, if a real society is in an equilibrium where people are following a specific strategy, people would be disposed to react effectively in line with this strategy.

Such a consideration leads to the following speculation. If human survival has depended on the existence of altruism, psychological tendencies congruent with an effective altruist strategy might have evolved in human history. The following psychological tendencies seem to be congruent with the altruism which such a strategy as the ingroup altruist strategy will bring about: Truly altruistic motivation (Batson, 1987); ingroup favoritism and discrimination against out members (Tajfel, 1982); a cognitive tendency to differentiate ingroup members[16] more than outgroup members (Park & Rothbart, 1982); liking similar others (Byrne, 1971); and conformity with a group standard and rejection of deviants (Schachter, 1951). An important point is that a combination of these psychological tendencies would result in behavior consistent with the strategies the generalized exchange perspective predicts. For example, truly altruistic motivation coupled with ingroup favoritism will lead to ingroup altruism or group centrism.

We Shall Not Live By a Communal Society Alone   Readers may feel that this chapter has depicted a strange picture of society. The society model that the generalized exchange perspective supposes is a *friendly but closed* one. Though ingroup members are benevolent, choices are restricted by group boundaries. One might think that a society can be based more on openness, freedom and universal principles.

However, what this chapter has depicted is one aspect of society, expected only in its communal sector. In contrast with the friendly and closed nature of a communal society, another aspect, an organic sector, can be characterized as a *cool and open* world of the division of labor. Stated simply, an organic sector will be so constructed that players can unrestrictedly take the opportunity to promote their own benefits. Here, group boundaries will be disregarded. On the other hand, players will not be protected from exploitation.

A real society will be a complex mixture of communal and organic sectors. The relationship between them will also be complex. Sometimes the two sectors will be in conflict with each other, since their principles are contradictory. If confined to a communal sector, one must endure opportunity costs (Yamagishi & Yamagishi, 1994). However, their relationship can be a collaborative one. In order for an organic sector to operate properly, public goods such as a market mechanism and a government will be required. As is argued in this chapter, the communal aspect of a society may facilitate the provision of these public goods.

ENDNOTES

[1] In the upper stratum, both the previous and new versions of I_Alt(10,10) survived. Because the upper stratum players did not find wealthier players, both strategies worked in exactly the same way.

[2] Takagi (1995a) describes the procedures and results of this simulation. I think this theme requires additional simulation analyses.

[3] The introduction of a club into the simulation model is equivalent to the assumptions that information on every player's strategy is disclosed and that no one can violate the rules of the club.

[4] One exception I know is an explanation by equity theorists, that insists that equity is required in order to maximize the group's outcome (Austin, Walster, & Utne, 1976; Walster, Berscheid, & Walster, 1973). However, this explanation seems implausible (cf. Homans, 1976), because, for example, a firm's maximizing behavior in a competitive labor market is not equal to the equity solution.

[5] This simulation was briefly described in Takagi (1994). The equity/equality issue also requires additional analyses.

[6] Under the assumptions of the following simulations, every player's payoff on a given round can be calculated from the payoffs on the first two trials, disregarding probabilistic errors. Thus, the repetition of 200 trials may be unnecessary. It is introduced here in order that the same simulation paradigm (Takagi, 1996) is utilized in the various forms of social exchange simulations.

[7] A strategy with G, G+, or G++ selects up to eight recipients randomly from the eligible players and rewards them equally.

[8] Strictly speaking, G strategies are equal to ingroup altruist strategies *whose giving level* and *standard of giving level* are the maximum of 10 (Takagi, 1996). This applies also to G+ and G++.

[9] Let $F(X_1, ..., X_i, ...) = (F_{X1}, ...F_{Xi}, ...)$ denote a frequency distribution of strategies, where X_i is a strategy, F_{Xi} is the frequency of X_i, and $\Sigma_i F_{Xi} = 100$. I then set the frequency distribution in the initial state as F[S(D,N), S(D,G), S(C,N), S(C,G)] = (25, 25, 25, 25).

[10] This simulation starts from F[S(D,N), S(D,G), S(D,G+), S(C,N), S(C,G), S(C,G+)] = (30, 10, 10, 30, 10, 10).

[11] S(C,G) players tend to increase more than S(C,G+) players because S(C,G) players get more benefits from S(C,G+) players than S(C,G+) players get from S(C,G) players. S(C,G) players give their resource even to S(D,G) players, while S(C,G+) players do not.

[12] The initial frequency distribution of strategies was such as F([S(D,N), S(D,G), S(D,G+), S(D,G++), S(C,N), S(C,G), S(C,G+), S(C,G++)] = (20, 10, 10, 10, 20, 10, 10, 10).

[13] The initial frequency distribution was F[S(D,N), S(D,G), S(D,G+), S(D,G++), S(C,N), S(C,G), S(C,G+), S(C,G++)] = (30, 20, 0, 0, 30, 10, 5, 5).

[14] This simulation also starts from such distribution as F[S(D,N), S(D,G), S(D,G+), S(D,G++), S(C,N), S(C,G), S(C,G+), S(C,G++)] = (20, 10, 10, 10, 20, 10, 10, 10).

[15] For both conditions, the initial distribution of strategies is such as F[S(D,N), S(D,G), S(D,GL), S(D,GLL), S(D,GH), S(D,GHH), S(CL,N), S(CL,G), S(CL,GL), S(CL,GLL), S(CL,GH), S(CL,GHH), S(CH,N), S(CH,G), S(CH,GL), S(CH,GLL), S(CH,GH), S(CH,GHH)] = (25, 5, 5, 5, 5, 5, 10, 3, 3, 3, 3, 3, 10, 3, 3, 3, 3, 3).

[16] For ingroup altruists, observing ingroup members' characteristics is more important than observing outgroup members. They can simply disregard out members because they do not need to interact with out members. However, they must observe ingroup members because ingroup members may turn out to be defectors.

Chapter 4

Emergence of Strategies in a Selective Play Environment with Geographic Mobility: A Computer Simulation

Yoriko Watanabe
Toshio Yamagishi

OVERVIEW

Strategies—decision rules that guide people's choices in social dilemmas—are one of the most important concepts in social dilemma research. Most of the research in this area has been centered around the factors—micropsychological as well as macrostructural—that affect people's use of strategies. Perhaps the most well known study of strategies in social dilemma research is Axelrod's (1984) investigation of the *tit for tat* (TFT) strategy. TFT is a set of rules that an agent facing an iterated prisoner's dilemma (PD) may adopt, according to which he or she cooperates in the first trial and thereafter simply repeats the partner's choice in the previous trial. Axelrod invited prominent game theorists to a computer tournament to determine the best strategies for playing iterated PD. The submitted strategies played an iterated PD game with each of the submitted strategies, and TFT was the best overall performer in this tournament.

A second similar tournament was held on a much larger scale. The participants of the

The research presented in this chapter was supported by a fellowship to the first author from the Japan Society for the Promotion of Science and Japanese Ministry of Education Scientific Research Grants to the authors.

second tournament knew the results of the first tournament. The overall winner in the second tournament was, again, TFT. Furthermore, through a series of "evolutionary" simulations, Axelrod (1984) demonstrated that a group of agents using the TFT strategy can successfully invade even a population of unconditional defectors and protect themselves against those defectors. While both experimental studies and computer simulations demonstrating the advantage TFT has in iterated PD games may be found both before and after Axelrod (1984), his study definitely had the greatest success in convincing social dilemma researchers of the strength and the robustness of the TFT strategy.

This chapter also presents a computer simulation related to TFT and other strategies. However, our goal differs from Axelrod's. What we are interested in is not how well TFT, or any other strategy, performs, nor why it does so. Rather, we are interested in whether or not, and how, a particular strategy such as TFT emerges. In Axelrod's simulation, the TFT strategy was given to a simulated player as a set of rules. The TFT strategy and the other strategies were creatures that came to life in their entirety. Even the evolutionary simulation by Axelrod was not really evolutionary in the sense that nothing evolved. The programmer-god created all the species at once, and then observed how some species came to prosper and the others became extinct. Our goal is to eliminate the programmer-god and see how natural selection creates strategies. Although we were not entirely successful in achieving this goal in this study we believe we were successful in starting a march in the right direction.

THE SOCIAL DILEMMA AS A COMPLEX SYSTEM

Our goal is to study the emergence of strategies and other properties in a world in which PD characterizes interpersonal relations. By *emergence* we mean a process through which a new property is created as an *unintended* or *nondesigned* consequence of actions among interdependent agents. Such a conception of emergence is not uncommon. For example, Reynolds (1987) built a computer simulation called *Boids* to investigate the essence and the emergence of the animal flocks. Each Boid had three simple rules for autonomous action:

1 Collision avoidance: Avoid collisions with nearby flockmates.
2 Velocity matching: Attempt to match velocity with nearby flockmates.
3 Flock centering: Attempt to stay close to nearby flockmates (p. 28).

Reynolds (1987) did not program Boids to flock. And yet, as an unintended consequence of these simple rules to act autonomously, flocks emerged. In this example of Boids, a new property of flocking emerged, not as a consequence of creation by design but as an unintended consequence of agents' behaviors who follow those simple rules. This *bottom-up* computer simulation is often cited as an early incident that laid foundations for the science of "complexity" (Kawata & Toquenaga, 1994; Waldrop, 1992).

Similar examples are abundant in the study of artificial life. For example, Ladd (1995) presents examples of Conway's Life-Game. In this game, cells are located on a two-dimensional lattice. Each cell has a state of *on* (alive) or *off* (dead). Three rules decide whether each cell is dead or alive on the next turn:

1 The rule of birth: A cell is born when just three *on* cells adjoin it.
2 The rule of overpopulation: A cell dies when four or more *on* cells adjoin it.
3 The rule of depopulation: A cell dies when one or zero *on* cells adjoin it.

Those three simple rules produce complicated patterns on the lattice, such that, for example, a similar pattern reappears in a cycle or a pattern moves across the lattice.

In the study of animal behavior, investigators developed a computer simulation program named ANIMAT to examine how macro patterns of animal social behavior emerge from interactions among animals whose behavior is based on simple principles (Maes, 1993; Stricklin, Zhou & Gonyou, 1995; Zhou, 1991; Zhou & Stricklin, 1992a, b). Each ANIMAT has lower level units to act autonomously. As an example in the social sciences, Yamamoto (1994) proposed an artificial society. He equipped each agent with rules for forming direct or indirect network ties and examined how complex network patterns emerged.

The studies presented above and similar studies of emergent properties may be thought of as studies whose primary goal is to examine the processes through which simple principles create complex phenomena. These programs are based on the understanding that complex patterns can be a product of interactions among simple agents, and convincingly demonstrate how this may be so. We share this supposition, and are further convinced that complex social phenomena can be fruitfully understood as emergent properties based on interactions among agents whose actions follow relatively simple principles (cf. Yamagishi, 1993). In the context of social dilemma research, we share this perspective with such researchers as Bibb Latane and associates (Latane & L'Herrou, 1996; Latane, Nowak, & Liu, 1994; Nowak, Szermrej & Latane, 1990). Our computer simulation presented below also represents an effort to construct tools for examining the processes through which complex patterns in terms of strategies and geographic distributions of agents emerge from interactions among agents whose behavior is based on simple principles.

SELECTIVE PLAY WITH GEOGRAPHIC MOBILITY MODEL

This study represents our first attempt at investigating the emergence of strategies used by geographically mobile people facing social dilemma situations. Our simulation program is called Selective Play with Geographic Mobility Model or SPGMM. In this model, each agent moves around autonomously on the computer display. The autonomous movements of the agents produce patterns in their geographic distribution.

Computer simulations have been used to examine the pattern of geographic distribution of the agents in other fields of study. For example, in Agui and Nagao's (1993) simulation program, several species of virtual animals located on a two-dimensional field moved around and looked for food. Those animals had a set of principles (to approach foods or not, to approach the same species or not, to approach the other species or not, and so on) that guided their movements. The animals moved in the vector that integrated the directions determined by those principles. Similarly, Kawata's (1997) virtual animals also moved around within their territories to seek food.

Thus, our simulation is not unique in letting agents have capacity for geographical movement. However, we believe we are the first to let agents move in response to the consequence of social interactions. Specifically, our agents move closer to another agent who cooperated with them in a prisoner's dilemma and move away from the one who defected. Because of this *social* nature of movement, we consider that the geographic distance in our computer simulation should be interpreted as representing *social distance* rather than real geographic distance.

The social distance between two agents determines the likelihood that the two interact, that is, play a PD. The closer two agents are located, the more likely they are to interact or play a prisoner's dilemma with each other. We represent the social distance, or the likelihood of social interactions, as a geographic distance in our simulation simply to help the user gain an intuitive grasp of the results. Although some two-dimensional lattice models (Axelrod, 1984, 1997b; Harada & Iwasa, 1994; Latane & L'Herrou, 1996; Latane, Nowak, & Liu, 1994; Morikawa, Orbell, & Runde, 1995; Nakamaru & Iwasa, 1997; Nakamaru, Matsuda, & Iwasa, 1996, 1997; Nowak & May, 1992, 1993; Nowak, Szermrej, & Latane, 1990; Ooura, 1992; Sato, Matsuda, & Sasaki, 1994) incorporate the social distance concept, our model is much more flexible.

In lattice models, the distance is binary; agents interact only with neighbors (direct neighbors or neighbors who can be reached in n steps along the lattice) and not with nonneighbors. Furthermore, agents in the lattice model do not move; they interact with the same set of neighbors throughout the entire duration of a simulation run. In this sense, they do not have freedom to choose partners. In contrast, our agents can move away (i.e., choose to interact less often) from the ones whom they do not like and approach (i.e., choose to interact more often) those whom they like. Using the terminology of Hayashi and Yamagishi (Hayashi & Yamagishi, in press; Yamagishi & Hayashi, 1996), the lattice model adopts the "forced play" paradigm and our model adopts the "selective play" paradigm.

In addition to this feature of geographic mobility, our agents differ from agents in the previous computer simulations of prisoner's dilemmas or social dilemmas in that our agents are not created by a programmer-god representing a special species endowed with a particular strategy. Instead of being endowed with a particular type of strategy such as TFT, our agents are endowed with abilities to detect signals that are displayed by the other agents. For the sake of simplicity, the simulation presented below uses only one kind of signal—the partner's previous behavior.

DESCRIPTION OF THE PROGRAM

Outline

1 Agents are initially distributed randomly on a two-dimensional geographic area (a computer display). As often used in computer simulations of lattice models or life games, the field is wrapped around on all sides, such that all of the four edges of the computer field are linked to the opposite edge forming a ball like structure.
2 One randomly selected agent is activated at a time. The activated agent selects interaction partners from others agents according to the distance. The closer a potential partner is located, the more likely the activated agent selects it as a partner with whom to play a PD game. The agent may select more than one partner per activation and thus play the PD game more than once, or the agent may not select any as a partner and thus does not play.
3 The activated agent plays a PD game once with each of the partners it has selected. In the PD game, each player decides between giving out one point to the partner (the choice of C or cooperation) and taking one point from the partner (the choice of D or defection). When a player chooses C, the partner receives two points. When a player chooses D, the partner loses two points. Thus, the resulting payoff structure in the matrix form is presented in Table 4.1.
4 Having played PD games with all the selected partners, the activated agent moves. The direction and the distance of the movement are determined by aggregating the results of the PD games it played during the activation period. More specifically, it approaches toward each of the partners who have cooperated and moves away from each of the

partners who have defected. The activated agent moves along the vector formed by adding all the approach or escape vectors.

5   The activated agent produces an offspring or its clone when it has accumulated a certain number of points. The location of the offspring is randomly determined. No mutation is included in this simulation, although the lack of mutation is not an inherent feature of SPGMM; it will be added in the future simulations. The activated agent dies when it loses all the points originally assigned to it.

All the changes in the agents (their moves, births, or deaths) are immediately shown on the computer display as agents are randomly activated one by one.

Agent's Behavior

The agent's behavior is controlled by a set of two types of "genes"—Type I and Type II. Each Type I gene has two values, and determines whether the agent detects a particular signal. When the value of the gene is 1 (or *on*), the agent can detect the state of a particular signal a partner exhibits. When the value is 0 (or *off*), the agent cannot detect the signal state. For example, the Type I-1 gene used in the simulation presented below determines whether or not the agent can detect (or remember) the behavior (C or D) the partner took in the last encounter. Although we only used this Type I gene in the simulation presented in this chapter, other Type I genes can easily be introduced in the future work, such as genes for detecting group identity and reputation. For each Type I gene, there are as many Type II genes as the number of signal states detectable by the owner of the corresponding Type I gene (i.e., whose corresponding Type I gene is *on*). Each Type II gene determines whether to cooperate or defect with the partner who has the corresponding signal state.

As mentioned earlier, only one Type I gene is used in this simulation. The Type I-1 gene used in the simulation determines whether or not the actor detects (or remembers) the partner's behavior in the last encounter. There are three signal states—N (the agent has never interacted with the partner), C (the partner cooperated in the previous encounter) and D (the partner defected in the previous encounter)—that can be detected by the agent whose Type I-1 gene is on. The corresponding Type II-1 genes are Type II-1n, Type II-1c, and Type II-1d. Each gene has two values, D for defection and C for cooperation. The value of C (D) for Type II-1n means that the agent cooperates (defects) with a newly encountered partner.

Similarly, the value of C (D) for Type II-1c means that the agent cooperates (defects) with a partner who cooperated in the last encounter. Finally, the value of C (D) for Type II-

Table 4.1   The payoff structure in the matrix form of the prisoner's dilemma used in the simulation.

		Choice of player B	
		C (giving one point to the partner)	D (taking one point from the partner)
Choice of player A	C (giving one point to the partner)	1	3
		1	-3
	D (taking one point from the partner)	-3	-1
		3	-1

1d means that the agent cooperates (defects) with a partner who defected in the last encounter. There are eight combinations of the three Type II-1 genes as shown in Table 4.2. In the ninth combination, the Type I-1 gene is off and thus the values of the Type II-1 genes does not affect the agent's behavior. When the value of Type I-1 gene is off, the agent randomly chooses between C and D with a 50-50 probability.

Some of the combinations represent familiar strategies. For example, Gene Set 1 is the unconditional cooperation strategy, Gene Set 8 is an unconditional defection strategy, and Gene Set 2 is the TFT strategy. Other combinations such as Gene Set 3 or 7 are highly unlikely to exist in the real world. The number of combinations used in this simulation is small, but it can get larger quickly as we start adding a few more Type I genes.

One of the major goals in the simulation is to examine which combinations emerge as the dominant behavior pattern. This goal may not seem to be much different from the goal of the earlier simulations—to examine which strategies come to prosper. The difference between the two—our simulation and the previous simulations—is in the way strategies are created. In the previous simulations, the programmer-god created the strategies. In our simulation, strategies are created by randomly combining behaviors toward the owners of particular signals. The difference does not seem significant in the above example with only nine combinations of genes. However, the number of combinations can easily exceed a thousand or even a million as we keep adding more Type I genes (or signals that may affect the behavior of the agent).

When the number of combinations exceeds the population size, not all combinations are present in the original population. And yet, a combination that is not present in the original population may emerge as a result of repeated mutations and may eventually dominate the population. For example, in an imaginary population of a thousand agents in which the number of gene combinations is a million, it makes sense to talk about the emergence of a particular gene combination or a strategy as an unintended consequence of agents' behavior over repeated interactions. The current simulation is only a first step toward this goal of examining the emergence of strategies in a more complicated environment.

Fertility and Mortality

The cloning method of reproduction used in this simulation is very simple compared to the reproduction method used in the more standard type of genetic algorithm (e.g. Agui &

Table 4.2 The combination of the two types of genes used in the simulation.

Gene Set	Type I-1	Type II-1n	Type II-1c	Type II-1d	
1	on	C	C	C	Unconditional cooperation
2	on	C	C	D	TFT strategy
3	on	C	D	C	Cooperate in the first encounter, defect with a previous cooperator, and cooperate with a previous defector
4	on	C	D	D	Cooperate in the first encounter, otherwise always defect
5	on	D	C	C	Defect in the first encounter, otherwise always cooperate
6	on	D	C	D	Defect in the first encounter, then play a TFT strategy thereafter
7	on	D	D	C	Defect in the first encounter, defect with a previous cooperator, and cooperate with a previous cooperator
8	on	D	D	D	Unconditional defection
9	off	can be any			random

Nagao, 1993; Davis, 1990; Goldberg, 1989; Holland, 1975, 1992; Mayer-Kress, 1989; Miller, 1996). The standard genetic algorithm has three basic rules: reproduction, cross-over, and mutation. In its simple version

(a) the initial population is provided,
(b) each agent's adaptive fitness is assessed,
(c) agents whose adaptive fitness levels are low are removed and those who have high levels of adaptive fitness produce their clones,
(d) agents in the next generation are matched and their genes are mixed,
(e) mutation occurs to some of the agents' genes, and
(f) the group as a whole is evaluated on overall fitness.

The simulation presented in this chapter is in this sense semievolutionary since agents produce their offspring or clones and die but no mutation or mixing of genes is included in the production of clones. The exclusion of mutation or gene mixing is only for the sake of simplicity rather than any theoretically relevant reasons. Mutation or gene mixing plays an important role when and only when a new species or genetic combination that was not present in the original combination or that died away emerges. Otherwise, it should not matter much if mutation or gene mixing is included or not. The current simulation represents the latter case in which mutation or gene mixing is expected not to play a major role.

The Simulation[1]

Initial Distribution of the Agents   Each simulation run started with the population of 3,000 agents randomly located in the 800 by 600 pixel square field (160×120 cells), each side of which was connected to the other side so that there was no border to the field. Each agent was represented by a 5 pixel by 5 pixel square or a circle with a diameter of 5 pixels.

Initial Allocation of Type I-1 Gene   The two values of the Type I-1 gene were randomly assigned to the original population of 3,000 agents with the ratio of 8 to 1 (i.e., 8 *on* genes for each *off* gene). The 8 to 1 ratio was to represent each combination evenly in the original population (see Table 4.2).

Initial Allocation of Type II-1 Genes   The three Type II-1 genes were assigned randomly to the original population of 3,000 agents.

Partner Selection   Once the initial assignments of the location and the two types of gene values were completed, agents were randomly activated one by one. Each simulation run lasted for 1.7 million activation periods.[2] Once activated, the agent first selected partners to play the PD game with according to the following procedure. First, the distance to each of the other agents was measured. Then, the probability of playing the PD game with each of the other agents was calculated according to the formula, $p = \alpha^{-d}$, where d is the distance using 5 pixels (the size of the agent displayed on the screen) as the unit of measurement. The value of α used in this simulation was 1.1, but it could be systematically varied to examine the effect of the strength of commitment formation tendency. According to this formula, for example, the probability of playing the PD game with another agent located side by side (i.e., with the distance of $d = 1$) is $1.1^{-1} = .91$.[3]

This procedure of selecting interaction partners is a generalized form of the out for tat (OFT) strategy used in the selective play situation (Yamagishi & Hayashi, 1996; Hayashi & Yamagishi, in press). OFT is a strategy used for selecting partners according to which a player keeps interacting with the same partner as long as the partner keeps cooperating. Once the partner defects, the player leaves the relationship. Since the distance in the current simulation represents the social distance which mostly reflects the past cooperativeness of the partner, choosing the partner according to the distance means interacting with those who have cooperated often in the past and not interacting with those who have defected often in the past.[4] The activated agent often selects more than one agent as interaction partners for the activation period. However, it is possible that an activated agent selects no one to interact with.

The PD Game Each agent was given an initial endowment of 3,000 points at the beginning of the simulation. The result of a PD game was added or subtracted from this resource pool. From the payoff matrix shown in Table 4.1, it can be seen that selecting someone who is likely to cooperate and not selecting the ones who are likely to defect is an effective strategy. This is in accordance with our intuitive understanding of social interactions, but is not necessarily true of payoff matrices whose entries are all zero or positive. Given such a payoff matrix, it is always better to select anyone for a PD partner since the worst outcome is zero or the status quo.

Geographic Movement After playing the PD game with all the partners it had selected, the activated agent moved following the procedure described earlier.

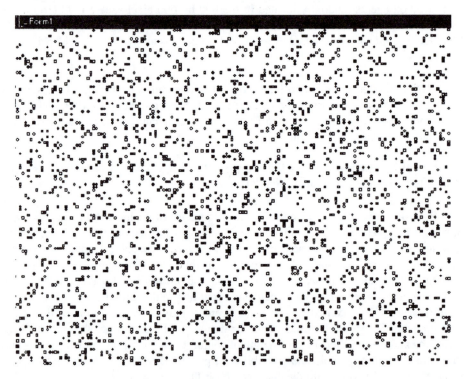

Figure 4.1 Randomly distributed agents

Reproduction and Removal of the Agent   When the resource pool expired or became negative, the activated agent died and was removed from the field. When the resource pool reached twice its original size of 3,000, those points were passed onto the agent's clone that appeared at a randomly determined location. The activated agent who produced a clone was then left with 3,000 fewer points. The upper limit of the population was set at 3,000.[5] That is, when the population size reached 3,000 agents, no more clones may be produced.

Results of the Simulation

Figures 4.1 through 4.3 are examples of screen displays taken from one simulation run. To make interpretations of the figures easier, the nine combinations of genes presented in Table 4.2 are aggregated into four groups, TFT players (Gene Sets 2 and 6), cooperators (Gene Sets 1 and 5), defectors (Gene Sets 4 and 8), and others (Gene Sets 3, 7 and 9). The symbol ■ is used to represent TFT players, ● to represent cooperators, ○ to represent defectors, and □ to represent others. In this example, agents were initially located randomly in a field (Figure 4.1).

In Figure 4.2, representing the field after 300,000 activations, we can see that some colonies of cooperators and TFT players started to form. Although we cannot see it in the figure, those colonies are not stable. Rather, they kept moving both in size and in location. The movement of the colonies seemed to be caused mostly by defectors who approached cooperators in the colonies. Although cooperators tried to move away from defectors, and thus causing the movements of the colonies of which members followed the fleeing coop-

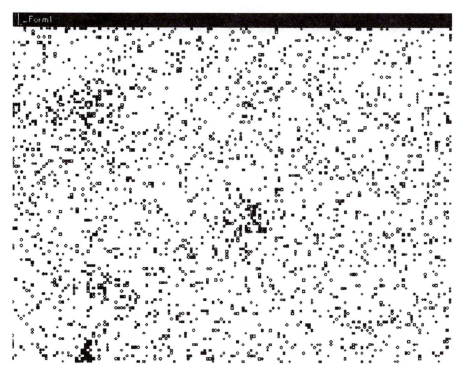

Figure 4.2   Colony formation after 300,000 activations

erators together with pursuing defectors, their efforts were not completely successful since they could not repel defectors as did TFT players who defected against defectors. Meanwhile, the other type of players whose strategies did not make much sense started to disappear from the field.

As more time passed, cooperators gradually disappeared because defectors exploited them. As the number of cooperators dwindled, defectors lost their prey and followed the pass to demise taken by cooperators. After 1.7 million activations (Figure 4.3), stable colonies of TFT players were established. The remaining lone defectors (they kept themselves away from both other defectors and TFT players) did not want to approach the colonies since the defectors had already had experiences of mutual defection with most of the TFT players.

Although the configuration shown in Figure 4.3 seems to suggest the possibility of coexistence of TFT players with defectors as in the results of Nowak and May's (1992, 1993) simulations, we do not consider the configuration as representing coexistence in any meaningful way. The lone defectors were surviving in the field because they did not interact with anyone and thus they did not lose points. Those defectors would have disappeared much earlier if an additional rule was introduced such that agents consume points for surviving. Figure 4.4 presents population sizes of the nine gene sets after 1.7 million activations based on 50 replications. The eventual pattern of colonies of TFT players with lone defectors always appeared.

DISCUSSION

The result that TFT players performed best and came to dominate the society of PD relations is no surprise. We all know, thanks to Axelrod (1984), that TFT players outperform

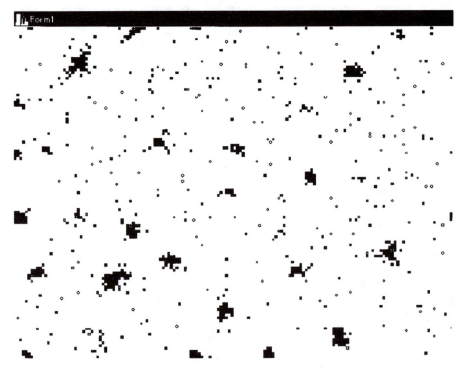

Figure 4.3 Stable colonies after 1.7 million activations

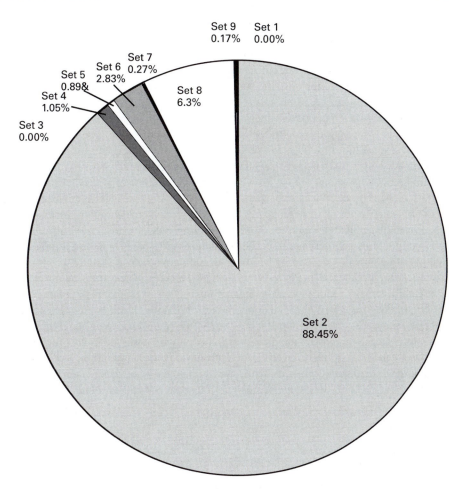

Figure 4.4 Relative frequencies of gene sets after 1.7 million activations based on 50 replications

any other strategy players even in the environment of total random matching. Another interesting finding that colonies of TFT players emerge is not new, either. For example, Axelrod placed four clones of each of the 63 strategies that participated in the second computer tournament in a 14 by 18 toroidal lattice field. Thus, all locations of the lattice field were occupied by one of the 63 strategies. Each player could interact (i.e., play a PD game) with only four immediate neighbors. High performers replaced low performers in their vicinity with their clones. Clusters of strategies, including clusters of TFT players, emerged in this simulation. Similarly, Morikawa, Orbell and Runde (1995) placed 10,000 agents in a 100 by 100 toroidal lattice field. The agents differed only in their cooperativeness. When the agents were not restricted in the choice of partners and the initial overall cooperation rate was low, high cooperators were replaced by low cooperators. However, when they were restricted to interact only with their neighbors, colonies of high cooperators emerged and survived.

Despite these similarities with previous simulations, our simulation and its results are different from their predecessors in very important respects. First, the strategies in our simulation were not creations of a programmer-god as in the previous simulations. As pointed out earlier, this difference is not salient in the particular simulation presented in this paper, but can be obvious in its future applications with a large number of signals to detect. Imagine a simulation using signals such as the partner's behavior in the previous encounter (the one used in the current simulation), the partner's group identity (either ingroup or outgroup), kinship with the partner (whether or not the partner is a closely related kin of the agent), various forms of reputation of the partner (e.g., overall cooperativeness of the partner; cooperativeness of the partner with ingroup members, with kins, or with friends who are located closely with the agent), and so on. The number of Type II genes is several times as large as the number of Type I genes, and the combinations of those genes will quickly become unmanageable for programmer-gods to think of any reasonable strategy. We can start with a few random combinations and let the process of mutation and reproduction select strategies that make sense in such an environment. Talking about emergence of strategies only makes sense in such a complex world.

Secondly, colonies emerged through different mechanisms in our simulation than those in previous simulations. In earlier simulations, colonies emerged through the conversion of neighbors. Conquering was the mechanism for colony making. In contrast, partner selection was the mechanism through which colonies were created in our simulation. Even in this simple initial simulation, interesting aspects of colony making processes were observed. For example, the role of cooperators for making the early colonies unstable has not been previously pointed out. We believe that the introduction of geographic mobility helps us examine more dynamic processes than could be observed in the previous simulations without such mobility. Overall, the current computer simulation, SPGMM, despite its lack of sophistication, gives us a glimpse of its potential power as a tool for examining emergence of not only strategies but also various patterns of social interactions.

ENDNOTES

[1] The simulation results have been reported in Watanabe and Yamagishi (1997a, 1997b).

[2] The simulation was run on PCs, and each run lasted 10 to 20 hours depending on the speed of the particular machine.

[3] To reduced computation time, this operation was done only for the agents who are located within the radius of $d = 48$ for which $p = .01$. This means that the activated agent never interacted with those outside this range.

[4] See the following studies as applications of the selective-play paradigm: Enquist and Leimer, (1993); Hayashi, (1993a, 1993b, 1995); Hayashi, Jin, and Yamagishi, (1993); Jin, Hayashi, and Shinotsuka, (1996); Macy, (1997); Marwell and Schmmit, (1975); Orbell and Dawes, (1991, 1993); Orbell, Schwartz-Shea, and Simmons (1984); Schuessler, (1989); Vanberg and Congleton, (1992); Watanabe, (1996); Watanabe and Yamagishi, (1997a, 1997b); Watanabe, Kosugi, and Yamagishi, (1994); Yamagishi, Hayashi, and Jin, (1994).

[5] With more than 3,000 agents in the field, it is hard to observe any pattern on the display.

Chapter 5

Social Dilemmas Embedded in Between-Group Competitions: Effects of Contest and Distribution Rules

Amnon Rapoport
Wilfred Amaldoss

INTRODUCTION

The ubiquity of relatively simple games such as the prisoner's dilemma, battle of the sexes, and chicken has shifted the focus of research on interactive decisions away from hierarchical organizations (Hausken, 1995b). In contrast to these simple games, in hierarchical organizations the within-group conflicts are embedded in higher levels of competition between the groups. Although a large body of research in social psychology suggests that individuals solve problems differently than groups and that individual and collective rationality do not always work in the same direction, there have been few theoretical attempts, and even fewer experimental studies, on how individuals make decisions in conflict situations when between-group effects are accounted for. This is due, in part, to the fact that rational choice models developed within economics and descriptive models developed

We thank Kjell Hausken for a careful reading of an earlier version of this chapter and for many constructive suggestions. We also thank the Hong Kong University of Science and Technology for supporting the research of the first author.

within social psychology often underplay the fact that in many social situations of interest a group operates in the context of other groups.

Our focus in this paper is on formal modeling of certain collective action problems in which groups compete for a divisible good. We propose a typology of this class of inter-group-intragroup problems and then offer theoretical results for two cases of interest. Our objective is to stimulate additional theoretical and experimental investigation. We use an example credited to Hausken (1995b) to motivate this class of collective action problems and then propose three dimensions for classifying them.

Criteria for Classification

Consider two islands separated from each other and isolated from any outside influence. Each island has developed a tax system to produce and distribute public goods (e.g., military defense, education, social welfare, cultural activities). Every member of the island incurs some cost of paying the taxes. By paying their taxes, individual members generate some public good that is distributed among all the residents of the island.

In the example described by Hausken (1995b), agents can choose between two actions: Pay their taxes (cooperate) or not pay any taxes at all (defect). In the more general and realistic case, agents can choose between more than two strategies (e.g., pay all of their taxes, pay half of their taxes, or not pay any taxes at all). Alternatively, their strategy space may be continuous, allowing them to pay any fraction of their taxes. If all the residents of the island pay taxes, the public good—whose value is assumed to exceed the total taxes paid—is provided. However, depending on the payoff structure, each agent has an incentive to free ride on the contributions of others. We shall refer to this problem as the *within-group conflict*. Problems of this type have been the major focus of experimental research on social dilemmas.

Consider next a natural extension of this parable that allows for competition between the islands. Instead of being completely isolated from each other, the islands have gradually come into closer contact (e.g., due to improvements in the technology of communication or transportation) which may lead to competition between them. The competition may be for status, for the right of extracting common resources around the two islands (e.g., mineral resources, fish, oil, etc.), or even for the right of intercepting and taxing ships passing by the two islands. The competition between the two islands may assume many forms. It may be violent, determined by military force or economic output, or purely technical, determined by the resources allocated to develop special technologies (e.g., machinery for underwater oil drilling). Whatever form this competition takes, its outcome is determined by the outputs (contributions, outlays, investments) of the individual members of each island. We shall refer to this problem as the *between-group competition*.

Generalizing from this example, we consider intergroup-intragroup collective action problems with the following characteristics:

(a) there are several groups, each of which facing a separate and possibly different social dilemma situation;

(b) these groups compete with one another for a single prize, which is a pure private good;

(c) only a single group can win the prize;

(d) the prize is divided among members of the winning group; and

(e) provided with the common knowledge how the prize will be divided among them, if they win the contest.

Individual members of each group decide voluntarily and independently on the level of their contribution (also known as rent-seeking effort). We propose to classify collective action problems of this kind in terms of three dimensions. For the sake of simplicity, we consider the case of two groups (islands) and two levels of hierarchy. For generalizations to higher level hierarchies and more than two groups, see Hausken (1995a, 1995b).

The first dimension concerns the *payoff structure of the game* chosen to model the within-group conflict. There are a variety of conflicts depending on the payoff structure (e.g., the tax system that evolved in the island, the distribution of the public goods generated by the taxes). In the present chapter, we assume that within-group conflicts are modeled either by the prisoner's dilemma game, where mutual defection of all the group members is the unique Nash equilibrium of the game, or by the step-level public-good game with binary actions (Rapoport, 1985, 1987; Van de Kragt, Orbell, & Dawes, 1983), which has multiple Nash equilibria. When considering the prisoner's dilemma game, we depart from the common (and, in our judgment, very restrictive) assumption that each strategy space includes only two elements (typically referred to as *cooperate* and *defect*) by considering spaces with a continuum of strategies.

The second dimension for characterizing this class of collective action problems concerns the *contest rule* used to determine the outcome of the between-group competition. We first distinguish between the case where the size of the prize being contested is fixed and exogenously determined, and the case where it is endogenously determined by some function of the difference between the total contributions of the two groups (e.g., Bornstein & Ben-Yossef, 1994). The second distinction is between deterministic and probabilistic rules. The literature has considered two extreme cases. The first case assumes a *deterministic* rule stipulating that the group investing most wins the contest with certainty. (If the strategy space is discrete, another rule is needed to break ties.) The second case assumes a *probabilistic* rule stipulating that the probability of a group winning the contest is proportional to its total investment. Patent races between two alliances of firms investing in R&D, competitions between communities for securing governmental concessions, and military competitions between alliances of nations are typically invoked to motivate either of these two rules. Other rules (e.g., where the probability of winning the contest is some function, not necessarily proportional, of the total group investment or of the difference between the total investments of the two groups) may better model the outcome of similar contests.

The third dimension concerns the profit-sharing or *distribution rule* for allocating the prize among members of the winning group. Prior knowledge of the profit sharing rule is important for every member of the competing groups when deciding what action to take (e.g., how much tax to pay in our previous example, how much effort to exert, or how much money to invest in interalliance patent races). The two most common distribution rules, which have received much attention from psychologists, economists, and philosophers, are the egalitarian (equality) and proportional (equity) rules. The former rule stipulates that the prize be shared equally among members of the winning group, regardless of the level of their contribution, whereas the latter rule divides the prize in proportion to the individual contributions. Other distribution rules are possible that combine in some way or another the egalitarian and proportional rules (e.g., Nitzan, 1991), or allow individual agents with relatively high levels of contribution to gain a share of the prize exceeding the proportion of their contributions (e.g., Hillman & Samet, 1987). Contest rules of this latter type may particularly apply in heterogeneous groups, where members of the group differ from one another in their status, capital, endowment, or physical strength, and therefore are not likely to agree about egalitarian or proportional distribution of the prize.

Previous Research

The approach that we espouse in this chapter builds on previous research conducted by economists and psychologists. Hart (1983) and subsequently Horn, Lang, and Lundgren (1995) examined the effects of product-market competition in reducing within-group free-riding. Building on the pioneering research on individual rent seeking by Tullock (1967, 1980) and others, Katz, Nitzan, and Rosenberg (1990); Lee (1995); Nitzan (1991); Baik and Lee (1997); and Baik and Shogren (1995); among others, have considered collective rent seeking which emphasizes the importance of collective goods in linking payoff structures at different levels of analysis. (See Nitzan, 1994, for a recent comprehensive review of the literature.) Putnam (1988) used the concept *two-level games* to refer to situations that can be interpreted as multilevel games. And Tsebelis (1988) coined the term *nested games* in discussing games with multiple payoffs, where the payoffs of each game in a principal arena are influenced by the situations occurring in other arenas. Within social psychology, Rabbie (1982), Stein (1976), Tajfel (1982a), Campbell (1965, 1972), and many others who studied intragroup conflicts noted that intergroup competition may enhance cooperation. Rapoport and Bornstein (1987), Bornstein and Rapoport (1988), and Bornstein, Rapoport, Kerpel, and Katz (1989) provided a formal analysis of a class of intergroup competitions for the provision of step-level public goods and the effects of communication between or within groups on the outcome of the competition. This early work was followed by Bornstein and his collaborators (Bornstein, 1992; Bornstein & Ben-Yossef, 1994; Bornstein, Erev, & Goren, 1994; Bornstein, Winter, & Goren, 1996), who started a systematic analysis of structural variables in a large class of intergroup conflicts modeled as team games by Palfrey and Rosenthal (1983) in their study of voting. Although influenced by this earlier research, our study builds more directly on the work of Nitzan (1991) on collective rent dissipation and, in particular, on the systematic analysis of the dynamics of within-group and between-group interaction by Hausken (1994, 1995a, 1995b, 1996a, 1996b, 1996c, 1996d).

BETWEEN-GROUP COLLECTIVE ACTION PROBLEMS WITH CONTINUOUS STRATEGY SPACES AND PROBABILISTIC CONTEST RULES

The first case that we consider is interest groups competing for a fixed, divisible, and exogenously determined prize. We assume that the players within each group are symmetric, strategy spaces are continuous, contest rule is probabilistic, and that each of the within-group conflicts is modeled as a prisoner's dilemma game.

   This section proceeds as follows. After presenting notation, we characterize the within-group conflict as an n-person prisoner's dilemma game with a continuous rather than discrete strategy space. We then present a one parameter family of distribution rules for solving the between-group competition that yields the egalitarian and proportional rules as special cases. The Nash equilibrium solution for the intergroup-intragroup conflict is presented next. Then, we solve explicitly for two cases, namely, two groups with equal number of members and two groups with unequal number of members. The focus of our analysis in both cases is on the comparison of the egalitarian and proportional distribution rules. We show that the separate within-group prisoner's dilemma games are solved in the sense that zero contribution is no longer the dominant strategy. We further show that the proportional rule (equity) has considerable advantage over the egalitarian rule (equality) for both cases of equal and unequal groups. Numerical examples are presented both to illustrate the magnitude of this advantage and suggest further experimentation.

Denote the number of groups by n ($n \geq 2$), the number of players in group i ($i = 1, 2, ..., n$) by $n(i)$, and the exogenously determined prize by S. The total number of players across all the n groups is denoted by N. We assume that each of the N players is endowed with some capital that we denote by y. Thus, although the number of players may vary from one group to another, all the N players are assumed to be symmetric.

Each member k of group i can invest (contribute) any fraction of his or her endowment. We denote the investment of player k of group i by X_{ki} ($0 \leq X_{ki} \leq y$), the total investment of group i (summed across its members) by X_i ($X_i = \Sigma_k X_{ki}$, and the total investment of all the n groups by X ($X = X_1 + X_2 + ... + X_n$).

In deciding how much to contribute, each player simultaneously affects the outcome of the within-group conflict and the outcome of the between-group competition. We assume that player k of group i, by investing X_{ki}, generates a (local) public good proportional to his or her investment. We further assume that the total public good generated by the $n(i)$ members of group i is distributed equally among the $n(i)$ members. Thus, the distribution rule assumed for the within-group conflict is always egalitarian, justifying our use of the term *public good*.

Moving from the within-group conflict to the between-group competition, we assume a probabilistic contest rule, where the probability of group i winning the contest, which we denote by Π_i, is proportional to the group's total contribution. In symbols:

$$\Pi_i = \left(\frac{X_i}{X} \right) \text{ for } i = 1, 2, ..., n. \tag{1}$$

By increasing his contribution, X_{ki}, player k of group i both increases the size of the public good to be distributed among the members of his or her group and the probability that his or her group will win the competition.

Modeling the Within-Group Conflict

Before specifying the family of distribution rules that we propose to study, we first turn to the resolution of the within-group conflict. Let g_i denote the public good that group i can generate, if each member contributes his entire endowment y. Then, the public good generated by group i is given by $(X_i/n(i)y)g_i$, and the payoff of player k in the within-group conflict is given by:

$$(y - X_{ki}) + \left(\frac{X_i}{n(i)y} \right) g_i . \tag{2}$$

We now prove the claim that if the public good, g_i, is smaller than the total group endowment $0 < g_i < n(i)y$, $i = 1, 2, ..., n$ then the equilibrium solution for each member k of group i is to contribute nothing $(X_{ki} = 0)$.

To prove this claim, consider a vector of $n(i)$ investments by all the members of group i: $X_{1i}, X_{2i}, X_{3i}, ..., X_{n(i)i}.$
Assume that player k unilaterally increases his contribution by some $\varepsilon > 0$. Then, the expected payoff of player k after increasing his contribution is given by:

$$(y - X_{ki} - \varepsilon) + \left(\frac{X_i + \varepsilon}{n(i)y} \right) g_i . \tag{3}$$

Subtracting Equation 3 from Equation 2 yields:

$$\varepsilon - \left(\frac{\varepsilon}{n(i)y}\right)g_i = \varepsilon\left(1 - \frac{g_i}{n(i)y}\right).$$

This expression is positive if $g_i < n(i)y$, implying that any increase in contribution by player i results in a loss. Therefore, the within-group conflict has the prisoner's dilemma property and each player k in group i should contribute $X_{ki} = 0$.

Example 1   To illustrate the structure of the within-group conflict, assume $n(i) = 5$, $y = 10$, and $g_i = 30$ (satisfying the condition $0 \leq g_i < n(i)$). Table 5.1 shows the expected payoffs of player k, if she contributes 0, 20%, 40%, 60%, 80%, and 100% of her total endowment for selected values of $X_i - X_{ki}$. The table shows that the dominant strategy is to contribute nothing ($X_i = 0$), in which case player k's payoff is 10. If, however, each of the five group members contributes his or her entire endowment, the expected payoff of each player is tripled. Hence the dilemma.

The Distribution Rule

Having specified the structure of the within-group conflict and the form of the contest rule, we turn next to a specification of the distribution rule—the procedure used to divide the prize S among members of the winning group.

We characterize the distribution rule, denoted by f, by the function:

$$f = \frac{X_{ki}^{c}}{X_i^{c}}, \tag{4}$$

where we use the notation

$$X_i^{c} = \sum_{k=1}^{n(i)} X_{ki}^{c}.$$

The power parameter c determines the degree of departure from equality in distributing the prize S. In the context of policy planning, it can also be interpreted as the incentive mecha-

---

Table 5.1   Player k's payoff in the within-group conflict satisfying the inequality $0 < g_i < n(i)y$.

			$X_i - X_{ki}$		
X_{ki}	0	10	20	30	40
0	10.0	16.0	22.0	28.0	34.0
2	9.2	15.2	21.2	27.2	33.2
4	8.4	14.4	20.4	26.4	32.4
6	7.6	13.6	19.6	25.6	31.6
8	6.8	12.8	18.8	24.8	30.8
10	6.0	12.0	18.0	24.0	30.0

Note: The maximum group contribution, excluding player k in group i, is $X_i - X_{ki} = 40$. Parameters: $n(i) = 5$, $g_i = 30$, $y = 10$.

nism used to enhance contribution. If $c = 0$, then each member k of the winning group i simply receives an equal share $1/n(i)$ of the prize S. We refer to this case as the *egalitarian* distribution rule. If $c = 1$, then each member receives the fraction X_{ki}/X_i of the prize. We refer to this case as the *proportional* distribution rule.

If $c > 1$, then players who contribute more than other members of their groups receive a proportion of the prize which exceeds their relative contribution, whereas if $c < 1$, then players making relatively small contributions receive a proportion of the prize exceeding their relative contribution. Note that if $c \rightarrow -\infty$, the distribution rule awards the entire prize to the player with the highest contribution, if such a player exists, whereas if $c \rightarrow -\infty$, it is the player with the smaller contribution who is awarded the entire prize. We refer to the two cases where either $c > 1$ or $c < 0$ as *discriminatory* distribution rules.

Example 2 To exemplify this class of distribution rules, assume that $n(i) = 5$, $y = 10$, and that the individual contributions of players 1 through 5 are 10, 5, 2, 2, and 1, respectively. Assume that group i wins the competition and receives the prize S. Then if $c = 1$, the fractions of the prize awarded to players 1 through 5 are .50, .25, .10, .10, and .05, respectively. If $c = 0$, each player receives 1/5 of the prize. If, for example, we set the parameter at $c = 8$, then these fractions of the prize are equal to .996, .004., 0, 0, and 0, respectively, essentially yielding the entire prize to the player with the highest contribution, whereas if we set the parameter at $c = -8$, then these fractions are equal to 0, 0, .004, .004, and .992, respectively, essentially yielding the entire prize to the player with the smallest contribution.

Equilibrium Analysis

Given the probabilistic contest rule (Equation 1) and the general distribution rule f (Equation 4), the expected payoff of player k of group i, having contributed X_{ki}, is given by[1]:

$$V_{ki} = \left(\frac{X_i}{X}\right)\left\{(y - X_{ki}) + g_i\left(\frac{X_i}{n(i)y}\right) + S\left(\frac{X_{ki}{}^c}{X_i{}^c}\right)\right\} + \left(\frac{X - X_i}{X}\right)\left\{(y - X_{ki}) + g_i\left(\frac{X_i}{n(i)y}\right)\right\}$$

$$= S\left(\frac{X_i}{X}\right)\left(\frac{X_{ki}{}^c}{X_i{}^c}\right) + g_i\left(\frac{X_i}{n(i)y}\right) + (y - X_{ki}). \tag{5}$$

The first order condition for global interior maximum of the expected value of player k of group i is:

$$\frac{\partial V_{ki}}{\partial X_{ki}} = \frac{S\left[XX_i{}^c X_i cX_{ki}{}^{c-1} - cXX_i X_{ki}{}^{2c-1} + X_i{}^c X_{ki}{}^c (X - X_i)\right]}{\left(XX_i{}^c\right)^2} + \frac{g_i}{n(i)y} - 1 = 0. \tag{6}$$

The second order condition is satisfied as it can be shown that V_{ki} is concave in X_{ki}.

Because the players in each group are symmetric, we construct a symmetric Nash equilibrium solution in which identical members of the same group receive the same payoff. We do so by simplifying the notation and writing:

$$x_i = X_{ki}, \text{ for every } i = 1, 2,..., n \text{ and } k = 1, 2, ..., n(i). \tag{7}$$

Using the new notation in Equation 7 and applying some algebra, the expression in Equation 6 can be rewritten as:

$$\frac{Sc[n(i)-1]}{n(i)X} + \frac{S}{n(i)X} - \frac{Sx_i}{X^2} = 1 - \frac{g_i}{n(i)y} \ . \tag{8}$$

We next solve explicitly for x_i in Equation 8 for two cases of interest.

Two Groups with Equal Number of Members

Consider first the case of two equal size groups (i.e., $n = 2$, $n(1) = n(2) = m$). If the two groups are symmetric, then $N = 2m$ and $X = Nx_i$. Substituting the latter expression for X in Equation 8, we obtain an explicit solution for x_i:

$$x_i = S \left[\frac{2c(m-1)+1}{N^2 \left(1 - \dfrac{2g_i}{Ny}\right)} \right]. \tag{9}$$

In the case of proportional distribution of the prize ($c = 1$), Equation 9 reduces to:

$$x_i = \frac{S(N-1)}{N^2 \left(1 - \dfrac{2g_i}{Ny}\right)}, \tag{10}$$

whereas if the distribution rule is egalitarian ($c = 0$), it reduces to:

$$x_i = \frac{S}{N^2 \left(1 - \dfrac{2g_i}{Ny}\right)}. \tag{11}$$

Finally, in the case of the discriminatory distribution rules, if $c \to \infty$, then $x_i \to y$, whereas if $c \to -1/2(m-1)$, then $x_i \to 0$.

Equation 9 shows that, in equilibrium, the contribution size is a linear function of c. Although while in equilibrium symmetric players contribute the same, the level of their contribution depends on the incentive mechanism that is controlled by the parameter c. In particular, Equation 9 shows that even if the prize is relatively small, there exists a discriminatory distribution rule with a sufficiently large value of c inducing all the players to contribute their entire endowment, and even when S is very large, there exists a discriminatory distribution rule with a sufficiently small value of c inducing all the players not to contribute at all. Equations 10 and 11 show that the contribution level under the proportional distribution rule is $N-1$ higher than under the egalitarian distribution rule (subject to the restriction that $x_i \leq y$). These are all experimentally testable implications of the effects of commonly known distribution rules.

Example 3   Assume that $n = 2$, $n(1) = n(2) = 5$, $y = 10$, $g_1 = g_2 = 30$, and $S = 40$. In equilibrium, each of the five players should contribute 9 units under the proportional distribution rule (Equation 10) and only a single unit under the egalitarian rule (Equation 9). The corresponding expected payoffs under these two rules (Equation 5) are 32 and 16, respectively. In other words, in equilibrium the proportional distribution rule for the present example elicits individual contributions that are nine times higher that those elicited by the egalitarian distribution rule. As a result, the expected payoff under the proportional rule is doubled. Experimental tests of these implications are warranted.

Two Groups with Unequal Number of Members

Consider next the case of two groups with an unequal number of members (i.e., $n(1) \neq n(2)$). Because of the symmetry of players within each group, we have $X = n(1)x_1 + n(2)x_2$. Using this fact, Equation 8 gives rise to two equations:

$$\frac{S\left[cX\big(n(1)-1\big)+X-X_1\right]}{n(1)X^2} = 1 - \frac{g_1}{n(1)y}, \tag{12}$$

and

$$\frac{S\left[cX\big(n(2)-1\big)+X-X_2\right]}{n(2)X^2} = 1 - \frac{g_2}{n(2)y}. \tag{13}$$

Noting that $X = X_1 + X_2$, we can solve for the total contribution of all the N players:

$$X = \frac{S\left[1+c(N-2)\right]}{N - \dfrac{(g_1+g_2)}{y}}. \tag{14}$$

Clearly, a solution exists only if $Ny > (g_1 + g_2)$ namely, if the sum of the endowments across all the N players in both groups exceeds the sum of the two public goods.

Once X is computed from Equation 14, x_1 and x_2 can be computed from:

$$x_1 = \frac{\left[ScX\big(n(1)-1\big)+SX-X^2\left(n(1)-\dfrac{g_1}{y}\right)\right]}{n(1)S}, \tag{15}$$

and

$$x_2 = \frac{\left[ScX\big(n(2)-1\big)+SX-X^2\left(n(2)-\dfrac{g_2}{y}\right)\right]}{n(2)S}. \tag{16}$$

In particular, if we further assume that $g_1/g_2 = n(1)/n(2)$, then it is easy to verify that:

$$x_1 - x_2 = X(1 - c)[1/n(1) - 1/n(2)].$$

This difference between x_1 and x_2 is equal to zero, if $c = 1$ (proportional rule). If $c < 1$, then the equilibrium solution implies that it is the *smaller* group which makes the *larger* contribution.

Example 4   Assume $n = 2$, $y = 10$, $n(1) = 4$, $n(2) = 2$, $g_1 = 20$, $g_2 = 10$ and $S = 30$. Note that in this example we set $g_1/g_2 = n(1)/n(2)$.

Consider first the case of proportional distribution of the prize ($c = 1$). Then, Equation 14 yields $X = 50$, and Equations 15 and 16 yield $x_1 = x_2 = 8.333$. With the probability of winning the prize being proportional to group size, the expected payoffs of individual members of groups 1 and 2 (Equation 5) are 23.333 and 15, respectively.

Consider next the case of the egalitarian distribution rule ($c = 0$). Then, Equation 14 yields $X = 10$, and Equations 15 and 16 yield $x_1 = 5/6$ and $x_2 = 20/6$. As noted earlier, under the egalitarian distribution rule, members of the smaller group contribute in equilibrium four times as much as members of the larger group (and all contribute less than players of both groups under the proportional distribution rule). This seems to be a counter-intuitive result that is experimentally testable. The expected payoffs of individual members of groups 1 and 2 (Equation 5) are 13.333 and 20, respectively.

Other expressions can be derived from Equation 8 for the case of more than two groups as well as for the case of groups differing from one another in their values of $n(i)$, g_i or both.[2]

BETWEEN-GROUP COLLECTIVE ACTION PROBLEMS WITH DISCRETE STRATEGY SPACES AND DETERMINISTIC CONTEST RULES

This section considers a second class of collective action problems combining the work on provision of step-level public goods conducted by Van de Kragt et al. (1983) and subsequently by Rapoport (1985, 1987), with the work on intergroup competition for the provision of public goods (IPG) originally conducted by Rapoport and Bornstein (1987). The collective action problem that we study in this section concerns two groups competing for a divisible prize S. Unlike Section 2, the winning group is not determined probabilistically. Rather, the group that contributes the most wins the competition with certainty and secures the prize. In case of a tie, each group receives a smaller prize equal to T ($0 \leq T \leq S / 2$).

Also in contrast to the previous section, the within-group conflict is no longer of the prisoner's dilemma type. Rather, it is an n-person generalization of the 2×2 game of chicken. The game reduces to the volunteer's dilemma, if only a single contributor is needed for the provision of the public good, and to the unanimity dilemma, if all the group members are required to contribute. Similarly to Section 2, our focus is again on the comparison of the proportional and egalitarian distribution rules. The comparison shows that for the class of collective actions under study the advantage of the proportional rule over the egalitarian rule is much smaller than for the class of conflicts examined in Section 2, and that it diminishes as the prize awarded to the winning group increases.

Modeling the Within-Group Conflict

As in Section 2, we denote by g_i the public good that group i generates when each of its members contributes his or her endowment y. The public good g_i is shared equally among the members of group i. The individual strategy space includes only two elements: $X_{ki} \in \{0,y\}$. In contrast to the cases studied in Section 2, players can either contribute their entire endowment or not contribute at all. The conflict is characterized by an exogenously determined cutoff point, or provision threshold, denoted by M ($M = 0, y, 2y, ..., n(i)y$), such that the public good g_i is provided if $X_i \geq M$ and is not provided, otherwise. Because of the symmetry of players within each of the groups, the provision rule can be stated in terms of the *number of contributors m* ($m = 0, 1, ..., n(i)$), such that the good is provided if $m \geq m^*$ and is not provided, otherwise ($m^* = 1, 2, ..., n(i)$).

Table 5.2 presents the individual payoffs of player k of group i associated with the possible outcomes of the conflict. Because the same payoff matrix characterizes the game played by each of the groups, reference to group i is omitted. Also, when the two groups are symmetric, we use the term n to denote the number of players in each group (earlier in Section 2, n was used to denote the number of groups). The assumption $g / n > y$, which we already invoked in Section 2, implies that the decision not to contribute is no longer a dominant strategy; rather, if $m^* - 1$ other members of his group contribute, player k is better off contributing than not contributing.

The step level (binary) public goods provision game in Table 5.2 has been investigated by Rapoport (1985, 1987), who showed that it has multiple equilibria where exactly m^* of the n group members contribute and another, more prominent, pure strategy equilibrium (if $m^* > 1$), where none of the players contributes. The game has at most two symmetric mixed-strategy equilibria depending on the relationship between the probability of being critical for the provision, which we denote by Q, and the ratio yn / g, where:

$$Q = \left(\frac{n-1}{m^*-1}\right)q^{m^*-1}(1-q)^{n-m^*}$$

(see Rapoport, 1987). If $Q < yn / g$, there exists no symmetric mixed-strategy equilibria. If $Q = yn / g$, there exists a unique equilibrium, where each member of the group contributes his or her entire endowment with probability $q = (m^* - 1)/(n - 1)$, and if $Q > yn / g$, there exists two symmetric mixed strategy equilibria, corresponding to the two solutions of the equation $Q = yn / g$.

There are two special cases of the conflict described by Table 5.2 that warrant discussion. If $m^* = n$, the conflict is a *unanimity dilemma,* as contribution of all the members is necessary for the good to be provided. This game has two pure strategies; in one of them no player contributes and in the other all n players contribute. It also has a mixed strategy equilibrium where each player contributes with probability q^*, the solution of:

$$q^* = \left(\frac{yg}{n}\right)^{\frac{1}{(n-1)}}. \tag{17}$$

Table 5.2 Payoff matrix for the within-group conflict for the provision of step-level public good.

Player k's Decision	Number of others contributing						
	0	1	...	m - 1	m	...	n - 1
Not contribute	y	y	...	y	$y + g/n$	...	$y + g/n$
Contribute	0	0	...	g/n	g/n	...	g/n

Note: Assume $g/n > y$.

If $m^* = 1$, the conflict is known as the *volunteer's dilemma* (Diekmann, 1985, 1986). This game has n multiple equilibria where exactly one of the n players contributes as well as a mixed strategy equilibrium, where each player contributes with probability q^*, the solution of:

$$q^* = 1 - \left(\frac{yg}{n}\right)^{\frac{1}{(n-1)}}. \tag{18}$$

Each of these two special cases eliminates one of the two motives for not contributing, namely fear and greed (see, e.g., Rapoport & Eshed-Levy, 1989). The unanimity dilemma eliminates greed, whereas the volunteer's dilemma eliminates fear.[3] As shown above, the mixed strategy equilibria of these two cases are related: The two equilibrium probabilities of contribution sum up to one.

Example 5   Assume that there are $n = 5$ members in the group, that $m^* = 3$ critical members are required for the good to be provided, and that $y = 5$. Then if $g = 50$, the game has no symmetric mixed strategy equilibria; if $g = 66.666$, there is a single mixed strategy equilibrium with probability $q^* = 0.5$; and if $g = 75$, then the game has two mixed strategy equilibria, namely $q^* = .211$ and $.789$. If we change the threshold by setting $m^* = n = 5$ while still holding $g = 50$, the mixed equilibrium solution (Equation 17) is $q^* = 0.841$. If we set $m^* = 1$ (and $g = 50$), it is $1 - .841 = .159$ (Equation 18).

We show below, as shown earlier in the previous section, that a structural solution to the separate within-group dilemmas about the provision of step level public goods can be achieved by embedding them in a between-group competition for a divisible private good.

Equilibrium Analysis

In the between-group competition, in addition to each group facing its own conflict for the provision of step level public good, the two groups compete for a prize S awarded by some outside agency in an attempt to enhance contribution. Like Rapoport and Bornstein (1987), we assume a deterministic contest rule: The group contributing the most wins the competition and receives the prize. In case of a tie, each group receives a prize T, which is also divisible among its members. Denoting the payoff to group i by G_i, the contest rule has the form:

$$G_i = \begin{array}{l} S, \; if \; m(i) > m(j) \\ T, \; if \; m(i) = m(j) \\ 0, \; if \; m(i) < m(j), \end{array}$$

where T satisfies $0 \leq T \leq S/2$. The two most common cases of tie investigated in the literature assume that either $T = S/2$ or $T = 0$.

We next show that if the prize S is sufficiently large, satisfying the inequality:

$$S - T > n(i)y, \tag{19}$$

and the distribution rule for each group is egalitarian, the between-group competition does not have a pure strategy equilibrium. To show this, assume on the contrary that there exists a pure strategy equilibrium in group i with $m(i)$ contributors. It can be shown that this assumption contradicts Equation 19. First, assume that $m(i) \geq m^* (i)$, where $m(i)$ is the provision threshold for group i. Then the equilibrium payoff to a noncontributor is given by $y + g_i / n(i) + T / n(i)$. If this player deviates, then his payoff is given by $g_i / n(i) + S / n(i)$. In equilibrium, it should be the case that: $y + g_i / n(i) + T / n(i) \geq g_i / n(i) + S / n(i)$. However, this inequality violates Equation 19. Next, consider the case where $m(i) = m^*(i) - 1$. The equilibrium payoff of a non-contributor is given by $y + T / n(i)$, whereas if he deviates, his payoff is given by $g_i / n(i) + S / n(i)$. The two inequalities $S > T$ and $g_i > n(i)y$ imply that: $g_i / n(i) + S / n(i) > y + T / n(i)$.

Finally, consider the case where $m(i) < m^*(i) - 1$. Then, the equilibrium payoff for a contributor is $T / n(i)$. If he deviates, his payoff increases to $S / n(i)$. Because unilateral deviation by player i is always beneficial, this completes the proof that no equilibrium in pure strategies exists if Equation 19 is satisfied.

Egalitarian Distribution Rule   To motivate and exemplify the derivation of the equations for the mixed-strategy equilibria under the egalitarian distribution rule, consider the case where $n(1) = n(2) = n = 5$ and $m^*(1) = m^*(2) = m^* = 3$. Assume that each player in group 1 contributes with probability p and each member of group 2 contributes with probability q. Table 5.3 shows the payoffs to player k of group 1 conditional on the number of other contributors in his group (denoted by $m(1)\backslash k$) and the number of contributors in group 2 (denoted by $m(2)$). For example, if $m(2) = 2$, the payoffs of player k are y, y, $y + T/n$, $y +g/n + S/n$, and $y + g/n + S/n$, if player k does not contribute (D) and the number of contributors in his group is 0, 1, 2, 3, and 4, respectively. If player k does contribute (C), his respective payoffs are 0, T/n, $g/n + S/n$, $g/n + S/n$, and $g/n + S/n$. The probability that m of the $n(2)$ members of the other group contribute is given by the binomial expression:

$$\binom{5}{m} q^m (1-q)^{5-m}, \, m = 0, 1, \ldots, 5$$

Generalizing from this example to arbitrary values of n and m^*, the expected payoff of player k in group i, if he does not contribute, is given by:

$$EV(D) = \sum_{m=0}^{n} \binom{n}{m} q^m (1-q)^{n-m} \left[\binom{n-1}{m} p^m (1-p)^{n-1-m} \left(\frac{T}{n}\right) + \sum_{v=m+1}^{n-1} \binom{n-1}{v} p^v (1-p)^{n-1-v} \left(\frac{S}{n}\right) \right]$$

$$+ \sum_{w=m^*}^{n-1} \binom{n-1}{w} p^v (1-p)^{n-1-w} \left(\frac{g}{n}\right) + y \tag{20}$$

The first expression in the braces is the expected payoff associated with a tie, and the second is the expected payoff associated with winning the contest. The next term is the expected payoff of the within-group conflict, and the following term is the endowment.

The expected payoff of player k in group i, if she does contribute his endowment, is given by:

$$EV(C) = \sum_{m=0}^{n} \binom{n}{m} q^m (1-q)^{n-m} \left[\sum_{v=m}^{n-1} \binom{n-1}{v} p^v (1-p)^{n-1-v} \left(\frac{S}{n}\right) \right] +$$

$$\sum_{m=1}^{n} \binom{n}{m} q^m (1-q)^{n-m} \left[\binom{n-1}{m-1} p^{m-1} (1-p)^{n-m} \left(\frac{T}{n}\right) \right] + \sum_{w=m^*-1}^{n-1} \binom{n-1}{w} p^w (1-p)^{n-1-w} \left(\frac{g}{n}\right) \tag{21}$$

Table 5.3 Payoff matrices for the provision of step-level public good under the egalitarian distribution rule ($n = 5$, $m^* = 3$).

| $m(2) = 0$ | Number of Others Contributing: $m(1)$\k | | | | |
	0	1	2	3	4
D	$y+T/5$	$y+S/5$	$y+S/5$	$y+g/5+S/5$	$y+g/5+S/5$
C	$S/5$	$S/5$	$g/5+S/5$	$g/5+S/5$	$g/5+S/5$
$m(2) = 1$					
D	y	$y+T/5$	$y+S/5$	$y+g/5+S/5$	$y+g/5+S/5$
C	$T/5$	$S/5$	$g/5+S/5$	$g/5+S/5$	$g/5+S/5$
$m(2) = 2$					
D	y	y	$y+T/5$	$y+g/5+S/5$	$y+g/5+S/5$
C	0	$T/5$	$g/5+S/5$	$g/5+S/5$	$g/5+S/5$
$m(2) = 3$					
D	y	Y	y	$y+g/5+T/5$	$y+g/5+S/5$
C	0	0	$g/5+T/5$	$g/5+S/5$	$g/5+S/5$
$m(2) = 4$					
D	y	y	y	$y+g/5$	$y+g/5+T/5$
C	0	0	$g/5$	$g/5+T/5$	$g/5+S/5$
$m(2) = 5$					
D	y	Y	y	$y+g/5$	$y+g/5$
C	0	0	$g/5$	$g/5$	$g/5+T/5$

Again this expression is the sum of three components. The first component is the expected payoff of a win, the second is the expected payoff of a tie, and the third is the expected payoff from the resolution of the within-group conflict.

In a symmetric Nash equilibrium $p = q$. Substituting p for q in Equations 20 and 21, equating the resulting two expressions, and simplifying, we obtain an expression from which the equilibrium mixed strategy can be computed numerically:

$$\sum_{m=0}^{n}\binom{n}{m}p^m(1-p)^{n-m}\left\{\binom{n-1}{m}p^m(1-p)^{n-1-m}\left(\frac{S}{n}-\frac{T}{n}\right)\right\}+$$
$$\sum_{m=1}^{n}\binom{n}{m}p^m(1-p)^{n-m}\left\{\binom{n-1}{m-1}p^{m-1}(1-p)^{n-m}\left(\frac{T}{n}\right)\right\}=y-\binom{n-1}{m^*-1}p^{m^*-1}(1-p)^{n-m^*}\left(\frac{g}{n}\right)$$

$$(22)$$

Example 6 Supposing there are three players in each group ($n = 3$) with the same provision threshold of two ($m^* = 2$). Then Equation 22 is given by:

$$\left[\frac{S-T}{3}\right]\left\{(1-p)^5+6p^2(1-p)^3+3p^4(1-p)\right\}+$$
$$\left(\frac{T}{3}\right)\left\{3p(1-p)^4+6p^3(1-p)^2+p^5\right\}=y-2p(1-p)\left(\frac{g}{3}\right)$$

Let $y = 5$, $g = 24$, $T = 0$, and $S > 15$. Note that because $2p(1-p) < 15/24$ for any value of p, there exists no mixed strategy equilibrium for the within-group conflict. When $S > 15$ (see Equation 19), there exists no pure strategy equilibrium for the between-group competition. However, there exists a symmetric mixed strategy equilibrium where each of the six players in both groups contributes with probability p. Figure 5.1 displays the values of p as a function of S.

Next we examine the effect of group size on the probability of contributing using Equation 22. We notice that as n increases the equilibrium values of p steadily decrease. But for any given n, as S increases the value of p increases. This is shown in Figure 5.2 for $n = 3$, 4, and 5, for values of S between 25 and 80, and for $y = 5$, $g = 24$, and $T = 0$.

Proportional Distribution Rule   To motivate and exemplify the equilibrium equations under the proportional distribution rule, consider the same example as before with $n(1) = n(2) = n = 5$ and $m^*(1) = m^*(2) = m^* = 3$. Assume as before that each member of group 1 contributes with probability p and each member of group 2 contributes with probability q. Table 5.4 shows the payoffs for player k of group 1 in the same format as Table 5.3. Under the proportional distribution rule, player k receives no share of the prize for a win (S) or a tie (T), if she does not contribute. However, if she contributes and her group either wins the prize S or T, her share of this prize is proportional to the number of contributors, m, in her group (rather than the total number of members, n, under the egalitarian distribution rule).

Generalizing from this example to arbitrary values of n and m^*, the expected payoff of player k, if she does not contribute (D), is given by:

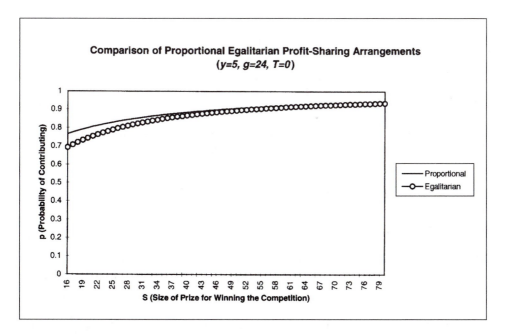

Figure 5.1   Comparison of proportional and egalitarian profit sharing rules

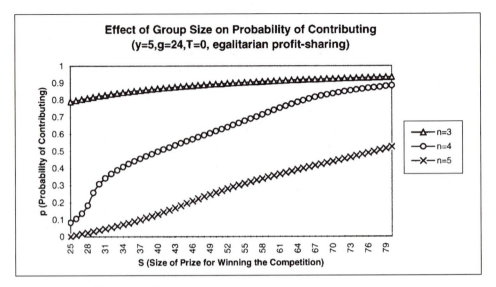

Figure 5.2   Effect of group size on probability of contributing

$$EV(D) = y + \sum_{w=m^*}^{n-1} \binom{n-1}{w} p^w (1-p)^{n-1-w} \left(\frac{g}{n}\right)$$

(23)

and her expected payoff, if she contributes (C), is given by:

$$EV(C) = \sum_{m=0}^{n} \binom{n}{m} q^m (1-q)^{n-m} \left\{ \sum_{v=m}^{n-1} \binom{n-1}{v} p^v (1-p)^{n-1-v} \left(\frac{S}{v+1}\right) \right\} +$$

$$\sum_{m=1}^{n} \binom{n}{m} q^m (1-q)^{n-m} \left\{ \binom{n-1}{m-1} p^m (1-p)^{n-m} \left(\frac{T}{m}\right) \right\} + \sum_{w=m^*-1}^{n-1} \binom{n-1}{w} p^w (1-p)^{n-1-w} \left(\frac{g}{n}\right)$$

(24)

Equating these two expressions after setting $p = q$, we obtain an equation from which the symmetric mixed-strategy equilibrium can be computed:

$$\sum_{m=0}^{n} \binom{n}{m} p^m (1-p)^{n-m} \left\{ \sum_{v=m}^{n-1} \binom{n-1}{v} p^v (1-p)^{n-1-v} \left(\frac{S}{v+1}\right) \right\} +$$

$$\sum_{m=1}^{n} \binom{n}{m} p^m (1-p)^{n-m} \left\{ \binom{n-1}{m-1} p^{m-1} (1-p)^{n-m} \left(\frac{T}{m}\right) \right\} = y - \binom{n-1}{m^*-1} p^{m^*-1} (1-p)^{n-1-m^*} \left(\frac{g}{n}\right)$$

(25)

The difference between the egalitarian and proportional distribution rules can be assessed by comparing the equilibrium probabilities of contribution computed from Equations 21 and 25.

   Example 7   Assume the same parameter values as in Example 6 (namely, $n = 3$ and $m^* = 2$). Then, Equation 25 simplifies in this case to the expression:

Table 5.4   Payoff matrices for the provision of step-level public good under the proportional distribution rule ($n = 5$, $m^* = 3$).

	Number of Others Contributing: $m(1)\backslash k$				
$m(2) = 0$	0	1	2	3	4
D	y	Y	Y	y+g/5	y+g/5
C	S/1	S/2	g/5+S/3	g/5+S/4	g/5+S/5
$m(2) = 1$					
D	y	Y	y	y+g/5	y+g/5
C	T/1	S/2	g/5+S/3	g/5+S/4	g/5+S/5
$m(2) = 2$					
D	y	Y	y	y+g/5	y+g/5
C	0	T/2	g/5+S/3	g/5+S/4	g/5+S/5
$m(2) = 3$					
D	y	Y	y	y+g/5	y+g/5
C	0	0	g/5+T/3	g/5+S/4	g/5+S/5
$m(2) = 4$					
D	y	y	y	y+g/5	y+g/5
C	0	0	g/5	g/5+T/4	g/5+S/5
$m(2) = 5$					
D	y	y	y	y+g/5	y+g/5
C	0	0	g/5	g/5	g/5+T/5

$$(1-p)^5\left(\frac{S}{1}\right)+2p(1-p)^4\left(\frac{S}{2}\right)+p^2(1-p)^3\left(\frac{S}{3}\right)+3p(1-p)^4\left(\frac{T}{1}\right)$$

$$+6p^2(1-p)^3\left(\frac{S}{2}\right)+3p^3(1-p)^2\left(\frac{S}{3}\right)+6p^3(1-p)^2\left(\frac{T}{2}\right)+3p^4(1-p)\left(\frac{S}{3}\right)$$

$$+p^5\left(\frac{T}{3}\right)=y-2p(1-p)\left(\frac{g}{3}\right)$$

Figure 5.1 displays the values of p for the same parameter values as in Example 6, namely, $y = 5$, $g = 24$, $T = 0$, and $S > 15$. A comparison of the mixed strategy solution under the proportional and egalitarian profit sharing arrangement suggests that at lower values of S the probability of contributing under the proportional profit sharing arrangement is much higher. But the difference is reduced as S increases.

CONCLUSION

In this paper we considered collective action problems often found in hierarchical organizations, where within-group social dilemmas are embedded in a between-group competition for a divisible private good. We have proposed three dimensions for classifying such social dilemmas: the payoff structure of the within-group conflict, the rule determining the outcome of the between-group competition, and the profit sharing rule for distributing the prize among members of the winning group. Technically, the two collective action problems considered in this chapter are single-shot, noncooperative, n-person games with complete information. We used Nash equilibrium, the basic solution concept of noncooperative game theory, to characterize the optimal behavior of completely informed, risk-neutral agents engaged in multilevel interactive decision making.

We formally examined the effects of changes in the incentive structure resulting from embedding the separate within-group conflicts in a between-group competition. In particular we compared the two most common rules for profit sharing: egalitarian and proportional distribution. The major benefit of this formal analysis is the quantification of the incentive to cooperate when a within-group conflict is embedded in a between-group competition. From a policy making perspective, introducing competition among groups, each of which is plagued by the problem of free-riding, is yet another structural mechanism for addressing social dilemmas that permeate our society (see Dawes, 1980, for alternative proposals to elicit or at least enhance cooperative behavior).

Although the finding (Sections 2 and 3) that the proportional distribution rule elicits higher levels of cooperation than the egalitarian rule is not particularly surprising, the magnitude of the effect and its dependence on the total number of members in all the groups have not been recognized. We show that as the size of the prize increases, the difference in cooperation levels elicited by the two distribution rules is reduced. The finding illustrated in Example 4, that when the distribution rule is egalitarian and the two competing groups are of unequal size, members of the smaller group should contribute considerably more in equilibrium than members of the larger group has not been anticipated. Experimental evidence is required to find out if, and to what extent, the equilibrium solutions can account for actual interactive behavior.

ENDNOTES

[1] Using a different notation, Hausken (1996b, 1996c, 1996c) has considered a more general model. It can be shown that Equation 5 in this chapter is equivalent to Equation 2.2 in Hausken (1996c), with the only modification being that Hausken allows public goods to be consumed globally, while we allow them to be consumed locally. Moreover, the distribution rule we use in Equation 4 is a special case of the one he uses.

[2] Nitzan (1991) and subsequently Lee (1995) and Hausken (1995a) considered another distribution rule, different from the one in Equation 4, that linearly combines equality and equity. This rule assumes the form:

$$f = \left[(1-a)\left(\frac{X_{ki}}{X_i}\right)\right] + \frac{a}{n(i)} \quad , \quad i = 1, 2, \dots, n \tag{26}$$

where a is a free parameter. If $a = 0$, then player k of group i receives the fraction X_{ki} / X_i of the prize S, if his group wins the competition. If $a = 1$, then he only receives $1 / n(i)$ of the same prize.

Given the probabilistic distribution rule in Equation 1 and the new distribution rule in Equation 26, the expected payoff of player k of group i from contributing X_{ki} to his group is given by:

$$V_{ki} = \left(\frac{X_i}{X}\right)\left\{(y - X_{ki}) + g_i\left(\frac{X_i}{n(i)y}\right) + S\left[(1-a)\left(\frac{X_{ki}}{X_i}\right) + \frac{a}{n(i)}\right] + \left(\frac{X-X_i}{X}\right)\left[(y-X_{ki}) + g_i\left(\frac{X_i}{n(i)y}\right)\right]\right\}$$

$$= S\left(\frac{X_i}{X}\right)\left[(1-a)\left(\frac{X_{ki}}{X_i}\right) + \frac{a}{n(i)}\right] + g_i\left[\frac{X_i}{n(i)y}\right] + (y - X_{ki}). \tag{27}$$

Differentiating V_{ki} with respect to X_{ki}, setting the derivative equal to zero, and noting again the symmetry of the N players, we obtain the following expression:

$$\frac{S(1-a)(X-x_i)}{X^2} + \frac{Sa(X-x_i)}{n(i)\,X^2} = 1 - \frac{g_i}{n(i)\,y}. \tag{28}$$

If we set $1 - a = c$, then it is easy to verify that Equation 28 is equal to Equation 8.

Originally, Nitzan (1991) and subsequently Lee (1995) adopted the restriction that $0 \leq a \leq 1$. However, as noted later by Baik and Lee (1997) and Hausken (1996b, 1996c, 1996d), there seems to be no a priori reason for such restriction. Therefore, the parameter a (and, similarly, the parameter c) may either be negative or exceed one. Relative individual contribution is encouraged if $c > 1$ (or $a < 0$) and discouraged if $c < 0$ (or $a > 1$).

[3] Whereas there have been several experiments designed to assess the differential effects of fear and greed by changing the payoff structure of the public goods game (see, e.g., Rapoport & Eshed-Levy, 1989), we are not aware of any experimental work which assesses the effects of these motives by directly comparing contribution levels in the volunteer's and unanimity dilemmas.

Chapter 6

Sequential Effects in Give-Some and Take-Some Social Dilemmas

Wing Tung Au
David V. Budescu

INTRODUCTION

A recurring theme in the study of social interaction is the conflict between maximizing individual and collective outcomes. This conflict is studied by social psychologists under the social dilemma paradigm (Dawes, 1980; Liebrand, 1984). Ledyard (1995) proposed that social dilemma experiments could be studied within a mechanism design framework that distinguishes between five components: the *environment* of the decision situation, the final *outcomes* of the participants, the *performance criteria* that induce an order over all possible outcomes, the *institutions (or protocols)* that define mechanisms for aggregating information and coordinating actions, and the *models of behavior* of the participants.

In this chapter we focus on the environmental and the institutional components of such dilemmas. The environmental element specifies the details of the situation and includes the description of the context and the scenario of the decision problem, the number of people, their endowments and preferences, and the physical constraints on behavior. Social dilemma environments can be divided into two broad classes—*give-some* or *take-some*—according to what constitutes a cooperative act (Dawes, 1980; Hamburger, Guyer, & Fox, 1975; Komorita & Parks, 1995). This distinction refers to the operational structure

We thank Drs. Xiao-Ping Chen, Amnon Rapoport, Michael Smithson, and Ramzi Suleiman for their careful reading of an earlier version of this chapter and their many useful comments.

of the games being implemented in typical experimental studies, independent of the actual context, or reality, that these games seek to model. However, the take-some and give-some games are usually presented as reasonable models for the study of public good and common pool resource dilemmas, respectively.

The institution element describes the mechanism by which players make their moves and it includes details such as the order of play and the nature and amount of information that is available to each player when he or she decides what action to take. Traditionally, researchers distinguish between simultaneous and sequential games. In this chapter we discuss several variants of the sequential protocol.

To begin, we review the literature on give-some and take-some games and the relations among them. Then, we discuss the simultaneous protocol of play and its generalization to the sequential case within each of the two classes of dilemmas. In this context we also describe two new models that focus on the effects of sequential play and provide some new data collected to test the validity of these models. We conclude with a short discussion of potentially interesting avenues of new research in this area.

Comparison of Give-Some and Take-Some Games

The give-some paradigm is typically described as a model of public good (PG) social dilemmas (Chamberlin, 1974; Marwell & Ames, 1979; see also the Glossary in this book). Real life examples include contributions to public broadcasting services (radio, television) and for the construction of public buildings (e.g., museums), blood donations, volunteering, and voting. The literature refers to take-some games as resource dilemmas (e.g., Budescu, Suleiman, & Rapoport, 1995), or common pool resource (CPR) problems (e.g., Gardner, Ostrom, & Walker, 1990). Examples of CPR include fishing grounds that can be accessed by all fishers in a region, or water resources from which everyone can pump for private consumption.

Research on PG and CPR social dilemmas has, for the most part, proceeded independently. However, there have been some theoretical and empirical efforts to study the two dilemmas jointly. Geotze (1995) proposed a broad theoretical framework that includes the PG, CPR and prisoner's dilemma (PD) games as different types of collective action dilemmas (CAD). The major unifying property of all the games is that their equilibrium outcome(s) are Pareto-deficient. All CADs can be described and equated by some return function that specifies the relation between the cost and benefit of the act of cooperation.

Empirical research has focused on how cooperation is altered if a game with the same payoff structure is framed as either a PG or a CPR. Most comparative analyses of PG and CPR are based on the concept of framing introduced in Kahneman and Tversky's (1979) original formulation of prospect theory (PT). In a PG dilemma, each individual begins with some positive endowment and the decision is whether to keep the endowment (defection) or to contribute it (cooperation) to provide a public good. In terms of PT the person has to decide whether to lose a sure thing (giving up the endowment) or to gamble for an uncertain future profit (getting the public good without contribution). Thus, the PG can be easily encoded as a loss. Conversely, the CPR dilemma is naturally encoded as a *gain*: Each person starts with nothing and faces a choice between requesting a small amount, or gambling for an uncertain bigger harvest (and risking busting the pool). In the language of PT the decision is between an (almost) sure gain (making a small request), and a risky gamble (making a large request, that has a lower probability of being granted).

The distinction between the domains of gains and losses proposed by PT implies that individuals in a loss frame (i.e., the PG dilemma) would behave in a risk seeking manner. Consequently they are more likely to gamble (defect) than to sustain a sure loss (contribute-cooperate). On the other hand, in a gain frame (i.e., a CPR dilemma), individuals should be aversive to taking risks, and should prefer the sure gain (cooperate by making a small request) to the gamble (defect by making a large request). This analysis predicts that cooperation should be more common in a CPR dilemma than in a PG situation if both have a common payoff matrix.

In the first empirical study comparing CPR and PG dilemmas, Brewer and Kramer (1986) used iterated games and manipulated the task structure. In the PG scenario, each person was endowed with 25 points at the beginning of every trial and had to decide how many points to contribute in order to maintain a diminishing common pool with some random replenishment rate. In the CPR scenario, each person could harvest up to 25 points from a common pool with the same replenishment rate. False trial by trial feedback informed participants of the status of the pool, the maximal and minimal individual requests/contributions, and the total group use/contribution. The false feedback was similar in both conditions. For example, if the feedback in the PG condition was that the group contributed 150 out of a possible maximum of 200 points, participants in the CPR condition were told that the group requested a total of 50 points, leaving 150 points in the common pool. As predicted by PT, participants cooperated more in the CPR than in the PG dilemma.

Fleishman (1988) used a similar design to study the interaction between framing and others' cooperation. He found that in the take-some frame (a CPR dilemma), individuals cooperated more when others cooperated, and cooperated less when others were less cooperative. An opposite pattern was found in the give-some frame (a PG dilemma): When others were more cooperative, people contributed less than when others were less cooperative. However, beyond this interesting interaction there was no effect of framing.

Recently Son and Sell (1995) and Sell and Son (1997) examined behavior in both PG and CPR dilemmas in static and dynamic contexts and found only partial support for Brewer and Kramer's (1986) findings. On the first trial people cooperated more in CPR than in PG games. However this initial difference dissipated in the dynamic context or with interactions among group members in the static context.

Parks and Hulbert (1995) suggested that the key difference between the PG and CPR dilemmas is fear. In a PG dilemma individuals fear the loss of contributions when the public good is not provided, whereas in a CPR one receives (at least a small) positive outcome with (near) certainty (Parks, 1994). Parks and Hulbert found that when this fear element was eliminated from the PG dilemma, cooperation rates in the PG and CPR dilemma were not significantly different.

In a slightly different context Van Dijk and Wilke (1995) studied how individuals with asymmetric endowments, asymmetric access to resources, or both, coordinate their behaviors (contribution or request) in one-shot games. Participants in PG dilemmas contributed proportionally to their endowments, whereas those in the CPR games focused on maintaining equality in their final outcomes.

It appears that at least some of the differences between the PG and CPR dilemmas can be attributed to the differential coordination rules they evoke. Salient aspects of the two dilemmas affect these rules in turn. As Van Dijk and Wilke (1995) suggested, the main focus of a CPR game is to achieve equal distribution of the resources, whereas the most salient feature of the PG dilemma is to secure sufficient contributions for the provision of the good. In many cases, this was achieved by a proportionality rule (i.e., participants contributed amounts proportional to their endowments). Indirect support for this observation comes from a study by Budescu, Rapoport and Suleiman (1990), who found that the requests of asymmetric players in CPR games were closer to equality than to proportionality. Rapoport and Suleiman (1993) obtained direct support in a PG game with unequal endowments.

McCusker and Carnevale (1995a) revised Brewer and Kramer's (1986) analysis of social dilemmas. Instead of formulating predictions based on attitudes towards risk, an approach that requires additional considerations of differential weighting of probabilities for gains and losses, they invoked only the concept of *loss aversion* (Tversky & Kahneman, 1991) which is more salient in the PG than in the CPR dilemmas. Their study, which was similar in many respects to that of Brewer and Kramer (1986), also found lower rates of cooperation in PG than in CPR dilemmas.

The attempt to use framing to analyze and model behaviors in PG and CPR games has not gone unchallenged. Rutte, Wilke and Messick (1987a) compared one-shot give-some and take-some games. Unlike Brewer and Kramer (1986), they did not find differences in cooperation rates between the two frames. Rutte et al. reasoned that it is unclear how risky choices should be defined in social dilemma studies. For example, requesting only a small amount in a resource dilemma could be considered as a risk averse or risk seeking choice, depending on whether it is compared with taking a large amount, or not requesting at all. Olson (1997) proposed an alternative PT analysis of social dilemmas in which the effects of framing (gain/loss) depend on the perceived cooperativeness of the others (and, indirectly, on the player's criticality). Two experiments involving 7-person games failed to uncover significant differences between the two games and did not support the PT analysis of social dilemmas either.

Finally, Schwartz-Shea and Simmons (1987) questioned the applicability of PT to social dilemma situations on different grounds. If one focuses on the *collective outcome*, depleting a common resource pool constitutes a group loss whereas providing a public good indicates a group gain. However, if one considers the *individual outcome*, cooperation in a CPR dilemma refers to an individual refusing an immediate gain, whereas in the PG dilemma cooperation is considered as accepting an immediate loss. It is unclear whether participants should consider a public good as a gain or loss. Schwartz-Shea and Simmons contend that the finding of no difference in cooperation rates between CPR and PG dilemmas (e.g., Messick, Allison, & Samuelson, 1988), and the finding that sometimes PG dilemmas induce higher cooperation rates (Allison & Messick, 1985; McDaniel & Sistrunk, 1991), could be explained by the ambiguity in the definition of a gain/loss frame.

SEQUENTIAL PROTOCOLS OF PLAY

Ledyard's (1995) five components (cf. the introductory chapter in this book) can be further divided into three distinct classes:

(a) *Environment, outcomes* and *performance criteria* characterize the incentive structure of the decision being modeled (the game), and jointly, they define a *model of the decision problem*.

(b) *Models of behavior* capture motives, values and expectations that drive the decisions of participants (Decision Makers—DMs). The focus of this section is on the third class that describes

(c) *Institutions* (or *protocols of play*)—the interface between DMs and the decision problem.

These protocols determine the order in which the decisions are made as well as the type and amount of information available to each DM. As such, they affect directly, and sometimes quite drastically, both the ability and the motivation of the players to coordinate their moves.

It is somewhat surprising that the importance of protocols of play was not fully recognized by researchers in this field. Practically all the work reviewed in the previous section was conducted under the *simultaneous protocol.* It is not necessarily that researchers deliberately focus on the simultaneous protocol, but rather it is a default choice that follows from the intuitive and natural structure of this protocol and the ease of its implementation in experiments. Although its label seems to emphasize the temporal relation among players, the key feature of the simultaneous protocol is that all DMs are symmetric (in terms of their information), and make their moves without any information about the decisions of other participants, even if not all decisions are made at the same time. An example is voting: In most democratic societies, polls are open for 12 hours and voters can cast their votes at any time during this designated period. No matter how late in the day one votes, however, he or she has no extra information about anyone else's votes. Thus, for all practical purposes, one can think of all the votes as being cast simultaneously. In contrast, sequential protocols involve special strategic issues because players in early positions can bind themselves, irrevocably, to defection and force subsequent rational players to cooperate.

Most real life dilemmas involve a temporal dimension, and players make their decisions sequentially. The broadest definition of a sequential protocol of play covers all cases where (a) not all moves are made simultaneously, and (b) there is some correlation between one's position and his or her information. In other words, players moving at different points in time are asymmetric in terms of their information. Sometimes the timing of the decision is determined by each DM according to private considerations such as expectations and information about the collective problem. For example, contributors to public radio may decide to contribute on the first day of a drive (to set an example and encourage others to do the same), or to wait until the last day of a drive (to determine if their contribution is necessary to meet the target sum). Similarly, some blood donors routinely time their donations according to holidays when the blood supply is known to run low. In other cases, organizational or societal rules and norms determine the timing and order of moves. For example, group members who are senior, respected, deserving, or needy may be allowed the privilege of an early access to the common pool. Indeed, some experiments have used ingenious methods to implement such norms (e.g., Hoffman, McCabe, Schachat, & Smith, 1994; Samuelson & Allison 1994; Suleiman, Rapoport, & Budescu, 1996).

However, in most experiments the order of moves is predetermined exogenously by the experimenters. We distinguish here between three variants of sequential play. In the *(full) sequential protocol* players (a) know their position in the sequence, and (b) have complete information about the decisions made by the previous players (e.g., see Rapoport, Budescu, & Suleiman, 1993, for CPR; and Experiment 1 in Erev & Rapoport, 1990, for PG). In the *positional protocol* players (a) know their position in the sequence, but (b) lack information about the decisions made by the previous players (e.g., see Budescu, Suleiman, et al., 1995, for CPR; and Rapoport, 1997, for PG). And in the *cumulative protocol* players (a) do not know their position in the sequence, but (b) have complete information about the decisions made by the previous players (e.g., see Budescu, Au, & Chen, 1997, for CPR; and Experiment 2 in Erev & Rapoport, 1990, for PG). Although all the various sequential protocols were used with take-some and give-some games, to the best of our knowledge there are no experiments in which the effects of order were examined in both frames simultaneously. In the next sections we review the literature on sequential effects in each type of game.

Sequential Effects in Give-Some Games (Step Level PG)

Erev and Rapoport (1990) and Rapoport and Erev (1994) report four step level PG (give-some) experiments involving groups of n players where the PG is provided if at least k ($k < n$) players cooperate. It is easy to see that in the sequential protocol the first $(n - k)$ DMs should defect and force the last k players to cooperate. Results indicate that the level of cooperation (i.e., the proportion of participants who contribute) in the sequential protocol was not higher than that in the simultaneous case. However, the provision of the PG in the sequential protocol was more efficient (it was provided in a larger proportion of groups). Furthermore, Rapoport (1997) demonstrated sequential effects even in the positional protocol. Somewhat surprisingly, the cumulative protocol (especially the version in which participants were only informed of the number of previous defectors) induced the most efficient patterns of contributions.

Chen, Au, and Komorita (1996) also studied the sequential protocol in PG, and manipulated the (target) player's criticality and uncertainty. A DM is said to be critical if his or her contribution is necessary for the provision of the PG. Uncertainty is a simple decreasing function of the DM's position in the sequence (the earlier one's position, the higher his or her uncertainty about the others' moves, simply because there are more of them). Chen et al. (1996) found that critical players contributed considerably more in low uncertainty situations, especially in the extreme case where one's cooperation is sufficient for (i.e., can guarantee) the provision of the PG. This is, obviously, consistent with the equilibrium solution described by Erev and Rapoport (1990). However, in cases of high uncertainty critical players did not contribute more than noncritical ones. They attributed this result to the effects of uncertainty on the players' perceived (self-reported) criticality (see also, Rapoport & Eshed-Levy, 1989).

Au, Chen, and Komorita (1998) proposed a probabilistic model for contributions to step level public goods under the sequential protocol. Extending Erev and Rapoport's (1990) game theoretical model, the probabilistic criticality model postulates that an individual's probability of contribution is a function of his or her perceived criticality. Empirically work has generally established that the probability of contribution increases with criticality (Kerr, 1989, 1992; Offerman, Sonnemans, & Schram, 1996; Rapoport, 1987). Let $p*$ denote the probability of contribution and π the probability of being critical for a given player, s. As a first approximation, Au et al. assume that $p*$ is a linear function of π:

$$p* = a + b\pi \tag{1}$$

where a and b are real valued parameters. The focal player's beliefs concerning other (subsequent) players' contribution decisions, $p*$, and probability of being critical, π, can then be derived through backward induction.

The parameter b can be conceptualized as a criticality impact parameter. As b increases, the weight of π increases; thus, a large value of b indicates that contribution behavior is heavily influenced by criticality. The parameter a can be interpreted as the base rate of contribution—the probability of contribution independent of the criticality of s. In the limiting case when the base rate contribution is zero ($a = 0$), and players determine their contribution solely by criticality ($b = 1$), the model reduces to Erev and Rapoport's

(1990) game theoretical model. The probabilistic model predicts quite well contribution behaviors not captured by the game theoretical model (including the data from Chen et al.'s, 1996 study), and it can be easily extended to situations with variable provision point or group size.

Au (1997) tested the model in the fixed and variable provision point situations. Both conditions involved nominal groups of size $n = 5$. In the fixed provision case, the PG was provided if at least $k = 3$ individuals contributed; in the variable provision point condition, the provision threshold was chosen randomly (and with equal probability) among three possible values ($k = 2$, 3, or 4). Results showed that provision point variability had only negligible effects on the overall individual contribution rates. However, when the provision point was fixed, the PG was provided much more often (i.e., more efficiently), than in the variable provision point case. Model fitting using nonlinear least square regressions showed that individual contribution rates were adequately described by the probabilistic criticality model in both the fixed and variable provision point situations: the (pseudo) R^2s were .81 and .86, respectively. A subsequent experiment examining interacting groups with a different task scenario replicated these results.

The probabilistic criticality model can also be extended to model sequential PG dilemmas with a variable group size. Au (in preparation) examined a game with a fixed provision point of three. Group size varied randomly between four and six persons with equal probability. Model fitting of individual contribution rates resulted in a (pseudo) R^2 of .81, which provided further support for the probabilistic criticality model. More interestingly, simulation analyses of PG provision rates found that the PG was provided 77% of the time in the sequential protocol, which was substantially higher than the 40% provision rate in the simultaneous protocol.

Sequential Effects in Take-Some Games (CPR)

Unlike the work on PG that focused on binary decisions (to contribute one's endowment, or not), this line of work focused on the continuous case (how many units do DMs harvest from a common pool of size S?). The first study to use the sequential protocol in this context was conducted by Rutte, Wilke, and Messick (1987b). They predicted that people would respond differently to resource shortages or surpluses, depending on the attribution they made for the sources of these shortages or surpluses. Groups of six participants played one-shot resource dilemma games and were led to believe that they would harvest in a randomly assigned sequential order. In actuality, they were all assigned to the fifth (second to last) position. Rutte et al. found that people harvested more when the resource was abundant than when it was scarce. Moreover, this difference was larger when abundance or scarcity was attributed to environmental factors (i.e., initial resource size), than when it was attributed to social factors (i.e., over- or under-harvesting by others in the group). They reasoned that people used a *social decision heuristic* to guide their harvest decisions. When participants could not make inferences about other group members' harvesting behaviors, they used the *equal share* rule to harvest the remaining resources. When participants inferred that others were overharvesting (in scarce resource) or underharvesting (in abundant resource), participants adopted similar rules (The reasoning being that group members considered such behavior fair and acceptable).

Rapoport et al. (1993) showed that two distinct models (the game theoretical equilibrium, and a modified equal share heuristic) predict a *position* effect, that is, an inverse relationship between one's position in the sequence and one's request. In other words, both models predict that early movers have an advantage over those placed in late positions, and should request more. This powerful intuition that order should induce asymmetry in requests is apparent in several studies in which participants were instructed to behave *as if they were (first or last) movers in larger (hypothetical) groups*. Allison, McQueen, and Schaerfl (1992), and Samuelson and Allison (1994) used this procedure to study various factors (group size, divisibility of the pool, assignment rules, etc.) that cause first movers to deviate from the social norm of equal requests from the resource; Messick and Allison (1987) used this setup to test the willingness of the last player to accept unfair allocations.

The various versions of the sequential protocol were explored and compared in a series of experiments using groups of size $n = 2$, 3, and, typically, 5 (see Budescu, Rapoport & Suleimen, 1995; Budescu, Suleiman, et al., 1995; Budescu et al., 1997; Rapoport, 1997; Rapoport et al., 1993; Suleiman et al., 1996; and a recent summary by Suleiman & Budescu, 1999).[1] As in the PG case, these studies found no significant differences between the overall levels of cooperation (i.e., the mean individual or group requests from the common pool) between the various protocols of play. The experimental evidence clearly supports the predicted position effect—in 90% of the relevant comparisons players in the advantageous positions requested, on the average, more than their counterparts assigned to a less favorable position (similar results were found for individual participants as well). Moreover, the amount that was requested in any given position was shown to vary according to the requests of the previous players, in a fashion consistent with the predictions of the rational model (subgame perfect equilibrium) (Budescu, Rapoport, et al. 1995). However, this asymmetric distribution of requests across players did not necessarily induce more efficient use of the resource. This result differs from the pattern observed in the PG games reviewed earlier. We think this difference can be attributed to the difference in the framing of the cooperation/defection mechanism. Whereas all the PG games reviewed called for simple binary decisions (contribute or not), the CPR games involved continuous decisions (request an amount between 0 and S) which are harder to coordinate.

Budescu, Suleiman, et al. (1995) and Budescu et al. (1997) found a position effect in the positional protocol as well. Although the effect is weaker in this case, it is remarkable that it appears at all in the absence of any relevant information that should effect rational action. It is, clearly, a reflection of strong social norms about the entitlements and implied privileges of "first comers (or movers)." This interpretation is supported by the *expectations* of the DMs regarding the behavior of their partners—in all cases participants think that the first X movers will request, jointly, more than the last X players ($X = 1, \ldots, n - 1$). Recently, Budescu et al. (1997) employed a design with controlled (false) feedback to compare the intensity of the positional effects under three distinct protocols. Interestingly, and consistent with the PG results, the positional effect was stronger in the cumulative protocol than in the positional protocol. In fact, in most cases, the cumulative results were indistinguishable from the (full) sequential case.

Returning to the (full) sequential protocol, note that although the position effect is robust and reliable, it falls considerably short of the predictions of the rational model. This model predicts that the player in the first position should request almost everything, say $S - (n - 1)\varepsilon$ (where ε is a small positive quantity), and the remaining DMs should get ε apiece. The underlying logic is that any rational DM would prefer ε to 0. Thus the first mover, who understands this, should request as much as possible subject to the constraint that all subsequent players can achieve a positive (nonzero) outcome. The fact that the first mover does not take full advantage of his or her strategic advantage is consistent with the results obtained in ultimatum games[2] (e.g., Camerer & Thaler, 1995; Güth, Schmittberger, & Schwartze, 1982). In fact, if $n = 2$ the sequential CPR is strategically equivalent to the ultimatum game (Larrick & Blount, 1997; Suleiman & Budescu, 1999).[3]

Budescu and Au (in preparation) developed a descriptive model for behavior in sequential CPR dilemmas. The model involves a single free parameter that captures the sequential effect. Let S be the size of a CPR to be shared by n players, and let r_j be the request of the player in the jth position. Assume that the first $(j-1)$ movers $(1 \leq j \leq n-1)$ requested, jointly, Σr_j. The model assumes that the jth player considers himself or herself to be the first mover in a reduced CPR game in which $n_j = (n-j+1)$ players share a shrunken pool of size $S_j = S - \Sigma r_j$. The model predicts that the request of the target player in the full sequential protocol, r^*_{js}, where the second subscript s denotes the sequential protocol, is:

$$r^*_{js} = S_j \frac{(n-j+1)^c}{\Sigma j^c} \tag{2}$$

and the sum goes from 1 to nj. In particular, for the first mover in the reduced dilemma (i.e., $j = 1$), this reduces to:

$$\frac{r^*_{is}}{S_j} = \frac{n^c}{\Sigma j^c} \tag{3}$$

The exponent, c, is a *position parameter* that captures the direction and intensity of the effect of the player's position on his or her request. Note that if $c = 0$, all players are expected to behave identically, regardless of their position (i.e., no position effect, just as in the symmetric and simultaneous cases). At the other extreme, as $c \rightarrow \infty$ the prediction approaches the game theoretical solution of the first mover taking (almost) everything. A meaningful anchor point is $c = 1$, where the requests are assumed to decrease as a linear function of one's position. Negative values of c, indicate a *reverse position effect* where the early movers take less than the late players. One attractive feature of this model is that c can be estimated from the DMs' requests under the positional protocol. A slight modification of the model for the sequential protocol yields the model for the request of the target player in the positional protocol, r^*_{jp}, where the second subscript p denotes the positional protocol, is:

$$r^*_{js} = S \frac{(n-j+1)^c}{\Sigma j^c} \tag{4}$$

and the sum runs from 1 to n. Note that, consistent with the assumptions of the positional protocol, this model depends only on the pool size (S), the group size (n), and the differential positioning of the players (j), but does not involve any information regarding the behavior of the other players.

Budescu & Au (in preparation) ran a study in which 62 participants stated their requests in 63 distinct CPR games to test the model. The first 15 games were played in the positional protocol and involved a variety of positions (ranging from being the first mover in a group of size $n = 3$ to the next to last mover in a group of size $n = 7$). The best fitting value of c was estimated separately for each participant by a nonlinear least square procedure. Eighteen participants (29%) had c values smaller than .01 (no position effect); 5 participants (8%) had parameters greater than .99 (more extreme than linear); and 39 participants (63%) were best fitted by parameters in the range $.01 < c < .99$. This indicates that most participants think that early movers are entitled to more and the rate of decrease is less than linear. The fit achieved was excellent with a median (pseudo) R^2 of .96. The mean c estimate for the 44 participants with $c > .01$ was .52. This value, close to .50, is meaningful and, in our opinion, it captures the implicit norm of positional privilege.

Interestingly, in the Budescu et al. (1997) study, players in the cumulative protocol were asked to guess the position to which they were assigned based on information about the joint requests of the previous (unknown number of) players in the sequence. Participants identified correctly their positions in 87% of the cases when the others' requests were generated by a model in which $c = 0.5$. The rate of correct guesses was considerably lower for $c = 1$ and 1.5.

In the next stage of the study the same participants played 48 games under the sequential protocol. The 48 games were embedded in a 4-way design that manipulated the number of previous and subsequent players in the group and the amount requested and left in the pool. Specifically, the number of previous players in the group was 1, 2, or 3; the number of subsequent movers was 1, 2, 3, or 4; the amount requested by the previous movers was 200 or 400; and the amount left in the pool was 200 or 400. Thus, the dilemmas facing the participants involved pools of size 400, 600, and 800 and groups ranging in size from 2 to 7. Using the previously estimated c values we predicted participants' requests in the sequential protocol. The fit was quite impressive: the median (pseudo) R^2 was .96, and the median Absolute Relative Error of Prediction (AREP) was 23%. The median relative error of prediction (REP) was –6%, indicating that the model slightly overpredicted the actual requests.

FINAL REMARKS

This chapter reviews a small domain of social dilemma research, namely, experimental studies of give-some and take-some games (Hamburger et al., 1975) involving small groups. In particular, we focus on studies that were designed to model behavior in public good and common pool resource dilemmas. In the first section we surveyed the literature comparing PG and CPR games directly. The bulk of this work is motivated by the distinction between gains and losses suggested by prospect theory (Kahneman & Tversky, 1979). CPR, being in a gain frame, facilitates *cooperation as a risk seeking behavior*. However, the PG situation, which can be considered as in a loss frame, facilitates *defection as a risk seeking behavior*. Thus, the gain/loss frame analysis predicts higher rates of cooperation in the CPR than PG games.

As in many other cases, the empirical results are mixed and provide only very limited support to this prediction. More important, the lucid analysis of Schwartz-Shea and Simmons (1987) points out, quite convincingly, that PT is a theory of *individual* choice under risk and any attempt to generalize and apply it to *social* decisions must address an important and difficult problem: Should the gain and loss frames be defined from the individual or the group perspective? Researchers in this field are not of one mind and, evidently, neither are the participants. We think this key criticism invalidates the conclusions of most studies that adopted, quite arbitrarily, one (typically the individual) of the two perspectives. At the same time, we share with the researchers in this field the belief that *framing* is a powerful and useful theoretical concept that can play an important role in this analysis. The key theoretical challenge seems to be the development of a *theory of social prospects* that embeds insights from the theory of individual choices within the social and strategic framework of social dilemmas.

A secondary, methodological, challenge is to design better and more natural ways of contrasting the two types of dilemmas. One experimental set up that comes to mind can be labeled *give-some AND take-some*. Consider a group of $2n$ players that are randomly divided into two equal subgroups. Participants in one group are endowed with e units apiece and offered the possibility to contribute to a common pool (just as in the regular give-some games), and participants in the second group can request various amounts from the common pool created by the givers (mimicking the regular take-some game). For example, one can think of the first group as donors to a community blood bank, whereas the second group represents patients who use this blood bank in time of medical needs. The most attractive feature of this game is the fact that it emphasizes the close relationship between the two dilemmas.

Most research on PG and CPR games was devoted to a simultaneous protocol of play involving symmetric DMs. In recent years, there has been an increased interest in the study of sequential protocols and their comparison with the simultaneous one. It is perhaps best to conceptualize the simultaneous game as a special case of the general sequential game that recognizes asymmetries in time and information. Evidently, a DM who makes an early decision, while lacking information about the others' choices, gains a temporal advantage. By binding himself or herself to an irrevocable action he or she can affect the decisions of the subsequent players in a direction that favors his or her interests. Conversely, a DM who decides late has more information, and can tailor his or her moves conditional upon the previous decisions, so as to maximize his or her outcomes subject to less uncertainty.

Our review of PG and CPR games under the various forms of the sequential protocol documents several robust empirical regularities. In give-some games the sequential protocol usually yields higher rates of provision rates than the simultaneous protocol. This finding, first reported in Erev and Rapoport's (1990) pioneering study, was recently replicated in a study of variable group size (Au, in preparation). In contrast, there is no strong evidence that the sequential protocol can enhance resource use/maintenance in take-some (CPR) games, as compared with a simultaneous protocol.

Any attempt to provide a theoretical explanation for this asymmetry between the two games must be qualified by the fact that all studies of sequential contributions to PGs examined discrete (binary) contributions to step level PGs, whereas all sequential studies of CPR focused on continuous requests. Thus, the higher efficiency achieved in the sequential give-some (PG) games may be due to this structural constraint that, undoubtedly, facilitates coordination, rather than to a framing effect. Some evidence supporting the conjecture that discrete and continuous decisions may induce differential levels of coordination can be found in the CPR literature. Allison et al. (1992) showed that, under the simultaneous protocol, compartmentalization of continuous resource units results in more efficient use of the resource. A definitive answer regarding the relative importance of

(a) the decision mechanism (discrete vs. continuous decisions),
(b) the protocol of play (simultaneous vs. sequential), and
(c) the framing of the decision (give-some vs. take-some), is another important challenge for students of behavioral dynamics in social dilemmas.

However, this requires a more sophisticated theoretical analysis of the various paradigms and protocols, as well as more complex experimental designs to unconfound the various effects.

A robust finding in the research of the sequential protocol in CPR games is the position effect. That is, the tendency of DMs in earlier positions to request more than the DMs in late positions. Most interesting of all is the finding of the position effect in the positional protocol, which is strategically equivalent to a simultaneous protocol. The chronological order of moves of the positional protocol conveys no useful strategic information and, therefore, should not affect behavior. Yet, the effect is replicated with groups of various sizes, and with fixed and random resources. We proposed a relatively simple, descriptive model that can account quite well for individual requests in the positional and the sequential protocols of play. One nice feature of the model is that it links elegantly, through one common parameter, c, between the requests in these two cases. Still lacking is a theoretical model to explain the sources—cognitive cues, beliefs, or social norms—underlying the position effect and its intensity, particularly in the positional protocol (Rapoport, 1997).

The c parameter, which can assume any real values, may be indicative of *an implicit norm of positional advantage* due to temporal priority. As c increases, a person takes increasing advantage of his or her early position and requests more. In the extreme case where $c \to \infty$, the first DM leaves (almost) nothing to the remaining players, consistent with the game theoretical equilibrium solution. In the special case where $c = 0$, a person disregards the temporal information and requests an equally divided share from the resource. At the opposite extreme where $c \to -\infty$, a reverse position effect occurs and the DM takes nothing and leaves all to the remaining players.

The c parameter can thus be considered as another index of social orientation specific to the *sequential* protocol. A positive c value may reflect an individualistic/competitive social orientation; a zero value suggests an egalitarian characteristic; and a negative c value is indicative of an altruistic disposition. Interestingly, our data showed that this alternative index of social orientation did not correlate with conventional measures of social orientation construct (in this case Liebrand's, 1984, Ring test). The Ring test is based on a series of forced choices among pairs of resource allocations in a *simultaneous* protocol context. These null results echo the weak effects of social orientation (as measured by the Ring test) on sequential games found in Budescu et al. (1997). It is possible that the DM's social orientation is affected by, or interacts with, the sequential framing of the game. And, perhaps, the c parameter is a better measure of *social orientation in sequential protocols* of play than the measures defined in the *simultaneous* context like the Ring test or decomposed games. Future research is called for to validate this conjecture and to examine the role and conceptualization of social orientation in the sequential protocol.

While research into the sequential protocol may still be in its infancy, and we do not fully understand behavior in the various protocols described above, our attention should also be directed towards other protocols of play. In all the sequential protocols that have been studied so far, it is advantageous to be in an earlier position (i.e., it is, in some sense, better to be in position p rather than in position $p + 1$). An intriguing question is whether there are variations of the sequential protocol that induce a reverse position effect, such that the information priority in position $p + 1$ gives an advantage over the temporal priority in position p. A possibility, that is perhaps also more ecologically valid than the sequential protocols that have been studied, is to have a random CPR (whose size is anywhere between a and b) with uncertainty decreasing over time, so that the range of the resource decreases from time t to $(t + 1)$: $[b(t) - a(t)] > [b(t + 1) - a(t + 1)]$.

Another type of sequential protocol that may also worth investigating is a *self-determined sequential* protocol. Recall that in the laboratory research on sequential protocols players are usually assigned to positions by an exogenous mechanism (for exceptions see Hoffman et al., 1994; Suleiman et al., 1996). This fact limits the ecological validity of these studies, because in many real life social situations the individual DMs determine by themselves *when* to decide and act. For example, people choose when to make a pledge to the public broadcasting services in the PG situation, and fishers decide when to hunt for whales in a CPR dilemma. In sociology similar ideas have been examined theoretically (e.g., Granovetter, 1978; Oliver & Marwell, 1988; Oliver, Marwell, & Teixeira, 1985) and by computer simulations (e.g., Macy, 1990, 1991a, 1991b). For both theoretical interests and real life applications, it is imperative to study systematically this self-determined sequential protocol.

ENDNOTES

[1] Another important variable in all these studies was the level of uncertainty regarding the size of the common pool. We do not discuss these results in this chapter (see Suleiman & Budescu, 1999, for a summary).

[2] An ultimatum offer is a *take it or leave it* proposition. A typical ultimatum game involves two parties A and B bargaining over a resouce of size x. Party A proposes an allocation—$x - b$ for himself or herself, and b to Party B. If Party B accepts this proposal, it is implemented; if Party B rejects the offer, both get nothing.

[3] To explain this nonrational behavior researchers invoke psychological concepts such as *fairness* (e.g., Kahneman, Knetsch, & Thaler, 1986), *expectations* (e.g., Suleiman, 1996) and *manners* (e.g., Camerer & Thaler, 1995).

Part Two

Control Systems and Structural Solutions

Chapter 7

Anonymity and Social Control in Social Dilemmas

Norbert L. Kerr

INTRODUCTION

You have all probably had the experience of reading something that sticks in your mind—which you keep coming back to as something of real significance. I had that experience when I read the following excerpt of a classic social-dilemma experiment, published over 20 years ago in the January, 1977, issue of *Journal of Personality and Social Personality* by Robyn Dawes, Jeanne McTavish, and Harriet Shaklee:

> . . . One of the most significant aspects of this study, however, did not show up in the data analysis. It is the extreme seriousness with which the subjects take the problems. Comments such as, "if you defect on the rest of us, you're going to have to live with it the rest of your life," were not at all uncommon. Nor was it unusual for people to wish to leave the experimental building by the back door, to claim that they did not wish to see the "sons of bitches" who doublecrossed them, to become extremely angry at other participants, or to become tearful. . . .
>
> The affect level also mitigates against examining choice visibility. In pretesting, we did run one group in which choices were made public. The three defectors were the target of a great deal of hostility ("You have no idea how much you alienate me!" one

The author would like to thank Mayu Ono and Toshihiko Matsuka for their assistance in data collection.

cooperator shouted before storming out of the room); they remained after the experiment until all the cooperators were presumably long gone. . . (Dawes et al., 1977, p. 7)

For me, this was one of those passages that says, something psychologically important is at work here. And that something is, I suspect, that group members often care about one another's behavior in social dilemma situations. They care most particularly, perhaps, when the group in question is a significant, long-term one (e.g., a work group, a family) and when they have had an opportunity to discuss the dilemma with one another. Members of such groups especially have expectations about one another's behavior in social dilemma contexts and are willing to punish one another if those expectations are violated. That is, there are prescriptive or injunctive (Cialdini, Kallgren, & Reno, 1991) social norms surrounding choice in a social dilemma (cf. Kerr, 1995a). This, in turn, suggests that what Dawes et al. (1977) called the *visibility* (or anonymity) of choice should also affect cooperative choice behavior in a social dilemma. If choices are completely anonymous, it is impossible for group members to determine who has violated norms and who should be socially sanctioned. When normative forces encouraging cooperation are thus neutralized, we can expect the incentive structure inherent in all social dilemmas to result in relatively high rates of defection. Indeed, every review of social dilemma research seems to confirm the latter prediction. Here is a sampling of these reviews:

"Three studies. . .all found higher rates of cooperation when choice was public" (Orbell & Dawes, 1981, p. 59).
". . .studies comparing private with public choice conditions in the NPD generally obtain higher rates of cooperation when choices are disclosed publicly" (Messick & Brewer, 1983, p. 26).
". . .the results of several studies [show that]. . .a higher level of cooperation was obtained when individual choices were disclosed publicly than when they were made anonymously" (Komorita & Parks, 1994, p. 47).
". . .the consistent finding is that public, identifiable choice in social dilemmas is more likely to be cooperative than private, anonymous choice. . ." (Kerr, 1995a, pp. 42–43).

To my eye, these reviews appear to become increasingly definite about the effect of the anonymity of choice. As we shall see, though, this may have less to do with an expanding and ever more conclusive database than with the tendency of later reviewers (including, I am embarrassed to admit, the last one cited above) to rely too strongly on early results and reviews.

Actually, the real focus of Dawes et al.'s (1977) classic study was not the effect of the visibility or anonymity of choice. The authors had concluded from a pilot study that the intense affect and interpersonal conflict that seemed to follow nonanonymous, public choice precluded direct manipulation of the anonymity of choice. The real focus of Dawes et al. was on the effects of group discussion on cooperative choice. They found that a period of group discussion about the dilemma substantially increased cooperation above the levels obtained in no discussion or task unrelated discussion control conditions. Since then, many investigators, with Dawes, Orbell, Van de Kragt, and their colleagues foremost among them (see, for example, Orbell, Dawes, & Van de Kragt, 1988; Orbell, Van de Kragt, & Dawes, 1991), have replicated and extended this finding. In the last few years, I have also done some research on this question, focusing primarily upon the psychological explanation for such group discussion effects. My preferred explanation is a normative one—that group members commit themselves and promise to act cooperatively during group discussion (also see Orbell et al., 1988, and Bouas & Komorita, 1996). Thereafter, a norm of commitment (Cialdini, 1984; Tedeschi, Lindskold, Horai, & Gahagan, 1969; Tedeschi, Powell, Lindskold, & Gahagan, 1969) enforces those promises. In a pair of papers (Kerr & Kaufman-Gilliland, 1994; Kerr, Garst, Lewandowski, & Harris, 1997), we have found that the effect of group discussion was not moderated by whether group members' choices were or were not anonymous. We have interpreted this pattern of results as indicating that the commitment norm is well internalized—that is, that the salient social sanctions for breaking a commitment are personal rather than social.

There was only one thing that has continued to nag me about the results of our recent studies—anonymity also had no effect on cooperation when there was no discussion (and hence, no promising). If, as I have argued elsewhere (Kerr, 1995a), there are norms prescribing cooperation in social dilemmas (that is, norms above and beyond the commitment norm engaged by promising during group discussion) and if group members really do care about the social consequences of violating these norms, why did we not find higher cooperation rates among those whose choices would be made public than those whose choices were anonymous, which appears to be the consistent finding in prior research? These puzzling results have led me to reexamine the effect of anonymity of choice in social dilemmas and to conduct some new research. In this chapter I first take another look at the empirical literature. Then I describe the results of two new studies that were stimulated by my reconsideration of the literature.

The Anonymity Literature Reconsidered

My search of the social dilemma literature came up with eight studies that have manipulated the anonymity of choice. In Table 7.1 I list these studies, along with information about the studies' methodologies and the key findings for the anonymity treatment. Examination of the *Results* column reveals that in only three of eight studies was any *negative* effect (reducing cooperation) for anonymity obtained (viz. in Bixenstein, Levitt, & Wilson 1966; Fox & Guyer, 1978; and Jorgenson & Papciak, 1981). It is noteworthy that these are among the earliest studies as well. In the early eighties, when the first social dilemma reviews appeared (e.g., Dawes, 1980; Messick & Brewer, 1983), it might have been sensible to conclude that most (3 or 4) of the then extant studies had found evidence that cooperation rates were lower with anonymous choice. However, none of the most recent studies have found that anonymity decreases cooperation, and one (viz. Flache & Liebrand, 1997) has even found some evidence for the opposite effect. This equivocal empirical record led us to reexamine the older studies more closely.

One point of interest is that the early anonymity effects only occurred under certain experimental conditions. In Bixenstein et al. (1966), no overall anonymity main effect was obtained. A simple effect of anonymity was obtained during the final two blocks and among those groups that *did* have group discussion. However, there was no effect during either early or later trials that were *not* preceded by group discussion. In Jorgenson and Papciak (1981), likewise, there was no overall anonymity effect. There was one significant anonymity simple effect, but in this study it occurred only when there was neither any trial by trial feedback nor any group discussion (ostensibly the opposite necessary conditions to those suggested by Bixenstein et al., 1966). In only one study (viz. Fox & Guyer, 1978) was there an overall anonymity main effect on cooperation.

Table 7.1   Summary of prior studies examining anonymity in social dilemmas.

Study	Task details	Results
Jerdee & Rosen (1974; *JPSP*)	5-person groups in NPD {where C=bid for contracts including all costs (e.g., pollution control) and D=cost-cutting bid (take quick profits)} 'Visibility' treatment: low=personal feedback only; high=every person's profits put up on blackboard	No effect of visibility
Bixenstein, Levitt, & Wilson (1966, *JCR*)	6-person iterated NPD 'Knowledge' treatment: K-all Ss' choices shown after every trial; NK-no such feedback. Also varied group discussion w/in Ss; 2 blocks w/out discussion; half discussed; then 2 more blocks	No Knowledge effect for groups w/out discussion; did get an effect (during last 2 blocks) for groups with discussion
Fox & Guyer (1978; *JCR*)	4-person NPD Anonymity treatment: Public-choice=initial meeting of group members where they give their names+visible to one another in mirrors during the experiment+trial-by-trial feedback; Anonymous=none of these treatments	More cooperation in the Public-choice condition (46.5%) than the Anonymous condition (34.5%), p<.05
Jorgenson & Papciak (1981, *JESP*)	4-person groups at resource/commons dilemma 2x2x2 design with communication x trial-by-trial feedback x identifiability. Identifiability: high=group members sat in sight of one another+personal (by name) choice feedback to group after each trial; low=visual isolation+no personal feedback to group	No effect of identifiability *except* when there was no communication and no feedback; under these conditions, commons preserved longer under high than low identifiability (p<.001)
Laury, Walker, & Williams (1995, *J. of Economic Behavior & Organization*)	4-person iterated give-some/public good game Anonymity treatment: control/low=Ss log in with name, play game in same room, receive payoff individually from E at the end of the session; hi=Ss randomly choose IDs, run in different locations, elaborate payoff procedure guaranteeing that neither E or other Ss know their choices	No effect of anonymity
Kerr & Kaufman-Gilliland (1994; *JPSP*)	5-person step-level public good game. Anonymity treatment: high=choices never shared with other Ss;Low=choices would be shared at the end of the experiment. Also varied group discussion.	No effects of anonymity, with or without discussion.
Kerr, Garst, Lewandowski, & Harris (1997, *PSPB*)	5-person step-level public good game. Anonymity treatment: high=choices never shared with other Ss;Low=choices would be shared at the end of the experiment. With group discussion.	No effect of S anonymity

Continued

Study	Task details	Results
Flache & Liebrand (1997)	5-person iterated AESD (approval embedded social dilemma) game: 5-person NPD & simultaneously playing 2-person NPD between all members of the 5-person group to simulate the giving or withholding of approval; veridical feedback of cooperative choices on the main game and approval choices. Anonymity treatment: C-A-A condition (non-anonymous)=before each trial, Ss given both cooperative choice on main game and approval choices on side, approval game for every other player, both for the last trial and accumulated across all previous trials; C-A (anonymous) condition=Ss given others choices on main game but not on the approval game, receiving only the approval data summed over other group members (not identified by members). No discussion	Got a marginal (p<.10) main effect for ano nymity, such that Ss were *more* coopera tive on the main game when their mutual ap proval decisions were anonymous.

Note: C=cooperative choice, D=defecting choice.

Moreover, the anonymity treatment was (or may well have been) confounded in 2 of the 3 studies which found any negative anonymity effect. In the Bixenstein et al. (1966) study, the manipulation of *knowledge* (i.e., anonymity) involved trial by trial feedback and occurred *before* group discussion. Thus, their NK (no knowledge, i.e., anonymous) participants knew before any group discussion that no group members' choices would ever be revealed, whereas their K (knowledge, i.e., nonanonymous) participants knew that all group members' choices would be known to all. It is quite possible that learning this *before* group discussion altered the content of the group discussion (e.g., participants may have been much more willing to make and extract promises to cooperate in the K groups). Recall that it was *only* in groups that had been allowed to have such a group discussion that an anonymity effect occurred. Thus, any simple *anonymity* effect might be attributed to differences in the content of group discussion between the K and NK groups. Unfortunately, Bixenstein et al. did not perform a content analysis on group discussions, so there is no way of determining the significance of this potential confound.

Fox and Guyer (1978) did obtain an anonymity main effect, but again, the anonymity manipulation was confounded (multiply). Fox and Guyer's *public choice* (i.e., nonanonymous) participants not only believed that their choices would be shared with other group members, but also (1) had met their fellow group members and given their names at the beginning of the session (i.e., anonymity of actors and anonymity of choice were confounded, cf. Roth, 1995), and (2) were visible to one another during the game itself. It is possible that the former confound increased group identification which has been shown in other research (e.g., Brewer & Kramer, 1986; Kramer & Brewer, 1984) to enhance prosocial behavior. And, it is possible that the latter confound increased individu ation which has also been shown to encourage prescribed behavior (e.g., Diener, 1980). Thus, again, there is no way of telling whether anonymity, per se, was responsible for the ostensible *anonymity* effect reported by Fox and Guyer (1978).

Finally, Jorgenson and Papciak (1981) also confounded the anonymity of choice with *visual separation* (or anonymity of actors). Members of their high identifiability (i.e., nonanonymous) groups were visible to one another throughout the game, whereas members of their low identifiability groups were visually isolated from one another. As argued above, this confounded variable might have altered levels of individuation, and thereby, contributed to the (isolated) *anonymity* simple effect observed.

Flache and Liebrand (1997) provide an interesting counterexample to the usual conclusion that anonymity decreases cooperation. They provide some empirical evidence that knowledge of one another's decisions to approve or disapprove can undermine cooperative behavior under certain conditions. It should be noted that Flache and Liebrand are investigating a much more complex dilemma (really, a joint set of dilemmas) than the simpler games considered in previous studies. On the other hand, their experiments capture certain features of actual groups that are lost in all the other simulations (most specifically, the dynamics of mutual, costly approval as an adjunct to the dynamics of the main social dilemma game itself). For our present purposes, anyway, their findings further undermine the generality of the usual conclusion about anonymity.

Thus, when one looks carefully at the empirical literature, it seems fair to conclude that

(a) public, nonanonymous choice increases levels of cooperation;

(b) the few effects that do occur emerge only under certain experimental conditions, implying the existence of important moderator variables; and

(c) methodological problems cast doubt on the actual cause of those few negative (simple) effects that have been observed.

Were I summarizing the literature today, in 1998, I would not have drawn as simple and definite a conclusion as the one cited above from Kerr (1995a).

Faced with this not so tidy picture, I and my colleagues have begun to look for the unknown moderators of the effect of anonymity of choice on cooperation in social dilemmas. Our two initial efforts are summarized below.

EXPERIMENT 1: GAME FRAMING AS A MODERATOR OF ANONYMITY EFFECTS?

The idea for this experiment was suggested by a recent study published by Eric Van Dijk and Henk Wilke (1997). They noted Fleishman's (1988) conjecture that the choices faced by group members in resource dilemmas (taking from a common resource) and public good dilemmas (contributing private resources toward a public good) may be conceptualized differently by group members. In particular, defection (i.e., declining to contribute) in a public goods problem may be seen as *not doing good*, whereas defection (i.e., harvesting resources) in a resource dilemma may be seen as *doing bad*. Recent work by J. Baron (e.g., 1996; Haidt & Baron, 1996) suggests that *doing harm* is proscribed far more than *not doing good*.[1] In this vein, Kerr and Kaufman-Gilliland (1997) have recently reported some evidence that such framing differences may have direct effects on cooperation (see Brewer & Kramer, 1986; Komorita & Parks, 1994; Schwartz-Shea & Simmons, 1995; or Sell & Son, 1997, for other evidence on the direct effects of how a dilemma is framed on cooperation rates). They found greater delayed[2] cooperation when a public good problem had been framed in terms of the *harm* done from defection to the group's chances of obtaining the public good than when the identical problem had been framed in terms of the *helpfulness* of a cooperative act.

This suggested the possibility that maybe people would be more concerned about the publicness of their choices in a resource dilemma (where taking from the common resource pool might be seen as inappropriate, proscribed behavior) than in a public good dilemma (where contributing might be seen as good behavior, but failing to do so might not be seen as an actively bad act). Thus, perhaps the way the social dilemma was framed might be one of those unknown moderators of the effect of the anonymity of choice.

I was encouraged in this hunch by noticing an apparent pattern in the literature (see Table 7.1). The most clear, least confounded effect of anonymity in the literature (viz. Jorgenson & Papciak, 1981) was for a resource dilemma. (Other studies that report any negative effect of anonymity all used N-person PD games.) On the other hand, my own and other (e.g. Laury, Walker, & Williams, 1995) recent failures to find anonymity effects all occurred for public good problems. (Flache & Liebrand's, 1997, paper involved a complex combination of an N-person PD and simultaneous 2-person PDs.)

Method: Experiment 1

To explore this possibility, I ran an experiment with a simple 2×2 design. One independent variable was the anonymity of group members' cooperate-defect choices. The other independent variable was the way in which the dilemma was framed (cf. Brewer & Kramer, 1986). About half of our participants received a public good/give-some framing. Under it, the social dilemma was described as an *investment game*. On each trial, each member of a 5-person group would receive some start up money (i.e., an endowment) which he or she could either invest or not. If enough people invested (i.e., a provision point was reached), a cash bonus would be paid to all group members. This is essentially the step level public good game I have used in several recent experiments (see Kerr, 1996, for a review).

The remaining participants were functionally playing the same step level game, but it was framed somewhat differently. In the resource dilemma/take-some frame condition, the experimental game was described as a *conservation game*. The group would begin each trial with a pool of shared money. Each member of the group would then have an option to either take for him or herself a certain amount (equal to the endowment in the public good framing) or leave that amount in the pool. If what remained in the pool was sufficiently large after all these choices, everyone in the group would receive a cash bonus.[3] Tests of participants' understanding insured that participants were familiar with the particular framing they had received.

Anonymity was manipulated as in several of our previous studies (e.g., Kerr & Kaufman-Gilliland, 1994; Kerr et al., 1997). Participants in the anonymous condition were told that no one in the group would ever be told any member's choices. Participants in the nonanonymous condition were told that everyone's choices would be displayed to the group as a whole at the end of the study. Note, however, that unlike Dawes et al. (1977), in our nonanonymous condition there had been no face to face interactions among group members prior to the point they made their choices (although they were led to expect such interactions later).

Participants were physically isolated from one another throughout the study in booths. They received all instructions and made all responses by computer. After receiving all instructions they played a series of trials of the investment or the conservation game.[4] The key dependent variable, of course, was participants' levels of cooperation, that is, the proportion of *invest* choices for the investment game and the proportion of *leave* choices for the conservation game.

Results and Discussion: Experiment 1

To begin with, I did find the typical framing effect (see Schwartz-Shea & Simmons, 1995). Participants were significantly (p < .02) more cooperative in the take-some/conservation game/resource dilemma than in the give-some/investment game/public goods dilemma (see Figure 7.1).

Consistent with our other recent work, I detected no hint (p=.85) of an overall main effect for anonymity. In stark contrast to the dramatic, confrontational dynamics described by Dawes et al. (1977) in their classic study, my participants generally seemed to be indifferent to whether or not their choices would subsequently be shared with their fellow group members. As Figure 7.1 indicates, this null effect could not be plausibly attributed to ceiling effects (i.e., nearly all participants were already cooperating even when nonanonymous).

Of course, the most important question for the present study was whether framing moderated any effects of anonymity—was there a Framing × Anonymity interaction effect? The answer was *no*. There was no indication that anonymity mattered more with the resource dilemma than with the public good framing; in fact, the nonsignificant (p = .25) trend was in precisely the opposite direction.

There are features of this study that would lead one to be somewhat cautious in accepting the latter null effect as conclusive. Foremost among these is the possibility that the framing manipulation was ineffective. The structure of the game in the present resource

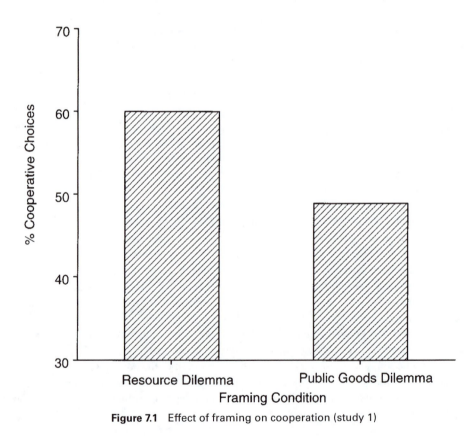

Figure 7.1   Effect of framing on cooperation (study 1)

dilemma was only superficially different from the present public good problem. In the former, the *shared pool* was really only a device for keeping track of collective cooperation. Unlike the prototypical resource dilemma, a participant who harvested in this conservation game did not directly reduce the resources available to his or her fellow group members. Rather, harvesting only affected the probability that a bonus would be earned. Thus, participants in this condition might well have continued to see the task for what it was—functionally a public good problem (cf. Keohane & Ostrom, 1995; Van Dijk & Wilke, 1997).

Clearly, my search for conditions under which group members care whether others know of their choices was not off to a rousing start.

EXPERIMENT 2: SOCIAL EXCLUSION AS A CONSEQUENCE OF KNOWN DEFECTION

A good point to return might be Dawes et al.'s (1977) observations, with which we began this chapter. They clearly suggest that their participants cared very much about one another's choices and were prepared to express their displeasure with others who chose to defect— that there were clear social norms prescribing cooperation. But in order for a social norm to alter an individual's behavior, certain things must be true. First, the individual must be aware of the norm. It may be significant in this regard that all the evidence Dawes et al. (1997) offer for the power of a procooperation norm involved groups in which discussion of the dilemma had taken place.[5] Of course, there is a good deal of evidence that explicit or implicit promises to cooperate are made during group discussion, and it thus may have been mutual awareness of the social norm of commitment which fueled Dawes et al.'s participants' comments.[6] Second, it must be the case that the anticipated sanctions for norm violations are both certain and salient. By *certain* I mean that the individual must be confident that someone will bother to enforce the norm—his or her subjective probability of sanctioning following norm violation must be reasonably high. We would not expect, for example, a small child to refrain from stealing cookies if she were only scolded once every twenty times she was caught. And by *salient* I mean that the costs for norm violation must be substantial enough. Even if our young cookie thief were scolded every time she was caught with her hand in the cookie jar (i.e., sanctions were quite certain), we would not expect her to reform her ways if the scolding was insubstantial (e.g., "tut tut, darling, too many cookies aren't good for you").

I am arguing that all these elements (high norm awareness, sanction certainty, and sanction salience) may be necessary for social norms to influence behavior. Absent any one, social norms can lose their power, and consequently, anonymity can lose its moderating effect on conformity to social norms. Thus, if any element were consistently missing in prior research on anonymity, we might be less surprised if participants did not seem to care whether or not others knew of their choices.

A couple of theoretical clarifications should be made at this point. First, my focus here is on *social norms*, for which others deliver sanctions to the actor, not on *internalized* or *personal norms*, for which the actor sanctions him or herself. The publicness or social anonymity of choice should not moderate the impact of well internalized norms. Second, I am suggesting that these three elements are all *necessary*—if any one is absent (i.e., at low enough levels), then the anonymity of one's choice should have no effect on cooperative behavior. I am not suggesting, however, that these conditions, individually or collectively, are *sufficient* to insure an anonymity effect. Cooperative choice (like nearly all behavior) is multiply determined, and even when social norms are known, certain, and salient, other incentives in a social dilemma (e.g., low temptation to defect, Komorita, 1976; highly salient internalized norms, Kerr & Kaufman-Gilliland, 1994) could vitiate the impact of such social norms. Thus, for example, anonymity may be irrelevant for choice if cooperation is dictated by salient internalized norms, even if one were aware of certain and salient social norms.

My reading of the anonymity literature, summarized in Table 7.1, suggests that one or more of these elements is routinely missing. In none of the studies examining anonymity have there been clear and explicit costs (social or otherwise) for violating a cooperation-promoting norm. The closest one comes is implicit threats for those violating a group commitment to cooperate. Sanction certainty and salience in these studies is either clearly low or highly ambiguous. Jerdee and Rosen (1974), in trying to explain why anonymity did not seem to matter for their no discussion groups make a similar point, ". . .when a social responsibility norm does not exist [i.e., no discussion], visibility of behavior may not have much effect *unless* (emphasis added) it is accompanied by some kind of legal sanction" (or, in our terminology, a certain and salient sanction) (p. 715).

The primary goal of this second experiment (Kerr, 1997) was to see if explicit risks of salient social sanctions would moderate anonymity effects. I expected that a group member would care much more whether other group members knew his or her choice in a social dilemma *if* there was a clear possibility of a substantial social sanction from those other group members for violating relevant social norms.

What might constitute such a substantial, salient social sanction? I have a candidate for the most substantial social sanction—the social death penalty—it is removing someone from the group. We might use any of several terms to describe such action—shunning, banishment, ostracism, exile, expulsion, rejection, disowning, or excommunication. Here, I will use the term *exclusion*. All of these terms connote that one is deprived of the support, the privileges, and even the human contact reserved for members of the group; one literally becomes an outsider. There is much empirical and theoretical work that testifies to the psychological impact of exclusion. For example, much early work on social communication and social comparison (Festinger, 1950; Schachter, 1951; see Levine's, 1980, review) suggests that the persistent deviate is eventually rejected from the group. Asch's (1956) classic work on conformity suggests that even simple disagreement carries an implicit threat of exclusion or social marginalization, a threat sufficient to lead many to comply with (descriptive) social norms. A more recent sociological analyses by Scheff (e.g., 1988) argues that even the possibility of not conforming to explicit or implicit social norms arouses strong emotions (e.g., shame), emotions likely to accompany social exclusion. More recent work by Williams on social ostracism (e.g., Williams, 1997) and Baumeister and Leary (1995) on belongingness[7] suggests that it is extremely aversive to be excluded from a group. Caporael, Dawes, Orbell, and Van de Kragt (1989) have even suggested that the threat to survival that accompanied exclusion from groups of early humans may have contributed to the evolution of a basic and profound human need to belong (or, conversely, not to be excluded).

Although it might validly be dismissed as less than anecdotal evidence, there are also many vivid and convincing literary illustrations on the power of social exclusion. My own favorite comes from the classic Yiddish play, *The Dybbuk* (An-Ski, 1926). A young girl is possessed with a dybbuk, a malignant spirit. The dybbuk successfully resists many varied attempts at exorcism. In desperation, a rabbi employs his most extreme and powerful threat— total exclusion from the community of believers, in this life and the next. In the Royal

Shakespheare Company production I saw, this threat of excommunication is concluded with all the actors silently turning their back on the dybbuk—a disturbing theatrical moment (at least to this playgoer). Faced with this dreadful threat, the dybbuk leaves the girl's body.

The goal in the second study described here (Kerr, 1997) was to explore whether and how the threat of exclusion from the group might deter defection. Before describing that study, another theoretical point needs to be clarified. Orbell and Dawes (1993) in a provocative paper, suggest that "recognizing and avoiding" (p. 789) defectors is not necessary to explain widespread cooperation. Such cooperation can result from the simple mechanism of defectors being less likely (than cooperators) to enter into any interdependent situation. However, even if they are right that social exclusion is not theoretically necessary for widespread cooperation, it may still be the case that cooperation could be further encouraged by the threat of exclusion for one's lack of cooperation. That is, perhaps a threat of exclusion is sufficient to deter defection, to some degree and under some conditions (e.g., when norm awareness and sanction certainty are also high). So, while groups may not have to recognize and avoid defectors to solve the tragedy of the commons, perhaps such recognition and avoidance contributes to a solution.

Method: Experiment 2

The base procedure was identical to those followed in one of the cells of the previous study. I used the resource dilemma (conservation game) framing. And participants' choices were not anonymous; all participants were told that all of their choices would be posted before and discussed by the group at the end of each block of trials. As before, though, participants were physically isolated when they were instructed and played the game.

Several experimental conditions were created that varied the group's ability to exclude a member as well as the nonsocial/game consequences of such an exclusion. Along with the social rewards of group membership (and social costs of exclusion), group membership is also often functional for achieving objective, nonsocial rewards. For example, if it takes a group to hunt and kill a buffalo, only those belonging to the hunting group get to eat the buffalo. If there is no other alternative to buffalo meat for food, we would not be too surprised to find that people placed a high value on belonging to the group. In such instances, not belonging to the group means that one must play a different game with different payoffs (with a different effective matrix, in Kelley and Thibaut's, 1978, terminology). I really was not interested in demonstrating that people would rather not be excluded from groups if such exclusion guaranteed poorer objective payoffs. Rather, I was particularly interested in seeing what kind of nonobjective, intangible value the prospect of social exclusion, per se, might carry. To explore this latter question, I systematically varied the objective costs of exclusion through a wide (and, I hoped, interesting range).

The cover story for the experiment was that the effect of group size on performance at the conservation game was being studied. Participants would first perform the task in a 5-person group. They would then leave their booths and examine and discuss one another's choices in the just completed game. Then, 4 of the 5 original participants would return to their booths and perform a parallel version of the game as a 4-person group—one of the original participants would be left out.

In this study, I did not vary the anonymity of choice, since several studies using the present paradigm (Kerr & Kaufman-Gilliland, 1994; Kerr et al., 1997; Experiment 1, above) had already demonstrated that anonymity of choice had no effect on cooperation when no social exclusion was possible. In this study, I wanted to see if adding the threat of such exclusion had any effect on the behavior of nonanonymous participants. The four experimental conditions of this study varied in the procedure used to determine who was excluded during the latter portion of the experiment, and what such exclusion meant in terms of objective game payoffs. These variations are summarized in Table 7.2. In the first (control) condition, participants were told that the experimenter would randomly choose which participant was excluded from the 4-person game. In the remaining three conditions, participants were told that after examining and discussing choices made during a 5-person version of the game, all 5 group members would rank order their preferences for those they would like to play with in a future 4-person version of the game. The person with lowest mean ranking would be excluded.

The other factor that distinguished the experimental conditions was the payoff that the excluded person would receive as a result of game play in the 4-person groups. In the control condition, participants were told that the excluded person would simply receive the average earned by the 4 persons playing the game. Thus, on average, those excluded would be no better or worse off in terms of actual objective rewards, than those who were included in the 4-person groups.

In the second condition (group vote/average), participants were told the same thing. Thus, the only thing distinguishing the first two conditions was whether chance or one's fellow group members excluded one from a group game. In terms of objective outcomes, there is little difference between the control and the group vote/average condition.[8] Differences in cooperative behavior in the 5-person version of this game, then, can reasonably be attributed to the social disutility placed on not being actively excluded by the rest of the group in the group vote/average condition.

In the third condition (group vote/none), the excluded person is economically as well as socially excluded. If he or she cannot play the game, he or she cannot receive any game payoffs. Like the prospective buffalo hunter, exclusion from the group is objectively costly. In this condition, exclusion carries both economic and social costs.

Finally, in the fourth condition (group vote/maximum), exclusion actually had an economic *benefit*. The excluded person would receive a payoff equal to the largest payoff received by a member of the 4-person group. This condition put economic and social incentives in conflict—it is better economically to be excluded, but perhaps not socially. The interesting question that this condition could shed light on was, "will participants sacrifice economic advantage to avoid social exclusion?"

As in a previous study (and most of our recent studies, see Note 4), I also varied the efficacy of a cooperative act within participants across trials. Sometimes, a cooperative act had little impact on earning the group bonus; at other times, it had much greater impact. On each trial, a 100-point pool was divided among the 5-group members. The only con-

Table 7.2 Experiment 2: Experimental concerns.

Condition	Procedure for selecting person to be excluded	Payoff to person excluded during 4-person version of the game
Control	Randomly by E	Average of earnings of those included
Group Vote/Average	By vote of group members	Average of earnings of those included
Group Vote/None	By vote of group members	No payoff
Group Vote/Maximum	By vote of group members	Maximum of earnings of those included

straint on this division was than no group member's share of these 100 points could exceed 50 points. Before making a choice, each participant would be told his share size, but would not be told any other member's share size (although he or she would know, of course, that the sum of his or her share and all the others' shares would equal 100). A decision to cooperate (i.e., leave $10 in the group resource pool) meant adding one's share to an accumulator. The bonus was earned if and only if the accumulated total of share points exceeded 50. By varying share size, I could manipulate the efficacy of a cooperative choice for providing the public good. (See Kerr, 1996, for a review of the research employing this efficacy paradigm.) In this study, share size was manipulated within participants across 8 trials or *plays* of the game. Share size took on the following values: 1, 5, 9, 13, 17, 21, 25, and 29.[9] The order of receiving these share sizes across trials was randomized separately for each participant.[10]

In summary I employed a 4 (condition; see Table 7.2) × 8 (efficacy) design, with repeated measures on latter factor. The primary dependent variable was level of cooperation (proportion that left the $10 in the group resource pool) in the 5-person group. (Note that participants never actually examined one another's choices or played the 4-person version of the game; the experiment ended after the 5-person block of trials.)

Results and Discussion: Experiment 2

The key question of this study was whether risk of exclusion and consequent implications for payoff would lead participants to cooperate more in the 5-person group so as to avoid being excluded in the subsequent 4-person group. Analysis of dichotomous cooperation choices (leave vs. take from the resource pool) yielded a significant Condition × Efficacy

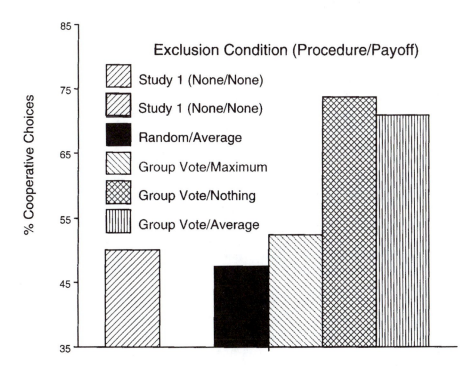

Figure 7.2 Effect of exclusion condition on cooperation (study 2). Maximum share size = 29.

interaction effect ($p < .03$). Tests of condition simple effects revealed that there were no reliable overall condition simple effects except when efficacy was maximal (i.e., the participant's share size = 29). Figure 7.2 shows the means for this significant simple effect, along with an interesting comparison condition from Experiment 1.

The first two means plotted are cooperation rates under comparable conditions of Experiment 1 (nonanonymous/resource frame) and the present control condition. The statistical equivalence of these two conditions verifies that just having a second block of trials with somebody (randomly) excluded did not systematically affect cooperation.

The next mean plotted is for the group vote/maximum condition. The cooperation rate in this condition does not differ significantly from the first two conditions plotted. This equivalence suggests that when being excluded actually guarantees good economic outcomes, participants did not cooperate more in 5-person group to avoid exclusion in the 4-person group. If a cost was attached to social exclusion, it was not high enough in this condition to deter defection. This might be because the clear and substantial rewards in this condition roughly compensate for the costs of such exclusion. But this could also mean that either participants attached little disutility or utility to the prospect of exclusion or that they believed that exclusion would not hinge on their level of cooperative behavior (e.g., their fellow group members would not base their rankings on levels of cooperative behavior). The results in the remaining conditions help speak to these latter possibilities.

The next condition plotted is the group vote/none condition. The level of cooperation in this condition was considerably and significantly ($p < .05$) higher than in the three previously considered conditions. Clearly, participants were sensitive to the prospect of exclusion in this condition, where being excluded socially also meant being excluded economically. However, it still remains unclear in this condition whether it is the social costs of exclusion, the economic costs of exclusion, or both which effectively deter defection.

The last and most interesting condition mean plotted is for the group vote/average condition. The rate of cooperation in this condition is also significantly above the baseline/control condition (and the group vote/maximal condition) but not significantly different from the group vote/none condition. This pattern of findings suggests that even when there is no overall economic cost to being excluded (because an excluded participant will receive the average payoff of those included in the 4-person group) there remains a real social cost of exclusion which participants prefer not to pay. If we assume that economic and social costs were additive, the present pattern of results implies that the social disutility of exclusion (present in both the group vote/none and group vote/average conditions) was much larger than the economic cost of exclusion in the group vote/none condition. Otherwise, we would have expected participants to cooperate more when they must suffer both costs than when they must only suffer the social costs. Of course, there are other possibilities. The combination of costs might not be additive. There might be a hierarchical consideration of costs (e.g., only consider one type of costs if the other is absent). My design does not allow us to choose between such possibilities. The data in this condition also render implausible a couple of possibilities raised earlier—that participants attached no social cost to exclusion or saw no contingency between their cooperative behavior and the probability of exclusion.

We may conclude from Experiment 2 that a risk of being excluded by the group can, under the proper conditions, prompt greater cooperation. Apparently, though, our participants believed that their cooperative choices had to have a reasonably strong impact on the group's welfare before they ran much of a risk of exclusion. It is not clear, however, whether this moderating effect is driven by norm awareness (i.e., the belief that others would not expect one to be cooperative unless that cooperation would have some substantial impact on the group), sanction certainty (i.e., the belief that others were not certain to sanction one's forgoing ineffectual cooperation), or sanction salience (i.e., the belief that others would probably not exclude one for defecting when cooperation did little good for the group), or some combination of these elements. I would like to assume that when the efficacy of cooperation is sufficiently high, all the purported necessary elements were satisfied in Study 2, but the present design does not allow us to analyze the precise moderating effect of the self-efficacy of cooperation, nor, for that matter, to directly test our working hypothesis (that norm awareness, sanction salience, and sanction certainty are all necessary for anonymity effects to emerge).

But, just for the sake of argument, let us assume that my assumption is justified. Several interesting conclusions then follow from these results. They indicate that group members are aware of an antidefection social norm; that they infer that other group members expect them to act cooperatively in a social dilemma, even when there has been no discussion of the dilemma. They indicate that group members expect others to pay attention to their behavior and to use the power to exclude to sanction norm violation. And, they indicate that the threat of exclusion, per se, can be a substantial and effective social sanction to discourage defection.

The data for the group vote/maximal condition demonstrates that the apparent aversion to social exclusion can be overcome by making it sufficiently worth one's while to be so excluded. For example, even if a fisherman agreed to observe catch limits, if he could make enough money by ignoring these limits, he might be willing to be a social pariah in the community of fishermen.

A number of interesting external validity questions remain. What other factors affect the disutility of exclusion? For example, might the costs of exclusion be even higher if the group were one that the members cared about (e.g., friends; a group with a long past and/or future)? Might the full power of the social costs of exclusion only emerge after one has experienced it? If so, participants in our group vote/maximum condition might have also increased their cooperation (relative to the control baseline) after having experienced actual social exclusion (and found it not to their liking). Another interesting question raised by our results is the boundary conditions of the moderating effect of the efficacy of a cooperative act. In our study, efficacy was manipulated within participants and there was no group discussion. The former meant that everybody in the group would at one time or another have opportunities to profit through defection (here, by taking resources from the resource pool) at little likely cost to the group (because their share size was relatively small). Under such conditions, group members may decide that a reasonable strategy for striking a balance between self- and collective-interest is to defect when cooperation is fairly ineffectual in helping the group, but cooperate when the cooperative act has relatively high impact on obtaining the public good. And indeed, in this (as in all our previous studies, see Kerr, 1996) there was a strong effect of efficacy on cooperation. As noted above, I suspect that this pattern of results can be understood in terms of purported necessary elements—that participants believed that other group members only expected cooperation when it was effectual, and would not be certain to punish one substantially (via exclusion) for defecting when the self-efficacy of one's cooperation was low. However, different beliefs might well arise under other conditions—for example, all group members' efficacies were constant or very low. And, if broad and binding promises to cooperate were made in group discussions, group members might well expect others to exclude anyone who defected, regardless of the efficacy of their cooperative act.

THE EFFECTS OF ANONYMITY ON COOPERATION—A REPRISE

With the acuity of hindsight, it may not be so surprising that anonymity, per se, does not have general or strong effects on cooperation in social dilemmas. Working roughly from an instrumentality value orientation, I have suggested that a number of conditions must be *simultaneously* met in order for normative social control of social dilemma behavior to be effective.

1   One must perceive that there is a social expectation or norm prescribing coopera-tion (or proscribing defection)—one has to believe that the rest of the group cares how one behaves. That is, norm awareness must be high.

2   One must be convinced that others can and will deliver sanctions for violation of that norm—one has to believe that the rest of the group can and will do something if one fails to act as expected. That is, sanction certainty must be high.

3   One must be convinced that others can, directly or indirectly,[11] monitor one's cooperative behavior. Others cannot effectively sanction what they cannot effectively monitor.

4   One must actively want to avoid the particular social sanctions likely to be lev-ied—one has to care about what the others in the group can do. That is, sanction salience must be high.

Experiment 2 suggests that one thing people do care about is being excluded from groups (even when that exclusion carries no other economic costs).

This analysis suggests that unless all of these conditions are met, social norms will not deter defection. So, one may not care whether one's choices are revealed to others if there are no clear normative expectations about cooperation, or other group members lack the means or will to enforce the norms or have no salient sanction to impose on defectors.

I have suggested that the reason that few studies have found any effects for anonymity is that very few studies have simultaneously met all of these purported necessary condi-tions. But, I would like to suggest further that life outside the lab may routinely satisfy all of these conditions, and that normative control of defection there is common. The scien-tific challenge is to provide clear and convincing empirical evidence for all these sugges-tions.

ENDNOTES

[1] Baron's findings, by the way, offer a tidy explanation of Mummendey's (e.g., Mummendey et al., 1992) findings that group favoritism in the minimal group paradigm occurs when one is deciding how many points to give to in- vs. out-group members, but not when one is deciding how many points to take away from in- versus out-group members. There may be social norms prescribing favoring ingroup members (cf. Tajfel, 1970), but there may be a more general prohibition against actively doing harm.

[2] These effects did not emerge on the initial public good problem considered by these participants, but rather on a subsequent one. See Kerr and Kaufman-Gilliland (1997) for some speculation on why such effects were delayed in their paradigm.

[3] Note that group members did not actually get to split the remains of the pool. One's outcomes were determined entirely by one's harvests and bonuses.

[4] The trials varied in the efficacy of a cooperative choice for providing the public good. This manipulation, which will be described in more detail in Experiment 2, did not qualify any of the key findings of Experiment 1 and will not be considered further here.

[5] The evidence was of two types. The first were comments made during group discussion that expressed strong expectations that defection was shameful behavior (e.g., "if you defect on the rest of us, you're going to have to live with it the rest of your life"). The other was hostile reactions of group members to defectors in a

pilot group in which choices were made public ("You have no idea how much you alienate me!"). It seems probable that group discussion of the dilemma preceded the revelation of members choices (R. Dawes, personal communication).

[6] As we've also noted, though, it may be the case that discussion engages an equally powerful internalized norm of commitment, which is sufficient to prompt greater cooperation even without public responding (Kerr et al., 1997).

[7] It is of interest that Baumeister and Leary's (1995) paper was preceded by another paper by Baumeister and Tice (1990) in which they argued (correctly, I believe) that the key incentive was not the reward of belonging, but the aversiveness of exclusion. In this vein, it is interesting that Flache & Liebrand's (1997) data justified a similar conclusion ["others' approval affects subjects' work behavior (i.e., cooperation) primarily when they are punished for shirking, while the potential loss of approval in the future does not seem to be effective in encouraging workers" (Flache, 1996; p. 195)].

[8] This assumes that participants don't presume that the overall level of outcomes earned by the 4-person teams will differ between the control and other conditions.

[9] Subjects were instructed that these game parameters would be suitably adjusted in the 4-person version of the game. Thus, in the 4-person game, the point pool had only 80 points. Since the pool of points had only 80 points, no group member would receive more than 40 points, and 41 points was the provision point.

[10] In most of our previous studies, share size had been manipulated through a wider range (e.g., from 1 to 50 points in 7-point increments; Kerr & Kaufman-Gilliland, 1994; Kerr et al., 1997). However, there were indications that a cooperation ceiling might be reached for the higher share size/efficacy levels. That was the reason why low to moderate share sizes were used in this experiment. As we shall see, this might have been a mistake in the present instance.

[11] Even when individual choices are not public, others may be able to make educated guesses about one's behavior from other information, such as the overall rate of cooperation (if overall water use hasn't dropped during a drought, one might infer that very few people are conserving) or indirect evidence of defection (even if one's water bills are not public, neighbors in a drought area can see if one's car is always clean or one's lawn is green).

Chapter 8

Solving Natural Resource Dilemmas through Structural Change: The Social Psychology of Metering Water Use

Mark Van Vugt

INTRODUCTION

A major challenge of modern society is to find solutions for dilemmas involving the distribution of limited natural resources such as water and energy. These problems are the result of an ever growing mismatch between resource supplies and demands. Whether due to a real shortage or to excessive usage, it is clear that long-term strategies are needed to cope with these problems, and these strategies should focus on changing resource consumption patterns (Stern, 1992). Among the various solutions available, the implementation of *technological devices*, such as meters for the use of water, gas, or electricity, seems to be a promising strategy to promote conservation structurally (Crabb, 1992). Little is understood, however, about the longer-term psychological effects of such interventions. So far, conservation programs have been designed primarily in response to an immediate resource crisis like a water shortage (see e.g., Berk et al., 1980).

The preparation of this chapter was supported by a grant from the Annual Grants scheme of the University of Southampton (A95/13).

For example, in 1995 the United Kingdom was hit by one of the worst droughts in recent history, which culminated in a severe water shortage during the summer months. Around the UK a variety of activities were organized to bring down consumption levels. Education campaigns were implemented to inform the public of the seriousness of the situation and to stress the need for domestic water conservation. In some areas, people were given practical information about how and when they should conserve water. In other parts of the country, actual bans were imposed on the use of sprinklers and hose pipes, and fines were issued when people failed to comply.

It is important to realize that these strategies were adopted in response to an *acute resource crisis* and that they were not intended to have any long lasting effects. Moreover, because of the time pressures involved there were no opportunities to systematically evaluate them. As a result, there still is great uncertainty among policy makers—representatives of government and water industry—concerning what needs to be done to promote efficient resource management. What seems evident is that intervention programs should be directed more toward the prevention and less toward the management of a shortage (OFWAT, 1996).

The current chapter examines the impact of a particular structural strategy to tackle resource problems, the installment of domestic *water meters*. I will present evidence that metering leads to a substantial reduction in water consumption rates. Moreover, I will show that the impact of this intervention produces numerous psychological side effects that facilitate the prevention and management of an acute resource crisis.

Resource Conservation as Social Dilemma: Theory and Findings

The reward structure underlying many natural resource problems shows similarities to an *N-person prisoner's dilemma game* (Dawes, 1980; Messick & Brewer, 1983). In this dilemma game, it is highly attractive for people to consume as much as they wish at their convenience. For example, most individuals want to be able to take a shower or water their garden whenever they like. However, if all or most individuals act accordingly, the resource is not likely to be sustained for long. Eventually, this could result in a situation whereby everyone is worse off than had all exercised some restraint. The conflict between the short-term individual interest not to conserve and the long-term collective interest to conserve is particularly salient during a *resource crisis*, such as a water shortage, because the situation requires conservation, but at the same time motivates people to consume as much as they can before the resource collapses (Kramer, McClintock, & Messick, 1986).

Social-psychological researchers have developed an experimental task, the so called replenishable resource dilemma paradigm (Messick et al., 1983; Samuelson, Messick, Rutte, & Wilke, 1984), to model resource shortages. In this computer controlled experiment, a group of (usually) six individuals are instructed to manage a common resource pool that consists of points representing a certain monetary value. Each of the participants takes a turn and harvests a number of points from the pool. Subsequently, the computer calculates the new pool size by subtracting the requested sum from the total number of points in the pool. The remaining points are then multiplied by a certain replenishment rate to establish the resource for the next trial—this process is analogous to a natural resource pool that also has a capacity to restore itself to a certain degree (e.g., a water reservoir). Feedback about the pool size is usually preprogrammed in these tasks in order to determine how people might, for example, respond to information about the state of the resource and harvest decisions of other consumers.

This line of research has identified *three* key motives that underlie people's consumption decisions (Messick et al., 1983; Samuelson & Messick, 1995; Samuelson et al., 1984; Wilke, 1991). First, people are motivated to consume as much as they can of a particular resource. This motive is inherent to the reward structure of the resource dilemma as it is, by definition, more attractive to consume than to exercise restraint. However, the desire to be *greedy* is constrained by two other motives that depart from people's immediate self-interest. They are also motivated to use the resource *responsibly* so that it remains intact for an extended time period. Finally, people are concerned with the distribution of resources between group members, which should be in line with their *fairness* expectations. Although all three motives—greed, responsibility, and fairness—influence harvest decisions to some extent, the dominant concern is greed (Wilke, 1991). It is therefore plausible that a resource is overused in the absence of initiatives to influence people's consumption decisions.

Behavioral Strategies to Promote Conservation

Strategies to influence decisions in resource dilemmas can be conveniently grouped according to which of these motives they focus. Following the greed motive, interventions to decrease consumption rates are aimed at changing the *personal reward structure* of the dilemma. The results of numerous laboratory studies show that this structural approach can be quite effective in solving dilemmas provided the rewards for conservation and punishments for nonconservation are sufficiently high (Komorita & Parks, 1994). In natural resource dilemmas this strategy usually comes about via a modification in the price setting of the resource units. For example, the standard price of water could be raised or households could be charged according to their demand of water.

A different set of strategies to promote conservation focuses primarily on promoting concerns with *responsible* resource management. This is usually achieved by social-psychological interventions that attempt to change the perceptions and motivations of people dealing with resources. Experimental research suggests at least four social-psychological factors that may contribute to conservation in resource dilemmas:

1   awareness of a shortage,
2   a responsibility to do something for the collective welfare,
3   a belief in the efficacy of an individual contribution,
4   a belief that other people in the community will also contribute (Komorita & Parks, 1994; Van Lange, Liebrand, Messick, & Wilke, 1992).

In the context of natural resource management, the social-psychological approach generally culminates in the implementation of *public education* campaigns, whereby people receive messages with details about the shortage and moral appeals to use the resource wisely (Gardner & Stern, 1996). These campaigns sometimes contain practical suggestions how to conserve. There is some indication that these campaigns help to promote water conservation, but only in the face of an acute shortage (Berk et al., 1980; Maki, Hoffman, & Berk, 1978). Under normal resource conditions such interventions do not seem to have an effect at all (e.g., Geller, Erickson, & Buttram, 1983; Thompson & Stoutemeyer, 1991).

What conclusions can we draw from these approaches to promote water conservation? First, it should be noted that the findings of experimental resource dilemma studies and actual resource management programs are not always compatible. Interventions that work in the laboratory do not necessarily produce the desired effects when implemented in practice (Van Vugt, Van Lange, Meertens, & Joireman, 1996). Whenever possible, resource management innovations should therefore be studied in both field and laboratory situations before being implemented in practice. Second, interventions tend to be focused on either greed or responsibility to conserve, but they seldom focus on both motives simultaneously. Yet there is good evidence from applied behavioral research that a combination of interventions may prove to be far more successful (Geller, Winett, & Everett, 1982). For example, analyses of the 1976/1977 California drought revealed that conservation efforts were substantial due to the *specific* combination of penalties and moral appeals (Berk et al., 1980).

In the present chapter I examine the effects of a structural intervention with social-psychological implications, the introduction of domestic *meters* for water use. I will first summarize briefly the results of two large scale metering projects that have been carried out in the US and UK. Subsequently, the various social-psychological consequences of metering will be discussed as well as the findings of two recent studies where I compared the conservation decisions and attitudes in households with and without meters. These studies were carried out in the UK, which has the lowest proportion of domestic water meters in Western society (i.e., about 90 % of properties in the UK were not equipped with a meter in '96; OFWAT, 1996). Most households in the UK pay a flat rate tariff that is unrelated to actual use.

The Effect of Meters on Water Demands

During the 1950s and 1960s large scale water metering projects were carried out in the US and have shown some dramatic changes in consumption patterns. Probably the best documented research was carried in Boulder, Colorado, where water meters were universally installed in 1962 (Hankle & Boland, 1971). From this date onwards customers were charged according to use level ($0.35 per 1000 gallons) instead of paying a standard charge. The water consumption data in Boulder had been gathered since 1955 and so a detailed time series analysis could be performed on the development of domestic water consumption patterns. The researchers examined the average consumption data in the period between 1955 and 1968 and found that water demands decreased by an average of *36%* after the installment of meters. Further analysis of the data revealed that the drop in water use could be attributed largely to a reduction in the use of garden hoses and sprinklers for such actions as lawn sprinkling, car washing, and filling swimming pools.

Similar metering programs were carried out in different locations in the UK in the early 1990s. These trials showed a more modest decrease in water demand of about 11% on average (Department of Environment, 1993). However, the effects varied substantially between regions that could be accounted for by the use of different tariff systems associated with meters. The best results were obtained in a district that introduced a so called seasonal tariff where the price of water (above a certain level) increased during the summer months and so high usage would lead to high costs. This area showed an average drop of 17.2% over a 3-year period. In areas where meters were introduced without a change in tariff system, the results varied from a reduction of 1.6% to 7.3% across different regions.

The Psychological Implications of Metering

The above results reveal that the introduction of meters can lead to a substantial reduction in domestic water consumption. Although this finding is impressive by itself, it does not tell us a great deal about the mediating psychological processes contributing to the metering effect (i.e., exactly why do people reduce water use when metered?) nor about conditions under which the effects of metering are more or less pronounced. Knowledge about possible mediating and moderating factors (cf. Baron & Kenny, 1986) will provide a better basis for prediction of the relative efficacy of different structural interventions. Below, I discuss various social-psychological explanations for the effects of metering and explore how the impact of metering varies with perceptions of a resource shortage.

Greed A first motive that presumably accounts for the positive effect of metering is greed. When water consumption is not individually metered households can use as much of the resource as they want without incurring additional costs. Charges are made according to a standard tariff, which is usually based upon the value of the property and household size (i.e., a so called flat rate tariff). This tariff system provides no direct incentive for conservation. The introduction of meters—and the associated change in tariff system—alters the reward structure of the dilemma dramatically. Suddenly, it becomes financially attractive for households to use as little water as possible. It follows logically from prior theorizing about social dilemmas (Dawes, 1980; Luce & Raifa, 1957; Wilke, 1991) that under these circumstances people will start to make conservation efforts as it is in their best interest.

Moreover, the greed motive will be particularly salient when people are facing a shortage. A crisis situation will highlight the conflict between people's self-interest and the interest of the community as a whole. From a collective viewpoint, individuals should increase their conservation efforts to contribute to the solution of the problem especially since the collective good is aligned with long-term individual self-interest. Yet many people might decide to increase their consumption rates while there is still an opportunity to do so (Kramer, McClintock, & Messick, 1986). This effect is likely to be attenuated, however, by the presence of a meter as metered households are penalized when they increase their water use. Accordingly, the availability of a meter and the associated contingent costs of consumption serve as a *buffer* against high levels of consumption during a shortage.

Feedback and Personal Efficacy The beneficial effects of metering may also be due to social-psychological factors. Metering introduces a *feedback* mechanism that allows people to regularly monitor their consumption pattern. Feedback about use levels is provided standard on the bills customers receive, but they also may inspect the meter themselves—provided it is located at a convenient place. There is considerable evidence that feedback works, both in the context of water (Aitken, McMahon, Wearing, & Finlayson, 1994; Geller, Erickson, & Buttram, 1983) and energy conservation (Samuelson, 1990; Seligman & Darley, 1977). But, precisely how it works remains unclear. The most likely explanation is that it enhances people's sense of *personal efficacy* as it allows them to determine if their conservation efforts have a noticeable effect on the size of their bills (Bandura, 1977).

An increased efficacy will help people to cope better during a shortage for various reasons. First, since they might know how to reduce their consumption level, they are presumably better able to adjust their behavior in case of a crisis. Also, unlike nonmetered households they might think that their conservation efforts make a real difference in tackling the collective problem (Kerr, 1996). Finally, the occurrence of a shortage may be interpreted as negative feedback for the efforts they are already making and they may therefore work harder on the task ("goal-relevant information"; Locke, 1968).

Concern with Responsible Resource Use   Metering may be effective because it promotes the concern for responsible use of water resources. Charging water according to a standard rate conveys to people that water resources are abundant and that they can engage in unrestrained consumption with no collective consequences. In contrast, the pay per unit system associated with meters communicates to customers that water is a valuable commodity and that it is each individual's responsibility to conserve, particularly when there is a collective threat in the form of a shortage (cf. Samuelson & Messick, 1995).

Trust   A fourth factor that may account for the success of metering programs is that metering increases expectations about the conservation efforts of other people in the community. Individuals may have good intentions to conserve water during a shortage, but it is clear that their efforts are futile unless sufficient other people in the community make an effort as well. Hence, to engage in conservation it is important that individuals develop reciprocal *trust* (Yamagishi, 1986b). Metering programs promote trust because in universally metered areas each community member realizes that others will be punished (i.e., by receiving a higher bill) if they do not restrain. This argument follows from the structural goal/expectation theory (Yamagishi, 1986b), which suggests that particularly in large scale social dilemmas structural changes (e.g., in the form of a sanctioning system) are necessary to assure people that their well intended behavior cannot be exploited by others.

Fairness   It may be considered fair that everyone pays according to what they use instead of paying a standard charge for water (cf. equity vs. equality rule; Deutsch, 1975). For example, people may regard it as unfair that they pay the same as their neighbors who are washing their car every day. Because a metered system may be more in line with people's fairness expectations, it might encourage them to make conservation efforts, particularly when it is collectively most desirable as in a shortage (Tyler & Degoey, 1995).

Accountability   Finally, people with meters may feel more accountable for their behavior as their consumption patterns can, in theory, be monitored by the water authorities. Rather than in nonmetered households, people in metered households may therefore feel more pressure to restrain themselves in case of a shortage (cf. Kerr, 1983).

EVIDENCE FOR THE PSYCHOLOGICAL IMPACT OF METERS

To examine the psychological and behavioral effects of metering I conducted a survey that was carried out in the summer of 1995, one of the UK's driest of the century. As indicated previously, all kinds of activities were initiated to promote conservation from the public, including media messages, leaflets, and hose pipe bans. Our research was conducted in Hampshire, an area in Southern England that was not subjected to any formal water use restrictions. This region was particularly suitable for our research purposes as it contained, within a largely nonmetered area, a community in which all households had been (involuntarily) equipped with a water meter as part of the national metering trials in the early 1990s. The households in this area paid, on top of a small standard fee, a variable fee which was dependent upon use (i.e., a volumetric tariff). By comparing responses in this community with those made in a similar but nonmetered community I was able to examine the impact of metering *ceteris paribus*.[1] Although the immediate resource crisis had been allayed at the time of our survey, it was still having a major impact on radio, television, and in the newspapers.

Participants and Procedure

Sixty questionnaires were distributed among residents in an area of Hampshire that was fully metered (i.e., Isle of Wight), whereas another 60 were distributed in a largely (but not fully) nonmetered area (i.e., Southampton). I approached these people in local supermarkets on two consecutive Saturday mornings in September. If they agreed to participate they received an envelope containing an introduction letter, a questionnaire, and a stamped return envelope.

Of the total number of distributed questionnaires, 36 were returned by people in the metered community (60%) and 40 by people in the nonmetered community (66.7%). The final sample consisted of 32 men and 44 women with an average age of 43 years.

Questionnaire

The questionnaire was subdivided into various sections. The first section contained a number of questions regarding household (e.g., size of household) and demographic characteristics (e.g., age, gender, etc.). The second section consisted of a series of statements (1 = *strongly agree*, 5 = *strongly disagree*) measuring the perceptions and motives of people during the shortage. For example, there were items related to greed, the severity of the shortage (e.g., "The water shortage had an important impact on me and the other members of my community"), concern with responsible use, trust in others (e.g., "The shortage was due to gardeners using too much water"), and the efficacy to do something about the problem (e.g., "I found it difficult to change my behavior and adapt to the dramatic situation"). The third and final section contained a series of ten statements about how people adapted their behavior to the shortage (e.g., "I only used the dishwasher when I had a full load," "I washed my car less than usual"). All constructs were measured reliably with Cronbach's alpha's between .72 and .75 (i.e., greed was measured by a single item).

Results

Conservation Decision   A hierarchical regression analysis was performed to examine the behavioral effects of metering. In a preliminary analysis I included various demographic variables in the equation (e.g., age, gender, household size) but these were dropped because they did not affect the conservation decisions.[2] The main analysis included the dummy coded metering variable (0 = not metered, 1 = metered) and estimated severity of the shortage as factors in the design, because I argued that the effects of metering would be *particularly* pronounced when people were indeed aware of the resource crisis.

This analysis revealed no main effect for metering (*beta* = 0.08, n.s.), but I did find evidence for a main effect of severity (β = 0.47, p <.001) and an interaction between severity and metering (β = 0.44, p < .001). This interaction is graphically displayed in Figure 8.1. It shows that, relative to nonmetered residents, metered residents were more responsive to perceptions about the severity of the shortage. They exhibited greater conservation when they perceived the shortage to be more, rather than less, severe; however, the nonmetered residents' beliefs about the severity of the shortage did not influence their conservation. The totally explained variance by the three factors amounted to almost 30% (*adjusted R^2 = .30*).

Psychological Effects of Metering   Although the analysis failed to obtain a straightforward effect of metering on conservation, I did find that metering had a beneficial impact when people were aware of the resource crisis. I now look at some of the psychological mechanisms that may account for the positive effects of metering: greed, personal efficacy, responsibility, and trust.

I argued previously that the beneficial effects of metering may be due to the fact that people will be punished if they do not restrain themselves during a shortage as they will receive a higher bill. An ANOVA on the greed question ("I remained reluctant to splash out for fear of large bills") revealed that people in the metered sample (*M* = 1.93) were indeed more concerned with their personal costs than people in the nonmetered sample (*M* = 3.33), $F(1, 75)$ = 19.46, $p < .001$. This difference was particularly pronounced when the shortage was perceived as severe as indicated by a significant interaction effect between metering and severity (i.e., the latter variable was dichotomized through a median split), $F(1, 75)$ = 4.53, $p < .05$. In the high severity condition the difference between metered (*M* = 1.64) and nonmetered residents (*M* = 3.47) was much larger ($p < .05$) than in the low severity condition (*Ms* = 2.29 vs. 2.62; n.s.).

The effects of metering might also be due to a greater *personal efficacy* to make conservation efforts. I analyzed the results of two questions ("I found it difficult to change my behavior and adapt to the dramatic situation" and "Looking back I could not have restrained myself more than I did") and found that metering influenced only the responses

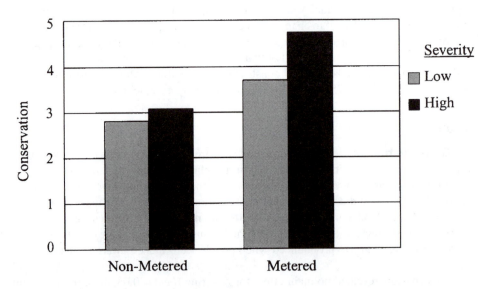

Figure 8.1   The influence of metering and perceptions about the severity of the shortage on conservation decisions during the 1995 UK shortage

to the second question. Relative to the nonmetered sample (M = 2.93), people in the metered sample thought they could have restrained themselves more during the shortage (M = 3.90), $F(1, 75)$ = 4.11, p <.05, which reveals a greater sense of efficacy to conserve. This was not further influenced by perceptions of the severity of the shortage.

A third advantage of metering might be that people become more concerned with responsible resource use. The analysis on a combined score of these items (e.g., "I felt that if I limit my water use this might have collective consequences") revealed no overall difference between the metered and nonmetered sample, $F(1, 75)$ < 1. However, metered residents showed a greater concern when the shortage was perceived as severe (M = 1.61) rather than insignificant (M = 2.72; p < .05), whereas this difference was less pronounced for nonmetered residents (Ms = 2.04 vs. 2.50; n.s.).

A final factor associated with metering might be that it enhances trust in the cooperation of others and prevents attributing the shortage to selfish others. I analyzed the results on a combined score of three questions related to trust (e.g., "The shortage was due to gardeners using too much water"). This analysis revealed that, as expected, residents in the metered sample (M = 2.86) were more trusting than residents in the nonmetered sample (M = 2.51), $F(1, 75)$ = 4.27, p < .05. This was not further influenced by perceptions about the severity of the shortage, $F(1, 75)$ = 1.34, n.s.

The above findings show that metering yields numerous psychological effects that may help to increase conservation. The availability of a meter appears to be associated with a greater concern about the personal and collective costs of water use, and it enhances feelings of efficacy, responsibility, and trust in others.

Mediators of the Impact of Metering During a Shortage   Which of these factors are most likely to account for the beneficial effects of metering during the experienced shortage? I performed several additional mediational analyses to examine which factors best account for the obtained behavioral effects. To establish mediation it has to be shown that these psychological mechanisms directly predict conservation decisions and that the effect of metering on conservation disappears or weakens when these factors are added as covariates (Baron & Kenney, 1986).

These additional analyses revealed that the most likely mediator of the impact of metering during the shortage is a concern with responsible water use. First, the previously reported analysis revealed that metered residents who perceived the shortage as severe were much more concerned with responsible resource use than the nonmetered residents. Furthermore, these concerns were positively and strongly related to people's conservation decisions (β = 0.57, p < .001). Finally, when these concerns were accounted for the interaction effect of metering and severity on conservation lost its strength (a 4% decrease in explained variance; β = 0.36 vs. 0.44 in the equation without the covariate). Hence, there is some evidence to suggest that the restraint shown by metered residents during the shortage was due predominantly to a greater concern with responsible resource management.

Water Consumption Records   In addition to the self-reported data from the survey, I analyzed the actual consumption records in the communities during the shortage period of 1995. Because I did not have specific consumption data available for the participants in the survey, I relied on the aggregated consumption data for the entire metered and nonmetered communities in which I recruited my participants. A comparison between the average consumption in these communities revealed a differential growth from the summer of 1994 to the dry summer of 1995. In the nonmetered community water demands increased by 12.3% compared to the previous year, whereas water demands rose by just 6.8% in the metered community. This supports our central claim that metering is particularly effective in moderating water demands in times of a shortage

CONCLUSIONS AND IMPLICATIONS

In this chapter I utilized insights from social dilemma research to understand the effects of domestic water metering. Having conceptualized metering as a techno-structural intervention in a natural resource dilemma, I examined the behavioral and psychological implications of this change. Our theoretical and empirical analysis lead to several conclusions.

Based upon a review of two large scale metering programs a first conclusion is that the installment of domestic water meters can have a dramatic impact on usage. Reductions in average demand of 11 and 36% per year were reported in studies conducted in the UK and US, respectively. The results revealed that these reductions remained fairly stable over the years. This suggests, with the introduction of meters, households develop new consumption patterns which become habitual after time. In this regard, it is interesting to note that there is a widespread idea in the research literature that the installment of conserving technological devices may lead to a "compensation" strategy (Geller et al., 1983), where use levels increase after a while to compensate for any financial savings (e.g., taking longer and more frequent showers). The current findings reveal no support for this theory with regard to metering as the usage remained consistently low once meters were introduced.[3]

What behavioral adjustments may account for the obtained reduction in water demand? It is not easy to answer this on the basis of these data because an extensive behavioral analysis is lacking. However, there is some preliminary evidence from the US study to suggest that water savings may have been largely due to one kind of behavioral change, a more restrained use of sprinklers. If this is true, I would expect the effects of metering to be most pronounced under a tariff system that makes excessive water use particularly unattractive during the summer months. A comparison between different tariff systems used in the UK metering trials indeed revealed that the greatest reduction in water demand was obtained in regions where metering was accompanied by a *seasonal* tariff (Department of Environment, 1993). Under this tariff households are charged extra for any water use in the summer which exceeds their usage in the winter. Accordingly, it is made less attractive for people to engage in activities during the summer that require large amounts of water, such as gardening or the use of swimming pools. Therefore our second conclusion is that metering is beneficial in promoting conservation but that the size of the effect depends, at least to some extent, on the nature of the *tariff system* that accompanies the meter.

Third, my own data indicate that the behavioral impact of water meters is influenced by perceptions about the state of the resources. In the face of a water shortage in their community, individuals in households with meters appeared to be more willing to make conservation efforts than households without meters. This difference was much smaller when there were no resource problems. These results were corroborated by looking at the actual consumption patterns in the two communities during the summer of 1995 when the shortage occurred. They showed a much stronger rise in water consumption in the nonmetered community than in the metered community compared to the summer period of 1994.

This result is important because it gives a strong justification for the widespread implementation of metering programs. Recall that, for example, in the UK just 10% of the properties are currently equipped with a meter. Following recent droughts, policy makers are increasingly concerned with finding solutions to cope with future shortages (OFWAT, 1996). Our findings suggest that the introduction of water meters may help to tackle future problems in two different ways. First, by decreasing water demands structurally, meters are instrumental in *preventing* a future shortage. Second, meters promote a better resource management during a shortage when there is an urgent need for conservation. To understand these multiple effects let us examine the various psychological processes associated with metering.

After theorizing about resource dilemmas (Messick et al., 1983; Samuelson et al., 1984), I proposed that metering works because it yields a personal incentive to conserve, promotes concern with responsible resource management, and is in line with people's fairness expectations. These motives are most salient during a water shortage. The analysis of my survey data revealed that the behavioral effects of metering during the shortage could be accounted for by concerns with collective well being. Compared with people in the nonmetered community, residents in the metered community were more concerned with responsible resource management, at least to the extent that they perceived the shortage as severe. As the resource problems in both communities were essentially the same, it is tempting to conclude that the availability of a meter evoked these concerns with the collective and longer-term personal interests.

How might this work? The presence of a meter perhaps conveys to people that water is a valuable and scarce resource which should not be wasted ("transformation of motivation"; cf. Kelley & Thibaut, 1978). Accordingly, metered households do not have to be told what to do when there is a collective threat. Although my mediational analyses suggest that this is the most likely explanation for the obtained effects, the social dilemma approach suggests alternative interpretations as well. First, as compared to nonmetered residents, metered residents might not need further instructions in a crisis as they probably know how to save water (personal efficacy; Bandura, 1977). This is perhaps why metered residents in my survey sample indicated they could have done more to restrain themselves during the shortage.

Second, in universally metered communities there presumably is greater trust in the conservation efforts of others as people realize that greedy others will receive higher bills (cf. structural goal/expectation theory; Yamagishi, 1986b). Preliminary evidence for this interpretation stems from my finding that, relative to the nonmetered sample, people in the metered sample attributed the cause of the shortage less to gardeners using too much water. Experimental research has indeed revealed that such attributions shape the way people behave in resource dilemmas (Samuelson, 1991).

Third, metering might be beneficial in saving water because the public might perceive it as a fairer method of distributing a valuable yet scarce resource such as water (OFWAT, 1996). That a metered charge might be considered fairer than a flat rate charge is in line with notions of equity because people pay more to the extent that they use more. The equity principle is commonly used in the transaction of economic or private goods (Deutsch, 1975). The strict application of this distribution rule in the domain of public goods or resources may, however, lead to an undesirable situation as vital goods or resources could be withheld from individuals who cannot afford to pay. This is a particular problem in countries or regions where water resources are insufficient, but many people are poor (e.g., developing countries). In these areas, the introduction of pay per use tariff systems is clearly not an appropriate strategy to tackle resource problems.

From a more theoretical perspective, my analysis of metering is important because it provides a conceptual framework to understand the nature and role of structural change in social dilemmas. Social dilemma theorists usually distinguish between individual-psychological and structural solutions and assume that the latter produce better results because they provide a direct incentive to cooperate (Messick & Brewer, 1983). The present analysis suggests, however, that a simple rational-economic model is too limited to explain the effects of structural change. First, the effectiveness of structural solutions is influenced by situational and group characteristics. As indicated in my studies structural interventions are more effective in the face of a resource shortage rather than abundance. Moreover, structural changes may also be more effective in low cohesive rather than high cohesive communities as people in weakly tied communities may not trust others to cooperate voluntarily.

Second, following a strictly rational approach, the primary motive in judging structural change is *greed*: "How does it affect my direct private outcomes?" However, the public acceptance of structural changes is also influenced by perceptions regarding their fairness, efficacy, and consequences for the collective interest (Samuelson & Messick, 1995; Van Vugt, 1997). These evaluations should be considered in order to understand why structural changes might sometimes fail. In a previous study, for example, I evaluated the implementation of a carpool lane in the Netherlands as a structural solution to the transportation dilemma (Van Vugt et al., 1996). From a purely rational perspective, this lane should have stimulated carpooling, because it gave people a huge time benefit relative to the normally congested lanes. Our longitudinal study revealed, however, that nobody in our sample of about 200 solo drivers switched to carpooling after the lane was opened. Our analyses indicated that car drivers resisted the change because they felt deprived from a benefit they thought they were entitled to—an extra lane to reduce traffic congestion (cf. "relative deprivation;" Cook, Crosby, & Hennigan, 1977). Also, they did not believe this lane would help in solving the collective problems associated with car use (i.e., environmental and congestion problems). These reactions could have been anticipated if policy makers had realized that the public does not evaluate structural changes purely in terms of immediate self-interest (e.g., a more favorable travel time).

Recommendations for Research and Policy

Based upon the previous discussion I would like to make some recommendations for further research into the effects of structural change in social dilemmas. One of the major goals of future research should be to develop a comprehensive theory of structural change, which takes into account the role of potentially important moderating and mediating psychological processes. Currently, a systematic theory for understanding the effects of structural change is lacking. Future research should evaluate structural interventions both in the real world as well as in the controlled laboratory environment. An important direction for applied research would be to examine the role of new technological developments, such as "power" showers, toilet dams, and cars on electricity because they may be important in saving natural resources (Kempton, Darley, & Stern, 1992). As Crabb (1992) pointed out in the *American Psychologist* some years ago: "Technological devices and products . . . are in themselves potent sources of behavior control, [and] play the key role in regulating depletion" (p. 815).

Finally, what lessons can we learn from the above for the development of resource management policies? A first lesson is that in the face of future shortages (in water or energy) it is undesirable to have charging systems in place where resource demand and costs are not or only weakly related. Accordingly, programs of metering should be implemented as soon as possible in places yet nonmetered, such as large areas in the UK and Ireland. Before implementing them, however, it is essential that there is sufficient public acceptance of meters as this will greatly facilitate their adoption (Stern, 1992). This could be achieved by public messages stressing the personal and collective advantages as well as fairness of metering. Moreover, once implemented people should be given intensive feedback about their use level, which can be achieved by sending regular bills and/or by locating the meter at a visible place in the house. For the short-term, the present findings suggest that educational activities during a forthcoming shortage must be targeted at households without a meter. They should receive messages telling them why they should and how they could save water since they may be lacking the motivation and skills to conserve.

ENDNOTES

[1] If one would compare nonmetered properties with properties that have been voluntarily metered it would be difficult to assess the impact of meters independent of existing differences between the households in, for example, family size, property value, and conservation attitudes. According to the UK tariff system metering is indeed relatively less attractive for larger families in cheaper accommodations.

[2] This may seem counterintuitive as these variables have been found to be important predictors of water consumption by other researchers (e.g., Aitken et al., 1994; Thompson & Stoutemeyer, 1991). However, the questions in my survey were primarily focused on how households *changed* their decisions during the shortage (e.g., "I washed my car less than usual") and there are no good reasons why this should be influenced by demographic characteristics, such as age or family size.

[3] An alternative explanation for the structural decrease in demand may be that water prices have risen systematically in the UK in the early 90s, thus making it more attractive for households with meters to save water.

Chapter 9

The Volunteer's Dilemma: Theoretical Models and Empirical Evidence

Axel Franzen

INTRODUCTION

Many interesting situations of public good provisions can be modeled as a volunteer's dilemma (VOD, Diekmann 1985). The most prominent example of a VOD game is helping behavior. Imagine a group of individuals watching an accident or a crime. Assuming the bystanders feel compassion for the victim, they obtain a benefit if the victim receives help. Since volunteering (that is helping the victim) is costly, even if it only means to call the police, every bystander might abstain from providing help, hoping for someone else to interfere. The phenomenon that bystanders of a crime or accident hesitate to help in the presence of others has inspired much research in social psychology. Darley and Latane (1968) labeled the reluctance of individuals in groups to help as "diffusion of responsibility."

Another example, discussed and analyzed by Brennan and Lomasky (1984), is voting behavior. Assume that a group of voters (e.g., members of a committee) has to make a decision on some proposal under unanimity rule. Acceptance of the proposal may increase the utility of outsiders but decrease the utility of the committee members. Every member prefers that someone use his or her right to veto the proposal. However, vetoing is costly

I am indebted to Norman Braun for helpful comments and discussions on this paper.

(e.g., the party that vetoes receives a bad reputation in the eyes of outsiders). Hence, the group needs a volunteer who is willing to veto in order to avoid a bad for the group.

A third example is the sanctioning dilemma. Assume a group of people whose utility is decreased because one member violates a norm (e.g., the norm not to smoke in a non-smoking restaurant or the norm to line up in a queue). In such a situation one member's expression of discomfort with the norm violation often suffices to restore the public good of clean air (or social order). However, providing the sanction is usually costly and so every member prefers someone else to do it.

These and other examples of volunteering behavior have been analyzed with game theoretical concepts. VOD is a special case of a public good, in which a single contribution of a player suffices to provide the good (or avoid a public bad). Public goods, once provided, are by definition open to usage by all players, even to noncontributors. Therefore, rational actors usually have an incentive not to contribute to the production of the good and to free-ride on the contribution of others. Because of this incentive problem rational actors might produce an inefficient outcome of collective goods.[1] Game theoretical analysis shows that rational actors have an incentive problem in the VOD. The game is therefore a special case of a social dilemma that is defined as a situation in which individual rational action leads to an inefficient collective outcome.[2]

Game theory is a normative theory. It tells us how individuals should behave if they are utility maximizers. But this does not necessarily exclude altruistic motives. Thus, the example of helping behavior demonstrates that altruism is included into the utility function which is subject to maximization. Actors can only derive utility from the fact that a victim receives help if they care for the well being of others. Therefore, they must be to some extent altruistic. Hence, whether altruistic motives are involved does not depend on the game theoretical model but rather on the nature of the public good.

The original formalization of the volunteer's dilemma is due to Diekmann (1985). Since then the game has received four major refinements which derive from the relaxation of major assumptions of the original game. This chapter is organized according to those refinements of the VOD. It describes the original model of the VOD. This game assumes that players have symmetric preferences concerning the outcome of the game, players have complete information about others' preferences, decisions are non-observable, and the production costs are indivisible. Thus, one extension of the game is achieved by relaxing the symmetry assumption. The chapter also discusses the consequences of introducing asymmetric preferences and then deals with the concept of time in the VOD. In the original model players have no opportunity to observe other players' decisions. However, the possibility to observe others' decisions makes time a crucial factor. Following this, the consequences of actors having only incomplete information about others' preferences are discussed. The penultimate section is concerned with cost sharing—that is, it examines the consequences of divisible production costs. Finally the theoretical and empirical research findings for the volunteer's dilemma are summarized.

THE VOLUNTEER'S DILEMMA

In its original version (Diekmann, 1985) a group of n individuals have equal interests in a public good. The good can be provided by the contribution of a single member. All individuals receive the same benefit (b) if the good is provided. Provision is costly (c) to the potential volunteer. Thus, the volunteer receives $b - c$ where $b > c$ and all noncontributors receive b. However, if no group member decides to volunteer all players will receive a payoff of 0. Thus, the game describes a symmetric binary choice situation in which all players have the option to provide the good or to free-ride on the provision of another player. The decision situation is depicted in Figure 9.1, where C denotes the decision to volunteer and D the option not to volunteer.[3]

If the players can communicate in the VOD they can agree on a mechanism (e.g., a lottery) to determine the volunteer. In such a case $N - 1$ players choose not to provide the good and one volunteers. Thus, there exist N asymmetric equilibria in pure strategies and all associated outcomes are Pareto-efficient.[4] Similarly, there is no obstacle to a Pareto-efficient solution if the game is iterated, since players could simply agree to take turns as a volunteer. However, if players have no opportunity to communicate in a one-shot VOD, there is no straightforward answer to the question of how rational actors should behave in the VOD. There exists a unique equilibrium solution in mixed strategies (Diekmann, 1985).[5] This equilibrium is found by calculating the expected payoff for a mixed strategy and determining that probability for which the payoff reaches a maximum. If q_i denotes the probability with which player i chooses not to volunteer then the expected payoff is given by:

$$E_i = q_i b \left(1 - \prod_{j}^{N} q_j \right) + (1 - q_i)(b - c) \text{ with } i \neq j \tag{1}$$

Taking the derivative with respect to q_i yields:

$$\frac{dE_i}{dq_i} = c - b \prod_{j}^{N} q_j \text{ with } i \neq j \tag{2}$$

Setting $dE_i/dq_i = 0$ ($i = 1, 2 \ldots N$) results in a system of simultaneous equations that yields the equilibrium strategy with the symmetric solution:

$$q_{VOD} = \sqrt[N-1]{\frac{c}{b}}. \tag{3}$$

Thus, the probability that utility maximizers will defect in the volunteer's dilemma is a function of group size (N) and the cost-benefit (c/b) ratio. The probability of defecting increases with group size and costs, but decreases with the benefit. Put differently, the probability that an individual volunteers decreases in larger groups and with larger costs,

C choices of other players

	0	1	2	...	N - 1
C	$b - c$	$b - c$	$b - c$	$b - c$	$b - c$
D	0	b	b	b	b

Figure 9.1 Volunteer's dilemma payoff matrix where C denotes volunteering and D not volunteering

and increases with larger benefits. Substituting Equation 3 into Equation 1 shows that the expected payoff of the equilibrium strategy is b – c. Hence, the expected payoff of the equilibrium strategy is not any larger than the payoff of the maximin strategy to volunteer. As a consequence a player may deviate from the equilibrium strategy towards a higher probability to volunteer without decreasing his expected payoff. Hence, the mixed equilibrium in the VOD may be called a weak equilibrium.

The probability that a public good will be provided by a group, which is not to be confused with the individual probability to volunteer, is given by:

$$P_{VOD} = 1 - q_{vod}^N \tag{4}$$

Substituting Equation 4 into Equation 3 yields:

$$P_{VOD} = 1 - \left[\frac{c}{b}\right]^{N/(N-1)} \tag{5}$$

From Equation 5 it is evident that a group of rational actors will always have a positive probability that no player volunteers and hence that the good will not be provided. Because of this characteristic, the volunteer's dilemma is a special case of a social dilemma, which by definition is a situation in which individual actions of rational players produce an inefficient collective outcome. The probability that a group has at least one volunteer decreases with the costs (c) and increases with the benefits (b). Furthermore, the derivative of P_{VOD} with respect to N is negative. Thus, the probability of public good provision decreases with larger group size.

The result that lower costs and higher benefits increase the individual as well as the macro probability of public good provision in the VOD conforms to intuition. It is also evident that larger groups have by definition a larger number of potential volunteers so that the individual probability to volunteer should decrease with N. However, the finding that larger groups have a lower likelihood of public good provision is rather counterintuitive. Thus, the effect that larger groups have more potential volunteers does not override the decreasing individual probability to volunteer. Therefore, according to game theoretic analysis, the chances that a victim receives help, that a norm violator will be sanctioned, or that an unfavorable proposition will be vetoed are larger in small groups than in large groups. On theoretical grounds the analysis of the volunteer's dilemma confirms, therefore, Olson's (1965) hypothesis that larger groups are less likely to obtain public goods.

The counterintuitive nature of the group size effect has inspired empirical research. One way to study the effect of group size is to construct field experiments. Examples include situations in which a confederate fakes an accident or constructs a helping situation and observes whether the presence of different numbers of bystanders influences the probability of public good provision (Darley & Latane, 1968; Latane & Nida, 1981). Another way is to conduct experiments in laboratories by describing the decision situation and by presenting payoff matrices similar to the one that is shown in Figure 9.1. Field experiments have the advantage of higher external validity, but the drawback is that not all factors are adequately controlled. Thus, in a field experiment a bystander's decision becomes immediately visible to all others. This actually changes the decision structure and calls for a refinement of the VOD model. Furthermore, in field experiments it is usually more difficult to control benefits and costs. Since costs and benefits are not observable in field experiments, the symmetry assumption of the original VOD might not be fulfilled. This calls for a further refinement of the game in order to submit game theoretic predictions to an empirical test in real life settings. Despite those differences most field experiments as well as laboratory studies on group size in the VOD find that individuals are less likely to volunteer with increasing group size but that the macro likelihood of public good provision increases contrary to game theoretic expectation.

This result was also observed in an experimental study by the author (Franzen, 1995).[6] The experimental results (see Figure 9.2) confirm the qualitative predictions derived from game theory. The proportion of participants who cooperate in the VOD decreases with increasing group size.[7] However, the prediction is not very accurate. The observed cooperation rates in all groups, particularly in the larger ones, are much higher than expected according to equilibrium behavior. That does not come as a great surprise since the mixed equilibrium is weak and deviations are not punished by smaller expected payoffs. As a consequence of the higher individual rates of volunteering, the macro probability of public good provision is much higher than hypothesized. If the observed rates are substituted into Equation 4 then 2-person groups would have provided the good with a probability of .88, 3-person groups with a probability of .93, 5-person groups with .94, 7-person groups with .87 and 9-person groups with a probability of .98. Thereafter the probability of public good provision is very close to 1. Thus, on the macro level the data contradict the game theoretical hypothesis. According to the mixed equilibrium the macro level probability should be .75 for the 2-person group and fall thereafter to .50 in the largest group. Instead, the data show that the probabilities of public good provision are increasing with group size. Hence, the experimental evidence actually suggests some doubts about Olson's (1965) analysis. Similar findings concerning the effect of group size are reported by Darley and Latane (1968), Diekmann (1986) and Murnighan, Kim and Metzger (1993).[8]

ASYMMETRIC PREFERENCES IN THE VOLUNTEER'S DILEMMA

The assumption of symmetric preferences is rather unrealistic in real life settings of public good provisions. Most likely, there is variance in costs of provision or utility derived from the good for different actors. Diekmann (1993) generalized the original game by introducing asymmetric costs and benefits. As in the symmetric case there are N equilibria in the asymmetric game in which one player volunteers and all others defect. Furthermore, there exists an equilibrium in mixed strategies that is given by allowing for different benefits and costs by substituting b_i and c_i into Equation 1:

$$E_i = q_i b_i (1 - \prod_{j \neq i}^{N} q_j) + (1 - q_i)(b_i - c_i) \tag{6}$$

Taking the derivative of Equation 6 with respect to q_i, setting the resulting N equations to zero, and rearranging yields the following equilibrium solution:

$$q_i^* = \frac{b_i}{c_i} \left(\prod_{j=i}^{N} \frac{c_j}{b_j} \right)^{\left(\frac{1}{N-1} \right)} \tag{7}$$

Analogously to the symmetric VOD, substitution of Equation 7 into Equation 6 gives the maximin payoff of $b_i - c_i$. The mixed equilibrium yields a rather counterintuitive result. If the costs (c) of providing a public good decrease for a player i or, alternatively, the benefits (b) increase then q_i^* increases. Thus a strong player with a relatively large interest in the

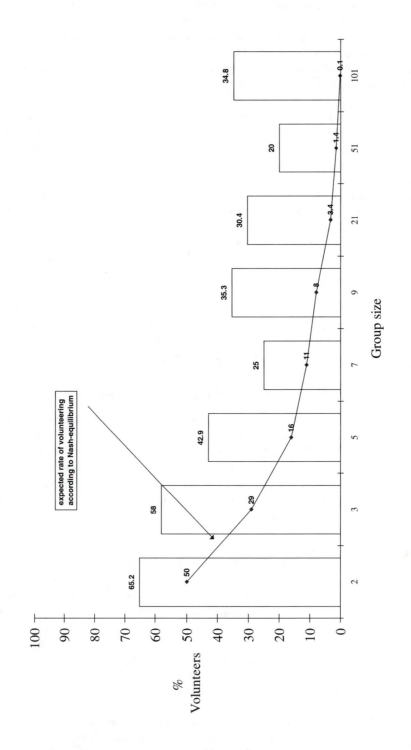

Figure 9.2 Group size effects in the volunteer's dilemma

good or relatively low production costs will be less likely to volunteer.[9] However, Schelling's (1960) concept of *focal equilibrium* in situations of conflict suggests that players will choose the asymmetric equilibrium in pure strategies. Particularly, if a single player is clearly the strongest actor, the prominent or focal solution would be that he or she volunteers. A similar conclusion can be derived from Harsanyi and Selten's (1988) theory of equilibrium selection. As in the symmetric VOD the individual probability to volunteer decreases for the mixed equilibrium with group size as well as the probability that the public good will be provided.[10]

Since the analysis of the asymmetric VOD produces rather counterintuitive results, experimental research is of particular interest. Diekmann (1993) tested the effect of strength and weakness on the probability of volunteering for 2- and 5-person groups.[11] The experimental results confirm the common sense expectation. Strong (weak) players have a higher (lower) probability to volunteer. Thus, in experiments participants tend to realize the asymmetric equilibrium in pure strategies, but do not adhere to the counterintuitive mixed equilibrium. Group size effects were found in two out of three test situations. Individuals in larger groups did defect more often than players in smaller groups.

TIMING IN THE VOD

Another extension of the volunteer's dilemma is the volunteer's timing dilemma (VTD) from Weesie (1993). Its starting point is that in reality (and in contrast to the volunteer's dilemma) individuals can very often observe others' choices. The decision is no longer to contribute or not contribute, but rather whether an actor should volunteer immediately or wait whether another actor volunteers. Assume further that the value (benefit) of the public good decreases with increasing time delay (e.g., the chance that a victim is rescued diminishes with the time delay). Though players' costs (c) for volunteering remain constant, the benefits decrease with increasing waiting time. Denote the probability of a successful public good provision by $\varphi(t)$. Then an actor receives a utility of $b_i\varphi(t) - c_i$ if he volunteers and $b_i\varphi(t)$ otherwise.

In the symmetric VTD all players have the same costs of providing the good and the same interest in receiving the good. There are N equilibrium sets in pure strategies in which one player volunteers immediately (at time delay 0) and all others free-ride on the provision of the volunteer. There is also an equilibrium in mixed strategies (Weesie, 1993):

$$q_{VTD} = \exp\left(\frac{c - b}{(N - 1)c}\right) \tag{8}$$

where q_{VTD} denotes the probability that a player does not volunteer at any time. This probability is positive and increases with group size (N), rises with increasing costs (c), and decreases with increasing benefits (b).[12] Thus, q_{VTD} and q_{VOD} are analogous with respect to the effects of group size and the cost benefit ratio. Also, the expected payoff in both games is b-c. However, the probability of defection is lower in the VTD than in the VOD.

The macro probability that the public good will be provided is (Weesie, 1993):

$$P_{VTD} = 1 - \exp\left(\frac{N}{N - 1} \cdot \frac{c - b}{c}\right) \tag{9}$$

It follows from Equation 9 that there is still a positive probability that the public good will not be provided. Because of this positive probability, the mixed equilibrium solution of

VTD is Pareto-inefficient as in VOD. However, the probability that no good will be provided is smaller in the VTD than in the VOD. But in the VTD volunteering might happen after a time delay, which by definition, decreases the value of the public good. It can be shown (Weesie, 1993) that the expected value of the public good is smaller in the symmetric VTD than in the VOD. Thus, applied to a rescue situation a victim is more likely to receive help when bystanders can observe each other's behavior. But the possibility of observation introduces a time delay that decreases the chance that the victim receives the help in time and thus makes helping less valuable.

Weesie (1993) analyzes the volunteer's timing dilemma with asymmetric preferences. It can be shown that if one player in the VTD has lower costs to provide the good or has higher benefits from it, and thus is a strong player, he or she will volunteer without any time delay. Hence, if players are able to observe each other's behavior in an asymmetric VTD then the equilibrium solution will be in line with common sense expectations. So far neither the volunteer's timing dilemma nor the VTD with asymmetric preferences have been empirically investigated.

INCOMPLETE INFORMATION IN THE VOLUNTEER'S DILEMMA

So far all variations of the VOD assumed that players have complete information on the costs and benefits of all other coplayers. But this assumption is not very realistic. Most likely players in real life situations of public good provision will not know each other's production costs or benefits. Thus, Weesie's (1994) introduction of incomplete information is a useful extension of the VOD. Incomplete information means that players only know their own cost-benefit ratio (c/b) but not that of others. Weesie (1994) assumes that players only know the distribution of others' cost-benefit ratios which in their simplest form is uniform with $U[(c/b) - \sigma, (c/b) + \sigma)]$. Thus, the larger σ, the larger the uncertainty about others' cost-benefit ratios in the volunteer's dilemma with incomplete information. For the VOD with uncertainty Weesie (1994) proves that the individual probability to defect (α_{vdi}) increases in σ if and only if $(1/2)^{N-1} < c/b$.

Unfortunately, Weesie (1994) misinterpreted the theorem. The effect of uncertainty in the VOD depends on the condition $(1/2)^{N-1} < c/b$. This condition is more likely to be fulfilled in large groups. Thus in large groups uncertainty increases the probability to defect. But in smaller groups the individual probability to defect (α_{vdi}) *decreases* with uncertainty. Hence, in small groups uncertainty may foster volunteering behavior.

The effects of uncertainty are completely reversed for the volunteer's timing dilemma. Weesie (1994) shows that the individual probability for unconditional defection (α_{vdi}) increases in σ if and only if $c/b < (c/b)\tilde{}_N$. The threshold $(db)\tilde{}_N$ decreases in N and satisfies $1/2(N-1) < (db)\tilde{}_N < 1/2$. Therefore, the probability of defection increases with uncertainty if groups are small. In larger groups uncertainty decreases the probability that a player will defect. Thus, in the volunteer's timing dilemma uncertainty fosters cooperation only in large groups. So far research on incomplete information in the VOD and VTD has been conducted analytically. But the hypotheses that are derived from game theoretical analysis have not been empirically tested.

COST SHARING IN THE VOLUNTEER'S DILEMMA

There is a fourth extension of the volunteer's dilemma, namely the introduction of cost sharing (Weesie & Franzen, 1998). In many settings the cost of public good provision is divided among players. For example, if a victim is in distress several bystanders could intervene and share each other's costs by coordinating their help. Another example is the maintenance of a community center. The latter depends on many voluntary contributions such as time spent on cleaning, renovating, or the organization of social activities. Clearly, most activities are divisible so that the provision costs for each actor decreases with the number of volunteers. Cost sharing may also take place in voting behavior under the unanimity rule. Suppose that a committee member who vetoes a proposal that is unfavorable to the committee members but favorable to outsiders receives a bad reputation if outsiders get to know his choice. The costs of receiving a bad reputation can be shared and thus decreased if others veto as well.

Assuming that all volunteers share costs, player i's utility function may be written as:

$$u_i(s;b,c) = \begin{cases} b - \dfrac{c}{k} & if \quad s_i = C_i \\ b & if \quad s_i = D_i \quad and \quad k \geq 1; \quad and \\ 0 & if \quad k = 0. \end{cases}$$

where k denotes the number of volunteers. Thus, the utility function that is given here assumes symmetry in the sense that all players have the same costs and benefits as well as that costs are shared equally among the volunteers. There exists a symmetric equilibrium in the VCS that is given by:

$$\alpha_{VCS} = \frac{\omega(b/c)}{N} + O(N^{-2}) . \tag{10}$$

where α_{VCS} denotes the probability to volunteer, $\omega(.)$ is a Riemann function, and $O(N^{-2})$ represents a residual term which can be neglected for large N. The probability to volunteer increases with benefits (b) and decreases with costs (c) and group size (N).[13] Moreover, the macro level probability that the public good will be provided is given by:

$$P_{VCS} = 1 - (1 - \alpha_{VCS})^N. \tag{11}$$

Substituting Equation 10 into Equation 11 yields:

$$P_{VCS} = 1 - e^{-\omega(b/c)} + O(N^{-2}). \tag{12}$$

Therefore, the probability that the good will be produced increases with b and decreases with c and group size N.

Further insights into the characteristics of the game are gained by a comparison between the volunteer's dilemma with and without cost sharing. Note that the qualitative characteristics of the volunteer's dilemma are analogous to the characteristics of the volunteer's dilemma with cost sharing. In both games the micro probability to cooperate as well as the macro probability that the good will be produced increase with benefits (b) and decreases with costs (c) as well as group size N. Thus, cost sharing does not affect the conclusion that larger groups have a lower probability of public good production despite the fact that larger groups have, by definition, more potential volunteers. However, cost sharing implies that the individual costs (c) for producing the good are lower in the VCS than in the VOD. Hence, costs are potentially reduced in the VCS and therefore α_{VCS} and P_{VCS} are strictly larger than α_{VOD} and P_{VOD} if the cost-benefit ratio and group size are held constant.[14] The difference between the micro level probabilities depend on the cost-benefit ratio and on group size. In large groups the probabilities are very small and, consequently, so are the differences.

To test the qualitative hypotheses of the volunteer's dilemma with cost sharing and its differences to the original volunteer's dilemma Weesie and Franzen (1998) conducted an experiment. Group size was varied between 2, 4, and 8 players. The benefits of the public good were set to 100 points ($b = 100$) while the costs of volunteering varied between a high cost ($c = 80$) and a low cost situation ($c = 40$).[15] To compare behavior in the VCS with behavior in the VOD both variations were also conducted for the symmetric volunteer's dilemma. Thus, the experiment is a three way factorial design: dilemma type (2) by group size (3) by cost-benefit ratio (2), with 12 experimental conditions. For each of the 12 conditions separate questionnaires were designed in which the decision task was verbally explained and presented in matrix form. Participants were told that a given number of other players received the same questionnaire and that their payoffs would be determined by the match of their own and others' decisions. Participants indicated their decision to volunteer or not volunteer. In addition they had to give an estimate of how many of their coplayers would choose either alternative. Furthermore, participants were asked to calculate their own payoffs given that their estimate on their coplayers choice as well as the payoffs coplayers would receive would be correct. This information was later used to determine whether participants properly understood the decision situation.

An equal number of copies of the 12 questionnaires were randomly assigned to a random sample of 850 first and third year students of the University of Berne in Switzerland. Four hundred and eighty-nine students returned the questionnaire of which 465 answered all control questions correctly. Since there was no selective influence of the conditions on the response rate there were between 33 and 45 participants in every experimental category. About half of the participants were female. A third of the students were enrolled in economic and law programs, one third in history and language programs and another third in medicine and natural sciences. Figure 9.3 depicts the results of the experiment.

It can be observed from Figure 9.3[16] that the qualitative hypotheses are mainly corroborated. The *individual* probability to cooperate was, as predicted, a decreasing function of group size. This replicates former findings about group size effects in the VOD. The group size effect is clear for all experimental conditions between group sizes 2 and 4. However, for larger groups ($N = 8$) the results are less clear cut. A minor drop of volunteering behavior can be observed for the VOD conditions. In the VCS condition, the effect is undetermined. There is a profound drop in the cooperation rate for the VCS with low cost between group sizes 4 and 8, but an increase for the VCS with high cost. In accordance with theoretical predictions is also that cooperation rates are always higher in the cost sharing condition than in the VOD. Furthermore, an increase in the provision costs (c) decreases the probability to volunteer with one exception in all conditions. These observations are confirmed by a logit-analysis in which all three effects were in the expected direction and are statistically significant.

Figure 9.4 shows that the observed values of the low cost conditions are rather close to the game theoretical predictions, particular for the VCS. However, for the high cost situation the experimental results deviate clearly from the predictions.[17] Overall, it can be concluded that the qualitative predictions, the direction of the main effects, were con-

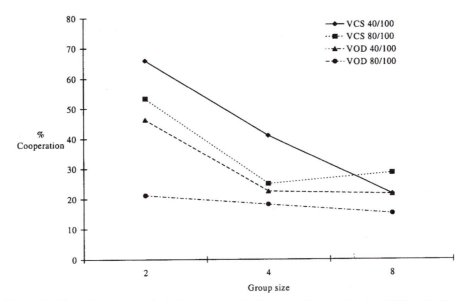

Figure 9.3 Experimental results in the volunteer's dilemma with cost sharing (VCS) and without cost sharing (VOD)

firmed by the experiment. However, the game theoretical model does not describe the observed frequencies very accurately.

CONCLUSIONS

The volunteer's dilemma is a game theoretical model of a class of social situations in which a single volunteer suffices to provide a public good. The game is a special case of a social dilemma, since rational players will produce only an inefficient amount of the good. The model explains a paradoxical phenomenon found in social life: Rational individuals who have sympathy with a victim, and are thus to some extent altruistic, may not help a victim, because they hope that someone else will provide the help. However, the model is more pessimistic than empirical findings suggest. It predicts, although as a *weak equilibrium*, not only that individuals decrease their propensity to help with increasing group size but also that larger groups are less likely to provide the good at all. Experimental evidence confirms the micro level prediction but sheds some doubts on the macro level conclusions. Thus, at least in experiments, participants show a higher probability to volunteer than is expected on the basis of the equilibrium strategy. As a consequence the good is produced more often than is predicted. Particularly, experimental evidence suggests that the (macro level) probability of public good production increases with group size.

The original model assumes symmetry in costs and benefits, complete information on those costs and benefits, and nonobservability of other players' decisions. During the last decade relaxing those assumptions refined the volunteer's dilemma. Asymmetric cost-benefit ratios, incomplete information, observability, and cost sharing were introduced. Analytically, most of these refinements do not alter the basic qualitative predictions—that volunteering is a decreasing function of the cost-benefit ratio and group size. There is, however, one exception. In an asymmetric volunteer's dilemma with complete information a stronger player (e.g., with lower costs or higher benefits) has, according to the mixed

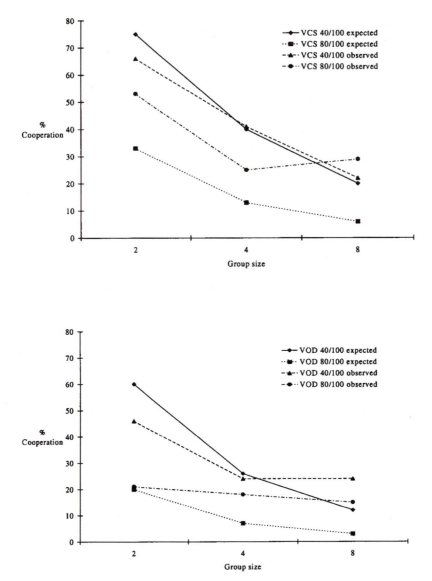

Figure 9.4   Expected and observed rates of cooperation in the VCS and VOD

equilibrium solution, a lower probability to provide the good than a weak player (i.e., someone with higher costs and lower benefits).

The introduction of observability and cost sharing both foster the individual propensity to volunteer as well as the group level chance that the good will be provided. The situation is somewhat more complicated when uncertainty about others' cost-benefit ratio is introduced. In the VOD uncertainty fosters volunteering when groups are small but it inhibits volunteering when groups are large. The effect of uncertainty is completely reversed for the volunteer's timing dilemma. In the VTD uncertainty increases the propensity to volunteer in large groups but decreases it in small groups.

So far experimental evidence is available for the symmetric and the asymmetric volunteer's dilemma as well as for the volunteer's dilemma with cost sharing. Up to now the effects of observability and uncertainty had not been experimentally assessed. Conducting such experimental research could be a fruitful route for further research on public good provisions.

ENDNOTES

[1] See Ledyard (1995) for a review and discussion of literature on public goods.

[2] Note that this definition of a *social dilemma* is broader than the one that was provided by Dawes (1980), who introduced the term. Dawes defined social dilemmas as situations in which every player has (a) a dominant strategy and in which (b) actors' uses of their dominant strategies result in an inefficient outcome. The symmetric equilibrium strategy in VOD is not a dominant strategy, but the symmetric equilibrium solution still results in an inefficient outcome.

[3] At first sight, the volunteer's dilemma seems to be a special case of the minimal contribution set (MCS) described by Van De Kragt, Orbell and Dawes (1983) and formalized by Rapoport (1985). In the MCS it is assumed that a group of k players ($1 < k < N$) suffices to provide a public good. However, the MSC explicitly excludes the possibility that one player ($k=1$) suffices to provide the good as is assumed in the VOD (Rapoport, 1985). This changes the strategic properties of the game. In the VOD ($k = 1$) volunteering is a maximin strategy whereas in the MCS cooperation is never maximin (see Diekmann, 1994).

[4] If a player i is determined by lottery or any other mechanism to volunteer then none of the N players (including i) has an incentive to deviate from that strategy combination. If there are N players then there are N possible strategy combinations in pure strategies and thus N asymmetric equilibria.

[5] A pure strategy tells a player to either play C or D. A mixed strategy is one that instructs an actor to mix C and D choices. In a one-shot game the term *mixed strategy* refers to a behavior in which an actor chooses C with a certain probability and plays D otherwise.

[6] To conduct the experiment 203 students of the University of Mannheim, Germany were arbitrarily recruited and randomly assigned to the different group size conditions. Thus, there were about 25 participants in every condition. Participants did not form real groups, instead, a separate questionnaire describing the situation and telling participants how many coplayers there were was constructed for every group size condition. Participants had to make their decision privately without communication or any other form of feedback. Cost (c) and benefits (b) were set to 50 and 100 points and were later transferred into money. For further detail see Franzen (1995).

[7] Group size has a statistical significant effect on the cooperation rate ($\chi^2 = 16.24$, $df = 7$, $p < .05$).

[8] These studies have different experimental designs. Darley and Latane (1968) use 2- and 5-person groups in a real life setting. Diekmann (1993) uses a similar design to the one reported. However, all participants ($N = 29$) had to made the decisions sequentially in all group size condition (2 through 10) so that decisions might not be independent. Murnighan et al. (1993) use hypothetical scenarios and no monetary payoffs with the drawback that participants might not take their decisions very seriously since they have no consequence. Taken together, however, experimental evidence is consistent.

[9] Weesie (1993) presents the same solution for the mixed equilibrium as Diekmann (1993); however, he misinterprets the results. The paradox of the asymmetric VOD exists in the fact that the stronger player would, according to the mixed equilibrium solution free-ride on the provision of the weaker player. Thus, the finding is not a rediscovery of Olson's (1965) assertion that sometimes strong players are exploited by weak players as Weesie suggests. The mixed equilibrium solution predicts quite the contrary.

[10] The probability that the good will be provided is given by

$$P = 1 - \left(\prod_{i=1}^{N} \frac{c_i}{b_i} \right)^{\left(\frac{1}{N-1} \right)}$$

The partial derivative of P with respect to N is negative. Thus, the probability P decreases with increasing N. It is, in contrast to Diekmann's (1993) assertion, a negative function of group size.

[11] The experimental procedure was very similar to the one described in Endnote 7. Participants were randomly assigned to different conditions. They were not part of real groups but received questionnaires which contained payoff matrices and written instructions on how many players would be assigned to the group. Decisions were then taken anonymously.

[12] Note that the implication of Equation 8 with respect to the cost benefit ratio is misinterpreted in Weesie (1993), but correct in Weesie (1994).

[13] Mathematical details and proofs may be found in Weesie and Franzen (1998).

[14] With $\alpha_{VOD} = 1 - q_{vod}$.

[15] Participants were informed that points would be transferred into monetary payoffs. One hundred points were transferred to 10 Swiss Francs (about $US 9).

[16] Benefits (b) were set to 100 points in all experimental conditions while costs (c) varied between 40 (low cost) and 80 (high cost) points. (Sample size = 465).

[17] This conclusion is confirmed by a test based on a deviance statistic. Note that the game theoretical predictions assume risk neutrality, thus it is assumed that money equals utility. For details see Weesie and Franzen (1998).

Chapter 10

Providing Step Level Public Goods Under Uncertainty: The Case of Probable External Supply

Ramzi Suleiman
Keren Or-Chen

INTRODUCTION

Following a talk on provision of public goods delivered by the first author at Al-Gish (an Arab village in northern Israel), one activist who was unfamiliar with the experimental literature in the field remarked that the basic experimental paradigms she had just learned, fail to capture certain situations that she and her colleagues encounter in fund raising for public projects. She mentioned cases in which the needed funds may be supplied by an external source (e.g., the central government), and raised concerns that the knowledge that a project might be supported externally might discourage the public from contributing for its provision. On a much wider scale, similar concerns were recently voiced in England, where several newspaper articles expressed concerns that publications concerning financial support for charities by the lotteries might reduce the amount of public donations to these charities.

This study was supported by a grant awarded to the first author by The Israel Science Foundation. We wish to thank the anonymous reviewer for his or her helpful remarks.

The possibility that public goods can be supplied externally was first alluded to by R. Hardin (1982) who distinguished between states of *internal supply*, where goods are supplied by the collective effort of the group members, and states of *external supply*, where the goods are supplied by an external agent. All existing research on public goods relates to the first category. The reason for this, most probably, is that the certain knowledge that the goods are to be supplied by an external source abates the social dilemma by completely eliminating the need for collective action. This is not the case for situations in which the external supply can not be secured with certainty; that is, when group members believe that external supply is probable, but not certain. Under such conditions, it is reasonable to assume that such information can affect the contributions of group members and their beliefs regarding the contributions of others.

The juxtaposition of internal and external sources of supply creates a variety of situations dependent on the type of goods (continuous, binary) and the ways by which the two sources add up for its provision. For example, the goods can be of a continuous nature and the relationship between the internal and external sources of supply can be a simple additive one. Such cases can be modeled by a simple variant of the n-person prisoner's dilemma (NPD) game. In other situations, the goods can be binary or "step-level"[1] (Hampton, 1987; Rapoport, 1987) as in the cases of railway lines or public roads, and the relationship between the two sources of supply can be additive. For such cases, the goods can be provided when the *cumulative* supply of the two sources (internal and external) exceeds the threshold. Alternatively, they can be provided when the supply from at least one of the sources, or from both, exceeds the threshold.

To illustrate, consider the case of a city neighborhood that seeks to raise contributions from its residents for building a public park. Notwithstanding the residents' contributions, there is a chance that the funds needed for the project might be given by the municipality. Receipt of the required sum from the external source (the municipality) will guarantee the realization of the project, regardless of the amount of money raised by voluntary contributions. If, on the other hand, the external source proves a disappointment and no money is received from the municipality, then the successful implementation of the project will depend solely on the money contributed by the residents themselves. For cases similar to the one described here, it is reasonable to assume that individuals' contributions will be affected by their subjective estimates that the goods can be supplied externally.

The present study focuses on such situations by investigating the effects of *social uncertainty* regarding the possibility that the goods might be supplied externally, regardless of the groups' efforts to secure their provision. Our main objectives are:

(a) to test the effect of the probability for external supply on individual and group contribution behaviors,

(b) to test the effects on contribution behavior of two individual attributes: social orientations and risk preferences, and

(c) to propose, and test, three theoretical models which may account for individuals' contribution behaviors.

Specifically, we derive extensions of three models: a subjective expected value (SEV) model, a game theoretic model, and a cooperative model for step level cases involving the possibility of external supply. We then compare the predictive power of these models based on experimental data.

In order to achieve these objectives, we first provide a brief description of step level public goods and summarize three previous theoretical models (a subjective expected value model, a cooperative model, and a game theoretical model) developed to account for individual contribution for step level goods. The next section provides a brief summary of two individual attribute variables—namely, social value orientation and risk preference. We then describe the experimental paradigm for the modified step level game with external supply, and extend the previously described models for the case of the modified game. Next we outline an experiment conducted to examine contribution behavior under various probabilities of external supply, and to compare the predictive power of the derived models. Finally, the study concludes with a discussion regarding the implications of the present research.

MODELING STEP-LEVEL PUBLIC GOODS

The social dilemma elicited by the public goods (PG) situation was originally modeled as an NPD game in which free-riding is a dominant strategy (Dawes, 1980). While such modeling might be appropriate for many PG situations, there exists a group of other situations that cannot be modeled as NPD games. In particular, some public goods are provided only after a minimal amount of resources (effort, money, etc.) has been contributed to their production. When provided, such goods do not increase in quality or quantity if more contributions are made. These goods have been termed *lumpy*, *binary*, or *pure step* goods. Examples of step level goods are railway lines, public roads, and bridges. Ecological systems such as rivers and forests may also be modeled as step level PGs, since they can often be exploited up to some critical level while retaining much of their use value. Once exploitation exceeds the critical threshold their use value may fall drastically.

A systematic investigation of the structural variables that affect voluntary contribution to the provision of step level goods was started by Van de Kragt, Orbell, and Dawes (1983). They proposed a paradigm that can be briefly described as follows: each member of a group N of n members receives an endowment of $\$e$ $(e > 0)$. Each member must then decide whether to contribute his or her entire endowment to the benefit of the group. If m or more players contribute their endowments, each of the n players receives a bonus (public good) worth $\$r$ $(r > e)$; otherwise, the public good is not provided. The game is played once, and the values of n, m, e and r are common knowledge.

Theoretical Models

Experimental research that utilized this paradigm (Dawes, Orbell, Simmons, & Van de Kragt, 1986; Poppe & Utens, 1986; Rapoport & Eshed-Levi, 1989; Rapoport & Suleiman, 1993; Suleiman & Rapoport, 1992) was partly motivated by three major theoretical models. The first is a strategic (game theoretical) approach proposed by Palfrey and Rosenthal (1984, 1988, 1991). The model solves for the equilibrium points of the game, where an equilibrium point is a solution (here a vector of all contributions) that, if reached, no single individual can benefit from deviating fit *unilaterally*. For the standard step level PG game with symmetric players, the model prescribes several equilibria in pure strategies (Palfrey & Rosenthal, 1984). One equilibrium point predicts that no one will contribute. The remaining pure-strategy equilibria predict that m out of the n players will contribute while $n - m$ will not. These are all the $n!/m!(n - m)!$ possibilities of forming a *minimal contribut-*

ing set (Van de Kragt et al., 1983). In a subsequent study, Palfrey and Rosenthal (1988) solved for a modified game in which they introduced an additive component to each player-payoff function to account for his or her private altruistic preference. An additional refinement of the strategic model is in the introduction of controlled communication, or "cheap talk" between players, through which each player can indicate whether he or she intends to contribute (Palfrey & Rosenthal, 1991).

A second approach for explaining individual contribution in step level PG situations is the SEV approach (Dawes et al., 1986; Rapoport, 1985; Taylor & Ward, 1982). According to this approach, the players' decisions whether to contribute or not are based on maximization of expected value considerations. Given the fact that noncontribution is not a dominant strategy, such considerations involve the participant's perceived likelihood (modeled by his or her subjective probability) that each of the other group members will contribute. Dawes et al. (1986) and Rapoport (1987) independently modified the SEV model to account for the *money back guarantee* (no fear) and the *fair-share* (no greed) *half dilemmas*. Another model was introduced by Suleiman and Rapoport (1992), who extended the theory and experimentation on step level public goods by removing the restriction that contribution is binary.

A third model for explaining individual contribution in step level PG situations with continuous contribution is a cooperative (C) model proposed by Suleiman and Rapoport (1992). Unlike the strategic and the SEV models, the C model assumes that individuals are not entirely selfish. Based on Kantian reasoning (see Laffont, 1975), it is assumed that individuals' strivings to maximize their payoffs are constrained by a tacit commitment to contribute their fair share. Experimental results from groups with symmetric and asymmetric endowments (Rapoport & Suleiman, 1993; Suleiman & Rapoport, 1992) showed that the C model's predictions of individual contributions outperformed the predictions of the SEV model.

INDIVIDUAL ATTRIBUTES

Social Orientations

Messick and McClintock (1968) defined social orientation as a general and relatively stable tendency to make consistent choices in social decision situations, in the hope of obtaining a desirable combination of own-other outcomes. Although many social values can be identified, the social-psychological literature has been traditionally concerned with three major orientations:

1 individualism, defined as the tendency to maximize one's own gains;
2 competition, defined as the tendency to maximize one's relative gains; and
3 cooperation, defined as the tendency to maximize joint gains.

Research on social orientations shows that these predict well the choices made in two-person, and in n-person social dilemma games. For example, McClintock and Liebrand (1988) found significant differences between the choices of cooperative, competitive, and individualistic participants in the prisoner's dilemma, chicken, trust, and leader games. Liebrand (1984) and Liebrand and Van Run (1985) reported that the amounts appropriated from a common pool in a multistage resource dilemma game were fully consistent with the participants' social orientations. In the present study, we test whether social orientations predict contribution behavior in a step level public goods game with possible external supply.

Attitudes Toward Risk

Predictions of individual and group performance in social dilemma situations can be improved if outcomes are evaluated in terms of their utilities (Suleiman & Rapoport, 1992). Notwithstanding, only a few previous studies have incorporated measurement of participants' risk preferences in social dilemma experiments (Parks & Godfrey, 1997; Rapoport & Suleiman, 1993; Suleiman & Rapoport, 1992). Parks and Godfrey found that the tendency for risk taking was a good predictor of the willingness to contribute to step level public goods. In the present study we test whether this holds true for situations involving the possibility of external supply.

STEP-LEVEL PUBLIC GOODS WITH PROBABLE EXTERNAL SUPPLY

The Van de Kragt et al. (1983) experimental paradigm and the theoretical models described in the previous section can be easily modified to account for the case of step level public goods with a probable external supply. The modified paradigm can be summarized as follows:

1   The game is played by a group N of n players.
2   Communication is prohibited.
3   Each player i ($i \in N$) receives a monetary endowment of e units ($e > 0$). He or she then decides independently and anonymously whether to contribute, or not contribute the entire endowment.
4   If the external supply is realized, the goods are provided, and each player receives a reward of size r ($r > e$) regardless of the number of contributors.
5   The external supply is provided with a probability q, which is common knowledge.
6   If the external supply is not realized, then the goods will be provided to all group members only if the number of contributors equals or exceeds a given threshold m. Otherwise, the goods will not be provided, and all contributors will lose their endowments.
7   Except for the final payoff, no feedback is given about the contributions of others.

Three Theoretical Models

A Subjective-Expected-Value Model   We now extend the SEV model proposed by Rapoport (1985) to account for the case of step level goods with probable external supply. Using Rapoport's notation, let P_{m-1} denote the i-th individual's subjective probability that exactly $m - 1$ others will contribute, and let P_{m+} denote his or her subjective probability that m or more others will contribute. Finally, denote the probability for external supply by q. The expected payoff matrix for player i is depicted in Table 10.1.

The expected value of contributing for individual i is given by:

$$EV(C) = qr(1 - P_{m-1} - P_{m+}) + r(P_{m-1} + P_{m+}) \tag{1}$$

and his or her expected value for not contributing is:

Table 10.1   Expected payoff matrix for player I.

Number of other contributors			Player's decision
$m+$	$m-1$	$m-2$	
r	r	$q \cdot r$	Contribute C
$e + r$	$e + q \cdot r$	$e + q \cdot r$	Not contribute $\bar{C}$

$$EV(\bar{C}) = e + qr + (1 - q)rP_{m+} \tag{2}$$

Defining $D = EV(C) - EV(\bar{C})$, we obtain:

$$D = (1 - q)rP_{m-1} - e \tag{3}$$

This yields the following decision rule:

Contribute if: $(1 - q) P_{m-1} > e/r$ (4)

Do not contribute if: $(1 - q) P_{m-1} < e/r,$

When equality holds, individual i should be indifferent between contributing and not contributing. For the case of $q = 0$, namely, when no external supply is possible, this decision rule reduces to the one proposed by Rapoport (1985).

A Cooperative Model   One approach to constructing cooperative and altruistic models is to incorporate a cooperative or altruistic component in the individual's utility function (c.f. Margolis, 1982; Palfrey & Rosenthal, 1988; Rapoport, 1987). While this approach recognizes factors other than selfishness, it does not eliminate selfishness entirely since it treats nonselfish motives as part of the individual's personal utility. By this, the individual's concern for the welfare of others is reduced to a matter of individual preference.

A different approach views cooperation as a behavior that is controlled by some form of *collective commitment*. According to this approach, the individual's interest in others' utilities is no longer a matter of personal preference, but of abiding to a social contract. As a basis for such commitment, Laffont (1975) suggested Kant's principle stating that "a typical agent assumes that other agents will act as he does, and he maximizes his utility function under this new constraint" (Laffont, p. 430). The generalization of the cooperative model described above to situations involving risk requires a restatement of the Kantian principle to account for risk. This can be obtained simply by stating that actors aim at maximizing their *expected* payoffs (instead of their payoffs), while adhering to the equality norm embedded in the Kantian principle.

Denote the contribution of individual i by x_i. Under the assumption that all contributions are equal (i.e. $x_i = x$ for all i, $i \in N$), the expected payoff, $E(x)$, for any player i who contributes x is given by:

$$E(x) = \begin{cases} e - x + qr & \text{if } x < M / n \\[2mm] e - x + r & \text{if } x \geq M / n \end{cases} \tag{5}$$

Where e is the endowment, r the reward from the public goods, M^2 the provision threshold, n the group size and q the probability of external supply.

For the case of binary contribution, it can be easily seen from equation 5 that the expected payoff for noncontribution, $E(x = 0)$, equals $e + qr$. For contribution, the expected payoff $E(x = e)$ equals qr when $e < M / n$, and r when $e \geq M / n$. This implies that for $e < M / n$ individuals should always refrain from contribution (and receive $e + qr$ in expected value). For $e \geq M / n$, individuals should contribute only if $r > e + qr$, and not contribute otherwise. This means that individuals should contribute if the size of their (equal) endowments equals or exceeds the (equal) cost, M / n, that each individual should bear for an optimal provision with no external supply.

A Game Theoretic Model   The SEV model introduced earlier assumes that the focal player holds certain beliefs regarding the total contribution of the rest of his or her group members (modeled by his or her subjective probability distribution). Underlying this model is the assumption that individuals' beliefs regarding others' actions are not different in nature from their perception of environmental uncertainty.

The approach suggested by game theory is qualitatively different. Rather than converting *strategic uncertainty* into environmental uncertainty, it tries to *solve* the game for all n players *simultaneously*. A *solution* here is a set of n actions, one for each player, with the property that once reached it stays in *equilibrium*, since no single player can benefit by changing his or her action unilaterally. This solution is known as the *Nash equilibrium solution* of the game.

To derive the equilibrium solution in pure strategies for the proposed game we note that the expected payoff matrix in Table 10.1 shows that if $e + qr \geq r$, then noncontribution is a dominant strategy. For the complementary case, $e + qr < r$, there is no dominant strategy. For this case, all possibilities of forming a *minimal contributing set*, with exactly m players contributing and the remaining $n - m$ not contributing, are in equilibrium. Another equilibrium point is when no one contributes. To summarize, the strategic model yields the following predictions: For $e + qr \geq r$, noncontribution is a dominant strategy. For the case where $e + qr < r$, there is no dominant strategy, and the set of equilibria in pure strategy are all $n!/m! (n - m)!$ possibilities of forming a minimal contributing set, in addition to the point at which no one contributes.

THE EXPERIMENT

The following experiment was designed to investigate the contribution behavior for step level public goods with various probabilities of external supply, and to test the predictions of the three theoretical models described in the previous section.

Method

Participants   Forty undergraduate students from the University of Haifa participated in the experiment. They all responded by writing their names and telephone numbers on a notice inviting students to participate in a "decision making experiment". They were told that they could earn as much as NIS 40 (about $12) depending on their performance. There were eight groups of five members each. Friends and acquaintances were not allowed to be in the same group.

Equipment   A Silicon Graphics Indigo 2 server was used to run and monitor the experiment. Five computers located in separate soundproof booths served as the participants' terminals.

Procedure   Participants were invited to the laboratory in groups of five. On arrival, each participant was admitted separately, seated in a booth, and given detailed written instructions explaining the experimental paradigm and the operation of the computer terminal. Special efforts were made to prevent participants from meeting, or even seeing, each other before the experiment. Before the experiment started, the experimenter made sure that all participants completely understood the game. The basic characteristics of the game, as emphasized in the instructions, were:

1   Five players in each group on each trial.

2   The experiment consisted of 16 independent trials, with no between trial to trial feedback.

3   No communication among players during the entire experiment.

4   Equal endowments of $e = 5$ NIS (about \$1.50), and a reward (public goods) of $r = 15$ NIS (about \$4.50).

5   At the beginning of each trial, each player was requested to decide privately and anonymously whether to contribute or not contribute his or her entire endowment. Following that, the computer conducted a random gamble with two possible results: a *star*, and a *circle*.

6   The reward (of 15 NIS) was provided to all group members if: (a) three ($m = 3$) or more players contributed (regardless of the outcome of the random gamble), *or* (b) the result of the random gamble was a star (regardless of the number of contributors).

7   Four conditions for the probability of a star outcome (i.e., the probability of external supply) were: $q = .00, .15, .50$ and $.85$. Each probability condition was repeated four times, for a total of 16 trials. In the first four trials, each condition for external supply appeared once (in a different order for each group). In the remaining 12 trials, each condition was iterated three times in a random order.

8   On half of the trials (8 trials), each participant was requested to estimate the likelihood (on a 0–100 scale) that less than two, exactly two, and more than two others contributed.

The participants were informed that at the end of the experiment, 2 out of the 16 trials would be chosen randomly and each participant would be paid his or her earnings on these trials.

At the beginning of each trial, participants received information about the trial number (1–16), and the probability of a star outcome. They were then requested to type in their decisions (to contribute or not) and wait patiently until the rest of their group members reported their decisions. When all participants finished this phase, the computer conducted the random gamble (with the specific probability of star for that trial), announced the termination of the gamble procedure, and moved to the next trial. No feedback about the contributions, the gamble results or the payoffs was given.

After the public goods part of the experiment was completed, each participant was asked to answer two questionnaires: a utility assessment questionnaire, and a social value orientations questionnaire. The *utility assessment* questionnaire served to assess the participant's utility function in the range (0, 20) NIS. The questionnaire implemented the successive bisection procedure for measuring utilities (e.g., Keeney & Raiffa, 1976; Schoemaker, 1980) in which the participant is asked to specify the certainty equivalent of a simple gamble yielding a *high* and *low* price (whose values are determined as a function of the participant's earlier response) with equal probabilities. This procedure elicited seven points that were used to approximate the participant's utility function by a continuous powerfunction. To measure the participant's *social orientation* we used a written version of the nine-item questionnaire developed by Van Lange (1995). This questionnaire enables the classification of participants into one of three social orientations: *individualism*, defined as the tendency to maximize one's gains; *competition*, defined as the tendency to maximize one's relative gains; and *cooperation*, defined as the tendency to maximize joint gains.

When the experiment ended, each participant was informed via the terminal about his or her earnings. Participants were requested to wait patiently for the experimenter, who then paid each one in his or her booth and released him or her from the laboratory. Care was taken that participants be sent out one at a time, thus preventing them from meeting after the experiment.

Results

Individual Contribution   Recall that all participants played four iterations of each probability of external supply condition. Figure 10.1 depicts the resulting mean proportion of contribution under all conditions of external supply.

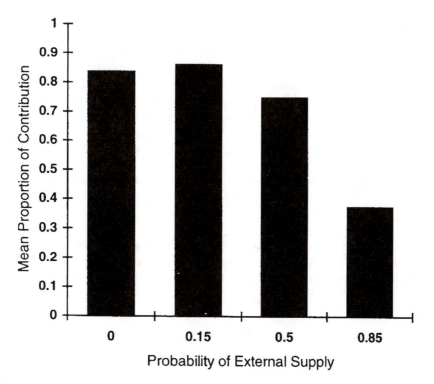

FIGURE 10.1   Mean proportion of contribution as a function of the probability of external supply

As shown by the figure, the mean proportion of contribution was significantly higher under the three lower probabilities of external supply (84%, 86%, and 75% for $q = .00, .15,$ and .50 respectively). The contribution rate dropped sharply (to 38%) under the highest probability of external supply ($q = .85$). A one-way ANOVA with repeated measures revealed a significant effect for the probability of external supply (q) on contribution [$F(3, 117) = 17.80, p < .0001$]. A post-hoc Scheffe test yielded a significant difference between the contribution rate obtained under the highest probability of external supply ($q = .85$) and all three rates that were obtained under q values of .00, .15, *and* .50. All other differences were not significant.

Estimates Following their contributions on half of the trials, participants were required to estimate the likelihood that the number of others contributing was less than two, exactly two, and more than two. These statistics are equivalent to the participants' estimates that they are futile, critical, and redundant, provided that the goods are supplied only by endogenous contributions.[3] Table 10.2 depicts the means (and standard deviations) of the three estimates, for each condition of probability of external supply (q).

As can be seen from the table, the mean estimates that less than two others contributed increased monotonically with q. Complementarily, the mean estimates that more than two others contributed decreased monotonically with q. The pattern observed for the mean estimates that *exactly* two others contributed was not monotonic. It increased up to a maximum of 38% for $q = .5$, and then decreased to 29% for $q = .85$. A one-way ANOVA on the mean subjective estimates that less than two others contributed revealed a significant effect [$F(3, 117) = 17.80, p < .0001$]. A Scheffe post-hoc test showed that the mean estimate obtained for $q = .85$ was significantly higher ($p < .01$) than the mean estimates obtained for $q = .00, .15,$ *and* .50. In addition, the mean estimate obtained for $q = .05$ was significantly higher ($p < .01$) than the mean estimate obtained for $q = .00$. All other differences were not significant. A similar analysis on the mean subjective estimates that more than two others contributed revealed a significant effect [$F(3, 117) = 12.63, p < .0001$]. The mean estimate obtained for $q = .85$ was significantly lower ($p < .01$) than the mean estimates obtained for $q = .00, .15,$ *and* .50. In addition, the mean estimate obtained for $q = .50$ was significantly lower ($p < .01$) than the mean estimate obtained for $q = .00$. All other differences between the mean estimates were not significant. Finally, a similar analysis on the mean subjective estimates that exactly two others contributed revealed a significant effect [$F(3, 117) = 8.98, p < .0001$]. The mean estimate obtained for $q = .50$ was significantly higher ($p < 0.01$) than the mean estimates obtained for $q = .00$ *and* for $q = .85$, and the mean estimate

Table 10.2 Means and standard deviations of players' subjective probabilities regarding the contributions of other group members for all conditions of probability for external provision.

| | | Subjective probability that the number of others contributing is: | | |
		< 2	= 2	> 2
Probability	0	.22 (.23)	.23 (.30)	.72 (.27)
of	0.15	.29 (.18)	.32 (.26)	.61 (.19)
External	0.5	.37 (.26)	.38 (.28)	.48 (.18)
supply	0.85	.55 (.21)	.29 (.22)	.41 (.23)

obtained for $q = .85$ was significantly higher ($p < .01$) than the mean estimate obtained for $q = .00$. All other differences were not significant.

Model Testing   The decision rules developed above were used to derive predictions from the SEV, the cooperative and the game-theoretic models. We start by testing predictions derived from the game-theoretic model. Recall that this model predicted that for $e + qr \geq r$, noncontribution is a dominant strategy, while for the complementary condition ($e + qr < r$), the equilibria set included all possibilities of forming a *minimal contributing set*, in addition to the equilibrium point at which no one contributes. For the parameter values of the present experiment ($n = 5$, $e = 5$, $r = 15$), this implies that all group members should not contribute under all q values greater than or equal to .67. This condition is satisfied only for the highest probability ($q = .85$). For the remaining three q conditions (.00, .15, .50), the model predicts that all possibilities in which exactly three group members will contribute, while the remaining two will not, are in equilibrium (in addition to one equilibrium prescribing noncontribution for all group members). In our experiment, eight groups played four trials under each of the four q conditions (a total of $8 \times 4 \times 4 = 128$ observations). To test the above predictions we counted for each q condition, the number of observations consistent with the models' prediction. The results were 7, 1, 12, 10 observations for $q = .00, .15, .50$ and .85 respectively (a total of only 30 correct predictions out of 128 observations). This low rate of correct prediction demonstrates the failure of the game theoretic model to predict the group's contribution behavior.

The predictions of the SEV and the cooperative models for all q conditions are summarized in Table 10.3.[4]

For the parameter values of our experiment, the SEV model predicts that in the absence of external supply, one should contribute only if the subjective probability that one is a critical player, P_{m-1}, exceeds .33. For probabilities of external supply of .15, and .50, the calculated critical values are respectively .39 and .67. For the highest probability of external supply ($q = .85$) the model predicts that one should not contribute regardless of one's probability estimate of being critical. The goodness of fit of the SEV model to the observed behavior was tested using the binominal test.[5] For q conditions of .00, .15, .50, three separate binominal tests yielded nonsignificant results ($p > .05$), which means that the model predictions were inconsistent with the observed behavior. For the highest probability of external supply ($q = .85$), the results of the binominal test were significant ($p < .05$) indicating that the model predictions were consistent with the observed data.

The cooperative model predicts that one should always contribute when $q = .00, .15, .50$, while for $q = .85$ it predicts that one should not contribute. A goodness of fit (using the binominal test) for the predictions of the cooperative model revealed that this model was quite satisfactory in accounting for the observed contribution behavior. The results of four

Table 10.3   Predictions of the SEV and the cooperative models

Probability of external supply	SEV model. Contribute if: P_{m-1}	Cooperative model
$q = 0$	> 0.33	Contribute
$q = 0.15$	> 0.39	Contribute
$q = 0.5$	> 0.67	Contribute
$q = 0.85$	> 1.00	Do not Contribute

tests (for the q conditions: .00, .15, .50 and .85) were significant ($p < .05$), suggesting that the cooperative model predictions were consistent with the observed data.

To further test the superiority of the cooperative model, we compared its predictions with those of the SEV model using the Cochran test for matched samples. For $q = .00$, the number of observations consistent with the SEV model was 15 (out of 80), as compared with 64 observations that were consistent with the prediction of the cooperative model. The Cochran test for this condition yielded a significant difference ($\chi^2 (1) = 36.5$, $p< .0001$), indicating that the cooperative model was superior to the SEV model. For $q = .15$, the number of observations consistent with the SEV and the cooperative models were 18 and 69 respectively, and for $q = .50$ the corresponding matches were 25 and 57 respectively. Two separate Cochran tests yielded significant differences ($p< .0001$), indicating that the cooperative model was superior to the SEV model for these conditions as well. Finally, the numbers of observations consistent with the SEV and the cooperative models' predictions under $q = .85$ were almost identical (50 and 49 respectively).

Social Orientations and Attitudes Toward Risk   In addition to model testing, we were interested in investigating the effects of social value orientation and risk preference on contribution. The classification to various social orientations (Van Lange, 1995) showed that out of 40 participants, 21 (52.5%) were classified as cooperative and 19 (47.5%) as individualistic. Figure 10.2 depicts the mean proportions of contribution for individualistic and cooperative participants as function of the probability of external supply (q).

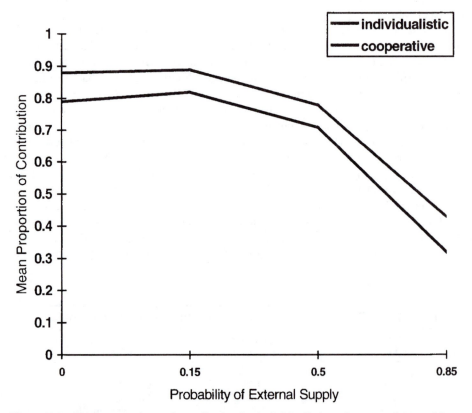

Figure 10.2   Mean proportions of contribution for individualistic and cooperative participants, as function of the probability of external supply

As can be seen, for both social orientation types, the mean proportions of contribution were fairly high for $q = .00$ and $.15$. They decrease slightly for $q = .50$, and then decreased sharply when the probability of external supply is highest ($q = .85$). The mean proportions of contribution were subjected to a 2×4 (Social Orientation × Probability of External Supply) mixed ANOVA. Neither the main effect due to social orientation, nor the interaction between social orientation and the probability of external supply were significant ($F < 1$).

To test the effect of the participants' risk preferences on their contributions, we used the results of the utility assessment test to approximate each participant's utility function by a power function of the form $u(x) = k\,x^c (c > 0)$. Each individual attitude toward risk is reflected by his or her estimated parameter such that risk aversion, risk neutrality and risk seeking correspond to $\alpha < 1$, $\alpha = 1$ and $\alpha > 1$ respectively. The frequency distribution of the estimated parameter α was negatively skewed with a range of $(0.35 - 1.55)$, mean of 0.898, and median of 1.00. Out of 40 participants, 17 were classified as risk averse, 12 as risk neutral, and 11 as risk seeking. To test the effect of the participants' attitudes toward risk on their contribution behavior, the individuals' mean proportions of contribution were subjected to a 3×4 (Attitudes Toward Risk × Probability of External Supply) mixed ANOVA. The analysis yielded a significant main effect for risk attitudes [$F(2, 37) = 3.55$, $p < .05$]. The interaction between the risk attitudes and the probability of external supply was not significant ($F < 1$). Table 10.4 depicts the mean proportions of contribution for risk averse, risk neutral, and risk seeking participants under all conditions of probability for external supply.

A Scheffe post-hoc test showed that the mean proportions of contribution were significantly higher for risk seeking than for risk averse participants (other differences were not significant). The finding that risk seeking participants contributed more than risk averse participants, coupled with the previously reported finding that cooperators contributed more than individualistic participants, raised the possibility that cooperativeness is correlated with risk seeking. To test this possibility, we compared the mean risk indices of cooperative and individualistic participants. The results of this comparison showed that cooperative participants were significantly more risk seeking than individualistic ones (means of $\alpha = 1.16$ and $\alpha = 0.81$, $t(38) = 2.74$, $p < .05$).

Table 10.4   Means and standard deviations of contribution proportions for risk averse, risk-neutral and risk-seeking participants under each condition of probability for external supply.

Type	Probability of external supply (q)				
	0	0.15	0.5	0.85	Across q conditions
Risk-Averse	.85	.88	.81	.44	.63
(n=17)	(.43)	(.39)	(.23)	(.85)	(.35)
Risk-Neutral	.78	.79	.66	.27	.74
(n=12)	(.33)	(.46)	(.33)	(.29)	(.35)
Risk-Seeking	.91	.95	.81	.48	.79
(n=11)	(.38)	(.39)	(.28)	(.35)	(.35)
Across types	.84	.86	.75	.38	.70
	(.78)	(.41)	(.3)	(.33)	(.35)

DISCUSSION

Recently, there has been a growing interest in investigating the effects of social and environmental uncertainties on individual and group behaviors in social dilemma situations (e.g., Budescu, Suleiman, & Rapaport, 1995; Messick, Allison, & Samuelson, 1988; Suleiman & Rapoport, 1988). While most of this research has focused on common pool resource dilemmas,[6] only a few studies have investigated the effects of sources of uncertainty on behavior in public goods dilemmas. Recently, Suleiman (1997) proposed three competing theoretical models (an SEV model, a game theoretical model, and a cooperative model) to account for the contribution behavior in step level PG situations with an unknown provision threshold, and Wit and Wilke (in press) reported the results of an experiment designed to investigate the effect of environmental uncertainty regarding the provision threshold on contribution.

The present study investigated the effects of a novel source of uncertainty related to the possibility that step level goods might be supplied by an external source, regardless of the group's efforts to secure its provision. Our results show that except for the low rate of contribution obtained under the 0.85 probability of external supply, the mean rates of contribution obtained under all other probabilities of external supply were impressively high (84%, 86% and 75% for probabilities of .00, .15, and .50 respectively). These results indicate that participants maintained very high levels of contribution, even when they were informed that there is a fair chance (up to 50%) that the goods will be supplied externally. Although there are no previous data to allow for a comparison with our results for external probabilities of $q \neq .00$, for the standard condition ($q = .00$) our results concerning the mean individual contribution are noticeably higher than the ones reported in previous studies. As example, for a step level game with $n = 7$, $m = 3$, $e = \$5$ and $r = \$15$, the mean proportion of contribution obtained by Dawes et al. (1986) was 51%. Under the same conditions, and a provision threshold of $m = 5$, the mean proportion of contribution reported by Dawes et al. was 64%. The contribution rates obtained in the present study were also significantly higher than those reported in previous studies based on the same participant pool from the University of Haifa. Under conditions of continuous contribution, and experimental parameters similar to the ones implemented in this study ($n = 5$, $m = 3$, $e = 5$ NIS and $r = 15$ NIS), Rapoport and Suleiman (1993),[7] and Suleiman and Rapoport (1992) reported mean proportions of contributions of 63.4% and 65.8%, respectively. We have no good explanation for the high levels of contribution obtained in our study. Nevertheless, we speculate that the depreciation in the values of endowment and expected rewards due to inflation rates since 1993 might have reduced the effects of fear and greed based motives, thereby allowing participants to contribute more generously and, perhaps, more cooperatively.

Social Value Orientation and Risk Preference

Previous research provides enough evidence showing that social value orientation is an important factor affecting the choices individuals make in social dilemmas (c.f., Liebrand & Van Run, 1985; McClintock & Liebrand, 1988). Contrary to these, and similar findings, we failed to detect a significant effect of social orientation on contribution. Notwithstanding, under all conditions of external supply, participants classified as cooperative contributed somewhat more than others who were classified as individualistic. Moreover, the nonsignificant interaction between social orientation and probability of external provision (q) indicate that the magnitude of q did influence the mean contribution of the various social orientation groups. The nonsignificant difference between the contributions of co-operative and individualistic participants may be attributed to the intermediate threshold implemented in this study. We suspect that the relatively weak effects of fear and greed under this threshold were insufficient for inducing individualistic motives. The inclusion of lower and higher thresholds may have succeeded in magnifying the effects of greed and fear, thus allowing for a better differentiation between the behaviors of individualistic and cooperative participants.

The most interesting findings of the present study are, perhaps, the ones showing that risk seeking participants contributed significantly more than risk averse participants, and that the readiness for risk taking correlated positively with the level of cooperativeness (as measured by the social orientation questionnaire). These results are consistent with findings by Parks and Godfrey (1997) indicating that the tendency for risk taking was a good predictor of the willingness to contribute to step level public goods. These findings support the argument made by Budescu, Rapoport and Suleiman (1990), according to which any decision to cooperate in social dilemma situations involves risk. Fearing the possibility that their contribution will be lost, risk averse (unlike risk seeking) participants might lower their contribution, or not contribute at all.

As noted before, no interaction was found between the participants' risk attitudes and the probability of external supply (q). This indicates that the participants' risk behavior was not influenced by the (commonly known) magnitude of q.

Model Testing

Our results were in agreement with the predictions of the cooperative model, but not with the predictions of the game theoretic, or the SEV models. The predictive power of the game theoretic model was very poor. We attribute this failure mainly to the multiplicity-of-equilibria problem alluded to in several previous studies (e.g., Palfrey & Rosenthal, 1984; Rapoport, 1985). In the absence of preplay communication, or sufficient opportunity for learning, participants could not coordinate their decisions to reach an equilibrium. It is reasonable to conjecture that the multiplicity of equilibria problem is intensified under conditions of uncertainty regarding various situational parameters (Suleiman, 1997). This conjecture is supported by the results obtained under all three conditions with $q \neq .00$.

Given the poor performance of the SEV model in generating satisfactory point predictions, a less conservative approach is to test its main qualitative prediction. This model prescribes that contribution should correlate positively with the participant's estimate that his or her contribution is critical. The resulting correlation between these variables was almost zero ($r_p = -0.05, p > .05$).

In contrast to the poor predictability of the game theoretic and the SEV models, our results yielded strong support for the cooperative model. This result adds to previous results (Rapoport & Suleiman, 1993; Suleiman & Rapoport, 1992) which demonstrated the superiority of the cooperative model over the SEV model under conditions of continuous contribution and binary provision. The results of the present study show that this superiority is maintained for situations in which the goods can be supplied externally.

The cooperative and game theoretic models disregard social uncertainty by imposing restrictive norms, or rules, on how others should behave. The only model that accounts for this source of uncertainty is the SEV model. The inspection of the decision rule generated by this model shows that the variables which represent the social and the external sources of uncertainty (P_{m-1} and $1 - q$, respectively) are not additive. Furthermore, the model predicts that as $1 - q$ increases, the threshold for contribution should decrease. On the other hand, the prediction regarding social uncertainty is nonlinear, and is based on considerations of futility, redundancy, and criticality (Dawes et al., 1986). Improving the SEV model, or the construction of other models that incorporate the two sources of uncertainty, calls for future experiments in which these two uncertainties could be separately manipulated.

The fact that the cooperative model was successful in predicting the *low* rate of contribution obtained under the highest probability of external supply ($q = 0.85$), and not only the high rates of contribution obtained under the lower three probabilities, provides insight for understanding the essence of Kantian cooperation for situations involving probable external supply. When external supply was highly probable, cooperative *and* rational participants recognized the possibility to free-ride over the external sources, and significantly reduced their contribution. In doing so, they did not deviate from the principle of conditional cooperation prescribed by the Kantian model.

ENDNOTES

[1] A detailed description of "step level" goods will be given in the following section. In principle, such goods are provided if, and only if, a certain amount of resources has been contributed to their production.

[2] For the case of binary contribution and equal endowments: $M = e\,m$, where e is the individual endowment and m is the critical number of contributors needed for providing the goods.

[3] Participants were not restricted to report estimates which add up to a total of one.

[4] The SEV model testing was based on the 80 observations which included the post decision probability estimates.

[5] We use the binominal test due to the fact that the samples are not independent, as we use repeated measures.

[6] For a more detailed review, see Suleiman and Budescu (in press).

[7] The Rapoport and Suleiman (1993) experiment was run on heterogeneous groups with regard to the endowment, but with a mean endowment equal to the one used in this study (5 NIS).

Chapter 11

Missing the Target?
Sanctioning as an Ambiguous
Structural Solution

Martin Beckenkamp
Axel Ostmann

SHARING RESOURCES

Contrary to Hardin (1968), the Tragedy of the Commons is not an unavoidable fate. History contains many examples of successfully managed commons. As Ostrom (1990) points out, self-governed organizations may provide effective facilities or institutions for negotiating, monitoring, and enforcing contracts. What distinguishes successful from unsuccessful resource management? Many authors favor sustainability as the criterion of success. Sustainability is usually interpreted to mean that the consumption of (renewable) resources should remain within the carrying capacity of the resource system, although it may have economic and social components as well.

While Ostrom (1990) does not explicitly refer to the sustainability criterion, her sets of conditions for successful management and institutional change incorporate comparable ideas. In Ostrom's view (p. 90), successfully managed commons are governed by fair rules for appropriation and provision, monitoring and sanctioning, as well as equipped with some mechanism for conflict resolution. Ostrom also stipulates (p. 94) that *fair monitoring* requires either that appropriators monitor each other, or that they hire an agent who is accountable to them. Likewise, *fair sanctioning* requires that appropriators or their agents apply sanctions against those who violate the rules and that the punishment is proportional to the offense.

From a scientific point of view, the effectiveness of a sanctioning system in promoting sustainability requires both theoretical and empirical assessments. A major theoretical issue is whether a sanctioning system is more efficient compared to a *baseline* condition. The usual argument states that rationally self-interested actors' violations of resource consumption agreements will be less likely if the probability of detection or the extent of punishment increases. This analysis must also consider provision and maintenance costs of the sanctioning system (Hechter, 1984).

The stylized models used in theory differ from the sanctioning systems found in practice, but even under experimental conditions it is an open question whether people behave in accordance with the rational actor model. In this chapter we will report behavior in laboratory experiments that does not conform to that model. Instead, participants show a palette of, say, limited rational responses to sanctioning events. The ensuing resource management outcomes are poor compared to the target derived under the rational actor model.

Understanding the role of institutions designed for resource management requires more than analyzing the incentive structure of the respective system or observing aggregate behavior. After all, fair rules of appropriation, provision, monitoring and sanctioning and, let us add group cohesion and homogeneity,[1] depend not only on objective facts but also on the perceptions and judgements of the persons involved. Nevertheless, we start with a model of the situation restricted to economic incentives and options. The rational actor solution will be used as our baseline for comparison with behavior in corresponding situations. The usual assumption made is that the rational actor solution for a social dilemma provides a worst case scenario with respect to cooperation levels.

Dilemma Games

From an economic point of view, *incentive structure* refers only to costs and returns. The collective product is distributed across users by some sharing rule. From the viewpoint of a single user the profit of an activity depends on the costs (or gains) of the activity and his or her share of the collective product. We define the *individual payoff* (u) as the individual share of a collective product minus private costs. The joint production and the physically or institutionally determined sharing rule gives rise to the *interdependence* of the users: The individual action exerts a positive or negative *externality* on others.

We shall restrict our considerations to the simplest case of resource dynamics: The resource is assumed to regenerate completely. In every period people face the same incentive structure. In this case it is enough to consider one-period models, which have special importance for regulated resource systems. If a monitoring and sanctioning regime is introduced, it is feasible to cap the maximum allowable usage at some sustainable level. The one-period model is a good approximation of such a system, and therefore we regard this model as central for our purposes. Although this model has many simplifications, real world counterparts do exist.

Mathematically the one-period incentive structure is represented by a *normal form game* with n players, action spaces, and a payoff function. Without much loss of generality we restrict our considerations to symmetric games in which every player can choose a *contribution* (x) whose value may range from 0 to an upper limit (w), called the actor's *endowment*. Let y denote the total contribution from all her or his n − 1 partners. Then the expression

$$u(x,y) = -cx + q(x,y)f(x + y) , c > 0 \tag{1}$$

represents the payoff the actor gets from the joint contribution profile (x,y).[2] The term *cx* represents (linear) private *cost* (c > 0), and f(x + y) is the *joint product* (e.g., as in a public good).[3] The function q(x,y) is a *quota* that determines how the joint product is to be divided among the players. It is also called the sharing rule. Constant (symmetric) quotas q = 1/n distribute the joint product equally among actors.

An important tool for determining game theoretic solutions is the *best reply* function. A best reply is an action that maximizes the payoff for given actions of all other players. In our symmetric set up it is enough to define best replies for the aggregate partners' contributions (y). Given our assumptions regarding the cost and production function, there is a unique best reply for every y. We get a best reply function B(y) by mapping y to its unique best reply. If the function B is constant, say B(y) = x, this action x is called a *dominant strategy*. The actor who chooses x maximizes her or his payoff, whatever the partners do.

Let us consider formula (1) once again. In economics this structure is used to represent conflicts in the provision of public goods. In general there is usually no dominant strategy; in the case of linear cost and linear production and cn > f(1) (unneglectable cost) it turns out that x = 0 (no contribution, or *free-riding*) is the dominant strategy. The dilemma arises from the fact that since f(0,0) gives the lowest possible outcome, if no one contributes then no one benefits.

Now, to represent collective interests we need to characterize a *welfare optimum,* that is, a total contribution that maximizes the total return. Suppose we denote the total contribution by s = x + y. Then the total return, U(s), is just the sum of individual payoffs, U(s) = −cs + f(s). It is independent of the shape of the vector of individual actions. Moreover, in our symmetric set-up U(s) can be allocated equally without redistribution of income if actors cooperate by contributing equally (i.e., everyone contributes x so that nx = s).

Now we turn from public goods to commons dilemmas. Here, subtractability (cf., Glossary) has the consequence that any individual's consumption decreases others' shares (i.e., *q*). The most popular version of this interdependence structure is the proportional rule[5] q = x/(x + y) = x/s. So public goods dilemmas involve two interdependent processes (namely costs and production) whereas commons dilemmas involve three (costs, production, and appropriation).

For a social scientist it is clear that, especially in situations that are characterized by massive externalities, humans are not exclusively motivated by self-interest.[6] Nevertheless, rational choice theory provides a valuable benchmark, since comparing actual behavior with it can help to measure the strength of other motives, the extent of limitations on human cognition, or both.[7] Here, we restrict our attention to two rationality standards, namely the conditioned standard and the (not fully specified) cooperative standard.

In game theory the Nash equilibrium corresponds to the conditioned rationality standard (cf., Glossary). Cooperative rationality, on the other hand, is usually interpreted in terms of binding agreements and contracts, and cooperation is established in a bargaining process. Without specifying the exact content and kind of cooperation it is clear that the welfare optimum defined earlier provides a cooperative rationality standard.[8] Since the welfare optimum (s*) maximizes the joint payoff (U), it can be used to provide an *efficiency* measure, eff(s) = U(s)/U(s*).

The nub of the commons dilemma in game theoretic terms is the following theorem: *For commons dilemma games the Nash equilibrium is unique and symmetric; but this equilibrium is inefficient compared to the (equally distributed) welfare optimum.* The usual interpretation of the theorem is that incentives and interdependence endanger the commons if actors follow their self-interest. Consequently the incentive structure may lead the actors to overuse. Moreover, since the resource regenerates each time, actors face the same incentive structure all the time.

Usually people react to a critical development in the commons by inventing institutional means such as communication. However, if communication does not alter the payoff structure, then players face the same game as before: If actors follow their self-interest, overuse is guaranteed.[9] In a second step actors may agree on individual use limits, and since usually the individual usage cannot be observed, in a third step they may install a control mechanism and sanctions for those who do not respect the limit. It is usually the latter step that changes the incentive structure. How this is done is shown in the next section.

Dimensions of Control and Sanctioning Regimes

Let us speak in terms of *internal control* if monitoring is done by the users themselves, and *external control* if an external agent is paid for inspection. In our formal model the introduction of internal control changes the action spaces of the players while external control leaves the action spaces unchanged. Monitoring and sanctions both incur costs. Perfect monitoring occurs only if every user's action is detectable with certainty. A complete list of who is controlled with which result is called the *control report*. We assume that the control report is published.[10] Moreover, we assume that sanctions depend only on the control report. *Sanctions* change payoffs, since they reduce the gain from violations. Prior knowledge of sanctions should therefore reduce the incentive for violations. In our view, a rational policy in designing sanctioning regimes can justify such a regime by stating the target of reaching the better equilibrium.

An *inspection game* includes monitoring and sanctions. The simplest example uses the n-prisoner's dilemma game as a base game. We define the base game by $u(x,y) = -x + 2s$ for $x = 0$ or 1. The efficiency of the equilibrium $x = 0$ is zero. In order to reach the target $x = 1$, we set the rule $x = 1$, a sanction (σ) for violating the rule, and a probability (p) of being inspected. Whereas an actor choosing $x = 1$ will get $2s - 1$ for sure, choosing $x = 0$ will result in a payoff of either $2s - \sigma$ (detected) or $2s$ (undetected). By computing expectations we can see that the equilibrium of the inspection game becomes $x = 1$ (hits the target) whenever $p\sigma > 1$.

Whereas under internal control it is a player's option to inspect another player, under external control the control agency may not be a player. Game theoretic models for binary decisions based on monitoring can be found in Weissing and Ostrom (1991) (internal control) and Weissing and Ostrom (1993) (external control). In this framework the incentives to monitor are explicitly modeled, whereas in our framework we assume that the external agency is called up for a predefined monitoring task that is carried out as contracted (at a given price). Another important difference in analysis is that mixed strategy extensions of the corresponding games are considered, that is, players are assumed to choose a probability distribution on the action space and evaluate the expected payoff given their and their partners' distributions. Thus, the corresponding equilibria of the above binary games specify stealing probabilities.[11] Such stealing rates can be compared with empirical data.

In our framework, having added monitoring and sanctions, the change in the incentive structure formally[12] can be covered by redefining the payoff structure in terms of *control events* and *transfers*. Transfers balance payments made and payments received;

they may include a cost share for financing the inspection; in case of a detection event the sanction to be paid may include payments to inspectors or partners. In the case of external control the sanction can be split in compensatory payments to partners and the payment of the inspection costs.

Adding external control we propose a rather general procedure based on the following four parameters: We set a *limit for individual use*, lambda (λ). We set a *maximum tolerated total usage,* eta (η). We determine *costs*, kappa (κ), for employing the inspection agency. Finally we set a *probability* (p) of being inspected. The inspection procedure is as follows:

> No control is carried out by the agent if total use does not surpass the threshold. If the threshold is surpassed, the agent chooses whom to inspect. Everyone has an equal chance of being inspected. There is no transfer without control. Sanctions are imposed only if the inspectee is reported to have extracted more than the limit for individual use.
>
> If the control takes place, costs for hiring the agent have to be paid. If no defector is detected, costs have to be carried by the public (in equal proportions). In the other case the defectors detected have to pay the costs in equal parts. Every actor who is not reported as defector gets a compensation fee from every defector. The compensation fee is equal to the extent of the defection multiplied with the sanctioning factor (σ).

The above regime of external control induces multiple asymmetric equilibria, that (in a large range) exhibit increasing efficiency for both more inspection and higher sanctioning. For a given inspection probability and a given sanctioning factor we interpret the interval of efficiency of the corresponding equilibria as the *target* set by introducing the control regime. The *baseline best reply* for the game base (n,w) (remember the parameter *n* stands for the number of players, *w* refers to the endowment) is a decreasing linear function within the boundaries of use: zero and w. Let us call the strictly declining linear segment within the boundaries the *inner line*.

Let us now consider the corresponding inspection game insp(n,w;λ,η,κ,p;σ). When the control regime is introduced the best reply function shows some change.[13] The general effect is in moving the inner line downwards. But additionally a region of *compliance* may be built. In this region use is equal to the individual use limit λ. Moreover a region of *tolerance* may come up. In this region total usage is η. With this new, *no longer continuous* structure of best reply, we can get *multiple asymmetric equilibria*.

In a game with 8 players, suppose only one[14] actor is inspected each time, so everyone has a probability of inspection of p = 0.125. We restrict our considerations to the family of games insp(8,25;5,46,40,0.125;s). The cost of inspection is κ = 40 and the upper limit on total usage is η = 46, so we tolerate (in total) 6 use units more than full compliance would allow.

We will skip[15] the derivations of best reply functions and equilibria. The use of sanctions and control reduces the equilibrium total usage from s = 64 (baseline without sanctions and control) to some lower level in proportion to the sanctioning factor. Since we get multiple equilibria in these games, the total usage in equilibrium for a give value of the sanctioning factor corresponds to an interval. For a sanctioning factor of σ = 0, the total usage equilibria are in the interval [60.25, 62.50]; whereas for σ = 1 the equilibria interval is [55.67, 58.80] and for σ = 2 it is [53.33, 56.00].

As discussed before, we interpret the efficiencies of the equilibra as a target set by introducing the respective control regime. In our case we get a [0.335,0.423] target for σ = 0, [0.475,0.578] for σ = 1, and [0.598,0.645] for σ = 2. The base line efficiency 0.395

can be called the *null policy target*. It is now an empirical question whether people follow the carefully tailored target or at least react in the intended direction—it would be fine if they do better.

A Set of Experimental Scenarios

In the next section we report an experimental test of the (strong) *rational actor hypothesis* that efficiency targets can be hit when an external control regime is added to a commons dilemma. The experiments also test the weaker hypothesis that actual results are no less efficient than the rational actor prescription. It is well known that in social dilemma games the strong hypothesis is usually rejected because costless communication enhances efficiency without changing the incentive structure. Let us call the observable efficiency gain surpassing the target[16] the *cooperation shift*. The weak hypothesis says that the cooperation shift is nonnegative.

Laboratory research based on the commons dilemma paradigm is mainly promoted by the Bloomington Group (Gardner, Ostrom, Walker and others). We decided to use the renewable resource experimental paradigm from Ostrom, Gardner, & Walker (1994) (hereafter abbreviated OGW) as our experimental baseline. In the OGW-setup a group of 8 participants has to perform a multiperiod task. In every period they face the same incentive structure. Up to a constant[17] additional individual payment the payoffs received are defined by the game base (8,w), w = 10 or 25. For the reason of comparability we drop the additional payment. After their anonymous decisions on individual usage the participants get as public information what amount of total usage was realized and as private information what payoff received. This procedure is repeated for 20 periods.[18] The repeated game can be interpreted as management conflict dealing with a totally renewable resource. Experiments show that without communication participants tend to follow the "path to hell."

We implemented monitoring and sanctioning in the OGW-setup in such a way that it conformed to the games described in the previous section. Four experiments were carried out: a preliminary study called OGWC0, a high inspection rate study called OGWC1, a study in which the sanctioning factor is varied (OGWC2), and its repetition, OGWC3. During the instructions participants had to learn how the procedure worked and how the materials (tables and figures) were used. They got protocol sheets to register their own actions, total usage, own payoffs before and after monitoring, and the state of their private account. In all experiments but OGWC0 participants sat at a workstation in a computer lab, completed entry forms, and received information on screen. After the last round participants were paid according to their private accounts. In the preliminary OGWC0 study we used paper and pencil entry forms, transferred data to the computer, and returned public information on the black board.

OBSERVATIONS AT THE AGGREGATE LEVEL

Results of the Earlier Experiments

Our preliminary study (OGWC0) was a classroom experiment with only one group of 10. After the instruction and a first phase of 8 periods in a seminar session the experiment was interrupted for two weeks. The experiment was completed with a second session of 16 periods. Various uncontrolled discussions had taken place between the two experimental sessions. Moreover before participants resumed they got explicit information on the welfare optimum.

The game behind the OGWC0 setup was insp(10, 25; 5, 50, 40, 0.2; 1). Since η was equal to 10 times λ there was no region of tolerance. Under these conditions the sanctioning is strong enough to give the incentive for full compliance: In equilibrium total usage is equal to 50. The corresponding target is 0.85. In the first part of the experiment (before communication) we observed an efficiency of 0.33 (mean total usage of 62). In all rounds inspection was called up. Astonishingly, even after the interruption, in half of the remaining periods inspection was called up (efficiency 0.69, mean total s = 52). Thus data from both parts do not conform to the weak rational actor hypothesis: We observed negative cooperation shifts in both parts. We concluded that the region of tolerance might compensate human errors especially if losses due to small deviations from full compliance are small. In order to make the results of the next experiment comparable to the base line result of OGW group size was set to eight.

In the next setup (OGWC1) we used the game insp(8, 25; 5, 46, 40, 0.25; 1). For this game we get two equilibria, a payoff superior one without inspection (it exhibits a total usage of η = 46 and an efficiency of 0.92) and another one showing a total usage of 54.39 (this corresponds to an efficiency of 0.64). Again, we observed negative cooperation shifts (even when the trial without payment is excluded). The observed efficiency was 0.37 (and 0.50 respectively). Moreover we observed lasting *oscillations* in total use without decrease in amplitude. Let us compare the OGWC1 result to the baseline with added communication facilities reported by OGW. The latter result (efficiency 0.73) meets the target for our control regime while the control regime empirically misses the target by far. Even with a communication cost equal to κ (same cost as for control), communication alone seems to perform better than the control regime. Having analyzed the results (see Beckenkamp & Ostmann, 1996; and Ostmann, 1998), we decided to reduce the unrealistically high value of inspection probability and to experiment with different sanctioning factors.

Results of the Sigma Setups

The first experiment varying the extent of sanctions was OGWC2, employing the games insp(8, 25; 5, 46, 40, 0.125; σ) that have been analyzed in the previous section. The results showed such remarkable patterns that we decided to repeat the experiment (OGWC3). By pooling the data of OGWC2 and OGWC3 we get a 2 × 3 × 3 design.[19] Since the first two factors show no important effects let us simply refer to the 6 × 3 design varying the sanctioning factor sigma. For each value of sigma (0, 1, and 2) we have six *trials* and observe 6 × 8 = 48 *participants*, 6 × 20 = 120 *periods* and 8 × 6 × 20 = 960 *individual decisions*.

Institutional Performance

The first impression from plots of the development of total usage is oscillations with different amplitudes and mean levels for the three different values of the sanctioning factor. For σ = 0 the usual overuse can be seen (mean total usage = 60.79, s.d. = 17.89), for σ = 1 we observe a reduction as planned (mean total usage = 53.49, s.d. = 17.02). Our problem starts with the observation that for σ = 2 the "old wildness" comes back (mean total usage = 57.96, s.d. = 17.67). Indeed a closer look reveals that for the moderate sanctioning regime (σ = 1) usage is significantly reduced compared with the other values of σ. Let us call this finding the *U-shaped effect*.

Mean rank statistics indicated that the U-shaped effect is significant, while the trial statistics result was near significance (see Table 11.1). Removal of an outlier trial for $\sigma = 2$ resulted in a somewhat stronger U-shaped trend. We collected additional data to investigate the significance of the U-shaped effect.

Efficiencies show strong differences[20] between the highly efficient moderate sanctioning regime (mean efficiency 0.612, s.d. 0.186) and rather inefficient extreme ones: for $\sigma = 0$ we get a mean efficiency of 0.303 (s.d. 0.265), but for $\sigma = 2$ we get a mean efficiency of 0.478 (s.d. 0.241). Remember, a positive cooperation shift means that participants are more cooperative than prescribed by the equilibrium standard. For $\sigma = 1$ the cooperation shift is weakly positive (mean shift 0.0855), whereas for $\sigma = 0$ the mean shift is –0.061 and –0.128 for $\sigma = 2$. At the trial level the mean rank statistic[21] shows a significant difference only after grouping extreme sanctioning versus moderate sanctioning.

A period statistic shows large differences in the performance of the three sigma regimes. In the "landscapes" for the sanctioning regimes shown in Table 11.2, every row shows the time series for one trial. Unshaded entries indicate periods without inspection. A bold entry stands for a negative cooperation shift or, in other words, for values above target. For every bold entry the sanctioning regime has failed to reach the target ($s > 62, 59$, resp. 55).

The friendly landscape with 28% of periods without inspection and only 25% beyond target corresponds to the moderate sanctioning regime. The institutional performance is extremely low in the case of high sanctions (61% beyond target if the outlier trial is dropped).

Deviation Patterns

The low institutional performance is produced by aggregate defection. With respect to trials the sanctioning factor explains neither a significant part of the variation of individual overuse nor the number of defections. On the decision level a U-shaped effect for the propensity to defect can be expected (mean rank statistics: $T = 19.2$, $p < 0.0001$).

The extent of defection shows another pattern. Here the weak sanctioning condition is clearly distinct from the other two conditions (mean individual overuse under the condition of defection: 6.06 for $\sigma = 0$, 4.55 for $\sigma = 1$, 4.78 for $\sigma = 2$, and 5.6 without the outlier trial). The rationale for undiminished overuse is that for $\sigma = 0$ sanctioning is not sensitive to the amount of overuse. The cumulative frequency distributions in Figure 11.1 show that the (conditioned) individual overuse in case of $\sigma = 0$ is (stochastically) larger than when $\sigma > 0$.

The weakness of the decision level defection statistics may reflect both the interdependence among decisions and the lack of a theory of how these decisions are made. In the following subsection we present some elements of such a theory that can be introduced without differentiating between types of participants.

Table 11.1   Mean rank statistics for total usage.

Sanctioning factor	0	1	2	Statistics
mean rank, trials	12.7	6.2	9.7	T = 4.46, p = 0.108
mean rank, decisions	1501	1366	1455	T = 14.7, p < 0.0001

Table 11.2 Institutional performance (N=340, without outlier trial).

sigma=0

46	48	46	44	48	63	46	48	49	55	45	54	67	55	46	61	45	47	46	52
53	62	37	80	69	78	36	41	68	61	63	78	59	60	78	78	54	78	62	78
52	47	69	93	49	50	59	55	75	63	67	60	66	63	61	61	69	62	61	74
40	52	49	45	48	64	57	70	75	44	50	47	47	62	60	84	61	61	57	68
46	73	70	78	57	88	88	41	66	70	60	72	61	82	54	79	68	70	74	72
48	58	47	53	80	55	59	73	84	72	70	46	55	64	62	71	63	55	64	66

sigma=1

41	42	42	43	52	41	44	45	45	46	45	41	44	46	48	50	48	48	50	47
44	45	46	44	48	50	61	44	50	59	43	45	47	58	52	46	54	46	60	56
47	56	44	50	47	65	60	46	49	57	55	44	43	58	63	52	50	61	44	51
50	67	59	61	61	59	57	64	40	44	66	61	67	77	40	65	45	63	63	48
67	32	48	65	53	61	50	54	48	60	67	42	40	55	73	60	68	62	60	74
53	68	55	53	53	58	49	56	57	51	53	65	65	72	73	69	57	53	58	57

sigma=2

35	66	69	60	62	76	79	55	72	82	52	58	42	70	61	44	68	72	60	78
53	51	47	50	52	52	57	52	46	72	57	56	57	56	54	48	52	71	51	52
39	58	48	62	76	65	74	55	54	64	67	66	65	67	59	57	68	61	61	62
64	56	70	58	47	64	70	66	77	77	55	61	54	66	52	46	47	58	50	52
55	62	57	67	51	44	57	53	55	67	56	50	71	49	69	62	48	67	73	55

Decision Elements

The importance of expectations and backward conjectures is widely acknowledged. In half of the trials participants had to report their estimation of total usage. Subtracting the amount used by each individual from their estimate of the total usage gives the predicted consumption by the other players (denoted by Y). This predicted consumption could motivate the individual to give a *best reply* (a game theoretic argument) or could trigger *social comparisons* (a social psychological argument). If best reply dominates, individual usage and the Y should be negatively related. If social comparisons dominate, then the correlation should be positive. An r^2 of 0.032 indicates that there is no clear trend in either direction.

It is reasonable to assume that the decision to defect or not can be separated from the decision of how much to take. Define D as a binary variable which represents defection (D = 1 iff x > 5). The second regression (see Table 11.3) yields a clear separation between defectors and cooperators (D = 1 and D = 0) resulting in a large increase in r^2.

For a further analysis it is useful to consider the variable pA = x −Y/7. The variable

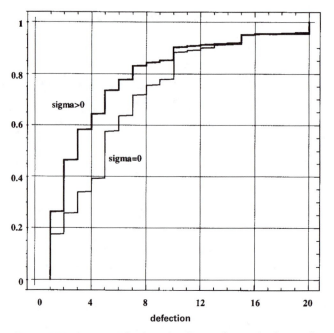

Figure 11.1 Larger defections for the weak sanctioning regime

pA is called *planned advantage*. Indeed an individual may try to get an advantage over the "average partner" by taking more than the estimated average. The mean planned advantage of 0.55 splits into –2.2 for compliance (D = 0) and 4.0 for defection (D = 1). The planned advantage can be compared with the variable rA = x – y/7, the *advantage realized*. It is remarkable that the difference between realized and planned advantage is small.

We now introduce history into our decision model. For the next regression we assume that decisions depend on the sanctioning parameter, planned advantage, the most recent advantage realized (rA), previous decisions (x before last) and on a crisis indicator (last s

Table 11.3   Regression analyses. Entries: parameter (s.e.).

	Regression 1	Regression 2	Regression 3
const	10.39 (0.56)	6.47 (0.38)	6.309 (0.114)
D	-	5.67 (0.17)	-
Y	–0.07 (0.01)	–0.04 (0.01)	-
pA	-	-	0.118 (0.001)
σ	-	-	–0.301 (0.042)
period	-	-	0.021 (0.006)
last rA	-	-	0.002 (0.001)
x before last	-	-	0.054 (0.009)
last s > 64	-	-	0.767 (0.074)
N	1380	1380	1246
r²	0.032	0.455	0.926
s.e.(residual)	4.23	3.18	1.18

Note: Significance levels below 0.001 (except for last rA: <0.05)

> 64). We also substitute the planned advantage pA for the decision to defect. The crisis indicator used is independent of σ, since it is based on the situation before the introduction of the sanctioning regime.

In the third regression we find a remarkable[22] fit, with r^2 being 0.926, and s.e.(residual) = 1.18. The regression coefficient for σ is negative, but the coefficient for the crisis indicator shows a large positive value. This fact is incompatible[23] with the oscillation pattern observed. We conclude from this model that the task of modeling actors' decisions must be passed on to a more adequate microanalysis.

Before we present a microanalysis of the decision process, let us again consider a period statistic of performance that uses the above crisis indicator (s > 64). We now compare the actual behavior to the equilibrium (s = 64) in the *preinstitutional state* (null policy target). For the corresponding landscapes we derive the following proportions of bold areas signaling a situation worse than the preinstitutional state: 35% for the weak sanctioning regime, 15% for the moderate one, and 32% for the strong regime.

THE INDIVIDUAL'S ROAD TO SUCCESS

In our experimental set-ups we confronted participants with a regime of external control and sanctions. Under all conditions but one we observed a behavior with persistent low performances which makes the structural solutions for resource dilemmas doubtful. The only condition for which the target was hit (in fact the performance was slightly better than the target) was moderate sanctions in the sigma setup. Moderate sanctions correspond to a modest target. But only relatively high inspection probabilities, high sanctions, or both, lead to targets that are close to the welfare optimum. This constitutes the *sanctioning dilemma*: Targets near the welfare optimum cannot be reached. It seems that a successful management of commons can not be implemented by merely adding external control and sanctions.

Individual commons in field experiments differ in various aspects from the models considered. But the rigorous introduction of the stylized incentive structure in the model and in the experiments make it possible to vary critical conditions and to identify some variables crucial for phenomena observed in the field. Our findings are consistent with observations from the field mentioned at the beginning of the chapter. Glick's (1970) report on relatively low fines being efficient meets our findings for the moderate sanctioning regime. Ostrom's (1990) principle of proportional sanctions should be compared not only with the theoretical effect on the efficiency of equilibria but also with the observed reduced amounts in case of defection if the sanctioning is not weak.[24] Moreover it can be conjectured that in case of strong sanctions at least some people would perceive the rules as unfair. But fairness of the rules is reported as another characteristic of successful long enduring management.

In our experiments individual behavior has been found to differ from the rational actor model. Our results show that the conditioned individual rationality (best reply) of the rational actor model can neither explain the social development nor the decision path of an individual. Nevertheless up to some degree the incentives set by the sanctioning regime influence behavior.

In order to get a better explanation for the behavior observed we can choose a *bounded rationality* approach.[25] In such an approach the rationality of the actors consists in more or less successful evaluation and decision procedures that have limited cognitive capabilities and may include sociocognitive, socioemotional or emotional processes. Observations can be used to tailor a set of rules that may generate decision patterns observed if the rules are combined in the right way. However, our data do not allow for a full specification of such rules. The corresponding internal processes of actors are not observable (not even by the actors themselves). Nonetheless, we may postulate a rule structure and test the performance of the corresponding multiagent system (the interaction of the agents are defined by the game and the corresponding information transfer). Simulation runs of the computerized multiagent system that mimic the participants' behaviors can be read as support for the postulated internal structure.[26]

Individuals strive for success. According to the bounded rationality approach the distant and vague goal success is operationalized in specific subgoals ready to use. It is plausible to consider *goal-directed behavior* as generated by rules that determine from the situation and the internal state of the agent what goal to activate. Moreover depending on what goal is activated the focus of attention may move. As an example in our context[27] consider (1) the goal to maximize one's own benefit and (2) the goal to maximize the benefit of the group. Since cooperation yields a higher benefit than pure self-interest, it is in the interest of an individual to motivate partners to cooperate. This derived (second order) goal can be seen as a strategic element in order to reach goal (1) from time to time. That is, sometimes participants try to calm the situation in order to make bigger benefits from a defection carried out in the calm period. The generated behavior creates a compromise between self-interest and group-interest and switches over time.

Besides the strategic derivation of a cooperative goal, the concept of bounded rationality allows for the activation of cooperative goals as primary goals. In many cognitive models, the *activation of goals* is among other things dependent on certain situational parameters. In cognitively oriented social-psychological experiments Hertel (1995) shows that the activation of prosocial and competitive goals can be primed. We may conjecture that the extreme sanctioning conditions activate more competitive goals than the moderate condition. Why they do so is an open question.

We suggest that two different mechanisms of evaluation of the situation operate in the low versus high sanctioning condition. If we compare the low sanctioning factor with the moderate one, it is plausible to assume that the moderate condition primes goals refering to group norms whereas in the weak condition these goals remain more in the background. Understanding the purpose of the sanctions, the focus of attention is shifted to cooperative goals. These goals seem to be internalized (in a weak sense): Violating the rules is usually interrupted after a successful control. The internalization fosters the feeling of being a member of a homogeneous group. Internalization of the rules is disturbed in the strong sanctioning regime. This condition seems to prime the goal: "Take care to not be detected." In this case the rules are not internalized and the purpose of the sanctioning regime is no longer reflected. This might lead to less orientation towards the group, with a feeling of "me and them." The result of this evaluation is motivation to "pay it back" and to "take my share."

The protocol sheets also give indications of how important participant-stable goals may be for the management of commons. We suggested different *types*. We may define a type as an agent with a set of goals that are stable over time and across situations. The strong sanctioning regime may activate goals that are adequate for those with little greed, but inadequate for most of the other participants, who feel inadequately punished. This suggestion can also be underpinned by Yamagishi's (1988a, 1988b, 1992) experimental results concerning second-order dilemmas. Following his argument, the composition of groups with different types would lead to different results.[28]

The difference in the evaluation of a situation between participants of different types may be crucial in times of crisis. The anger of cooperative participants about the defections of other members of the group may activate the goal to defect. Some comments in the protocol sheets show that this kind of self-justification may avoid a moderation of defections. Competitors getting insight in the usefulness of restraint behavior are rejected in revenge by participants who were cooperative until they found a calmer opportunity to strike back. This defection reactivates the competitive goals: The commons remain in a bad state.

Let us draw some conclusions from our experiments with respect to judging the practicability of monetary sanctions to ensure sustainability. If economic incentives were sufficient then monetary sanctions would guarantee sustainable use of (renewable) resources. Theoretical analysis suggests that both the ecological and the economic goals of sustainability could be achieved by correspondingly high fines. However, the social aspect of sustainability can be endangered by fines that surpass a certain limit of acceptability. In this case the social objective of sustainability is missed: the objective that the social structures, including systems of governance, should effectively propagate and sustain the values by which people wish to live. By missing this goal the two other objectives of sustainability are also endangered. The social issue of sustainability, which might seem to be some kind of rather irrelevant accessory with respect to the real objective of sustainability, proves to be decisive.

Our experimental series suggest that structural solutions are not sufficient to ensure sustainability in the government of a common. From our point of view external control alone is not sufficient because *responsibility* for the commons is delegated to an anonymous instance. The sanctions introduced may weaken the feeling to be responsible and may disrupt ingroup solidarity especially in the case where sanctioning is perceived as inadequate, unfair, or unacceptable. Probably the acceptance of the rules introduced is one reason for successful self-responsible government of commons over centuries which is described in Ostrom (1990). In any case, the hope that drastic fines may lead to nondefective behavior is an illusion. It seems more likely that drastic fines lead to ingenious efforts to defect without fearing detection.

APPENDIX

The basic normal-form game is defined by the action space $x \in [0,w]$ and the payoff function

(1) $$u(x,y) = -cx + qf(x + y)$$

with some cost parameter c and a production function (f) such that

$$c > 0, \ f(0) = 0, \ f'(0) > c, \ f'' < 0$$

For a given y an action b is called best reply if

(2) $$u(b,y) = \max \{u(x,y); 0 \le x \le w\}$$

In commons dilemma games actors are rivals, formally expressed by the quota

(3) $q = x/(x + y)$.

The welfare optimum s^* fulfills

(4) $c = f'$, respectively $s^* = nw$ if the endowment restricts

In case best replies are not bound by the restriction $x \leq w$ the equilibrium has to fulfil the following fundamental equations in x

(5) $(n - 1)(f' - f/s) = n(f' - c)$ for all players

The simplest functional form for the production function is quadratic, that is, $f(s) = (a - bs)s$, $a, b > 0$. Formula (5) reduces to

(6) $-(n - 1)bs = n(a - 2bs - c)$

or

(7) $(n + 1)x = (a - c)/b$

This important subclass of commons dilemma games is parametrized by the scalars a, b, c, w, and n. It turns out that the efficiency of the respective equilibrium (s^*) is a function of n alone. We get an efficiency decreasing in n:

(8) $eff = 4n / (n + 1)^2$

Formula (8) specifies the well known *group size effect* for standard commons dilemma situations.

Introducing sanctions and random inspection we have to redefine the payoff as a random variable adding control events $h = K(s, \omega)$ and transfers $t(x, h)$:

(9) $U(x, \omega) = u(x) + t[x, K(s, \omega)]$

We get the following structure of best reply (let m be the number of defectors):

Type	Best Reply x = B(y)	Range of y
Take all	$x = 25$	$y < 21$
Up to the limit	$x = 46 - y$	$21 \leq y \leq L(m, \sigma)$
Inner	$4x = 144 - 2y - 7\sigma$	$L(m, \sigma) \leq y \leq R(\sigma)$
Comply	$x = 5$	$R(\sigma) \leq y \leq 62$
Reduce	$2x = 72 - y$	$62 \leq y \leq 72$
Withdraw	$x = 0$	$72 \leq y$

The left and right boundaries of the *inner* region can be found by solving the respective equation of payoffs. It is easy to see that $L(m, \sigma)$ and $R(\sigma)$ are functions of m and σ respective of σ alone. By testing all constellations we can determine the equilibria.

The following table shows all equilibria for a selection of sigma values.

Entries: Total Use(s); and Defector's Usage (x)

m	σ = 0	σ = 1	σ = 2
2	-	55.667; 12.833	53.333; 11.667
3	60.25; 11.75	57.625; 10.875	55; 10
4	61.6; 10.4	58.8; 9.7	-
5	62.5; 9.5	-	-

The corresponding payoff values are given in the next table.

Entries: Payoffs (Total Return and in Brackets: Defectors' Payoffs; Compliants' Payoffs)

m	σ = 0	σ = 1	σ = 2
2	-	187.30	208.89
		(37.778; 18.625)	(35.694; 22.917)
3	136.98	167.09	193.75
	(26.391; 11.563)	(27.285; 17.047)	(28.125; 21.875)
4	120.16	154.04	-
	(19.54; 10.5)	(22.16; 16.35)	
5	108.438	-	-
	(15.688; 10)		

ENDNOTES

[1] With respect to institutional change Ostrom (1990) discusses sociopsychological factors like group cohesion and homogeneity.

[2] This corresponds to the *give-some frame* in so far as the individual gives away x facing costs receiving a return $qf(x + y)$ from the pooled amounts. The model is quite general because there is a duality for the *take-some frame* translating the formal results.

[3] As usual in our context the production function is assumed to be concave and normal (i.e., $f(0) = 0$, "no product without effort").

[4] If we substitute a binary choice for the continuous action space we get the famous n-prisoner's dilemma game.

[5] Only a few other sharing rules are investigated. Both fixed equality and proportional rule belong to the following (nonlinear) family of quotas (see Rapoport & Amaldoss, 1997a): Define $g(a): = a^c$, $c > 0$ and let X be the vector of individual actions x; now the generalized rule is given by $q(x,y) = g(x) / \Sigma g(X_i)$; for $c = 0$ we get fixed equality and for $c = 1$ the proportional rule.

[6] cf Mansbridge, 1990.

[7] For such an approach we have to specify the procedures of evaluation and planning that allow the agent to interact with the respective environment. This branch of limited rationality research started with the introduction of the satisficing principle and the procedural rationality by Simon (1955, 1976) and produced a diversity of artificial intelligence methods. Conceptualized as a processing unit in a multiagent system the agents apply weak rationality principles to search in a dynamic knowledge base for a satisficing reply under the goal activated. Limited cognitive resources, memory filters, and even emotional filters can be modeled. Using a computer-implemented version the simulated behavior can be compared to behavior empirically found. Methods to test the validity of the inner constructs are discussed in Beckenkamp and Ostmann (1996).

[8] Cooperative-rationality standards and the corresponding cooperative-solution concepts are investigated in cooperative game theory. For the analysis of cooperative games that are induced by normal-form games see Aumann (1967) and Ostmann (1988). For the special context of commons dilemma games see Meinhardt and Ostmann (1996).

[9] The game theoretically motivated, cheap-talk hypothesis states that in such situations without change in the incentive structure the introduction of communication will produce no noticeable effect.

[10] In fact we implemented a semianonymous setting. Control reports were published with the participants' numbers, but the assignment of the numbers to the individual participants was unknown.

[11] A typical result is that the parameter space splits up in regions defined by the kind of equilibria. A first region shows intermediate stealing rates and intermediate monitoring rates. The three other regions exhibit a maximal stealing rate. This maximal stealing rate is combined with no, intermediate, and complete monitoring respectively.

[12] For a formal treatment of the general case see Ostmann (1997).

[13] For a rigorous analysis see Ostmann, Wojtyniak and Beckenkamp (1997) and Ostmann (1998).

[14] For two inspectees an analysis of insp(8,25;5,46,40,0.25;1) is found in Ostmann (1998).

[15] See appendix.

[16] In case of multiple equilibria the cooperation shift is a signed distance to the target.

[17] The constant used was equal to cw.

[18] In some experiments another number of periods is set.

[19] (study) ×(participant pool) × (sigma) = $2 \times 3 \times 3 = 18$. The first two factors are *study* (OGWC2 and OGWC3) and *participant pool* (students of psychology, business administration, and jurisprudence respectively). For the two studies different computer programs have been used; for OGWC3 we used a program that allowed parallel treatment of groups.

[20] The corresponding rank statistics over trials reveals a significant difference between the three sanctioning conditions (T = 4.69, p = .0096).

[21] The corresponding statistics over trials and (0,2) vs. 1 exhibits mean ranks of 7.9 and 12.7 (T = 3.17, p = .075).

[22] The regression model uses confounded variables that in part explain the large r^2. Nevertheless the moderate correlations and the small standard error of the residual indicate that it is fair to use it for getting some heuristics for a rule-based hierarchical agent model—the validity of which can be tested in simulations independent of the regression analysis.

[23] The pure effect of the difference equation $x(t) = ax(t-1) + bx(t-2) + ct$ can be represented by a limiting (stationary) action of about $x = 0.021t + 6.65 - 0.3\sigma$ not surpassing the crisis indicator $s > 64$ within the time limit of $t = 20$. Adaptation is monotonic. Inhomogeneous plans, pA, may produce inhomogeneous realizations, rA, but their possible effect is small. With the above model the enduring oscillations can only be explained by an adequate set of (externally given) negative values for pA.

[24] In our set-ups weak sanctioning (sanctioning factor 0) means that sanctions do not include a component proportional to the offense.

[25] Cf. Selten (1990, 1994) and Ostmann (1990).

[26] In Beckenkamp and Ostmann (1996) and Ostmann and Beckenkamp (1997) a multiagent system related to our sanctioning dilemma scenario is specified and discussed. In this model total usage observed triggers the emotional state of the agent. The main variable of the state can be interpreted as *charge* or accumulated anger. A second variable can be interpreted as *inhibition* or indulgence and is used to represent the different types of individuals like the greedy one and the restrained one. In an evaluation procedure that depends on the emotional state the action of the agent is determined. Finally as a consequence of the action the emotional state of the agent is changed (e.g., when revenge can be taken there will be a considerable change in the emotional state). The discharge can be interpreted as catharsis.

[27] In the experimental games tradition situations that prompt humans to this kind of two-fold goal setting have been called mixed motive situations.

[28] Such effects of type can be conjectured for our experimental data: As in many other studies we found clear differences between participants studying psychology and participants studying economy and law.

Chapter 12

Work Team Cooperation: The Effects of Structural and Motivational Changes

Xiao-Ping Chen

INTRODUCTION

Members of work groups often encounter a conflict between maximizing individual interests (defection) or working for the good of the team as a whole (cooperation). This is particularly true in organizations that have adopted work groups as a basic organizational unit. For instance, a member in a research project team must decide how much time and effort to devote to a project to make it successful. On the one hand, the member can choose not to do anything about the project, hoping others will do all the work so that she can enjoy the benefits of success at minimal cost. On the other hand, if every member chooses to do so, the project will fail and no one benefits from it. Motivating members to work hard for the group project is a major concern for many managers and supervisors in organizations, especially with the increasing emphasis on the importance of teams for organizational success in the modern economy.

The situation described above is a typical example of the *free-rider* problem (Olson, 1965) or a social dilemma (Dawes, 1980; Komorita & Parks, 1995; Messick & Brewer, 1983). Social dilemmas have been studied extensively in social psychology, economics, sociology, and political science. Among the many approaches proposed to solve the problem, the motivational approach and the structural approach are the most prominent ones.

The motivational approach focuses on changing participants' perceptions of the social environment (e.g., expectations of others' behaviors, feelings of group identity, trust, perceived self-efficacy), and therefore their motivation for cooperation. Motivational solutions include:

(a) introducing face to face communication before engaging in the task (Bouas & Komorita, 1996; Dawes, McTavish, & Shaklee, 1977; Edney & Harper, 1978a; 1978b; Jerdee & Rosen, 1974; Kerr & Kaufman-Gilliland, 1994);

(b) informing participants about the negative consequences of defective actions (Alock & Mansell, 1977; Caldwell, 1976; Edney & Harper, 1978a; Foddy & Veronese, 1996); or

(c) manipulating participants' expectations about other members' behaviors (Alock & Mansell, 1977; Fox & Guyer, 1977; Komorita, Hilty, & Parks, 1991).

Structural approaches, on the other hand, focus on the effects of the parameters of the dilemma (e.g., the k' index by Komorita, 1976; or the *d/m* parameter by Schelling, 1973; group size) on individual behavior. Structural solutions often include:

(a) changing the payoff matrix (Komorita, Chan, & Parks, 1993; Marwell & Ames, 1979, 1980);

(b) introducing sanction systems (Caldwell, 1976; Sato, 1984; Yamagishi, 1986);

(c) reducing group size (Fox & Guyer, 1977; Komorita & Lapworth, 1982b); or

(d) assigning a group leader (Foddy & Crettenden, 1994; Messick, et al., 1983; Wit & Wilke, 1988).

However, motivational and structural approaches cannot be absolutely separated because structural solutions may work through their effects on motives and expectations. For example, the reason that high k' (Komorita, 1976) social dilemma games induce higher rates of cooperation than low k' games may be that members feel safer to invest for the collective interest in the high k' games. Similarly, the reason that introducing a sanction system leads to more cooperation may be that it makes people realize that being cooperative is the right thing to do. Moreover, the reason why members in smaller groups are more willing to cooperate may be due to the fact that they feel that their contributions are more critical to help the group reach its goal (Kerr, 1989, 1992). As Komorita and Parks (1994) pointed out in their book, "group size by itself does not seem to affect individual behavior" and "individual contributions seem to be affected only when something else changes along with group size" (p. 63). Therefore, when investigating the effects of structural changes, we also need to investigate the associated motivational changes. This chapter will describe a study that examined the effects of structural changes on members' cooperative behavior and their corresponding motivational changes. Then by discussing the relationship between the structural and motivational approaches, I will propose a combined approach in searching for more solutions to this ubiquitous problem.

The study I will discuss in this chapter investigated the effects of reward allocation rules and task difficulty on group members' cooperative behavior. It also examined group members' perceptions of fairness, group identity, and perceived criticality induced by different allocation rules and tasks. In particular, three types of reward allocation rules were assigned to various groups: the equity rule, the equality rule, and the mixed rule (a combination of equity and equality). Moreover, each group was given three different tasks with different difficulty levels at three times. The main purpose of the study was to examine if the effects of allocation rules would be invariant when members' individual performances and rewards were contingent upon the group product (a social dilemma situation), and what the underlying mechanisms were to explain these effects.

The Research Scenario

The research scenario used in this study was an adaptation of the incremental collective goods paradigm described by Hampton (1987) or the paradigm used in Suleiman and Rapoport (1992). According to Hampton, collective goods can be defined as goods that benefit a collective and that are *indivisible* or *in joint supply*, that is, making them available to one person in the community makes them available to all. The incremental collective goods, on the other hand, can "vary from being quite 'steppy' so that a certain fairly large contribution level must be reached in order for an increment of the good to be produced (e.g., the construction of railway lines connecting small towns), to being completely continuous such that any contribution, no matter how small, will result in some increase in the good (e.g., clean air or clean water)" (Hampton, p. 249). In this study, participants were asked to analyze three management cases with their group members throughout a semester. They were informed that their group paper must achieve a certain *contribution level* (or *provision level*) to earn course credit, and that after the contribution level was reached, more contribution would increase the value (credit) of the group paper.

This research scenario mimics a situation often observed in work units of organizations. The payment system introduced in the classical Hawthorne studies—*group piecework*—is a typical example (Homans, 1998). Under this system, the department as a whole counted as a unit. When the department output exceeded a certain requirement level, the more equipment completed and shipped by the whole department, the more pay each employee received. When the department output did not reach that requirement level, each received fixed pay. Thus, members could increase their earnings *only if* the output of the department as a whole increased. In this situation, members' performance interdependently determined the departmental output, which in turn determined each member's level of pay. This situation possesses the characteristics of the incremental collective goods scheme described above because (a) members could contribute any amount of their time and effort to produce the departmental output; and (b) when the departmental output exceeded the required level, more output brought more earnings.

Similar situations can be observed in many modern organizations too. Imagine a shoe factory in which 500 pairs of shoes are the minimum amount (provision level) to balance production cost. If fewer than 500 pairs are produced, no profit will be earned and all the effort will be wasted. However, if more than 500 pairs are produced, the more produced, the higher the earnings for the factory (as well as for the workers), with the constraint that these shoes must be out in the market within a short period of time. In this example, there is a required provision level (500 pairs) for the factory to earn profit; and moreover, after the provision level is reached, more pairs bring more profits. Thus, it also represents an incremental collective goods dilemma, assuming the profits are shared.

This situation presents a dilemma problem regardless of what reward allocation rules are used. At the time a worker makes his or her decision as to how much time and effort to invest, or how many pairs of shoes to produce, there is always uncertainty about whether or not the departmental output will exceed the required level (e.g., 500 pairs). Therefore, doubt will be cast on whether his or her contribution will be wasted or bring him or her more profits. In general, if the departmental output does not exceed the requirement, the payoff for contribution is always smaller than for noncontribution, no matter what distribution rule is used. This situation induces fear of wasting one's contribution among group members (Dawes, Orbell, Simmons, & Van de Kragt, 1986; Rapoport & Eshed-Levy, 1989). If the departmental output exceeds the requirement, on the other hand, whether the situation still remains a dilemma problem depends on what reward rule is used. In particular, if equality is the allocation rule, it will still be a dilemma because regardless of the amount of contribution, everyone receives the same payoff. Under the equity rule, however, it will no longer be a dilemma because the payoff will be contingent upon one's contribution (i.e., it removes *greed* from members). Under the mixed rule it will remain a dilemma, but to a lesser degree because only part of the collective good will be distributed according to contributions. Therefore, introducing different allocation rules to the problem changes the structure of the game.

Cooperation can be operationalized in two ways using this research scenario. First, because group members can contribute any amount of their resources to the group paper, the mean percentage of the total resources contributed (mean Pc) is an index of cooperation. Second, because there is a provision level for the group paper to earn course credit, the mean success rate of the group paper (mean Sr as measured by whether groups met the minimum criteria for success or not) serves as another index of cooperation.

Reward Allocation Rules and Cooperation

The results of previous studies on the effects of reward allocation rules on individual performance have consistently supported equity theory (Pritchard, Dunnette, & Jorgenson, 1972). However, very few studies have looked at how allocation rules affect individual, as well as group performance in a situation in which there is interdependence between individual members' performance, and between individual and group performance. The relevant research we could find is Rapoport and Amaldoss' (1997b) formal theoretical demonstration (see Chapter 5 in this book) and Suleiman and Rapoport's (1992) empirical study. Rapoport and Amaldoss demonstrated mathematically that the equity rule should be more effective than the equality rule or the mixed rule in inducing cooperation. Suleiman and Rapoport found that participants contributed more to the collective good when the contribution was incremental rather than when it was all or none. They hypothesized that the equity principle might have been evoked when contribution was incremental so that the participants could fix the level of contribution at k/n, where k = provision level and n = group size.

Indeed, one of the explanations for the effectiveness of the equity rule is the fairness hypothesis (Adams, 1965; Greenberg & Cohen, 1982). That is, members work harder or cooperate more under the equity rule because they perceive that it is a fairer rule. Fairness has also been found to be a mediating variable between leader behaviors and subordinates' organizational citizenship behaviors (OCB) (Farh, Podsakoff, & Organ, 1990): the fairer the subordinates perceive their leaders' behaviors, the higher their levels of OCB exhibited. OCB refers to those organizationally beneficial behaviors and gestures that can neither be enforced on the basis of formal role obligations nor elicited by contractual guarantee of recompense (Bateman & Organ, 1983), so they can be viewed as special types of cooperative behaviors in organizations.

In the incremental collective goods dilemma described earlier, under all three allocation rules, people will be uncertain about the likelihood that the public good will be provided (thus both the fear that contribution may be wasted and the fear of failure of attuning provision will be affected). However, will people exert more effort toward the collective good if they believe that the reward allocation rule is fair? To put it more precisely, will a fair allocation rule attenuate people's fear of losing their contribution and getting less than others will? Based on our theoretical reasoning and suggestive evidence from previous studies, we hypothesized that group members would contribute more to the collective goods when the reward was distributed proportionally to contributions than when the reward was distributed equally, or when a mixed rule was applied.

Task Difficulty and Cooperation

Task difficulty has been identified as one of the parameters under which individuals will or will not exert high effort when working in groups (Shepperd, 1993). In this study, we operationalized it by varying the required provision level: Higher required provision level represented difficult tasks and lower provision level represented easy tasks. We hypothesized that greater cooperation would be observed when group members were given difficult tasks than when they were given easy tasks. This hypothesis was based on two reasons. First, when facing difficult tasks, members would be more likely to believe that their individual contribution was important in the provision of the collective good than when facing relatively easy tasks. Suleiman and Rapoport (1992) reported a significant increase in the mean individual contribution as a function of the provision level. Also, Harkins and Petty (1982, Experiment 1) examined the effects of task difficulty and identifiability on members' contributions of ideas to the group, and found that regardless of whether contributions could or could not be identified, individuals working on a difficult task exerted higher effort. Shepperd (1993) interpreted these results in terms of perceived criticality. He reasoned that when the task was difficult or challenging, members would perceive that "their contributions were unlikely to be duplicated by fellow workers" (p. 74), thus developing a sense of importance of their own contributions. Empirical findings (Chen, 1997; Chen, Au, & Komorita, 1996; Kerr, 1989, 1992; Rapoport, 1988) have shown that perceived criticality significantly enhances cooperation. Second, the literature on goal setting (Latham & Yukl, 1975; Locke, 1968; Locke & Latham, 1990) consistently suggests that difficult goals, when accepted, result in higher performance than easy goals. Because higher required provision levels set difficult goals for members to achieve, whereas lower levels set relatively easy goals, members' contributions should be greater when performing difficult tasks than when performing easy tasks.

On the other hand, because a higher provision level set an objectively higher requirement to establish a collective good, we hypothesized that the success rate of the group paper would decrease with task difficulty (mean Sr would be lower when the provision level was high than when it was moderate or low).

THE STUDY

In order to test these hypotheses, a quasi-experiment was conducted. One hundred and sixty undergraduate business students (70 male and 90 female) who were enrolled in an introductory management course participated. The design of the quasi-experiment was a 3 (reward allocation rules: equity, equality, or mixed rule) × 3 (required contribution level: 30%, 50%, or 70%, nested within groups) factorial. The design is presented in Table 12.1.

Table 12.1　Design of the experiment.

Required contribution levels	Reward allocation rules		
	Equity	Equality	Mixed
30%	30%-Equity	30%-Equality	30%-Mixed
50%	50%-Equity	50%-Equality	50%-Mixed
70%	70%-Equity	70%-Equality	70%-Mixed

At the beginning of the semester, students were randomly assigned to 1 of the 35 4–6 person groups formed to conduct group exercises during the semester. Among them, 12 groups were randomly assigned to the equity rule condition, 12 groups to the equality rule condition, and 11 groups to the mixed rule condition. Upon the formation of the groups, all students were asked to introduce themselves to other group members. Later in the semester, they were asked to complete three case analyses in which they could earn course credit. They were told that the points they earned from these group exercises would be counted toward their final grade, which was about 15% of the total points they could earn for the course.

In each group exercise, students were first given a management case to read. They were then asked individually to answer questions about the case. The questions were asked in a way so that answers could be tabulated as a list of ideas (e.g., what are some explanations for the success of Microsoft?). This list of ideas was referred to as their *individual paper* and the quantity, as well as the quality of these ideas were emphasized. All students were informed that the number of ideas they listed on their individual paper (no matter how many there were) was worth 100 points, and that they must decide how many ideas from the list they would like to contribute to the group paper. If more than $k\%$ of the group members' total ideas were presented on the group paper (if two members had identical ideas, as long as the idea was on the group paper, it was counted as two ideas), members would receive certain bonus points, in addition to the percentage of ideas they kept for their own. However, if less than $k\%$ of the total ideas were presented on the group paper, all the ideas contributed to the group paper would be wasted and each member would retain *only* the percentage of points he or she kept for herself. They were then asked to write down, on a small piece of paper (a) the total number of ideas they wrote down in their individual paper, and (b) the number of ideas they would like to contribute to the group paper.

After collecting this piece of paper from each individual, group members were allowed to discuss the case and write their group paper together. Before starting group discussion, they were given written instructions (in which distribution rules were explicitly explained) on how to proceed with the group exercise. They were then asked to complete a questionnaire individually. The questionnaire was designed to assess their group identity and perceived criticality.

No feedback or discussion was given after each case analysis. However, all students were fully debriefed after the three case analyses were completed. The debriefing was combined with a lecture on the social dilemma topic, and students were informed that a full mark (credit) was given to every student who participated in the group exercise, no matter which distribution rule was assigned to their group.

Research Conditions

There were three research conditions in the study: the equity rule, the equality rule, and the mixed rule. The provision level $k\%$ represents task difficulty.

To describe these conditions explicitly, let Pi and Qi denote the percentage of ideas contributed by member *i* to the individual and group paper, respectively (Pi + Qi = 100), and let T denote the total percent of ideas contributed to the group paper (T = ΣQi). Then, if we let *k%* denote the required provision level and *n* denote the group size, the three conditions can be described as follows:

The Equity Rule Condition   Participants in this condition were informed that if *k%* (vary across tasks) or more of the total individual ideas were presented in the group paper, the group paper would receive twice the total contribution (2T) points, and each member's gain from the group paper would be *proportional* to what he or she had contributed. However, if less than *k%* of the total individual ideas were presented, all the ideas contributed to the group paper would be lost. The formula for calculating the individual outcome was:

Individual outcome = Pi + (Qi/T) (2T) = Pi + 2Qi   if *T/n* ≥ *k;*
Individual outcome = Pi   if *T/n* < *k*

The Equality Rule Condition   Participants in this condition were also informed that *k%* or more of the total individual ideas were needed for the group paper to earn any points. If *k%* or more ideas were presented, the group paper would receive twice the total contribution (2T) points. Each member would then receive an *equal* share of points from the group paper, regardless how many ideas he or she had contributed. However, if less than *k%* of the total individual ideas were presented, all the ideas contributed to the group paper would be lost. The formula for calculating individual outcome was:

Individual outcome = Pi + (2T) / *n*   if *T/n* ≥ *k;*
Individual outcome = Pi   if *T/n* < *k*

The Mixed Rule Condition   Mixed rule refers to the mixture of the equity and equality rules. Participants in this condition were informed that *k%* or more of the total individual ideas were necessary for the group paper to earn any points. If the group paper contained *k%* or more of the total ideas, the group paper would receive 2T points from which each member could get 40 points,[1] regardless of his or her contribution. The remaining points would be allocated to each member proportional to their contribution. However, if less than *k%* of the total individual ideas were presented, all the ideas contributed to the group paper would be lost. The formula for calculating the individual outcome was:

Individual outcome = Pi + 40 + (Qi/T) (2T - 40*n*)   if *T/n* ≥ *k;*
Individual outcome = Pi   if *T/n* < *k*

Measures of Group Identity, Perceived Criticality, and Perception of Fairness

In order to examine the correspondent feelings induced by the structural changes of the game, three related feelings were measured. Group identity was measured using a modified Group Identification Scale (GIS) by Hinkle, Taylor, Fox-Cardamone, and Crook (1989). Perceived criticality was measured using two statements on a 9-point Likert scale (1 = *strongly disagree*; 9 = *strongly agree*): (1) "I felt that my input to the group paper was very important" and (2) "I see myself as an important part of this group." Perception of fairness about the reward allocation rules, however, was measured separately. At the beginning of the semester, a questionnaire containing two scenarios was distributed to all students. One scenario described a situation in which five members of a new group (low group identity) were involved in a distribution of $1,500 for a well done group task. Students were asked to indicate a fair way to allocate this reward. Four responses were provided:

1   every member receives the same amount (equality rule);
2   distribute the reward according to the number of hours each member contributed to the group task (equity rule);
3   randomly distribute the reward; and
4   every member receives a certain amount of money, with the rest distributed according to number of hours spent on the group task (mixed rule).

The other scenario described a situation in which the members of a four-person group were all good friends (high group identity) and they needed to choose a fair way to allocate 100 points for the group project they completed. They were again provided with these four responses. The majority choice was considered to be the perceived fair allocation rule for each scenario.

RESULTS

Mean Proportion of Total Ideas Contributed to the Group Paper

The mean proportion of total ideas contributed (mean Pc) to the group paper was used as an index of cooperation. Table 12.2 presents the mean Pc in each condition. A two-way ANOVA (Allocation Rule × Required Provision Level, with repeated measures on required provision level) revealed a significant main effect of allocation rule, $F(2, 32) = 8.96$, p < .001. Neither the main effect of required provision level nor the two-way interaction was significant at the .05 level.

These results support the hypothesis that the reward allocation rule has a strong impact on group members' contributions. Specifically, members in the equity rule condition contributed a significantly higher proportion of their ideas to the group paper across the three tasks (mean Pc = .93) than members in the equality rule condition (mean Pc = .74) or the mixed rule condition (mean Pc =.80).

Table 12.2   Mean proportion of ideas (Pc), mean group identity (GI), and mean perceived criticality (PC).

| Required Provision Levels | Reward allocation rules | | | | | | | | | | | |
| | Equity-rule | | | Equality-rule | | | Mixed-rule | | | Mean | | |
	Pc	GI	PC	Pc	GI	PC	Pc	GI	PC	Pc	GI	PC
30%	.90	7.54	6.64	.64	7.38	6.75	.78	7.18	6.53	.77	7.36	6.64
50%	.92	7.86	6.91	.72	7.63	6.86	.83	7.31	6.71	.82	7.60	6.83
70%	.96	7.74	7.00	.84	7.83	7.59	.79	7.63	7.02	.86	7.73	7.23
Mean	.93	7.71	6.85	.74	7.61	7.07	.80	7.37	6.75			

Separate one-way ANOVAs for each required provision level yielded significant effects of allocation rule when it was 30% [$F(2, 32) = 5.10$, p < .05] and 50% [$F(2, 32) = 6.30$, p < .01]. However, the effect was not significant at the .05 level when it was 70%. These results suggest that the effects of reward allocation rules may be generalized to tasks with low or moderate difficulties. However, when the task is very difficult (i.e., the required provision level is 70%), the effects seem to be diminishing (mean Pc was .96, .84, and .79 across the three reward conditions, respectively).

On the other hand, these results do not support the hypothesis that mean Pc will be greater when the task is difficult than when it is easy. The mean Pc was not significantly greater when the provision level was 70% than when it was 50% or 30%, although it was in the predicted direction (mean Pc = .86, .82, and .77, respectively).

Mean Proportion of Successful Group Papers

Table 12.3 presents the mean percentage of group papers that successfully met the requirement ($k\%$) in each condition. Because the mean success rate (mean Sr) is a dichotomous variable, three separate logistic regression analyses (using mean Sr as the dependent variable, allocation rule, provision level and the interaction term as the covariates, respectively) were performed. These analyses yielded a significant main effect of provision level [Wald (df = 1) = 8.74, p < .01] and a significant interaction effect [Wald (df = 2) = 4.55, p < .05]. However, the main effect of allocation rule was not significant at the .05 level.

These results suggest that whether a public good can be successfully provided is affected by task difficulty. We found more successful group papers when the provision level was low (100% successful) than when it was moderate (94.6% successful) or high (71% successful). In this study (as predicted) the easier the task, the more likely the group was to attain success.

Nevertheless, the significant interaction between provision level and allocation rule suggests that the main effect of provision level needs to be explained with caution. To further examine the nature of the interaction, separate chi-square analyses for each provision level and each allocation rule were performed. These analyses revealed that (a) when the provision level was 70%, mean Sr was significantly higher in the equity rule condition (91.7%) than in the mixed rule condition (54.5%), $\chi^2(1) = 3.92$, p < .05, and (b) when the allocation rule was equality or mixed, mean Sr was significantly higher in the 30% condition (100% and 100%, respectively) than in the 70% condition (66.7% and 54.5%, respectively), $\chi^2(1) = 4.82$, $\chi^2(1) = 8.39$, p < .01, respectively. All other effects were not significant at the .05 level.

These results suggest that the equity rule is more effective in producing qualified group papers compared to the equality and mixed rules, especially when the task require-

Table 12.3   Percentage of successful group papers.

| Provision Levels | Reward allocation rules | | | |
	Equity	Equality	Mixed	Mean
30%	100	100	100	100
50%	100	83.3	100	94.4
70%	91.7	66.7	54.5	71.0
Mean	97.2	83.5	84.5	

ment is high. Moreover, when the equity rule is applied, the success rate of group papers becomes insensitive to provision levels, that is, the impact of task difficulty becomes minimal when the benefits are to be distributed in proportion to contributions—participants uniformly cooperated across three provision levels. Overall, only one out of twelve groups failed to provide a qualified group paper in the equity rule condition.

Mean Group Identity and Perceived Criticality

The mean scores on group identity and perceived criticality are also presented in Table 12.2. Two separate two-way ANOVAs (Allocation Rule × Required Provision Level, with repeated measures on required provision level) were performed on group identity and perceived criticality, respectively. The analyses revealed significant main effects of required provision level on both group identity [$F(2, 64) = 7.86$, $p < .001$] and perceived criticality [$F(2, 64) = 7.83$, $p < .001$]. Other effects were not significant at the .05 level.

An examination of Table 12.2 reveals that group identity increased with the required provision level: group identity was lowest when the required provision level was 30% (mean GI = 7.36), moderate when it was 50% (mean GI = 7.60), and highest when the required provision level was 70% (mean GI = 7.73).

The pattern of results for perceived criticality is identical to that for group identity: Perceived criticality was highest when the required provision level was 70% (mean PC = 7.20), moderate when it was 50% (mean PC = 6.83), and lowest when it was 30% (mean PC = 6.64). These results suggest that participants' feelings of the criticalness of their own contribution to the group paper was determined, at least in part, by task difficulty: Higher requirements for the group paper generated higher levels of perceived criticality among group members than lower requirements.

These results also suggest some reasonable explanations for the insignificant effect of allocation rule on mean Pc when the provision level was 70%. Seventy percent of the total individual ideas to be presented in the group paper is a rather high requirement for the group paper to earn points; thus, members' feelings of importance of their contributions to the group paper and their identifications to the group were aroused because of this high requirement. The combination of these two feelings (group identity and perceived criticality) has been repeatedly demonstrated to be effective in inducing cooperation in social dilemmas (Chen, 1996, 1997). These results provide another piece of supporting evidence to this conclusion because the strong effect of allocation rule seems to be overridden when both group identity and perceived criticality reached a high level.

Perception of the Fair Distribution Rule

The percentage of responses to the two scenarios are presented in Table 12.4. It is clear that the equity rule was considered to be a fair rule in the first scenario (57.6%) in which group members were new to one another (low group identity), whereas the equality rule was considered to be the fair rule in the second scenario (62.6%) in which group members were friends (high group identity). These results indicate that participants make distinctions between good friends and acquaintances in terms of reward allocations. In other words, perception of fairness of the distribution rule is a function of levels of group identity.

These results also suggest a glimpse as to why the allocation rule failed to affect mean Pc when the required provision level was 70%. Because group identity increased

**Table 12.4   Percentage of preferred responses
to the three allocation rules**

| | Allocation rules | | | |
Scenarios	Equality	Equity	Random	Mixed
Nonfriends	24.2%	57.6%	1.0%	13.1%
Friends	62.6%	14.1%	3.0%	13.1%

with the required provision level and reached a high degree when it was 70%, at which time the equality rule might have been seen as fair as (if not fairer than) the equity rule. Therefore, the effect of the allocation rules on mean Pc may have diminished.

DISCUSSION AND CONCLUSIONS

The primary goal of this study was to investigate the effectiveness of reward allocation rules in changing people's cooperative behavior when facing conflict between maximizing individual welfare and maximizing collective welfare. The results of the study support the notion that reward allocation rules affect members' cooperation in an incremental collective goods dilemma as significantly as they do in the other (mostly organizational) settings in which they've been studied. In particular, the equity rule was more effective than the equality or the mixed rule in eliciting cooperation, in terms of both individual level contribution and collective good provision. Moreover, this effect seems to be stable across tasks within a certain range of difficulties.

Another goal of this study was to investigate the motivational changes induced by structural changes and to provide explanations for the effects of reward allocation rules on behavior in mixed motive situations. Three factors associated with these structural changes that could have a significant impact were examined: group identity, perceived criticality, and perception of fairness. All three factors provide reasonable explanations for the findings of this study.

From what has been found in this study, it is clear that structural changes are accompanied by motivational changes and that the latter may provide a deeper understanding of human behavior under the structural changes. The inseparability of the two types of changes calls for a third approach to the social dilemma problem—a combination of the structural and motivational approaches. I propose a framework and explain why this approach will lead to a more fruitful research in this field.

As discussed earlier, the structural approach focuses on the change of the parameters of the dilemma such as payoff structure, allocation rules and group size and their direct effects on behavior. A motivational approach on the other hand emphasizes the importance of psychological feelings in influencing behavior. The framework I propose here is the combined approach, which advocates that I should study both the structural and motivational effects at the same time. This approach can broaden our view because it looks at the problem from both perspectives simultaneously. First, this approach can start with the structural changes to find out the motivational changes evoked, study the effects of these changes on cooperation and the effective solutions to the problem (the dashed lines on Figure 12.1). At the same time, it can start with the motivational factors that have been found to be important in cooperation induction, search for possible structural changes that

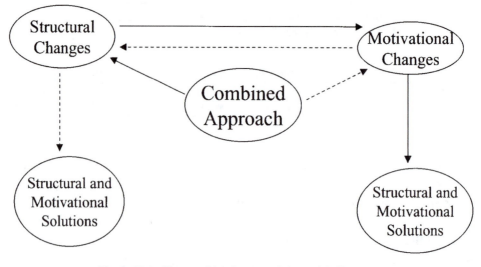

Figure 12.1   The combined approach to social dilemmas

would lead to these motivational changes and thus the effective solutions to the problem (the solid lines on Figure 12.1).

This combined approach has important implications for solving social dilemmas in general and the free-rider problems in the work place in particular. Using this approach, we will be able to give advice to managers about the practical structural changes that may be introduced to the organization, as well as the explanations (from the employees' subjective feelings perspective) as to what extent and why they will be effective. Moreover, we will be able provide suggestions to managers as to what feelings are important in inducing cooperation among team members and what are the practical things that we can do to evoke these feelings at the same time. For example, one piece of advice that can be drawn from the study described in this chapter is that difficult tasks are not necessarily obstacles for motivating employees and the reason is that these tasks may induce employees' feelings of importance as well as their identifications as part of the group. Another is that managers need to be sensitive to employees' fairness concerns, because perception of fairness seems to be a good explanation for the effectiveness of the equity rule, and also because employees' perceptions of what constitutes a fair reward allocation rule change when they interact with different people at different times.

ENDNOTES

[1] Any points below 60 were applicable to the three case analyses with different required provision levels: 30%, 50%, and 70%, because when the provision level was 30%, at least 60 points could be equally distributed to each member if the collective good is established. It was an arbitrary choice to allow 40 points to be divided equally among group members.

Chapter 13

Decision Contexts for Structural Change in Social Dilemmas: A Preliminary Framework

Janine Webb

Social dilemmas are situations in which individuals receive a higher payoff from a socially defecting choice than from a socially cooperative choice, but all individuals are better off if all cooperate than if all defect (Dawes, 1980). The idea that people voluntarily cooperate for the implementation of needed structural change, to resolve social dilemmas, is termed *instrumental cooperation* (Yamagishi, 1986b). This article is concerned with the discrepancy that exists between the representation of structural change decisions in this area of research and the sociopolitical processes that surround such decision making in real world social dilemmas. To help bridge this gap, a preliminary taxonomy of social structures is proposed to assist in generating further research into potential solutions of social dilemmas and in related research areas.

IDENTIFYING SOLUTIONS TO SOCIAL DILEMMAS

There have been two major theoretical approaches to the solution of social dilemmas: the *rational structural* approach and the *goal/expectation* approach (Yamagishi, 1986a; 1986b). The rational-structural approach holds that the only solution to social dilemmas is to (externally) modify the structure of the dilemma itself, to achieve a state where it is in the individual's self-interest to cooperate, because group and individual interests become aligned (Yamagishi, 1986a; 1986b). In contrast, the goal/expectation approach assumes that social dilemmas are resolved by altering individuals' cognitions about the type of situation and the degree of conflict that exists between individual and group interests (Yamagishi, 1986b).

Dissatisfied with both of these approaches, Yamagishi (1986b) coined the term instrumental cooperation to refer to the idea that people *voluntarily* cooperate for the implementation of needed structural change to resolve social dilemmas. The importance of this concept was that it bridged a previously ignored feedback loop between the structure of the social dilemma (configuration of outcomes and associated form of interdependence) and the actions of individuals (Yamagishi, 1988a). It served to capture how actors in real world situations voluntarily introduce structural change to resolve social dilemmas and actively transform the dilemma structure itself (Yamagishi, 1988a). (cf. The observations of authors such as Buckley, Burns, & Meeker, 1974; Burns & Meeker, 1974; Liebrand, 1984; and Ostrom, 1988, 1990.)

In recent years, research by political scientists and economists into the solution of common pool resources has further recognized that all actors do not have equal access to the decision making process and that heterogeneity among actors can affect decisions about structural change. In her detailed case descriptions of institutional decision making in common pool resources, Ostrom (1990) highlighted how decisions about structural change can serve vested interests. She described, for example, how some farmers in an irrigation development project in Sri Lanka had privileged access to central officials who could help obstruct the impartial enforcement of rules (see also the earlier observations of Crowe, 1969).

Ostrom (1990) also emphasized the importance of the sociopolitical context on an actor's experience of a given structure and on decision making about structural change. She made this point in the context of her discussion of how data, such as benefits and costs (summary variables), can affect decision making and how there may be situational variables that affect summary variables. According to Ostrom, the type of external political regime that is in place is one of these situational variables. Regimes may be either supportive or nonsupportive and may enable, via such means as bribery, some actors to gain rules or exceptions to rules that advantage them over others.

Keohane and Ostrom (1995) and colleagues extended Ostrom's (1990) earlier analysis. They called for consideration of how heterogeneity among actors in the common pool resource dilemmas can affect collective action and preference for institutional arrangements. These authors (e.g., Libecap, 1995; Martin, 1995) stressed the need to consider the effect of differences in preferences, goals, capabilities, and information and beliefs on cooperation among people with access to common pool resources. These authors also described how institutional changes alter the structure of the situation and the incentives and behaviors of actors.

INEQUALITIES AND DECISIONS ABOUT STRUCTURAL CHANGE

The inequality that exists under structural arrangements in the distribution of resource outcomes across the group is one form of heterogeneity that is of central importance to decisions regarding structural change. More specifically, inequalities in the distribution and transformation of resource allocations provide the decision context in which actors make their decisions about structural change. (See, for example, the argument of Buckley et al., 1974, that the social structural context of decision making influences responses to a given situation.)

Each type of status quo and alternative structure can be characterized as a distribution of one or more variables (e.g., fines, voting influence, access to shared resources, and bonuses) across the members of the group. The different combinations of these variables produce many different types of structures (e.g., different types of leadership, as recognized in leadership studies such as those by Bianco & Bates, 1990; or sanctioning systems as acknowledged by Sato, 1987), and a range of different types of group experiences of structural change. Moreover, given that the type of status quo structure that is in place can vary over time (Ostrom, 1990; Samuelson & Messick, 1995), groups can be moved through a large range of outcomes over time.

Parallel to this group level experience, huge inequalities may be experienced by the individual members of the same group because different individuals can occupy quite different *positions* (i.e., receive very different shares of the group distributed variables, depending on past behavior or previous allocations) within each type of structural arrangement. For example, when the status quo structure is leadership and the distribution of variables across the group is unequal, one individual group member (the leader) may be in a structural position where she or he receives none of the distributed fines but all of the distributed access, bonuses, and voting influence. At the same time, another individual *within the same group* may be in a position where she or he receives all of the distributed fines but none of the distributed access, bonuses, or voting influence.

The particular combination of status quo and alternative structure(s) that is in place determines the type of change that can occur to these positions, at one or more points in time. For example, if a newly introduced status quo structure provides those with low access to the shared resource with a higher level of access, their relative disadvantage in the group can be diminished. Likewise, if a newly introduced status quo structure imposes a fine on those who have taken the fewest resources, group members with few resources can face the prospect of becoming even more disadvantaged than in the past.

A single decision about structural change at a particular time can thus direct self and others to any one of numerous possible points within a network of positions (cf. Kelley's, 1984b, transition lists). For some group members, structural change will represent the opportunity to obtain further gain for self. For others, structural change will provide few prospects or even unwanted outcome transformations, and create increased inequalities between group members over time. Structural change can even serve to exclude some actors from certain courses of outcome transformation and constrain their ability to alter their own destiny.

At a higher order level, agenda setting, or the decision to alter the number or type of structures from which people can choose, can perpetuate or further these inequalities. Such agenda setting often seems to occur in real world social dilemmas (e.g., by means of lobbying or legislative challenges).

Decisions for and against structural change thus occur within a context of outcome inequalities and within a context of potential change to these outcomes. An actor's position in structural arrangements can affect his or her ability to secure certain outcomes, perception of structural alternatives, and subsequent structural change preferences. (This idea represents an extension of Komorita & Chertkoff's, 1973, theoretical approach. They argued that people with different levels of resources would emphasize and advocate different norms of equity in order to maximize profit for self.) At the level of structural change, for example, influential parties may not participate in collective action when they cannot see prospects of their private welfare being improved (Libecap, 1995, p. 188). Similarly, they may reject structural change that resolves a social dilemma, when such change threatens to undermine their current status within the existing structure.

Framing changes to the structural properties of social dilemmas as a complex and political decision making process centering on very real inequalities within structural arrangements has not been a popular approach to the study of instrumental cooperation. There is a clear opportunity to extend this area of research.

EMPIRICAL STUDIES INVESTIGATING THE CONDITIONS OF INSTRUMENTAL COOPERATION

In the empirical studies investigating the conditions of instrumental cooperation, participants have been presented with a choice between a status quo social dilemma structure and one or more alternative structures.

The status quo structures, presented to participants, have been social dilemmas and have usually been systems where all actors have equal and free access to the shared resource or where there are no sanctions on harvesting behavior. In contrast, the alternative structures have represented solutions to the status quo social dilemma situation. More specifically, they have represented a change either to the incentive structure to make cooperation more attractive (e.g., sanctioning systems), or the elimination of interdependence among individuals with access to the shared resource (e.g., the appointment of a leader to make the harvesting decisions) (Foddy & Crettenden, 1994; Rutte, 1990; Samuelson & Messick, 1986a).

Consistent with the observations of authors such as Ostrom (1990) and Ostrom, Gardner and Walker (1994), researchers have accepted that the solution to social dilemmas can rest with the coordinated actions of individual group members. Although political scientists such as Keohane and Ostrom (1995) have noted the importance of heterogeneity of actors in larger scale, real world settings, heterogeneity among actors and the positioning of actors within structural arrangements has not been a central feature of any of the major theoretical accounts or empirical studies in this research area.

Past research has emphasized solutions which, on first inspection, seem to restore equality within the group, rather than introduce inequality within and between groups. For example, Sato (1987) presented participants with two types of fining systems: one that distributed costs equally among group members and another that fined the greatest defector. Similarly, other researchers (such as Messick et al., 1983; and Rutte & Wilke, 1984) seem to have assumed that appointed leaders will prefer to make equitable distributions of the shared resource. There is some evidence that this is the case (see Foddy & Hogg, this volume).

While variables such as the level of access to shared resources, rate of resource use and variance in the harvests of fellow group members were manipulated, researchers have frequently omitted details of the type of outcome transformation (and restrictions on outcome transformation) that will occur with the structural change. In several studies (e.g., Messick et al., 1983; Rutte & Wilke, 1984; Rutte & Wilke, 1992, and Rutte, Wilke & Messick, 1987a), participants were asked if they wished to elect a leader, but they were given no indication, *at the time of voting*, of the relative weight of their vote on the final decision about the form of any structural change which might follow. Once the political context of decisions was specified, there was also little variability across studies in the type of voting influence distribution that was represented in structural arrangements. Indeed, while Rutte and Wilke (1985) presented participants with a choice of structures involving different distributions of voting influence, most studies placed participants in a majority rule political system. Included in this category are the studies by Messick et al. (1983), Rutte and Wilke (1984), Samuelson (1991, 1993), Samuelson and Messick (1986a,1986b), Samuelson, Messick, Rutte and Wilke (1984), and Sato (1987).

Nonetheless, Samuelson and Messick (1986b) did make a distinction between different types of structures. They classified structures as either equality restoring (leadership and equal division of the shared resource) or not equality restoring (free access to the shared resource and proportional division of the resource). These authors reasoned that, relative to a status quo structure of free access, leadership and equal division would tend to promote equality in harvest outcomes among group members once they are instituted. In contrast, free access and proportional division allow the inequalities of the past to continue into the future.

This classification was utilized in two of Samuelson and Messick's empirical studies. They argued that the equal territorialization of resources would serve to advantage low users of a shared resource but disadvantage high users, while proportional division would perpetuate the advantage of high resource users (Samuelson & Messick, 1986a). Further, these authors proposed that low access, compared with high access, participants would prefer equality restoring structures on the grounds that equality restoring structures would be of greater personal benefit to the low access group members (Samuelson & Messick, 1986b). Both of these studies focussed on how inequalities in resource outcomes may arise with decisions to make structural changes. There remains the opportunity, however, to explore how a much wider range of inequalities may be created or perpetuated by means of structural changes made by decision makers. The impact of inequalities in variables such as fines, bonuses, and voting influence on decisions about structural change still awaits investigation.

Researchers could also investigate higher order processes such as agenda setting. To date, the range of alternatives available to decision makers at different times has not been explored extensively (Van Lange & Veenendaal, 1992, cited in Van Lange, 1994), despite its importance to decisions about structural change. Instead, a voluntarist position has been adopted to represent the relationship of structure and power. In other words, the constraints facing choice making agents have been minimal and the only structural constraints have been external to the choosing agent (Lukes, 1977). This means that the full range of structural alternatives remains unspecified.

Thus, the next challenge is to explore how inequalities under structural arrangements can provide a decision-context for structural change decisions. A framework is needed that recognizes that structural change decisions can be used to *introduce* inequalities (rather than solve them), and prevent certain actors from influencing the form of structural change that occurs. The development of a comprehensive taxonomy of social structures in this research area is the first step toward making the systematic investigation of characteristics such as political agendas in real world social dilemmas possible.

There are related theoretical approaches which might provide the basis for such a taxonomy. The framework provided by Kelley and Thibaut (1978) provides one way of classifying the different impacts of structures (e.g., fining systems) on the outcomes derived by self and others (as well as the utility of such outcomes). However, further theoretical development is required before it will be possible to link the payoff matrices, central to this approach, with arrangements such as leadership, fining systems, or equal territorialization.

Presumably, the resulting classification of structures from such an exercise would be very broad. In particular, few details would be provided about the way in which incentive structures, such as Chicken or Prisoner's Dilemmas, evolve. As noted by Ostrom et al. (1994), simple inspection of a matrix of outcomes does not make apparent the rule responsible for constituting that matrix (where rule is defined as the prescription that defines the actions and outcomes which are required, prohibited or permitted).

Ostrom et al. (1994) identified seven broad types of rules that may operate configurally (e.g., payoff rules, such as whether a farmer may sell the water received from an irrigation system). They presented a theoretical framework for representing how rules affect what they term action situations and the underlying game structure. Ostrom et al. recognize, for example, that small changes in the type of rule utilized may have an impact on the structure of a game but that in certain contexts, a rule change may not lead to any change in outcomes.

This work represents an important advance on Ostrom's (1990) earlier work. A comprehensive taxonomy of social structures is, however, still required (Samuelson, 1993) if researchers are to investigate how inequalities provide a context for structural change decisions and thereby affect the resolution of social dilemma situations. In the next section, a preliminary framework is provided for representing such contexts and the various implications of structural change decisions. Future research could extend and modify this approach and link it to a theoretical approach such as the one offered by Ostrom et al. (1994).

EXTENDING THE THEORETICAL FRAMEWORK

A preliminary taxonomy of structures is provided by defining structure in terms of *two* distributions: (1) the actual or probable distribution of variable(s) in the group, and (2) each individual's percentage share of those variables. This taxonomy allows *for the simultaneous representation of inequalities at both the group and individual levels.*

Table 13.1 shows how different types of group level experiences are created when status quo and alternative structures are classified in terms of whether there is an equal or unequal distribution of structure defining variables, such as fines, bonuses, access to shared resources, and even influence over the decision making process. Table 13.1 also reveals that individuals in the same group may have quite different experiences. It is possible to construct an array of values representing each individual's share of the variables distributed across the group; all individuals may have the same array, or it may differ across individuals.

Thus, for any single group level experience, there are many different ways that the outcomes may be shared between individual group members. Consider for example, the four cases displayed in Table 13.2. Each case represents a group of four individuals with an unequal distribution of fines and access to the shared resource.

Three of these cases (Groups 1, 3, and 4) might be classified as being in the same *type of structure* because across these groups, there are the same combinations of percentage share of fines and access, albeit in different orders. In Groups 1 and 3, the person who receives 100% of the distributed fine and 10% of the distributed access is group member A. In Group 4, this person is group member D. Groups 1, 3 and 4 could also be considered to be in the same type of structure, despite the fact that the particular allocations received by group members B and C are different in Group 3 compared with Groups 1 and 4. Group 2, in contrast, could be classified as representing a totally different type of structure because the positions held by group members are quite different to those held in groups 1, 3,

Table 13.1   Some of the possible features of a structure.

Type of variable	Type of distribution across the group as a whole [a]	Percentage share of the distributed variable that is received by each group member
access to shared resources (The maximum amount that can be harvested from the shared resource)	equal or unequal	*range*: 0–100% of all distributed access
fine (A cost that may be contingent or non-contingent on other variables)	equal or unequal	*range*: 0–100% of all distributed fines
bonus (A gain that may be contingent or non-contingent on other variables)	equal or unequal	*range*: 0–100% of all distributed bonuses
voting influence (The level of influence over the type of structure that is adopted by the group. Different levels correspond to different political systems.)	equal or unequal	*range:* 0–100% of all distributed voting influence

Note: [a] The level of variables can also vary

Table 13.2   The distribution of fines and of access to shared resources in four different groups.

Case/group number	Group member's identification	Percentage share of distributed fine	Percentage share of distributed access
1	A	100%	10%
	B	0%	60%
	C	0%	30%
	D	0%	0%
2	A	100%	60%
	B	0%	10%
	C	0%	30%
	D	0%	0%
3	A	100%	10%
	B	0%	30%
	C	0%	60%
	D	0%	0%
4	A	0%	0%
	B	0%	60%
	C	0%	30%
	D	100%	10%

and 4. Instead of one group member receiving 100% of the distributed fine and 10% of distributed access, the group member who receives 100% of the distributed fine stands to receive 60% of the access to shared resources that is distributed across the group. From the point of view of certain individuals making choices about preferred structures, each of the four structures is quite different, and one would expect that individuals A, B, C, and D might not have consensus about the most desirable structure.

Assuming a group size of four, Table 13.3 provides further examples of the different kinds of distributions that can be obtained when structures are classified in terms of both group level and individual level experiences. This table reveals the wide range of inequalities that could exist under structures such as equal division of the shared resources, leadership, or free access. It is also apparent that many structures that were previously considered quite different from one another may appear similar when viewed in terms of the proposed classification system. For example, a punishment rule can share many of the structural features of leadership. Furthermore, contrary to Samuelson and Messick's (1986b) reasoning, leadership and equal division of shared resources need not always be equality restoring structures.

Of course, to generate predictions from this taxonomy, assumptions are necessary about the underlying motivation of decision makers, and the reference point that is used. Presumably, the structural alternative that maximizes a particular person's goal will be a function of the particular combination of status quo and alternative structure(s) that is presented. Within this particular decision context, individuals can be expected to act to increase the probability that their preferred structure remains in place, becomes the status quo structure, or (in the case of agenda setting), is presented as a structural change option to others.

Some examples of possible voting behavior are provided in Table 13.4, where for purposes of illustration, it has been assumed that

(a) there is only one structural alternative available to the members of a two person group,
(b) the status quo and alternative structures distribute the same level of fine and access to shared resources, and
(c) individuals maximize narrow self-interest.

Table 13.4 exemplifies how the decision context might systematically alter the voting behavior of individuals and emphasizes that, *for any one group experience*, there are many different decision contexts facing individual decision makers. It is also apparent that the preferences of individual group members occupying various positions within structural arrangements might collectively result in a particular group preference for structural change. For example, when there is a majority rule system, the majority of group members may have low access, and collectively, their preferences may ensure that a fining system targeting low access participants is not introduced. Given a different distribution of voting influence, however, the first structural change preference of such actors might not be so easily secured for the group.

FUTURE RESEARCH DIRECTIONS

The preliminary framework presented in this chapter allows for a broader approach to be taken for the investigation of the conditions under which structural change decisions are made to resolve social dilemma situations.

Table 13.3   Some examples of different types of structures.

The descriptive term that was either used in past research or consistent with past research	Type of structure	
	Type of group experience in the structure	Positions held in the structure
Equality rule	– Equal distribution of access – Equal distribution of voting influence – Equal distribution of fines	Each group member has 25% of distributed access; 25% of the vote; 25% of distributed fines.
Equality rule	– Unequal distribution of access – Unequal distribution of voting influence – Equal distribution of fines	One group member has 100% of distributed access; 100% of the vote; 25% of distributed fines. Each other group member has 0% access; 0% of the vote; 25% of distributed fines.
Punishment rule	– Equal distribution of access – Equal distribution of voting influence – Unequal distribution of fines	One group member has 25% of access; 25% of the vote; 100% of distributed fines. Each other group member has 25% of access; 25% of the vote; 0% of distributed fines.
Punishment rule	– Unequal distribution of access – Equal distribution of voting influence – Unequal distribution of fines	One group member has 0% of distributed access; 25% voting influence; 100% of distributed fines. Each other group member has 33.33% access; 25% voting influence; 0% of distributed fines.
Punishment rule or Leadership	– Unequal distribution of access – Equal distribution of voting influence – Unequal distribution of fines	One group member has 100% of access; 25% voting influence; 0% of distributed fines. Each other group member has 0% access; 25% voting influence; 33.3% of distributed fines.
Leadership	– Unequal distribution of access – Unequal distribution of voting influence	One group member has 100% of distributed access and 100% of the vote. Each other group member has 0% of distributed access and 0% voting influence.
Free access	– Equal distribution of access – Unequal distribution of voting influence	Each group member has 25% of the distributed access. However, one group member has 100% of the distributed voting influence, while others have 0% voting influence.
Free access	– Unequal distribution of access – Equal distribution of voting influence	One group member has 50% of the distributed access and 25% of the voting influence in the group. Each other group member has 16.6% of the distributed access and 25% of the voting influence.

(*Continued*)

Table 13.3 *Continued*

The descriptive term that was either used in past research or consistent with past research	Type of structure	
	Type of group experience in the structure	Positions held in the structure
Equal division of the shared resource	– Equal distribution of access (or unequal distribution if consideration is given to the grouping before equal division) – Equal voting influence	All group members have 100% access to their own share (or 25% of the total pool of resources). Each group member has 25% of the voting influence.
Equal division of the shared resource	– Equal distribution of access (or unequal) – Unequal voting influence	All group members have 100% access to their own share (or 25% of the original pool of resources). One person has 100% of the voting influence and others have none.

In particular, this approach assists researchers to systematically specify and then vary the type of context in which decisions are made, and facilitates exploration of how decisions in the group's interests might coincide with the maximization of self-interest. Rather than simply investigating preference to introduce a fining system, researchers might, for example, investigate whether such preference depends on who will get fined and whether the fine represents an increase, decrease, or no change in the amount of fine previously incurred under the status quo structure. The relative proportions of actors in each of the structural positions becomes a critical factor which needs to be taken into account, as does the relative power of these subgroups to control the range of alternatives being considered.

Another interesting possibility concerns the structural change decisions of people with different social values. Since social values represent different levels of concern for one's own and others' outcomes, it seems likely that preferences for structural change may also differ as a function of where a person is located in a status quo structure, and the implications of alternative structures for the outcomes for self and others. As an example, a prosocial person who held high voting influence, and who was in a structure which distributed outcomes very unevenly across participants, might be more in favor of a change to a more equal distribution system than would a similarly influential person with proself values. However, neither of them would choose an alternative that reduced or removed their voting influence. The proposed framework outlines an initial set of concepts to describe more systematically the ways in which structures may vary, and takes into account the importance to the individual of their location in the status quo and alternative structures.

The taxonomy could also be used to reexamine and extend the results of previous empirical studies. By specifying and manipulating both the position of actors within structural arrangements and the form of outcome transformation that would occur with structural change, a comparison of findings with earlier studies would shed light on the assumptions that participants in these earlier studies may have been making.

Researchers may wish to investigate further Samuelson and Messick's (1986b) finding that low access participants favor equality restoring structures more than high access

Table 13.4   Some examples of possible voting behavior with various decision-contexts (for a two-person group).

Type of status quo structure		Type of alternative structure		Structure maximizing allocations to self	Expected voting behavior
Group experience	**Individual positions**	**Group experience**	**Individual positions**		
Unequal distribution of access, equal distribution of fines	*Person A* 80% access, 50% of distributed fines	Unequal distribution of access, unequal distribution of fines	*Person A* 80% access, 0% of distributed fines.	*Person A* Alternative structure	*Person A* Alternative structure
	Person B 20% access, 50% of distributed fines		*Person B* 20% access, 100% of distributed fines	*Person B* Status quo structure	*Person B* Status quo structure
Unequal distribution of access, unequal distribution of fines	*Person A* 80% access, 100% of distributed fines	Equal distribution of access, unequal distribution of fines	*Person A* 50% access, 100% of distributed fines	*Person A* Status quo structure	*Person A* Status quo structure
	Person B 20% access, 0% of distributed fines		*Person B* 50% access, 0% of distributed fines	*Person B* Alternative structure	*Person B* Alternative structure
Unequal distribution of access, unequal distribution of fines	*Person A* 80% access, 100% of distributed fines	Equal distribution of access, unequal distribution of fines	*Person A* 50% access, 0% of distributed fines	*Person A* Depends on actual amount of distributed fines and access	*Person A* Either
	Person B 20% access, 0% of distributed fines		*Person B* 50% access, 100% of distributed fines	*Person B* Depends on actual amount of distributed fines and access	*Person B* Either
Equal distribution of access, equal distribution of fines	Both group members have 50% of distributed access, 50% of distributed fines	Equal distribution of access, unequal distribution of fines	*Person A* 50% access, 0% of distributed fines	*Person A* Alternative structure	*Person A* Alternative structure
			Person B 50% of access, 100% of distributed fines	*Person B* Status quo structure	*Person B* Status quo structure
Equal distribution of access, equal distribution of fines	*Person A* 50% access, 50% of distributed fines	Unequal distribution of access, unequal distribution of fines	*Person A* 80% access, 0% of distributed fines	*Person A* Alternative structure	*Person A* Alternative structure
	Person B 50% access, 50% of distributed fines		*Person B* 20% access, 100% of distributed fines	*Person B* Status quo structure	*Person B* Status quo structure

participants, or Samuelson's (1993) observation that participants' evaluations of a leadership option were determined by the interaction between individual differences in social values and past experience of the resource.

Researchers might also reconsider Sato's (1987) research in the light of the proposed framework. Sato reasoned that people who experience "poor group performance" in a deficient structure will realize the need for a sanctioning system and, when given the opportunity, be more willing to implement a sanctioning system than those who did not have such an experience. It is possible that the structural change preferences of participants in her study were a reflection of their (individual level) positions within structural arrangements. Rather than responding to the experience of poor group performance in a "deficient structure," individuals may have been responding to a range of individual level experiences of the structural arrangements in this study. For example, it was possible for one group member to face a choice between receiving 100% of a distributed fine and 25% of a distributed fine, while another member *of the same group* faced a choice between receiving 0% of a distributed fine and 25% of a distributed fine. Collectively, the maximization of individual goals within these individual level decision contexts may have created the illusion that the group as a whole was responding to the experience of "poor group performance."

The impact of differences in the experience of structural arrangements is not, however, the only possible focus for future research: the investigation of *common* experiences may also be fruitful. Assuming that some of these common experiences will be salient to actors (common fate), an actor's group identity could vary as a result of structural change decisions and researchers could explore the changes that occur to an actor's social group identity by means of structural change. In certain circumstances, the decision to replace an inequitable fining system with an equitable fining system could mean, for example, that some actors who previously did not have a sense of a shared fate, develop a sense of group identity. This line of work would be consistent with Kramer and Goldman's (1995) calls to investigate the relationship between individuals' social identifications, motivational orientations, and responses to various kinds of structural change.

Researchers could also identify the particular sequence of structural alternatives that are experienced over time and could explore the impact of each sequence on individual and group experiences and outcomes, including processes such as coalition formation. The history of decision making and higher order processes that precede a given decision or inability to make a decision about structural change may also be of particular interest (c.f. Yamagishi's, 1988a, earlier investigation of the feedback loop between instrumental and elementary cooperation).

Another possible application of the proposed approach is to extend the research that has been conducted into preference for an equality rule when using shared resources. (See for example, Allison & Messick, 1990; Rutte, Wilke & Messick, 1987b; and Samuelson & Allison, 1994.) While research by Van Dijk and Wilke (1993) makes a start in this direction, further research is needed. The use of an equality rule by cooperators (who prefer to maximize joint gain) could, for example, depend on the particular structural arrangements that are in place when actors make resource use decisions. The approach taken also offers one way of extending the studies linking research into the solution of social dilemmas with research on decision framing. (See for example, Aquino, Steisel & Kay, 1992; and McCusker & Carnevale, 1995b.)

This chapter thus provides researchers with a framework that can be used to study how structured inequalities affect decision making and opportunities for decision making within social dilemmas. It also lends support to the calls of other researchers (e.g., Aquino, Steisel & Kay, 1992; and Tyler & Degoey, 1995) to forge closer links between research concerned with the solution of social dilemmas and research into topics such as allocation decisions, procedural justice, decision framing, distributive justice, and network analysis. For example, the work of authors such as Cook and Hegtvedt (1983; 1986) on reactions to injustice and the work of Blalock (1991) and Mikula (1980) might be linked more closely with research into the solution of social dilemmas (see the chapter in this book by Messick). The current framework also encourages further exploration of the underlying motivation for the introduction of structural solutions to social dilemmas and the aggregate level consequences of individual level processes.

Perhaps the most important point to be made is that the characterization of what constitutes a structure, and thus a structural alternative, is more complex than has been previously recognized. This takes us to the core of our understanding of the nature of social structure itself, and highlights the need for a conceptual framework that will allow us to assess when, and in what respects, one structural alternative differs from another. The question immediately arises, whether the theoretical distinctions among structures made by social scientists represent meaningful alternatives for the people who will make choices among them.

Part Three

Linking Individual and Group Processes

Chapter 14

Models of Decision Making in Social Dilemmas

David M. Messick

In this chapter, I explore the different models of decision making that are evoked in real world social dilemmas. To begin, let me describe several real world dilemmas that I will use to illustrate the range of situations that are involved.

FIVE REAL CASES

Coke-Pepsi Price War

On June 12, 1997, the *Wall Street Journal* reported that Summerfield K. Johnston and Henry Schimberg, the chief executive and president, respectively, of Coca-Cola Enterprises, had sent a memo to executives on June 5 stating that Coca-Cola, after July 4, would "attempt to increase prices" (Deogun, 1997, p. A3). Heavy price discounting, in competition with Pepsi Cola, their chief rival, had cut deeply into their profit margins and this move was an effort to restore prices to profitable levels.

OECD Ministers Ban Bribery

Several days before the Coke-Pepsi article, on May 27, 1997, the *Wall Street Journal* ran a story on the announcement made in Paris, France that the 29 member states of the Organization for Economic Cooperation and Development (OECD) had agreed to negotiate a binding agreement that would criminalize bribery and outlaw the practice of paying government officials in order to get business contracts (Bray, 1997). This agreement was described as the first step in the creation of a network of laws and regulations that would eliminate bribes and corruption and thereby "level the playing field" for firms from all nations in the international business arena.

Naval Flight Instructor Dumps Jet Fuel

A student, Michael, in one of my business ethics classes, described the following practice. Michael was a naval flight instructor. His job was to train naval pilots to fly jets and to take off and land on aircraft carriers. He wrote an assignment that described the practice of taking his squadron up at the end of each month, with all fuel tanks full, and dumping the squadron's jet fuel into the atmosphere. It was, he claimed, the only responsible thing to do.

Northwestern University Benefits Forms

Last year I called the Northwestern University benefits office to request a form to change the tax being withheld from my paycheck. I got a telephone menu that told me what to push if I wanted forms. After following the instruction, I was told that the forms could be downloaded from the N.U. homepage and was given the internet address to access. It took three tries to get the full address. I attempted to download the forms from the website but failed several times. Finally I walked over to the benefits office, a quarter of a mile from my office, and picked up the forms.

The Plant Manager

A student, Dave, in one of my executive classes, wrote about a problem in the plant that he managed in Greensburg, TN, a fictitious city. His plant was large with the capacity to employ more than 800 employees. The problem was that there were only about 650 employable persons in the area. Once he got more than this number, problems like absenteeism began to skyrocket. So Dave improved efficiencies to make do with 650 employees. The regional economic development council initiated a policy to attract new businesses to the Greensburg area and offered tax breaks to attract new companies. Several moved in. Dave found that these new companies were offering higher wages than his (due to the tax break among other things) and that the newcomers were hiring his employees who were leaving his plant for the new better paying jobs.

WHY SOCIAL DILEMMAS?

Why have I called these situations social dilemmas? Each of these cases is nicely modeled by a social dilemma. The Coke-Pepsi competition is a good illustration of a repeated or iterated two-party prisoner's dilemma (PD) in which the moves are to compete (reduce price) or to cooperate (do not reduce price). In this and many others similar cases, firms compete via price for market share, losing sight of the fact that such competition may not increase profitability (Armstrong & Collopy, 1996). The point may be reached in which both firms realize that they are bleeding money in the competition, but they may see no way to break out of the competitive trap.

Coke (and surely Pepsi too) would prefer to be competing at higher prices where the profit margins are higher. How can an executive get from the low margin competition to the higher level? The Coke strategy can be seen as implementing a version of Axelrod's (1984) tit for tat strategy. As Axelrod has noted, one of the most important features of this successful strategy is that it is "nice," which is to say that the one that implements it will not be the first to defect (drop prices in this case). The Coke memo went on to say that Coke had no motivation to reduce prices "except in response to a competitive initiative." What this says is that Coke will not be the first to drop prices. Yet, the memo also says that Coke will not stand by and allow Pepsi to take market share without a fight. In other words, the Coke memo is using tit for tat—we will not be the first to defect but we will retaliate if the other does—as its strategy for breaking out of the pricing war with Pepsi.

One further important point to note about this case is that the intended audience for the memo is not Coke executives but rather Pepsi's strategists. It would be a violation of antitrust laws for Coke to call Pepsi and suggest that they coordinate prices, but there is nothing against the law in sending a memo to your own people and, perhaps, to the *Wall Street Journal.* This is because the tit for tat strategy is not exploitable if discovered. In other words, it is of no benefit in a game of undefined length, to conceal the fact that you are using a tit for tat strategy. On the contrary, disclosure allows the competitor to coordinate and tacitly cooperate.

The situation with the OECD ministers is a completely different type of social dilemma. In this case there are 29 actors (nations) each of which has an economic advantage if they can get international business through bribery while the others refrain from bribery. However, all parties would prefer to see a world with no bribes than a world of unanimous bribery because the costs of doing business with bribery are greater than of doing business without the practice. Thus this situation is a good illustration of what Messick and Brewer (1983) called a symmetric social trap. All parties are tempted to bribe and when they all do they are all worse off than if they all did not.

Tit for tat is not a feasible strategy in a 29-person game. How can the actors solve this dilemma? When all of the parties are made aware of the dilemma nature of the interdependence, they may realize that the only realistic strategy for managing the dilemma is to make a structural change, in this case to create a superordinate legal authority that will enforce the ban on bribery and oversee the prosecution of parties that violate the ban. According to the article, some nations refused to sign the agreement unless all industrialized nations also signed it. In other words, these nations refused to place themselves in the possible roles of suckers to other nations who could exploit their self-restraint. Contingent agreements ("I will cooperate only if everyone else agrees to cooperate") are useful in these contexts because they create the type of incentives that Van de Kragt, Orbell, and Dawes (1983) refer to as *minimal contributing sets.* Reaching the desired collective outcome, mutual restraint from paying bribes, is achieved only if all parties agree to restrain themselves. The collective agreement, in other words, hangs on *each* party's agreement.

The naval flight instructor is faced with a soul wrenching dilemma in which he must choose between the interests of the pilots he is training and the interests of the organization, the United States Navy, which he and the pilots serve. The heart of this dilemma resides in the fact that the fuel allocation to the squadrons is based, at least in part, on the amount of fuel burned in the previous month. Thus, following a month in which the weather had been poor, making training flights few and brief, relatively little fuel would have been burned. If the following month was blessed with good weather, allowing for extensive training, the rationing of fuel based on the last month's use could lead to fewer training flights than the weather itself would have permitted. Limited training could expose the pilot trainees to unnecessary hazards in the event that hostilities broke out and the pilots were called into a battle situation. Therefore, the moral choice was to dump fuel in order to insure a full allocation for the coming month.

The social dilemma here resides in the fact that the flight instructor knows that all flight instructors do the same thing in order to train their charges responsibly. The collective outcome for the U.S. Navy is that far more fuel is burned (or dumped) than is necessary to exploit all opportunities for training. The allocation system makes fuel dumping the rational, as well as moral, choice for the instructors, but it is not the best outcome for the Navy.

A similar but less dramatic organizational principle is reflected in the case of the benefits forms. The effort to use a technological solution to answer employee requests for forms of various sorts is well intended. If forms can be downloaded, the benefits office can function with a reduced staff, saving money for the university. However, if the new system merely shifts the costs from one part of the organization to another, the benefits office may reduce its costs but those costs will pop up in some other part of the organization. Therefore, the overall efficiency of the organization may not improve, or it may actually diminish. The question is posed in the present illustration of whether the university is better off financially by having a relatively highly paid professor spend an hour to get a form instead of having a relatively low paid employee answer the phone and send forms in the campus mail. If the number of professors who must take time from their research and teaching to get these forms is large, and if value is placed on their time, then the university may not be better off with the new technology than it was when a clerk answered the phone and mailed forms to other employees. In this case costs are not being reduced, they are being redistributed, partly to places where it is difficult to measure them.

In our final illustration, Dave, our plant manager, is faced with the dreary prospect of having to increase his wage scale in order to keep the employees he trained. If he does not increase his salaries, he will have to hire the employees who know the least about holding a job, and his training costs will go up. If he does increase his wages, he may keep the employees he trained, at least for the time being, but he also increases the incentives for the new firms to offer higher wages to attract the best local employees, who currently work for Dave. So Dave may initiate a wage spiral. Whatever the prevailing level of wages may be, there are incentives for all firms to attract the best workers by offering higher wages than competitors. This incentive drives wages up for all employees. How should Dave manage this problem?

I have several reasons for beginning this chapter with these real cases. First, I want to illustrate the variety of manifestations that social dilemmas exhibit in the real world. Second, the cases allow me to outline some of the important dimensions along which social dilemmas vary. Finally, the cases illustrate the fact that solutions to social dilemmas must be highly contextualized. What I mean by this is that the details of the context are exceedingly important. Theoretical ideas about solutions must be tailored to the details of the context. In the following sections I will try to make these points clear.

Temporal Perspective

One important issue on which these five cases differ is the extent to which they are explicitly motivated by future considerations. Repeated games have very different structures and solutions from one-shot games and this dimension is a crucial one. The Coke-Pepsi case is explicitly a temporal problem that has been modeled as an iterated prisoner's dilemma. A price reduction by one player will be met by a price reduction by the other, making such price wars appear as examples of Axelrod's (1984) tit for tat strategy. One of the valuable features of this strategy, a feature that appears to have been employed in the Coke approach to the problem, is that the strategy is publicizable. This is to say that a party that plans to use the tit for tat strategy can publicly proclaim the fact and not suffer. In other words the strategy can not be exploited to the disadvantage of the party using it. To the contrary, announcing the strategy may provide a coordination opportunity allowing the parties to either avoid or to break out of a competitive spiral.

The plant manager's problem is similar but there are more than two parties involved, making tit for tat less applicable. The plant manager understands that there are multiple time periods, so to speak, and that the game is not over with a single move. A crucial consequence, therefore, or the decision to raise wages or not, is the impact that decision will have on the decisions of the other actors sharing the labor pool.

Future considerations enter in a somewhat different pattern in the flight instructor's dilemma. Here the planning is not a strategic plan foreseeing the choices of other strategic players, but rather a plan that uses a time dependent allocation system to achieve the flight instructor's goal of giving his pilots the most and best training possible. The allocation system that uses past fuel consumption as a determinant of future allocations is used more as an impersonal feature of the environment than as a rational, strategic party. In other words, this problem is not well modeled by game theory whereas the first two discussed here can be modeled as repeated games.

Both the OECD decision and the N.U. benefits problems are essentially one-shot situations. In both cases, learning may occur about the consequences of various policies, but the conditional agreements that require unanimity for a collective agreement, in the case of the OECD, and the cost reduction effort of the benefits office, do not have strategic temporal aspects.

Collective Perspective

Some of these problems are explicitly collective while others are essentially individual problems. The OECD case has a solution that can only be defined collectively so solutions to the international bribery problem cannot be found through individual efforts alone. All of the ministers to the conference understand that the solution requires unanimous agreement that no nation will agree to restrain their corporations unless all nations do. Otherwise, a niche would be created for unscrupulous nations to exploit those with scruples.

Likewise, the Coke-Pepsi spiral is a collective problem. Neither side can solve the problem alone, without risking a disastrous business outcome. Both parties understand that the problem is one that grows from the dynamics of their interaction and that profitability can be achieved only through their collective efforts.

Likewise, the plant manager sees that his labor problem is rooted in the dynamics of the local labor market. The choices he has individually, to increase wages or to refrain from so doing, will not solve the problem. If he does not increase wages he will predictably lose valuable employees. If he does, he may retain the employees for a while but other firms will probably increase their wages and he will be back in the same situation, only with increased costs.

The flight instructor and the N.U. benefits office, however, are not dilemmas that have an inherently collective perspective. In both of these cases, the dilemma stems from a badly designed incentive or allocation system, and the decision makers are behaving rationally within the context of the systems. The flight instructor is concerned about the skill level of his pilots and will make decisions to achieve this goal. It turns out that dumping fuel is a way to guarantee an ample fuel supply for the next month so that is what he does. He does not have to think about the actions of any other players in the system. The solution to the problem will come from a change in the allocation system.

Likewise, the head of the benefits office is, presumably, responding to requests to reduce the costs of her operations and is therefore seeking ways to reduce the number of employees working in her department. Replacing them with a phone menu system makes perfectly good sense from her perspective. Her costs are reduced. She can externalize the costs that the new system places on others in the university because they do not show up on her books. If those costs are greater than her savings, however, the university is not better off, although her department is. Moreover, if the time of employees whose activities are not measured or monitored (like professors) is considered, either implicitly or explicitly, to be free, then making these employees use their time to get the forms they need is sensible. They will merely do less of the other things they do which includes teaching, research, and, of course, wasting time. The problem is that it is hard to know which of these activities the time taken to get forms will substitute for. To determine whether the university is better or worse off with the new phone system, someone with a broader view of the university will have to determine whether the costs imposed on others by eliminating the form/clerk(s) is worth the money saved. The head of the benefits office cannot make that determination. She will do her job as best she can and reduce her costs.

MORAL OR LEGAL CONCERNS

These five cases differ to the extent that a model of decision making must include moral concerns, legal concerns, or both. These concerns are important in that when moral issues are involved, decisions may become more rule-based than outcome-based (Messick & Kramer, 1998). The very basis of the decision may be different. Legal issues also add constraints that may exclude certain types of strategies that would otherwise make the resolution of the problem easy. In the Coke-Pepsi case, for instance, antitrust laws prohibit Coke and Pepsi executives from discussing a collaborative pricing strategy. This constraint hinders the use of communication, noted by Messick and Brewer (1983) and Ostrom (1998) as a means for solving social dilemmas, as an efficient tool. If communication is to occur, it must be public communication that can be broadcast to all parties. So the legal context of this problem makes the resolution of the dilemma more difficult.

The OECD case, on the other hand, deals explicitly with a problem, namely bribery, that is both immoral and illegal. The solution to this pervasive problem, is also a legal solution, a contractual agreement and all members of OECD will agree to eschew bribery if all other members agree as well. So this case has both legal and moral features as central elements.

Another of the cases that is inherently about moral issues is the flight instructor case. The overriding consideration in this case is to protect the lives of the pilots being trained by the instructor. This was, in his mind, his absolute moral duty. Dumping fuel was necessary in order for him to be able to prepare his pilots to the best of his ability.

Legal and moral considerations entered in a more complex way for the plant manager. First, Dave felt that it was unfair for authorities to encourage more firms to establish themselves in the Greensburg area without being sure that there was an adequate labor pool. He had entered without incentives and he had worked to train the local people about what it meant to hold a job. Now, it seemed to him, he was going to be punished for having been a moral pioneer. Others were going to exploit the investment he had made and he would be penalized.

Furthermore, the action was being taken by a legal body, the local Economic Development Council. This agency had the authority to offer tax reductions and other economic incentives to firms who established operations in the region. If justice was to be served, and a solution to the dilemma found, it would have to be with the cooperation of this Council.

The case of the benefits office illustrates the fact that real social dilemmas need not involve legal or moral considerations. This case deals simply with cost reduction in an organization and the question of whether the use of telephone technology to provide forms for employees is truly cost reduction or cost reallocation. There seem to be no obvious legal or moral issues associated with this case.

OUTCOMES

The final dimension that I want to highlight with regard to these cases deals with what is at stake. Most psychological research that is conducted in laboratories use money or points that are exchangeable for money as the outcomes for participants choices. The five cases described here indicate that the range of outcome variables is quite wide and is also more complex than imagined in experimental research. While the Coke-Pepsi case is not complex, it does illustrate that there are at least two factors influencing decision making, the desire to increase market share, which leads to price competition; and profitability which often suffers as a result of price competition.

Money, of course, is also crucial in the N.U. benefits case, but here the issue is cost reduction. The question is raised whether a focus on cost frames decisions differently from a focus on profits. Questions of outcome framing have been popular research questions recently, and these real examples demonstrate the importance of the issue.

Yet a different type of cost emerges in the OECD case. Here the issue is the fear of losing business to firms willing to pay bribes if your firm refuses to do so. Thus the question of opportunity costs is raised and with it, questions about whether opportunity costs are psychologically different from out of pocket costs.

For the plant manager, the crucial issue is the maintenance of an adequate supply of labor. Cost is an issue but the plant cannot function without employees who are trained and reliable. Moreover, Dave has the perception that the employees he now has are, in some sense, his, and that the threat is that they will be lured away to another employer. So while the labor supply is a type of shared, common resource, Dave was the first plant in the region, and he feels that this entitles his employees to protection from the newcomers.

Perhaps the most dramatic outcome of these five cases is that concerning the flight instructor. He is concerned with protecting the lives of his pilots. Money is not an issue. Saving lives is the issue. It is not accidental that this is also the case that is most involved with moral issues.

From a theoretical perspective, the question that is posed by these five cases is "what type of psychological theory can be used to clarify these cases?" There is not space here to develop a complete answer to this question, but I will sketch one possible answer to this question.

I have argued elsewhere (Messick, in press) that social psychology needs a new way to think about decision making in social contexts like social dilemmas. The approach I have advocated is grounded on the theoretical ideas developed by March (1995). March's approach involves three broad categories of concepts. The first is the perception of appropriateness. The second involves issues of personal (or organizational) identity. Finally, he argues for the importance of rule-based decision processes, in addition to (not *instead of*) consequence-based processes. Rules, he argues, are often more important than outcomes. A convenient way to summarize March's theory, is to propose that decisions are made by answering the question, "in a situation like this (Appropriateness), what does a person like me (Identity), do (Rule)?" The acronym I have used to refer to this theory is the AIR approach.

The heart of the AIR approach to decision making resides in the perception of the situation, in the way in which a person answers the question, "what kind of situation is this?" Little has been written or studied about this process within social psychology. One thoughtful, conceptual article was published by Forgas (1982) but little empirical or theoretical research has followed from this insightful paper. In the study of social dilemmas, the question of "what kind of situation is this?" may be the central conceptual question that theorists tackle. For instance, is a social dilemma an individual decision making task, or is it a group problem solving task? The way in which we answer this question will have a huge impact on the type of theory we create to model decision processes. For instance, if we conceive of social dilemmas as individual decision tasks, it becomes natural to employ models that summarize choices as a function of payoffs, like expected utility models, or in terms of individual choice heuristics, like *tit for tat*, *win-stay*, or *lose-change*. Seeing the dilemma as a group task, on the other hand, may entail answering the question, "what is my role in the group?" or "what is my duty?" The initial perception or decision about the nature of the task will have a large impact on permissible or desirable behavioral alternatives.

Part of the decision about appropriateness deals with the perception of the temporal structure of the situation. Is this a task that is extended in time or a task that has a past and a future? If the task has a future the decision must deal with forecasts. We remind ourselves not to eat our seed corn, and to temper today's consumption with concern for tomorrow's harvest. Sometimes we do this well and sometimes poorly. We will surely do it poorly if we ignore tomorrow. Sustainability is important when we are dealing with a temporal process in which tomorrow's resources and options depend on today's actions. When the future casts a shadow on the decision of the present, the perception of appropriateness is altered.

The perception that the problem is inherently a collective problem is also crucial. The OECD case, for instance, is clearly a case that can only be solved with the unanimous agreement of all the parties. One is forced to view the problem from a collective perspective and to deal with the issue of encouraging cooperation and compliance from the other parties. While each party has a national perspective, each also must see the collective structure as well. Likewise, in the Coke-Pepsi spiral, each participant must realize that the only solution to the price war is a collective restraint on the part of both parties. The means of ensuring compliance are very different from the OECD case, but there must be recognition of the collective nature of the situation.

In contrast to these two cases, there is no reason to think that the manager of the N.U. benefits office sees any hint of interdependence with other components of the university. To her, this is purely an individual policy to reduce costs. There is no collective dimension and the problem becomes simplified in the manager's mind as a result. Because the manager does not perceive a collective dimension does not, of course, mean that there is not one. Only that it does not influence her decision making.

When moral or legal concerns are perceived, the decision context is radically changed. The major change is that moral or legal rules are imposed that must be obeyed. The presence of moral or legal considerations not only evokes thoughts about possible future outcomes (what will happen if others find out?) but also thoughts about the adherence to appropriate rules of behavior. Much of legal and moral thought is deontological in nature, which is to say it is concerned with rules rather than the outcomes of action. Bribery, for instance, is illegal nearly everywhere and even if paying bribes facilitates business, it should be avoided, if possible, because it is wrong. The legal prohibition against price fixing prevents the executives of Coke and Pepsi from calling each other on the phone to discuss pricing. Communication must be disguised and price coordination must be implicit rather than explicit to meet the requirements of the law. The flight instructor decided that saving lives was more important than any other consideration in his decision so he dumped fuel monthly. The plant manager, Dave, thought that his labor problem involved an issue of fairness that motivated him to seek a solution to the employee dilemma that would be beneficial to all involved.

Finally, what is appropriate may depend on whether we are dealing with profits, costs, jobs, or lives. The nature of the outcomes that are involved in the decision may influence how we interpret the situation. We may be comfortable making tradeoffs between profit and cost, for instance, but we may not consider it right to make tradeoffs between lives and costs. Michael did not think that it was proper to think about the tradeoff between environmental harm and the mortal risks to his students when deciding how to manage his fuel allocations. Risk of life dominated his deliberations. And Dave thought about jobs, with their implications for the welfare of the citizens of Greenburg, differently from the way he might have thought about other types of costs, like transportation or power that had fewer human connotations. The point is that different types of outcomes evoke different ways of thinking about solutions to social dilemmas.

I have mentioned four classes of features that can influence the perception of appropriateness in social dilemmas but I do not mean to suggest that these are the only features that are important. Personal aspects of the decision maker will influence the perception of appropriateness. Social orientation provides a good illustration. The difference between cooperators and competitors is not only in the choices they make, but also in the way they perceive the social world. Cooperators see the cooperation/competition distinction as a moral dimension, whereas competitors see it as morally neutral (Liebrand, Jansen, Rijken & Suhre, 1986). Cooperators think that smart people in social dilemmas will cooperate, whereas competitors think that smart people will compete (Van Lange, 1992). Who we are influences how we see the situation and the question of the social identity of the decision maker must also be addressed.

The concluding point that I want to make is that only a theory with the richness and flexibility of the AIR conceptualization can help us understand and explain decisions in social dilemmas that are as diverse and varied as those with which I began this chapter. I claim that we need a model of decision making that has the flexibility to allow us to understand decision behavior in a wide variety of situations, but that still has the descriptive parsimony that allows the theory to be tested. The five examples with which I began this chapter must be seen as special cases of a more general theory that captures underlying commonality of social dilemmas as well as their unique and individuating qualities.

Chapter 15

Managing Uncertain Common Resources

Tommy Gärling
Mathias Gustafsson
Anders Biel

INTRODUCTION

A major difficulty faced by society in managing common resource pools is that the size or quality of the pool is seldom known with certainty. This problem besets both resources contributed by people such as retirement funds and resources consumed such as oil.

In social dilemma experimental research (Dawes, 1980; Komorita & Parks, 1995) there are two aspects of uncertainty: uncertainty about what others will do, or social uncertainty; and lack of knowledge of features of the resource such as its size, or resource uncertainty (Biel & Gärling, 1995; Liebrand, Messick, & Wilke, 1992). In most of this research the size of the resource has been known by participants, whereas they have had no knowledge of what others will do. However, as noted, lack of knowledge about the size of the resource pool may be the more salient feature of societal resource management problems. In this chapter, we selectively review social dilemma research showing overharvesting effects due to resource uncertainty and propose some possible explanations of these effects. We conclude with implications for real life resource management problems.

The authors' research reported in this chapter was financially supported by grant #94-0012:01 from the Bank of Sweden Tercentenary Foundation. We are grateful to a reviewer for valuable suggestions.

OVERHARVESTING DUE TO RESOURCE UNCERTAINTY

Messick, Allison, and Samuelsson (1988) introduced the concept of resource uncertainty in studies of behavior in resource dilemmas. In subsequent research, Budescu, Rapoport, and Suleiman have been particularly instrumental in increasing our knowledge of the effects of resource uncertainty. Suleiman and Rapoport (1988) offered testable hypotheses about the effects of resource uncertainty. Budescu, Rapoport, and Suleiman (1990) introduced an experimental paradigm in which the task of managing replenishable but nonexcludable resources is reduced to its essential characteristics.

Participants in a one-shot resource dilemma are told that they are members of a group in which each is free to request what they want from a common resource pool. They are informed that the initial size of the resource is a uniformly distributed random variable. On each trial information about resource size is then conveyed by defining a lower and upper bound of the distribution (e.g., from 250 to 750 money units). Resource uncertainty is manipulated by varying the width of the interval (e.g., 250–750 vs. 0–1000). If the total amount requested by participants does not exceed the resource size each will receive what they request, otherwise none will receive anything.

Budescu et al. (1990) investigated both the effects of resource uncertainty and asymmetric payoffs. The main result was that as resource uncertainty increased so did the size of the requests, resulting in overharvesting (i.e., total requests exceeding the mean of the distribution). Their findings have been replicated several times. For instance, Rapoport, Budescu, Suleiman, and Weg (1992) found an overharvesting effect, and observed that it was augmented by individual differences in risk taking tendencies. Since the payoffs were symmetric, the effects of social uncertainty appeared to be eliminated by adhering to an equal share norm (e.g., Allison & Messick, 1990; Messick & Schell, 1992).

Likewise, Gustafsson, Biel, and Gärling (1997a, Experiment 1) replicated the overharvesting effect. However, Gustafsson, Biel, and Gärling (1997b) noted a problem with defining resource uncertainty as an interval width since it directs participants' attention to the lower and upper bounds. Instead, they presented numbers representing resource size in a random sequence. Uncertainty was defined as the variance of the sequence. Under these conditions, overharvesting also increased with resource uncertainty.

A different line of research (Allison, McQeeen, & Shaerfl, 1992; Herlocker, Allison, Foubert, & Beggan, 1997) has investigated participants' performance when asked to share resources which are either easy to divide (e.g., square blocks) or difficult to divide (e.g., sand). In the former case it is simple to apply a norm such as equal share, whereas in the latter case it is difficult due to uncertainty about how much an equal share is. Overharvesting increased when the resource was difficult to divide. A moderating factor was group size since overharvesting was confined to large groups.

In addition to uncertainty about the size of a resource, Hine and Gifford (1996) investigated the impact of uncertainty about the replenishment rate of the resource in an iterated resource dilemma. They found that unless information about replenishment rate was consistently provided, overharvesting was observed. However, in disagreement with Rapoport et al. (1992), Hine and Gifford found no correlation between risk seeking and overharvesting under conditions of high resource uncertainty.

Several other factors have been investigated in conjunction with resource uncertainty. Budescu, Rapoport, and Suleiman (1992) compared simultaneous and sequential requests. The simultaneous protocol is identical to that employed in experiments already described, whereas in the sequential protocol participants make requests in a prespecified order (see the chapter in this book by Au and Budescu), and are informed about their position in the sequence as well as about total prior requests. Although both uncertainty and position effects on overharvesting were found, they operated independently. The independence of the overharvesting effect due to resource uncertainty and the position effect has later been replicated (Budescu, Suleiman, & Rapoport, 1995; Suleiman, Budescu, & Rapoport 1994; Suleiman, Rapoport, & Budescu, 1996).

Wit and Wilke (1998) conducted a study of a step level public good dilemma in which both social and resource uncertainty were varied in comparable ways. On the basis of social comparison theory (Festinger, 1954), Wit and Wilke hypothesized that when people are uncertain about the resource size they may become more sensitive to what others will do. The results showed that when resource uncertainty was high, participants underestimated the provision threshold. That is, an error was observed in the *opposite* direction from those observed in resource dilemmas. In addition, in line with their social comparison hypothesis, Wit and Wilke found an interaction showing that the effect of high resource uncertainty was reduced by reduction of social uncertainty. However, Gustafsson et al. (1997a, Experiment 2) failed to find such an interaction effect in a step level resource dilemma. A possible reason is that social uncertainty is not as salient in a resource dilemma as it is in a public good dilemma.

In summary, it appears that social uncertainty does not result in less cooperation because it is reduced by fairness norms such as, for example, the equal share principle (De Vries & Wilke, 1992; Rutte, Wilke, & Messick, 1987b). However, resource uncertainty has invariably been found to reduce cooperation. This holds across different definitions of resource uncertainty (interval, variance, replenishment rate, and dividable), single stage and multistage resource dilemmas, public good and resource dilemmas, and step level and continuous resource dilemmas. Furthermore, the effect seems to be largely independent of other factors such as whether the dilemma is symmetric or asymmetric, the type of protocol, and, possibly, the degree of social uncertainty. Why does resource uncertainty so consistently result in overharvesting? Some explanations of the phenomenon which have been offered will be reviewed in the next section.

EXPLANATIONS

Two possible explanations of the overharvesting effect due to resource uncertainty were offered by Rapoport et al. (1992). First, overharvesting may occur because participants perceive a positive relationship between measures of central tendency (e.g., the mean) and variability. Under increasing resource uncertainty, this would thus lead participants to overestimate the size of the resource and therefore to request too much. Such a *perceptual* explanation is in line with the so called big pool illusion (Messick & McClelland, 1983) that a resource of uncertain size is perceived as larger than a resource of known size.

The second explanation starts with the assumption that participants weight the upper and lower bounds of the interval when estimating the resource size. It is further assumed that they overweight the upper bound resulting in an upward shift of their estimates and requesting too much. In contrast to the first explanation, motivational reasons are highlighted such as optimism or risk taking. The explanation is therefore consistent with research demonstrating a tendency to judge desirable outcomes as more likely (Buckley & Sniezek, 1992; Budescu & Bruderman, 1995; Fischer & Budescu, 1995; Olsen, 1997; Weinstein, 1980; Zakay, 1983). Terms for this effect include optimism bias, outcome desirability bias or wishful thinking.

Neither explanation takes into account the fact that in a resource or public good dilemma the individual outcomes depend on others' decisions. Wilke (1991) proposed the so called constrained egoism hypothesis stating that although individuals try to maximize their own outcomes, their greed is constrained by the motives to maintain the resource efficiently and to achieve fairness among the group members.

In line with this hypothesis, an equal share fairness norm may feel less compelling when the size of the resource is uncertain. Participants may therefore want to request more than an equal share of the resource. At the same time they may not believe that a sufficient number of others will request less than the equal share. Thus, the goal of efficient resource use is in conflict with egoism. Nevertheless, an egoism bias may also result in *misperceptions* of the resource size when the outcomes depend on others' decisions that lead to unintentional overharvesting. This supposition is not unreasonable if previous research, demonstrating egoism biases in how payoffs are perceived (e.g., Kelley & Thibaut, 1978), generalizes to an uncertain resource size. Evidence for this claim was provided by De Vries and Wilke (1992). Under conditions of resource uncertainty, overharvesting was observed in a resource dilemma but not in a coordination game where overharvesting resulted in lower payoffs to participants.

Is there a way of disentangling the three explanations proposed thus far? If a perceptual bias is the explanation of overharvesting under resource uncertainty, the effect should emerge irrespective of whether the outcomes are desirable or not. If the overharvesting effect is found only under conditions where the resource represents value to participants, then an explanation in terms of egoism or optimism seems more reasonable. Support for an egoism explanation would be obtained if interdependence were a necessary condition for the overharvesting effect. On the other hand, if the effect emerges under conditions where no interdependence is present, an explanation in terms of optimism bias seems more reasonable.

In a program of research (Biel & Gärling, 1995; Gustafsson et al., 1997a, 1997b, 1998) our objective has been to establish which factors underlie overharvesting of resources of uncertain size. A series of experiments was conducted with between-participants conditions in which different groups of undergraduate students either made perceptual estimates of resource size when it was uncertain, requested from an uncertain resource when the outcome depended only on the resource size, or requested from an uncertain resource when the outcome depended both on the resource size and the requests by others.

Estimates were generally accurate, thereby falsifying the perceptual bias explanation. Yet, the usual overharvesting effect was found when the outcome depended only on resource size. In support of an outcome desirability bias, the overharvesting effect did not increase when the outcome also depended on others' requests. Consistent with the results of Rapoport et al. (1992), under high resource uncertainty, participants requested more than an equal share when they were free to request any amount from the resource (a sum of money).

In contrast to our results, Rapoport et al. (1992) found that participants overestimated the resource. However, in their experiments, the same participants who requested from the resource also estimated its size. Therefore, the possibility that they tailored their estimates to fit their requests cannot be ruled out. We found that the degree of bias in the estimates decreased if the resource did not represent value to the participants. In another experiment we replicated the overharvesting effect in a step level resource dilemma, despite the fact that participants did not overestimate the uncertain provision threshold.

Since the results of De Vries and Wilke (1992) appeared to support an egoism bias explanation of overharvesting due to resource uncertainty, we conducted further investigations into this possible explanation. In one experiment (Gustafsson et al., 1998; Experiment 1) participants were informed about the other group members' estimates of the resource. When these estimates were lower than participants' estimates, an egoism bias would lead them to exploit the other group members by requesting more than an equal share. However, an average estimate by the other group members below the expected resource size made participants *reduce*, rather than increase, their requests in a resource dilemma. In a public good dilemma they increased their contributions. The same results were also obtained when participants knew that the estimates of the resource size by some other group members (although not the average) were larger than the expected size.

Since these results clearly indicated an important role for an *individual* outcome desirability bias, we sought further evidence of its nature. In addition to the earlier outcome desirability bias demonstration (Zakay, 1983), Buckley and Sniezek (1992) found that optimism in individual predictions of desirable outcomes increased with the uncertainty of the outcomes. However, in a series of recent experiments, Bar-Hillel and Budescu (1995) examined participants' probability estimates in several different experimental tasks without being able to demonstrate an outcome desirability bias. Bar-Hillel and Budescu therefore suggested that the bias may come into play at a prior stage when relevant information is recalled. Thus, the bias in evaluation may be due to biased recall.

In real life resource dilemmas such as the energy crisis, information about the size of a resource is usually made available over time. An outcome desirability bias may in such situations primarily reflect selective remembering. In Gustafsson et al. (1997b, Experiment 1) participants were presented with sequences of numbers representing the size of a resource (a sum of money). This information was either presented sequentially, so that participants would have to remember the information, or simultaneously so that there was no demand on memory. Uncertainty of resource size (variance) was either low or high. On the basis of Bar-Hillel and Budescu's (1995) findings we reasoned that if an outcome desirability bias accounts for the overharvesting effect, a stronger effect would be observed when information about resource size was presented sequentially than when it was presented simultaneously.

In a between-participants (individual request) condition participants could request an amount from the resource which represented a sum of money. They would receive a bonus proportional to their request if it did not exceed the resource. By comparison with another (individual guess) condition, in which participants predicted the size of the resource from the time series without knowing what the numbers represented, it was determined that a necessary condition for the recall bias to occur was that the outcomes were perceived as desirable. An additional attempt at refuting the egoism bias (De Vries & Wilke, 1992) entailed a third between-participants request condition in which participants' outcomes also depended on the requests by four others.

Table 15.1 displays participants' mean requests and guesses. As expected, participants requested more in the individual and group request conditions when the resource was presented sequentially and resource uncertainty was high. Only for sequential presentation and high resource uncertainty, did the mean requests exceed the available resource. When participants guessed the amount of the resource, type of presentation and resource uncertainty had no apparent effect. Thus, the results confirmed the prediction that when participants recalled information about resource size from memory, they requested more from the resource than if the same information was available to inspect. Again, no differences in request sizes were found when the outcome depended only on resource size and

Table 15.1   Mean requests and guesses in different conditions related to type of presentation and resource uncertainty (after Gustafsson et al., 1997a).

| | Type of presentation and resource uncertainty | | | |
| | Simultaneous | | Sequential | |
Group (n's = 16)	Low	High	Low	High
Individual-guess[a]	979.1	982.0	968.8	989.9
Individual-request[a]	891.2	918.2	928.0	1017.7
Group-request	852.0	922.9	909.0	1071.5

Note: [a]The means are in these conditions divided by 5

when it depended on both resource sizes and how much others requested. These findings lend further support to the claim that the overharvesting effect in resource dilemmas with unknown sizes is an individual outcome desirability bias.

Figure 15.1 summarizes the main features of our results. When resource size is known with certainty, there is no bias in estimates of its size. Overharvesting may then depend on social uncertainty (e.g., not conforming to an equal share norm). On the other hand, when the individual outcome is positive, the size of an uncertain resource is overestimated (or underestimated in public good dilemmas).

CONCLUSIONS

Social uncertainty in resource dilemmas may not result in less cooperation because it is reduced by fairness norms (De Vries & Wilke, 1992; Rutte et al.,1987b). In contrast, resource uncertainty appears to invariably reduce cooperation. We believe that our program of research has clarified why this occurs. An outcome desirability bias (Zakay, 1983) is a key factor: If people do not know the size of a resource with certainty and hence have to estimate it, they will be too optimistic when the resource is valuable to them. As a result, they will overuse the resource. Our experiments rule out alternative explanations such as a perceptual bias (Rapoport et al., 1992) or an egoism bias (Wilke, 1991; De Vries & Wilke, 1992).

It is not possible from our experiments to infer that the outcome desirability bias is intentional. Likewise, it is unclear whether it arises from motives such as greed or fear.

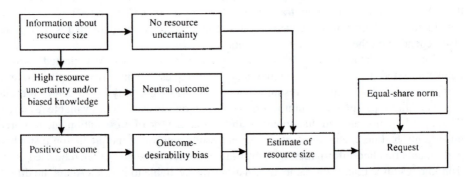

Figure 15.1   Factors affecting requests in a resource dilemma with unknown resource size

However, the issue of the motivational structure underlying the bias is certainly an important one deserving further attention. Budescu et al. (1990) showed that participants also expected others to request more when resource size was uncertain. Since everyone should realize that no one obtains his or her share if they request too much, this finding suggests that the outcome desirability bias may be unintentional, perhaps similar to a perceptual bias. At the same time it seems difficult to avoid the conclusion that such a perceptual bias is not influenced by motives.

An important question to address for societal resource management is what can be done to curb or possibly eliminate the overharvesting effect due to resource uncertainty. One possibility was demonstrated in one of our experiments (Gustafsson et al., 1997b, Experiment 1). When participants had access to all information simultaneously, this considerably reduced the overharvesting effect. However, this condition is unlikely to occur in real life resource dilemmas.

Another promising finding is reported in Gustafsson et al. (1998, Experiment 1) where participants were informed about others' estimates. As already noted, when these estimates were below the expected resource size, participants did not overharvest. However, the effect of resource uncertainty was not completely eliminated. The most likely reason was that participants anchored their requests to their biased estimates of the uncertain information about the resource.

In another experiment (Gustafsson et al., 1998, Experiment 3), the overharvesting effect of uncertainty was eliminated when the information about the others' estimates preceded the uncertain information about the resource. In line with recent research on the anchoring and adjustment heuristic (Chapman & Johnson, 1994), the information on which people anchor may crucially determine how they judge uncertain resources. Shared information, however fallible and whether from experts or fellow resource consumers, may alleviate the sense of uncertainty that engenders overly optimistic estimates of the size of the resource pool.

Chapter 16

Mood Effects in Social Dilemmas: What We Know So Far

Guido Hertel

AN OVERVIEW

About 20 years ago, Dawes, McTavish, and Shaklee (1977) observed in their social di-lemma studies that participants not only adapted cooperative decisions according to their assumptions about other people's behavior, but also reacted very emotionally to others' choices. This was especially true when the other people were acting uncooperatively. The authors took this as evidence that participants were very involved in the games, despite the fact that monetary incentives were rather small. However, a more thorough analysis of such affective reactions and their possible influences on cooperative decisions was post-poned for several years.

When investigating decision processes in social dilemmas and related exchange con-flicts, scholars traditionally focused on cold cognitive factors in accordance with the game theoretical background of this research field. Whereas cognitive cost-benefit analyses are of course crucial factors in understanding individuals' behaviors in social dilemmas, affec-tive influences might be important as well. People deciding between cooperation and de-

The preparation of this chapter was supported by a postdoctoral grant (He 2745/1-1) funded by the Deutsche Forschungsgemeinschaft. Christy Brandt and Norbert Kerr are thanked for their helpful suggestions on earlier versions of this paper. Address correspondence to Dr. Guido Hertel, Department of Psychology, University of Kiel, Olshausenstrasse 62, Kiel, Germany, 24098.

fection are not in an emotional vacuum, but constantly experience certain feeling states. For example, people can feel angry about the behavior of others, guilty about their own exploitive choices, elated because they managed to obtain high profits, or even thankful for others' cooperation. These feeling states might strongly affect cooperative behavior, whether they are caused by events within or outside the exchange conflict situation.

Indeed, happiness is often described as emotion of cooperation, whereas negative feeling states are associated more with noncooperation (Deutsch, 1973; Oatley & Jenkins, 1996). However, beyond this rather general assumption, there exists very little direct research concerning affective influences on cooperation in general, and on affective effects in social dilemmas in particular. Moreover, as will be shown here, the theoretical implications as well as current empirical evidence are far from clear.

In this chapter I will review what we already know about affective influences in social dilemmas. I will restrict the focus to effects of mood differences, because only these have been investigated in controlled experimental studies. In addition, it is reasonable to start with more basic affective influences (positive vs. negative feelings) before one tries to understand effects of more complex emotions like guilt, anger, or thankfulness (see Clore, Schwarz, & Conway, 1994, for a review on social aspects of complex emotions). Although I will restrict the focus on mood effects, I will broaden the scope and include not only studies of social dilemmas in the classical meaning (Dawes, 1980)—but with a somewhat looser definition—but also social exchange situations that are only broadly related to social dilemmas (i.e., negotiation tasks) when no social dilemma studies are available to address the question at hand. Although this might appear somewhat unorthodox, it will help to achieve a more general impression of mood influences in interdependent social situations.

In accordance with recent definitions (Clore et al., 1994; Frijda, 1993; Schwarz & Clore, 1996), mood is considered to be an affective state that is rather enduring, lacks a clear referent or target, and has a rather low intensity compared to concrete emotions. In contrast, emotions are shorter in duration, have a clear referent or target, and are usually high in intensity. However, mood states have been shown to influence a variety of cognitions and social behaviors that are relevant to social dilemmas, such as helping behavior (Bierhoff, 1988; Schaller & Cialdini, 1990), person perception (Forgas & Bower, 1987), problem solving (Isen, Daubman, & Nowicki, 1987), or mode of information processing (Bless, Clore, et al., 1996; Schwarz & Clore, 1996). Moreover, they often affect the evaluation of situations with respect to their goodness or badness (Fiedler, 1988; Schwarz, 1990; Schwarz & Clore, 1996). Accordingly, we can assume that different mood states are an important determinant of people's behaviors in social dilemma conflicts.

As already mentioned, there exist popular assumptions about a simple relationship between mood and cooperation, suggesting that investigating mood effects on cooperative behavior is rather trivial. According to this "common knowledge," as well as some recent reviews in social or applied psychology, positive mood simply leads to more cooperative behavior than negative mood (e.g., Baron, 1993; Isen & Baron, 1991; Oatley & Jenkins, 1996). However, although some studies of social dilemmas and related conflicts found that negative mood decreased cooperative behavior (Carnevale & Isen, 1986; Forgas, 1998; Knapp & Clark, 1991), others did not (Hertel & Fiedler, 1994; Hertel, Neuhof, Theuer, & Kerr, in press; Vollmeyer, 1994). At least for experimental social dilemmas, the relationship between affect and cooperation seems to be more complex and less conclusive than often assumed.

Consulting general theories of mood and social behavior, one can think of (at least) three different principles of mood effects on cooperative behavior that are relevant for social dilemmas. I will briefly outline these three principles and discuss the available empirical evidence.

Associative Approach

Based on spreading activation models of human memory (Bower, 1991; Collins & Loftus, 1975), this approach asserts that different mood states activate associated cognitive concepts (schemas, scripts) that have been learned in the past. Assuming that positive mood is more likely associated with concepts such as trust, friendship, or helpfulness and negative mood is more strongly connected with concepts such as hostility, conflict, or competition, it is expected that positive mood activates cooperation related concepts more likely than negative mood. In accordance with research demonstrating that decisions in social exchange conflicts are influenced by cognitive concepts that are available at the time of the decision (Hertel, 1995; Hertel & Fiedler, 1994, 1998), such *affective priming* might indeed lead to different amounts of cooperation in social dilemmas.

Alternatively, or in addition to the outlined reasoning that mood might affect the availability of different behavior concepts (cooperating or competing) or situational schemas (team or competition), affective priming might also alter the perceptions of interaction partners (Forgas & Bower, 1987; Sinclair & Mark, 1992) in a social dilemma, and in turn affect cooperative decisions based on these perceptions. Since trust is a major influence in most social dilemma conflicts (Pruitt & Kimmel, 1977; Yamagishi, 1986b), a more positive perception of interaction partners might increase the probability of cooperative behavior. Although there is yet no direct evidence available that mood congruency processes affect the assessment of other persons in social dilemma experiments, research has shown that other variations in partner perception in a prisoner's dilemma game indeed moderated the amount of cooperation that participants showed in the game (Herr, 1986; Neuberg, 1988).

Moreover, recent experiments by Forgas (1998) provided evidence for mood congruency processes in negotiation tasks. Participants in positive and negative moods took the role of students or university faculty members who debated the psychology curriculum. The results revealed that participants in a positive mood planned and later reported to have applied more cooperative negotiation strategies than participants in a negative mood. The author interpreted this as evidence for mood congruency processes on participants' expectations and judgments, in that good mood led persons to form more favorable expectations about the ease of the negotiation task as well as the cooperativeness and reliability of the other participants.

Although very similar processes are conceivable in social dilemmas, in which people also form expectations about the task and the cooperativeness and reliability of their interaction partners, a generalization of the results of Forgas (1998) should be made carefully since the author only analyzed self-report data that might have been biased by participants' mood states. Moreover, the induction of mood was somewhat confounded with a manipulation of self-efficacy that might explain the differences in self-reported (and more risky) cooperative bargaining strategies just as well as mood differences. In order to generalize the reported mood congruency effects to social dilemmas these studies should be replicated, manipulating mood more unambiguously and measuring cooperative behavior more directly.

Besides the lack of clear empirical evidence, another problem of an associative approach to explain mood effects on cooperation is that the assumed memory link between positive mood and cooperation is questionable. Especially in social dilemma conflicts, one can easily find examples in which cooperation is more strongly associated with negative affect, depending on the idiosyncratic experiences of the individual. For example, cooperation can be connected with feelings of disappointment or annoyance about being exploited by others, or with regret about lost opportunity costs. Competition, on the other hand, can be associated with elated feelings, such as in the context of sports when someone enjoys his or her success in a tournament.

The association between valence of mood and cooperation or defection seems to be ambiguous and more or less dependent on the learning history of each individual, so that clear predictions are rather difficult. Adding further evidence to this notion, a trait oriented perspective did not provide confirming data for a simple correlation between positive affect and cooperative attitudes. As part of a larger screening questionnaire given to undergraduate students at Michigan State University (Hertel & Kerr, 1997), positive and negative affectivity (Watson, Clark, & Tellegen, 1988) as crystallized mood differences were correlated with social orientations as predictors of behavior in social dilemmas (Kuhlman & Marshello, 1975; Van Lange & Kuhlman, 1994). The results revealed no significant relationship between positive affectivity and social orientations and only a very low negative correlation between negative affectivity and social orientations, $r(829) = -.08, p < .05$. Cooperative participants had rather low scores in negative affectivity. However, this correlation explained less than 1% of the variance.

Another ambiguity that is unique to social dilemmas is the unclear implication of mood congruency effects on person perception for behavioral decisions in mixed motive conflicts. In most social dilemma structures the defecting choice is especially tempting when other participants are expected to cooperate because the outcome for oneself in such a situation is a maximum. For example, in the classic prisoner's dilemma game (Luce & Raiffa, 1957; see also Smithson's chapter in this volume) the highest outcome can be achieved when the other person cooperates and oneself defects. Thus, perceiving other persons in a social dilemma as friendly and trustworthy does not automatically imply personal cooperation, and could lead to defection as well. This ambiguity may even increase in some related games such as the chicken dilemma (see below) or the volunteer's dilemma (Diekman, 1985), where it is often rational to choose the cooperative option when everybody else is expected to defect in order to prevent bigger losses for one's self. In general, the consequences of mood congruency effects on person perception can be very complex, so that predictions of related cooperative behavior become complicated and depend strongly on prior experiences, as well as on the structure of the given exchange conflict (see also Hertel, 1995).

Motivational Approach

A second principle for explaining how mood might affect cooperative behavior in social dilemmas is based on motivational models of mood management (Knapp & Clark, 1991; Vollmeyer, 1994). This approach states that people are hedonistic in nature and generally strive to stay in a positive emotional state. As a consequence, people in positive moods try to maintain their emotional state by avoiding unpleasant thoughts or behaviors, whereas people in negative moods try to improve or repair their moods by engaging in behaviors that lead to positive outcomes (Isen, 1987; Wegener, Petty, & Smith, 1995; but see also Parrott, 1993). Based on the idea that cooperation in social dilemmas often implies sacrificing gains (at least in the short run) and that negative mood often causes a shorter delay of gratification (Mischel, Ebbesen, & Zeiss, 1972; Schwarz & Pollack, 1977), it is deduced that negative mood should lead to lower cooperation than positive or neutral mood states (Knapp & Clark, 1991).

Indeed, a study by Knapp and Clark (1991) provides some evidence for this line of reasoning. In this study, participants read a happy, neutral, sad, or annoying story about a fictitious person to induce different mood states. In an alleged second experiment, they then played a multitrial resource dilemma game. Congruent with the outlined motivational assumption, participants in negative mood states (angry, sad) exploited a common resource more, especially in the first trials. In a second experiment, Knapp and Clark only contrasted neutral and sad mood states and found again that sad participants exploited a common resource more than participants in a neutral mood condition.

Although these results are consistent with an explanation that mood affects the level of cooperation directly, the studies contain some problems that restrict a clear interpretation and generalization. First, the manipulation of mood using stories with different contents somewhat confounded the induction of mood states with the activation of cooperation related cognitive concepts. For example, the anger inducing story ended with an unjust treatment of the protagonist, which might have strongly activated *retaliation* concepts in this condition. Later experiments using a very similar dilemma paradigm but different mood manipulations could not replicate the reported main effects of mood on the level of cooperation (Vollmeyer, 1994).

Second, the authors only *assumed* that the differences in cooperation scores were based on motivational differences. Additional process data that supported this assumption more thoroughly were not reported. As a consequence, alternative explanations are possible. For example, since the replenishing rate of the resource pool was not explicitly explained in the beginning of the game, and since cooperation was concluded from participants' success in maintaining the common resource, the result pattern can also be interpreted as demonstrating mood effects on problem solving and creativity (cf. Isen, 1987; Isen et al., 1987) rather than on individual cooperation.

Third and more generally, it can be questioned from a theoretical perspective whether sad people really perceive higher exploitation of a common resource as a way to improve their emotional state. Exploiting a resource pool and causing a crisis of the common team project can just as well evoke negative feelings of guilt, shame, or hopelessness that depress current mood states rather than elevate them. Moreover, recent research has shown explicitly that cooperation is often perceived as socially more positive and desirable than competition (Hertel & Fiedler, 1998). On the other hand, being cooperative in a social dilemma implies the risk of being exploited. Given that people in positive mood are concerned with maintaining their pleasant mood state, these persons should have a sound motive for choosing defection rather than cooperation.

A simple way to test whether exploitation or, more generally, egoistic choices in social dilemmas actually lead to elevated mood states would be to ask people in a dilemma situation directly about the affective consequences of different behavior options. Unfortunately, there are no such data available at the moment. Moreover, rather than assuming universal emotional implications of cooperation and defection, it seems more plausible that emotional consequences of behavior in a social dilemma situation are a function of whether individuals' goals are maintained or not (cf. Clore et al., 1994). Since people's goals in social dilemmas are determined by complex influences such as social value orientations, situational demands, or salient social norms, motivational analyses of mood management processes have to be qualified by these different influences.

Processing Approach

Alternatively to the outlined *associative* and *motivational* principles stating rather direct effects of mood on the level of cooperation, different feeling states might also have indirect influences on decisions in a social dilemma. According to recent models in social psychology, mood states especially affect the *processing mode* people apply in social judgments. Happy moods generally increase heuristic processing strategies, whereas sad moods are more associated with a systematic elaboration of information (e.g., Schwarz & Clore, 1996). Although earlier accounts attributed these differences to different amounts of cognitive capacity or mood maintenance motivations, recent research suggests that signaling functions of mood explain this relationship more conclusively (Bless, Clore, et al., 1996).

According to this account, negative affect signals that the current psychological situation is problematic and insecure. Positive affect, on the other hand, signals that the current situation is benign and rather secure. As a consequence of these attribution or simple associative learning processes, negative feeling states prompt more detail oriented, systematic processing in order to cope with the problematic situation. Positive mood, however, signals that no problem solving is needed, so that individuals may rely on simple heuristics and save cognitive capacity until it is needed (see Bless, Clore, et al., 1996; Schwarz, 1990; Schwarz & Clore, 1996, for more detailed discussion). In a similar way, the *sufficiency principle* in the heuristic-systematic model of information processing (e.g., Maheswaran & Chaiken, 1991) describes subjective experiences of confidence as a crucial moderator between heuristic and systematic processing modes. Applying this account to social dilemmas provides an interesting alternative perspective on affective influences on cooperative behavior. As mentioned earlier, social dilemmas are very complex situations (not only in the laboratory) and people probably choose or develop certain heuristics or simplifications to handle these situations. However, individuals might also differ in the degree to which they use these simplifications. In addition to personal preferences and situational constraints, one moderator of reliance on heuristic strategies to handle a social dilemma might be the individual's current mood state.

Usually social dilemmas are defined as situations where, everything else being equal, each defective option dominates each cooperative option (Dawes, 1980). As a consequence, a systematic or rational analysis (rational in the sense of maximizing own gains) might more often yield defection, whereas cooperative choices are more probable when persons are in a heuristic-processing mode. Investigating mood effects on cooperation in such a setting makes it difficult to discriminate between direct effects of mood on cooperation and indirect effects mediated by different processing styles. To distinguish between direct and processing effects of mood on cooperation, it would be advantageous to have a dilemma structure where systematic or heuristic decision modes are not confounded with cooperation per se, but allow variation in both directions.

In order to provide such a dilemma structure, we loosened the definition of social dilemmas slightly (viz., "there is at least one case where defection dominates cooperation;" cf. Liebrand, 1983) and chose a dilemma paradigm where it is rational to cooperate as well as to defect depending on contextual factors. This is given in a so called *chicken dilemma* (Liebrand, 1983; Van Vugt, Meertens, & Van Lange, 1994; see also Smithson's chapter in this volume). The classical example for a chicken dilemma is the test of courage played by American teenagers of the 1950s and 1960s. Two persons, each in their own car, drive towards each other at high speed. The one who swerves away first is the *chicken*. Although it is socially rewarding not to swerve away in order to demonstrate one's boldness and courage, it is much more costly for each driver if neither one swerves or the game ends in a crash of the two cars. Contrary to the better known prisoner's dilemma structure, in a chicken dilemma defection (i.e., not swerving first) does not dominate in all cases, but only when others are cooperating. When other involved persons also defect, defection leads to even higher losses than the cooperative choice. As a consequence, in a chicken dilemma, it is rational to defect when others are cooperating, but to cooperate when others are defecting.

Chicken dilemmas not only exist in teenager games but also accurately describe many cooperation dilemmas. For example, in work teams the outcome of each group member depends on the cooperation of the other group members. At the same time, there is often the opportunity to free-ride, especially when people can not control the contribution of each of the other group members. While it might be rational to maximize one's own outcomes by decreasing contributions to the common good while others' cooperation is high, the same rationality prescribes increasing one's own cooperation when others' contributions are low. This would prevent a failure of the group's goal that might lead to more severe consequences for everybody (e.g., loss of the job) than being exploited by other group members. In general, chicken dilemmas are an interesting version of social exchange conflicts with important theoretical and applied implications. At the same time, a chicken game contains the specific qualities required in order to distinguish between direct and indirect mood effects on cooperation. In the following section I present three experiments that demonstrate the impact of mood on persons' processing modes and their implications on cooperative behavior in chicken dilemma conflicts.

THE EXPERIMENTS

Experiment 1

In the first study (Hertel & Fiedler, 1994), the effects of participants' moods were investigated in a chicken type 4-person public good game. The game simulated a group of four hobby pilots that jointly possess an airplane to reduce costs. To upkeep the plane, it was necessary to do some maintenance work. Each of the pilots had to decide in the following trials (weeks), how many out of ten available hours he or she wanted to spend for the maintenance work. Each hour of maintenance work yielded two points (collective gain, i.e., lower attrition and value increase of the plane) that were divided equally among all four players. Each hour not invested in the maintenance work led to an individual gain of one point that did not have to be shared with the other players (i.e., time for other activities).

Note that according to these rules, the dilemma game is a social dilemma game in the classic sense since, in all possible combinations of others' choices, defection (i.e., not investing time for maintaining the plane) results in higher gains than cooperation (investing hours for the maintenance work). In order to change this game into a chicken dilemma, an additional rule was added explaining that the four players together must invest at least eight hours of maintenance work in each trial (week) in order to upkeep the minimum basic functions of the plane. If less than eight hours were invested in one trial, the plane would crash and each player would lose all gains accumulated so far. (The pilot would have a parachute, so no person would lose more than the others.) As a consequence of this rule, when others were spending only a few or no hours for maintaining the plane, it was more rational for one to invest hours for the common good in order to prevent a crash instead of defecting and risking the loss of all gains accumulated so far (see also Table 16.1).

The mood of participants was varied using short film excerpts. In the positive mood condition participants saw a funny film about a baby bear doing his first clumsy steps outside of the cave. In the negative mood condition, participants saw a depressing documentary about a man in prison waiting for his execution. Whereas neither of the two films had any apparent associations with cooperation or competition, the manipulation check revealed highly significant differences of participants' mood states after the films. In order to prevent mood effects on the understanding of the experimental game, the instructions for the game were given before the participants saw the films.

To discriminate between associative, motivational, and processing mood effects we also manipulated the accessibility of cooperation related concepts with a priming technique as a second between-participant factor. According to an associative approach, we would expect that different mood states should increase accessibility effects of the priming manipulation in congruent conditions. If positive mood is really more strongly associated with cooperation than negative mood, effects of cooperative priming should have been increased when persons were in positive moods, but decreased when persons were in negative moods. According to a motivational approach we would expect direct effects of mood on cooperation without moderation by the priming because a negative mood should lead to a decrease in delay of gratification and to higher exploitation of others' cooperation. Finally, according to a processing approach, we expected no direct effects of mood on the level of cooperation, but rather on the way in which persons decided what to do. Given that a positive mood causes rather heuristic decision behavior compared to negative mood, positive mood persons might use rather unsystematic trial and error strategies or decide impulsively, whereas persons in a negative mood should apply more systematic decision strategies. These different decision strategies should be visible in different variability scores of people in positive and negative moods.

The results of the study clearly confirmed the expectations of the processing account. Whereas the cognitive priming manipulation significantly moderated the cooperation scores, $F(1, 60) = 6.51$, $p < .05$, the mood manipulation had no effect on the average cooperation scores, $F < 1$. Analyses of the standard deviations of each person during the 12 trials of the game revealed the expected main effect of mood on the variability of participants' decisions. Persons in positive moods showed a significantly higher standard deviation than persons in negative moods, $F(1, 60) = 14.92$, $p < .001$ (see also Vollmeyer, 1994, for similar results).

No indication of any direct motivational mood effects occurred in the results. Better recall of cooperation related priming material while in a positive mood and competition

Table 16.1   Experiment 1: Case examples of the exchange matrix in the experimental chicken game.

Own maintenance	Average maintenance work of others		
	0 hours	5 hours	10 hours
0 hour	0/0	17.5/12.5	25/15
10 hours	5/15	12.5/17.5	20/20

Note: Values before the slash refer to own outcomes. Values after the slash refer to outcomes for each of the other participants. Persons were allowed to choose any number between 0 and 10.

related concepts while in a negative mood showed at least some evidence for a stronger association between positive affect and cooperation, and negative affect and competition in participants' memories. However, this association had no effect on the cooperative behavior of participants. In summary, the results confirmed the assumption that mood states can vary the cognitive processing style in a social dilemma, leading to a rather superficial *trial and error* mode in positive mood compared to a more consistent and presumably more concept driven behavior strategy of participants in negative mood.

Whereas trial and error strategies, or deciding by chance, might be an appropriate heuristic when no useful clues are at hand, this should change when valid cues are available. One popular heuristic cue in social interaction is the behavior of other people in the same situation. That people follow such a *consensus heuristic* has been shown in social communication (e.g., Chaiken, Liberman, & Eagly, 1989), person perception (Bodenhausen, Kramer, & Susser, 1994; Macrae, Milne, & Bodenhausen, 1994), and in the early work on group conformity (e.g., Asch, 1951; Festinger, Schachter, & Back, 1950). In social dilemmas, people may also use the perceived behavior of others to define what behavior is appropriate. Indeed, many experiments have demonstrated that people often imitate the perceived behavior of other participants in these settings (Allison & Kerr, 1994; Dawes et al., 1977; Hertel & Fiedler, 1994; Hertel & Klinkner, 1998; Schroeder, Jensen, Reed, Sullivan, & Schwab, 1983).

However, if the use of simple heuristic strategies varies according to the current mood of persons, their reaction to the perceived behavior of others should be moderated by their mood states. A positive mood should lead to the impression that the current situation is safe and benign, so that one can just do as others do. As a consequence, positive mood persons should often follow a consensus heuristic and simply imitate others' behaviors. Negative mood, on the other hand, should lead to an interpretation of the current situation as problematic and should prompt a more systematic and rational decision strategy. As explained earlier, in a chicken dilemma this should yield choices that are contrary to the perceived behavior of other group members.

A third factor in Experiment 1 was the manipulation of the perceived behavior of the other three game players with a false feedback procedure among participants (see Hertel & Fiedler, 1994). After the fourth trial, participants were informed that the average cooperation of the group was very high (7.0 hours/person), whereas after the eight trials the average cooperation seemed to be very low (3.125 hours/person). Besides these extreme feedback statements, two additional moderate feedback statements were given after the sixth (6.75 hours/person) and tenth trials (3.5 hours/person) in order to make the perceived development of others' perceived behavior more plausible. Analyzing the first decisions after the two extreme feedback statements (from the fourth and eighth trials) provides a first test as to whether the reactions to others' behaviors are moderated by participants' mood states as outlined above.

The results of this analysis indeed revealed a marginal interaction effect of mood and the perceived cooperation of other participants in the game, $F(1,62) = 3.95$, $p < .06$.[1] As expected, participants in positive moods tended to imitate others' perceived behaviors, showing relatively high investments for the common good when others seemed to be cooperative, but low investments when others seemed to be uncooperative. Participants in negative moods did not exhibit such reactions to the feedback (see also Figure 16.1). This result provided first evidence that positive mood leads to an increased use of a *consensus heuristic* when such heuristic cues are available.[2] Participants in negative moods, in contrast, behaved more consistently and stable, presumably because they followed a more system-

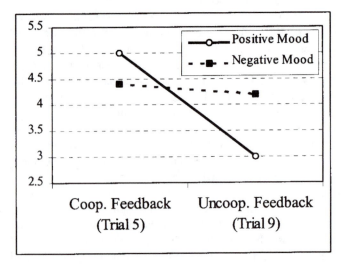

Figure 16.1 Mean cooperative decisions after cooperative feedback and uncooperative feedback as a function of mood in Experiment 1

atic strategy. In order to further elaborate these results we conducted a second study varying mood and the perceived behavior of others using another chicken dilemma game. To obtain more refined process data, this time the experiment was run on personal computers.

Experiment 2

In this experiment (Hertel et al., in press, Exp. 1) two different sources of information about others' behaviors were varied in addition to the mood manipulation. Whereas a manipulation of descriptive norms varied the general expectations of behavior in the given dilemma situation, a preprogrammed feedback procedure similar to Experiment 1 varied more detailed information about the perceived behavior of the concrete interaction partners.

Cooperative behavior was again measured in a chicken type public good game. This time the game was explained as a simulation of four students running a taxi business together. Each student had to decide how many of a total of nine hours[3] to invest driving the taxi in each trial. As in the pilot game, each hour invested for the common good yielded two points that were distributed equally among all four participants. Each hour not spent for the common project resulted in a one point gain that need not be shared with the others. Again, a minimum threshold of eight hours had to be provided by the group in each trial to maintain the taxi business. This time, it was explained that eight hours were the minimum amount a taxi has to be driven in order to maintain the taxi license. If the group invested less than eight hours in one trial, the game would be finished immediately and each participant would lose all gains accumulated so far in the game.

Moods of participants were again varied by short film excerpts. This time, positive mood was induced by a short, funny film about ostriches roaming through the African steppe. Negative mood was induced by a sad film about a cruel killing of a tiger. Descriptive social norms representing the more general or categorical information about others' behaviors were varied as part of the game instruction. The experimenter casually told half of the participants that former participants usually invested about six hours in each trial, whereas the other half got the information that former participants usually invested three hours in each trial. The second, more detailed information about others' behaviors was manipulated by a false feedback procedure during the game. After the fourth trial, participants were given very cooperative feedback ("during the last trials, the other players invested an average of 7.5 hours"), whereas after trial eight the feedback was very uncooperative (average of 2.4 hours). As in Experiment 1, two additional feedback statements were included that showed a more moderate tendency in order to increase the plausibility of the development of the perceived behavior of others (average of 6.9 hours after the sixth trial, average of 3.0 hours after the tenth trial).

According to the considerations outlined earlier, we expected that positive mood leads to subjective security, which in turn prompts a rather heuristic mode of information processing. Negative mood, on the other hand, should prompt feelings of insecurity that should lead to rather systematic and rational decision processes. These different processing modes should moderate the reactions to expected (general norms) and perceived behavior (false feedback) of other people in the same situation. It is noteworthy that we did not form specific hypotheses about the absolute amount of heuristic and systematic processing in each mood condition. This would require additional assumptions about the defaults of processing styles in a given conflict structure and participant sample that are not relevant to our model. Instead, we mainly expected an interactional pattern showing that positive mood leads to relatively more heuristic processing than negative mood (see also Hertel et al., in press).

The results confirmed our expectations. First of all, the mood manipulations not only led to significant differences in the valence ratings of current feeling states, but also in the ratings of subjective security. Participants in the positive mood condition rated themselves as feeling significantly more secure than participants after the negative mood induction did. Second, induced positive mood led to significant shorter decision latencies than the negative mood induction, especially in the first four trials, indicating a rather heuristic mode of decision making. Third and most important, the results confirmed the expectation that mood differences moderated the reaction to others' perceived behaviors. Focusing only on the first four trials where no feedback was given and only the descriptive norm information was available, participants in a positive mood mainly imitated the given norm. When the norm suggested that usually persons in earlier experiments invested six hours per trial, happy participants invested an average of 4.8 hours per trial. When the norm suggested that other persons usually invested three hours per trial, the mean investment of happy participants was 3.8 hours per trial, $t(76) = 1.70$, $p < .05$ (one-tailed). Participants in a negative mood, however, showed no such simple effect for the norm manipulation but invested relatively few hours in both norm conditions ($Ms = 3.9$ and 3.8 hours, respectively; see also Figure 16.2).

Whereas negative mood did not show an effect for the norm manipulation, sad participants did exhibit the expected opposite reaction to others' perceived behaviors when receiving the more concrete feedback information. Focusing on the first decisions after the extreme cooperative and uncooperative feedback (viz., Trial 5 and Trial 9) showed the expected interaction, $F(1, 72) = 4.00$, $p < .05$ (see also Figure 16.3). Whereas participants in a positive mood were not strongly affected by the feedback manipulation, obviously because they already followed the more general norm information, participants in a negative mood reacted strongly to the perceived actual behaviors of their group members. In accordance with what is rational in the given game, the direction of these reactions was

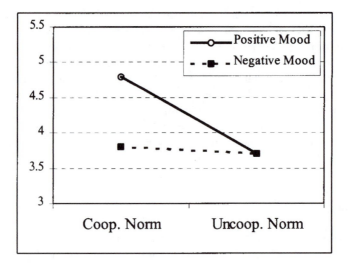

Figure 16.2 Mean cooperative decisions in Block 1 (Trial 1—4) as a function of mood and descriptive norms in Experiment 2

contrary to the perceived behaviors of others—and contrary to reactions of positive mood participants. When others appeared to cooperate, negative mood participants invested relatively few hours for the common good. However, when others seemed to invest only a few hours so that the common project was close to a breakdown (loss of the taxi license), people in negative moods, but not participants in positive moods, showed relatively high cooperation trying to compensate others' low investments.

These results are in accordance with our assumption that positive mood leads to more heuristic decision behavior that imitates others' perceived behaviors, whereas negative mood prompts rather rational, systematic processing modes that, given the logic of a chicken

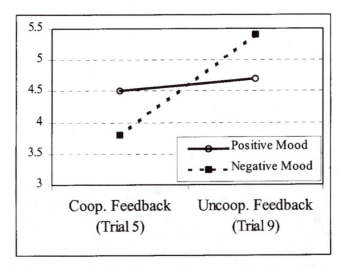

Figure 16.3 Mean cooperative decisions after cooperative feedback and uncooperative feedback as a function of mood in Experiment 2

dilemma, led to defection when others were cooperating, but to increased investments for the common project when others' cooperation seemed to be low. Analysis of strategy descriptions further supported our conclusion, with a significantly higher proportion of participants describing the rational inverse reactions to others' behaviors when participants were in negative moods than in positive moods.

Surprisingly, we did not find a significant interaction between mood and descriptive norms in the first four trials of the experiment. Whereas participants in positive moods imitated descriptive norms as expected, those in negative moods did not show a reversed reaction pattern. One explanation is that this result might indicate differences in the informational sensitivity of persons experiencing positive versus negative moods. Recent research has shown that a positive mood leads to stronger processing of general, categorical information, whereas negative mood prompts rather data driven processing styles oriented mainly on piecemeal information (Bless, Schwarz, & Wieland, 1996; Schwarz & Clore, 1996). Considering descriptive norms as general, *theory-based* information about others behaviors and the feedback information as rather concrete and *piece-meal* information, the reported results are in accordance with this account.

However, a second and more simple explanation suggests that the manipulation of descriptive norms was not extreme enough. Please note that the uncooperative norm manipulation in Experiment 2 did not imply serious problems for the common project. When everybody else in a four-person group was expected to invest three hours for the common enterprise, the minimum threshold of eight hours per trial was still maintained even when oneself did not invest at all. Thus, it was still rational to show only low levels of cooperation under this condition. Increasing one's own investments in order to save the common project was only necessary (and rational) when the group's investment seemed to drop below the eight hour threshold. Consistent with this explanation Experiment 1 participants in a negative mood showed no different reactions to the concrete (although false) feedback information when the uncooperative feedback (3.125 hours/person) was above the critical threshold of 2.7 hours (8 necessary hours/3 persons). However, when the other's perceived behaviors dropped below this critical threshold, as given after the uncooperative feedback in Experiment 2 (2.4 hours/person), participants in a negative mood suddenly increased their investments for the common good, which is consistent with the outlined reasoning. In order to replicate these results and to further test our process assumptions we conducted a third experiment.

Experiment 3

The general procedure of this experiment was similar to Experiment 2. The main goal of Experiment 3 (Hertel et al., in press, Exp. 2) was to test the assumption that subjective security is a crucial mediator of mood effects on processing modes, which are in turn moderating reactions to others' behaviors in a chicken dilemma. In order to do this, we developed a procedure that manipulated subjective security directly instead of assuming it to be based on mood variations. In the *insecurity condition* participants were told that during the game a surprising event might happen that could be either positive or negative. In addition, they might be observed through one-way mirrors that were visible in the lab. In the *security condition* participants were assured that nothing unforeseen would happen, and that everything would be explained thoroughly. The one-way mirrors were handled as if they were part of other experiments.

A second purpose of this experiment was to test whether insecure feelings can also exhibit compensating tendencies to more general information about others' behaviors when this information is more crucial for the maintenance of the common project. As already mentioned, the descriptive norm manipulation in Experiment 2 did not suggest serious problems for the maintenance of the common project, thus it was still rational to show only low levels of cooperation. This might change when the expected behavior of others is below the minimal investment required to maintain the common good. In Experiment 3 we increased the descriptive norm variation by telling participants that usually persons invested 2 (or 7, respectively) hours in the game. Now, the uncooperative norm suggested that the taxi business would break down when the participant does not invest at least a moderate amount of hours. Under this condition, we expected insecure, but not secure participants, to show compensating cooperation as a consequence of rather systematic and rational decision processes.

The results strongly supported our hypotheses. First, the manipulation of subjective security was successful. Participants in the security condition rated themselves as significantly more secure than those in the insecurity condition, without significant differences in the valence ratings of mood. Second, similar to Experiment 2, these different feelings of security led to differences in decision latencies indicating rather heuristic decision processes when participants felt secure, but rather systematic processes when they felt insecure. Third, subjective security moderated the reactions to others' expected behaviors in the predicted way, expressed in a significant interaction between the subjective security and the descriptive norm manipulation, $F(1, 76) = 4.98, p < .02$. In the first four trials before any false feedback, secure feeling participants exhibited relatively high cooperation when descriptive norms were cooperative ($M = 4.7$ hours), but relatively low cooperation when descriptive norms were uncooperative ($M = 3.4$ hours). However, the opposite was true for insecure participants. While acting rather uncooperatively when the descriptive norm was cooperative ($M = 3.8$ hours), these participants showed relatively high cooperation scores when the descriptive norm was uncooperative so that the common project seemed to be in serious trouble if no person invested more than the norm ($M = 4.5$ hours; see also Figure 16.4). Both of these strategies are rational given the structure of the chicken dilemma game. More specifically, the results confirmed our expectation that insecure feelings can lead to compensating reactions after more general information about others' behaviors (descriptive norm) when this information indicates that the maintenance of the common project is in danger.

Further analyses replicated the finding that insecure, but not secure feeling participants, showed compensating cooperation when the maintenance of the common project was at stake also according to the behaviors of the others in the game. Similar to Experiment 2, after extreme uncooperative feedback (Trial 9) insecure participants showed relatively high cooperation both in the uncooperative norm and cooperative norm conditions. Secure feeling participants in the uncooperative norm condition, on the other hand, did not show such compensating behaviors after uncooperative feedback.

In general, the results of the reported three experiments provided strong evidence for processing effects of mood in social dilemmas and their impact on cooperative behavior. Positive feeling states prompted heuristic processing modes that led to higher decision variability and more trial and error strategies when no clear heuristic cues were available. However, when heuristic cues such as information about others' behaviors were available, positive feeling states increased the tendency to simply follow these cues. Negative mood, on the other hand, prompted more systematic and rational processing modes that led to lower decision variability indicating more concept driven behavior strategies, as well as

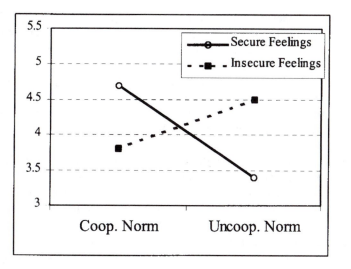

Figure 16.4   Mean cooperative decisions in Block 1 (Trial 1—4) as a function of subjective security and descriptive norms in Experiment 3

reactions to others' behaviors that not simply imitated others but were consistent with a rational analysis of the given chicken dilemma structure. The similar result patterns in Experiments 2 and 3 suggest that these processes are at least partly mediated by the subjective security signaled by current mood states.

Besides these rather indirect mood effects, none of the reported chicken dilemma experiments revealed a main effect of mood on the level of cooperation. At least in situations where cooperation is not confounded with the rationality of decision behavior, the popular assumption that positive mood simply increases cooperation is not true. Instead, the implications of mood effects on the amount of exhibited cooperation depend on additional social factors such as social norms and others' perceived behaviors.

SUMMARY AND FURTHER RESEARCH

This review of experimental studies has demonstrated that affective influences in social dilemmas are rather complex and can not be easily predicted by assumptions of simple effects. This is not surprising given that social dilemmas are very complex situations in themselves, containing many different processes where affective factors can come into play. From the three discussed approaches to understanding mood effects on cooperation, the most compelling evidence has been found for the processing account, namely that mood states influence the way people make their decisions more than the level of cooperation per se. However, this does not imply that the other two approaches might not be predictive under certain conditions. At least according to an associative principle there exists preliminary evidence that mood congruency processes might contribute to cooperative decisions when memory and perceptual processes are involved. Although clear evidence for motivational effects of mood on cooperation is lacking, it would be too early to exclude this possibility based only on the few studies that are currently available.

Rather than contrasting these three different accounts in an *"either-or"* approach, it might be more fruitful to integrate the different processes in multiprocess or multilevel models as proposed in recent approaches on affect and cognition (e.g., Fiedler, 1990; Forgas, 1995). In social dilemma situations, people engage in many different perceptual and decisional processes, for example, analyzing what kind of situation they are in, evaluating whether the situation is safe or not, preconsciously switching to different processing modes that seem to be appropriate, retrieving scripts from their memory that indicate how to handle this situation, and evaluating their interaction partners. Most of these processes can be affected by current mood states. In order to make sound predictions about mood effects on cooperation one has to not only understand how moods affect these different processes, but also how these processes interact with each other. Whereas this complexity might sound discouraging at first, the reported research suggests that there are some general principles that can simplify the complex picture.

This review also demonstrated that we have only begun to understand affective influences in social dilemmas, and that there are many open questions that await further research. As a potential way to structure the field for next steps, it might be helpful to conceptualize behavior in a social dilemma as a multiphasic process (cf. Barry & Oliver, 1996; Schwarz & Bohner, 1996). In the first phase, people try to orient themselves in the social dilemma situation. During this *orientation process*, they categorize the dilemma situation and the behavior options they have, evaluate how problematic the situation is, try to retrieve appropriate behavior scripts, and assess their interaction partners. Since these activities involve mainly memory-based and perceptual processes, they should be mostly prone to mood congruency effects based on biased retrieval. However, processing effects of moods, for example different reliance on stereotypes (e.g. Bodenhausen et al., 1994; Macrae et al., 1994), can also come into play.

In a second, *decisional phase*, people deliberate what they want to do based on the results of the first step in the process model. In this phase, effects of mood on the processing styles of persons are presumably the most important affective influence. However, it is noteworthy that the implications of different processing strategies depend on the results of categorization and retrieval processes of the first step. For example, the reliance on simple behavior scripts as a consequence of a heuristic processing mode has different implications depending on whether a person remembered cooperative or competitive behavioral schemas. Or, using perceived sympathy for interaction partners as another heuristic cue, the resulting cooperative behavior can be influenced by mood effects on the perception of interaction partners earlier in the process (cf. Forgas & Bower, 1987). In addition, considering feeling states as devices that can set priorities between different possible goals (Schwarz & Clore, 1996; Simon, 1967; Tomkins, 1995), motivational effects of more concrete emotions might occur during this phase. However, these motivational effects should be qualified by the social orientation of a person as well as by prior categorizations of the situation (cf. Lanzetta & Englis, 1989) and the behavior options (Hertel, 1995).

A third phase involves *evaluation processes* after each decision in a social dilemma. Whereas mood congruent processes might bias the perception of feedback information, affective influences can also moderate the reactions to feedback as demonstrated in Experiments 1–3. Finally, the evaluation process can produce emotional reactions that vary the current mood-state of a person as well as following behavior decisions. In the long run, the accumulation of these evaluation processes should establish certain attitudes and social orientations as permanent associations of affect and cooperation relevant concepts that determine behavior in later social dilemmas (Van Lange, de Bruin, Otten, & Joireman, 1997).

Another extension line for further research refers to the source of feeling states. In this review I focused on effects of feeling states that are unrelated (or incidental, cf. Bodenhausen, 1993) to the social dilemma situation. Although this research provides important insight on basic affective processes, it is only the first step in understanding how interactions and decisions in social exchange conflicts are moderated, structured, or even directed by the emotions of the persons involved. As a next step in the research process, it would be interesting to focus more on affective reactions that are elicited by the social interaction itself (integral effects, cf. Bodenhausen, 1993). For example, the mood ratings in Experiments 2 and 3 revealed that the uncooperative descriptive norm information affected the moods of participants in addition to the main mood manipulation (see Hertel et al., in press, for more details). In another study, using a very similar chicken dilemma as in Experiments 2 and 3, participants were asked to rate their feelings after each of several cooperative and uncooperative (false) feedback statements about others' cooperation. The results showed that participants reacted consistently with elated moods when others seemed to cooperate, but with depressed moods when others seemed to act uncooperatively (Hertel & Klinkner, 1998; see also Vanman, Paul, Ito, & Miller, 1997). Given that negative feelings prompted more systematic and rational processing strategies as well as compensating behaviors (i.e., high investments for the common good) when the groups' project was close to a crisis, these results might indicate an important function of feeling states in self-stabilizing processes of small groups (cf. Fiedler, 1988, for related considerations on the individual level).

Finally, it is of course desirable to understand the role of more complex emotions that occur during interactions in social dilemmas, such as anger about or fear of being exploited, thankfulness about others' cooperation, or guilt of one's own defection. Given that social dilemmas are one of the most central paradigms to investigate complex behavior within and between social groups, research on emotional effects in social dilemmas not only furthers our understanding of the interplay of affects and cooperation, but also demonstrates the function emotions have to structure social behavior in general. At the moment, we are only at the beginning of such a thorough understanding. Framing it in a positive way, there are a lot of fascinating research questions awaiting. The considerations outlined in this chapter suggest further steps in this direction.

ENDNOTES

[1] This result is not reported in Hertel and Fiedler (1994) but is based on a later reanalysis of the data set.

[2] Please note that the stronger reactions to the feedback in positive mood were not the only reason for the higher decision variability reported earlier. The difference in decision variability was already significant in the first four trials before the first feedback was given, $F(1,60) = 8.43$, $p < .01$.

[3] In order to measure the decision latencies as indicated by the first key stroke of participants, we only allowed one-digit response options and reduced the amount of available hours to nine.

Chapter 17

Norm Perception and Cooperation in Large Scale Social Dilemmas

Anders Biel
Chris Von Borgstede
Ulf Dahlstrand

INTRODUCTION

Many large scale problems faced by societies can be approached by a social dilemma analysis. A societal social dilemma is a situation in which the personal interests of citizens are at odds with the interest of the public at large. The dilemma arises because the payoff to the individual is higher from a selfish than from a nonselfish behavior, while the public at large is worse off if most citizens act selfishly.

Many environmental problems are of this kind. Individuals often prefer to commute by car rather than going by public transport because the car saves time, is more convenient, or more comfortable. In order to resolve such dilemmas, people have to engage in cooperative actions. If the theorists who assume that people are motivated by rational self-interest are correct (e.g., Von Neumann & Morgenstern, 1947), there would not be any cooperation. Nevertheless, more recent experimental research has shown that people may forsake their private interests in favor of the collective (for reviews, see Dawes, 1980; Komorita & Parks, 1995; Van Lange, Liebrand, Messick, & Wilke, 1992).

Potential solutions to the large scale societal problems such as preservation of natural

This research was financially supported by grant #95-1439:2 from the Swedish Council for Planning and Coordination of Research. We are grateful to a reviewer for valuable comments.

resources have inspired much of the experimental social dilemma research. However, the external validity of the experimental research has been questioned (e.g., Nemeth, 1972). At the same time there is a strong defense for the experimental realism of these studies (Van Lange et al., 1992). Participants are highly engaged and motivated. Dawes (1995) recalled an older participant who called him in the middle of the night and wanted to pay back the money he had taken from the common pool, despite the fact that his choice was anonymous to the rest of the group. Furthermore, Dawes (1980) assumes that ". . . the psychological factors that lead to defection or cooperation in small scale dilemmas are roughly the same as those that influence behavior in large dilemmas." (p. 189).

This argument is supported by Ostrom's (1990) field studies of common pool resources. Ostrom's studies have a direct link to Hardin's (1968) *Tragedy of the Commons* in that she has studied local resources where the number of persons involved is rather small, they are all dependent upon the resource for economic returns, and they live close together. However, both localized commons dilemmas and small scale, laboratory-based, dilemmas may differ significantly from large scale societal dilemmas. In local and laboratory dilemmas it is made explicit that a group of people has access to a common resource; be it water, land, points, or dollars. In ongoing interactions between appropriators, or in repeated games, where feedback about the size of the resource is provided, it is evident that participants' choices have consequences. Thus, it is quite clear that one is facing a dilemma and the interdependent nature of the situation is plain. In larger scale, societal dilemmas it may not be obvious to the individual that the choice he or she makes is a choice whether to cooperate or to defect with society's welfare. Rather, one goes by car to save time or out of sheer habit. Hence, factors that motivate cooperation in small scale dilemmas may not be experienced in large scale dilemmas.

NORMS

In contrast to sociobiological models of cooperative behavior (e.g., Alexander, 1987), Caporael, Dawes, Orbell and Van de Kragt (1989) argued that humans have always been social. Thus, not only egoistic but also social incentives motivate people's actions. People not only want to benefit themselves, they also care for the well being of others. This is not a claim that individuals are prepared to sacrifice their own good in every instance. In social interdependence situations the cost for the individual must not be too high or the collective good will not be promoted (Dawes, 1980). This implies that in social interdependence situations there may be a conflict between individual and collective outcomes. For my own comfort, I keep the indoor temperature high. On the collective level, such a behavior might risk the energy supply. An energy campaign signals that keeping the thermostat low is a proper behavior. As a citizen, saving energy is the right thing to do. If such a message reaches a consensual standard, a social norm is established. Thus, we regard social norms as obstacles whose function is to deemphasize egoistic incentives—on behalf of a choice that is better for the collective.

The aim of this chapter is to investigate which factors contribute to norm perception, and to show that people will adapt their behaviors in accordance with norm strength. In situations where people perceive that a norm about proper behavior exists and is strong, they will be more inclined to cooperate for the common good than in situations where norms are weak or absent.

Unless otherwise stated, by norm we mean an injunctive norm or a moral standard. This is the *ought* meaning of a norm, in contrast to a descriptive norm that tells what is typical (Cialdini, Kallgren, & Reno, 1991). The latter kind of norm reflects what most people do and has an informative value about what could be an effective or adaptive behavior. An injunctive norm specifies what is the right thing to do and may be regulated by social sanctions. It is also quite common to make a distinction between personal norms, norms that have been internalized, and social norms where the consequences of norm violation are administered by others (Schwartz, 1977). Notice that this is not a distinction between idiosyncratic and social standards. In both cases the norm has a social origin, but in the former case it has a personal value for the individual to act accordingly while in the latter case the individual may adopt to standards in order not to be punished by others. Thus, both personal and social norms can be regarded as injunctive norms.

Despite their importance, social norms have drawn little attention in research on social dilemmas (Kerr, 1995b). Kerr proposed several reasons as to why this has been the case. One is the theoretical tradition from game theory and economics which deemphasizes subjective rewards, such as social sanctions. Another is the methodology developed to study dilemmas. To a large extent most studies have been experimental where the experimenter instructs participants to collect as many points or dollars for themselves as possible. Thus, the payoffs—the salient outcomes and behavior, which normally might be prescribed by norms—might not be activated.

Kerr's own research shows that commitment is an important norm enhancing cooperation in social dilemmas (Kerr, Garst, Lewandowski, & Harris, 1997; Kerr & Kaufman-Gilliland, 1994). However, like Ostrom (1990) the studies by Kerr are performed in situations where a smaller number of persons are involved, where communication has an important part to play, and where the nature of the dilemma is plain. Can norms encourage cooperation in large scale dilemmas? In large scale dilemmas, people act under high anonymity, low group solidarity, little communication, and with low personal efficacy (Kerr, 1995b). He further points out: "These are conditions under which one might expect social norms to have their least impact. . ." (p. 35). Our suggestion is that injunctive norms about what one ought to do as a citizen, *social duty*, rather than norms governing interpersonal interactions, may encourage cooperation in large scale dilemmas.

What, then, contributes to a norm being perceived as morally binding? A proviso is that people regard that you and others ought to perform a certain behavior, or refrain from performing a behavior. According to Schwartz's norm activation model (1968a; 1968b), individuals have to be aware that their action, or inaction, may have consequences for the well being of others. Furthermore, individuals have to ascribe to themselves responsibility for these acts and their consequences. When individuals feel a high degree of awareness and responsibility, their personal norms will be activated and govern their behavior (Schwartz, 1977).

In addition, we suggest that when a valued collective resource is being threatened by the aggregate effects of individuals' actions, people may realize a need for behavioral change. If, for example, citizens place a high value on a clean environment and perceive that certain behaviors are detrimental to the environment, then a common perception that such behaviors should be restricted or banned might develop. This common perception or norm about proper behavior will in turn lead people to cooperate in a social dilemma.

A SURVEY STUDY

Four common everyday situations were described in a questionnaire. They concerned commuting by car or by public transport, reducing electricity consumption, recycling, and buying ecological products such as organic food. The problem for each of the four situations respectively was air pollution, electricity supply, waste products, and the use of pesticides. Using electricity consumption as an example, the questionnaire is described below. The same set of questions was used for all four situations.

One group of questions tapped the gravity of the problem at hand and the necessity for behavioral changes. Five questions were asked about the need for changes in society (e.g., to reduce electricity usage in offices). These scales were pooled into a *need* variable. Three questions measuring the importance of behavioral changes among the respondents themselves and various groups in society formed an *importance* variable. Another two questions concerned the seriousness of the problem today and the seriousness in 10 years time. These were pooled in a *seriousness* variable. All questions were rated on 9-point scales except for the seriousness questions where a 4-point scale was used.

Another set of questions referred to responsibility. Three aspects of the respondent's own responsibility for the potential situational problem formed an index variable, *own responsibility*. A single question measured to what extent it was *politicians' responsibility* to solve the problem. We assumed that if it were considered the responsibility of politicians to solve the problem, this would oppose norm development.

Two aggregated scales measuring the significance of various consequences were formed. One concerned situational effects and the well being of others—arguments for *reducing the problem*. The other scale contained individual inconveniences from cooperation, arguments for *avoiding inconveniences*. In a social dilemma, egoistic incentives may counteract cooperation. Thus, this variable was expected to be negatively related to norm strength.

The variables above were all independent variables in the analyses that follow. They will be related to the dependent variable *norm perception* that in turn will be correlated with *likelihood of changing behavior towards cooperation*. For each situation respondents were asked two questions regarding to what extent they perceived that an injunctive norm existed. In the case of electricity consumption, participants were asked to rate on a scale ranging from *No, hardly* to *Yes, absolutely* if they ought to reduce their electricity consumption in their home as compared to their present consumption. This question was intended to measure personal beliefs in a social norm. It was explained that *ought* implied that they and others should act in a certain manner and unless not, their behavior would be met with disapproval. They were also asked to what extent their friends and acquaintances thought that they themselves should reduce their electricity consumption. The same scale format was used. This question measured the perceptions of social acceptance of a social norm. The two norm questions were combined into *norm perception*. Finally, *likelihood of changing behavior* was measured by a single item question. In the case of electricity consumption the question read: "Do you believe that you will reduce your energy consumption at home during the year to come" with the end-points *No, hardly* and *Without doubt*.

The questionnaire was addressed to a random sample of 500 Swedish adult citizens, aged eighteen to seventy-five. The response rate of completed questionnaires after two reminders was 51%. Fifty-two percent of the respondents were women. The mean age was 44 years. Just over one third of the respondents resided in households with children under the age of 18.

Results

Variations in norm perception across situations as well as across individuals will be analyzed in separate sections. We will mainly focus on the question "what factors covary significantly with norm perception?" If the same pattern of relationships can be found across situations and across individuals, the suggested factors contributing to norm perception will be more compelling.

Variation Across Situations The perceived norm, measured as what one ought to do, varied substantially across the four dilemma situations. An inspection of Table 17.1 reveals that the most strongly held social norm refers to recycling, followed by buying organic food, reducing electricity consumption, and commuting by public transport instead of a car. The means for "to what extent respondents believed that they would act in line with the cooperative choice" (likelihood of changing behavior) showed a similar but less dispersed pattern.

Variables listed below norm perception in Table 17.1 were introduced as factors that potentially contribute to norm perception. It is quite clear that the means of estimated need to act in order to reduce the problems covary strongly with norm perception across situations. This is also true for arguments for reducing the problem and the importance of changing *behavior.*

In order to correlate variation across situations in norm perceptions with other variables, a difference value was computed for each participant. Recycling and buying organic food, the two situations with means for norm perceptions above the midpoint of the scale, were grouped together. In a similar manner, saving electricity and commuting by public transports were grouped together since a norm was less likely to be activated in these situations, that is, their means were below the midpoint.[1]

The difference value between the two groups of situations was computed for each variable for each individual according to the following formula: (recycling + organic food) − (electricity + commuting). Using these difference values, Table 17.2 shows correlation coefficients between norm perception, likelihood of changing behavior towards cooperation and the independent variables. There is a rather strong relationship to likelihood of changing behavior and importance of behavioral change. Need for changes in society, own responsibility, and arguments for reducing the problems have somewhat weaker relationships to norm perception, while no relationships can be found for the seriousness of the problem, individual inconveniences from cooperation, and politicians' responsibility.

Table 17.1 **Means[1] of norm perception, likelihood of changing behavior, and seven other variables for four different situations.**

Variable	Situation			
	Recycling	Organic food	Electricity	Commuting
Likelihood of changing behavior	6.79	6.09	4.59	3.46
Norm perception	6.90	5.36	3.44	2.77
Need	8.29	7.17	5.15	4.89
Importance	8.06	6.42	6.10	6.50
Seriousness	3.35	3.23	2.70	3.21
Reducing the problem	7.32	6.87	5.28	6.21
Inconveniences	4.50	5.20	4.92	6.00
Own responsibility	6.64	5.87	5.31	5.25
Politicians' responsibility	5.87	5.72	5.38	4.54

Note: [1]All variables were measured on a 9-point scale except seriousness where a 4-point scale was used.

Table 17.2   Correlation coefficients, beta weights, student's t-values, and significance levels in multiple regression analyses with norm perception as dependent variable.

Variable	r	β	t	p
Likelihood of changing behavior	.47			
Need	.39	.19	3.00	.003
Importance	.49	.31	4.38	.000
Seriousness	.12	−.01	−.14	.892
Reducing the problems	.32	.11	1.62	.108
Inconveniences	−.05	−.00	−.08	.939
Own responsibility	.37	.15	2.38	.018
Politicians' responsibility	.05	.01	.22	.824

These variables, with the exception of likelihood of changing behaviors, are regarded as predictor variables for norm perception in a multiple regression analysis. Since these variables to a certain extent share the same variance, using multiple regression analysis enables sorting out which variables make unique contributions to norm perceptions while holding other variables constant. Results from this analysis are also presented in Table 17.2. Three variables have significant effects on norm perception, namely, importance, need, and own responsibility. These results suggest that, across situations, variation in these variables may explain variation in norm perception. Altogether, the model explained 32% of the total variation.

Variation Across Individuals   Not only might situations vary in norm strength, individuals may also differ with regard to norm perception. In this section we analyze why it is likely that an injunctive norm is perceived by some but not by others. Data in the analyses were aggregated across situations. This was possible since the same questions were posed for each situation.

As shown in Table 17.3, three variables, importance to act, one's own responsibility, and the seriousness of the potential problems, correlate substantially with norm perception. The need variable also has a strong relationship with norm perception across individuals. Inconveniences and politicians' responsibility have very weak negative correlations with norm perceptions. Finally, norm perception and likelihood of changing behavior correlates rather strongly with each other. If an injunctive norm is perceived, people are likely to report they will act in a cooperative manner.

Results from a multiple regression analysis, corresponding to the analysis for variations across situations (above), are also presented in Table 17.3. The seven predictor variables explained 38% ($R^2 = .38$) of the total variation in norm perception. The need and own responsibility variables were the only two variables that uniquely contributed to norm perception.

CONCLUSIONS

With regard to norm perception, there was quite a difference between the four situations. Thus, most respondents thought that one ought to recycle but not necessarily to commute

Table 17.3   Correlation coefficients, and beta weights, student's *t*-values, and significance levels in multiple regression analyses with norm perception as dependent variable aggregated across situations.

Variable	r	β	t	p
Likelihood of changing behavior	.60			
Need	.51	.18	2.30	.022
Importance	.56	.12	1.10	.272
Seriousness	.47	.10	1.33	.185
Reducing the problems	.46	.07	.83	.406
Inconveniences	−.16	.00	.00	.998
Own responsibility	.54	.26	3.50	.001
Politicians' responsibility	−.14	−.01	−.12	.907

by public transport rather than by car. Why? All four situations held serious problems. It was also agreed that cooperation in all four would result in positive consequences for others and the environment. What differed in, and contributed to, variations in norm perception were the perceived necessity for behavioral changes and personal responsibility for the problems at hand. The analysis of individual differences with regard to norm perception pointed in the same direction. Thus, factors that contribute to why one ought to cooperate in one situation rather than in another can also account for why individuals differ in norm perception in the same situation. Taken together, the similarity in results between these two sources of variance, situational and individual, points to the importance of these factors for the activation of an injunctive norm.

These results partly support Schwartz's (1977) norm activation theory in that ascribed responsibility accounted for individual variations in norm perception. The results also support our suggestion that people's evaluations of the need for and importance of behavioral changes influence the perceived significance for normative control. However, our data do not account for why behavioral changes should be more important when it comes to recycling or buying organic food rather than electricity consumption or commuting by car. Detrimental consequences from car emissions are often emphasized in media. One possibility is that public campaigns supporting recycling and consumption of organic food have been common during the last years. In Sweden, people have been informed about how to recycle and which labels indicate ecological foods. Similar campaigns have not been carried through for electricity use or commuting. Thus, information signals that it is important for people to stand up for the common good and recycle and choose ecological foods. One ought to perform such activities. At the same time, need for and importance of behavioral changes become more directly linked to people's everyday behavior. When, as a citizen, one can contribute, it raises the question of personal responsibility.

Rather to our surprise, personal inconveniences did not seem to block norm perception. One could imagine that if people perceive that a certain behavior implies personal sacrifices and at the same time experience that they ought to perform this behavior, an undesirable dissonance would be aroused. Neither did we find an effect of politicians' responsibility on norm perception. Hence, it was *not* the case that the more politicians were held responsible for solving the problems, the weaker the normative pressure was perceived to be. At the same time, the correlations between personal inconveniences and politicians' responsibility, and norm perception were negative and thus in the expected direction. However, these effects were overshadowed in the regression analysis across situations. One possibility is, of course, that the expected relationships simply are not there. Another possibility is that these effects are nonexistent until a certain threshold is reached. Then people may pass the buck to the politicians—"You put us in this situation so now you have to take us out of it." The present situation in Russia with a new political system and a falling currency seems to foster such thoughts. Citizens may also feel the request is asking too much—"It is all right to spend another 15 minutes on the bus, but one hour? Never!"

Once norms are activated or perceived, they are assumed to help individuals achieve collective action. The strong correlation between norm perception and likelihood of changing behavior toward cooperation speaks in favor of such an assumption. We further believe that this relationship indicates another kind of injunctive norm in addition to commitment (Kerr et al., 1997) or reciprocity (Ostrom, 1998) that has been identified previously to promote cooperation in social dilemmas. It is not the case that we deny the importance of the commitment and the reciprocity norms for levels of cooperation in social dilemmas. Rather, we believe their influence to be stronger in dilemmas that involve and affect smaller groups with a probability of communicating face to face. In larger scale societal dilemmas certain behaviors might be included in the moral sphere in the sense that this is what the individual, as a good citizen, ought to do. If people realize that their present behaviors put important values at stake, they might see a need for changes and take on a personal responsibility for changes to come about.

It is certainly not the case that a single survey study investigating a few situations by means of scales that are not firmly rooted in a theory of norm development, activation, and maintenance can claim any definite answers. Of course, we also have to measure behavior in large scale societal dilemmas more accurately. In this research intended behavior is self-reported but compliance with social norms may, in some instances, also be directly observed. However, we can not put all of society into a laboratory to test injunctive norm theories. We have to rely on more circumstantial evidence. In due time we will develop better means to conceptualize and measure societal injunctive norms more accurately in order to understand their mediating effect on behavior. This is important not only for potential solutions to environmental dilemmas but also to understand the legitimacy of and support for public policies and initiatives.

ENDNOTES

[1] This procedure was also motivated by statistical reasons, that is, to avoid nonindependence of errors.

Chapter 18

Curbside Recycling: Does It Promote Environmental Responsibility?

Sherry Schneider
Jim Sundali

Urban governments have increasingly become involved in encouraging and administering recycling programs. In the early 1990s the price paid for recyclable materials fell to the point that many of these government sponsored programs became money-losing efforts. Administrators of such programs have been forced to weigh the costs and benefits of operating them. Although the short-term costs of recycling are immediate and defined for a local community, many of the benefits of recycling are intangible and accrue over the long term (such as more efficient use of landfill space). The recycling issue is a classic social dilemma: As long as everyone else is recycling it makes little rational sense for an individual to make the effort to collect, store, and dispose of recyclables; yet, if everyone were to come to this conclusion, there would be negative consequences for all.

The contribution of this research is that it utilizes a research design that allows us to test whether there are broader social benefits to government supported recycling efforts beyond the immediate financial value of the materials collected. In particular, this methodology involves analyzing both the attitudinal and behavioral effects that accrue from individuals' participation in a recycling program, paying special attention to the hypothesis that there may be a priming effect from recycling to other environmentally responsible behaviors (Cialdini, Reno, & Kallgren, 1990). Hence, can participation in everyday recycling efforts lead to increased environmentally responsible behavior in other domains?

SOCIAL DILEMMAS

There have been two basic approaches in promoting cooperative behavior in social dilemmas (Messick & Brewer, 1983). The first approach addresses changing the payoff structure of the dilemma. A change in the basic rewards and punishments of cooperative and defecting behaviors could easily alter the incentive structure of the dilemma, thereby eliminating the conflict (Kelley & Grzelak, 1972; Komorita, Sweeney, & Kravitz, 1980). For example, in energy conservation, apartment dwellers will reduce consumption when provided with financial incentives to conserve (Newsom & Makranczy, 1977–78; Slavin, Wodarski, & Blackburn, 1981). As applied to recycling, researchers have found that rewards, such as contests, prizes, and raffles, can increase participation in a recycling program (Geller, Chaffee, & Ingram, 1975; Jacobs & Bailey, 1982–1983; Luyben & Bailey, 1979; Luyben & Cummings, 1981–1982; Witmer & Geller, 1976). Lowering the cost of recycling by increasing the availability of containers also reduces the dilemma by altering the payoff structure (Luyben & Bailey, 1979; Reid, Luyben, Rawers, & Bailey, 1976).

Unfortunately, these simple solutions become more complex when we ask who can alter the payoffs and how this might be done on a larger scale in the community. Typically, implementation of structural change has been done by government agencies, and the method adopted is usually negative coercion (Yamagishi & Sato, 1986). There are many problems associated with this approach, including prohibitive costs in changing the payoffs, reduced efficiency of the economic system, the ability of stakeholders to get around set rules, and the lack of consensus both within and between governments to agree on common solutions. Crowe (1969) stated that coercion is both inefficient and rarely effective in the long term, for it requires a continued stability in the government entity applying the coercion, which is not consistent with the nature of political organizations.

The second approach to social dilemmas has been to broaden the concept of payoffs, from simple monetary rewards into more complex individual utility functions. Individual utility functions encompass monetary rewards along with mediating norms and values, which can have significant effect on a decision to cooperate with the collective good. This line of thought has sought ways to increase the salience of values such as fairness and altruism to influence cooperative behavior. Although psychological variables, such as personal values, have been found to promote cooperation in laboratory settings (see the introductory chapter of this volume for a review), much less research has assessed their generalizability to more natural settings. Samuelson (1990) reviewed the findings from field research concerning social dilemmas and concluded that the following clusters of psychological variables reduce energy conservation among consumers:

1 *Modeling*—showing the participant how to conserve energy reduced energy consumption (Aronson & O'Leary, 1983; Winett et al., 1982);

2 *Social diffusion*—informal social networks provide the critical information on which individual technological innovation decisions are made (Darley, 1978; Darley & Beniger, 1981; Leonard-Barton, 1981; Stern & Aronson, 1984). For example, both independently and together, modeling and social diffusion can encourage recycling if neighborhood block leaders share information with their neighbors and remind them to recycle (Hopper & McCarl-Neilsen, 1991).

3 *Public Commitment*—home owners who made public commitments to conserve energy were more likely to do so than individuals who made private commitments (Pallak, Cook, & Sullivan, 1980; Pallak & Cummings, 1976; and similarly, Kerr, this volume). Overall, commitment to recycling has been found to increase its likelihood (Burn & Oskamp,

1986; Katzev & Pardini, 1987–1988; McCaul & Kopp, 1982; Pardini & Katzev, 1983–1984).

4 *Feedback*—frequent, credible, meaningful feedback to home owners about their energy use resulted in significant energy savings (Becker, 1978; Hayes & Cone, 1981; Seligman & Darley, 1977; Winett, Neale, & Grier, 1979; and Van Vugt, this volume).

5 *Perceptions/Attitudes*—perceptions and attitudes of consumers toward energy conservation moderate the effectiveness of the previously mentioned variables (Hummel, Levitt, & Loomis, 1978; Olsen, 1981). DeYoung and Associates (DeYoung, 1985–1986; DeYoung, 1986; DeYoung & Kaplan, 1985–1986) reported that many people cite personal satisfaction as their main reason for recycling. In another study, social norms mediated by moral attitudes and awareness of environmental consequences predicted recycling (Hopper & McCarl-Niesen, 1991).

If, as these findings suggest, cooperative behavior in social dilemmas can be increased by carefully constructing the structural and psychological variables in the environment, then we may ask: Are changes in the behavior of consumers transitory or permanent? And, as mentioned previously, does the conserving behavior generalize to other domains? The classic social psychological paradigms on attitudes and norms provide some possible answers to these questions.

ATTITUDES AND NORMS

Self-perception theory (Bem, 1967) argues that people infer their attitudes from their behaviors. For example, a person who complies with a legitimate request from a government authority to recycle may think, "I am the sort of person who recycles." This self-observation would then result in more commitments being made to later and larger requests on environmental issues, once a "foot in the door" has opened the initial threshold (Freedman & Fraser, 1966). The foot in the door technique of encouraging initial small commitments has been used successfully to induce recycling in consumers (Arbuthnot et al., 1976–1977).

Historically, the alternative to self-perception theory in explaining behavior change has been cognitive dissonance (Festinger & Carlsmith, 1959). Cognitive dissonance theory states that incongruities between attitudes and behaviors produce a state of discomfort, which gives rise to activity aimed at reducing or eliminating this state. For example, a person who holds favorable attitudes towards recycling but who does not recycle is likely to feel guilty. Such discomfort will induce the person to either begin recycling or to alter their attitude about recycling.

The research of Ajzen and Fishbein (1977, 1980) allows us to be even more specific with regard to the effects of positive environmental attitudes on behavior. Their research has shown that although there appears to be a weak correlation between attitudes and behaviors, attitudes predict behavior when they are matched in levels of specificity: that is, specific attitudes predict specific behaviors and general attitudes predict overall behaviors. Weigel and Newman (1976) demonstrated this matched-specificity hypothesis in the domain of environmental attitudes and behaviors. They found that a person's general attitude about the environment was predictive of subsequent environmental behaviors as measured by a comprehensive behavioral index. While Weigel and Newman could not predict what specific behaviors an individual with a positive environmental attitude would engage in, they demonstrated a strong correlation between general environmental attitudes and overall environmental behavior.

Directly related theoretical support for the relationship between specific attitudes and behavior change can be found in a series of studies by Cialdini et al. (1990). In a series of experiments on littering behavior of individuals in natural settings, Cialdini et al. showed that the decision to litter or not can be manipulated by altering the salience of social norms. For example, by controlling the number of pieces of litter in the environment or by altering the message on a handbill (do not litter, turn out lights, vote) a relationship was found between the salience of the norm which was primed and the amount of littering that occurred. Therefore, a relevant and salient norm is effective in reducing public littering.

In the recycling literature, a priming effect that has been shown to be somewhat successful in increasing recycling is providing reminders to recyclers (Jacobs & Bailey, 1982–1983; Luyben & Bailey, 1979; Luyben & Cummings, 1981–1982; Reid et al., 1976). The important contribution of Cialdini and colleagues (1990), however moves beyond simple priming. These researchers demonstrated that cognitive priming of a specific social norm could focus that individual's attention on a related concept, which then prompts related behaviors. An explanation for this effect is that cognitive priming leads to internal activation or spreading from one concept to other semantically or conceptually related concepts (Anderson, 1983). Cognitive priming thus suggests that the concept of recycling will spread internally in an individual to other related environmentally responsible concepts, that is, a norm regarding a specific behavior may generalize to other related domains. The purpose of this study is to test whether such response generalization leads to overall positive increases in environmentally responsible attitudes and behaviors.

METHOD

Participants and Setting

At the time of this research, a midsize U.S. city was considering implementing a citywide curbside recycling program. The plan entailed the collection of various recyclable goods (aluminum, glass, plastic, and newspaper) from residential locations on a weekly basis. Initially, the city began operating pilot curbside recycling programs in various neighborhoods. Residents of an ordinary, middle class neighborhood chosen for the pilot program served as the primary participants in this study. Those who lived in the targeted pilot neighborhoods were instructed to place their recyclable materials in special blue plastic trash bags. The city picked up these blue bags once a week as an extension of normal trash pick up.

Data on the target pilot program neighborhood were gathered from telephone surveys of neighborhood residents. Telephone surveys were implemented with a quasi-experimental pre-post, post-only design with comparison groups (Campbell & Stanley, 1966). This entailed survey measurements of residents living inside and outside the selected pilot recycling program neighborhood before and after the operation of the program. In order to validate against testing effects, a post-only group of residents living in the recycling neighborhood was also surveyed. Finally, one of the unique contributions of this study is independent verification of self-reported behavior. The trash collectors on the city trucks recorded whether each house in the target neighborhood put out the special blue recycling bags for collection during each week of the pilot program.

All of the interviews were conducted over the telephone. There were a total of 254 individual residences in the targeted pilot neighborhood. In the initial survey, 27 were randomly selected and contacted. Next, random samples of 37 and 44 residences were contacted to serve as comparison groups from what we believed to be two demographically similar neighborhoods (which we later confirmed when we found no significant differences between neighborhoods on the survey's demographic questions). In the initial survey, a total of 138 individuals living in the designated areas were contacted, and of these 78% completed the survey.

Four months later, the same individuals who responded to the first survey were contacted again. As the city had then discontinued weekly pick up of recyclable materials, individuals who wished to continue recycling had to find other means of disposal. Of the 108 in the initial survey, 65 (60%) completed the follow-up, with about equal numbers from the pilot neighborhood and the two comparison neighborhoods. Finally, 18 additional individuals residing in the pilot neighborhood who had not completed the initial survey completed the follow-up survey.

The Surveys

The questionnaire used for the first telephone survey asked questions about the extent to which an individual engaged in, and held positive attitudes toward, environmentally cooperative behaviors. Questions on the initial survey ranged from inquiries about very simple behaviors to several behaviors that would require substantial effort and commitment. Examples included such things as installing low flow water devices in one's home, using environmentally safe laundry detergent, recycling plastic, installing water heater insulation, and contributing financially to environmental causes. The second, follow-up survey had additional questions to ascertain the extent to which respondents discussed the pilot program with others, as well as several operational questions concerning the pilot program to evaluate the program's effectiveness and to gauge respondent's knowledge of the program.

The surveys were designed to test several specific hypotheses generated from the social dilemmas and attitudes literatures described previously.

> Hypothesis 1. Changing the payoff structure of the social dilemma by lowering the costs to individuals of recycling will encourage cooperation. Specifically, curbside pickup will increase recycling.
>
> Hypothesis 2. The pilot recycling program will create a priming and the foot in the door effect. There will be response generalization to other environmentally cooperative behaviors in addition to recycling. Specifically, individuals who have been induced into recycling by the pilot program are likely to continue recycling and other related environmentally responsible behaviors even after the inducements have been removed.
>
> Hypothesis 3. Individuals who have been involved in the curbside recycling program will experience cognitive dissonance. Specifically, individuals in the pilot program neighborhood will feel guiltier when they do not recycle than those who do not have curbside pick up.
>
> Hypothesis 4. Individuals who have positive attitudes toward recycling are more likely to recycle.
>
> Hypothesis 5. Public commitment, modeling and social diffusion will each predict recycling. In the present research, the blue recycling bags outside residences in the pilot neighborhood served both as a weekly measure of public commitment and as a measure of a neighbor's cooperation. It is expected that those who paid attention to these blue bags were more sensitive to the construct of public disclosure and were more aware of who else was participating in the program. Thus, they were more likely to participate in the recycling program than those who did not notice the blue bags. We also expected to

find a positive relationship between a participant's beliefs concerning how many of their neighbors were recycling and their own recycling behavior. Specifically, individuals who were aware that others were recycling were more likely to recycle than those who were not aware of others' participation.

RESULTS

After the follow-up survey a comparison was made of those in the recycling neighborhood that had responded to both surveys versus those in the recycling neighborhood that had only responded to the follow-up survey. There were no significant differences between these groups, which showed there were no effects attributable to the initial survey instrument. Therefore, we collapsed these two groups into *one program neighborhood* or *program group*. A comparison was also made between the two *control* neighborhoods. The two groups differed significantly on only one survey question. Therefore, the two groups outside the recycling neighborhood were combined to create one *comparison group*.

> Hypothesis 1. The first hypothesis addressed whether participants increased their recycling behaviors during the operation of the curbside program. The recycling collectors counted the number of weeks during the twelve-week program that each household set out a blue recycling bag for pick up. The average number of blue bags put out by each household during the program was 4.8. As some households may only have needed to put out a bag every few weeks, this number may underestimate participation. In our sample, a large majority of the respondents (80.5%) left out a blue bag for collection at least once during the program. For the entire neighborhood of 254 households, 75.4% of the residences participated at least once during the program.

In addition to the number of blue bags set curbside, self-reports on three survey questions directly assessed participation in the pilot programs. Participants were asked to report the amount of glass, plastic, and aluminum they recycled before the program began, during the operation of the program, and after curbside pick up had been discontinued. These self-report measures are summarized in Figure 18.1, which suggests that reducing

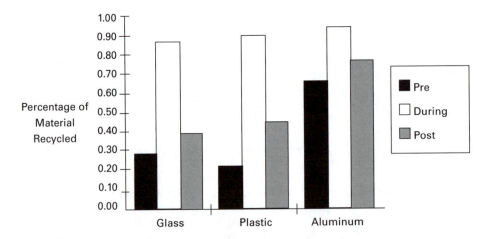

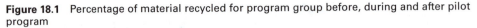

Figure 18.1   Percentage of material recycled for program group before, during and after pilot program

the costs of recycling by providing curbside pick up significantly increased the amount of recycling that occurred.

Hypothesis 2. To test whether recycling would continue, we compared the mean pre- and post-responses of those in the pilot neighborhood to those in the comparison neighborhood. We expected no significant differences on the initial measures and, on the second set of measures, we hypothesized that the program group would report higher participation in environmental behaviors than the comparison group. There was strong support for the first expectation and little support for the second.

If there was a strong effect for the pilot recycling program, we would see positive increases on the variables for the program group and these increases would be consistently above any increases seen for the comparison group. This pattern is not apparent in Tables 18.1 and 18.2. These results do not provide evidence that there was any strong effect attributable to the pilot recycling program after the program was discontinued.

The results suggest that participants increased their level of recycling behavior during the operation of the curbside program, but that once the program was discontinued, they quickly returned to their previous levels of recycling behavior (see Figure 18.1). However, it is possible that while no long-term behavioral changes were apparent, the program may have affected participants' attitudes towards the environment.

Hypothesis 3. One interesting measure is the amount of guilt felt when participants do not recycle (see Figure 18.2). Figure 18.2 shows that on the second survey, the amount of guilt felt increased for the program group. The resulting difference between the program and comparison groups on the second survey was not significant but in the predicted direction, $t(80) = 1.71$, $p < .10$. These results provide weak support for Hypothesis 3;

Table 18.1 Mean responses from telephone surveys for program and comparison groups on behavioral and attitudinal questions.

Measurement variable	First survey		Second survey	
	Program	Comparison	Program	Comparison
Behaviors:				
Recycle Plastic	0.9	0.7	1.8	0.9*
Reuse Grocery Bags	0.6	1.0	0.7	2.0*
Recycle Glass	1.2	0.7	1.6	1.0
Recycle Aluminum	2.7	2.5	3.1	3.0
Water Conservation	2.6	3.0	2.9	3.2
Financial Contributions	1.6	1.2	1.1	1.2
Attitudes:				
Guilt Felt When Not Recycling	1.2	1.5*	1.9	1.4
Environment Improved	1.1	1.6*	.9	1.0
Importance of Recycling	2.9	2.9	2.8	2.8
Notice Blue Bags	—	—	3.3	0.8*
Product Packaging Concern	1.3	1.4	1.3	1.7
CFC Concern	1.8	2.2	2.1	2.2
Change in Recycling Attitude	—	—	1.0	0.5*
Current Recycling Attitude	—	—	1.5	1.5
Neighbors Currently Recycling	—	—	1.6	0.8
Awareness of Neighbors	—	—	2.9	—

Note: The values represent mean responses to questions on a 0-4 scale. 0 = None or 0%, 4 = All or 100%.
   *$p < .05$.

Table 18.2 Percentage of respondents who report engaging in specified activities for program and comparison groups

Measurement variable	First survey		Second survey	
	% program	% comparison	% program	% comparison
Use Alternative Transportation	48.0	28.0*	37.8	29.3
Use Envir. Laundry Detergent	46.2	48.1	41.0	43.2
Volunteer Time to Envir. Causes	61.5	43.0	26.7	11.4
Don't Use CFC	42.3	53.8	51.3	61.4
Contribute to Public T.V.	46.2	45.6	60.5	50.0
Insulate Water Heater	42.3	26.3	20.7	8.7
Install Lo-Flow Water Devices	20.0	35.1	17.1	8.3
Turn Off Air Conditioner	—	—	65.7	72.7
Buy More Expensive Product if Envir. Sensitive	—	—	65.8	72.7

Note: The values represent the percentage of "yes" responses when asked if they engage in the specified activity.
*$p < .05$.

participation in the pilot curbside recycling program may have led participants to feel more guilty when they did not recycle than participants who did not have such a low effort option available to them.

Hypothesis 4. The fourth hypothesis was that individuals who have positive attitudes toward recycling are more likely to recycle. Participants were asked how important they felt it was that people recycle materials that can be recycled. From the research of Ajzen and Fishbein (1977, 1980) discussed earlier, a general attitude such as importance should not predict any one specific environmental behavior. When we ran regressions for each of the continuous behavioral measures from Table 18.1 (aluminum, plastic, glass, water conservation, reuse grocery bags, and contribute financially to environmental causes), the importance of recycling did not predict any one of these behavioral measures very well. However, when we created a composite measure of environmental behavior from these

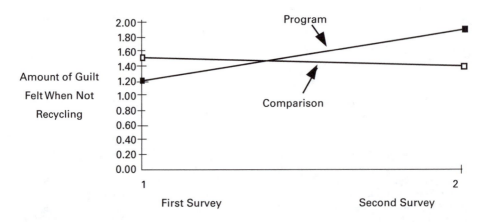

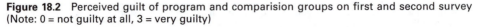

Figure 18.2 Perceived guilt of program and comparision groups on first and second survey (Note: 0 = not guilty at all, 3 = very guilty)

variables by adding them together and then regressed it on the reported importance of recycling, the participant's general environmental attitude of importance was a significant predictor of the overall environmental behavior for both the initial survey ($R^2 = .11, p < .01$) and the follow-up survey ($R^2 = .07, p < .01$). Although the variance explained is small, the perceived importance of recycling significantly predicted an overall measure of environmental behaviors in both the first and second surveys. Specifically, we have shown that overall environmental behaviors can be predicted from global environmental attitudes.

Hypothesis 5. It was argued previously that awareness of the special blue recycling bags in front of neighboring houses serves as one measure of public disclosure and commitment to the program. Thus we expected a positive relationship between awareness of these blue bags and recycling behavior. We also expected to find a positive relationship between respondents' estimates of how many others in their neighborhood were recycling and their own recycling behavior. Whether individuals who were aware that others were recycling were more likely to recycle was tested by regressing three awareness measures on the composite measure of environmental behavior. The three measures were participants' (1) awareness of the blue recycling bags left out for collection, (2) estimates of how many in their neighborhood they believed to have actively participated in the program, and (3) estimates of how many others in their neighborhood were currently recycling after the pilot program ended. Perceived current participation of neighbors was not related to the composite recycling measure, $R^2 = .13$, $p = .07$, and no single predictor was significant.

DISCUSSION

In summary, the hypothesis that active participation in the curbside recycling program would lead individuals to increase the frequency of recycling behavior was supported. The hypothesis that participation in the pilot program would lead to long-term increases in other environmentally responsible behaviors was not supported. The remaining hypotheses concerning attitude and cognitive measures provided evidence that the pilot program had an effect on participants.

The three major findings of this study are that

1   a curbside program increases recycling for the duration of the program,
2   a curbside pilot recycling program initiated by a city government will cause individuals to report more concern with their actions when they do not recycle, and
3   general environmental attitudes are predictive of a composite measure of environmental behaviors.

Our research did not confirm our major hypothesis, however. Participation in a recycling program did not directly cause response generalization to other similar behaviors. These findings have important implications for both theory and public policy.

From a theoretical perspective, these findings suggest that participation in certain environmental activities can lead to increases in other environmentally responsible behavior. The process is not directly a priming effect, but instead is mediated by the social activation and spreading of more general internal attitudes, norms, and behaviors. Specifically the findings suggest that induced social cooperation will affect the emotions and attitudes of individuals—that changes in attitudes are the first step in changes of behavior.

From a public policy perspective, first and foremost, the program was successful at inducing residents in the pilot neighborhood to recycle. As the literature on social dilemmas has shown (Kelley & Grzelak, 1972; Komorita, Sweeney, & Kravitz, 1980), changing the payoff structure by reducing personal costs increases social cooperation. Our hopes for this research were more ambitious than evaluation of the current city program, however. Our findings provide some evidence (albeit weak evidence) that political entities should be concerned with more than just the short-term costs and benefits of environmental programs. If the programs affect the attitudes and beliefs of the public they are designed to serve, then there is tremendous potential for increasing social cooperation in many other domains. It may be possible that a well designed, implemented and operated program will eliminate the need for numerous other programs, or a least increase the effectiveness of other similar programs.

We expected, perhaps too optimistically, that the introduction of a pilot curbside recycling program would lead quickly to significant improvement in participants' environmental responsibilities. In retrospect, it is more realistic to posit that such changes occur over a much longer time span. Extending the survey period over longer periods of time would go far in improving upon the results reported here.

CONCLUSION

The driving force behind this research was the notion that individuals who engage in "good" behaviors are more likely to continue to do so and will also most likely expand the scope of such behaviors. Each of us does not wake up one day and say: "From here on I am going to be environmentally aware and only engage in behaviors that are socially responsible." Rather, most of us probably begin on a very small scale such as white paper recycling at work and then expand our social responsibility from there. In this research, the goal was to determine whether such a process does in fact occur, the strength of the process, and whether or not the beginning of the process can be induced by outside agents like governments. More field research on social policy implementation theoretically grounded in the social science disciplines could go a long way in guiding policy makers and advocating attempts to solve our environmental social dilemmas.

Chapter 19

Choice of Transportation Mode: Factors Influencing Drivers' Willingness to Reduce Personal Car Use and Support Car Regulations

Jörgen Garvill

The choice between using cars and alternative modes of transportation (e.g., public transportation) can be seen as a social dilemma (Van Vugt, Meertens, & Van Lange, 1995). Depending on choice of transport mode, a trip will produce different levels of individual outcomes (e.g., monetary cost, travel time, flexibility, and comfort) and collective outcomes (e.g., air pollution, noise, and energy consumption). In an earlier study (Garvill, Laitila, & Brydsten, 1994), it was found that cars were seen as better than buses and bicycles in terms of travel time, flexibility and comfort. The car was seen as worse in terms of contributing to air pollution, noise, and energy consumption. It was also found that most individuals judged the individual outcomes to be more important than the collective outcomes. Thus, the choice to commute by car (a noncooperative choice) maximizes individual benefits, but contributes to negative collective outcomes.

Researchers have distinguished between two types of solutions to dilemmas (Messick & Brewer, 1983; Samuleson, Messick, Rutte, & Wilke, 1984; Yamagishi, 1986b). The first focuses on changing the individual's attitudes and beliefs that influence the choice between cooperation and noncooperation. The other is a structural solution, which focuses on changing the structure of interdependence, effectively eliminating the dilemma. This suggests that we can distinguish between two types of cooperation, cooperation in the first-order dilemma and cooperation in a second-order dilemma. Yamagishi (1986b) has labeled cooperation in the first-order dilemma *elementary cooperation*, and in the second-order dilemma *instrumental cooperation*, or the decision to introduce structural constraint. Yamagishi suggested that the two forms of cooperation are not necessarily correlated, and indeed, may be predicted from different sets of variables. In this study, a number of predictors were examined for their ability to predict cooperation. These are grouped into two classes: *fundamental* and *specific* factors, as outlined below.

Behavior in social dilemmas has usually been studied in laboratory experiments where a number of factors that influence individuals' willingness to show elementary cooperation have been identified (see Van Lange, Liebrand, Messick, & Wilke, 1992 for an overview). In this study, some of these results were extended to a real life social dilemma, where elementary cooperation was represented by a willingness to reduce use of the automobile for daily trips, and instrumental cooperation was shown by support for the introduction of regulations to constrain the use of cars in the city.

The study was conducted as a survey of car owners living in five Swedish midsize cities (about 100,000 inhabitants). The reason for choosing car owners from cities of this size was to include respondents that actually had a choice between different modes of transportation for daily trips within the city. In Swedish cities of this size, public transport and bicycles are realistic options because distances are short.

FUNDAMENTAL FACTORS

Environmental Concern

Klandermas (1992) argues that for people to be motivated to cooperate in a social dilemma, they must believe that there are collective problems that need to be solved and that their decision to cooperate is relevant to the solution of these problems. In this study, it was predicted that the stronger an individual's concern about environmental problems (air pollution, noise, and energy consumption), and the more they believed that commuting by car contributes to these problems, the more willing they would be to cooperate by reducing their own automobile use and to support the introduction of regulations reducing use of cars within the city.

Values

Environmental concern and proenvironmental behavior may be affected by different underlying values. Stern, Dietz, and Kalof (1993) postulated three types of environmental concern based on different value orientations: *egoistic*, where the person believes that some environmental conditions are harmful for him or herself, so proenvironmental behavior benefits self; *altruistic,* where the person believes that some environmental conditions have adverse consequences for other people; and *biospheric*, where the concern is not with human beings, but with the whole biosphere or the ecosystem. Stern et al. found that all three types of environmental concerns independently predicted willingness to take political action for environmental protection. In the present study, the three types of environmental concerns were included as independent variables.

Willingness to cooperate has also been shown to be related to the individuals' social value orientations, defined as preferences for specific distributions of outcomes to oneself and to others (McClintock, 1978; Messick & McClintock, 1968). Three social value orientations are usually distinguished, namely cooperation, individualism, and competition, although the latter two are sometimes collapsed into *proself*, and contrasted to the *prosocial* cooperative motive. Cooperators prefer to maximize own and others' outcomes, individualists tend to maximize own outcomes without reference to other's gain, and competitors prefer to maximize the relative advantage of self over others. Social value orientation has been seen as a relatively stable individual difference variable (Liebrand, 1984; Van Lange, 1992). It is measured by offering the individual choices among alternatives which vary the distributions of resources between self and another person (e.g., points or money) (Kuhlman & Marshello, 1975; Messick & McClintock, 1968). It has been shown that social value orientation is related to an individual's priorities concerning more general human values (Gärling, 1997). It follows that priorities in values may also be important determinants of behavior in social dilemmas.

According to Schwartz and Bilsky (1987), human values can be defined as concepts or beliefs that

(a) pertain to desirable end states or behaviors,
(b) transcend specific situations,
(c) guide selection or evaluation of behavior and events, and
(d) are ordered by relative importance.

Schwartz and Bilsky (1987, 1990) have shown that there is a universal structure of human values but that individuals and nations differ with regard to the importance attributed to different values. They have also shown that human values can be divided into more individually oriented, or selfish, values (e.g., achievement, pleasure) and more collectively oriented values (e.g., equality, social justice). In this study, human value orientation was measured by asking individuals to rate the importance of a number of individual and collective values. It was predicted that the more importance given to collective values, the more willing the individual should be to engage in elementary and instrumental cooperation. Conversely, the more weight given to individual values, the less willing the individual should be to cooperate.

One way to account for the effect of social value orientation on cooperation in social dilemmas is to assume that individuals assign different weights to the individual and collective outcomes and make choices according to these transformed or subjective outcomes (Kelley & Thibaut, 1978). Van Vugt et al. (1995) applied this conceptualization to the study of decisions to use public transportation. They found that proself people, as compared with prosocials, are more influenced by the effects on their own interests (e.g., convenience, comfort), and less affected by the outcomes for others. In a similar way, it can be argued that more general human values that reflect a tendency to weight individual and collective values differentially might also lead to different transformations of the objective individual and collective outcomes of a particular dilemma. In field studies, objective outcomes for any one individual's particular choice are difficult or impossible to ascertain. However, as already mentioned, it has been found that most individuals judge commuting by car as better than the alternative modes of transportation with regard to individual outcomes and worse with regard to collective outcomes (Garvill et al., 1994). Garvill et al. also found that the importance attributed to the individual and collective outcomes varied as a function of value orientation. Thus, it was predicted that the more weight individuals gave to collective values, the more weight they should give to the collective travel consequences and the more willing they should be to cooperate. Furthermore, the more weight

given to individual values, the more weight they should give to the individual travel consequences, and the less willing they should be to cooperate. It was also assumed that the
more environmentally concerned the individuals were and the more they believed that
commuting by car contributed to the environmental problems, the more weight they would
give to the collective travel consequences.

Perception of the Cause of the Environmental Problem

The need for elementary or instrumental cooperation does not arise if a resource is not
perceived as threatened (Yamagishi, 1986b). Further, the need to engage in a particular
form of cooperation (here, restraint of car use) will not be apparent if individuals do not
perceive a relationship between a behavior and the environmental problem. If the car is not
seen to be an important contributor to the problem of pollution, for example, then use of
alternative transport modes is irrelevant. Thus, a necessary condition for cooperation is a
belief that there is a substantial causal link with improvement in the problem.

The three factors, environmental concern, value orientation, and belief that traffic
contributes to environmental problems are labelled as *fundamental*, in that they are enduring, trans-situation variables. It is now argued that they have their effect on cooperation
through their effect on more specific, contextual factors.

SPECIFIC FACTORS

Efficacy Beliefs

As Klandermas (1992) points out, it is not enough that people believe that there is a problem that needs to be solved; they need to believe that their own cooperation will contribute
to a solution. The more effective individuals feel their cooperative behavior to be, the more
motivated to cooperate they should be (Kerr & Bruun, 1983; Van de Kragt, Orbell, &
Dawes, 1983). It has also been found that perceived efficacy is inversely related to group
size (Kerr, 1989). The larger the group, the lower the perceived efficacy.

In this study, the group consists of all individuals commuting by car in a particular
city, so of course the size of this group is large. Objectively, the contribution of a single
individual to the solution of the city's pollution problems is therefore negligible. However,
other studies have shown that, although each individual's contribution to the collective
goal is very small, many still believe that their contribution is important (Opp, 1986). In
the present study, perceived efficacy was measured as the perceived importance of one's
own reduction of use of the car for the reduction of the environmental problems caused by
car traffic. This type of efficacy is relevant for elementary cooperation (personal reduction
in car use) rather than instrumental cooperation (support for introduction of car use regulations).

Expectations of Others' Cooperation

The environmental problems caused by motorized traffic are collective problems in the
sense that they are the result of many individuals' choices to act in their own interests. To
solve such dilemmas, it is necessary that a sufficient number of individuals change their
behavior and act in the interest of the collective. An important factor may be expectations
of others' cooperation. If individuals have high expectations of others' cooperation they

should be more willing to engage in elementary cooperation. A number of studies have shown that expectations of others' cooperation are related to one's elementary cooperation (Messick et al., 1983; Schroeder, Jensen, Reed, Sullivan, & Schwab, 1983; Van Lange & Liebrand, 1989). Thus, it was predicted that the more the individuals believed that other car drivers were willing to reduce their use of an automobile, the more willing they should be to reduce their own car use.

The relationship between expectations of others' cooperation and instrumental cooperation is less clear. Rutte and Wilke (1992) extended goal/expectation theory (Pruitt & Kimmel, 1977) to a second-order dilemma. Rutte and Wilke supported their hypotheses that participants with a cooperative goal and noncooperative expectations should be more willing to support a structural solution than participants with a cooperative goal and cooperative expectations. Furthermore, individuals with cooperative goals were more willing to cooperate than participants with noncooperative goals (regardless of their expectations). However, Yamagishi (1992) found that, in a larger group, high trusters (presumably individuals with cooperative expectations) were more willing to contribute to a structural solution than low trusters. In this study we can compare these predictions (i.e., positive effect of expectations of others' cooperation on instrumental cooperation, versus interaction between goal orientation and expectations).

Moral Obligation

In social dilemmas, the choice between acting in one's own interest or in the interest of the collective implies a conflict between an individualistic and a collectivistic rationality. According to individual rationality, one should act in one's own interest because this leads to higher individual outcomes regardless of others' choices. According to collective rationality, one should act in the interest of the collective, since everyone will be better off if all cooperate then if all do not cooperate. Thus, as Van Lange (1992) concludes, there is no objectively rational solution to guide one's decision. However, the choice between cooperation and noncooperation can also be seen as a moral choice, where cooperation is seen as "good" or "the right thing to do" (Dawes, 1980; Liebrand, Jansen, Rijken, & Suhre, 1986; McClintock & Van Avermaet, 1982). This would imply that an individual could be motivated to cooperate even if the probability to attain the collective goal is low (Kerr & Harris, 1996).

It was expected that the higher the perceived personal moral obligation to cooperate, the more willing the individuals would be to engage in elementary cooperation, since the choice between cooperation and noncooperation in the first-order dilemma is a personal choice. It was also expected that the higher the perceived collective moral obligation, the more willing the individuals would be to engage in instrumental cooperation. If it is believed that reduction in the use of the car is the right thing to do for everyone, there should be less opposition to the introduction of regulations with that aim.

Consequences for the Collective and the Individual

As shown by Van Lange et al. (1992) and Van Vugt et al. (1995), people with different value orientations place differential weights on outcomes to self and the collective. In the case of restrictions to use of the car, it is important to identify the particular outcomes that may be perceived as relevant to self and to others. High weight on individual outcomes should reduce willingness to cooperate, both in an elementary and an instrumental way.

Perceived Seriousness of the Problem

Except in cases where people see no relationship between a particular behavior and environmental problems, it seems reasonable to assume that willingness to act will be a direct function of the perceived seriousness of the threat to the environment.

RELATIONSHIP BETWEEN FUNDAMENTAL AND SPECIFIC FACTORS

In this survey, a rather large number of factors were included as they all were expected to have an effect on the individuals' willingness to cooperate in the real life social dilemma. In addition to the predictions made for each factor separately, one aim of the study was to see to what extent these factors independently predicted willingness to cooperate when they were considered together. The fundamental factors (environmental concern, belief that commuting by car contributes to environmental problems, and collective and individual values) were expected to influence the individuals' willingness to cooperate *indirectly* through the specific factors, as well as having a direct influence on the two forms of cooperation. According to Schwartz (1977) and Homer and Kahle (1988), one can expect that values influence more specific attitudes and beliefs that, in turn, influence intentions and behavior. Thus, it was expected that the effects on cooperation of the fundamental factors—environmental concern, value orientation, and the belief that car traffic contributes to the environmental problems—would be mediated by their effects on the specific factors.

More specifically, environmental concern was predicted to correlate with the extent to which individuals regarded cooperation as a moral issue and with perceived seriousness of the problem. Perceived contribution of car traffic to environmental problems was expected to predict the more specific factors of need for immediate reduction of environmental problems caused by car traffic, perceived efficacy of own reduction of use of an automobile, and expectations about others' willingness to reduce use of their automobiles. It is also possible that the fundamental factors are correlated with each other. Figure 19.1 shows the general relationship between fundamental factors, specific factors, and willingness to cooperate.

THE SAMPLE

Questionnaires were mailed to 2,000 car owners between the ages of 20 and 65. Usable questionnaires were obtained from 1,562 respondents, a response rate of 52%. The mean age of the sample was 41.9 years. Thirty percent were women. Of the respondents, 43% had children under the age of 18 living in the household. About 70% had secondary school qualifications or higher. The median reported distance from home to work was 5 kilometers, to a shopping center was 1.5 kilometers, and to a bus stop was 200 meters. Ninety percent had access to a bicycle.

THE SURVEY

Background Information and Travel Habits

The respondents answered background questions about gender, age, household, education, occupation, income, and distance from home to place of work, nearest shopping center, and nearest bus stop. There were questions about access to bicycles, number of cars in the

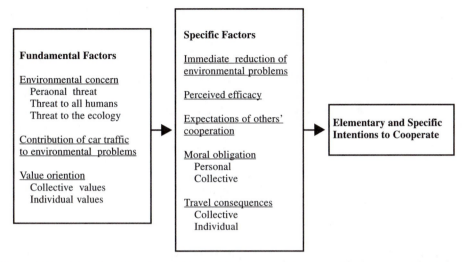

Figure 19.1 General relationships between fundamental factors, specific factors, and intentions to cooperate (specific hypotheses described in text)

household, and annual driving distance. Questions about frequency of use of an automobile, a bus, and a bicycle for traveling to work, shopping, and for other trips within the city were also asked. Finally, respondents rated how possible they thought it was to use the automobile, bus, and bicycle for the different types of trips (totally impossible to totally possible).

Fundamental Factors

Environmental Concern   Three types of environmental concern were measured. The respondents judged to what extent (on a scale from 1, *not serious at all,* to 7, *very serious*) they thought that air pollution, noise, and energy consumption were a serious threat to their own health and well being, to all humans' health and well being, and to the balance of the ecological system.

Value Orientation   To measure how much weight the individuals gave to individual and collective values, the respondents rated how important 10 human values were to them in their lives (1, *not at all important,* to 7, *very important*). The values were adapted from Rokeach (1973), and were selected to represent individual and collective values as described by Schwartz and Bilsky (1987, 1990). The individual values were achievement, stimulation, excitement, and pleasure; the collective values were equality, social justice, security for everyone, and loyalty. Two values, not included in the individual or collective values, were health and a good environment.

Perceived Contribution of Car Traffic to Environmental Problems   The respondents rated the extent to which they believed that car traffic in the city contributed to air pollution, noise, and energy consumption, from 1 (*very little*) to 7 (*very much*).

Specific Factors

Seriousness of the Environmental Problems Caused by Car Traffic   The respondents rated to what extent they thought that air pollution, noise, and energy consumption caused by car traffic in the city should be reduced immediately (1; *no, not at all;* to 7; *yes, to a high degree*).

Individual and Collective Travel Consequences   To assess how much weight the individuals gave to individual and collective travel consequences, the respondents were asked to rate how important six consequences of travel, within the city, were to them (1, *not at all,* to 7, *very much*). The three individual consequences were travel time, flexibility, and comfort; and the three collective consequences were air pollution, noise, and energy consumption.

Perceived Efficacy   On a scale from 1 (*not at all*) to 7 (*very much*), the respondents judged the perceived efficacy of how important they believed that their own reduction of the use of their automobiles in the city would be for the reduction of air pollution, noise, and energy consumption caused by car traffic in the city.

Expectations of Others   The respondents' expectations of others' cooperation were also measured. They rated how much they believed that other car drivers were willing to reduce their use of their automobiles in the city in order to contribute to the reduction of the environmental problems caused by car traffic. The rating was expressed as percent reduction of the normal use of their automobile.

Perceived Moral Obligation   The extent to which the individuals saw cooperation as a moral issue was measured in terms of their perceived personal moral obligation to reduce their commuting by car in order to reduce the environmental problems. They also rated to what extent they thought that it was a moral obligation for all commuters to reduce their use of automobiles in the city in order to reduce the environmental problems. The ratings were made on 7-point rating scales ranging from 1 (*to a very low degree*) to 7 (*to a very high degree*).

Willingness to Cooperate   Finally, the respondents stated to what extent they were willing to reduce their own use of their automobile in the city in order to reduce air pollution, noise, and energy consumption. For each type of travel (work, shopping, and other) they stated, in percent of current driving distance, how much they were willing to reduce their use of the automobile. They also rated the extent to which they were willing to support the introduction of regulations with the aim of reducing the possibility to use a car in the city (all ratings on 7-point scales).

RESULTS

Travel Habits and Perception of Car, Bus, and Bicycle as Possible Modes of Transport

For travel to work and for shopping and other purposes, there was not much difference between respondents' uses of their cars. The majority of the respondents used the automobile most of the time (around 75%) for all three types of tasks. About a third of the respondents used a bicycle, regardless of the purpose of their travels. The bus was rarely used (about 5% overall), except to get to work (12%). When asked to consider possible transportation modes for different purposes, over 90% of respondents reported cars as highly possible to use, with bus and bicycle being listed by between 50 and 60% of the sample, with very little variation in mode of transportation for different purposes.

Measures of Values, Travel Consequences, and Willingness for Elementary Cooperation

The importance ratings of the human values were submitted to factor analysis to assess whether there would be separate factors with different weights given to individual and collective values respectively. A principal component analysis followed by varimax rotation was performed on the ratings for the eight values assumed to represent individual and collective values. The analysis revealed two factors that explained 61.3% of the variance. The first factor was described by social justice (factor loading of .87), equality (.84), security (.79), and loyalty (.73). The second factor was described by excitement (factor loading of .83), pleasure (.75), stimulation (.70), and achievement (.65). Thus, the collective values and the individual values were combined into index variables with $\alpha = .83$ and $\alpha = .71$, respectively.

The same procedure was followed for the importance ratings of the six travel consequences. A principal component analysis with varimax rotation yielded two factors that explained 69.4% of the variance. The first factor was described by the collective travel consequences, air pollution (factor loading of .92), energy consumption (.91), and noise (.89). Questions that loaded on the second factor were the individual consequences of flexibility (factor loading of .78), travel time (.76), and comfort (.70). The mean importance ratings for collective consequences ($\alpha = .89$) and for individual consequences ($\alpha = .60$) were then calculated for each respondent.

Finally, the mean of the three ratings (travel to work, shopping, and other) of how much the respondents were willing to reduce the use of automobiles in order to reduce the environmental problems were calculated for each respondent ($\alpha = .79$).

Mean Ratings for Each Variable in the Study

The means and standard deviations for the respondents for each variable in the study are summarised in Table 19.1. As can be seen, the environmental concern was rather high, with the largest threat perceived to the ecology. With regard to value orientation, it is evident that the respondents as a group rated the collective values as more important than the individual ones. The respondents also believed, to a high degree, that the environmental problems caused by car traffic should be immediately reduced. The rating of the perceived efficacy was higher than could have been expected if they had rated the objective effect of own reduction of use of automobile. With regard to elementary cooperation, it can be seen that overall, the respondents were willing to reduce their use of the car for travel in the city by approximately 27% of their current driving distance. For willingness to engage in instrumental cooperation (i.e., support car use regulation) the mean is slightly above the midpoint of the rating scale.

Relations Between Fundamental Factors, Specific Factors, and Elementary and Instrumental Cooperation

To test the different predictions made about relationships between (a) the fundamental factors and willingness to cooperate, (b) the fundamental factors and the specific factors,

Table 19.1   Means and standard deviations for the fundamental and specific factors and for elementary and instrumental intentions to cooperate.

Factor	M	SD
Fundamental factors		
Environmental concern		
Personal threat	5.04[a]	1.55
Threat to all humans	5.45[a]	1.35
Threat to the ecology	5.80[a]	1.30
Contribution of car traffic to environmental problems	5.41[a]	1.40
Value orientation		
Collective values	6.12[a]	.95
Individual values	5.51[a]	.93
Specific factors		
Immediate reduction of environmental problems	5.29[a]	1.56
Perceived efficacy	3.57[a]	1.97
Expectations of others' cooperation	25.89[b]	18.40
Moral obligation		
Personal	4.61[a]	1.80
Collective	4.95[a]	1.65
Travel consequences		
Collective consequences	5.08[a]	1.44
Individual consequences	5.48[a]	1.11
Intentions		
Reduce own car use	27.80[b]	24.66
Support car regulation	3.82[a]	2.01

Note: [a] Ratings on a scale ranging from 1 to 7
[b] Ratings given in percent of current driving distance

and (c) the specific factors and willingness to cooperate, a series of multiple regression analyses were performed. The expectation that the effects of the fundamental factors on willingness to cooperate should be mediated by their effects on the more specific factors was tested according to the logic proposed by Baron and Kenny (1986).

Fundamental Factors and Intentions to Cooperate

Table 19.2 shows that when examined separately, a significant proportion of the variance in elementary and instrumental cooperation intentions can be predicted from the three types of environmental concerns and that each of these types significantly contributes to the prediction of the dependent variables.

It was expected that the more weight the respondents gave to collective values, the more willing they would be to cooperate and that the more weight they gave to individual values, the less willing they would be to cooperate. As can be seen in Table 19.2, a small but significant proportion of the variance in elementary and instrumental cooperation intentions can be predicted, and both collective and individual values independently contribute to the prediction. Since environmental concern is supposed to be based on different values, a question is whether it measures the same thing as value orientation. As can be seen in Table 19.2, when examined together, both environmental concerns and value orientation significantly contribute to the prediction of elementary and instrumental cooperation intentions, although the increase in proportion of predicted variance is small.

Table 19.2 Regression of elementary and instrumental cooperation intentions on fundamental factors.

| | Intentions | | | |
| | Elementary Cooperation | | Instrumental Cooperation | |
Fundamental Factors	Beta	t	Beta	t
Environmental Concern (E.C.)				
Personal threat	.06	1.40	.05	1.49
Threat to all humans	.09	1.91	.07	1.54
Threat to ecology	.08	2.12*	.09	2.37*
Contribution of car traffic to environmental problems	.16	5.53***	.32	12.00***
Value Orientation (V. O)				
Collective values	.13	5.03***	.13	5.25***
Individual values	−.06	−2.36*	−.08	−2.76**
R² for Both E.C. & V.O.[a]	R^2=.13***		R^2=.19***	
R² for E.C. regression only[a]	R^2=.12***		R^2=.17***	
R² for V.O. regression only[a]	R^2=.05***		R^2=.07***	

Note: * p<.05, ** p<.01, *** p<.001
[a]All individual variables contributing to E.C. and V.O. were significant until "Contribution of car traffic" was added to the regression equation.

When the final fundamental factor *perceived contribution of car traffic to the environmental problems* was added to the environmental concern and value orientation regression it increased the explanatory power of the model for both elementary and instrumental cooperation (R^2 = .15 and .26, respectively). However, the environmental concern values of personal threat and perceived threat to humans no longer significantly predicted cooperation intentions in the social dilemma.

Fundamental and Specific Factors

It was expected that environmental concern and perceived contribution of car traffic to environmental problems should have an effect on the extent to which the respondents thought that the environmental problems should be reduced immediately. It was further expected that the perceived contribution of car traffic to environmental problems should have an effect on the perceived efficacy of one's own willingness to reduce the use of the automobile. It was also expected that environmental concern, perceived contribution by car traffic to the environmental problems, and weight given to collective values should influence expectations of others' cooperation, since without specific information about the others, the respondents could be expected to assume that the others perceive the situation the same way as they themselves do.

With regard to perceived moral responsibility to cooperate, it was expected that environmental concern, perceived contribution of car traffic to the environmental problems, and weight given to collective values should have an effect. Finally, it was expected that environmental concern, contribution of car traffic to environmental problems, and weight given to collective and individual values should influence the weight given to collective and individual travel consequences. To test these expectations, each of the specific factors was regressed on the fundamental factors in a number of multiple regression analyses. The results from these analyses are summarized in Table 19.3. They show that the fundamental factors significantly explain some of the variance in the specific factors. Perceived contribution of car traffic to environmental problems predicts a significant proportion of each of the specific factors. With regard to value orientation, it is clear that weight given to *collective* values predicts all of the specific factors with the exception of weight given to individual travel consequences. Weight given to *individual* values is only related to weight given to individual travel consequences. The results also show that for perceived efficacy, expectations of others' cooperation, and weight given to individual travel consequences the proportion of explained variance is rather low.

Specific Factors and Intentions to Cooperate

The expectations that the specific factors should influence elementary and instrumental cooperation intentions were tested in separate multiple regression analyses for these two variables (see Table 19.4). In the table, it can be seen that for elementary cooperation all of the specific factors (except perceived collective moral obligation to cooperate) contribute significantly to the prediction of intentions to cooperate. The most important factors seem to be expectations of others' cooperation and perceived personal moral obligation to cooperate. For instrumental cooperation, all factors, with the exception of perceived efficacy, contribute significantly to the prediction of willingness to cooperate. The most important factors for instrumental cooperation seem to be the perceived need for immediate reduction of the environmental problems and perceived collective moral obligation to cooperate. There is also a positive effect of expectations of others' cooperation on instrumental cooperation, although it is much smaller then the effect on elementary cooperation. It can also be seen that the effect of perceived personal moral obligation to cooperate is much smaller for instrumental as compared to elementary cooperation, while the reverse is true for perceived collective moral obligation.

Fundamental Factors, Specific Factors, and Intention to Cooperate

Multiple regression analyses with willingness to elementary and instrumental cooperation as dependent variables and with both fundamental and specific factors as independent variables were performed. According to the logic of Baron and Kenny (1986), the expectation was that beta weights for the fundamental factors in these analyses should be nonsignificant or reduced compared to the beta weights obtained when the fundamental factors were the only predictors of willingness to cooperate. As can be seen in Table 19.5, for elementary cooperation, none of the fundamental factors have significant beta weights. For instrumental cooperation there are still significant effects of collective and individual values, but the beta weights are lower than when the fundamental factors were the only predictors. The beta weights for the specific factors are, for both elementary and instrumental cooperation, almost the same as when they were the only predictors. Thus, the results support the hypothesis that the effects of the fundamental factors on willingness to cooperate are mediated by their effects on the specific factors.

DISCUSSION

This study has been concerned with individuals' intentions to reduce their use of their cars in the city where they live, and to support the introduction of regulations to limit car use in

Table 19.3 Regression of specific factors on fundamental factors.

Independent variables	Immediate reduction	Perceived efficacy	Expectations of others	Moral personal	Moral collective	Collective consequences	Individual consequences
Environmental concern							
Personal threat	.11***	.24***	.10*	.21***	.13***	.29***	.00
Threat to all humans	.05	-.03	.04	.03	.08*	.05	-.05
Threat to ecology	.08**	-.05	.05	.09**	.11***	.07*	.01
Contribution of car traffic to environmental problems	.56**	.25***	.10**	.33***	.35***	.14***	-.13***
Social value orientation							
Collective values	.06**	.07**	.13***	.16***	.15**	.21***	-.03
Individual values	.01	.03	.00	.01	.00	.03	.20***
R²	.52***	.16***	.10***	.39***	.40***	.34***	.06***

Note: * p<.05, ** p<.01, *** p<.001
Note. Read vertically down the table for standardized regression coefficients and R² for each analysis.

Table 19.4   Regression of elementary and instrumental cooperation intentions on specific factors.

	Intentions			
	Elementary cooperation		Instrumental cooperation	
Independent variable	Beta	t	Beta	t
Immediate reduction of				
Environmental problems	.12	4.16***	.32	12.40***
Perceived efficacy	.06	2.32*	.01	.71
Expectations of others'				
Cooperation	.33	14.20***	.07	3.16**
Moral obligation				
Personal	.21	5.21***	.07	1.97*
Collective	−.03	−.77	.21	5.66***
Travel consequences				
Collective consequences	−.07	−2.61**	−.14	−6.83***
	R^2=.35***		R^2=.42***	

Note: * p<.05, ** p<.01, *** p<.001

order to reduce city pollution. One aim of the study was to test some of the factors found to influence cooperation in laboratory social dilemma experiments in a real environmental dilemma facing Swedish citizens. A second aim was to compare the effects of those factors on elementary and instrumental cooperation intentions, and a third aim was to test the hypothesis that the effects on intentions of more fundamental or general factors like value orientation and environmental concern are mediated by their effects on more situational or specific factors. These specific factors were then hypothesized to have direct effects on behavioral intentions.

Of the fundamental factors proposed, three types of environmental concern were found to influence elementary and instrumental cooperation intentions. As also found by Stern et al. (1993), environmental concern can be viewed as a mixture of egoistic, altruistic, and ecocentric motives which motivate people to act proenvironmentally. It was also found that value orientation, measured as the importance attributed to collective and individual values, also influenced elementary and instrumental cooperation intentions. Although measured in a different way, the results for value orientation are in accordance with the results usually obtained for social value orientation in experiments on social dilemmas. It was also shown that a third fundamental factor, the belief that car traffic actually contributes to environmental problems, had significant effects on elementary and instrumental cooperation intentions. It stands to reason that if individuals did not believe that car use causes environmental damage, reducing one's own car use would not be seen as necessary.

Since value orientation and environmental concern are broad or general orientations that transcend specific situations, they were expected to influence willingness to cooperate mainly through their effects on the more situation specific factors. As predicted, the fundamental factors were found to influence the specific factors. The belief that the environmental problems caused by car traffic needed to be reduced immediately was mainly influenced by the extent to which car traffic was believed to contribute to these problems, and

Table 19.5   Regression of elementary and instrumental cooperation intentions on fundamental and specific factors.

| | Intentions | | | |
| | Elementary cooperation | | Instrumental cooperation | |
Independent variable	Beta	t	Beta	t
Fundamental factors				
Environmental concern				
Personal threat	−.05	−1.47	−.04	−1.27
Threat to all humans	.08	1.79	.02	.42
Threat to ecology	.02	.64	.03	.87
Contribution of car traffic to				
environmental problems	−.01	−.47	.03	1.03
Value orientation				
Collective values	.04	1.49	.05	2.02*
Individual values	−.03	−1.39	−.04	−1.97*
Specific factors				
Immediate reduction of				
Environmental problems	.11	3.42***	.31	9.99***
Perceived efficacy	.07	2.54*	.01	.24
Expectations of others'				
Cooperation	.33	13.95***	.07	2.95**
Moral obligation				
Personal	.20	4.96***	.06	1.60
Collective	−.05	−1.28	.20	5.30***
Travel consequences				
Collective consequences	.06	2.18*	.06	2.39*
Individual consequences	−.13	−5.81***	−.14	−6.43***
	$R^2 = .36$***		$R^2 = .42$***	

Note: * $p < .05$, ** $p < .01$, *** $p < .001$

also by the extent to which the environmental problems were seen as a personal threat and as a threat to the ecology, and by the weight given to collective values.

Perceived efficacy was, as expected, influenced by the belief that car traffic contributes to environmental problems. Respondents believed that their own reduction in car use would be much more effective in reducing environmental pollution (3.56 on a 7-point rating scale) than could be objectively expected. This may have occurred because respondents confused the perceived importance of doing anything to improve the environment (Opp, 1986), with the actual effects that their behavior would have on the problem. The specific factor, *expectations of others' intentions to reduce their car use* was influenced by the fundamental factors of perceived personal threat, contribution of car traffic to the environmental problems, and belief in collective values. In congruence with the experimental social dilemmas literature (Messick, et al., 1983; Schroeder, et al., 1983; Van Lange & Liebrand, 1989), when individuals lack specific information about others, they will assume that the others perceive the situation in the same way they do.

The importance of the fundamental factors was further illustrated by the significant relationship between the majority of those factors and an individual's specific beliefs regarding both society's moral obligations, and one's own *personal* moral obligations to reduce car use. These results indicate that individuals who are environmentally concerned and give priority to collective values tend to see the choice to cooperate more as a moral choice then individuals who do not share these fundamental values. This finding is congruent with experimental social dilemmas research which has found that cooperators see cooperation as the right thing to do (McClintock & Liebrand, 1988).

The specific factor of *weight given to collective and individual travel consequences* was also influenced by most of the fundamental factors. The effect of value orientation on beliefs concerning collective and individual travel consequences is congruent with the proposed explanation that social value orientation transforms how individuals evaluate the importance of individual and collective outcomes (McClintock & Liebrand, 1988).

However, it should be pointed out that although the relations between the specific factors and the fundamental factors are significant, for some of the specific factors the proportion of variance predicted by the fundamental factors is rather small. This indicates that there may be important underlying values that were not measured in this study.

Most of the specific factors were shown to influence elementary and instrumental cooperation intentions. The most important factors for elementary cooperation were expectations of others' cooperation and perceived personal moral obligation to cooperate, while the most important factors for instrumental cooperation were perceived need to reduce the environmental problems immediately and perceived collective moral obligation to cooperate. In the first-order dilemma it is necessary that a sufficient number of individuals chose to cooperate in order to solve the collective problem and thus expectations of others' cooperation should be important. Since the choice to cooperate in the first-order dilemma is an individual choice, it is reasonable that perceived personal moral obligation is the important factor rather than perceived collective moral obligation.

In experiments on experimental resource dilemmas it has been found that if the participants perceive that the resource is overused, they were more willing to accept a structural solution (Messick, et al., 1983; Samuelson, et al., 1984). In this study, the specific factor of *perceived need to reduce the environmental problems immediately* can be seen as an indication of the individuals' beliefs that the environment is being overused and is in need of protection. Thus, this factor was hypothesized (and found) to be an important determinant that influences intentions to cooperate.

In the second-order dilemma the choice is between supporting or not supporting regulations that would constrain everyone's freedom of choice. In this situation it was reasonable to assume that perceived collective moral obligation to cooperate is more important than feelings of personal moral obligation. This was the case.

According to Yamagishi (1992), second-order instrumental cooperation (support for car use regulations in this study) is a function of both individuals' desires to cooperate with the collective and their beliefs about whether others will cooperate as well. Individuals with a cooperative goal and low expectations of others should be more in favor of external regulation than individuals with a cooperative goal and high expectations or individuals who do not wish to cooperate. This hypothesis was not confirmed. The results in this study show that individuals with high expectations are more willing to accept regulation than individuals with low expectations, regardless of their own intentions to cooperate.

When both fundamental and specific factors were entered into the regression equation, none of the fundamental factors influenced the elementary cooperation intentions, while the effects of the specific factors were the same as before. Approximately the same results were obtained for instrumental cooperation. This indicates that the effects of the fundamental factors on intentions were mediated by their effects on the specific factors.

These results show that environmental concern and value orientation can influence willingness to cooperate in several different ways. They influence the weights given to individual and collective consequences of the choice, they influence the extent to which the choice is seen as a moral choice, and the expectations of others' cooperation.

The results of the present study clearly indicate that the results obtained in laboratory experiments on social dilemmas have external validity and can be generalized to real life situations. The results also show that the social dilemma paradigm is useful for the analysis of an individual's choice of transportation mode when, collectively, that choice can have an impact on a real, pervasive, and difficult environmental problem.

Chapter 20

The Reduction of the Interindividual-Intergroup Discontinuity Effect: The Role of Future Consequences

John Schopler
Chester A. Insko

The research program we have guided for the past decade has been divided into three phases, which were each defined by a different question. The first question can be paraphrased: "Do decent people behave indecently when they are banded together in a group?" Under certain, specific conditions the answer is a resounding "yes." The second question was: "Why do decent people behave indecently when banded together in groups?" After addressing this question, we turned to the third question: "What are the conditions which will make intergroup behavior as decent as interindividual behavior?" Although this chapter will focus on the progress made toward answering the last question, it will first be necessary to summarize the work relevant to the first two questions.

DEFINING THE DISCONTINUITY EFFECT

The indecency of behavior by people in groups has been noted by various persons in different contexts. We have gleefully gathered some of these expressions, which go back in time as long ago as Plato. ("Had every Athenian citizen been a Socrates, every Athenian assem-

The research reported in this chapter was supported by NIMH grant MH53258 to both authors.

bly would still have been a mob.") Many of our gathered quotes contrasted individuals' behaviors in groups with their behaviors when they were alone. It was evident from the outset that indecent behavior can not take place in isolation. Observing it requires an inter-personal, rather than a single individual, context, thus, establishing the phenomenon typi-cally involved comparing intergroup behavior with interindividual, or dyadic, behavior. We also restricted our observations to behaviors in a mixed-motive situation, typically to prisoner's dilemma outcome arrays. (See Figure 20.1 for a prototype matrix.). The discon-tinuity effect then refers to the greater amount of competitive responding in intergroup, compared to interpersonal, interactions.

There are additional characteristics to the prototypical situation we created to assess discontinuity. We defined *group* in terms of people who have some functional relation to each other. They form a unit or an entity (see Gaertner & Schopler, 1998) and interact with another entity. Furthermore, they are required to make simultaneous, irrevocable responses after they have been trained on the meaning of matrix outcomes and after they have com-municated with the other side. With the exception of one study, the outcomes are always symmetrical and are always defined in monetary terms. In the prisoner's dilemma game (PDG) this means that mutual cooperation has a higher joint payoff than mutual competi-tion. The PDG outcome array is also characterized by what Thibaut and Kelley (1959)

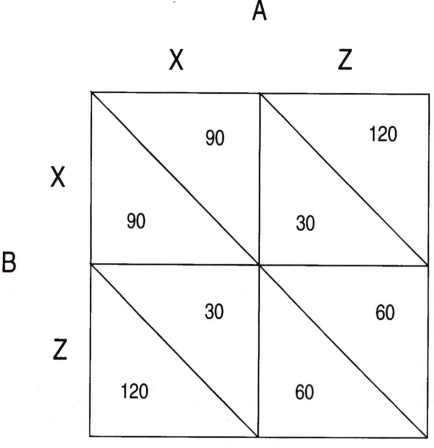

Figure 20.1   A PDG matrix

term *noncorrespondence of outcomes*. Basically, this term refers to outcome arrays in which one person's outcomes are negatively correlated with the outcomes of the other side. If the two sets of outcomes are positively correlated (are "correspondent") no conflict exists and discontinuity is irrelevant. Under the conditions specified above, the discontinuity effect has been extremely robust.

THE RELIABILITY AND GENERALITY OF DISCONTINUITY

Beginning with McCallum, et al., (1985) and proceeding through Insko et al., (1988); Insko, Pinkley, Harring, et al., (1987); Insko, Pinkley, Hoyle et al., (1987), these studies all found a statistically significant and descriptively large tendency for intergroup relations to be more competitive or less cooperative than interindividual relations. Following Roger Brown (1954) we have termed this phenomenon a discontinuity effect. It appears to be very robust because it has held over variations among and within studies.

Restricting attention to the domain of mixed-motive situations, we have demonstrated that the discontinuity effect occurs for females as well as for males (McCallum et al., 1985, Experiments 1 & 2; Insko, Pinkley, Hoyle, et al., 1987), and for a variety of forms of contact or communication between individuals or groups (Insko, Pinkley, Hoyle, et al., 1987). We have also found that discontinuity generalizes across a number of group sizes. These data revealed that two-on-two relations were markedly more competitive than were one-on-one relations, with three-on-three and four-on-four relations producing progressively smaller increases. (This study, incidentally, makes it particularly apparent why the term *discontinuity* is appropriate. There is indeed a discontinuity between interpersonal and intergroup relations involving the smallest possible group size.)

More recent generality studies demonstrated discontinuity whether there were positive or negative outcomes in the PDG matrix (Schopler, Insko, Graetz, Drigotas & Smith, 1991, Experiment 1) or whether the outcome size was increased 10 times the typical size (Schopler et al., 1991, Experiment 3). We have also examined the effect of the usual equal power matrix in contrast to a matrix in which one player was unable to influence the outcomes of the other player (Schopler et al., 1991, Experiment 2). The results indicated that there was no effect of power on the magnitude of the discontinuity effect within the first block of 5 trials, but that within the second block of 5 trials the discontinuity effect was nonexistent on the unequal power matrix. Perhaps the failure of the high-power groups to continue to exploit their low-power opponents is related to the fact that they had to face them repeatedly in trial after trial.

We have also demonstrated that the discontinuity effect holds whether the interactions are over many trials or restricted to a single trial (Schopler et al., 1993) and whether the interactions involve the standard PDG or a 3-choice matrix (Insko, Schopler, Hoyle, Dardis & Graetz, 1990). Discontinuity also occurs whether the participants are recruited from Ft. Bragg, NC (Brazil, 1992) or from campus advertisements (Insko, et al., 1994). Furthermore, all of the studies used groups homogeneously composed by gender and, except for single trials, have never found gender differences.

An additional study in this series involved contrasting the standard PDG with generalizations to *n-person games* (Insko et al., 1994). As played between two groups, these *n*-person games involve separate investment decisions by individual group members which collectively determine the overall choice of each group. As played between two individuals, the individual player decides the total number of notes that his or her side invests. Our experiment used two different games, the intergroup public goods game (Rapoport &

Bornstein, 1987), and the intergroup prisoner's dilemma game (Bornstein, 1992). With the former game the outcomes are said to be *step level* and with the latter *continuous*. All participants were separated in different rooms and communicated via an intercom that was configured to allow for appropriate discussion (within group, between groups, or between individuals) across two trials. The results indicated that groups invested more promissory notes (i.e., competed more) than did individuals. Thus, discontinuity is not restricted to situations requiring a group consensus. Relevant to the possibility of fear and greed mediation, content analysis of the tape recorded discussions indicated significantly more fear statements and greed statements in the discussions between groups than in the discussions between individuals.

Finally, we have expanded the generality of the discontinuity effect by showing its presence in a mixed-motive setting that did not involve matrix representations. In one instance we borrowed a procedure from a previous experiment (Insko et al., 1980) such that two groups (or individuals) each folded some origami products (either rabbits or swans) which could be exchanged. The procedure for 3-person groups will be described below. The numbers for the interindividual condition were proportionately reduced.

For any given trial each group folded 12 origami products. At the end of each trial representatives from each side met to discuss whether to exchange half of their own products. After returning to their own room each side made a simultaneous and irrevocable decision by placing their own products (6 or 0) in a box which was then to be delivered to the other side. These decisions in combination with the rules for the monetary value of pairs of figures created a PDG outcome array. A pair of identical products was worth 10 cents, while a pair composed of different products was worth 15 cents. Thus, mutual competition (both sides choosing to trade 0 products) resulted in 60-cent payments, while mutual cooperation (both sides trading 6 products) produced 90 cents for each side. If one side chose to trade 0 while the other side chose to trade 6 products, the former earned 120 cents and the later earned 30 cents. This outcome array has already been presented in Figure 20.1.

In addition to a manipulation of groups versus individuals and genders of participants the experiment included a factor which involved three conditions: matrix only, matrix and origami products, and origami products only. In the matrix and the matrix and origami condition the participants folded and exchanged origami products, but were also shown a matrix describing the four possible outcomes. The only significant effect was a main effect for groups versus individuals such that groups competed more than individuals. Using a matrix does not artifactually produce the discontinuity effect. The small descriptive difference among the conditions, in fact, indicated a slightly larger discontinuity effect in the two origami conditions.

Two nonlaboratory studies were also completed to assess whether the discontinuity effect had any basis in experience (Pemberton, Insko, & Schopler, 1996). These studies used the Rochester-Interaction Record (RIR, Reis & Wheeler, 1991) to investigate this possibility. Participants were asked to carry a small booklet with them for a period of one week. In this booklet they recorded all two-minute interactions that were one-on-one, within group, one-on-group, group-on-one, or group-on-group, and classified them as cooperative or competitive. An interaction was defined as any situation involving two or more parties in which the behavior of each interacting party involved a verbal response to the other party. Merely being in the presence of another party, as, for example, in a class, did not qualify.

Since most participants did not experience, or record, examples of all five types of interaction during the single week, the data were analyzed in two steps. In step one we analyzed just the data for those participants who reported examples of each of the five types of interaction. In step two we combined the data for the interactions with another group (one-on-group, group-on-one, group-on-group), and separately combined the data for the one-on-one and within group conditions (which generally did not differ). Thus it was possible to do a comparison of almost all participants of the interactions involving individuals with interactions involving groups. Fortunately, both analyses yielded the same conclusion—that group interactions were generally experienced as more competitive than were individual interactions. This was true both in the first study (in which interactions were rated for degree of competitiveness) and in the second study (in which interactions were simply categorized as competitive or cooperative). Furthermore, this result remained significant after all interactions relating to sports, or games, were removed from the data sets.

We also should note that our discontinuity framework is beginning to be validated by others whose studies do not use a matrix format. For example, Polzer (1996) has shown that negotiations conducted between teams, compared to between individuals, are more competitive and less trusting (p. 694) and Platow, Hoar, Reid, Harley and Morrison (1997), using scenario formats with intact groups, have reported results consistent with our social support predictions (p. 487).

THREE INTERPRETATIONS OF WHY DISCONTINUITY OCCURS

Our analysis of the discontinuity effect involves identifying the different processes instigated by intergroup versus individual interactions. The effect appears to be due to the three intergroup mechanisms of fear, greed, and nonidentifiability, which are absent, or reduced, in dyadic interactions.

The Fear Interpretation

The *schema based distrust* or *fear* interpretation argues that group members hold an outgroup schema that is weighted with negative traits. According to this interpretation, groups are more competitive than individuals because of learned beliefs, or expectations, that intergroup relations, compared to interindividual relations, are competitive, unfriendly, aggressive, and so on. (See Hoyle, Pinkley & Insko, 1989 for a description of one study indicating that other groups are generally more distrusted than are other individuals, and a second study indicating that in our laboratory setting participants, regardless as to whether they are in a group or are alone, are more distrustful of another group than of another individual.) In the context of the PDG, the assumption that the other group will be competitive rationally implies that one's own group should be competitive. Otherwise one's own outcomes will be reduced in the short run and, consistent with a tit for tat strategy (Axelrod, 1984), also in the long run.

The Greed Interpretation

The *social support for shared self-interest* or *greed* interpretation accounts for the discontinuity effect in terms of the social support that group members provide each other for acting in a manner that is consistent with immediate self-interest or greed, although contrary to norms of equity, equality, and reciprocity (Gouldner, 1960) as well as own long term self-interest. Such social support, of course, is necessarily absent for individuals. Greed is assumed to arise in a context in which the opponent is assumed to be cooperative and is therefore vulnerable, while fear is assumed to arise in a context in which the opponent is assumed to be competitive and is therefore dangerous.

The Identifiability Interpretation

The fear and greed interpretations are based on two differences between intergroup and interindividual relations: the fact that group opponents are more distrusted than individual opponents, and the fact that group members can provide each other with social support for self-interested choices, while individuals have no such source of support. The *identifiability* interpretation is based on still a third difference between intergroup and interindividual relations. This is the fact that membership in a group provides a degree of anonymity regarding personal responsibility for self-interested behavior. According to the identifiability interpretation, a group member's recognition that he or she cannot be held personally responsible by the other group will increase the group member's tendency to act in a self-serving manner. Anecdotal evidence consistent with this third interpretation comes from our repeated observation that the competitive choice is frequently blamed on "those other two," when a group representative meets with his or her counterpart after his or her own group has competed on the previous trials.

STUDIES OF THE FEAR, GREED, AND IDENTIFIABILITY MEDIATION

The first study providing support for the fear and greed interpretation compared the behavior of groups and individuals with the usual PDG matrix and a new PDG-Alt matrix (Insko et al., 1990, Study 2). The PDG-Alt matrix (see Figure 20.2) contains a third choice—a safe choice that provides intermediate outcomes regardless of the opponent's choice. We refer to this third choice as withdrawal. In keeping with the fear hypothesis, the data with the PDG-Alt matrix indicated that groups indeed withdrew more than did individuals. Furthermore, on the PDG matrix and on the PDG-Alt matrix the usual pattern of groups competing more than individuals was found. The tendency of groups to compete more than individuals was less marked on the PDG-Alt matrix than on the PDG matrix, but the effect was still present. Even when a safe defensive choice was available, groups still competed more than individuals. This result provides evidence for greed.

The second study correlated the number of competitive choices made by a group with instances of within group discussion of distrust of the other group (Insko et al. 1990, Study 1). Within group discussion of distrust of the other group was assessed both by ratings of audiotapes of the discussion and by real time observers. For each assessment, it was found that the greater the discussed distrust of the other group the greater the number of competitive choices, as predicted by the fear hypothesis.

The third study addressed a potential ambiguity in the results from the first study with the PDG-Alt matrix (Schopler et al. 1993, Experiment 1). This ambiguity results from the fact that the participants played multiple trials, introducing the possibility that the observed withdrawal was more tactical than noncombative (and thus more greed related than fear related). In order to eliminate all such ambiguity the participants in the third study played only one trial and knew that they were going to be playing only one trial. Hence, all tactical considerations related to withdrawal were rendered irrelevant. This study again revealed that groups both withdrew more and competed more than did individuals.

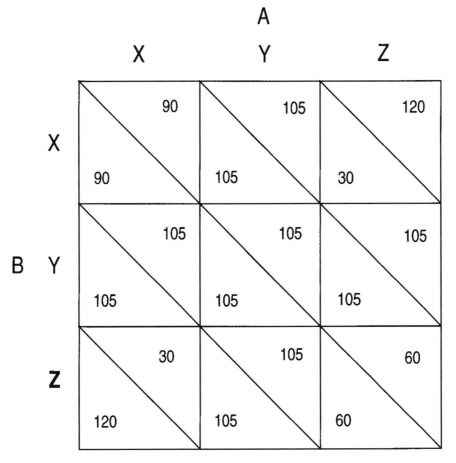

Figure 20.2   A PDG-Alt matrix

The greed hypothesis depends on two processes: first, the belief that the opponent is vulnerable to exploitation; and, second, social support for acting in accordance with immediate self-interest to take advantage of the opponent. On the other hand, the fear hypothesis depends only on the belief that the opponent is dangerous. Social support is not necessary for the occurrence of defensive competitiveness because reciprocal competitiveness is consistent with both short- and long-term self-interest, as well as with norms of reciprocity, equality, and equity. To provide a further test of these hypotheses, the fourth study placed role players in the groups, and arranged for the role players to be the group representatives (Schopler et al. 1993, Experiment 2). Because it was the group representatives who met in the center room, the use of role players as representatives allowed for the ready manipulation of the other group's apparent choices, which were portrayed as consistently cooperative, consistently competitive, or mixed. A second independent variable related to the suggestions that the role players made to their fellow group members regarding the choices that the group should make. These suggestions were either always cooperative or always competitive. Suggestion was intended as a manipulation of social support and feedback was intended as a manipulation of the vulnerability or dangerousness of the opponent. Our hypotheses predicted an interaction between these two variables, and that is exactly what happened. In the context of a cooperative and vulnerable opponent, social support had a large effect on group behavior; but, in the context of a competitive and dangerous opponent, social support had a significantly smaller effect.

The fifth study was a follow-up of the fourth (Schopler et al., 1993, Experiment 3). This study added a no-suggestion condition to the competitive and cooperative suggestion levels of the social support variable, and was conducted with just cooperative feedback. No suggestion and competitive suggestion groups did not differ in competitive choices, but both showed significantly higher levels of competition when compared to groups that had experienced a cooperative suggestion. This pattern of results is consistent with the assumption that, in the presence of a vulnerable opponent, participants themselves provide social support for exploitation. Suggestion from a role player is not necessary. This tendency can be contravened, however, by the introduction of social support for cooperation.

The sixth study had two purposes (Insko et al., 1993). One purpose was to explore the hypothesis that the high (90 to 95%) cooperation rates found between individuals in our research differs from the much lower rates characteristic of findings in the traditional PDG literature at least partially because we have allowed direct trial by trial communication between participants. The other purpose was to test two predictions flowing from the fear and greed hypotheses relating to the interaction of groups versus individuals and communication versus no communication. The first prediction is a fairly direct implication of the outgroup schema. Given that groups tend not to trust each other, it follows that communication between them should be of low credibility and, whether or not they communicate with each other, should have less effect than whether or not individuals communicate with each other. Stated more simply, groups should tend to distrust each other's stated intentions to a greater extent than should individuals. Thus the first prediction was that communication would increase cooperation between individuals more than cooperation between groups. But given that individuals who do not communicate tend not to trust each other and do not cooperate, what should they do? On a PDG matrix, of course, they would have no alternative but to compete. However, on a PDG-Alt matrix they could conceivably either compete or withdraw. Our second prediction was that they would withdraw. Stated more formally, the second prediction was that a lack of communication would increase withdrawal more for individuals than for groups. The rationale for the prediction is quite simple. According to our greed hypothesis, without social support the competitive response is unlikely to occur because it runs counter to existing norms concerning equality and reciprocity. Stated more simply, since individuals lack social support from fellow group members, they are unlikely to compete because of the concern that such behavior would be judged unfair and greedy. Both predictions were supported. Communication increased cooperation for individuals to a greater extent than for groups, and a lack of communication increased withdrawal to a greater extent for individuals than for groups. It was also found that communication increased the expectation of cooperation, particularly if the opponent was an individual—thereby supporting the trust mediation hypothesis.

The seventh study (Schopler et al., 1995) provided support for the hypothesized mediation of discontinuity by the individual anonymity (or nonidentifiability) inherent in group decisions. In this experiment individual group members anticipated reporting their preferences, or votes, for one of the three PDG-Alt choices to the experimenter over an intercom when each participant was called by his or her first name. In the identified condition the group members anticipated that their individual votes would be overheard by the other group, whereas in the nonidentified condition the group members anticipated that their votes only would be heard by the experimenter (and, of course, own group members). Consistent with the identifiability interpretation, identified groups made fewer competitive choices and more cooperative choices. A variety of assessments, including some obtained by the coding of tape recorded discussions, provided evidence for the fear and greed interpretations.

Floyd Allport (1924) argued that the relationship of the individual and the group is the master problem of social psychology. We believe that we have contributed to progress in the study of this problem by exploring both the robustness of the discontinuity effect and the mechanisms responsible for its occurrence.

THE REDUCTION OF DISCONTINUITY

Even a brief review of the historical background of discontinuity makes it clear that many early thinkers such as Schiller and LeBon did not hold very high opinions of groups and, by implication, of intergroup relations. It is, of course, abundantly clear that in some contexts intergroup relations are unfortunate and even tragic. This conclusion is buttressed by the survey results reported by Farrington, Berkowitz, and West (1982). These investigators interviewed 389 youths who were asked to give accounts of fights. When the descriptions were categorized by whether they were individual or group fights, the expected differences emerged. Group fights were significantly more likely to involve weapons (40% vs. 15%), to create injuries (54% vs. 32%), and to involve police intervention (24% vs. 4%). Beyond this, if it is true that prejudice is better understood as a problem between groups than between individuals, it is clear that an understanding of procedures for reducing discontinuity would be highly desirable.

As we have noted elsewhere (Schopler & Insko, 1992) there are two distinct research traditions that address overcoming ingroup ethnocentrism. There is an older literature that tended to specify remedial interventions in terms of interactive behavior between two groups. These interactive behaviors differed in various ways, but especially in terms of the comprehensiveness of the behavior. At one extreme were such global recommendations as joint interactions to attain superordinate goals (Sherif, Harvey, White, Hood & Sherif, 1961) while at the other extreme were the specific behavioral rules contained in Osgood's (1962) graduated and reciprocated initiatives in tension-reduction (GRIT). The newer literature focuses on the cognitive mechanisms presumed to be antecedents to intergroup bias, and seems to vary with respect to the directness with which the intervention affects relevant cognitions. The most direct methods are those that degrade the categorized representation by such methods as recategorization (Gaertner, Mann, Dovidio, Murrell & Pomare, 1990; Gaertner, Dovidio, Anastasio, Bachman & Rust, 1993) or criss-crossing category membership (Brewer, Ho, Lee & Miller, 1987). With the exception of modeling GRIT (e.g., Lindskold, 1983), both traditions tested for a reduction in ethnocentrism with measures of individual perceptions of ingroup and outgroup members. To our knowledge no one has attempted to assess whether the intervention was successful in increasing such behaviors as intergroup cooperation. The recent ethnic strife in Eastern Europe provides obvious reasons why, as Messick and Mackie (1989) state, degrading the category may not always be possible or even desirable. We believe the ultimate effectiveness of any technique resides in its ability to create intergroup cooperation between intact groups.

Two Failures

We have come to this point of view only after pilot testing some recategorization procedures that were spectacular failures. The pilot studies began with the formation of four 3-person groups, who were subsequently combined into two rivalrous 6-person groups or, in a different version, two, independent, 6-person groups each working cooperatively on a task. The recategorization worked as expected in terms of increasing liking for former outgroup members and creating satisfactory working relations with them. The problem arose when we regrouped participants into their initial 3-person groups and asked them to interact on a PDG with another group, composed of previous group members. In these circumstances their rate of competition was just as large as the rate for groups whose members were never recategorized. All of which makes us suspect that if, at the end of camp, Sherif and his associates (Sherif et al., 1961) had put the Eagles and Rattlers into a mixed-motive situation they would have been just as competitive as at the height of their tournament. Quite possibly Sherif and others have underestimated the power of the social setting.

Discontinuity Reduction Via Concern for Future Outcomes

We have completed two studies that address the important matter of the reduction of discontinuity (Insko, et al. 1998). Both of these studies were inspired by Axelrod's (1984) book, *The Evolution of Cooperation*. In this book Axelrod argues that the social situation confronting the Allied and German troops on the Western front in World War I was described accurately by the PDG (see p. 75), Furthermore, and of particular interest from the standpoint of reducing intergroup conflict, Axelrod cites extensive documentary evidence (Ashworth, 1980) that in sector after sector of the front lines the troops ceased to fight with each other, despite orders to the contrary by the commanding officers. The troops, for example, fired over each other's heads, or shelled only certain safe targets at certain times of the day.

Axelrod's (1984) interpretation of the troops' behavior is that the permanence of the front lines led to an enlarging of the "shadow of the future" (p. 126) or to an understanding of the long-term mutual benefits of reciprocal cooperation. Quoting directly: "What made this mutual restraint possible was the static nature of trench warfare, where the small units faced each other for extended periods of time" (p. 21). Taken at face value this idea suggests that there should be a difference on the first trial if we compared groups and individuals who knew that trial was the only trial with groups and individuals who anticipated playing additional trials. We have never conducted such an experiment, but we have conducted experiments in which the participants have known there was to be only one trial and experiments in which participants anticipated playing multiple trials, and our impression is that anticipated playing of only one trial leads to increased competitiveness, particularly for groups. On the other hand, it is obvious that anticipating additional trials is no panacea for inducing mutual cooperation. It is clear from numerous investigations that the level of competitiveness is still very high when groups anticipate playing, and in fact do play, additional trials.

Still, we suspect that Axelrod's (1984) emphasis on future consequences is correct. It is just that something else—something other than the anticipation of extended interaction—is involved. A crucial aspect of that something else may be that the troops apparently engaged in reciprocal behavior that was not a pure form of tit for tat. Axelrod is very explicit about avoiding a "narrow focus on a pure tit for tat strategy" (p. 61). He states that "the strategy was not necessarily tit for tat. Sometimes it was two for one" (p. 60), and then goes on to cite evidence that in the French sector at least two shots were always fired for one. Axelrod does argue that the two for one strategy has two obvious similarities with tit for tat: first, both strategies are nice in the sense that neither is ever the first to compete (or defect); second, they both retaliate after a competing (or defecting) response by the opponent.

Tit for tat appeals to us as an interesting procedure for creating trust without at the same time making one's self (or group) totally vulnerable to exploitation by the opponent and also of stimulating the opponent to consider the future consequences of one's choice. Nowak and Sigmund (1993), however, have run computer simulations over many trials, with some built in randomness, and report that tit for tat did not endure. Instead an alternative strategy, which they call Pavlov, emerged as stable. Pavlov is a direct application of Kelley, Thibaut, Radloff, and Mundy's (1962) *win stay-lose change* strategy. According to this strategy a player wins (and stays with the previous response) after receiving either of the two highest outcomes and loses (and changes the previous response) after receiving either of the two worst outcomes. Using the outcome array in Figure 20.1 as an example, each player would stay with the previous response if it produced an outcome of 90 or 120 and would change if the outcome was 30 or 60. Other investigations of Pavlov, or win stay-lose change, who do not find it particularly robust are by Kraines and Kraines (1989, 1993, 1995), Wu and Axelrod (1995), and Messick and Liebrand (1995).

The importance of a future orientation in mediating a reciprocal strategy has also been emphasized by Parks and Komorita (1997). Based on their computer simulation of the survival of reciprocal strategies in large groups, they state: "We would predict that a person with a long-term outlook will be more likely to adopt a reciprocal strategy than those with a short-term outlook, an easily testable proposition" (p. 321). Although we concur with the prediction, its testability has posed some difficulties. Recall that Parks and Komorita have extended to large groups what was typically found for smaller units in what are essentially intragroup simulations. The prediction should, thus, apply with equal force to interindividual or intergroup interactions in mixed-motive settings. How then is this relevant for reducing the discontinuity effect by increasing intergroup cooperation? It is our speculation that the key revolves around the conditions that build credibility and trust. With our set of operations, particularly prior communication before making an irrevocable choice, interindividual interactions create credibility and trust through communication. Thus, fear of being suckered by responding cooperatively is minimized and high rates of cooperation are obtained, whether or not there is future interaction. As previously mentioned, prior communication between groups does not build credibility or trust (Insko, et al., 1993). Attributions about the other group are made primarily on the basis of prior choices and outcomes. It will be easier for a group to risk making a cooperative response if it is assured of future interactions because it will then be possible to reciprocate defections as well as cooperation. Thus, the long-term outlook is essential for intergroup cooperation, but not for interindividual cooperation.

Two between-participant variables were important in our first experiment. These were a three level strategy factor including a tit for tat condition, a Pavlov condition, and a normal, control condition which were crossed with a groups versus individuals variable. In the tit for tat and Pavlov conditions the participants (groups or individuals) played against an opponent who followed one of the specified strategies.

A three factor analysis of variance for the proportion of competitive choices resulted in a significant main effect for groups versus individuals, a significant main effect for strategy, and a significant groups versus individuals by strategy interaction. The means for the relevant conditions are displayed in Table 20.1. Combining all strategies, groups were more competitive than individuals, and, combining groups and individuals, the most competition occurred in the Pavlov condition, and the least occurred in the tit for tat condition.

Table 20.1 Mean proportions of competitive choices in experiment 1.

Pavlov		Tit for Tat		Control	
Groups	Individuals	Groups	Individuals	Groups	Individuals
.41	.17	.08	.16	.28	.09

Note: Proportions were calculated over 15 trials.

Both of these main effects were qualified by the interaction. The results indicated that the tendency of groups to be more competitive than individuals was reduced in the tit for tat condition relative to the Pavlov and control conditions. Within the tit for tat condition the discontinuity effect was, in fact, nonsignificantly reversed in direction. The differences, however, were totally in the groups condition. Tit for tat virtually eliminated the tendency for groups to compete. We regard this result as very significant.

Why did the groups become less competitive? We believe that it is because the tit for tat procedure focused concern on long-term outcomes, or to use Axelrod's (1984) phrase, increased the shadow of the future. The basic idea is straightforward. Note that in the context of a single trial each player is better off competing if the other player cooperates and is also better off competing if the other player competes. In the long run, however, both players will be worse off if they each compete than if they each cooperate. Thus the adoption of a future orientation reduces competitiveness, and facing a tit for tat opponent directs attention to the future consequences of an immediate own choice. Coding of post-experimental responses to a question regarding the reason for past choices indeed indicated a greater tendency, for groups in the tit for tat condition, to make statements having to do with the consequences of their own choices.

The second experiment investigated another procedure that theoretically should have focused attention on the consequences of one's choices—a comparison of the usual simultaneous responding with successive responding and strict turn taking. The successive turn taking procedure is one in which the opponents (groups or individuals) take turns responding first with the understanding that the opponent who responds second will learn of the other side's choice before making a choice. Such a procedure makes it apparent that regardless as to whether one responds first or second it is functional to think about the opponent's subsequent choice.

There is an interesting connection between the possible role of successive responding and Axelrod's (1984) discussion of World War I trench warfare. We began by arguing that, while we agreed with Axelrod's shadow of the future interpretation, we did not believe that the simple knowledge of additional trials was sufficient to have a large impact on competitiveness. Something else was involved. In the World War I situation that something else, if not strict tit for tat, was something much like tit for tat. We now make the further observation that something else beyond even tit for tat was involved. That something else, if not strict successive turn taking, was something much like successive turn taking. Axelrod's recounting of events suggests that much of the responding was successive. He, in fact, referred to the echoing of one side by the other. Of course, if actual fighting broke out, quite likely what began as successive quickly became simultaneous.

The second experiment compared simultaneous responding with successive responding, groups versus individuals, and gender of participant in a session (all male or all female). In addition to a main effect for groups versus individuals, there was an interaction with successive versus simultaneous responding such that the tendency of groups to be more competitive was less (by half) with successive than with simultaneous responding. It is interesting that the tendency for less competitiveness with successive responding was present on the very first trial—even for the group that responded first. A direct assessment indeed indicated that participants were more likely to think ahead with successive than with simultaneous responding.

The violent resolution of intergroup conflict has plagued the world for all of known history. The major focus of the present chapter was identifying ways to increase cooperativeness in intergroup interactions. By contrasting the consequences that occur when someone is behaving as part of a group, compared to behaving as an individual, we have previously established a clear discontinuity. That is, using a mixed-motive paradigm and face to face interaction, repeated group-on-group interactions typically produce high rates of competition, whereas interactions of two people from those groups are typically characterized by high rates of cooperation. Such discontinuity occurs even though competition yields worse results than mutual cooperation. Two techniques designed to increase intergroup cooperation were assessed in two separate experiments. Experiment 1 reduced discontinuity with a tit for tat strategy (versus other strategies), while the reduction in Experiment 2 occurred by successive (versus simultaneous) responding. The results are interpreted as being mediated by the induction of a concern for the future.

Chapter 21

Interdependence, the Group, and Social Cooperation: A New Look at an Old Problem

Brenda Morrison

INTRODUCTION

People are sustained and divided by the many interdependencies that define their social relations. We belong to many groups and categories including gender, occupation, ethnic, and national identities. It seems reasonable to assume that individuals will feel interdependent with different social groups at different times. How can we best understand the dynamics of these interdependencies and how they relate to cooperation and competition within and among social groups? These questions are important in order to an understand social dilemmas, which pose a conflict not only between individual and group, but between different groups. The focus of this chapter is an examination of the conceptual relationship between interdependence, the group, and cooperation, three important constructs in the analysis of social dilemmas.

Through the work of students of Kurt Lewin, the relationship between these constructs has been conceptualized as follows: *cooperation* among *interdependent* individuals produces the *group*. Functional interdependence and a common fate are seen to be the necessary preconditions for group formation, arising through acts of cooperation. This will be termed the *functional interdependence* position (e.g. Deutsch, 1949; Thibaut &

Kelley, 1959). On the other hand, self-categorization theory (Turner, Hogg, Oakes, Reicher, & Wetherell, 1987) states that the psychological salience of the *group* is the necessary precondition for perceived *interdependence* and *cooperation*. This will be termed the *social identity* position. Does interdependence produce the group or is the group the basis of interdependence? Does cooperation arise as a product of the functional interdependence of individuals or the psychological salience of the group?

This chapter does not aim to answer these questions in any definitive sense. Good work has been done within each framework. The purpose of this chapter is to provide a brief summary of the social psychological literature that defines the relationship between interdependence and the group in terms of these two perspectives: functional interdependence and social identity. The social dilemma literature, central to the study of social cooperation, will provide a common context for the examination of the conceptual relationship between interdependence, group salience, and cooperation. Finally, the results of a field study are reported, in which functional interdependence was held constant and psychological salience of group boundaries was varied, in an attempt to demonstrate the effect of such variable salience on levels of cooperation, as well as on perceptions of interdependence, and shared values and needs.

Lewin (1939, 1952) stated that "It is not similarity but a certain interdependence of fate that constitutes a group" (p. 147). This theme has been taken up by researchers in the development of interdependence theory (Deutsch, 1949; Kelley, 1984a; Thibaut & Kelley, 1959; Rusbult & Van Lange, 1996; Johnson & Johnson, 1998).

INTERDEPENDENCE THEORY

Kelley (1997) recently stated:

> Interdependence theory is cast in the broad formula stated by Kurt Lewin (1946), that behavior is a function of the person and the environment. Because we are interested in interaction, the theory must include at least two persons (A and B) and, on the behavior side, their interaction. The environment is described in terms of situations of interdependence, hence the label for the theory. The property of interdependence, which was Lewin's (1951) prime candidate for the essential features of groups, simply means that each situation specifies ways in which one or both persons are dependent on (under control of) the other with respect to outcomes, movement, or both. The theory identifies the kinds of interpersonal dispositions . . . relevant to each situation. Then, the dispositions of A and B, together with the situation, are assumed to determine their interaction. (p. 144)

Thus, behavior is predicted to be a function of the objective outcome interdependence structure that defines the situation and the transformational processes brought to the situation by individuals. The functional interdependence of individuals is central to this analysis because all individuals are socially (and thus functionally) *interdependent* with respect to the amount of control each individual has over the outcomes received. The core assumption is that individuals are motivated to maximize their *subjective* utility within the specified interdependence structure.

The interdependence model makes use of the structure and properties of a 2×2 ANOVA model: two individuals make a choice between two alternatives. While the theory is formally based on this simple 2×2 model, its principles are applied to interactions within larger groups of individuals as well as to intergroup behavior.

The given interdependence structure can take many forms: positive interdependence (players outcomes are aligned, suggesting cooperative relations); negative interdependence (players outcomes are antagonistic, suggesting competitive relations) and mixed motive interdependence (players outcomes are both aligned and antagonistic; e.g. prisoner's dilemma, chicken, and leader and trust game structures). The alternatives open to each player, and the outcomes associated with them, are represented in the form of matrix games (see glossary definition of social dilemmas).

It is further assumed that individuals transform the objective (or given) matrix into a subjective (or effective) matrix. Subjective utility is gauged by the transformed outcomes rather than the objective outcomes. It differs from economic models in its claim that subjective utility includes as a variable weighted outcomes to other(s) as well as to self, where the weightings are construed as individual differences in situations of interdependence. It is now understood that transformational processes of individuals account for the variance in behavior that the outcome structure on its own cannot. The most widely studied, and understood, transformational factor has been individuals' social value orientations (to be reviewed below) but others have also been distinguished.

Rusbult and Van Lange (1996) have proposed two motivational categories of transformational tendencies: distal and proximal. Distal determinants include interpersonal dispositions, relationship macromotives and social norms which are embodied in stable interpersonal orientations. Proximal determinants include cognitive interpretations and emotional reactions that underlie self-presentation. The transformed matrix, termed the effective matrix, is assumed to be more closely aligned to individuals' actual behaviors in situations of interdependence

Given the importance of individual variables in the transformation of the given outcome matrix, much attention has been directed to understanding the orientation that individuals bring to situations. Using decomposed games, Messick and McClintock (1968) developed the first measures of these three orientations originally identified by Deutsch (1949). Griesinger and Livingston (1973) developed a continuous measure based on vectors in a two-dimensional space defined by the weights placed on one's own and others' interests. The measurement of social value orientations is now a dominant tool in interdependence research, the assumption being that within any given context, the expression of a particular value orientation remains relatively stable over time (Kuhlman, Camac, & Cunha, 1986; McClintock, 1978; McClintock & Liebrand, 1988; McClintock & Allison, 1989; Van Lange, de Bruin, Otten, & Joireman, 1997). In summary, interdependence theory acknowledges the importance of both the outcome interdependence structure of groups and the transformational processes of individuals in understanding human decision making and behavior. While it admits the importance of relations with others in the calculation of utility for cooperative and competitive actions, it still places primary emphasis on the nature of the structure of interdependence in which the individuals are located.

Interdependence theorists have also been influenced by game theory, (Luce & Raiffa, 1957; Von Neumann & Morgenstern, 1944) because, as Deutsch put it:

> Game theory has made a major contribution to social scientists by formulating in mathematical terms a problem which is central to the various social sciences: the problem of conflict of interests. . . . its core emphasis [being] that the parties in conflict have interdependent interests, that their fates are woven together. (1980, p. 61)

For interdependence theorists, game theory represented a formal and systematic approach to the study of conflicts of interest, where individuals are outcome interdependent. The fact that the interdependence structure could be systematically specified and manipulated was compelling. The gaming paradigm flourished in the 1960s and 70s, with an early review estimating that over 1,000 published studies were done in this time (Pruitt & Kimmel, 1977). This work has been significantly influential in the study of conflict, cooperation, and social dilemmas. Following this tradition, the structure of social dilemmas was formalized by Dawes (1975, 1980). The emphasis on outcome interdependence remains evident in his definition:

> [Dilemmas] are defined by two simple properties: (a) each individual receives a higher payoff for a socially defecting choice (e.g. having additional children, using all the energy available, polluting his or her neighbours) than for a socially co-operative choice, no matter what the other individuals in society do, but (b) all individuals are better off if all cooperate than if all defect. (Dawes, 1980, p. 169)

Social Dilemmas and Cooperation

The best known game is the 2-person prisoner's dilemma (see glossary). This game has a mixed motive structure and is taken from the early work of Luce and Raiffa (1957). The scenario has the following structure. A district attorney has two felons in custody. While she is unable to prove their guilt for a major robbery, she can provide evidence for a minor offense. Holding the two felons in separate rooms, she tempts each of them to confess to the major robbery for a lesser conviction. If neither confesses both will get a light sentence. If one confesses, and the other doesn't, the one that confesses will get off for turning state's evidence while the other will get a heavy sentence. However, if they both confess the payoff is worse than if they both keep quiet. Hence the dilemma; mutual individual rationality, which would seek to minimize the sentence, leads to collectively worse outcomes—both get a heavier sentence.

In experiments studying these mixed motive settings, competition is indeed more common than cooperation. This finding has lead researchers to try to identify factors that increase cooperation in these situations. Interdependence theory and the related "goal-expectation" (Pruitt & Kimmel, 1977) approach suggest there will be factors that somehow affect the subjectively expected utility of cooperative and competitive choices. For example, variables which affect the *expectations* that others will cooperate—such as communication with other group members, or a binding commitment to cooperate—will also affect levels of cooperation (Bouas & Komorita, 1996; Dawes, McTavish, & Shaklee, 1977).

Social value orientations alter the objective outcomes, because one's own *utility* is a weighted combination of one's own and others' outcomes. Thus, cooperators will gain greater Subjectively Expected Utility (SEU) from a joint cooperative choice, while competitors will estimate the SEU of competition to be higher. There is some evidence that shared group membership also increases the value of joint gain (Kramer & Goldman, 1995). The incorporation of others' interests in the calculations of one's own utility sets the interdependence approach apart from strict economic utility maximization, but there is still a general acceptance of the assumption that this (modified) individual utility is the fundamental unit of analysis.

A recent meta-analysis by Sally (1995) found 23 independent variables that accounted for cooperation. These variables fell into several broad categories: content of experimenters' instructions to participants (e.g. cooperate/compete, maximize individual/collective gain); participants' anonymity; salient group identification; communication between participants; monetary compensation for playing; and whether participants were economists. The relevant point is that many of these variables are examples of the *tranformational* influences identified by interdependence theorists as those which determine the final outcome matrix affecting participants' decisions to cooperate or compete. In the final analysis, however, this approach assumes that cooperation, and group formation, occur when individuals perceive their own fates to be intertwined with those of others. Changes toward greater cooperation will occur only when there are changes in the effective outcome matrix.

Sherif's Field Studies

Sherif's (1966) summer camp studies of intergroup rivalry and group cooperation provide a bridge between the interdependence and social identity approaches. In this well known field research, boys attending a summer camp were formed into groups who were initially isolated from each other, and within which a strong group identity developed. When placed in contact with one another, the task and goal interdependence of the groups was arranged so that rivalry and competition were encouraged through zero-sum games. Attitudes towards the ingroup became more positive, and those toward the outgroup more negative; ingroup bias in judgments was evident. In a final stage, a common threat to both groups was created. Cooperation between the groups emerged to overcome the threat and reach a superordinate goal. In terms of interdependence theory, cooperative behavior occurred because the outcome matrix changed: the imposition of a superordinate goal that had "a compelling appeal for members of each group, but that neither group can achieve without the participation of the other" (Sherif, 1966, p. 89).

    While Sherif emphasized common fate, he also drew attention to the cognitive processes of comparison and contrast:

> . . . the mere awareness of other groups within the range of our desires generates a process of comparison between "us" and the others. This tendency seems to be one of the fundamental facts in the psychology of judgment. Through this comparison process, we evaluate and categorize other groupings of people, comparing them with our notions of ourselves, our conceptions of our place in life and the places of others. (Sherif, 1966, p. 3)

The question taken up by Tajfel, Flament, Billig, & Bundy (1971) was whether group formation and intergroup relations were the result of the correspondence of outcomes (see Glossary), or whether they had a causal role in determining the perceived interdependence structure.

SOCIAL IDENTITY TRADITION

The social identity tradition rejects individualistic theories of human nature. This theoretical perspective aims to account for the underlying psychological processes that contribute to the emergent properties of individual and group life (Tajfel, 1972; Tajfel & Turner, 1979, 1986; Turner, 1975). Tajfel was intrigued (Tajfel, 1970; Tajfel et al., 1971) by the findings of Sherif's summer camp studies. Specifically, Tajfel was interested in rethinking the process by which ingroup morale developed, and how it was related to negative evaluations of the outgroup and rivalrous behavior between the groups. The starting point for a line of research was to examine the minimal conditions needed to generate intergroup phenomena.

The *minimal group paradigm* requires participants to allocate resources to members of two arbitrary, completely unknown groups with no prior history of interaction or reward dependence (Tajfel et al., 1971). When groups were stripped down and chosen by arbitrary means, participants still discriminated in favor of their ingroup. This occurred despite the lack of group goals (such as an objective current conflict of interests between groups), personal reward (that may lead to a simple assertion of individual self-interest for instrumental gain), history of hostility between groups, and face to face interaction. This surprising "empty situation" (Tajfel, 1972, p. 298) of intergroup behavior established the importance of social categorization as a primary psychological process.

These findings from the minimal group studies remain significant as the results indicated a seemingly deliberate strategy of ingroup favoritism under these minimal conditions. Tajfel and colleagues (1971) concluded that: "Social categorization is not just an 'organizing principle' used in the absence of other guideposts; it is capable of creating deliberate discriminatory behavior" (pp. 162–163). Tajfel and colleagues concluded that the results:

> . . . also point to the possibility that discriminatory intergroup behaviour cannot be fully understood if it is considered solely in terms of an 'objective' conflict of interests or in terms of deep-seated motives that it may serve. . . . The crucial aspect of this situation was that it contained a socially derived and discontinuous categorization of people into an in-group and an out-group. (p. 176)

The psychological reality of the group membership brings distinct social meaning and significance to the perceiver, and these social identities bring a unique understanding to the nature of intergroup relations. *A social identity is conceptualized as the psychological link between the self and the collective that emerges through the psychological process of categorization.* As stated by Tajfel (1978), social identity is "that part of an individual's self-concept which derives from his knowledge of his membership of a social group (or groups) together with the value and emotional significance attached to that membership" (p. 63). This analysis later became social identity theory (Tajfel & Turner, 1979, 1986), which provides a theoretical explanation for behavior in the minimal group paradigm. The basic hypothesis is "that pressures to evaluate one's own group positively through in-group/out-group comparisons lead social groups to attempt to differentiate themselves from each other" (Tajfel & Turner, 1986, p. 16; see also Tajfel, 1978; Turner, 1975). There are three defining classes of variables that are important to this analysis: (1) categorization, (2) identification, and (3) social comparison. The conclusion was drawn that *social categorization* of oneself, even in terms of a minimal group, led to an *identification* process that resulted in *intergroup comparisons* which were self-evaluative and thus became the basis for social competition.

Social competition, as exhibited by participants in these studies, is conceptually different from instrumental (zero-sum) cooperation and competition. In other words, social cooperation and competition *arise* out of the perceived intergroup situation; they do not create intergroup cooperation or intergroup conflict and identification. Objective goals are not absolute ends in themselves, they are relative and emerge in terms of relevant social comparisons that are based on social identifications that reflect social structure. Thus, social behavior is not based on individuals' motivations to attain absolute or instrumental ends, as the economic self-interest model would argue. The minimal group findings suggest that social categorization, per se, can provide a sufficient basis for the psychological reality of group formation (while not denying the importance of other group level processes).

The Continuum Model of the Self

As a theory of intergroup behavior it was important to make a qualitative distinction between group-based behavior and interindividual behavior. Tajfel (1981) suggested a continuum model with each pole representing one of these extremes. All behavior at the interindividual level was seen to be determined by interpersonal relationships, and all behavior at the intergroup level was determined by intergroup relationships. However, Tajfel (1981) argued that "one of these extremes—the interpersonal one—is absurd, in the sense that no instance of it can conceivably be found in 'real life' " (p. 240). To some degree, an interpersonal encounter (even within the most familiar relationships) will be determined by the various mutual social groups to which the individuals belong. For social identity theory, the emphasis was on the real social implications that arose from categorizing a person at an intergroup level of abstraction, vis-a-vis an interpersonal level.

Building on this early work by Tajfel and colleagues, Turner (1981) and Worchel (1979) did some early work on *decreasing* the salience of intergroup boundaries to promote intergroup cooperation. Turner (1985) concluded that "whereas interdependence theory states that positive interdependence leads to cooperation, which in turn leads to the formation of a psychological group, the evidence implies that psychological group formation may be the necessary intervening process before objective interdependence can be transformed into cooperative activity" (p. 88). The conclusion is that social cooperation does not arise in any straightforward way from the pursuit of individual self-interest. With the development of self categorization theory, Turner and colleagues stated: "instead of social cooperation producing the group, it may well be that, psychologically, the group is the basis of cooperation" (Turner et al., 1987, p. 34). Individual interests become collective interests through the transformation of the self along the continuum between individual and collective life. We cooperate with others included in our self-definition.

Social Identity and Social Dilemmas

There are mixed findings as to the role of social identification within the social dilemma literature. The work of Dawes and colleagues provides a good example of the increasing interest in the role of identity processes in social dilemmas (Dawes, McTavish, & Shaklee, 1977; Dawes, Van de Kragt, & Orbell, 1990; Tyler & Dawes, 1993). These authors concluded that: "developing a group's identity is central to willingness to act in the group's interest rather than one's own. The key psychological question is why this effect occurs. Is group membership important because groups provide their members with a sense of social identity, or are groups important because they provide resources?" (Tyler & Dawes, p. 93).

Brewer's work represents the most systematic approach to applying a social identity analysis to the understanding of social dilemmas (e.g. Brewer & Schneider, 1990). This work is closely tied to Brewer's analysis of the social self (e.g. Brewer & Gardner, 1996). As they state: "Central to this new perspective is the idea that connectedness and belonging are not merely affiliations or alliances between self and others but entail fundamental differences in the way the self is construed" (Brewer & Gardner, p. 83). Given this variability of the self, Brewer (1991) postulated, "when the definition of self changes, the meaning of self-interest and self-serving motivations also change accordingly" (p. 476).

Brewer and Kramer (1986) and Kramer and Brewer (1984) provided evidence that by making a superordinate category membership salient, higher levels of cooperation were obtained in a deteriorating resource dilemma, than when subgroup boundaries were salient (the intergroup condition), or only individual identities were focused on. These effects occurred despite the fact that the actual interdependence structure of the dilemma was the same across the categorization conditions.

The work reported below examines the contextual aspects of social identity processes more closely. The study shows support for the prediction that social cooperation may a be product of a salient social identity. Recall that interdependence theorists argue that *objective interdependence* is the necessary and sufficient precondition for social cooperation to ensue between individuals. In contrast, the following field study examined whether a *salient group membership* is the basis for social cooperation and perceived interdependence with others.

Experimental Field Study

The study reported here examines social cooperation within a field setting, where a social dilemma was established. The objective interdependence that created the social dilemma was held constant, and the salience of social identities that made up the objective state of affairs was manipulated across conditions. The study tests the prediction that level of cooperation is the product of a salient social identity and that the emergence of a psychological group transcends the objective interdependence structure that defines the social dilemma. Further, the salience of the psychological group is then predicted to *define the interdependence with others that is perceived by the individual.*

The salience of a psychological group is in part determined by the contextual frame of reference (see Oakes, Haslam, & Turner, 1994). Identity salience was systematically varied in this study through manipulating the comparative frame of reference (e.g., social comparison based on provincial, regional, or national identification). An important aspect of this study is that it utilizes mutually inclusive frames of reference (provinces within regions; regions within a nation). Given that the objective interdependence structure was held constant, it was possible to examine the effects of varying the comparative frame of reference on levels of cooperation and perceptions of similarity and interdependence with others. Any variation in cooperation must then be due to the variation in inclusiveness of identification, since it cannot be due to differences in levels of objective functional interdependence. Perceptions of similarity, as well as shared needs and values, were also predicted to vary with identity salience. Expectations of other's levels of cooperation were also examined; it was predicted that others included in the same self-category of membership would be expected to act in the same cooperative manner.

METHOD

The identity salience of 135 Papua New Guineans was manipulated in the context of an environmental social dilemma. Given that self-interest is argued to vary on a continuum between individual and collective level of identification, the following identifications are possible. At the individual level any one of the participants in this study could define themselves as a unique individual, differentiating themselves from others on many relevant dimensions. Yet, these same individuals could also define themselves in terms of relevant collective similarities with others who were members of various geographical areas. As well as being a unique individual, each participant could be defined in terms of three increasingly inclusive identities: provincial, regional, and national. Each participant shared with some other individual in the sample one of 19 provincial identities; at the next level of abstraction, each participant also shared a regional identity, which is geographically inclusive of the provincial area but not definitive of this area; and still more inclusively, they shared their national identity as Papua New Guineans.

In Papua New Guinea (PNG), each region contains four to five provinces, and the nation is made up of four regions. Within each of these three levels of abstraction of identity, both intragroup and intergroup cooperation were measured. *Intragroup* cooperation is defined as cooperation with other ingroup members, whatever the level of inclusiveness of the category. *Intergroup* cooperation is defined as cooperation with relevant outgroup members. At each salient level of abstraction of the self, intragroup, and intergroup cooperation were measured; that is, cooperation was measured *within* and *between* the three levels of social identification manipulated: provincial, regional, and national. These six comparisons make up the six conditions of this study. Cooperation was examined using three dependent measures; participants' levels of intended cooperation, participants' expectations of ingroup members levels of cooperation, and participants' expectations of outgroup members levels of cooperation. The essence of the dilemma was based on a conflict of interest between the individual and the collective. The collective was represented by a nameless nonprofit environmental agency asking for voluntary assistance in a project to protect the rainforest from a noxious insect that was destroying the forest. This agency either represented a comparative ingroup or an outgroup. If the participant volunteered to assist they would join an expedition team in which they would spend a number of days in the dense rainforest locating and destroying the insects. Participants were asked to volunteer for this project during their limited holiday time during their midyear holiday back in PNG, a time the participants looked forward to spending with their families and friends after their studies in Australia. The dilemma was thus structured in terms of their personal interests in spending time with family and friends versus the interest of protecting the rainforest for the collective.

As previously mentioned, this design allows interesting comparisons to be made, given that the four regions could also be objectively defined by the provinces that make them up and that the nation could be defined by the four regions. Thus, the same geographical areas can be objectively defined in two different ways. For example, the area that is not shaded in Figure 21.1 may be defined in two ways: as the region Momase or the four provinces Morobe, Madang, East Sepik, and West Sepik (Sandaun). Either way they define the same objective area. Thus for a given resource dilemma, the problem could be defined as affecting these four provinces, or the region as a whole.

This enabled the comparison of *provincial intergroup* cooperation (between a number of subordinate groups) with *regional intragroup* cooperation (within a larger superordinate group), given that independently these make up the same objectively defined geographic area. Likewise, *regional intergroup* cooperation was compared with *national intragroup* cooperation.

The following experimental predictions were made: a main effect for frame of reference (intragroup or intergroup) at all three levels of abstraction, with intragroup cooperation being predicted to be greater than intergroup cooperation in each case. The same pattern of results was expected when the participants were predicting what they expected other ingroup members to do, given that, in line with self-categorization theory, they would be expected to be perceived as interchangeable perceptions of self. For example, when the

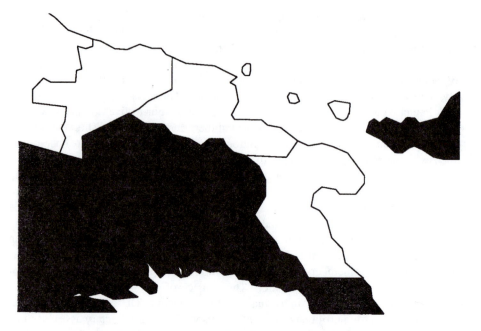

Figure 21.1   Madang, Morobe, East Sepik, and West Sepik (Sandaun)

Momase regional identity was salient, participants would expect the people of Momase to be very willing to cooperate when it is an ingroup problem and less willing to cooperate when it is perceived as an outgroup problem. Finally, participants were also asked what they expected outgroup members to do. It was predicted that, if the problem was perceived as an outgroup problem then they would expect high levels of cooperation within that outgroup.

Two planned comparisons were also carried out: intergroup cooperation, when provincial identities were salient, were compared to intragroup cooperation when regional identities are salient; and intergroup cooperation, when regional identities were salient, was compared to intragroup cooperation when the national identity was salient. Thus, for the same objectively defined geographical area, intragroup cooperation was predicted to be greater than intergroup cooperation. This same pattern of results was predicted for measures of similarity, needs and values, and interdependence of individuals.

Participants in each of the six conditions were given a relevant map of their province, region, or nation and made either intra or intergroup comparisons in the context of a resource dilemma vignette. Within each condition, participants were presented with a resource dilemma vignette that corresponded to the relevant identity and the appropriate comparative (intra and intergroup) frame of reference which was to be made salient for a given condition.

Experimental Results

The results supported the predictions for each of the measures of cooperation, similarity, needs and values, and interdependence. Supporting the primary prediction, it was found that participants were more willing to volunteer their time in the intragroup condition than the intergroup condition regardless of the level of abstraction of the self (or social identity)

[F (1, 129) = 4.20, $p < .05$; Intragroup: $M = 6.16$, $SD = 1.78$; Intergroup: $M = 5.48$, $SD = 2.02$].

Further, when participants were asked what they expected other members of their ingroup would do in the same situation, the same effect was found: anticipated intragroup cooperation was greater than anticipated intergroup cooperation [F (1, 129) = 11.00, $p < .001$; Intragroup: $M = 6.42$, $SD = 1.57$; Intergroup: $M = 5.50$, $SD = 1.85$]. The results also supported the predictions for anticipated outgroup members' responses. When the resource dilemma was framed as an ingroup problem, participants did not expect as much cooperation from outgroup members; however, if it was an outgroup member's resource problem (that could affect them in the long term) they expected high levels of intragroup cooperation by the outgroup members [$F(1, 129) = 57.91$, $p < .001$; Intragroup: $M = 4.77$, $SD = 2.24$; Intergroup: $M = 7.25$, $SD = 1.38$]. In other words, participants expected people to look after their own ingroup.

As Table 21.1 shows, planned comparisons were also carried out between the provincial intergroup condition and the regional intragroup condition, as these were objectively interchangeable in terms of being at environmental risk and thus all individuals within each of these conditions were functionally interdependent. The same was done with the regional intergroup condition and the national intragroup condition. All comparisons were significant, indicating that for the same objectively defined area the comparative frame of reference had a significant effect on social identification and thus level of cooperation.

Perceptions of Similarity   Whatever the level of identification, participants perceived relevant ingroup members to be similar to other ingroup members and outgroup members to be similar to other outgroup members. As above, planned comparisons were

Table 21.1   Mean ratings and planned comparisons of dependent variables across three levels of identification and two comparative frames of reference.

Frame of reference of request	Level of identification			Planned comparisons	
	Provincial	**Regional**	**National**	**Comparison 1**	**Comparison 2**
	M (SD)	**M (SD)**	**M (SD)**	**t (1, 40)**	**t(1, 46)**
Participants' behavioral intentions					
Ingroup	5.86 (1.74)	6.00[b] (2.02)	6.50[d] (1.61)	1.72*	2.09**
Outgroup	5.00 [a](1.72)	5.33[c] (2.25)	6.00 (1.92)		
Expectation of in-group members' behavior					
Ingroup	6.76 (1.51)	6.27[b] (1.54)	6.30[d] (1.64)	1.68*	3.21**
Outgroup	5.40[a] (2.04)	5.05[c] (1.89)	5.92 (1.64)		
Expectation of out-group members' behavior					
Ingroup	4.86 (2.01)	4.45[b] (2.39)	4.93[d] (2.33)	23.34***	18.19***
Outgroup	7.55[a] (1.00)	7.33[c] (1.14)	6.96 (1.76)		

Note: Superscript denotes means compared in Comparison 1: Interprovincial/Intraregional comparison (a vs. b); and means compared in Comparison 2: Interprovincial/Intraregional comparison (c vs. d).
*** $p < .001$; ** $p < .01$; * $p < .05$

carried out with the similarity measures. While the people of provinces that make up the regions are not perceived to be very similar when a provincial identity is salient ($M = 4.78$, $SD = 2.10$), the people of the same region are perceived to be similar when the regional identity is salient ($M = 7.02$, $SD = 1.78$). This same pattern of results is also borne out at the next level of abstraction. The people of the regions that make up the nation are not perceived to be very similar when a regional identity is salient ($M = 3.44$, $SD = 1.66$); however, they are perceived to be similar when the national identity is salient ($M = 6.45$, $SD = 2.03$). Each of these differences was found to be significantly different [$t (1, 40) = 19.59$, $p < .001$; $t (1, 46) = 23.98$, $p < .001$].

Perceptions of Shared Needs and Values   When participants were asked about the needs and values of the people of the ingroup and outgroup at each level of abstraction, the same pattern of results was found. Planned comparisons parallel to those used for the primary dependent measures produced similar results. The people of provinces that make up the regions were not perceived to share the same needs and values when a provincial identity was salient ($M = 5.30$, $SD = 1.32$). In contrast, the people of the same region were perceived to share the same needs and values when the regional identity was salient ($M = 6.82$, $SD = 1.14$). The same pattern of results was found at the next level of abstraction. The people of the regions that make up the nation were not perceived to share the same needs and values when a regional identity was salient ($M = 4.79$, $SD = 1.67$), however they were when the national identity was salient ($M = 6.10$, $SD = 1.86$). Both of these differences were found to be significantly different [$t (1, 40) = 3.12$, $p < .01$; $t (1, 46) = 2.98$, $p < .01$].

Perceptions of Interdependence   Individuals varied systematically in terms of the same pattern of results as similarity and needs and values, as well as reflecting the cooperation measures. Regardless of level of inclusiveness, when the ingroup was salient, perceptions of interdependence of individuals did not vary across conditions ($M = 6.33$, $SD = 1.88$). In other words, perceptions of interdependence were constant regardless of group size. The same was found for the outgroup ($M = 6.21$, $SD = 1.45$).

Again the planned comparisons were revealing. People of the provinces that make up the regions were perceived to be less dependent upon each other to satisfy their individual needs when a provincial identity was salient ($M = 5.15$, $SD = 1.34$), than when the regional identity was salient ($M = 6.01$, $SD = 1.21$). The same results were found at the next level of abstraction. The people of the regions that make up the nation are perceived to be less dependent upon each other to satisfy their individual needs when a regional identity was salient ($M = 5.30$, $SD = 2.14$) than when the national identity was salient ($M = 6.50$, $SD = 1.42$). Both of these differences were found to be significantly different [$t (1, 40) = 1.96$, $p < .01$; $t (1, 46) = 2.05$, $p < .01$]. These findings clearly show that perceived interdependence with others varied with identity salience.

Discussion of the Field Study

The results clearly support a self-categorization theory analysis: Cooperation varied as a function of the level of abstraction of the self, that is in terms of the inclusiveness of the social identification that was salient. Specifically, it was found that intragroup cooperation was greater than intergroup cooperation at each level of abstraction: provincial, regional, and national. Further, social cooperation varied systematically with levels of identification. In particular the planned comparisons revealed results that are important to the social dilemma literature. Given that the same geographical area was defined in terms of one region or a number of provinces (or one nation or a number of regions), and that the environmental dilemma related to this geographical region as a whole, the different levels of cooperation illustrate the point that the psychological level of identification has a significant impact on cooperative behavior in a social dilemma. Intergroup cooperation at the provincial level was significantly lower than intragroup cooperation at the regional level. Intergroup cooperation at the regional level was significantly lower than intragroup cooperation at the national level. In terms of both comparisons, the dilemma was defined to affect the same geographical area. In other words objective outcome interdependence was not the direct criterion for group-based behavior; in fact, perceptions of interdependence arose in line with identity salience. This was predictive of group-based behavior.

The primary and follow-up questions reveal remarkable consistency. Perceptions of similarity, shared needs and values, and interdependence varied with category salience, and commitment to cooperate, regardless of level abstraction of the category. In line with these findings, each of these outcomes is argued to be a product of categorization processes of individuals. Thus, for any given salient category, perceptions of similarity, shared needs and values, and interdependence will follow. The findings are particularly important given that interdependence theorists first emphasize the interdependence structure that objectively defines the social dilemma and then look at factors to increase the level of cooperation. Here, the mechanism of social identification has served as a systematic conceptual link between the objective and perceived state of affairs. Given that each individual can, of course, define themselves to be interdependent with many different social groupings, it seems pertinent to fully understand the functional dynamic of this link between the objective and perceived nature of interdependence.

Social identity theory states that categorizations are comparative judgments, and that perceptions of the outgroup and their expected behavior vary systematically with ingroup judgments. Thus, just as the ingroup was perceived to be similar, to share the same needs and values, and be interdependent at each level of abstraction, so too do these perceptions reflect categorization of the outgroup. These, in turn, reflect the levels of expected cooperation for the outgroup. In other words, categorization, and thus social cooperation, emerged as an essentially comparative process. As such, the frame of reference in which a social dilemma is perceived contributes to the pattern of behavior that emerges.

In summarizing these experimental results one can make the following points. Social dilemmas are traditionally defined in terms of discrete individuals interacting within a social system, wherein conflicts of interest between the individual and society are inherent. The paradigm clearly pits the individual against society. Yet in terms of everyday life, we do cooperate to a remarkable degree and act in terms of a large number of social identities. These identities too, can come into conflict and define a conflict of interest. And while conflicts of interests may always be an inevitable aspect of life, we often do not act in terms of our individual self-interest. Often the interests of the collective and the individual, as this study has suggested, are one and the same—there is no dilemma, as there is no conflict of interests. Self-interest is collective interest.

A few caveats are in order. In this study, the objective interdependence structure was held constant in order to evaluate the impact of variable category boundaries on cooperation. It is no doubt the case that some categories are made salient *because* their boundaries are aligned with outcome dependencies—people fighting for national identity are also often fighting for the land and resources with which this identity is associated. While there is consistent evidence that mere categorization can produce ingroup bias, it is important to emphasize that the theory acknowledges that individuals do live in a world where group membership is frequently associated with valued resources. Future research will need to systematically investigate the ways in which such reward interdependencies strengthen or weaken psychological processes of identification.

Although a sharp contrast has been drawn between interdependence theory and social identity theory, it is also the case that an interdependence analysis of the Papua New Guinean study could make predictions about the effects of activating particular levels of identity. Stressing membership in an ingroup may increase the value placed on outcomes for others within one's own group, and increase cooperation. However, at present, interdependence theory, being based more on the individual's perceptions of own utility, does not have as extensive a conceptual framework for predicting the effects of identification with members of a range of subgroups, nor does it deal with the effects of changing the comparative frame. If anything, one might expect cooperation to *decrease* as group size increased from province to nation, due to lowered perceptions of efficacy of a single individual and weaker ties to the larger group.

CONCLUSION

Many recent conflicts around the world highlight the importance of the collective to the individual. In each case these groups fight to maintain the essence of themselves as a distinct people. The security of the identity, as a collective, seems to be the primary aim despite the high costs: Hutu and Tutsi face each other with murderous contempt in their eyes; Northern Irish Catholics mobilize themselves internationally against the British, as represented by the Northern Irish Protestants; the Quebecois rally for their self-determination in Canada with little concern for the loss of economic security. In each of these cases there is a clearly differentiated *us* and *them*. Yet differentiating us and them can also be variable, as witnessed in the ongoing conflicts of interests within former Yugoslavia. The striking reality is that Serbs and Croats, Serbs and Muslims, and Croats and Muslims have each defined the conflict at times. Analysis of how such identities are activated and changed in social dilemma settings may yield important insights about their resolution.

Chapter 22

Impact of Leaders on Resource Consumption in Social Dilemmas: The Intergroup Context

Margaret Foddy
Michael A. Hogg

The structure of interdependence defining a social dilemma applies to a wide range of relationships among people, where the central feature is the incompatibility of individual and collective interests. Use of shared fish stocks, provision of public radio, and accessing the internet are all seemingly disparate cases which present individuals with a choice of acting to maximize one's own gain, or taking less. Despite predictions of collective disaster resulting from the pursuit of individual self-interest, humans have devised many and varied ways to ensure behavior that favors the collective. Some of these solutions emerge unplanned and unrecognized (e.g. Axelrod, 1984; Macy, 1995). Others may arise through implicit or explicit acknowledgment of the need for constraint (Keohane & Ostrom, 1995, p. 2). Norms, practices, sets of rules and institutions may be implemented to alter the reward structure, in recognition of the unreliability of elementary cooperation (Hardin,

The research reported in this chapter was supported by grants from the Australian Research Council. We wish to thank James Willis, Danny Bryant, and Katrina Pernat for helping conduct the studies, Sherry Schneider for her comments on the design and operationalization of some of the studies, and Marilynn Brewer for comments on an early draft of the chapter. Some of these data were presented by the first author at the 7th international conference on social dilemmas in Cairns, Australia, 1997, and at the meetings of the Society of Australasian Social Psychologists, Wollongong, Australia, 1997.

1968; Messick & Brewer, 1983; Ostrom, 1990; Samuelson, Messick, Rutte, & Wilke, 1984; Yamagishi, 1986b).

Once altered by such *structural solutions*, the situation may no longer meet the definition of a dilemma, or may be one in which the difference in reward associated with cooperation and relative to noncooperation is reduced (Foddy & Crettenden, 1994; Rutte, 1990). Privatization of a resource such as land is an example of the former (the social dilemma is removed), whereas imposition of surcharges for high water consumption illustrates the latter (behavior with noncooperative consequences is relatively more costly than behavior with cooperative consequences). A third structural solution which may be particularly effective with replenishable common resource pools is the appointment or election of a leader to manage consumption of the resource on behalf of group members.

LEADERS AS A STRUCTURAL SOLUTION

There has been surprisingly little research on leaders as structural solutions to social dilemmas. Initial research indicated that although imposing a leader was not particularly popular with participants (Van Vugt & de Cremer, in press; Rutte & Wilke, 1984; Samuelson & Messick, 1986a; Wilke, Rutte, Wit, Messick, & Samuelson, 1986; Wit & Wilke, 1992), under conditions in which the resource deteriorated rapidly due to overuse, participants were more likely to vote to give control of resource consumption to a single individual, compared with conditions where there was optimal or underuse (Rutte & Wilke, 1985; Samuelson, 1991; Samuelson & Messick, 1986b). Furthermore, a single leader-manager was more effective in conserving a simulated resource than were aggregates of individuals (Messick et al., 1983; Rutte & Wilke, 1984).

There are many reasons why a leader may be able to resolve the conflicting pressures between individual and collective interests that social dilemmas create. Let us consider the simplest case where the leader accesses the resource on behalf of the group, and then distributes it among group members, or has the right to designate how much an individual may take from a common resource. We leave aside the more complex case in which all group members have access and the leader is assigned the job of constraining their use (see Bianco & Bates, 1990).

First, leaders are likely to have more information about the overall state of the resource. For example, individual fishers may have limited information about the large scale movement of fish stocks or level of harvesting by others. Leaders or managers are more likely to have access to such information and be able to fine tune levels of consumption (e.g., by imposing quotas) to take such information into account. Second, the leader may be able to coordinate actions of group members. This is important for many dilemmas, where the main problem is sequencing of use, or designation of a minimal contributing set (Caporael, Dawes, Orbell, & Van de Kragt, 1989; Diekmann, 1985). Third, constraint in use of the resource is simply individual constraint on the part of the leader, albeit influenced by expectations of the constituents—there is no longer a social dilemma because only one person actually accesses the pool (e.g., Messick and McClelland, 1983). Fourth, the role of leader itself may invoke a leader schema (a cognitive representation of contextually relevant leadership-defining features—cf., Fiske & Taylor, 1991) which creates normative pressure to be fair and responsible. Research on leadership suggests that leaders are generally expected, among other things, to be procedurally and distributively fair (e.g., Bass, 1990; Chemers, in press; Frolich & Oppenheimer, 1996; Kerr & Stanfel, 1993; Lord, Foti, & DeVader, 1984; Nye & Simonetta, 1996; Platow, Reid, & Andrew, 1998; Rutte &

Wilke, 1984). Finally, making a person responsible for the outcomes of others may invoke a superordinate social orientation (i.e., a shared social identity or common ingroup orientation) (e.g., Gaertner, Dovidio, Anastasio, Bachman, & Rust, 1993; Hogg & Abrams, 1988; Kramer, 1991) where concern for the welfare of the group as a whole may lead to constraint in the dilemma setting. Thus, in many ways, simple assumption of a leader role transforms the orientation and thus the behavior of the person in the role.

These potential sources of leader effectiveness may be realized only if they are relevant to the reasons that elementary cooperation (Yamagishi, 1986b) is difficult to attain from the aggregate of individuals in the group. A leader may be more effective when the social dilemma involves a relatively simple coordination problem, such as the volunteer's dilemma, which requires contributions from a subset of actors (Caporael et al., 1989), although no empirical research has been reported relevant to this possibility. In contrast, a leader may have no impact if deterioration of a resource is due to ecological factors beyond the control of anyone. In other words, the dilemma structure must be one that offers affordances to leaders that allow them to behave in ways that produce different outcomes than would emerge from the combination of individual actions.

LEADERS OF SUBGROUPS WITH ACCESS TO COMMON RESOURCES

An additional complication is presented by the fact that in many cases there are two or more leaders accessing a pool on behalf of quite separate groups or subgroups. Heads of corporations may act on behalf of the members of their organization in a social field with a small number of other representatives who may decide, for example, whether to increase or decrease production. There are also many natural groups, such as fishing communities and users of water supplies (Ostrom, 1990), who may appoint a small number of representatives to access a common resource and to negotiate with other groups about shared access. The appointment of leaders in this case does not dissolve the dilemma, but retains its defining features (dominance of the noncooperative choice, deficiency of the dominant strategy, etc.). Will leaders of subgroups be as positive a force as leaders of the entire collective? This has been a neglected focus of research in social dilemmas.

Foddy and Crettenden (1994) provided an initial analysis of factors which might make leaders or representatives of subgroups more or less effective in managing common resources. (Although provision of public goods was not examined, there is no reason to believe that the same analysis would not be relevant.) They analyzed the case in which there are only two groups who access the same resource. According to Foddy and Crettenden, many of the reasons leaders of a single group are effective also apply to leaders of subgroups. When there is only one other person accessing the resource, the subgroup leader will still be in a better position to see the impact of the aggregate demand of the (sub)group members, than will individual group members. The leader will be better able to designate solutions to coordination problems and will have similar advantages in being able to restrain access. If one thinks of the case of subgroup leaders in terms of a two-person dilemma, research has shown that feelings of efficacy are higher. Cooperation by an individual has greater impact, and cooperative intent can be signaled to the other if there is repeated interaction (e.g., Komorita & Lapworth, 1982a; Pruitt & Kimmel, 1977). In two-person or small-n dilemmas, low anonymity (i.e., elevated identifiability) diminishes the likelihood that the subgroup leader will free-ride (see Kerr, 1983). Activation of a leader schema might produce the same effects as for the leader of an entire group, but we will discuss reasons why the *subgroup leader* schema might have some important differences.

Finally, in addition to these structural reasons why subgroup leaders might be more cooperative, Foddy and Crettenden also argued from social identity theory that the nature of the leader's relationship to his or her own subgroup, and to the other subgroup, was important.

Thus far, our discussion of the role of leadership in social dilemmas paints a somewhat different picture to that of a collection of individuals accessing a limited or diminishing resource. Leaders represent or speak for groups, and access or manage resources on behalf of people who belong to groups. In many cases a number of leaders, all representing different groups may access or manage a resource—in which case intergroup relations will influence their behavior. A proper analysis of leadership in social dilemmas needs to be conceptually framed by a more general understanding of psychological group membership, group and intergroup behavior, and leadership as a group process. Social identity theory provides one such conceptual frame.

SOCIAL IDENTITY THEORY

Social identity theory is a social cognitive theory of group membership, group behavior and intergroup relations. Originating in the work of Henri Tajfel and developed by John Turner and colleagues, social identity theory is described in detail elsewhere (e.g., Hogg, 1996; Hogg & Abrams, 1988; Tajfel & Turner, 1979; Turner, 1982; Turner, Hogg, Oakes, Reicher, & Wetherell, 1987). While the early emphasis was on intergroup relations (e.g. Tajfel, 1978, 1982b; Tajfel & Turner, 1979) the theory has been developed to provide an analysis of a wide array of group phenomena. These include discrimination, prejudice, stereotyping, social perception, solidarity, conformity, norms, leadership, group structure, and attitude polarization (Abrams & Hogg, 1990, in press; Hogg, 1992; Hogg & Abrams, 1988, 1993; Hogg & Terry, in press; Oakes, Haslam, & Turner, 1994; Robinson, 1996; Spears, Oakes, Ellemers, & Haslam, 1997; Tajfel, 1978, 1982b; Terry & Hogg, in press; Turner, 1991).

Social identity theory starts from the premise that humans have a strong inclination to categorize the social world into meaningfully simplified representations of groups of people. These representations are generally organized as prototypes—fuzzy sets of a relatively limited number of category defining features that not only define one category but serve to distinguish it from other categories.

The social categorization process forms prototypes according to the principle of metacontrast (maximization of the ratio of intergroup difference to intragroup difference), and then accentuates perceived prototypical similarities within and differences between groups. This process is intimately tied to the immediate or more enduring social comparative context of people and social goals. This process involves the self—almost all social categorizations are made with reference to self—and thus we construct ingroups and outgroups where self is categorized as an ingroup member. It is the process of self-categorization that actually generates group behavior; through it, self is assimilated to the contextually salient ingroup prototype which both describes and prescribes cognition, affect, and behavior (Turner, 1985; Turner et al., 1987). For example, categorization of self as a conservationist, particularly in contrast to loggers, would make salient beliefs about environmentally sensitive behaviors, and influence evaluations of both the ingroup and the outgroup.

Self-categorization is thus responsible for self-definition as a group member, and is seen to be the basis for normative behavior, conformity, differential intergroup behavior, ethnocentrism, ingroup bias, and stereotyping. Because groups furnish social identity and thus self-definition, prototypes are not only descriptive and prescriptive, but above all they are evaluative. They not only tell us who we are and how we should think, feel, and act; but also prescribe our worth in relation to other people and other groups. People strive to acquire and maintain a relatively positive self-concept, and they do this in intergroup contexts by striving for evaluatively positive social identity via positive distinctiveness for their own group relative to relevant outgroups (see Abrams & Hogg, 1988, 1998; Hogg & Abrams, 1990; Rubin & Hewstone, 1998). Depending on the perceived nature of the status relations between groups, people adopt different types of strategies to do this (e.g., Ellemers, 1993; Tajfel & Turner, 1979).

An important feature of self-categorization theory is that categorizations are seen to vary in terms of inclusiveness (Turner, 1991, p.155). At the individual level, people define themselves in terms of differences from other people. At the intermediate ingroup level, the individual focuses on similarities of self and the ingroup, and differences with some salient outgroup. Some groups are more inclusive than others, and so more *superordinate*; the highest level of inclusion would be the superordinate group, *humanity*. An important implication for social dilemmas is that all people with access to a resource may categorize themselves as members of the same superordinate group; there may be two or more subgroups accessing it; or resource users may see themselves as an aggregate of distinct individuals.

SOCIAL IDENTITY, COOPERATION, AND SOCIAL DILEMMAS

Social identity theory has direct relevance to an analysis of social dilemmas. The central idea is that as a collection of people increasingly define themselves as members of a common social group, the welfare of the collective should increasingly prevail over self-interest, and their behavior should become more cooperative: ". . . cooperation will follow from the shared and mutual perception by in-group members of their interests as interchangeable" (Turner et al., 1987, p.65). Research using the minimal group paradigm shows that people who define themselves as members of the same social group show marked ingroup favoritism in resource allocation, even if there exists an alternative intergroup allocation strategy that does not favor the ingroup over the outgroup but yields a greater absolute allocation to the ingroup (see discussions by Bourhis, Sachdev, & Gagnon, 1994; Diehl, 1990).

By questioning the premise that actors always perceive themselves as separate individuals rather than as parts of a social group with a shared identity, a fresh impetus is provided for examining voluntary restraint as a solution to social dilemmas. If the crux of the conflict in resource dilemmas resides with the level at which identification occurs, then the resolution will rely on finding methods for instilling compatible levels of social identity. In particular, if the construal of self can be shifted from the personal to the group level, the utility of acting on behalf of the group should be enhanced. Furthermore, when group welfare is aligned with the preservation of a common resource, collective orientation may promote resource conservation.

Reflecting directly on social dilemmas, Brewer and Kramer (1986) suggest that behavior in social dilemmas may rest upon ". . . whether individuals . . . think of themselves as single and autonomous individuals or whether, in contrast, they regard themselves as sharing a membership in and identification with a larger aggregate or social unit" (p. 545). Indeed, how people treat a shared resource may depend critically upon whether those people identify themselves and relate to one another as individuals, a single inclusive group, or two or more subgroups.

Kramer and Brewer (1986) argued that when superordinate common group identity is salient, "subgroup comparisons become less relevant and impactful, thus reducing or eliminating intergroup competition (for the common resource). Under these conditions, more cooperative decisions are likely" (p. 229). According to their analysis, individual level identity would produce levels of cooperation intermediate between the superordinate and subgroup levels. In a dilemma situation the individual tendency to maximize self-gain is intensified through the desire to distinguish the subgroup (self) from the outgroup. Because the range of behavioral and symbolic options available to do so are limited, group members become *even more selfish* on behalf of other group members. Thus, level of categorization transforms the meaning of individual self-interest.

Social identity theory suggests the depersonalization associated with group identification makes individuals desire gain for all ingroup members because ingroup favoritism is inseparable from self-favoritism. In the social dilemma setting with several subgroups, this translates into a desire for one's own group members to gain *more* than the outgroup. This would cause groups to compete against one another for access to the pool, and would probably produce severe overuse of the common resource (see Kramer, 1991, for a similar account in the context of organizational dilemmas). The dilemma setting, however, contains a paradox—if you plunder the resource to prevent the outgroup from benefiting from it, then you also harm the ingroup. It is not clear what is in the subgroup's best interest—to cooperate with an outgroup (unreliable, particularly given that there is generally little trust across group boundaries) or to compete with the outgroup, at the risk of destroying the resource for one's own group as well as for the others.

A superordinate group orientation removes the conflict, because it aligns individual interests with those of all people accessing the pool. However, it is often difficult to establish such an orientation, particularly in very large groups, as Brewer and Schneider (1990) and others have noted. The problem is that people generally have a large repertoire of identities they can use to define themselves (e.g., race, ethnicity, gender, religion, political affiliation), and it can be very difficult to arrange circumstances that enduringly maintain a superordinate identity. Indeed, according to Brewer's (1991) optimal distinctiveness theory, people in large groups strive to categorize themselves at the subgroup level because that optimally satisfies conflicting motives for distinctiveness and assimilation.

Brewer and Kramer (1986) examined the prediction that subgroup identification would exaggerate selfish tendencies on behalf of the ingroup, and that superordinate group orientation would lead to more cooperation. They conducted a series of experiments using a simulated resource, from which participants were able to harvest points. When the resource was deteriorating rapidly, they found that superordinate or collective orientation did indeed produce greater restraint compared with a condition in which subgroup identity was stressed, and intergroup comparisons were salient. This was so, whether the salient level of identity was induced by drawing attention to natural category memberships (e.g., *university students* as superordinate, compared with *psychology students* versus *economics students* as two subgroups), or using a *common fate* manipulation which emphasized subgroup or superordinate group boundaries. Brewer and Kramer (1986) also contrasted superordinate and individual levels of identity, using the common fate manipulation, and found higher levels of cooperation in the superordinate condition, in a take-some dilemma (see also Brewer & Schneider, 1990; de Cremer and Van Vugt, 1998).

In this research, all three levels of identification were not simultaneously compared; the overall pattern suggests that the subgroup condition produced the most competitive behavior. In the contrast of superordinate group and subgroup orientations, the participants with subgroup salience took between 10 and 20% more than those with a superordinate categorization; the difference between individual and superordinate orientation was smaller in a similar experiment, although the figures are not directly comparable. However, there was little evidence that the effects found in these studies were mediated by levels of iden-tification—measures of perceptions of others and expectations for their behavior did not vary as a function of induced categorization level, and did not correlate with behavior (see also de Cremer & Van Vugt, 1998).

While this work points to clearly different influences of subgroup and superordinate orientations, the distinctions may not always be so clear in the dilemma setting. The ef-fects associated with *superordinate* group identity have been found to diminish in inten-sity and duration as they are applied to broadening bands of social categories (Brewer & Schneider, 1990; Dawes, 1975; Kerr, 1989; Messick & McClelland, 1983). Furthermore, *subgroup* identity may not always *reduce* cooperation. In particular, if the group norm prescribes fairness or cooperation, then high levels of group identification may enhance such tendencies. As the very term *social dilemma* suggests, there is no obvious *group benefiting* choice to be made at the subgroup level. Is the benefit of fellow group members best served by attempting to gain more than an outgroup, at the risk of depleting the com-mon resource? Or, by acting in a way that will sustain the resource? In comparison with an individual orientation, focus on *either* the subgroup or superordinate group may make salient the interdependence of actors' outcomes, which in itself may promote cooperation (Dawes, 1980; Foddy & Crettenden, 1994; Lichbach, 1996; Pruitt & Kimmel, 1977).

On the basis of the work by Brewer, Kramer, and others, we can conclude that social categorization may affect behavior in social dilemmas. Further research is needed to specify exactly what the effect is, how it varies in different dilemma structures, and most impor-tantly, how the processes underlying the effect operate. Researchers to date have had lim-ited success in demonstrating that greater cooperation under group categorization is corre-lated with subjective reports of identification or attraction to group members (Bouas & Komorita, 1996; de Cremer & Van Vugt, 1998).

SOCIAL IDENTITY THEORY AND LEADERS OF SUBGROUPS WITH ACCESS TO COMMON RESOURCES

Having explored the role of group membership as social identity in social dilemmas, let us now return to our main theme—the role of leaders in social dilemmas. A social identity analysis of leadership has only recently been elaborated (Fielding & Hogg, 1997; Hains, Hogg, & Duck, 1997; Hogg, 1996, in press; Hogg, Hains, & Mason, 1998; see also Turner & Haslam, in press). In salient groups, behavior conforms to the group prototype, and thus the individual who happens to occupy the contextually most prototypical group position appears to exercise influence. This process is particularly pronounced where the group exhibits high entitativity (Campbell, 1958; Sherman, Hamilton, & Lewis, in press), and thus where people identify strongly and have a consensual prototype that endures due to a stable comparative context. This is a passive process—the leader does not actively lead, but merely embodies the aspirations, attitudes, and behaviors of the group as they are represented by the group prototype. Over time, however, people who occupy the most prototypical position may acquire the ability to actively influence: (a) they become so-cially attractive, consensually liked as prototypical group members (Hogg, 1992), and thus able to secure ready compliance with their suggestions, requests, and orders; and (b) they are imbued with charismatic/leadership personalities, due to attribution processes that cause members to attribute the leader's apparent influence to the person and to person-ality rather than to the prototypicality of the position—that is, a fundamental attribution error (Ross, 1977) or correspondence bias (Gilbert & Jones, 1986) occurs (also see Gilbert & Malone, 1995; Trope & Liberman, 1993).

Research on this model of leadership has provided relatively good support from a field study (Fielding & Hogg, 1997) and three laboratory experiments (Hains et al., 1997; Hogg et al, 1998) for the idea that as people identify more strongly with a group they base their leadership perceptions and endorsements more strongly on group prototypicality, and that prototypicality itself is an interactive function of identity salience and the social comparative frame of reference. When group membership is salient, effective leadership rests significantly on being a prototypical group member (and thus someone who identi-fies strongly with the group), because only then will the group validate and recognize one's leadership position (Platow, Reid, & Andrew, 1998). One implication of the fact that group leaders are likely to view themselves as prototypical group members, is that they will identify relatively strongly with the group and will thus be particularly motivated to serve what they perceive to be the best interests of the group as a whole (because group interest is strongly linked to self-interest). Both leaders and followers expect leaders to favor the ingroup over the outgroup while treating all ingroup members fairly (see Platow et al., for empirical evidence to support this idea). So, in social dilemmas, a *superordinate* group leader will be particularly conserving of a shared resource. However, where sub-groups exist, a *subgroup* leader will be caught in the paradox described earlier in which intergroup competitiveness and subgroup loyalty conflicts with the benefit of all (includ-ing the subgroup).

Both these effects will be accentuated where the leader knows that he or she is ac-countable to or under surveillance by the relevant ingroup. Research on accountability of representatives to constituencies shows that accountability causes leaders to behave in ways that are markedly ingroup favoring. This can be a serious obstacle if leaders of differ-ent groups need to compromise to reach a mutually beneficial intergroup outcome (e.g., Carnevale, 1985; Rubin & Brown, 1975; Tetlock, 1992). In the area of social identity theory, as in the study of social dilemmas, little research has focused on the perceptions and behaviors of leaders—there has been more work on the expectations and preferences of followers.

To recap: Leaders for whom a superordinate identity is equally or more salient than subgroup identity should show greater concern for the welfare of all members of the col-lective than for self, or for the subgroup, and should act to enhance collective utility. To the extent that collective gain is enhanced by cooperation in social dilemmas, the leader with a superordinate orientation would be expected to be more resource conserving (Kramer & Brewer, 1984, 1986; Schopler & Insko, this volume). Here, the transformation of indi-vidual self-interest effected by the leader role and superordinate categorization work in the same direction, toward conservation of the scarce resource. In contrast, identification with, and accountability to subgroups would produce a different effect (Foddy and Crettenden, 1994). Salience of a strong subgroup identity would produce ingroup favoring behavior on the part of the subgroup leader. In many social dilemmas, actions to favor an ingroup might be equivalent to selfish or noncooperative choices. Further, if a strong psychological tie with a subgroup were accompanied by accountability to the subgroup, the leader might well assume that group members expected the leader to act to distinguish the subgroup from the outgroup, and this would further accentuate the effect. In subgroup contexts, it may well be the case that resource conservation is best served by leaders who

(a) are not very subgroup prototypical,

(b) do not identify very strongly with their subgroup, and

(c) are not highly accountable to their subgroup.

RESEARCH ON SOCIAL IDENTITY, LEVEL OF CATEGORIZATION, AND LEADERSHIP IN SOCIAL DILEMMAS

There is remarkably little research assessing the relative impact of subgroup and superordinate group leaders on resource consumption in social dilemmas. Although we have already seen that there is research on levels of social categorization in social dilemmas that does not deal with leadership (e.g., Kramer & Brewer, 1984, 1986), and some on leaders and social dilemmas that does not deal with social identity (e.g., de Cremer & Van Vugt, in press; Rutte & Wilke, 1984; Wit & Wilke, 1992), there is only one study, to our knowledge, which puts all this together to look at subgroup and superordinate group leaders from the perspective of social identity theory (Foddy & Crettenden, 1994). Foddy and Crettenden conducted a study which suggested that leaders, whether from an ingroup or an outgroup, were much more successful in managing a social dilemma requiring coordinated restriction of demand on a shared resource, than were individual members. The authors pointed out that their experiment had created conditions in which subgroup leaders were likely to take a superordinate point of view: they were appointed at random, were not accountable to their group members, and there was a prominent solution to the coordination problem. They concluded that future work should explore variables that might produce different behaviors in subgroup leaders.

In order to take up this lead we formulated a set of hypotheses and designed a series of studies to investigate them (Foddy & Hogg, 1994). We reasoned that if there are two groups accessing a common resource, then competitive tendencies will be emphasized— the leader would assume that there is an expectation that he or she will favor the ingroup. Under conditions of high ingroup identification and competitiveness between groups it may in fact be better if leaders are *less* accountable, since they will be more likely to consider more complex and integrative solutions to the commons problem. However, it is clear that in order to predict whether leaders will be more or less conserving than individuals, it is necessary to attend to the nature of their relationship to the group.

As outlined above, we believe this includes:

(a) the *psychological* relationship to the group (do the leaders see themselves as prototypical or not; does the group provide an optimally distinctive identity, how strongly do they identify with the group),

(b) the *structural* relationship of the representative to the rest of the group (accountability), and

(c) the *intergroup context* that determines the level of social identity that is salient (individual, ingroup, or superordinate group).

It is quite possible that the three variables are not entirely independent: representative group leaders who are also accountable to the subgroup may be incapable of adopting a superordinate group perspective. Furthermore, there are many different structural arrangements that vary the ways in which the leader is related to the group, and in which the subgroups are related to one another. Similarly, the psychological relationship of the leader to the group, and the groups to one another, may vary along the dimensions of importance, relevance, and duration. Finally, the opportunities for the leaders of subgroups to have an effect will vary with the affordances offered by features of the dilemma itself.

Our own research could only address a subset of these possibilities. We conducted a series of experiments in which we varied the salience of existing nested category memberships (types of university student). We assigned half the participants to the role of leader, in some cases varying the accountability of the leaders to their constituents. The standard design in all of these experiments is a 2 × 3 factorial design (see Table 22.1) which crosses leader/solo role, with one of three levels of salient self-categorization or social category orientation: individual, intergroup, and superordinate group. Level of self-categorization was manipulated by making salient participants' existing category memberships—category memberships referred either to a subgroup that was part of a larger group (e.g., students living in colleges who were also part of a superordinate category of university students), or to the superordinate category. Measures were taken of the extent to which participants identified with the relevant group(s), and in the case of leaders, we measured the extent to which they endorsed features of the leader schema (responsibility, fairness, influence over outcomes).

It is important to note that we focus on the case in which a leader *is always a leader of a subgroup*, not a single leader of one single group, as has been the case in previous research (e.g. Rutte & Wilke, 1984). We took this approach in part because we believed that the task of the subgroup leader in the intergroup context is more complex than that of the overall leader. However, this meant that subgroup identification was likely to be salient, and that we would have to devise methods to induce self-categorization (a psychological state), at the three different levels—individual, subordinate group, superordinate group.

We employed two different dilemma settings: (1) a one-shot take-some game, similar to that used by Foddy and Crettenden (1994), and (2) a deteriorating resource dilemma, modeled after Kramer and Brewer (1984), and Brewer and Kramer (1986).

Study 1: Library Dilemma

Our first study (Foddy & Hogg, unpublished) was an extension of Foddy and Crettenden (1994), who devised a one-shot dilemma framed as competition to use scarce library resources. Participants were psychology students who believed they were taking part in a university library study of alternative ways to deal with high CD-ROM demand. Their task was to book hours for themselves (solo condition) or on behalf of themselves and 5 other people (leader condition) in order to complete an assignment. They believed that 12 people (seated at different terminals across the campus) had access to the pool of 16 hours but that each person really needed 1.5 hours—if too many hours were booked the system would crash and no one would get any hours. Participants were referred to as individuals (individual condition), as La Trobe University students (superordinate condition), or as six

Table 22.1   General experimental design.

| Social category | Role | |
orientation	Leader	Solo
Individual	A	B
Intergroup	C	D
Superordinate group	E	F

psychology students taking part with six students across the campus from another faculty (intergroup condition). To further strengthen the salient level of categorization, a common fate manipulation was also employed—each individual would receive either AU$1.00 or AU$5.00 on the basis of a coin toss for each individual, a single coin toss for the group of 12 University students as a whole, or a single coin toss for the su' group of six psychology students as a whole. Participants booked hours for themselves (solo condition) or for themselves and five other students—self and a random selection of five individuals (individual leader), self and a random selection of five university students (superordinate group leader), or self and the five other psychology students (intergroup leader). Leaders were not accountable to their group—their booking was only seen by themselves and the other leader.

We measured group identification with a set of 14 questions adapted from previous research by Brown, Condor, Mathews, Wade, and Williams (1986), and Kashima and Kashima (1992). For participants in the intergroup condition the target group was psychology students, and for participants in the superordinate condition the target group was La Trobe University students. In the individual condition half the participants were given the psychology questionnaire and the other half the university questionnaire. The primary dependent measure was the number of hours booked. Because fractions of hours could not be booked, any booking greater than one hour in the solo conditions represented noncooperative behavior. If all participants booked one hour then 12 of the available 16 hours would be booked, but if all participants booked two hours then 24 hours would be booked and the system would crash. In the leader conditions, any booking that exceeded 1.33 hours per group member (i.e., 8 hours total for a group of six people) represented a noncooperative choice, which would cause the system to crash if both leaders behaved the same way. The major potential for the leader in this task lay in being better able to identify and implement a prominent solution (take half the hours), and to exercise restraint in what was effectively a two-person dilemma.

We predicted that leaders would be more resource conserving than solo participants (Hypothesis 1), that participants in the superordinate identity condition would be more conserving than participants in the individual conditions (Hypothesis 2), and that intergroup participants would be least conserving (Hypothesis 3). We also predicted an interaction in which intergroup leaders would be least conserving and superordinate leaders most conserving (Hypothesis 4). We expected measured identification to reflect the manipulations—superordinate and intergroup participants would identify with their respective groups more than comparable individuals. In addition, assignment to the leader role was expected to elevate group identification relative to solos, particularly in the intergroup condition.

Our principal analysis was a 3 (social orientation) $\times$ 2 (role) ANCOVA on hours booked (the number of hours booked by the leader was divided by six to make this comparable to the solo condition—solos only booked for self, whereas leaders booked for six people). The covariate was number of hours booked in a preliminary practice trial, before the role manipulation, but after the social orientation manipulation (3 $\times$ 2 ANOVA revealed no effects on the practice trial). The ANCOVA revealed (a) that leaders were more conserving than solos ($F(1, 111) = 127.94, p < .001$). However, across all social orientation conditions leaders took more for themselves ($M = 1.45$) than they gave to the other five group members ($M = 1.18$. $t(59) = 3.98, p < .001$); (b) that superordinate group participants were more conserving than individuals (intergroup was not significantly different to either) ($F(2, 111) = 4.98, p < .01$), and (b) that the role effect was more pronounced in the individual self-categorization condition than other conditions ($F(2, 111) = 7.77, p < .01$)—see Figure 22.1.

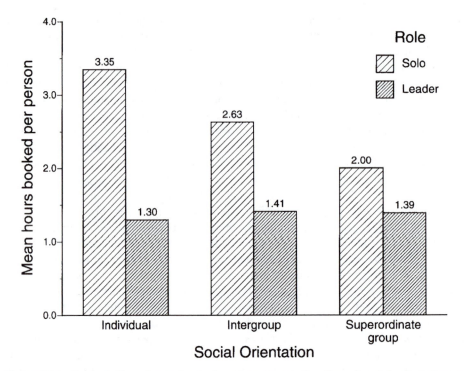

Figure 22.1 Study 1: Mean hours booked per person as a function of social orientation and role. *Notes:* There were 16 hours available to be used by a total of 12 individuals; means greater than 1.33 indicating non-coopreative, non-resource-conserving behavior.

Overall leaders behaved as predicted under Hypothesis 1—they were more conserving than solos in all social orientation conditions. Hypothesis 2 was also supported—participants in the superordinate identity condition were more conserving than participants in the individual conditions. Hypotheses 3 and 4 were not supported—intergroup participants and intergroup leaders were not the least conserving and superordinate leaders were not the most conserving.

Analysis of the identification measures did not support the idea that cooperation was mediated by identification. Against a background of relatively high identification (cell means ranged from 5.01 to 5.51, scale midpoint = 4) there were no significant differences among conditions. Thus, unless the identification measures are insensitive in this context, the effects of the independent variables on resource consumption are not mediated by self-reported identification or by level of self-categorization. However, bivariate correlation of identification and hours booked revealed a nonsignificant relationship for solos ($r = .15$, $n = 55$), but a significant negative relationship for leaders ($r = -.36, p = .005$, 1-tailed ($n = 60$). The more strongly leaders identified with either sub or superordinate group the *less* they took from the pool (or vice versa). This is consistent with the idea that leaders are more resource conserving because depersonalization renders self-interest isomorphic with collective interest. However, yet again, the intergroup leaders did not appear to behave as we initially hypothesized—for them, identification should have been negatively related to conservation.

We have learned from this first study that: (a) Leaders are more conserving than solos, and more conserving leaders are those who identify more with their subgroup or superordinate group; and (b) people, particularly solos, for whom a superordinate identity has been made salient are more conserving than people for whom individual identity has been made salient. The intergroup orientation did not accentuate competitiveness of solos or leaders—this condition was intermediate to individual and superordinate group orientation conditions. This is quite possibly because of the paradox discussed earlier—intergroup competitiveness in a social dilemma setting harms the ingroup, whereas in the traditional nonzero sum structures used in minimal group studies, intergroup competition does not have to harm the ingroup. Hence a social dilemma is also a psychological dilemma for social identity contingent displays of ingroup favoritism—it is quite possible that this dilemma may actually reduce ingroup identification because people are ambivalent over how to demonstrate or express preferential ingroup ties. This is an intriguing idea that should be tested in subsequent research. Another possibility is that the subgroups made salient did not invoke a strong sense of competitiveness or rivalry because the subgroup (discipline major) and superordinate group (university student) are similar in many respects. In our next study, we varied the extent of identification with the ingroup, and the degree of accountability to assess whether these factors would undermine the effectiveness of the leader.

Study 2: Deteriorating Resource Dilemma (DRD)

Study two was actually a set of three experiments. Each experiment adopted the basic design shown in Table 22.1, but used a repeated trial resource dilemma that added an extra within-participants factor. This yielded a 3 (social orientation) × 2 (role) × 5 (blocks of two trials) design. In the three experiments, there were differences in the extent to which participants identified with, or were accountable to, the subgroup. Thus, in some of the analyses below there is a further factor, referred to as *sample*, in the design. The dilemma paradigm was modeled closely on the second phase of the replenishing resource dilemma used by Kramer and Brewer (1984); also see experiments by Messick et al. (1983). Participants harvested from a pool of points, which although replenished at a rate of 11% of the points remaining at the end of each trial, continued to deteriorate because simulated others overharvested.

Participants, believing they were in a study of how groups of people manage limited resources, individually sat at terminals they believed were networked with two other terminals in adjoining rooms and three terminals at another location on the campus. In reality, all feedback was programmed. The limited resource was a pool of 300 points each worth AU$0.04, that was replenished after each trial at the rate of 11% of the points remaining at the end of the trial. If everyone took 5 points per trial or less, the resource would be sustained.

The objective was to harvest as many points as possible during the course of the experiment. On each trial, solos could take between 0 and 10 points, and leaders, who harvested on behalf of themselves and two others, between 0 and 30 points. It was explained that making the resource last would increase the number of points available to harvest. The study was to run until the pool was exhausted or there had been 24 trials—whichever came first. At the end of each trial there was textual and graphic feedback on the number of points taken by others and on the cumulative take of self and others. There appeared to be a high ($M = 7.83$ points/trial), medium (7.04) and low (6.08) harvester at the remote location, and a high (7.79) and low (6.17) harvester in the adjoining rooms.

Participants were aware of three possible levels of categorization

1   six individuals forming
2   two three-person subgroups (different locations/labs) nested within
3   a six person superordinate university student group.

The social orientation manipulation involved making one level of categorization relatively more salient than the others. We did this by an amalgam of verbal and written instructions as well as posters, computer feedback presentation, and a category priming task in which participants were instructed to focus on the relevant level of categorization. These methods were based on other social identity studies (e.g. Hains et al., 1997; Hogg & Hains, 1996; Kramer & Brewer, 1984). Solos harvested on behalf of themselves, whereas leaders harvested on behalf of themselves and the two other people in adjoining rooms. They were responsible for distributing the points within their group, described in the instructions as *three individuals*, *three subgroup members*, or *three La Trobe University students at this location*. Leaders believed they had been randomly selected and that only they and the leader at the other location would have access to the pool.

Our principal dependent measure was points taken per person. We also asked participants about the fairness of their choices for their subgroup and the entire group of six, as well as their feelings of responsibility and efficacy. Leaders were asked how they would distribute points within their three-person group. Subjective level of self-categorization was measured by prevalence of individualistic or category-based self-descriptions given by participants as part of the category priming task. To assess *degree* of identification, we also administered two 9 item chronic group identification questionnaires (based on Brown, Condor, Mathews, Wade, & Williams, 1986)—one referring to the subgroup, and the other to the superordinate group. Participants also indicated whose interests had been most important to them during the session:

(a) own versus subgroup,
(b) own versus superordinate group,
(c) subgroup versus superordinate group

a measure of *situational* identification with the actual group of students present in the session, in contrast to chronic identification with an enduring social category.

Using these methods we conducted three experiments. For the first experiment (called *day standard experiment*) participants were *day* students (students who do not live in colleges on campus), and the outgroup (i.e., participants at the remote site) was college students (students living in halls of residence). For the second experiment (called *college experiment*) participants were college students and the outgroup was day students. For the third experiment (called *day accountable experiment*), participants were day students while college students were the outgroup, but in this experiment, unlike the other two, solos and leaders were accountable to their group. They had to provide written justifications of their take from the pool (leaders also believed that members of their group might meet them face to face where the leaders would have to justify their behavior).

The three experiments act as a manipulation of the level of commitment to the group by the leader. Relative to the day standard experiment, solo participants in the college experiment should have higher chronic subgroup identification, because their group is smaller and more distinctive. The college students should thus show greater ingroup bias and higher consumption, especially in conditions where subgroup identity is made salient. College students are a relatively distinct group on campus (only 5% of students live at the college and they tend to overrepresent rural, younger, and full time students), with higher entitativity (e.g., Sherman et al., in press) and consensual prototype clarity providing a more salient social identity than is the case for day students (largely a nebulous default category). In the day accountable experiment, while chronic group identification might not be higher than in the standard day experiment, the immediate sense of responsibility to the subgroup should be higher, and should lead to less conserving behavior. Our analysis of the competing forces operating on the leader suggests that when ingroup identification is high, or leaders are accountable to subgroups, their effectiveness in conserving the re-source will be reduced. Given the results of the library dilemma study, it is possible that resource consumption might follow a similar pattern here—individually oriented partici-pants being least conserving, with lower consumption among those oriented to the sub-group or superordinate group. Generally, as importance of subgroup membership increases (college students), or accountability to the group increases (accountable day experiment), there is greater ingroup bias in the subgroup conditions, and leaders of subgroups in all conditions are less likely to be resource conserving.

Analysis of the chronic identification measures across the three experiments revealed

(a) that college students identified more strongly with their subgroup ($M = 6.75$) than did day students ($Ms = 5.40$ and 5.36 for the standard and accountable experiments respec-tively [main effect for sample, $F (2, 353) = 15.33, p < .001$]);

(b) that chronic subgroup identification was greater than superordinate (University) identification (main effect for questionnaire, $F (1, 353) = 118.2, p < .001$); and

(c) that subgroup and superordinate group identification were more closely associ-ated for day ($r = .80$) than college students ($r = .34$).

Although the social orientation manipulation within experiments did not affect chronic identification, it did affect the *situational* self-description measures. Content analysis of self-descriptions revealed them to be consistent with the relevant level of salient categori-zation as an individual, a day student, a college student, or a superordinate university student. The measure of degree of situational identification also confirmed the effective-ness of the manipulation within the experiments—Table 22.2 shows means, collapsed across the three experiments, for each measure in each cell of the 3 × 2 design. Solos and leaders preferred

(a) subgroup over individuals more strongly in the subgroup than individual condi-tion,

(b) superordinate group over individuals in the superordinate group than individual condition, and

(c) superordinate group over subgroup in the superordinate group than subgroup con-dition.

However, leaders in both the subgroup and superordinate group conditions generally pre-ferred the subgroup to a greater degree than the superordinate group. The indices of orien-tation to both subgroup and superordinate group were higher for the leaders compared with the solos (note that the third question compared subgroup and superordinate group interests, so low scores indicate subgroup orientation).

Points taken per trial, averaged over pairs of trials across the first 10 trials and divided by three for leaders, were analyzed by 3 (social orientation) × 2 (role) × 5 (trial block) ×

Table 22.2 Mean situational identification by role and social orientation situational identification by role and social orientation: Study 2.

Social orientation	Role	
Measure	Solo	Leader
Individual		
Individual-subgroup	3.81	5.77
Individual-superordinate group	4.35	4.50
Subgroup-superordinate group	4.76	3.04
Subgroup		
Individual-subgroup	4.67	6.40
Individual-superordinate group	4.14	5.17
Subgroup-superordinate group	3.40	2.95
Superordinate group		
Individual-subgroup	4.56	5.80
Individual-superordinate group	4.94	5.04
Subgroup-superordinate group	5.09	3.72

Note: Answers to three post-experimental questions concerning whose interests were more important: individual versus subgroup; individual versus superordinate group; subgroup versus superordinate group; rated on a 9-point scale with 1 favoring the label on the left and 9 the label on the right.

3 (experiment) ANOVA. Figure 22.2 shows the mean take per block by experiment for solo participants, and Figure 22.3 shows the same information for leaders. Of most interest to us were the two-way interactions of role with block [F (4, 1392) = 12.09, $p < .001$], and role with experiment [F (2, 348) = 3.58, $p < .05$]. Leaders' takes declined over trials whereas that of solos fluctuated and showed a sharp rise on the last block of trials—this pattern for solos has occurred in other studies (e.g. Kramer and Brewer, 1984; Messick, et al., 1983).

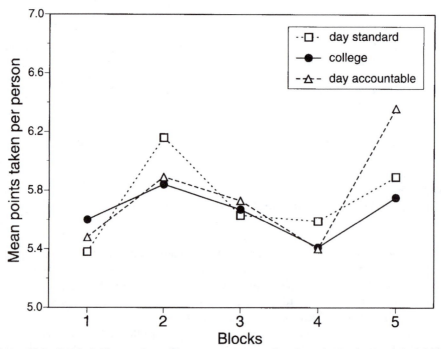

Figure 22.2 Study 2: Mean points taken per person as a function of experiment and trial block, for solo participants

Table 22.3 Mean take per person by role and social orientation for each of three experiments.

| Experiment | Role | |
Social orientation	Solo	Leader
Day standard		
Individual	5.71	5.33
Intergroup	5.52	5.16
Superordinate	5.98	5.13
College standard		
Individual	5.94	5.99
Intergroup	5.55	5.56
Superordinate	5.42	5.69
Day accountable		
Individual	5.78	5.89
Intergroup	6.03	5.88
Superordinate	5.51	5.83

Notes: Maximum take per person is 10 points per trial.

It probably reflects a panic reaction as the resource declined. Resource conservation was also significantly greater for leaders in the standard day experiment than leaders or solos in the other experiments. Although induced level of categorization within experiments did not significantly affect take per person, inspection of means in Table 22.3 shows a tendency for leaders in the standard day experiment to take less than solo participants, particularly in the superordinate condition. One implication of this is that the advantage of the

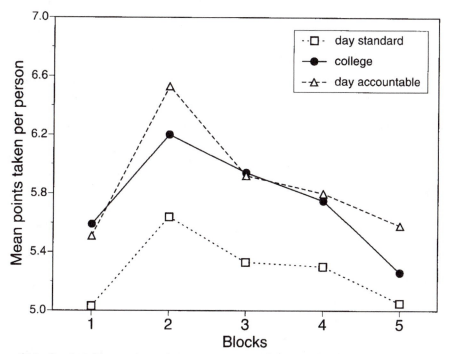

Figure 22.3 Study 2: Mean points taken per person as a function of experiment and trial block, for leaders

leader as a structural solution to overuse is compromised when the leader is more highly identified with the subgroup (standard college experiment) or more accountable to members of the subgroup (day accountable experiment). Interestingly, across conditions and experiments, leaders reported that they had behaved more responsibly and fairly towards members of their subgroups and the group of six (superordinate group) than did solos.

We also performed some correlation and regression analyses. If degree of identification with the subgroup leads to higher consumption, then there should be a positive correlation of ingroup identification and take per person. In contrast, high identification with the superordinate group should produce lower consumption, and negative correlations with take per person. However, the correlations of the chronic group identification measures with mean take per person were not significant in any of the conditions in any of the experiments, although there was a trend for those who identified more strongly with the subgroup to consume more.

The more contextually sensitive measures of situational identification were more promising. Recall that these situational identity questions asked participants to rate whose interests were more important to them during the session:

(a) their own individual interests versus the interests of the subgroup,
(b) their own individual interests versus the interests of the superordinate group,
(c) the interests of the subgroup versus the interests of the superordinate group.

The correlation among the three measures in all three samples did not reveal the expected negative relationship between subgroup and superordinate group interests. Overall, the correlation of the first two questions was .58 (lowest in the college sample). Thus, for these participants, subgroup orientation did not preclude superordinate group orientation, probably because they were *nested* subgroups with similar interests and characteristics.

We assessed the relationship between degree of situational identification and resource consumption. Initial correlations suggested that lower consumption was associated with both high subgroup and high superordinate group identification. Because subgroup and superordinate identification were also correlated, we performed regression analyses where we entered both situational measures as predictors of consumption separately for the three samples. This allowed us to control for the shared variance of subgroup and superordinate group identification. No significant relationships were found for the day accountable sample, probably reflecting the strong influence of the expectation that the participants would have to explain their actions to their constituents. However, in the day standard and college student samples, an interesting pattern emerged. For *leaders* in both the day standard and college samples, high identification with the *subgroup* (question a) was a significant predictor of *higher* resource consumption (beta = .266, $p < .01$). At the same time, high identification with the superordinate group (question b) predicted lower consumption (beta = $-.375$, $p < .001$). For solo participants, the regression analysis revealed no significant predictors for the day standard sample, but a relatively strong tendency in the college sample for identification with the subgroup to be associated with lower consumption (beta = $-.368$, $p < .01$).

In the case of leaders, this analysis helps to explain the puzzling pattern of results, which suggests that both subgroup and superordinate group orientation are associated with lower consumption (higher cooperation). It appears that subgroup identification does, as predicted by social identity theory, predict higher consumption on behalf of the subgroup. However, higher levels of identification with the superordinate group are associated with lower consumption. Since subgroup and superordinate group identification are not mutually exclusive, (rs ranging from .46 for college leaders, to .755 for solo day standard), the resultant effect is lower consumption by higher identifiers, regardless of whether the group orientation was to the subgroup or the superordinate group; partialing out the overlap of the measures shows that it is superordinate group orientation that accounts for higher levels of cooperation.

These results are complex, but generally consistent with findings from Study 1, the library dilemma. Identification with the subgroup or the superordinate group leads to greater conservation than does an interest in one's own outcomes, and concern for the superordinate group has more impact than concern for the subgroup. The within experiment manipulation of level of salient categorization did not affect chronic measures of identity but did affect our more situation specific measures. This is not surprising, but it does have implications for social identity theory—social identification should be measured at the same level of transience as the manipulation (see similar discussion concerning measurement of identity related to self-esteem—e.g., Abrams & Hogg, 1988; Hogg & Abrams, 1990; Rubin & Hewstone, 1998). Finally, it should be noted that participants in all three of these experiments were resource conserving (taking between 5 and 6 points per trial when they could take up to 10) relative to the simulated others, who took on average 7 points per trial. This may be unremarkable—90% of participants were subsequently classified as cooperators on the basis of their responses to a social value orientation questionnaire (McClintock & Liebrand, 1988; also see Kramer & Goldman, 1995). Given the similarity in procedures to the studies conducted in the U.S., we can only conclude that Australian participants were generally more cooperative than their American counterparts, both in social value orientation and behavior.

GENERAL DISCUSSION

Do leaders who take resources on behalf of a group provide an effective structural solution to a social dilemma? Our analysis of the leader's perception of the expectations of followers, and the leader's own aspirations for the group, suggested that as the importance of the subgroup, and accountability to the subgroup increases, leaders will be less affected by the leader schema, which emphasizes responsible resource use and restraint. They will be more likely to act according to group norms and expectations, and to try to facilitate a positive group identity in ways consistent with these norms. As a result, any differences between how the leader and group members behave should decrease. We had originally thought that the more highly identified or accountable leader would become *less* conserving than individuals in the subgroup on the grounds that the leader would be expected, and would wish, to take a high level of resources on the group's behalf. However, if doing so were to make the common resource collapse, the leader might be seen to be acting *against* the interests of the group members, especially if the norms of the group included cooperation and conservation. Thus, the social dilemma interdependence structure creates a more complex decision for the leader than the typical zero sum setting normally used to examine ingroup bias. In zero sum structures, whatever is gained by the ingroup is a loss for the outgroup. In dilemma settings, such a result occurs only if the other side cooperates in the face of defection, an unlikely outcome. The more common result is mutual defection, leading to an equally poor outcome for both sides. If excessive consumption to advantage the ingroup produces negative outcomes for ingroup *and* outgroup members (effectively equating them in a lose-lose sense), the leader will not realize a positive advantage for his or her group. In a group where members adhere to values of fairness and cooperation (as ours did), a leader who delivered a kamikaze outcome would not be well received.

Our results suggest that the impact of the subgroup leader may be different in different dilemmas. The library dilemma, which is essentially a coordination problem, puts the leader in a much better position than the subgroup of 6 (noncommunicating) individuals to identify and implement the prominent solution. Levels of self-categorization were apparently neutralized in this setting for the leader, despite their having clear effects in the solo conditions. This setting was a one-shot dilemma, and thus the behavior of the leader could only be influenced by expectations about (not experience with) the other leader. Presumably in this case, participants in the leader role felt sufficiently confident that the other leader would also cooperate (or that the participant did not wish to have responsibility for the destruction of the common resource).

On the other hand, in the environment created by our Deteriorating Resource Dilemma (DRD), the other group leader and individuals were programmed to be unrelentingly noncooperative, and so a strategy of unconditional cooperation was not feasible. It appears then, that the leader's response to these conflicting pressures was to act similarly to individual group members in the conditions in which identification or accountability were high (although we have no direct evidence that the leader anticipated either behavior or expectations of other group members). In the standard version, the leader schema appeared to have a greater impact, although the contrast between the leader and solo conditions was much less marked than in the library dilemma. Thus, we need to be cautious in claiming either that (subgroup) leaders will provide an effective structural solution to social dilemmas in general, or that they will plunder the resource on behalf of their groups. Systematic research is needed to allow specification of the conditions under which leaders will have positive and negative effects. In our view, it is important to assess the nature of the relationship between subgroups (Are they mutually exclusive or aligned? Do they have a history of conflict or cooperation? Have they shared the resource for a long time or is one group invading the resource previously accessed by the other, as occurs in mergers of companies? Are the leaders closely identified with one subgroup, the superordinate group, or neither?).

The assumption that subgroup and superordinate group identity and interests are in opposition needs closer examination. The positive correlation of subgroup and superordinate group identity on both chronic and situational measures is an interesting new finding, given the tendency in the literature to assume that these two levels of categorization are somehow mutually exclusive (Rapoport & Bornstein, 1987; Turner, 1991). The sign and degree of relationship among identities are important variables which have not been systematically investigated in the area of social dilemmas, or more generally. Extrapolating from our results, we might speculate that as the correlation between two identities decreases or becomes negative, intergroup competition might become more salient and manifest itself in greater resource consumption, even though this would have negative effects for the collective, as noted earlier. A history of negative intergroup relations, or a reward structure which defines subgroups in terms of mutually exclusive interests (Bornstein, 1992; Insko & Schopler, 1987) has been shown to produce such effects; future work will need to outline the relevant differences in the structures of interdependence used in studies employing different category memberships.

Our results have implications for social identity theory. First, we based our predictions on the assumption that perceptual salience of a common category is sufficient to align personal behavior to group concerns, and to lead to ingroup favoring behavior. Earlier work by Brewer and Kramer (1986) indicated that subgroup identification would be associated with higher resource consumption, while relative salience of the superordinate group would produce lower consumption. In our first study, we did not find this effect; subgroup and superordinate group salience both lead to more cooperation than did an individual orientation in the solo condition.

In our second study, well established methods for inducing levels of self-categorization failed to produce any systematic effect on consumption in the solo conditions. While free response measures at the beginning of the session indicated that the manipulation of self-categorization had been effective, by the end of the session such differences did not register on the chronic or situational measures of identification. Subgroup, compared with superordinate, group identification was generally higher across conditions (although the two were positively correlated). This probably reflects an *optimal distinctiveness* effect (especially for the college students). However, rather than producing high levels of competition with the outgroup, subgroup identification was overall negatively correlated with consumption, and significantly so for those in the more optimally distinctive (college) group. But we found that when the correlation of sub and superordinate group identity was controlled for, subgroup identification of leaders was related to higher consumption. When these two sources of "other-regardingness" are combined (Lichbach, 1996), it may be that the net effect is to produce cooperative or conserving behavior. If the key to these varied findings is in the degree of alignment of identities, then the principle of metacontrast may be developed to provide predictions about lack of discrimination, as well as its presence.

We will not comment in detail on other results of these initial studies of the impact of leaders on resource consumption in an intergroup dilemma setting. Instead, we will indicate what we have learned from our research about conceptual tasks which need to be addressed in this area. These observations arise in part from the design decisions we made while conducting the research, which showed us the wide array of research questions waiting to be tackled.

First, we have begun with a very simple case in which a leader is designated by the experimenter, an outside authority. The results from the accountability condition of the DRD suggest that the relationship of the leader to the group is an important determinant of his or her behavior. However, the characterization of this relationship is in its early stages, theoretically. Aside from the issues of leader prototypicality and identification with the group alluded to earlier, the *structural* relationship of the leader is also important. For example, does it matter how the leader is selected (informally, formally—if formally, by what rule?). What is the source of legitimacy of the leader? What may undermine this legitimacy? If the leader does not have veto power over constitutents, how can decisions be enforced on group members?

In our studies, it was left unstated how the leader would benefit, relative to group members; the leader's fate was clearly tied up with subgroup outcomes. In many cases where a leader is assigned, that person's outcomes may be independent of the fate of the group members (as indicated in the frequent preference for the *impartial leader*). The nature of the relationship between leader's payoff and group membership is clearly important to the prediction of leader behavior, and leader effectiveness.

Another set of questions concern the basis of leader/follower expectations and trust. What is the leader expected to do? What is the basis of these expectations? How much consensus exists between expectations of leaders and followers? Do followers expect the leader to be impartial and fair to ingroup and outgroup, or to show favoritism to the ingroup? Does the leader know of the relevant group expectations? The domain of social dilemmas provides a rich testing ground for the comparison of models of leadership which stress the leader schema or "leader role" (Kerr & Stanfel, 1993; Lord, et al., 1984), and those which focus on the leader who emerges as prototypical of the group members (Hogg, in press; Turner & Haslam, in press).

The detailed nature of the intergroup context is important to whether it will produce cooperation or competition. Our results suggest that mere categorization of people into subgroups will not necessarily produce intergroup competition dangerous to the common resource, or that superordinate categorization necessarily leads to higher levels of cooperation. Clearly, an important consideration is the relationship among the various identities, not only in terms of the mutual inclusiveness or exclusiveness, but also the degree of correspondence of their outcomes (Insko & Schopler, 1998). This, and factors such as the relevance of the group categories to the resource and the past and present reward interdependence, are all likely to be important determinants of whether the intergroup context will produce collective disaster. Future research needs to consider how the intergroup context transforms the perception of individual self-interest, how the leader role transforms individual self-interest, and how these two combine.

Chapter 23

Social Dilemmas and Social Evolution

Marilynn B. Brewer
Sherry Schneider

In their introductory chapter, Smithson and Foddy provide an overview of the epistemological status of theory and research paradigms in the study of social dilemmas as represented by the contributions to this anthology. We seek to complement their perspective by considering the implications of these contributions for advancing our understanding of the nature of human sociality. The starting point of our discussion is the recognition that social dilemmas constitute part of the fabric of human existence, one of the fundamental conditions that shaped the course of human evolution. From this perspective, social dilemmas are aspects of a dynamical system, rather than discrete problems to be solved. The strength of the present volume lies in the acknowledgment and development of this systems approach that emerges from every chapter.

DIMENSIONS OF A DYNAMIC VIEW

The transition from static to dynamic perspectives on social dilemmas influences theory and research paradigms along many dimensions. These include:

(a) increasing the importance and salience of *temporal* considerations in defining the structure of social dilemmas and the nature of the decision making process;

(b) *contextualizing* the decision process in terms of complex interactions among structural, group, and individual level variables;

(c) assessing the behavior of the *system as a whole*, including emergent properties, system learning, and the role of exogenous influences; and

(d) enhancing the value of *multimethodological programs* that capitalize on the complementarity and interrelationships among simulations, laboratory experiments, and field studies in applied settings.

Each of these dimensions of a dynamical perspective is well illustrated in the preceding chapters of this volume.

The Temporal Dimension: Shadows Cast by the Past and the Future

Temporal factors are important at every level of analysis of social dilemmas. Some dilemmas are themselves temporal in nature (Messick & Brewer, 1983), involving implicit or explicit trade off between immediate and long-term outcomes. Time is one of the structural features of dilemma classification systems, including the distinction between single and repeated play games, and between simultaneous and successive or sequential choice modes (Au & Budescu, this volume). As we've seen in this volume, dilemmas are also embedded in environmental systems with their own temporal features (Smithson), and in systems of social interrelationships that extend over time (Chen; Kerr; Morrison; Rapoport & Amaldoss; Schopler & Insko; Takagi). At the individual level, the decision process can be conceptualized in terms of sequential stages (Hertel, this volume), heavily influenced by the time perspective (present or future orientation) that the individual brings to the dilemma situation. In fact, time perspective can be added to the psychological transformations (Kelley & Thibaut, 1978; Webb, this volume) that qualify the relationship between the objective structure of the dilemma and the effective structure of the participant's subjective representation of the situation.

One of the strengths of the contributions to the present volume is the refreshing emphasis on the influence of the shadow of the future on behavior, in contrast to the more traditional behavioral models which characterize learning as an adaptation to past outcomes (e.g., Axelrod, 1984; Rapoport & Chammah, 1965). This shift of orientation is most explicit in Smithson's (this volume) treatment of the exogenous dynamics of public goods and resource dilemmas. Smithson's experiments with different dynamic regimes convincingly demonstrate that human participants are preemptive and forward looking in responding to change patterns and not just to current levels of the resource, and that such strategies are predictive of long-term survival. However, the positive effects of future orientation hinge on the accuracy with which the future state of the resource can be projected. Three chapters in this volume specifically examine the effects on ability to predict the future. In Smithson, the capacity to project the future state of the resource affects an individual's urgency to act. Gärling, Gustafsson, & Biel review the research on the effects of resource uncertainty on behavior and conclude that uncertainty is associated with overoptimism about future availability. Finally, Messick describes how decisions in four organizational social dilemmas were differentially motivated by future considerations. Messick's organizational examples illustrate how various strategies guiding decisions in repeated play games differ in their sensitivity to past versus future outcomes.

Stochastic learning models (e.g., Macy, 1990) and rules such as win stay-lose change rely solely on remembering and learning from past outcomes. By contrast, the effectiveness of *reciprocal* tit for tat strategies may depend not only on responding to past behaviors of the other but also on the anticipated influence of one's own choices on the other's future behaviors (Schopler & Insko, this volume). In Webb's (this volume) extension of Kelley and Thibaut's (1978) theory of psychological transformations to social dilemmas, expectations of the future transform the subjective perception of the objective social dilemma structure, and it is this subjective perception which influences future behavior. Parallel effects at the group level are evident in the relative effectiveness of group norms and sanctions that establish contingencies between one's own immediate behavior and future outcomes (Kerr, this volume).

Complex Interactions: Context and Contingency

Among the inevitable consequences of taking a dynamic systems approach to any area of study is that main effects give way to interactions, both within and between levels of analysis. Broad classes of variables relevant to the study of social dilemmas include social and physical environmental context; structural features of the dilemma itself; the structure of incentives, payoffs, and outcome distributions; information and communication; group behavior, norms, and standards; and individual values, motives, expectancies, and attributions. Early paradigmatic research in this field tended toward systematic experimental variation of each of these dimensions considered one at a time, to assess their independent effects on decision making and collective outcomes. As the field matured, more complex experimental designs, field research, and computer simulations replaced simple parametric variations. The consequence is a growing body of knowledge about contingent relationships whereby the effects of changes in any one domain are moderated and constrained by the state of other variables in the system.

Again, the chapters in this volume provide a rich sampling of the higher order interactions that characterize a complex system. Smithson's chapter illustrates how an exogenous factor (resource renewal function) interacts with an endogenous factor (size of the collective) to determine system stability and resource sustainability. Rapoport and Amaldoss' chapter demonstrates how payoff structure and outcome distribution rules interact to create different decision spaces and equilibria, and how the nature of intragroup conflict is changed when embedded in intergroup competition. The Chen, Morrison, and Foddy and Hogg chapters all deal with the functional dynamic between the interdependence structure and social identity. Chen's experiment demonstrates that an exogenous factor (difficulty of the provision level) influences group cohesion and social identification and the relative effectiveness of equality versus equity allocation rules. (In the latter respect, the effects of task difficulty parallel effects of intergroup competition on intragroup dynamics.) On the other hand, in the other two chapters, the researchers manipulate social identity as an independent variable. Both works demonstrate that the social identity which is salient in a particular context alters the perception of the situation as an ingroup or intergroup dilemma, with significant consequences for cooperative intent.

The difference between the dynamics of intragroup and intergroup dilemmas is also well illustrated by Schopler and Insko's (this volume) programmatic research on the discontinuity effect. Again, holding objective interdependence structure constant, participants are consistently more cooperative when making decisions as individuals (interpersonal context) than when making decisions as members of groups (intergroup context). More importantly, the contingencies required to motivate and sustain cooperative choices by individuals appear to be different from those required by groups. As Schopler and Insko suggest in their chapter, the role of the shadow of the future may be particularly important for intergroup dilemmas.

Several other chapters also document significant interactions between structural variables and individual psychological states as determinants of cooperative behavior or intent. Foddy and Hogg, for example, demonstrate that taking on the role of group leader alters motivation and hence behavior. Likewise, Hertel shows in his chapter how a participant's mood alters the effect of information about others' cooperation on his or her own choice. In a particularly elegant experimental paradigm, Beckenkamp and Ostmann's chapter documents an important interaction between sanctioning regime and participants' values that reveals the potentially paradoxical effects of negative sanctions. Participants who are already oriented toward restraint and group interests are affected relatively little by variations in the severity of sanctions for noncooperation, but the U-shaped function generated by greedy players illustrates that high sanctions can backfire in the presence of self-interested motives.

Three of the chapters involving field studies, Van Vugt, Garvill, and Schneider and Sundali demonstrated how structural properties interact with individual values to affect orientation towards group interests. Van Vugt's field experiment demonstrates that the effectiveness of a control mechanism (metering) to increase willingness to conserve water depended critically on residents' beliefs in the severity of the water shortage. In the absence of perceived urgency, metering (and associated fee structure) has little or no effect on intended consumption. Similarly, the other two chapters reported that understanding the interaction between situational context and values was important in predicting behavior in social dilemmas involving the environment.

The chapters in this volume which emphasize how structural and psychological contexts interact to influence behavior are typical of the experimental analysis of variance research that has been the traditional preference of social psychologists studying social dilemmas. However, many of the contributions to this book, through new theoretical approaches and experimental designs, adopt a more dynamical systems approach to the study of social dilemmas.

A Systems Gestalt: The Whole is More than the Sum of its Parts

Specific interaction effects may be integrated into a larger picture when social dilemmas are viewed as a multilevel system. From environmental states to interdependence structures to group dynamics to individual psychology, causal influences flow in both directions (as illustrated schematically in Figure 23.1). From this perspective, cross level interactions and dynamic relationships are of particular interest.

A number of chapters in this volume indicate that in dilemma situations, individual behavior is more responsive to information about the state of the collective than to information about other individuals' behavior (Au & Budescu, Biel, von Borgstede, & Dahlstrand; Gärling et al., Garvill, Smithson, Van Vugt). This responsiveness to the state of the resource suggests that group members are able to construe social dilemmas as collective rather than interpersonal conflict situations. This has important implications for theoretical models of cooperative choice, particularly with respect to the effects of group size, framing, and the applicability of reciprocal strategies such as tit for tat (cf. Parks & Komorita, 1997). It also has important practical implications for how persuasive campaigns and incentive systems can best be designed. Van Vugt's (this volume) review of water metering and fee structures, for example, illustrates the importance of tying incentive systems to

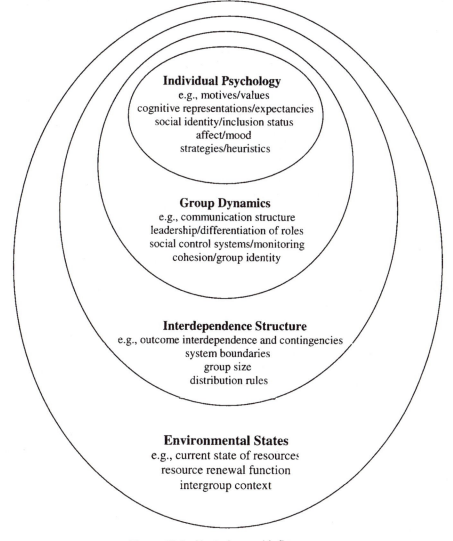

Figure 23.1   Nested causal influences

variations in the state of the resource and demands on the collective good. As Van Vugt shows, providing accurate information about the state of collective resource can serve both motivational and coordinating functions.

The importance of collective perspectives in dilemma situations also helps explain the mediating role of social identity in responding to social dilemmas. As Morrison (this volume) compellingly argues, the essence of group identification is an extension of self-interest to the outcomes of the group as a whole. When the group comprises a cohesive, bounded ingroup—a collective we—the situation is defined as an interaction between this collective self and the external environment rather than an interaction among (potentially competing) individuals within that environment. What is critically important here is whether the psychological representation of the collective ingroup corresponds to the objective structure of interdependence with respect to the shared resource or public good. If the boundaries of group identification are less inclusive than the network of interdependence, the situation is transformed into an intergroup dilemma with corresponding changes in the system dynamics.

As mentioned earlier, the structure of interdependence and the engagement of group identity stand in dynamic relation to each other. While the intensity of interdependence can create group cohesion or alter group boundaries (Chen, this volume; Schopler & Insko, this volume), the salience of group boundaries and corresponding social identities can affect the perception of interdependence and, ultimately, its actual structure (Morrison, this volume). The behavior of leaders of subgroups embedded within a collective, for example, was dependent upon leader perception of which level of categorization was most important, the superordinate collective or the subgroup.

Understanding social dilemmas in terms of the relationship between individual and collective levels of representation also sheds new light on the effects of sanctions and incentive structures in regulating individual behavior. In many cases, incentive systems may work as expected, but not because of their effect on individual calculation of rewards and costs. As manifestations of the collective will, sanctions and rewards provide information about the severity of the collective problem and the state of the resource. For example, Schneider and Sundali (this volume) report that participation in a recycling program depended on whether the city initiated curbside pickup, perhaps signaling the importance of recycling. Even though most participants in the pilot program reported that their attitudes to recycling had changed as a result of the program, when the curbside pickup was discontinued, most reverted to throwing out their recyclable goods. Hence, structural contingencies are likely to be domain specific. As such, their effectiveness depends not on their appeal to individual self-interest but on their perceived legitimacy and credibility as a source of information and (ironically) on the degree of *collective* concern among group members. As a number of the studies reported in this volume indicate, sanctions and other control mechanisms can backfire if they are not perceived to reflect real collective interests. Furthermore, even when sanctions do send a message about the severity of the resource dilemma, this information can motivate strategic competition rather than cooperation for group members who view the situation in terms of individual self-interest rather than collective outcomes (Beckenkamp & Ostmann, this volume). Finally, the symbolic social approval or disapproval implicit in incentives and sanctions carries weight only to the extent that individuals seek inclusion or fear exclusion from the collective as a social group (Kerr, this volume).

The transformation of institutions and structural arrangements through individual meaning systems represents one form of interaction between the social system and individual psychology. Other interactions come in the form of emergent properties, where the aggregation of individual decisions and behaviors gives rise to structural properties at the group level that are not commensurate with their meaning at the individual level. In a sense, social dilemmas themselves represent an emergent product of self-interested individual decision making. But some psychological mechanisms serve to sustain significant rates of cooperation at the group level even in the absence of collective concern or explicit coordination. For instance, a series of simulation studies by Messick & Liebrand (1995, 1997) and Paese & Stang (1998) demonstrate how variations in the application of the win stay-lose change decision rule at the individual level can dramatically alter the prevalence of cooperative choices over generations of prisoner's dilemma game (PDG) play within a population. Subtle psychological biases in the evaluation of outcomes as wins or losses (e.g., the overevaluation of one's own outcomes in comparison to others' and the asymmetry in rate of adaptation to gains versus losses) have the cumulative effect of fostering cooperation in large groups. In the present volume, Takagi's generalized exchange model and Watanabe and Yamagishi's model of selective play demonstrate how individual strategies of contingent altruism and selective association can give rise to cooperative communities. It is interesting to speculate how emergent properties that contribute to group survival may play a role in selection of traits and preferences at the individual level.

Methodological Synergies: Simulations and Experiments are Complementary

Laboratory experimentation using university students as participants has allowed social psychologists to understand the complex interactions between many different types of independent variables that affect behavior in social dilemmas. More and more frequently, however, psychologists are exploring social dilemmas in situations beyond the boundaries of the traditional laboratory experiment. Recent field experimental work on real environmental dilemmas reported in this volume (Biel, Garvill, Schneider & Sundali, and Van Vugt, this volume) demonstrates that the principles refined in the laboratory have external validity and generalizability to populations other than students.

While traditional experimental field and laboratory paradigms are invaluable for developing what we know as a discipline about behavior in social dilemmas, this approach has always had limitations. For mostly practical reasons, these studies are necessarily limited to manipulation of two or three independent variables at a time. The 2×2 ANOVA design limits the ability of social psychologists to describe and understand how social dilemmas operate as complex, dynamic, and social systems. While the addition of field research outside of the laboratory is a desirable trend, it would seem even more important in field settings to try to capture the interactive, temporal, and dynamic aspects of the social dilemma under study. Until recently, the dynamic systems approach to social dilemmas had been exclusively the domain of other academic disciplines such as political science and sociology. This volume, we believe, demonstrates that there is a widespread shift towards more dynamic systems approaches.

A systemic approach to the study of social dilemmas has methodological as well as substantive implications, as illustrated throughout this volume. In current research programs, simulations serve a role similar to that of formal game theory models in both hypothesis generation and theory testing. Simulations transcend the limitations of human experiments in the number of parameters that can be varied simultaneously and the number of iterations of play that can be tracked. But far from making analogue experiments obsolete, the results of simulation runs provide new motivation and structure for laboratory and field experimentation. As Smithson's chapter elegantly illustrates, simulations can be used to establish the range of parametric variations that are worth pursuing experimentally, as well as suggesting new dependent variables for comparing actual to theoretical behavior at the individual and system levels.

We see simulations as particularly complementary to field experimentation. As experimental hypotheses based on simulations and mathematical modeling can take many more parameters into account than more traditional hypothesis testing, they should be able to rapidly generate new explanations for the behavior of individuals in real social dilemmas. In addition, using simulations in conjunction with both field and laboratory experiments allows for the testing of more comprehensive models of social dilemmas, including the relationships among the antecedents, mediators, and moderators of cooperative behavior.

AN EVOLUTIONARY PERSPECTIVE

Anthropological evidence indicates that *homo sapiens* are unique among primate species in their achievement of large scale social coordination that does not depend on spatial proximity or face to face interaction (Kuper, 1994; Rodseth, Wrangham, Harrigan, & Smuts, 1991). Human sociality rivals that of the social insects but is remarkable because—unlike the social insects—it involves cooperation among genetic competitors (Campbell, 1975, 1983). From this perspective, the very existence of stable human groups and society itself implies the successful resolution of social dilemmas of trust and exchange. The question to be addressed is not how *can* social dilemmas be resolved, but how *do* they get resolved on an ongoing basis. What are the evolved mechanisms that make large scale cooperation and interdependence possible despite the temptations of defection in the service of individual self-interest?

The position we take here is that social dilemmas have always played a vital role in the coevolution of human biological and social systems. Dilemmas of interdependence are not only pervasive but also highly variable in form, intensity, and duration. Because dilemmas vary in the size of the collective involved (some interdependence structures are highly localized, others far reaching), no single group size or definition of group boundaries is likely to be functional across all situations. Furthermore, within a given collective, dilemmas vary in terms of the intensity and rate of cooperation required to optimize collective goods. This is a particularly interesting feature of different dilemmas that has important implications for how social systems are maintained.

By definition, dilemmas are situations in which 100% defection is optimal at neither the collective nor the individual level. However, in N-person dilemmas (unlike two-person PD games), 100% cooperation is usually also suboptimal at the collective level. Shared resources are not optimized if no one takes anything from the commons, compared to moderate usage which sustains the commons while affording the benefits of consumption. Similarly, most public goods are not benefited by overcontribution—too many volunteers or excessively large contributions reduce the total benefit to be realized at the collective level (Franzen, this volume). This means that social systems must have some range of tolerance for variability of individual cooperative behavior—both within and between dilemmas—but at the same time mechanisms for constraining tolerance so as not to tip the system toward 100% defection. Furthermore, the system must be sensitive to information from the environment that signal changes in the level of demand for cooperative effort and must have mechanisms for communicating that information within the collective.

The fact that social dilemmas are pervasive, variable, and characterized by exogenous and endogenous uncertainty requires the existence of *multiple, redundant mechanisms* for sustaining sufficient levels of cooperation across time. As Lichbach (1996) emphasizes, any one solution must be an incomplete explanation of collective action, and some combination of solutions must be required. Some of the mechanisms are social structural, some individual psychological, and some involve coordination between levels. From this perspective, single dilemmas are always embedded in a larger metagame that regulates individual connection and attachment to social groups. One message that comes across clearly from an evolutionary perspective on human nature is that we must abandon that notion that the genetic raw material of individual humans is unsocialized, unconstrained self-interest (a claim supported by results of simulations and tournaments). The idea that social systems have evolved *in opposition to* biological dispositions (Campbell, 1975) is just not a viable explanation for the achievements of human sociality.

On the other hand, the notion that individuals come into the world with specific predispositions for noncontingent altruism is not viable either. Conflicts between survival and reproductive success at the individual and collective levels do exist; these conflicts vary in scope and intensity across situations and domains; and no specific disposition will resolve the conflict adequately across all situations of interdependence. Instead, what we need to look for in human nature are general dispositions that make responsiveness to collective needs possible. As a number of chapters in this volume have suggested, one such generic mechanism is a strong need for inclusion (or as Kerr, this volume, suggests, a *fear of exclusion*). A motivation to maintain connectedness with social groups makes the individual exquisitely sensitive to signals that either the viability of the group as a whole is threatened or that the individual's inclusion within the group is tenuous. When either signal is strong, concern for group interests (and expression of cooperation) should increase; when these signals are weak, collective concerns are relaxed and attention to individual self-interest dominates. Humans are driven neither by unmitigated individual selfishness nor by unconditional altruism, but instead show the capacity for variable motivation and behavior patterns contingent on the state of the environment.

To be viable, social groups must be willing and able to exclude individuals from membership contingent upon their cooperation, and at the same time allow enough slack to make the pursuit of individual self-interest possible. The importance of balance between individual and collective needs makes sense of social complexity characterized by potentially conflicting norms and standards and situational flexibility in sanctions.

For example, it is interesting to consider that social systems can achieve this balance in one of two ways—either allowing each individual a limited degree of expression of self-interest over collective interests, or allowing some individuals virtually unlimited exploitation privileges while others are constrained toward 100% altruism. Historically, it is clear that the latter strategy in its extreme can sustain social coordination in the short-term but is highly vulnerable to internal collapse. Some combination of intraindividual and interindividual variability in level of cooperation is more likely in the long run.

Rules and Construals

Given this analysis, an adaptive social system will be characterized by multiple redundant mechanisms at individual and collective levels that are activated probabilistically rather than deterministically. Individuals are attuned to their state of inclusion or acceptance by relevant social groups and have a limited tolerance for risk of exclusion or isolation. By this account, social life can be characterized as something of "a perpetual juggling act— maintaining the integrity of individual identity, interpersonal relationships, and collective interests simultaneously" (Brewer, 1997, pp. 57–58). In order to negotiate conflicting demands, individuals learn rules that match situations to acceptable trade offs between self and collective interests. This notion of heuristic rules and situational construals resembles closely March's (1995) appropriateness-identity-rules (AIR) theory of adaptive decision making discussed by Messick in this volume.

The principles underlying AIR generate the properties of an adaptive system for coping with social dilemmas as we have outlined. Because of the subjective nature of construals and judgments of appropriateness, AIR allows for interindividual variability in response to any given interdependence situation and for intraindividual variability across situations. But at the same time, both sources of variability are constrained by identity concerns that hold individuals to personal and social standards of behavior. To be sure, individuals will be motivated to construe situations in the most self-serving way possible, but this bias will be tempered by the need to avoid any large discrepancy between one's own behavior and the expectations of others (i.e., *shared* construals). Autistic construals are outside the range of tolerance of the social group. The coordination between individual and social levels is achieved through the rules that are learned within the social system (which vary in response to environmental exigencies) and the shared definition of social situations.

The Role of Vigilance and Understanding

Lest we end on too optimistic a note about human nature and social coordination, let us hasten to emphasize that the existence of successful social systems reflects only *past* adaptations. There is no built in match between individual psychology and collective needs. Because rules must be learned, because construals are subjective, because signals are ambiguous, because group boundaries and environmental exigencies change across time, there is no guarantee that the resolution of social dilemmas will be sufficient to sustain large scale social coordination into the future. There is a role here for planning and conscious control at both the individual and collective levels.

The more we know about the characteristics of social dilemmas; the state of the environment; the nature of individual motivations, needs, and values; and the effects of signals from the social system on individual decision making; the better position we are in to design social policies that enhance the possibility of effective coordination in the future. From this perspective, it is encouraging to note that there is evidence of compatibility between results of laboratory studies and field experiments in how individuals respond to different configurations of dilemmas (e.g., Garvill, this volume; Van Vugt, this volume). This means that individuals do not treat the novel laboratory situations as isolated social events but bring with them the influences of the wider social context in which such decisions are usually embedded. To the extent that this is true, well designed laboratory and field experiments in conjunction with simulations can help us understand both the invariants of human motivation and the implicit rules and construals that have been acquired in a particular societal environment. Given the ever widening scope of social interdependence in today's world, such understanding of adaptations from the past will be crucial to managing the future.

References

Abrams, D., & Hogg, M. A. (1988). Comments on the motivational status of self-esteem in social identity and intergroup discrimination. *European Journal of Social Psychology, 18*, 317–334.

Abrams, D., & Hogg, M. A. (Eds.). (1990). *Social identity theory: Constructive and critical advances.* Hemel Hempstead, England: Harvester Wheatsheaf.

Abrams, D., & Hogg, M. A. (Eds.). (in press). *Social identity and social cognition.* Oxford, England: Blackwell.

Adams, J. S. (1965). Inequity in social exchanges. In L. Berkowitz (Ed.), *Advances in experimental social psychology* (pp. 267–300). New York: Academic Press.

Agresti, A. (1990). *Categorical Data Analysis.* NY: Wiley.

Agui, T., & Nagao, T. (1993). *Genetic algorithm.* Tokyo: Shokodo.

Ainslie, G. (1975). Specious reward: A behavioral theory of impulsiveness and impulse control. *Psychological Bulletin, 82*, 463–496.

Aitken, C. K., McMahon, T. A., Wearing, A., & Finlayson, B. L. (1994). Residential water use: Predicting and reducing consumption. *Journal of Applied Social Psychology, 24,* 136–158.

Ajzen, I., & Fishbein, M. (1977). Attitude-behaviors relations: A theoretical analysis and review of empirical research. *Psychological Bulletin, 84,* 888–918.

Ajzen, I., & Fishbein, M. (1980). *Understanding attitudes and predicting social behavior.* Englewood Cliffs, NJ: Prentice Hall.

Alexander, R. D. (1987). *The biology of moral systems.* Hawthorne, NY: Aldine de Gruyter.

Allison, P. D. (1992) The cultural evolution of beneficent norms. *Social Forces, 71,* 279–301.

Allison, S. T., McQeeen, L. R., & Shaerfl, L. M. (1992). Social decision making processes and the equal partionment of shared resources. *Journal of Experimental Social Psychology, 28,* 23–42.

Allison, S. T., & Messick, D. M. (1985). Effects of experience on performance in a replenishable resource trap. *Journal of Personality and Social Psychology, 49,* 943–948.

Allison, S. T., & Messick, D. M. (1990). Social decision heuristics in the use of shared resources. *Journal of Behavioral Decision Making, 3*, 195–204.

Allison, S. T., & Kerr, N. L. (1994). Group correspondence biases and the provision of public goods. *Journal of Personality and Social Psychology, 66,* 688–698.

Allport, F. H. (1924). *Social psychology.* Boston: Houghton–Mifflin.

Alock, J. E., & Mansell, D. (1977). Predisposition and behavior in a collective dilemma. *Journal of Conflict Resolution, 21*, 443–457.

Anderson, J. R. (1983). *The architecture of cognition.* Cambridge, MA: Harvard University Press.

An-Ski, S. (1926). *The dybbuk: A play in four acts.* New York: Boni & Liveright.

Aquino, K., Steisel, V., & Kay, A. (1992). The effects of resource distribution, voice, and decision framing on the provision of public goods. *The Journal of Conflict Resolution, 36,* 665–687.

Arbuthnot, J., Tedeschi, R., Wayner, M., Turner, J., Kressel, S., & Rush, R. (1976–1977). The induction of sustained recycling behavior through the foot-in-the-door technique. *Journal of Environmental Systems, 6,* 355–368.

Armstrong, J. S., & Collopy, F. (1996). Competitor orientation. Effects of objectives and information on managerial decisions and profitability. *Journal of Marketing Research, 33,* 188–199.

Aronson, E. (1992). The return of the repressed: Dissonance theory makes a comeback. *Psychological Inquiry, 3,* 303–311.

Aronson, E., & O'Leary, M. (1983). The relative effectiveness of models and prompts on energy conservation: A field experiment in a shower room. *Journal of Environmental Systems, 12,* 219–224.

Asch, S. E. (1951). Effects of group pressure upon the modification and distortion of judgment. In H. Guetzkow (Ed.), *Groups, leadership, and men* (pp. 177–190). Pittsburgh: Carnegie.

Asch, S. (1956). Studies of independence and submission to group pressure: I. On minority of one against a unanimous majority. *Psychological Monographs, 70,* (9, Whole No. 417).

Ashworth, T. (1980). *Trench Warfare, 1914–1918: The Live and Let Live System.* New York: Holmes & Meir.

Au, W. T. (1997). *Elicitation mode effects on group decision making in a step–level public good social dilemma.* Unpublished doctoral dissertation, University of Illinois, Urbana–Champaign.

Au, W. T. (in preparation). *The effect of group size variability on step-level public good.* Manuscript in preparation.

Au, W. T., Chen, X. P., & Komorita, S. S. (in press). A probabilistic model of criticality in a sequential public good dilemma. *Organizational Behavior and Human Decision Processes.*

Aumann, R. (1967). A survey of cooperative games without side payments. In M. Shubik (Ed.), *Essays in mathematical economics* (pp. 3–27). Princeton, NJ: Princeton University Press.

Austin, W., Walster, E., & Utne, M. K. (1976) Equity and the law. *Advances in Experimental Social Psychology, 9,* 163–190.

Axelrod, R. (1984). *Evolution of cooperation.* New York: Basic Books.

Axelrod, R. (1986). An evolutionary approach to norms. *American Political Science Review, 80,* 1095–1111.

Axelrod, R. (1997a). *The complexity of cooperation: Agent–based models of competition and collaboration.* Princeton, N.J.: Princeton University Press.

Axelrod, R. (1997b). The dissemination of culture: A model with local convergence and global polarization. *Journal of Conflict Resolution, 41,* 203–226.

Baik, K. H., & Lee, S. (1997). Collective rent seeking with endogenous group size. *European Journal of Political Economy, 13,* 121–130.

Baik, K. H., & Shogren, J. F. (1995). Competitive-share group formation in rent-seeking contests. *Public Choice, 83,* 113–126.

Bandura, A. (1977). Self–efficacy: Toward a unifying theory of behavioral change. *Psychological Review, 84,* 191–215.

Bar-Hillel, M., & Budescu, D. (1995). The elusive wishful thinking effect. *Thinking and Reasoning, 1,* 71–103.

Baron, J. (1996). Do no harm. In D. Messick (Ed.), *Codes of conduct: Behavioral research into business ethics* (pp. 197–213). New York: Sage.

Baron, R. M., & Kenny, D. A. (1986). The moderator-mediator distinction in social psychological research: Conceptual, strategic, and statistical considerations. *Journal of Personality and Social Psychology, 51,* 1173–1182.

Baron, R. A. (1993). Affect and organizational behavior. When and why feeling good (or bad) matters. In K. J. Murnigham (Ed.), *Social psychology of organizations: Advances in theory and research* (pp. 63–88). Englewood Cliffs, NJ: Prentice Hall.

Barry, B., & Oliver, R. L. (1996). Affect in dyadic negotiation: A model and propositions. *Organizational Behavior and Human Decision Processes, 67,* 127–143.

Bass, B. M. (1990). *Bass and Stogdill's handbook of leadership: Theory, research and managerial applications.* New York: Free Press.

Bateman, T. S., & Organ, D. W. (1983). Job satisfaction and the good soldier: The relationship between affect and employee "citizenship." *Academy of Management Journal, 26,* 587–595.

Bates, R..H. (1988). Contra–contractarianism: Some reflections on the new institutionalism. *Politics and Society, 16,* 387–401.

Batson, C. D. (1987). Prosocial motivation: Is it ever truly altruistic? *Advances of Experimental Social Psychology, 20*, 65–122.

Baumeister, R., & Leary, M. (1995). The need to belong: Desire for interpersonal attachments as a fundamental human motivation. *Psychological Bulletin, 117*, 497–529.

Baumeister, R., & Tice, D. (1990). Anxiety and social exclusion. *Journal of Social and Clinical Psychology, 9*, 165–195.

Beckenkamp, M., & Ostmann, A. (1996). A member's view of a common: Cognitive and socio-cognitive factors. In Christine Roland-Lévy (Ed.), *Social and economic representations* (pp. 1203–1220). Paris: IAREP 1996; Université René Descartes.

Becker, L. J. (1978). The joint effect of feedback and goal setting on performance: A field study of residential energy conservation. *Journal of Applied Psychology, 63*, 428–433.

Bem, D. J. (1967). Self perception: An alternative interpretation of cognitive dissonance phenomenon. *Psychological Review, 74*, 183–200.

Berger, J., & Zelditch, M., Jr. (1993a). Orienting strategies and theory growth. In: J. Berger, & M. Zelditch, Jr. (Eds.), *Theoretical research programs: Studies in the growth of theory* (pp. 3–19). Stanford, CA: Stanford University Press.

Berger, J., & Zelditch, M., Jr. (1993b). *Strategies, theories, and models.* Unpublished Working Paper 100-6, Stanford University.

Berk, R. A., Cooley, T. F., LaCivita, C. J., Parker, S., Sredl, K., & Brewer, M. (1980). Reducing consumption in periods of acute scarcity: The case of water. *Social Science Research, 9*, 99–120.

Bianco, W. T., & Bates, R. H. (1990). Cooperation by design: Leadership, structure, and collective dilemmas. *American Political Science Review, 84*(1), 133–147.

Biel, A., & Gärling, T. (1995). The role of uncertainty in resource dilemmas. *Journal of Environmental Psychology, 15*, 221–233.

Bierhoff, H. W. (1988). Affect, cognition, and prosocial behavior. In K. Fiedler & J. P. Forgas (Eds.), *Affect, cognition and social behavior* (pp. 167–182). Toronto, Canada: Hogrefe.

Bixenstein, V. E., Levitt, C. A., & Wilson, K. V. (1966). Collaboration among six persons in a Prisoner's Dilemma game. *Journal of Conflict Resolution, 10*, 487–496.

Blalock, H. M., Jr. (1991). *Understanding social inequality: Modelling allocation processes.* Newbury Park, CA: Sage Publications.

Blau, P. M. (1964). *Exchange and power in social life.* New York: Wiley.

Bless, H., Clore, G. L., Schwarz, N., Golisano, V., Rabe, C., & Wölk, M. (1996). Mood and the use of scripts: Does a happy mood really lead to mindlessness? *Journal of Personality and Social Psychology, 71*, 665–679.

Bless, H., Schwarz, N., & Wieland, R. (1996). Mood and the impact of category membership and individuating information. *European Journal of Social Psychology, 26*, 935–959.

Bodenhausen, G. V. (1993). Emotion, arousal, and stereotypic judgments: A heuristic model of affect and stereotyping. In D. M. Mackie & D. L. Hamilton (Eds.), *Affect, cognition, and stereotyping. Interactive processes in group perception* (pp. 13–37). San Diego, CA: Academic Press.

Bodenhausen, G. V., Kramer, G. P., & Susser, K. (1994). Happiness and stereotypic thinking in social judgment. *Journal of Personality and Social Psychology, 66*, 621–632.

Bornstein, G. (1992). The free rider problem in intergroup conflicts over step-level and continuouos public goods. *Journal of Personality and Social Psychology, 62*, 597–602.

Bornstein, G., & Ben-Yossef, M. (1994). Cooperation in intergroup and single group social dilemmas. *Journal of Experimental Social Psychology, 30*, 52–67.

Bornstein, G., Erev, I., & Goren, H. (1994). The effect of repeated play in the IPG and IPD team games. *Journal of Conflict Resolution, 38*, 690–707.

Bornstein, G., & Rapoport, A. (1988). Intergroup competition for the provision of step-level public goods: Effects of pre-play communication. *European Journal of Social Psychology, 18*, 125–142.

Bornstein, G., Rapoport, A., Kerpel, L., & Katz, T. (1989). Within and between group communication in intergroup competition for public goods. *Journal of Experimental Social Psychology, 25*, 422–436.

Bornstein, G., Winter, E., & Goren, H. (1996). *Experimental study of repeated team games* (Discussion Paper # 95). The Hebrew University of Jerusalem, Israel. Center for Rationality and Interactive Decision Theory.

Bouas, K. S., & Komorita, S. S. (1996). Group discussion and cooperation in social dilemmas. *Personality and Social Psychology Bulletin, 22*, 1144–1157.

Bourhis, R. Y., Sachdev, I., & Gagnon, A. (1994). Intergroup research with the Tajfel matrices: Methodological notes. In M. Zanna & J. Olson (Eds.), *The psychology of prejudice: The Ontario symposium* (Vol. 7, pp. 209–232). Hillsdale, NJ: Erlbaum.

Bower, G. H. (1991). Mood congruity of social judgement. In J. Forgas (Ed.), *Emotion and social judgement* (pp. 31–54). Oxford, England: Pergamon Press.

Bray, N. (1997). OECD ministers agree to ban bribery as a means for companies to win business. *Wall Street Journal*, Tuesday, May 2, p. A2.

Brazil, D. (1992). *Discontinuity with intact groups*. Unpublished master's thesis, University of North Carolina, Chapel Hill.

Brennan, G., & Lomasky, L. (1984). Inefficient unanimity. *Journal of Applied Philosophy, 1*, 151–163.

Brewer, M. B. (1991). The social self: On being the same and different at the same time. *Personality and Social Psychology Bulletin, 17*, 475–482.

Brewer, M. B. (1997). On the social origins of human nature. In C. McGarty & S. A. Haslam (Eds.), *The message of social psychology* (pp. 54–62). Oxford, England: Blackwell.

Brewer, M. B., & Gardner, W. (1996). Who is this "we"?: Levels of collective identity and self-representations. *Journal of Personality and Social Psychology, 71*, 83–93.

Brewer, M. B., Ho, H., Lee, J., & Miller, N. (1987). Social identity and social distance among Hong Kong school children. *Personality and Social Psychology Bulletin, 13*, 156–165.

Brewer, M. B., & Kramer, R. M. (1985). The psychology of intergroup attitudes and behavior. *Annual Review of Psychology, 36*, 219–243.

Brewer, M. B., & Kramer, R. M. (1986). Choice behavior in social dilemma: Effects of social identity, group size, and decision framing. *Journal of Personality and Social Psychology, 50*, 543–549.

Brewer, M. B., & Schneider, S. K. (1990). Social identity and social dilemmas: A double-edged sword. In D. Abrams, & M. Hogg (Eds.), *Social identity theory: Constructive and critical advances* (pp. 169–184). London: Harvester Wheatsheaf.

Brown, R. (1954). Mass phenomena. In G. Lindzey (Ed.), *Handbook of social psychology* (Vol. 2, pp. 833–876). Cambridge, MA: Addison-Wesley.

Brown, R., Condor, S., Mathews, A., Wade, G., & Williams, J. (1986). Explaining intergroup differentiation in an industrial organisation. *Journal of Occupational Psychology, 59*, 273–286.

Buckley, T., & Sniezek, J. (1992). Passion, preference, and predictability in judgmental forecasting. *Psychological Reports, 70*, 1022.

Buckley, W., Burns, T., & Meeker, L. D. (1974). Structural resolutions of collective action problems. *Behavioral Science, 19*, 277–297.

Budescu, D. V., Au, W. T., & Chen, X. P. (1997). Effects of protocol of play and social orientation on behavior in sequential resource dilemmas. *Organizational Behavior and Human Decision Processes, 69*, 179–193.

Budescu, D. V., & Au, W. T. (in preparation). *A descriptive model of behavior in sequential CPR dilemmas*. Manuscript in preparation.

Budescu, D. V., & Bruderman, M. (1995). The relationship between the illusion of control and the desirability bias. *Journal of Behavioral Decision Making, 8*, 109–125.

Budescu, D. V., Rapoport, A., & Suleiman, R. (1990). Resource dilemmas with environmental uncertainty and asymmetric players. *European Journal of Social Psychology, 20*, 475–487.

Budescu, D. V., Rapoport, A., & Suleiman, R. (1992). Simultaneous vs. sequential requests in resource dilemmas with incomplete information. *Acta Psychologica, 80*, 297–310.

Budescu, D. V., Rapoport, A., & Suleiman, R. (1995). Common pool resource dilemmas under uncertainty: Qualitative tests of equilibrium solutions. *Games and Economic Behaviour, 10*, 171–201.

Budescu, D. V., Suleiman, R., & Rapoport, A. (1995). Positional order and group size effects in resource dilemmas with uncertain resources. *Organizational Behavior and Human Decision Processes, 61*, 225–238.

Burn, S. M., & Oskamp, S. (1986). Increasing community recycling with persuasive communication and public commitment. *Journal of Applied Social Psychology, 16*, 29–41.

Burns, T., & Meeker, L. D. (1974). Structural properties and resolutions of the prisoner's dilemma game. In A. Rapoport (Ed.), *Game theory as a theory of conflict resolution* (pp. 35–62). Dordrecht, Holland: D. Reidel Publishing.

Byrne, D. (1971). *The attraction paradigm*. New York: Academic Press.

Caldwell, M. D. (1976). Communication and sex effects in a five-person prisoner's dilemma. *Journal of Personality and Social Psychology, 33*, 273–281.

Calhoun, C. (1991). The problem of identity in collective action. In J. Huber (Ed.), *Macro-micro linkages in sociology* (pp. 51–75). Newbury Park, CA: Sage.

Camerer, C., & Thaler, R. (1995). Anomalies: Ultimatums, dictators and manners. *Journal of Economic Perspectives, 9*, 209–219.

Campbell, D. T. (1958). Common fate, similarity, and other indices of the status of aggregates of persons as social entities. *Behavioral Science, 3*, 14–25.

Campbell, D. T. (1965). Ethnocentric and other altruistic motives. In D. Levine (Ed.), *Nebraska Symposium on Motivation*. Lincoln, NE: University of Nebraska Press.

Campbell, D. T., & Stanley, J. C. (1966). *Experimental and quasi-experimental designs for research.* Chicago: Houghton Mifflin Company.

Campbell, D. T. (1972). On the genetics of altruism and counter-hedonic components in human culture. *Journal of Social Issues, 28*, 21–37.

Campbell, D. T. (1975). On the conflicts between biological and social evolution and between psychology and moral tradition. *American Psychologist, 30*, 1103–1126.

Campbell, D. T. (1983). On two distinct routes beyond kin selection to ultrasociality: Implications for the humanities and social sciences. In D. Bridgeman (Ed.), *The nature of prosocial development: Theories and strategies* (pp. 11–41). New York: Academic Press.

Caporael, L., Dawes, R. M., Orbell, J. M., & Van de Kragt, A. (1989). Selfishness examined: Cooperation in the absence of egoistic incentives. *Behavioral and Brain Science, 12*, 683–739.

Carnevale, P. J. D. (1985). Accountability of group representatives and intergroup relations. *Advances in Group Processes, 2*, 227–248.

Carnevale, P. J. D., & Isen, A. M. (1986). The influence of positive affect and visual access on the discovery of integrative solutions in bilateral negotiation. *Organizational Behavior and Human Decision Processes, 37*, 1–13.

Cashdan, E.A . (1980). Egalitarianism among hunters and gatherers. *American Anthropologists, 82*, 116–120.

Cashdan, E. A. (1985). Coping with risk: Reciprocity among the Basarwa of Northern Botswana. *Man (N.S.), 20*, 454–474.

Casti, J. (1994). *Complexification.* New York: Harper Collins.

Chaiken, S., Liberman, A., & Eagly, A. H. (1989). Heuristic and systematic information processing within and beyond the persuasion context. In J. Uleman, & J. Bargh (Eds.), *Unintended thought* (pp. 212–252). New York: Guilford.

Chamberlin, J. (1974). Provision of collective goods as a function of group size. *American Science, 18*, 424–428.

Chapman, G. B., & Johnson, E. J. (1994). The limits of anchoring. *Journal of Behavioral Decision Making, 7*, 223–242.

Chemers, M. M. (in press). Leadership effectiveness: An integrative review. In M. A. Hogg & R. S. Tindale (Eds.), *Blackwell handbook of social psychology* (Vol. 3: Group processes). Oxford, England: Blackwell.

Chen, X. P. (1996). The group-based binding pledge as a solution to public goods problems. *Organizational Behavior and Decision Making Processes, 66*, 192–202.

Chen, X. P. (1997). *The effects of past group performance on cooperation: Conformity, group identity and perceived criticality.* Paper presented at the annual meeting of the Judgment and Decision Making Society, November, Philadelphia.

Chen, X. P., Au, W. T., & Komorita, S. S. (1996). Sequential choice in a step–level public goods dilemma: The effects of criticality and uncertainty. *Organizational Behavior and Human Decision Processes, 65*, 37–47.

Cialdini, R. B. (1984) *Influence: How and why people agree to do things.* New York: Morrow.

Cialdini, R. B., Kallgren, C. A., & Reno, R. R. (1991). A focus theory of normative conduct: A theoretical refinement and reevaluation of the role of norms in human behavior. In M. Zanna (Ed.), *Advances in experimental social psychology* (Vol. 24, pp. 201–234). New York: Academic Press.

Cialdini, R. B., Reno, R. R., & Kallgreen, C. A. (1990). A focus theory of normative conduct: Recycling the concept of norms to reduce littering in public places. *Journal of Personality and Social Psychology, 58*, 1015–1026.

Clore, G. L., Schwarz, N., & Conway, M. (1994). Cognitive causes and consequences of emotions. In R. S. Wyer, & T. K. Srull (Eds.), *Handbook of social cognition* (2nd ed., pp. 323–417). Hillsdale, NJ: Erlbaum.

Coleman, J. S. (1986). Micro-foundations and macrosocial theory. In: S. Lindenberg, J. S. Coleman & S. Nowak (Eds.), *Approaches to social theory* (pp. 345–363). New York: Russell Sage.

Collins, A. M., & Loftus, E. F. (1975). A spreading-activation theory of semantic processing. *Psychological Review, 82*, 407–428.

Cook, K. S., & Hegtvedt, K. A. (1983). Distributive justice, equity, and equality. *Annual Review of Sociology, 9*, 217–241.

Cook, K. S., & Hegtvedt, K. A. (1986). Justice and power. An exchange analysis. In H. W. Bierhoff, R. L. Cohen, & J. Greenberg (Eds.), *Justice in Social Relations* (pp. 19–41). New York: Plenum Press.

Cook, T. D., Crosby, F., & Hennigan, K. M. (1977). The construct validity of relative deprivation. In J. M. Suls, & R. L. Miller (Eds.), *Social comparison processes* (pp. 307–333). Washington, DC: Hemisphere.

Crabb, P. B. (1992). Effective control of energy depleting behavior. *American Psychologist, June*, 815–816.

Crowe, B. (1969). The tragedy of the commons revisited. *Science, 166*, 1103–1107.

Danielson, P. (1992). *Artificial morality: Virtuous robots for virtual games.* London: Routledge.

Darley, J. M. (1978). Energy conservation techniques as innovations, and their diffusion. *Energy and Buildings, 1*, 339–343.

Darley, J. M., & Beniger, J. R. (1981). Diffusion of energy–conserving innovations. *Journal of Social Issues, 37*, 150–171.

Darley, J. M., & Latane, B. (1968). Bystander intervention in emergencies: Diffusion of responsibility. *Journal of Personality and Social Psychology, 8*, 377–383.

Davis, L. (1990). *Handbook of genetic algorithms.* New York: Thomson International Publishing.

Dawes, R. M. (1975). Formal models of dilemmas in social decision making. In M. F. Kaplan, & S. Schwartz (Eds.), *Human judgment and decision making* (pp. 87–108). New York: Academic Press.

Dawes, R. (1980). Social dilemmas. *Annual Review of Psychology, 31*, 169–193.

Dawes, R. M., McTavish, J., & Shaklee, H. (1977). Behavior, communication, and assumptions about other people's behavior in a commons dilemma situation. *Journal of Personality and Social Psychology, 35*, 1–11.

Dawes, R. M., Orbell, J. M., Simmons, R. T., & Van de Kragt, A. J. C. (1986). Organizing groups for collective action. *American Political Science Review, 80*, 1171–1185.

Dawes, R. M., van de Kragt, A. J. C., & Orbell, J. M. (1990). Cooperation for the benefit of us—not me, or my conscience. In J. J. Mansbridge (Ed.), *Beyond self-interest* (pp. 97–110). Chicago: The University of Chicago Press.

de Cremer, D., & Van Vugt, M. (1998). Collective identity and cooperation in a public goods dilemma: A matter of trust or self-efficacy? *Current Research in Social Psychology, 3*, 1–9

Deogun, N. (1997). Coke & Pepsi may call off pricing battle. *Wall Street Jounral*, Thursday, June 12, p. A3.

De Vries, S., & Wilke, H. (1992). Constrained egoism and resource management under uncertainty. In W. Liebrand, D. M. Messick, & H. Wilke (Eds.), *Social dilemmas: Theoretical issues and research findings* (pp. 81–99). Oxford, England: Pergamon Press.

Department of Environment (1993). *Water metering trials: Final report.* London: Department of Environment.

Deutsch, M. (1949). A theory of cooperation and competition. *Human Relations, 2*, 129–152.

Deutsch, M. (1973). *The resolution of conflict.* New Haven, CT: Yale University Press.

Deutsch, M. (1975). Equity, equality, and need: What determines which value will be used as the basis for distributive justice? *Journal of Social Issues, 31*, 137–149.

Deutsch, M. (1980). Fifty years of conflict. In L. Festinger (Ed.), *Retrospections on social psychology* (pp. 46–77). Oxford, England: Oxford University Press.

DeYoung, R. (1985–1986). Encouraging environmentally appropriate behavior: The role of intrinsic motivation. *Journal of Environmental Systems, 15*, 281–292.

DeYoung, R. (1986). Some psychological aspects of recycling: The structure of conservation satisfactions. *Environment and Behavior, 18*, 435–449.

DeYoung, R., & Kaplan, S. (1985–1986). Conservation behavior and the structure of satisfactions. *Journal of Environmental Systems, 15*, 233–242.

Diehl, M. (1990). The minimal group paradigm: Theoretical explanations and empirical findings. *European Review of Social Psychology, 1*, 263–292.

Diekmann, A. (1985). Volunteer's dilemma. *Journal of Conflict Resolution, 29*, 605–610.

Diekmann, A. (1986). Volunteer's dilemma: A social trap without a dominant strategy and some empirical results. In A. Diekmann & P. Mitter (Eds.), *Paradoxical effects of social behavior: Essays in honor of Anatol Rapoport* (pp. 187–197). Heidelberg, Wien: Physica-Verlag.

Diekmann, A. (1993). Cooperation in an asymmetric volunteer's dilemma game: Theory and experimental data. *International Journal of Game Theory, 22*, 75–85.

Diekmann, A. (1994, August). *The limits of rationality solutions in a volunteer's dilemma game.* Paper presented at the American Sociological Association Meeting, Los Angeles, CA.

Diener, E. (1980). Deindividuation: The absence of self–awareness and self–regulation in group members. In P. Paulus (Ed.), *Psychology of group influence* (pp. 209–242). Hillsdale, NJ: L. Erlbaum.

Durkheim, E. (1950). *Les regles de la methode sociologique.* Paris: Press Universitaires de France.

Durkheim, E. (1893). *De la division du travail social [The Division of Labor in society].* New York: Free Press.

Edney, J. J., & Harper, C. S. (1978a). The effects of information in a resource management problem: Social trap analog. *Human Ecology, 6*, 387–395.

Edney, J. J., & Harper, C. S. (1978b). Heroism in a resource crisis: A simulation study. *Environmental Management, 2*, 523–527.

Ellemers, N. (1993). The influence of socio-structural variables on identity management strategies. *European Review of Social Psychology, 4,* 27–57.

Enquist, M., & Leimer, O. (1993). The evolution of cooperation in mobile organisms. *Animal Behavior, 45,* 747–757.

Erev, I., & Rapoport, A. (1990). Provision of step-level public goods: The sequential contribution mechanism. *Journal of Conflict Resolution, 34,* 401–425.

Farh, J-L., Podsakoff, P. M., & Organ, D. W. (1990). Accounting for organizational citizenship behavior: Leader fairness and task scope versus satisfaction. *Journal of Management, 16,* 705–722.

Farrington, D., Berkowitz, L., & West, D. J. (1982). Differences between individual and group fights. *British Journal of Social Psychology, 21,* 323–333.

Festinger, L. (1950). Informal social communication. *Psychological Review, 57,* 271–282.

Festinger, L. (1954). A theory of social comparison processes. *Human Relations, 7,* 117–140.

Festinger, L., & Carlsmith, J. M. (1959). Cognitive consequences of forced compliance. *Journal of Abnormal Psychology, 58,* 203–210.

Festinger, L., Schachter, S., & Back, K. (1950). *Social pressures in informal groups: A study of a housing community.* New York: Harper.

Fiedler, K. (1988). Emotional mood, cognitive style, and behavior regulation. In K. Fiedler, & J. P. Forgas (Eds.), *Affect, cognition, and social behavior* (pp. 100–119). Toronto, Canada: Hogrefe.

Fiedler, K. (1990). Mood-dependent selectivity in social cognition. In W. Stroebe, & M. Hewstone (Eds.), *European review of social psychology* (Vol. 1, pp. 1–32). Chichester, England: Wiley.

Fielding, K. S., & Hogg, M. A. (1997). Social identity, self–categorization, and leadership: A field study of small interactive groups. *Group Dynamics: Theory, Research, and Practice, 1,* 39–51.

Fischer, I., & Budescu, D. V. (1995). Desirability and hindsight biases in predicting results of a multiparty election. In J–P. Caverni, M. Bar–Hillel, F. H. Barron, & H. Jungerman (Eds.), *Contributions to decision making.* (pp. 193–211). North Holland: Elsevier.

Fiske, S. T., & Taylor, S. E. (1991). *Social cognition* (2nd ed.). New York: McGraw-Hill.

Flache, A. (1996). *The double edge of networks: An analysis of the effect of informal networks on cooperation in social dilemmas.* Amsterdam: Thesis Publishers.

Flache, A., & Liebrand, W. (1997, July). *The double edge of networks.* Paper presented at the Seventh International Conference on Social Dilemmas, Cairns, Australia.

Fleishman, J. A. (1988). The effects of decision framing and others' behavior on cooperation in social dilemma. *Journal of Conflict Resolution, 32,* 162–180.

Foddy, M., & Crettenden, A. (1994). Leadership and group identity as determinants of resource consumption in a social dilemma. In U. Schulz, W. Albers, & U. Mueller (Eds.), *Social dilemmas and cooperation* (pp. 207–232). Berlin: Springer-Verlag.

Foddy, M., & Hogg, M.A . (1994). *Intergroup dimensions of resource consumption in social dilemmas: The role of group leaders.* Latrobe University and University of Queensland, unpublished research proposal to the Australian Research Council.

Foddy, M., & Hogg, M. (1999). *The impact of subgroup leaders on resource consumption in a social dilemma: Coordination of access in an information dilemma.* Manuscript submitted for publication.

Foddy, M., & Veronese, D. (1996). Does knowing the jointly rational solution make you want to pursue it? Motivational orientation, information, and behavior in two social dilemmas. In W. B. G. Liebrand, & D. M. Messick (Eds.), *Frontiers in social dilemmas research* (pp. 135–155). Heidelberg and New York: Springer, 1996.

Forgas, J. P. (1982). Episode Cognition: Internal representations of interactive routines. In L. Berkowitz (Ed.), *Advances in experimental psychology* (15, pp. 59–103). New York: Academic Press.

Forgas, J. P. (1995). Mood and judgment: The Affect Infusion Model (AIM). *Psychological Bulletin, 116,* 39–66.

Forgas, J. P. (1998). On feeling good and getting your way: Mood effects on negotiator cognition and bargaining strategies. *Journal of Personality and Social Psychology, 74,* 565–577.

Forgas, J. P., & Bower, G. H. (1987). Mood effects on person perception judgements. *Journal of Personality and Social Psychology, 53,* 53–60.

Fox, J., & Guyer, M. (1977). Group size and others' strategy in an n-person game. *Journal of Conflict Resolution, 21,* 323–338.

Fox, J., & Guyer, M. (1978). "Public" choice and cooperation in n–person prisoner's dilemma. *Journal of Conflict Resolution, 22,* 469–481.

Franzen, A. (1995). Group size and one-shot collective action. *Rationality and Society, 7,* 183–200.

Freedman, J. L., & Fraser, S. C. (1966). Compliance without pressure: The foot-in-the-door technique. *Journal of Personality and Social Psychology, 4,* 195–202.

Frijda, N. H. (1993). Moods, emotion episodes, and emotions. In M. Lewis, & J. M. Haviland (Eds.), *Handbook of emotions* (pp. 381–403). New York: Guilford Press.

Frohlich, N., & Oppenheimer, J. A. (1996). Experiencing impartiality to invoke fairness in the n-PD: Some experimental results. *Public Choice, 86,* 117–135.

Gaertner, S. L., Dovidio, J. F., Anastasio, P. A., Bachman, B. A., & Rust, M. C. (1993). The common ingroup identity model: Recategorization and the reduction of intergroup bias. In W. Stroebe & M. Hewstone (Eds.), *European review of social psychology* (Vol. 4, pp. 1–26). Chichester, England: John Wiley & Sons.

Gaertner, S. L., Mann, J. A., Dovidio, J. F., Murrell, A. & Pomare, M. (1990). How does cooperation reduce intergroup bias? *Journal of Personality and Social Psychology, 59,* 692–704.

Gaertner, S. L., & Schopler, J. (1998). Ingroup entitativity and intergroup bias: An interconnection of self and others. *European Journal of Social Psychology, 28,* 963–980.

Gardner, G. T., & Stern, P. C. (1996). *Environmental problems and human behavior.* Needham Heights, MA: Allyn & Bacon.

Gardner, R., Ostrom, E., & Walker, J. (1990). The nature of common-pool resource problems. *Rationality and Society, 2,* 335–358.

Gärling, T. (1997, July). *Value priorities, social value orientation, and cooperation in social dilemmas.* Paper presented at the 7th Conference on Social Dilemmas, Cairns, Australia.

Garvill, J., Laitila, T., & Brydsten, M. (1994). *Values and choice of transportation mode.* Umeå University, Transportation Research Unit, Sweden.

Gauthier, D. P. (1986). *Morals by agreement.* Oxford: Oxford University Press.

Geller, E. S., Chaffee, J. L., & Ingram, R. E. (1975). Promoting paper recycling on a university campus. *Journal of Environmental Systems, 5,* 39–57.

Geller, E. S., Erickson, J. B., & Buttram, B. A. (1983). Attempts to promote residential water conservation with educational, behavioral and engineering strategies. *Population and Environment, 6,* 96–112.

Geller, E. S., Winett, R. A., & Everett, P. B. (1982). *Preserving the environment: New strategies for behavior change.* New York: Pergamon Press.

Geotze, D. (1995). Comparing prisoner's dilemma, commons dilemma, and public goods provision designs in laboratory experiments. *Journal of Conflict Resolution, 38,* 56–86.

Gilbert, D. T., & Jones, E. E. (1986). Perceiver-induced constraint: Interpretations of self-generated reality. *Journal of Personality and Social Psychology, 50,* 269–280.

Gilbert, D. T., & Malone, P. S. (1995). The correspondence bias. *Psychological Bulletin, 117,* 21–38.

Glance, N. S., & Huberman, B. A. (1993). The outbreak of cooperation. *Journal of Mathematical Sociology, 17,* 281–302.

Glick, T. F. (1970). *Irrigation and society in medieval Valencia.* Cambridge, MA: Harvard University Press.

Goldberg, D. (1989). *Genetic algorithms in search, optimization, and machine learning.* Reading, PA: Addison-Wesley.

Gouldner, A. W. (1960). The norm of reciprocity: A preliminary statement. *American Sociological Review, 25,* 161–178.

Granovetter, M. (1978). Threshold models of collective behavior. *American Journal of Sociology, 83,* 1420–1443.

Greenberg, J., & Cohen, R. L. (Eds.). (1982). *Equity and justice in social behavior.* New York. Academic Press.

Griesinger, D. W., & Livingston, J. W., Jr. (1973). Toward a model of interpersonal motivation in experimental games. *Behavioral Science, 18,* 173–188.

Gustafsson, M., Biel, A., & Gärling, T. (1997a). *Optimism and overharvesting in resource dilemmas* (Göteborg Psychological Reports, 27, No. 10). Göteborg, Sweden: Göteborg University, Department of Psychology.

Gustafsson, M., Biel, A., & Gärling, T. (1997b). *Overharvesting of resources of unknown size* (Göteborg Psychological Reports, 27, No. 9). Göteborg, Sweden: Göteborg University, Department of Psychology.

Gustafsson, M., Biel, A., & Gärling, T. (1998). *Test of an egoism explanation of noncooperation in social dilemmas with resource uncertainty* (Göteborg Psychological Reports, 28, No. 1). Göteborg, Sweden: Göteborg University, Department of Psychology.

Gûth, W., Schmittberger, R., & Schwartze, B. (1982). An experimental analysis of ultimatum bargaining. *Journal of Economic Behavior and Organization, 3,* 367–388.

Haidt, J., & Baron, J. (1996). Social roles and the moral judgment of acts and omissions. *European Journal of Social Psychology, 26,* 201–218.

Hains, S. C., Hogg, M. A., & Duck, J. M. (1997). Self–categorization and leadership: Effects of group prototypicality and leader stereotypicality. *Personality and Social Psychology Bulletin, 23,* 1087–1100.

Hamburger, H., Guyer, M., & Fox, J. (1975). Group size and cooperation. *Journal of Conflict Resolution, 19,* 503–531.

Hampton, J. (1987). Free–rider problems in the production of collective goods. *Economics and Philosophy, 3,* 245–273.

Hankle, S. H., & Boland, J. J. (1971). Water requirements or water demands? *Journal of the American Water Works Association, 63,* 677–682.

Harada, Y., & Iwasa, Y. (1994). Lattice population dynamics for plants with dispersing seeds and vegetative propagation. *Research in Population Ecology, 36,* 237–249.

Hardin, G. (1968). The tragedy of the commons (The population problem has no technical solution; it requires a fundamental extension in morality). *Science, 162,* 1243–1248.

Hardin, G. (1982). Discriminating altruisms. *Zygon, 17,* 163–186.

Hardin, R. (1982). *Collective action.* Baltimore: The Johns Hopkins University Press.

Harkins, S. G., & Petty, R. E. (1982). Effects of task difficulty and task uniqueness on social loafing. *Journal of Personality and Social Psychology, 43,* 1214–1229.

Harsanyi, J. C., & Selten, R. (1988). *A general theory of equilibrium selection in games.* Cambridge, MA: M.I.T. Press.

Hart, O. (1983). The market mechanism as an incentive scheme. *Bell Journal of Economics, 74,* 366–382.

Hausken, K. (1994). *Dynamic hierarchical game theory.* Unpublished doctoral dissertation, The University of Chicago.

Hausken, K. (1995a). The dynamics of within-group and between-group interaction. *Journal of Mathematical Economics, 24,* 655–687.

Hausken, K. (1995b). Intra-level and inter-level interaction. *Rationality and Society, 7,* 465–488.

Hausken, K. (1996a). Dynamic multilevel interaction. Unpublished manuscript. Max-Planck Institute, Cologne, Germany.

Hausken, K. (1996b, August). *Leadership struggle and intergroup competition.* Paper presented at the European Economic Association, Istanbul, Turkey.

Hausken, K. (1996c, July). *Repeated within-group games with discounting in a multi-group environment.* Paper presented at the International Conference on Game Theory, State University of New York, Stony Brook, NY.

Hausken, K. (1996d). *The technology of conflict in dynamic multi–group environment.* Paper presented at the University of Dorthmund, Germany.

Hayashi, N. (1993a). From tit-for-tat to out-for-tat. *Sociological Theory and Method, 8,* 19–32.

Hayashi, N. (1993b, October 30–31). *Prisoner's dilemma networks: Study of strategies, II.* Paper presented at the 34th Annual Meetings of the Japanese Social Psychological Association. Tokyo.

Hayashi, N. (1995). Emergence of cooperation in one-shot prisoner's dilemmas and the role of trust. *Japanese Journal of Psychology, 66,* 184–190.

Hayashi, N., Jin, N., & Yamagishi, T. (1993). Prisoners dilemma networks: A computer-simulation of strategies. *Research in Social Psychology, 8,* 33–43.

Hayashi, N., & Yamagishi, T. (in press). Selective play: Choosing partners in an uncertain world. *Personality and Social Psychology Review.*

Hayes, S. C., & Cone, J. D. (1981). Reduction of residential consumption of electricity through simple monthly feedback. *Journal of Applied Behavior Analysis, 14,* 81–88.

Hechter, M. (1984). When actors comply: Monitoring costs and the production of social order. *Acta Sociologica, 27,* 161–183.

Hechter, M. (1991). From exchange to structure. In J. Huber (Ed.). *Macro-micro linkages in sociology* (pp. 46–50). Newbury Park, CA: Sage.

Herlocker, C. E., Allison, S. T., Foubert, J. D., & Beggan, J. K. (1997). Intended and unintended overconsumption of physical, spatial and temporal resources. *Journal of Personality and Social Psychology, 73,* 992–1004.

Herr, P. M. (1986). Consequences of priming: Judgment and behavior. *Journal of Personality and Social Psychology, 51,* 1106–1115.

Hertel, G. (1995). *Kognitive und affektive Einflüsse auf kooperative Verhaltensentscheidungen* [Cognitive and affective influences on cooperative behavior decisions]. Aachen, Germany: Shaker.

Hertel, G., & Fiedler, K. (1994). Affective and cognitive influences in a social dilemma game. *European Journal of Social Psychology, 24,* 131–145.

Hertel, G., & Fiedler, K. (1998). Fair and dependent versus egoistic and free: Effects of semantic and evaluative priming on the "ring measure of social values." *European Journal of Social Psychology, 28,* 49–70.

Hertel, G., & Kerr, N. L. (1997). [Correlations between social orientation, affectivity, need for cognition, and ratings of universal values] Unpublished raw data.

Hertel, G., & Klinkner, A. (1998). *Effects of perceived others' cooperation in a chicken dilemma game*. Manuscript in preparation.

Hertel, G., Neuhof, J., Theuer, T., & Kerr, N. L. (in press). Mood effects on cooperation in small groups: Does positive mood simply lead to more cooperation? *Cognition and Emotion*.

Hillman, A. L., & Samet, D. (1987). Dissipation of contestable rents by small number of contenders. *Public Choice, 54*, 63–82.

Hine, D. V., & Gifford, R. (1996). Individual restraint and group efficiency in commons dilemmas: The effects of uncertainty and risk-seeking. *Journal of Applied Social Psychology, 26*, 993–1009.

Hinkle, S., Taylor, L., Fox-Cardamone, D. L., & Crook, K. (1989). Intragroup identification and intergroup differentiation: A multi-component approach. *British Journal of Social Psychology, 28*, 305–317.

Hobbes, T. (1651/1939). *Leviathan*. New York: Modern Library.

Hoffman, E., McCabe, K., Schachat, K., & Smith, V. (1994). Preferences, property rights and anonymity in bargaining games. *Games and Economic Behavior, 7*, 346–380.

Hogg, M. A. (1992). *The social psychology of group cohesiveness: From attraction to social identity*. Hemel Hempstead, England: Harvester Wheatsheaf, and New York: New York University Press.

Hogg, M. A. (1996). Intragroup processes, group structure and social identity. In W. P. Robinson (Ed.), *Social groups and identities: Developing the legacy of Henri Tajfel* (pp. 65–93). Oxford, England: Butterworth-Heinemann.

Hogg, M. A. (1999). *A social identity theory of leadership*. Unpublished manuscript, submitted for publication. University of Queensland.

Hogg, M. A., & Abrams, D. (1988). *Social identifications: A social psychology of intergroup relations and group processes*. London: Routledge.

Hogg, M. A., & Abrams, D. (1990). Social motivation, self-esteem and social identity. In D. Abrams & M. A. Hogg (Eds.), *Social identity theory: Constructive and critical advances* (pp. 28–47). Hemel Hempstead, England: Harvester Wheatsheaf, and New York: Springer–Verlag.

Hogg, M. A., & Abrams, D. (Eds.) (1993). *Group motivation: Social psychological perspectives*. Hemel Hempstead, England: Harvester Wheatsheaf, and New York: Prentice Hall.

Hogg, M. A., & Abrams, D. (1998). Social identity and social cognition: Historical background and current trends. In D. Abrams & M. A. Hogg (Eds.), *Social identity and social cognition* (pp. 1–25). Oxford, England: Blackwell.

Hogg, M. A., & Hains, S. C. (1996). Intergroup relations and group solidarity: Effects of group identification and social beliefs on depersonalized attraction. *Journal of Personality and Social Psychology, 70*, 295–309.

Hogg, M. A., Hains, S. C., & Mason, I. (1998). Identification and leadership in small groups: Salience, frame of reference, and leader stereotypicality effects on leader evaluations. *Journal of Personality and Social Psychology, 75*, 1248–1263.

Hogg, M. A., & Terry, D. J. (Eds.). (in press). *Social identity processes in organizational contexts*. Philadelphia, PA: Psychology Press.

Holland, J. H. (1975). *Adaptation in natural and artificial systems*. Ann Arbor, MI: The University of Michigan Press.

Holland, J. H. (1992). Genetic algorithms, *Scientific American, 7*, 66–72..

Homans, G. C. (1976). Commentary. *Advances in Experimental Social Psychology, 9*, 231– 244.

Homans, G. G. (1998). The bank wiring observation room. In G. L. Carter (Ed.), *Empirical approaches to sociology* (2nd ed., pp. 21–29). Boston, MA: Allyn and Bacon.

Homer, P. M., & Kahle, L. R. (1988). A structural equation test of the value-attitude-behavior hierarchy. *Journal of Personality and Social Psychology, 54*, 638–646.

Hopper, J. R., & McCarl-Nielsen, J. (1991). Recycling as altruistic behavior: Normative and behavioral strategies to expand participation in a community recycling program. *Environment and Behavior, 23*, 195–220.

Horn, H., Lang, H., & Lundgren, S. (1995). Managerial effort incentives, x-inefficiency, and international trade. *European Economic Review, 39*, 117–138.

Hoyle, R. H., Pinkley, R. L., & Insko, C. A. (1989). Perceptions of behavior: Evidence of differing expectations for interpersonal and intergroup interactions. *Personality and Social Psychology Bulletin, 15*, 365–376.

Hummel, C. F., Levitt, L., & Loomis, R. J. (1978). Perceptions of the energy crisis: Who is blamed and how do citizens react to environment-lifestyle trade-offs? *Environment and Behavior, 10*, 37–88.

Insko, C. A., Hoyle, R. H., Pinkley, R. L., Hong, G., Slim, R., Dalton, G., Lin, Y., Ruffin, P. F., Dardis, G. J., Bernthal, P. R., & Schopler, J. (1988). Individual-group discontinuity: The role of a consensus rule. *Journal of Experimental Social Psychology, 24*, 505–519.

Insko, C. A., Pinkley, R. L., Harring, K., Holton, B., Hong, G., Krams, D. S., Hoyle, R. H., & Thibaut, J. (1987). Beyond categorization to competition: Expectations of appropriate behavior. *Representative Research in Social Psychology, 17,* 5–36.

Insko, C. A., Pinkley, R. L., Hoyle, R. H., Dalton, B., Hong, G., Slim, R., Landry, P., Holton, B., Ruffin, P. F., & Thibaut, J. (1987). Individual-group discontinuity: The role of intergroup contact. *Journal of Experimental Social Psychology, 23,* 250–267.

Insko, C. A., & Schopler, J. (1987). Categorization, competition, and collectivity. In C. Hendrick (Ed.), *Review of Personality and Social Psychology: Group Processes, 8,* 213–251.

Insko, C. A., & Schopler, J. (1998). Differential distrust of groups and individuals. In C. Sedikides, J. Schopler, & C. A. Insko (Eds.), *Intergroup cognition and intergroup behavior* (pp. 75–107). Mahwah, NJ: Erlbaum.

Insko, C. A., Schopler, J., Drigotas, S. M., Graetz, K. A., Kennedy, J., Cox, C., & Bornstein, G. (1993). The role of communication in interindividual-intergroup discontinuity. *Journal of Conflict Resolution, 37,* 108–138.

Insko, C. A., Schopler, J., Graetz, K. A., Drigotas, S. M., Currey, D. P., Smith, S. L., Brazil, D., & Bornstein, G. (1994). Individual–intergroup discontinuity in the Prisoner's Dilemma Game. *Journal of Conflict Resolution, 38,* 87–116.

Insko, C. A., Schopler, J., Hoyle, R. H., Dardis, G. J., & Graetz, K. A. (1990). Individual-group discontinuity as a function of fear and greed. *Journal of Personality and Social Psychology, 58,* 68–79.

Insko, C. A., Schopler, J., Pemberton, M. B., Wieselquist, J., McIlraith, S., Currey, D. P., & Gaertner, L. (1998). Long-term outcome maximization and the reduction of interindividual-intergroup discontinuity. *Journal of Personality & Social Psychology, 75,* 695–710.

Insko, C. A., Thibaut, J. W., Moehle, D., Wilson, M., Diamond, W. D., Gilmore, R., Solomon, M. R., & Lipsitz, A. (1980). Social evolution and the emergence of leadership. *Journal of Personality and Social Psychology, 39,* 431–448.

Isen, A. M. (1987). Positive affect, cognitive processes, and social behavior. In L. Berkowitz (Ed.), *Advances in experimental social psychology* (Vol. 20, pp. 203–253). San Diego, CA: Academic Press.

Isen, A. M., & Baron, R. A. (1991). Positive affect as a factor in organizational behavior. *Research in Organizational Behavior, 13,* 1–53.

Isen, A. M., Daubman, K. A., & Nowicki, G. P. (1987). Positive affect facilitates creative problem solving. *Journal of Personality and Social Psychology, 52,* 1122–1131.

Jacobs, H. E., & Bailey, J. S. (1982–1983). Evaluating participation in a residential recycling program. *Journal of Environmental Systems, 12,* 141–152.

Jerdee, T. H., & Rosen, B. (1974). Effects of opportunity to communicate and visibility of individual decisions on behavior in the common interest. *Journal of Applied Psychology, 59,* 712–716.

Jevons, W. S. (1871/1911). *The theory of political economy.* London: Macmillan.

Jin, N., Hayashi, N., & Shinotsuka, H. (1996). An experimental study of prisoner's dilemma network. *Japanese Journal of Experimental Social Psychology, 35,* 292–303.

Johnson, D. W, & Johnson, R. T. (1998). Cooperative learning and social interdependence theory. In T. R. Scott, and L. Heath (Eds.), *Theory and Research on Small Groups: Social Psychological Applications to Social Issues, 4,* 9–35.

Jorgenson, D. O., & Papciak, A. S. (1981). The effects of communication, resource feedback, and identifiability on behavior in a simulated commons. *Journal of Experimental Social Psychology, 17,* 373–385.

Kahneman, D., Knetsch, J. L., & Thaler, R. (1986). Fairness and the assumptions of economics. *Journal of Business, 59,* S285–S300, S329–S354.

Kahneman, D,& Tversky, A. (1979). Prospect theory: An analysis of decision under risk. *Econometrica, 67,* 263–291.

Kashima, E., & Kashima, Y. (1992). *Self typicality.* Unpublished manuscript, Swinburne Institute of Technology, Melbourne, Australia.

Katz, E. S., Nitzan, S., & Rosenberg, J. (1990). Rent seeking for pure public goods. *Public Choice, 65,* 49–60.

Katzev, R. D., & Pardini, A. U. (1987–1988). The comparative effectiveness of reward and commitment approaches in motivating community recycling. *Journal of Environmental Systems, 17,* 93–117.

Kawata, M. (1997). Exploitative competition and ecological effective abundance. *Ecological Modeling, 94,* 125–137.

Kawata, M., & Toquenaga, Y. (1994). From artificial individuals to global patterns. *Trends in Ecology and Evolution, 9,* 417–421.

Keeney, R. L., & Raiffa, H. (1976). *Decisions with multiple objectives.* New York: John Wiley & Sons.

Kelley, H. H. (1984a). Interdependence theory and its future. *Representative Research in Social Psychology, 14,* 2–15.

Kelley, H. H. (1984b). The theoretical description of interdependence by means of transition lists. *Journal of Personality and Social Psychology, 47*(5), 956–982.

Kelley, H. H. (1997). The "stimulus field" for interpersonal phenomena: The source of language and thought about interpersonal events. *Personality and Social Psychology Review, 1*, 140–169.

Kelley, H. H., & Grzelak, J. (1972). Conflict between individual and common interest in an n-person relationship. *Journal of Personality and Social Psychology, 21*(2), 190–197.

Kelley, H. H., & Thibaut, J. W. (1978). *Interpersonal relations: A theory of interdependence.* New York: Wiley.

Kelley, H. H., Thibaut, J. W., Radloff, R., & Mundy, D. (1962). *The development of cooperation in the "minimal social situation"* (Psychological Monographs, 76, No. 19). Washington, DC: American Psychological Association, Inc.

Kempton, W., Darley, J. M., & Stern, P. C. (1992). Psychological research for the new energy problems: Strategies and opportunities. *American Psychologist, 47,* 1213–1223.

Kent, S. (1993). Sharing in an egalitarian Kalahari community. *Man (N.S.), 28,* 479–514.

Keohane, R. O. & Ostrom, E. (Eds.). (1995). *Local commons and global interdependence: Heterogeneity and cooperation in two domains.* Thousand Oaks, CA: Sage.

Kerr, N. L. (1983). Motivation losses in small groups: A social dilemma analysis. *Journal of Personality and Social Psychology, 45,* 819–828.

Kerr, N. (1989). Illusions of efficacy: The effects of group size on perceived efficacy in social dilemmas. *Journal of Experimental Social Psychology, 25,* 287–313.

Kerr, N. L. (1990). Applied perspectives on social and temporal dilemmas: An introduction. *Social Behavior, 5,* 201–205.

Kerr, N. L. (1992). Efficacy as a causal and moderating variable in social dilemmas. In W. Liebrand, D. Messick, & H. Wilke (Eds.), *A social psychological approach to social dilemmas* (pp. 59–80). New York: Pergamon Press.

Kerr, N. L. (1995a). Norms in social dilemmas. In D. Schroeder (Ed.), *Social dilemmas: Perspectives on individuals and groups* (pp. 31–47). Westport, CT: Praeger.

Kerr, N. L. (1995b). Norms in social dilemmas. In D. Schroeder (Ed.), *Social dilemmas: Social psychological perspectives* (pp. 31–47). New York: Pergamon Press.

Kerr, N. L. (1996). Does my contribution really matter? Efficacy in social dilemmas. In W. Stroebe, & M. Hewstone (Eds.), *European review of social psychology* (pp. 209–240). Chichester: Wiley.

Kerr, N. L. (1997). *Social exclusion as a deterrent to defection in social dilemmas.* Unpublished manuscript, Michigan State University.

Kerr, N. L., & Bruun, S. E. (1983). Dispensability of member effort and group motivation losses: Free-rider effects. *Journal of Personality and Social Psychology, 44,* 78–94.

Kerr, N. L., Garst, J., Lewandowski, D. A., & Harris, S. E. (1997). The still, small voice: Commitment to cooperate as an internalized versus a social norm. *Personality and Social Psychology Bulletin, 23,* 1300–1311.

Kerr, N. L., & Harris, S. E. (1996). Why do cooperators cooperate?: Efficacy as a moderator of social motive effects. In W. B. G. Liebrand, & D. M. Messick (Eds.), *Frontiers in social dilemma research* (pp. 101–115). Berlin: Springer-Verlag.

Kerr, N. L., & Kaufman-Gilliland, C. M. (1994). Communication, commitment, and cooperation in social dilemmas. *Journal of Personality and Social Psychology, 66,* 513–529.

Kerr, N. L., & Kaufman-Gilliland, C. (1997). Rationalizing defection in social dilemmas. *Journal of Experimental Social Psychology, 33,* 211–230.

Kerr, N., & Stanfel, J.A. (1993). Role schemata and member motivation in task groups. *Personality and Social Psychology Bulletin, 19,* 432–44.

Klandermas, B. (1992). Persuasive communication: Measures to overcome real-life social dilemmas. In W. B. G. Liebrand, D. M. Messick, & H. A. M. Wilke (Eds.), *Social dilemmas: Theoretical issues and research findings* (pp. 3–28). Oxford, England: Pergamon Press.

Knapp, A., & Clark, M. C. (1991). Some detrimental effects of negative mood on individuals' ability to solve resource dilemmas. *Personality and Social Psychology Bulletin, 17,* 678–688.

Komorita, S. S. (1976). A model of the N-person dilemma-type game. *Journal of Experimental Social Psychology, 12,* 357–373.

Komorita, S. S., Chan, K–S., & Parks, C. D. (1993). The effects of reward structure and reciprocity in social dilemmas. *Journal of Experimental Social Psychology, 29,* 252–267.

Komorita, S. S., & Chertkoff, J. M. (1973). A bargaining theory of coalition formation. *Psychological Review, 80,* 149–162.

Komorita, S. S., Hilty, J., & Parks, C. D. (1991). Reciprocity and cooperation in social dilemmas. *Journal of Conflict Resolution, 35*, 494–518.

Komorita, S. S., & Lapworth, C. (1982a). Cooperative choice among individuals versus groups in an n-person dilemma situation. *Journal of Personality and Social Psychology, 42*, 487–496.

Komorita, S. S., & Lapworth, C. W. (1982b) Alternative choices in social dilemmas, *Journal of Conflict Resolution, 26*, 692–708.

Komorita, S. S., & Parks, C. D. (1994). *Social dilemmas*. Madison, WI: WCB Brown & Benchmark.

Komorita, S. S., & Parks, C. D. (1995). Interpersonal relations: Mixed-motive interaction. *Annual Review of Psychology, 46*, 183–207.

Komorita, S. S., Sweeney, J., & Kravitz, D. A. (1980). Cooperative choice in the n-person dilemma situation. *Journal of Personality and Social Psychology, 38*(3), 504–516.

Kraines, D., & Kraines, V. (1989). Pavlov and the prisoner's dilemma. *Theory and Decision, 26*, 47–79.

Kraines, D., & Kraines, V. (1993). Learning to cooperate with Pavlov: An adaptive strategy for the prisoner's dilemma with noise. *Theory and Decision, 35*, 107–150.

Kraines, D., & Kraines, V. (1995). Evolution of learning among Pavlov Strategies in a competitive environment with noise. *Journal of Conflict Resolution, 39*, 439–466.

Kramer, R. M. (1991). Intergroup relations and organizational dilemmas: The role of categorization processes. *Research in Organizational Behavior, 13*, 191–228.

Kramer, R. M., & Brewer, M. B. (1984). Effects of group identity on resource use in a simulated commons dilemma. *Journal of Personality and Social Psychology, 46*, 1044–1057.

Kramer, R. M., & Brewer, M. B. (1986). Social group identity and the emergence of cooperation in resource conservation dilemmas. In H. A. Wilke, D. M. Messick, & C. G. Rutte (Eds.), *Psychology of decisions and conflict: Experimental social dilemmas* (pp. 205–234). Frankfurt, Germany: Verlag Peter Lang.

Kramer, R. M., & Goldman, L. (1995). Helping the group or helping yourself? Social motives and group identity in resource dilemmas. In D. A. Schroeder (Ed.), *Social dilemmas: Perspectives on individuals and groups* (pp. 49–67). Westport, CT: Praeger.

Kramer, R., McClintock, C. G., & Messick, D. M. (1986). Social values and cooperative response to a simulated resource conservation crisis. *Journal of Personality, 54*, 101–117.

Kuhlman, D. M., Camac, C. R., & Cunha, D. A. (1986). Individual differences in social orientations. In H. Wilke, D. Messick, & C. Rutte (Eds.), *Experimental social dilemmas* (pp. 151–176). New York: Peter Lang.

Kuhlman, D. M., & Marshello, A. (1975). Individual differences in game motivation as moderators of preprogrammed strategic effects in prisoner's dilemma. *Journal of Personality and Social Psychology, 32*, 922–931.

Kuhn, T. S. (1962). *The structure of scientific revolutions*. Chicago: University of Chicago Press.

Kuper, A. (1994). *The chosen primate: Human nature and cultural diversity*. Cambridge, MA: Harvard University Press.

Kurlansky, M. (1997). *Cod: A biography of the fish that changed the world*. London: Jonathon Cape.

Ladd, S. R. (1995). *C++ simulations and cellular automata*. New York: M & T Books.

Laffont, J. J. (1975). Macroeconomic constraints, economic efficiency and ethics: An introduction to Kantian economics. *Economica, 42*, 430–437.

Lakatos, I. (1963). Proofs and refutations. *British Journal for the Philosophy of Science, 14*, 1–25, 120–139, 221–243, 296–342.

Lanzetta, J. T., & Englis, B. G. (1989). Expectations of cooperation and competition and their effects on observers' vicarious emotional responses. *Journal of Personality and Social Psychology, 56*, 543–554.

Larrick, R. P., & Blount, S. (1997). The claiming effect: Why players are more generous in social dilemmas than in the ultimatum game. *Journal of Personality and Social Psychology, 72*, 810–825.

Latane, B., & L'Herrou, T. (1996). Spatial clustering in the conformity game: Dynamic social impact in electronic groups. *Journal of Personality and Social Psychology, 70*, 1218–1230.

Latane, B., & Nida, S. (1981). Ten years of group size and helping. *Psychological Bulletin, 89*, 308–324.

Latane, B., Nowak, A., & Liu, J. H. (1994). Measuring emergent social phenomena: Dynamism, polarization, and clustering as order parameters of social systems. *Behavioral Science, 39*, 1–24.

Latham, G. P., & Yukl, G. A. (1975). A review of research on the application of goal setting in organizations. *Academy of Management Journal, 18*, 824–845.

Laury, S. K., Walker, J. M., & Williams, A. W. (1995). Anonymity and the voluntary provision of public goods. *Journal of Economic Behavior and Organization, 27*, 365–380.

Ledyard, J. O. (1995). Public goods: A survey of experimental research. In J. H. Kagel & A. E. Roth (Eds.), *Handbook of experimental economics* (pp. 111–195). Princeton, NJ: Princeton University Press.

Lee, S. (1995). Endogenous sharing rules in collective-group rent-seeking. *Public Choice, 85,* 31–44.

Leonard-Barton, D. (1981). The diffusion of active residential solar energy equipment in California. In A. Shama (Ed.), *Marketing solar energy innovations* (pp. 243–257). New York: Praeger.

Levine, J. M. (1980). Reaction to opinion deviance in small groups. In P. Paulus (Ed.), *Psychology of group influence* (pp. 375–429). Hillsdale, NJ: L. Erlbaum.

LeVine, R. A., & Campbell, D. T. (1972). *Ethnocentrism: Theories of conflict, ethnic attitudes, and group behavior.* New York: Wiley.

Lewin, K. (1939). Field theory and experiment in social psychology. *American Journal of Sociology, 44,* 868–897 .

Lewin, K. (1952). *Field theory in social science.* London: Tavistock.

Libecap, G. D. (1995). The conditions for successful collective action. In R. O. Keohane & E. Ostrom (Eds.), *Local commons and global interdependence. Heterogeneity and cooperation in two domains.* (pp. 161–190). London: Sage.

Lichbach, M.I. (1996). *The cooperator's dilemma.* Ann Arbor, MI: University of Michigan Press.

Liebrand, W. B. G. (1983). A classification of social dilemma games. *Simulation and Games, 14,* 123–138.

Liebrand, W. B. G. (1984). The effect of social motives, communication and group size on behavior in an n-person multi-stage mixed-motive game. *European Journal of Social Psychology, 14,* 239–264.

Liebrand, W. B. G., Jansen, R. W. T. L., Rijken, V. M., & Suhre, C. J. M. (1986). Might over morality: Social values and the perception of others in experimental games. *Journal of Experimental Social Psychology, 22,* 203–215.

Liebrand, W. B. G., Messick, D. M., & Wilke, H. A. M. (1992). Current theoretical issues. In W. Liebrand, D. M. Messick, & H. Wilke (Eds.), *Social dilemmas: Theoretical issues and research findings.* (pp. 29–43). Oxford, England: Pergamon Press.

Liebrand, W. B. G., & Van Run, G. J. (1985). The effects of social motives on behavior in social dilemmas in two cultures. *Journal of Experimental Social Psychology, 21,* 86–102.

Locke, E. A. (1968). Toward a theory of task motivation and incentives. *Organization Behavior and Human Performance, 3,* 157–189.

Locke, E. A., & Latham, G. P. (1990). *A theory of goal setting and task performance.* Englewood Cliffs, NJ: Prentice Hall.

Lomborg, B. (1996). Nucleus and shield: The evolution of social structure in the iterated prisoner's dilemma. *American Sociological Review, 61,* 287–307.

Lopes, L. L. (1981). Decision making in the short run. *Journal of Experimental Social Psychology: Human Learning and Memory, 7,* 377–385.

Lord, R. G., Foti, R. J., & DeVader, C. L. (1984). A test of leadership categorization theory: Internal structure, information processing, and leadership perceptions. *Organizational Behavior and Human Performance, 34,* 343–378.

Luce, R. D. (1997). Several unresolved conceptual problems of mathematical psychology. *Journal of Mathematical Psychology, 41,* 79–87.

Luce, R. D., & Raiffa, H. (1957). *Games and decisions: Introduction and critical survey.* London: John Wiley and Sons.

Lukes, S. (1977). *Essays in social theory.* London: The MacMillan Press.

Luyben, P. D., & Bailey, J. S. (1979). Newspaper recycling: The effects of rewards and proximity of containers. *Environment and Behavior, 11,* 539–557.

Luyben, P. D., & Cummings, S. (1981–1982). Motivating beverage container recycling on a college campus. *Journal of Environmental Systems, 11,* 235–245.

Macrae, C. N., Milne, A. B., & Bodenhausen, G. V. (1994). Stereotypes as energy-saving devices: A peek inside the cognitive toolbox. *Journal of Personality and Social Psychology, 66,* 37–47.

Macy, M. W. (1990). Learning theory and the logic of critical mass. *American Sociological Review, 55,* 809–826.

Macy, M. W. (1991a). Chains of cooperation: Threshold effects in collective action. *American Sociological Review, 56,* 730–747.

Macy, M. W. (1991b). Learning to cooperation: Stochastic and tacit collusion in social exchange. *American Journal of Sociology, 97,* 803–843.

Macy, M . W. (1995). Pavlov and the evolution of cooperation. *Social Psychology Quarterly, 58,* 74–87.

Macy, M. W. (1997). Trust and cooperation between strangers [On-line]. Available: http://www.people.conel.edu/pages/mwm14/

Maes, P. (1993). Behavior-based artificial intelligence. In J. A. Meyer, H. L. Roitblat, & S. W. Wilson (Eds.),

From animals to animats 2: Proceedings of the second international conference on simulation of adaptive behavior. (pp. 2–10). Cambridge, MA: MIT Press.

Maheswaran, D., & Chaiken, S. (1991). Promoting systematic processing in low-motivation settings: Effect of incongruent information on processing and judgment. *Journal of Personality and Social Psychology, 61,* 13–25.

Maki, J. E., Hoffman, D. M., & Berk, R. A. (1978). A time series analysis of the impact of a water conservation campaign. *Evaluation Quarterly, 2,* 107–118.

Mansbridge, J. (Ed.). (1990). *Beyond self-interest.* Chicago: University of Chicago Press.

March, J. G. (1995). *A primer on decision making.* New York: Free Press.

Margolis, H. (1982). *Selfishness, altruism and rationality.* Cambridge, MA: Cambridge University Press.

Markus, H., & Kitayama, S. (1991). Culture and the self: Implications for cognition, emotion, and motivation. *Psychological Review, 98,* 224–253.

Martin, L. (1995). Heterogeneity, linkage and commons problems. In R. O. Keohane, & E. Ostrom (Eds.), *Local commons and global interdependence. Heterogeneity and cooperation in two domains.* (pp. 71–91). London: Sage.

Marwell, G., & Ames, R. E. (1979). Experiments on the provision of public goods I: Resources, interest, group size, and the free–rider problem. *American Journal of Sociology, 84,* 1335–1360.

Marwell, G., & Ames, R. E. (1980). Experiments on the provision of public goods. II: Provision points, experience, and the free–rider problem. *American Journal of Sociology, 85,* 926–937.

Marwell, G., & Schmitt, E. R. (1975). *Cooperation: An experimental analysis.* New York: Academic Press.

Mayer-Kress, G. (1989). *A nonlinear dynamical systems approach to international security.* Technical Report LA-UR-89-1355, Los Almos National Laboratory.

McCallum, D. M., Harring, K., Gilmore, R., Drenan, S., Chase, J., Insko, C. A.,& Thibaut, J. (1985). Competition between groups and between individuals. *Journal of Experimental Social Psychology, 21,* 301–320.

McCaul, K. D., & Kopp, J. T. (1982). Effects of goal setting and commitment on increasing metal recycling. *Journal of Applied Psychology, 67,* 377–389.

McClintock, C. G. (1978). Social values: Their definition, measurements and development. *Journal of Research and Development in Education, 12,* 121–137.

McClintock, C. G., & Allison, S. T. (1989). Social value orientation and helping behavior. *Journal of Applied Social Psychology, 19* (4), 353–362.

McClintock, C. G., & Liebrand, W. B. G. (1988). Role of interdependence structure, individual value orientation, and other's strategy in social decision making: A transformational analysis. *Journal of Personality and Social Psychology, 55,* 396–409.

McClintock, C. G., & Van Avermaet, E. (1982). Social values and rules of fairness: A theoretical perspective. In V. Derlage & J. L. Grzelak (Eds.), *Cooperation and helping behavior: Theories and research* (pp. 43–71). New York: Academic Press.

McCusker, C., & Carnevale, P. J. (1995a). Frame and loss aversion in social dilemmas. *Organizational Behavior and Human Decision Processes, 61,* 190–201.

McCusker, C., & Carnevale, P. J. (1995b). Framing in resource dilemmas: Loss aversion and the moderating effects of sanctions. *Organizational Behavior and Human Decision Processes, 61*(2), 190–201.

McDaniel, W. C., & Sistrunk, F. (1991). Management dilemmas and decisions: Impact of framing and anticipated responses. *Journal of Conflict Resolution, 35,* 21–42.

Meeker, B.F. (1971). Decisions and exchange. *American Sociological Review, 36,* 485–495.

Meinhardt, H. & Ostmann, A. (1996). *Competition for the first move in cooperative TU-CPR games.* Discussion Paper, Department of Economics, University of Saarland, Saarbrücken.

Messick, D. M. (in press). Alternative logics for decision making in special settings. *Journal of Economic Behavior and Organization.*

Messick, D. M., & Allison, S. T. (1987) Accepting unfairness: Outcomes and distributions. *Representative Research in Social Psychology, 17,* 39–50.

Messick, D. M., Allison, S. T., & Samuelson, C. D. (1988). Framing and communication effects on group members' responses to environmental and social uncertainty. In S. Maital (Ed.), *Applied behavioral economics* (Vol. 2, pp. 677–700). Brighton, England: Wheatsheaf Books.

Messick, D. M., & Brewer, M. B. (1983). Solving social dilemmas: A review. In L. Wheeler & P. Shaver (Eds.), *Review of personality and social psychology* (vol. 4, pp. 11–44). Beverly Hills: Sage.

Messick, D. M., & Kramer, R. M. (1998). *Trust as a form of shallow morality* (Working Paper). Center for the Study of Social Issues in Management, Kellogg Graduate School of Management, Northwestern University.

Messick, D. M., & Leibrand, W. B. G. (1995). Individual heuristics and the dynamics of cooperation in large groups. *Psychological Review, 102,* 131–145.

Messick, D. M., & Liebrand, W. B. G. (1997). Levels of analysis and the explanation of the costs and benefits of cooperation. *Personality and Social Psychology Review, 1,* 129–139.

Messick, D. M., & Mackie, D. M. (1989). Intergroup relations. In M. R. Rosenzweig, & L. W. Porter (Eds.), *Annual review of psychology* (pp. 45–81). Palo Alto, CA: Annual Reviews.

Messick, D. M., & McClelland, C. L. (1983). Social traps and temporal traps. *Personality and Social Psychology Bulletin, 9,* 105–110.

Messick, D. M., & McClintock, C. G. (1968). Motivational bases of choice in experimental games. *Journal of Experimental Social Psychology, 4,* 1–25.

Messick, D. M., & Schell, H. (1992). Evidence for an equality heuristic in social decision making. *Acta Psychologica, 80,* 311–323.

Messick, D. M., Wilke, H. A. M., Brewer, M. B., Kramer, R. M., Zemke, P. E., & Lui, L. (1983). Individual adaptations and structural change as solutions to social dilemmas. *Journal of Personality and Social Psychology, 44,* 294–309.

Metzger, M. A. (1994). Have subjects been shown to generate chaotic numbers? Commentary on Neuringer and Voss. *Psychological Science, 5,* 111–114.

Mikula, G. (1980). On the role of justice in allocation decisions. In G. Mikula (Ed.), *Justice and social interaction: Experimental and theoretical contributions from psychological research* (pp. 127–166). Bern, Switzerland: Hans Huber.

Miller, J. H. (1996). The coevolution of automata in the repeated prisoner's dilemma. *Journal of Economic Behavior and Organization, 29,* 87–112.

Mischel, W., Ebbesen, E., & Zeiss, A. (1972). Cognitive and attential mechanisms in delay of gratification. *Journal of Personality and Social Psychology, 21,* 204–208.

Morikawa, T., Orbell, J. M., & Runde, A. S. (1995). The advantage of being moderately cooperative, *American Political Science Review, 89,* 601–611.

Morris, M. W., Sim, D. L. H., & Girotto, V. (1998). Distinguishing sources of cooperation in the one-round prisoner's dilemma: Evidence for cooperative decisions based on the illusion of control. *Journal of Experimental Social Psychology, 34,* 494–512.

Mummendey, A., Simon, B., Dietze, C., Grunert, G. H., Haeger, G., Kessler, S., Lettgen, S., & Schaferhoff, S. (1992). Categorization is not enough: Intergroup discrimination in negative outcome allocation. *Journal of Experimental Social Psychology, 28,* 125–144.

Murnighan, J. K., Kim, J. W., & Metzger, A. R. (1993). The volunteer dilemma. *Administrative Science Quarterly, 38,* 515–538.

Nakamaru, M., & Iwasa, Y. (1997, November). *Can cooperators coexist with non–cooperators?* Paper presented at the 24th Meeting of the Japanese Association for Mathematical Sociology, Chiba, Japan.

Nakamaru, M., Matsuda, H., & Iwasa, Y. (1996). Evolution of cooperation in a lattice group. *Bussei Kenkyu (Kyoto), 67,* 257–285.

Nakamaru, M., Matsuda, H., & Iwasa, Y. (1997). The evolution of cooperation in a lattice–structured population. *Journal of Theoretical Biology, 184,* 65–81.

Nemeth, C. (1972). A critical analysis of research utilising the prisoner's dilemma paradigm for the study of bargaining. *Advances in Experimental Social Psychology, 6,* 203–234.

Neuberg, S. L. (1988). Behavioral implications of information presented outside of conscious awareness: The effect of subliminal presentation of trait information on behavior in a prisoner's dilemma. *Social Cognition, 6,* 207–230.

Neuringer, A., & Voss, C. (1993). Approximating chaotic behavior. *Psychological Science, 4,* 113–119.

Newsom, T. J., & Makranczy, U. J. (1977–1978). Reducing electricity consumption of residents living in master-metered dormitory complexes. *Journal of Environmental Systems, 7,* 215–235.

Nitzan, S. (1991). Collective rent seeking. *The Economic Journal, 101,* 1522–1534.

Nitzan, S. (1994). Modeling rent-seeking contests. *European Journal of Political Economy, 10,* 41–60.

Nowak, A. S. J., Szermrej, J., & Latane, B. (1990). From private attitude to public opinion: A dynamic theory of social impact. *Psychological Review, 97,* 362–376.

Nowak, M. A., & May, R. M. (1992). Evolutionary games and spatial chaos. *Nature, 359,* 826–829.

Nowak, M., & May, R. (1993). The spatial dilemmas of evolution. *International Journal of Bifurcation and Chaos, 3,* 35–78.

Nowak, M. A., & Sigmund, K. (1993). A strategy of win-stay, lose-shift that outperforms tit for tat in the prisoner's dilemma game. *Nature, 364,* 56–58.

Nye, J. L., & Simonetta, L. G. (1996). Followers' perceptions of group leaders: The impact of recognition-based and inference-based processes. In J. L. Nye, & A. M. Bower, (Eds.), *What's social about social cognition: Research on socially shared cognition in small groups* (pp. 124–153). Thousand Oaks, CA: Sage.

Oakes, P. J., Haslam, S. A., & Turner, J. C. (1994). *Stereotyping and social reality.* Oxford, England: Blackwell.

Oatley, K., & Jenkins, J. M. (1996). *Understanding emotions.* Cambridge, MA: Blackwell.

Offerman, T., Sonnemans, J., & Schram, A. (1996). Value orientations, expectations and voluntary contributions in public goods. *The Economic Journal, 106,* 817–845.

OFWAT (1996). Annual Report 1995. London: HMSO.

Oliver, P. E., & Marwell, G. (1988). The paradox of group size in collective action: A theory of critical mass, II. *American Sociological Review, 53,* 1–8.

Oliver, P. E., Marwell, G., & Teixeira, R. (1985). A theory of critical mass, I. Interdependence, group heterogeneity, and the production of collective action. *American Journal of Sociology, 91,* 522–556.

Olsen, M. E. (1981). Consumers' attitudes towards energy conservation. *Journal of Social Issues, 37,* 108–131.

Olsen, R. A. (1997). Desirability bias among professional investment managers: Some evidence from experts. *Journal of Behavioral Decision Making, 10,* 65–72.

Olson, M. (1965). *The logic of collective action: Public goods and the theory of groups.* Cambridge, MA: Harvard University Press.

Olson, M. J. (1997). *Necessary and sufficient criticality in a minimal cooperative set dilemma: A revised application of prospect theory.* Unpublished doctoral dissertation, University of Illinois, Urbana-Champaign.

Ooura, H. (1992). Simulation of social change by a cell-automaton model: Effects of individual differences in conformity on macroscopic social change. *Japanese Journal of Experimental Social Psychology, 85,* 515–528.

Opp, K.-D. (1986). Soft incentives and collective actions: Participation in the anti-nuclear movement. *British Journal of Political Science, 16,* 87–112.

Orbell, J. M., & Dawes, R. M. (1981). Social dilemmas. In G. Stephenson & J. H. Davis (Eds.), *Progress in applied social psychology* (Vol. 1, pp. 37–65). Chichester, England: Wiley.

Orbell, J. M., & Dawes, R. M. (1991). A cognitive miser theory of cooperators' advantage. *American Polical Science Review, 85,* 515–528.

Orbell, J. M., & Dawes, R. M. (1993). Social welfare, cooperators' advantage, and the option of not playing the game. *American Sociological Review, 58,* 787–800.

Orbell, J. M., Dawes, R. M., & Van de Kragt, A. J. (1988). Explaining discussion induced cooperation. *Journal of Personality and Social Psychology, 54,* 811-819.

Orbell, J. M., Schwartz-Shea, P., & Simmons, R. T. (1984). Do cooperators exit more readily than defectors? *American Political Science Review, 78,* 147–162.

Orbell, J. M., Van de Kragt, A. J., & Dawes, R. M. (1991). Covenants without the sword: The role of promises in social dilemma circumstances. In K. Koford & J. Miller (Eds.), *Social norms and economic institutions* (pp. 117–133). Ann Arbor, MI: University of Michigan Press.

Osgood, C. E. (1962). *An alternative to war or surrender.* Urbana, IL: University of Illinois Press.

Ostmann, A., & Beckenkamp, M. (1997). *Agentenmodelle zum Umgang mit vollständig erneuerbaren Gemeingütern.* In C. G. Jung, K. Fischer & S. Schacht (Hrsg.) [Distributed cognitive systems – Proceedings of the VKS'97 Workshop] (S. 19–31). Saarbrücken: DFKI (German Research Institute for Artifical Intelligence).

Ostmann, A. (1988). Limits of rational behavior in cooperatively played normal form games. In R. Tietz, W. Albers, & R. Selten (Hrsg.), *Bounded rational behavior in experimental games and markets* (Lecture Notes in Economics and Mathematical Systems 314, S. 317–332). Berlin: Springer.

Ostmann, A. (1990). On rationality issues in the bargaining context. *Journal of Institutional and Theoretical Economics / Zeitschrift für die gesamte Staatswissenschaft, 146,* 481–492.

Ostmann, A. (1997). When to defect in commons. In P. Kleinschmidt, A. Bachem, U. Derigs, D. Fischer, U. Leopold-Wildburger, & R. Möhring (Eds.*), Operations Research Proceedings 1995* (pp. 505–510). Berlin: Springer.

Ostmann, A. (1998). External control may destroy commons. *Rationality and Society, 10,* 135–154.

Ostmann, A., Wojtyniak, B. & Beckenkamp, M. (1997). *Control and sanctions may destroy commons: Experimental results and some microanalytical explications.* (Working Paper in game theory and experimental economics 7). Institut für Statistik und Mathematische Wirtschaftsforschung. Universität Karlsruhe.

Ostrom, E. (1987). Institutional arrangements for resolving the commons dilemma: Some contending approaches. In B. J. McCay & J. M. Acheson (Eds.), *The questions of the commons* (pp. 250–265). Tucson: University of Arizona Press.

Ostrom, E. (1990). *Governing the commons: The evolution of institutions for collective action.* Cambridge; New York: Cambridge University Press.

Ostrom, E. (1998). A behavioral approach to the rational choice theory of collective action. *American Political Science Review, 92,* 1–22.

Ostrom, E., Gardner, R., & Walker, J. (1994). *Rules, games, and common-pool resources.* Ann Arbor, MI: The University of Michigan Press.

Paese, P. W., & Stang, S. J. (1998). Adaptation-level phenomena and the prevalence of cooperation. *Social Psychology Quarterly, 61,* 172–183.

Palfrey, T. R., & Rosenthal, H. (1983). A strategic calculus of voting. *Public Choice, 41,* 7–53.

Palfrey, T. R., & Rosenthal, H. (1984). Participation and the provision of discrete public good: A strategic analysis. *Journal of Public Economics, 24,* 171-193.

Palfrey, T. R., & Rosenthal, H. (1988). Private incentives and social dilemmas: The effects of incomplete information and altruism. *Journal of Public Economics, 28,* 309–332.

Palfrey, T. R., & Rosenthal, H. (1991). Testing the effects of cheap talk in public goods games with private information. *Games and Economic Behavior, 3,* 183-220.

Pallak, M. S., Cook, D. A., & Sullivan, J. J. (1980). Commitment and energy conservation. In L. Bickman (Ed.), *Applied social psychology annual* (Vol. 1, pp. 235–253). Beverly Hills, CA: Sage.

Pallak, M. S., & Cummings, W. (1976). Commitment and voluntary energy conservation. *Personality and Social Psychology Bulletin, 2,* 27–31.

Pardini, A. U., & Katzev, R. D. (1983–1984). The effect of strength of commitment on newspaper recycling. *Journal of Environmental Systems, 13,* 245–254.

Parfit, D. (1984). *Reasons and persons.* Oxford, England: Oxford University Press.

Park, B., & Rothbart, M. (1982). Perception of out-group homogeneity and levels of social categorization. *Journal of Personality and Social Psychology, 42,* 1051–1068.

Parks, C. D. (1994). The predictive ability of social values in resource dilemmas and public goods game. *Personality and Social Psychology Bulletin, 20,* 431–438.

Parks, C. D., & Godfrey, K. J. (1997). Cooperative choice in social dilemmas as risk-taking behavior. Unpublished manuscript.

Parks, C. D., & Hulbert, L. G. (1995). High and low trusters' responses to fear in a payoff matrix. *Journal of Conflict Resolution, 39,* 718–730.

Parks, C. D., & Komorita, S. S. (1997). Reciprocal strategies for large groups. *Personality and Social Psychology Review, 1,* 314–322.

Parrott, W. G. (1993). Beyond hedonism: Motives for inhibiting good moods and for maintaining bad moods. In D. M. Wegener, & J. W. Pennebaker (Eds.), *Handbook of mental control* (pp. 278–305). Englewood Cliffs, NJ: Prentice Hall.

Pemberton, M. R., Insko, C. A., & Schopler, J. (1996). Memory for and experience of differential competitive behavior of individuals and groups. *Journal of Personality and Social Psychology, 71,* 953–956.

Platow, M. J., Hoar, S., Reid, S., Harley, K., & Morrison, D. (1997). Endorsement of distributively fair and unfair leaders in interpersonal and intergroup situations. *European Journal of Social Psychology, 27,* 465–494.

Platow, M. J., Reid, S., & Andrew, S. (1998). Leadership endorsement: The role of distributive and procedural behavior in interpersonal and intergroup contexts. *Group Processes and Intergroup Relations, 1,* 35–47.

Polzer, J. T. (1996). Intergroup negotiations: The effects of negotiating teams. *Journal of Conflict Resolution, 40,* 678–698.

Poppe, M., & Utens, L. (1986) Effects of greed and fear of being gypped in a social dilemma situation with changing pool size. *Journal of Economic Psychology, 7,* 61–73.

Poundstone, W. (1992). *Prisoner's dilemma.* New York: Anchor Books.

Pritchard, R. D., Dunnette, M. D., & Jorgenson, D. O. (1972). Effects of perceptions of equity and inequity on worker performance and satisfaction. *Journal of Applied Psychology, 56,* 75–94.

Pruitt, D. G. (1972). Methods for resolving differences of interest. *Journal of Social Issues, 28,* 133–154.

Pruitt, D. G., & Kimmel, M. (1977). Twenty years of experimental gaming: Critique, synthesis, and suggestions for the future. *Annual Review of Psychology, 28,* 363–392.

Pryor, F. L. & Graburn, N. H. H. (1980). The myth of reciprocity. In K. J. Gergen, M. S. Greenberg, & R. H. Willis (Eds.), *Social Exchange.* (pp. 215–237). New York: Plenum Press.

Putnam, R. D. (1988). Diplomacy and domestic politics: The logic of two–level games. *International Organization, 42,* 429–460.

Rabbie, J. M. (1982). The effects of intergroup competition on intragroup and intergroup relationships. In V. J.

Derlega & J. Grzelak, (Eds.), *Cooperation and helping behavior: Theories and research* (pp. 123–149). New York: Academic Press.

Rachlin, H. (1989) *Judgment, decision, and choice: A cognitive-behavior synthesis.* NY: W. H. Freeman.

Rapoport, A. (1960). *Fights, games, and debates.* Ann Arbor, MI: University of Michigan Press.

Rapoport, A. (1967). Optimal policies for the prisoner's dilemma. *Psychological Review, 74,* 136–148.

Rapoport, A. (1985). Provisions of public goods and the MCS experimental paradigm. *The American Political Science Review, 79,* 148–155.

Rapoport, A. (1987). Research paradigms and expected utility models for the provision of step-level public goods. *Psychological Review, 94,* 74–83.

Rapoport, A. (1988). Provision of step-level public goods: Effects of inequality in resources. *Journal of Personality and Social Psychology, 45,* 432–440.

Rapoport, A. (1997). Order of play in strategically equivalent games in extensive form. *International Journal of Game Theory, 26,* 113–136.

Rapoport, A., & Amaldoss, W. (1997a). *Comparison of difference* (Talk held in Cairns). 7th Congress on Social Dilemma Research, Cairns.

Rapoport, A., & Amaldoss W. (1997b). *Social dilemmas embedded in between-group competitions: Effects of contest and distribution rules* (Working paper).

Rapoport, A., & Bornstein, G. (1987). Intergroup competition for the provision of binary public goods. *Psychological Review, 94,* 291–299.

Rapoport, A., Budescu, D.V., Suleiman, R., & Weg, E. (1992). Social dilemmas with uniformly distributed resources. In W. Liebrand, D. M. Messick, & H. Wilke (Eds.), *Social dilemmas: Theoretical issues and research findings* (pp. 43–57). Oxford: Pergamon Press.

Rapoport, A., Budescu, D. V., & Suleiman, R. (1993). Sequential requests from randomly distributed shared resources. *Journal of Mathematical Psychology, 37,* 241–265.

Rapoport, A., & Chammah, A. M. (1965). *Prisoner's dilemma: A study in conflict and cooperation.* Ann Arbor, MI: University of Michigan Press.

Rapoport, A., & Erev, I. (1994). Provision of step-level public goods: Effects of different information structures. In U. Schultz, W. Albers, & U. Mueller (Eds.), *Social dilemmas and cooperation* (pp. 147–171). Berlin, Germany: Springer-Verlag.

Rapoport, A., & Eshed-Levy, D. (1989). Provision of step–level public goods: Effects of greed and fear of being gypped. *Organizational Behavior and Human Decision Processes, 44,* 325–344.

Rapoport, A., & Suleiman, R. (1993). Incremental contribution in step–level public goods games with asymmetric players. *Organizational Behavior and Human Decision Processes, 55,* 171–194.

Reid, D. H., Luyben, P. D., Rawers, R. J., & Bailey, J. S. (1976). Newspaper recycling behavior: The effects of prompting and proximity of containers. *Environment and Behavior, 8,* 471–482.

Reis, H. R., & Wheeler, L. (1991). Studying social interaction with the rochester interaction record. In M. P. Zanna (Ed.), *Advances in experimental social psychology* (Vol. 24, pp. 269–318). New York: Academic Press.

Reynolds, C. W. (1987). Flocks, herds, and schools: A distributed behavioral model. *Computer Graphics, 21,* 25–34.

Robinson, W. P. (Ed.). (1996). *Social groups and identities: Developing the legacy of Henri Tajfel.* Oxford, England: Butterworth-Heinemann.

Rodseth, L., Wrangham, R.W., Harrigan, A. M., & Smuts, B.B. (1991). The human community as a primate society. *Current Anthropology, 12,* 221–254.

Ross, L. (1977). The intuitive psychologist and his shortcomings. *Advances in Experimental Social Psychology, 10,* 174–220.

Roth, A. E. (1995). Bargaining experiments. In J. Kagel, & A. Roth (Eds.), *The handbook of experimental economics* (pp. 253–348). Princeton, NJ: Princeton University Press.

Rubin, M., & Hewstone, M. (1998). Social identity theory's self-esteem hypothesis: A review and some suggestions for clarification. *Personality and Social Psychology Review, 2,* 40–62.

Rubin, Z., & Brown, B. R. (1975). *The social psychology of bargaining and negotiation.* New York: Academic Press.

Rusbult, C. E., & Van Lange, P. A. M. (1996). Interdependence processes. In T. Higgins, & A. Kruglanski, (Eds.), *Social psychology: Handbook of basic principles.* New York: Guildford.

Rushton, J. P. (1995). *Race, evolution, and behavior.* New Brunswick, NJ: Transaction.

Rutte, C. G. (1990). Solving organizational social dilemmas. *Social Behavior, 5,* 285–294.

Rutte, C. G., & Wilke, H. A. M. (1984). Social dilemmas and leadership. *European Journal of Social Psychology, 14,* 105–121.

Rutte, C. G., & Wilke, H. A. M. (1985). Preference for decision structures in a social dilemma situation, *European Journal of Social Psychology, 15,* 367–370.

Rutte, C. G., & Wilke, H. A. M. (1992). Goals, expectations and behavior in a social dilemma situation. In W. B. G. Liebrand, D. M. Messick, & H. A. M. Wilke (Eds.), *Social dilemmas. Theoretical issues and research findings* (pp. 289–305). Oxford, England: Pergamon Press.

Rutte, C. G., Wilke, H. A. M., & Messick, D. M. (1987a). The effects of framing social dilemmas as give-some or take-some games. *British Journal of Social Psychology, 26,* 103–108.

Rutte, C. G., Wilke, H. A. M., & Messick, D. M. (1987b). Scarcity or abundance caused by people or the environment as determinants of behavior in the resource dilemma. *Journal of Experimental Social Psychology, 23,* 208–216.

Sahlins, M. D. (1965). On the sociology of primitive exchange. In M. Banton (Ed.), *The relevance of models for social anthropology.* New York: Praeger.

Sahlins, M. D. (1972). *Stone age economics.* Chicago: Aldine.

Sahlins, M. (1976). *Culture and practical reason.* Chicago, Illinois: University of Chicago Press.

Sally, D. (1995). Conversation and cooperation in social dilemmas: A meta-analysis. *Rationality and Society, 7,* 58–92.

Samuelson, C. D. (1990). Energy conservation: A social dilemma approach. *Social Behavior, 5,* 207–230.

Samuelson, C. D. (1991). Perceived task difficulty, causal attributions, and preferences for structural change in resource dilemmas. *Personality and Social Psychology Bulletin, 17,* 181–187.

Samuelson, C. D. (1991). Perceived task difficulty, causal attributions, and preferences for structural change in resource dilemmas. *Personality and Social Psychology Bulletin, 17*(2), 181–187.

Samuelson, C. D. (1993). A multiattribute evaluation approach to structural change in resource dilemmas. *Organizational Behavior and Human Decision Processes, 55,* 298–324.

Samuelson, C. D., & Allison, S. T. (1994). Cognitive factors affecting the use of social decision heuristics in resource-sharing tasks. *Organizational Behavior and Human Decision Processes, 58,* 1–27.

Samuelson, C. D., & Messick, D. M. (1986a). Alternative structural solutions to resource dilemmas. *Organizational Behavior and Human Decision Processes, 37,* 139–155.

Samuelson, C. D., & Messick, D. M. (1986b). Inequities in access to and use of shared resources in social dilemmas. *Journal of Personality and Social Psychology, 51*(5), 960–967.

Samuelson, C. D., & Messick, D. M. (1995). When do people want to change the rules for allocating shared resources? In D. Schroeder (Ed.), *Social dilemmas: Perspectives on individuals and groups* (pp. 143–162). New York: Praeger.

Samuelson, C. D., Messick, D. M., Rutte, C. G., & Wilke, H. A. M. (1984). Individual and structural solutions to resource dilemmas in two cultures. *Journal of Personality and Social Psychology, 47,* 94–104.

Sato, K. (1987). Distribution of the cost of maintaining common resources, *Journal of Experimental Social Psychology, 23,* 19–31.

Sato, K., Matsuda, H., & Sasaki, A. (1994). Pathogen invasion and host extinction in lattice structured populations, *Journal of Mathematical Biology, 32,* 251–268.

Schachter, S. (1951). Deviation, rejection, and communication. *Journal of Abnormal and Social Psychology, 46,* 190–207.

Schaller, M.. & Cialdini, R. B. (1990). Happiness, sadness, and helping: A motivational integration. In E. T. Higgins, & R. M. Sorrentino (Eds.), *Handbook of motivation and cognition* (Vol. 2, pp. 265–298). New York: Guilford Press.

Scheff, T. J. (1988). Shame and conformity: The deference-emotion system. *American Sociological Review, 53,* 395–406.

Schelling, T. C. (1960). *The strategy of conflict.* London: Oxford University Press.

Schelling, T. C. (1973). Hockey helmets, concealed weapons, and daylight saving. *Journal of Conflict Resolution, 17,* 381–428.

Schoemaker, J. H. (1980), *Experiments on decisions under risks.* Boston: Martinus Nijhoff Publications.

Schopler, J., & Insko, C. A. (1992). The discontinuity effect: Generality and mediation. In W. Stroebe, & M. Hewstone (Eds.), *European review of social psychology* (pp. 121–151) London: Wiley.

Schopler, J., Insko, C. A., Drigotas, S. M., Wieselquist, J., Pemberton, M. B., & Çox, C. (1995). The role of identifiability in the reduction of interindividual-intergroup discontinuity. *Journal of Experimental Social Psychology, 31,* 553–574.

Schopler, J., Insko, C. A., Graetz, K. A., Drigotas, S. M., & Smith, V. A. (1991). The generality of the individual-group discontinuity effect: Variations in positivity-negativity of outcomes, players' relative power, and magnitude of outcomes. *Personality and Social Psychology Bulletin, 17,* 612–624.

Schopler, J., Insko, C. A., Graetz, K. A., Drigotas, S. M., Smith, V. A., & Dahl, K. (1993). Individual-group discontinuity: Further evidence for mediation by fear and greed. *Personality and Social Psychology Bulletin, 19,* 419–431.

Schroeder, D. A., Jensen, T. D., Reed, A. J., Sullivan, D. D., & Schwab, M. (1983). The actions of others as determinants of behavior in social trap situations. *Journal of Experimental Social Psychology, 19,* 522–539.

Schuessler, R. (1989). Exit threats and cooperation under anonymity. *Journal of Conflict Resolution, 33,* 728–749.

Schwartz, S. H. (1968a). Awareness of consequences and the influence of moral norms on interpersonal behavior. *Sociometry, 31,* 355–369.

Schwartz, S. H. (1968b). Words, deeds, and the perception of consequences and responsibility in action situations. *Journal of Personality and Social Psychology, 10,* 232–242.

Schwartz, S. H. (1977). Normative influences on altruism. In L. Berkowitz (Ed.), *Advances in experimental social psychology* (Vol. 10, pp. 221–279). New York: Academic Press.

Schwartz, S. H., & Bilsky, W. (1987). Toward a universal psychological structure of human values. *Journal of Personality and Social Psychology, 53,* 550–562.

Schwartz, S. H., & Bilsky, W. (1990). Toward a theory of the universal content and structure of values: Extensions and cross-cultural replications. *Journal of Personality and Social Psychology, 58,* 878–891.

Schwartz-Shea, P., & Simmons, R. (1987). Social dilemmas and perceptions: Experiments on framing and inconsequentiality. In D. Schroeder (Ed.), *Social dilemmas* (pp. 87–103). New York: Praeger.

Schwartz-Shea, P., & Simmons, R. T. (1995). Social dilemmas and perceptions: Experiments on framing and inconsequentiality. In D. Schroeder (Ed.), *Social dilemmas: Perspectives on individuals and groups* (pp. 87–103). Westport, CT: Praeger.

Schwarz, N. (1990). Feelings as information: Informational and motivational functions of affective states. In R. M. Sorrentino, & E. T. Higgins (Eds.), *Handbook of motivation and cognition: Foundations of social behavior* (Vol. 2, pp. 527–561). New York: Guilford Press.

Schwarz, N., & Bohner, G. (1996). Feelings and their motivational implications: Moods and the action sequence. In J. A. Bargh, & P. Gollwitzer (Eds.), *The psychology of action: Linking thought and motivation to behavior* (pp. 119–145). New York: Guilford.

Schwarz, N., & Clore, G. L. (1996). Feelings and phenomenal experiences. In E. T. Higgins, & A. Kruglanski (Eds.), *Social psychology: A handbook of basic principles* (pp. 433–465). New York: Guilford.

Schwarz, J. C. & Pollack, P. R. (1977). Affect and delay of gratification. *Journal of Research in Personality, 11,* 147–164.

Seligman, C., & Darley, J. M. (1977). Feedback as a means of decreasing residential energy consumption. *Journal of Applied Psychology, 62,* 363–368.

Sell, J., & Son, K. (1997). Comparing public goods with common pool resources: three experiments. *Social Psychological Quarterly, 60,* 118–137.

Selten, R. (1990). Bounded Rationality. *Journal of Institutional and Theoretical Economics, 146,* 649–658.

Selten, R. (1994). New challenges to the rationality assumption: Comment. *Journal of Institutional and Theoretical Economics, 150,* 42–44.

Shepperd, J. A. (1993). Productivity loss in performance groups. *Psychological Bulletin, 113,* 67–81.

Sherif, M. (1966). *In common predicament: Social psychology of intergroup conflict and cooperation.* Boston: Houghton Mifflin.

Sherif, M., Harvey, O. J., White, B. J., Hood, W. R., & Sherif, C. (1961). *Intergroup conflict and cooperation: The robbers cave experiment.* Norman, OK: University Book Exchange.

Sherman, S. J., Hamilton, D. L., & Lewis, A. C. (1998). Perceived entitativity and the social identity value of group memberships. In D. Abrams, & M. A. Hogg (Eds). *Social identity and social cognition* (pp. 80–110). Oxford, England: Blackwell.

Shubik, M. (1970). Game theory, behavior, and the paradox of the prisoner's dilemma: Three solutions. *Journal of Conflict Resolution, 14,* 181–193.

Simon, H. A. (1955). A behavioral model of rational choice. *Quarterly Journal of Economics, 69,* 99–118.

Simon, H.A. (1967). Motivational and emotional controls of cognition. *Psychological Review, 74,* 29–39.

Simon, H. A. (1976). From substantive to procedural rationality. In S. J. Latsis (Ed.), *Method and appraisal in economics* (pp. 129–148). Cambridge, MA: Cambridge University Press.

Sinclair, R. C., & Mark, M. M. (1992). The influence of mood state on judgment and action: Effects on persuasion, categorization, social justice, person perception, and judgmental accuracy. In L. L. Martin, & A. Tesser (Eds.), *The construction of social judgment* (pp. 165–193). Hillsdale, NJ: Erlbaum.

Slavin, R. E., Wodarski, J. S., & Blackburn, B. L. (1981). A group contingency for electricity conservation in master-metered apartments. *Journal of Applied Behavior Analysis, 14*, 357–363.

Smith, A. (1970). *The wealth of nations.* London: Penguin.

Smith, E. A. (1988). Risk and uncertainty in the 'original affluent society': Evolutionary ecology of resource-sharing and land tenure. In T. Ingold, D. Riches, & J. Woodburn. (Eds.) *Hunters and gatherers: History, evolution, and social change* (pp. 222–252). Oxford, England: Berg.

Smithson, M. (1997). Judgment under chaos. *Organizational Behavior and Human Decision Processes, 69*, 59–66.

Son, Y., & Sell, J. (1995). Are the dilemmas posed by public goods and common pool resources the same? In L. Freese (Ed.), *Advances in human ecology* (Vol. 4, pp. 69–88). Greenwich, CT: JAI Press.

Spears, R., Oakes, P. J., Ellemers, N., & Haslam, S. A. (Eds.) (1997). *The social psychology of stereotyping and group life.* Oxford, England: Blackwell.

Stein, A. A. (1976). Conflict and cohesion: A review of the literature. *Journal of Conflict Resolution, 20*, 143–172.

Stern, P. C. (1992). Psychological dimensions of global environmental change. *Annual Review of Psychology, 43*, 269–302.

Stern, P. C., & Aronson, E. (Eds.). (1984). *Energy use: The human dimension.* New York: Freeman.

Stern, P. C., Dietz, T., & Kalof, L. (1993). Value orientations, gender, and environmental concern. *Environment and Behavior, 25*, 322–348.

Stricklin, W. R., Zhou, J. Z., & Gonyou, H. W. (1995). Selfish animates and robot ethology: Using artificial animals to investigate social and spatial behavior. *Applied Animal Behavior Science, 44*, 187–203.

Suleiman, R. (1996). Expectations and fairness in a modified ultimatum game. *Journal of Economic Psychology, 17*, 531–554.

Suleiman, R. (1997). Provision of step-level public goods under uncertainty: A theoretical analysis. *Rationality and Society, 9* (2), 163–187.

Suleiman, R., & Budescu, D. V. (in press). Common pool resource dilemmas with incomplete information. In D. V. Budescu, I. Erev, & R. Zwick (Eds.), *Games and human behavior: Essays in honor of Amnon Rapoport.* Hillsdale, NJ: Lawrence Erlbaum Associates.

Suleiman, R., Budescu, D. V., & Rapoport, A. (1994). The position effect: The role of a player's serial position in a resource dilemma game. In U. Schultz, W. Albers, & U. Mueller (Eds.), *Social dilemmas and cooperation* (pp. 55–73). Berlin, Germany: Springer Verlag.

Suleiman, R., & Budescu, D. V. (1999). Common pool resource (CPR) dilemmas with incomplete information. In D. V. Budescu, I. Erev, & R. Zwick (Eds.), *Games and human behavior: Essays in honor of Amnon Rapoport* (pp. 387–410). Hillsdale, NJ: Erlbaum.

Suleiman, R., & Rapoport, A. (1988). Environmental and social uncertainty in single trial resource dilemmas. *Acta Pcychologica, 68*, 99-112.

Suleiman, R., & Rapoport, A. (1992). Provision of step–level public goods with continuous contribution. *Journal of Behavioral Decision Making, 5*, 133–153.

Suleiman, R., & Rapoport, A., & Budescu, D. V. (1996). Fixed position and property rights in sequential resource dilemmas under uncertainty. *Acta Psychologica, 93*, 229–245.

Tajfel, H. (1970). Experiments in intergroup discrimination. *Scientific American, 223*, 96-102.

Tajfel, H. (1972). Social categorisation, English manuscript of 'La categorisation sociale.' In S. Moscovici (Ed.), *Introduction a la Psychologie Sociale, 1.* Paris: Larousse.

Tajfel, H. (1978). *Differentiation between social groups: Studies in the social psychology of intergroup relations* (European Monographs in Social Psychology, 14). London: Academic Press.

Tajfel, H. (1981). Social stereotypes and social groups. In J. C. Turner and H. Giles (Eds.), *Intergroup behavior* (pp. 144–167). Oxford, England: Basil Blackwell.

Tajfel, H. (1982a). Social psychology of intergroup relations. *Annual Review of Psychology, 33*, 1–39.

Tajfel, H. (Ed.) (1982b). *Social identity and intergroup relations.* Cambridge, England: Cambridge University Press.

Tajfel, H., Flament, C., Billig, M. G., & Bundy, R. F. (1971). Social categorization and social behaviour. *European Journal of Social Psychology, 1*, 149–177.

Tajfel, H., & Turner , J. C . (1979). An integrative theory of intergroup conflict. In W. G. Austin, & S. Worchel (Eds), *The social psychology of intergroup relations* (pp. 33–47). Chicago: Nelson-Hall.

Tajfel, H., & Turner, J. C. (1986). The social identity theory of intergroup behaviour. In S. Worschel, & W. G. Austin (Eds.), *Psychology of intergroup relations 2nd ed.* (pp. 7–24). Chicago: Nelson-Hall.

Takada, Y. (1922). *Principles of sociology* [in Japanese]. Tokyo: Iwanami.

Takagi, E. (1994). The evolutionary giving game: A computer simulation paradigm for the study of social exchange [in Japanese]. *Saitama University Review, 30*, 23–55.

Takagi, E. (1995a). *The evolution of altruism: A generalized exchange perspective.* Paper presented at the 6th International Conference on Social Dilemmas.

Takagi, E. (1995b). The group-centrism puzzle [in Japanese]. *University Review, 31,* 17–40.

Takagi, E. (1996). The generalized exchange perspective on the evolution of altruism. In W. B. G. Liebrand, & D. M. Messick (Eds.), *Frontiers in social dilemmas research* (pp. 311–336). Berlin, Germany: Springer-Verlag.

Tanaka, J. (1980). *The San, hunter-gatherers of the Kalahari: A study in ecological anthropology.* Tokyo: Univ. of Tokyo Press.

Taylor, M. (1990). Cooperation and rationality: Notes on the collective action problem and its solutions. In K. S. Cook, & M. Levi (Eds.). *The limits of rationality* (pp. 222–240). Chicago: University of Chicago Press.

Taylor, M., & Ward, H. (1982). Chickens, whales, and lumpy goods: Alternative models of public-goods provision. *Political Studies, 30,* 350-370.

Tedeschi, J. T., Lindskold, S., Horai, J., & Gahagan, J. P. (1969). Social power and the credibility of promises. *Journal of Personality and Social Psychology, 13,* 253–261.

Tedeschi, J. T., Powell, J. Lindskold, S., & Gahagan, J. P. (1969). The patterning of "honored" promises and sex differences in social conflicts. *Journal of Social Psychology, 78,* 297–298.

Terry, D. J., & Hogg, M. A. (Eds). (in press). *Attitudes, behavior, and social context: The role of norms and group membership.* Mahwah, NJ: Erlbaum.

Tetlock, P. (1992). The impact of accountability on judgment and choice: toward a social contingency model. *Advances in Experimental Social Psychology, 25,* 331–376.

Thibaut, J. W., & Kelley, H. H. (1959). *The social psychology of groups.* New York: Wiley.

Thompson, S. C., & Stoutemeyer, K. (1991). Water use as commons dilemma: The effects of education that focuses on long–term consequences and individual action. *Environment and Behavior, 23,* 314–333.

Tomkins, S. S. (1995). *Exploring affect: The selected writings of Sylvan S. Tomkins* (E. V. Demos). New York: Cambridge University Press.

Tönnies, F. (1887). *Gemeinshaft und Gesellschaft.* Leipzig: Fues's Verlag.

Trope, Y., & Liberman, A. (1993). The use of trait conceptions to identify other people's behavior and to draw inferences about their personalities. *Personality and Social Psychology Bulletin, 19,* 553–562.

Tsebelis, G. (1988). Nested games: The cohesion of French electoral coalitions. *British Journal of Political Science, 18,* 145–170.

Tullock, G. (1967). The welfare costs of tariffs, monopolies, and theft. *Western Economic Journal, 5,* 224–232.

Tullock, G. (1980). Efficient rent-seeking. In L. M. Buchanan, R. D. Tollison, & G. Tullock (Eds.), *Toward a theory of rent-seeking society* (pp. 97–112). College Station, TX: Texas A&M University Press.

Turner, J. C. (1975). Social comparison and social identity: Some prospects for intergroup behavior. *European Journal of Social Psychology, 5,* 5–34.

Turner, J. C. (1981). The experimental social psychology of intergroup behavior. In J. C. Turner, & H. Giles (Eds.), *Intergroup behavior* (pp. 66–101). Oxford: Basil Blackwell and Chicago: University of Chicago Press.

Turner, J. C. (1982). Towards a cognitive redefinition of the social group. In H. Tajfel (Ed.), *Social identity and intergroup relations* (pp.15–40). Cambridge, England: Cambridge University Press.

Turner, J. C. (1985). Social categorization and social concept: A social cognitive theory of group behaviour. In E. J. Lawler (Ed.) *Advances in group processes* (Vol 2, pp. 77–122). Greenwich, CT: JAI Press.

Turner, J. C. (1991). *Social influence.* Buckingham, England: Open University Press.

Turner, J. C., & Haslam, S. A. (in press). Social identity, organizations and leadership. In M. E. Turner (Ed.), *Groups at work: Advances in theory and research.* Hilldale, NJ: Erlbaum.

Turner, J. C., Hogg, M. A., Oakes, P. J., Reicher, S. D., & Wetherell, M. S. (1987). *Rediscovering the social group: A self-categorization theory.* Oxford, England: Blackwell.

Tversky, A., & Kahneman, D. (1991). Loss aversion in riskless choice: A reference dependent model. *Quarterly Journal of Economics, 106,* 1039–1061.

Tyler, T., & Dawes, R. M. (1993). Fairness in group: Comparing the self-interest and social identity perspectives. In B. A. Mellers, & J. Baron (Eds.), *Psychological perspectives on justice: Theory and application* (pp. 87–108).Cambridge, England: Cambridge University Press.

Tyler, T. R., & Degoey, P. (1995). Collective restraint in social dilemmas: Procedural justice and social identification effects on support for authorities. *Journal of Personality and Social Psychology, 69,* 482–497.

Van de Kragt, A. J. C., Orbell, J. M., & Dawes, R. M. (1983). The minimal contribution set as a solution to public good problems. *The American Political Science Review, 77,* 112–122.

Van Dijk, E., & Wilke, H. (1993). Differential interests, equity, and public good provision. *Journal of Experimental Social Psychology, 29*, 1–16.

Van Dijk, E., & Wilke, H. (1995). Coordination rules in asymmetric social dilemmas: A comparison between public good dilemmas and resource dilemmas. *Journal of Experimental Social Psychology, 31*, 1–27.

Van Dijk, E., & Wilke, H. (1997). Is it mine or is it ours?: Framing property rights and decision making in social dilemmas. *Organizational Behavior and Human Decision Processes, 71*, 195–209.

Van Lange, P. A. M. (1992). Rationality and morality in social dilemmas: The influence of social value orientations. In W. B. G. Liebrand, D. M. Messick, & H. A. M. Wilke (Eds.), *Social dilemmas: Theoretical issues and research findings* (pp. 3–28). Oxford, England: Pergamon Press.

Van Lange, P. A. M. (1994). Toward more locomotion in experimental games. In U. Schulz, W. Albers & U. Mueller (Eds.), *Social dilemmas and cooperation* (pp. 25–43). Berlin, Germany: Springer–Verlag.

Van Lange, P. A. M. (1995), *Social value orientation: A brief note*. Unpublished manuscript.

Van Lange, P. A. M., Otten, W., de Bruin, E. M. N., & Joireman, J. A. (1997). Development of prosocial, individualistic, and competitive orientations: Theory and preliminary evidence. *Journal of Personality and Social Psychology, 73*, 733–746.

Van Lange, P. A. M. & Kuhlman, D. M. (1994). Social value orientations and impressions of partner's honesty and intelligence: A test of the might versus morality effect. *Journal of Personality and Social Psychology, 67*, 126–141.

Van Lange, P. A. M., & Liebrand, W. B. G. (1989). On perceiving morality and potency: Social values and the effects of person perception in a give-some dilemma. *European Journal of Personality, 3*, 209–225.

Van Lange, P. A. M., Liebrand, W. B. G., Messick, D. M., & Wilke, H,. A. M. (1992). Introduction and literature review. In W. Liebrand, D. Messick, & H. Wilke (Eds.), *Social dilemmas: Theoretical issues and research findings* (pp. 3–28). Oxford, England: Pergamon.

Van Vugt, M. (1997). Concerns about the privatization of public goods: A social dilemma analysis. *Social Psychology Quarterly, 60*, 355–367.

Van Vugt, M. & de Cremer, D. (in press). Collective action in social dilemmas: The impact of group identification on the selection and cooperation with leaders. *Journal of Personality and Social Psychology,*

Van Vugt, M., Meertens, R.M., & Van Lange, P.A.M. (1994). Commuting by car or by public transportation? An interdependence theoretical approach. In U. Schulz, W. Albers, & U. Mueller (Eds.), *Social Dilemmas and Cooperation* (pp. 291–309). Berlin, Germany: Springer.

Van Vugt, M., Meertens, R. M., & Van Lange, P. A. M. (1995). Car versus public transportation? The role of social value orientations in a real-life social dilemma. *Journal of Applied Social Psychology, 25*, 258–278.

Van Vugt, M., Van Lange, P. A. M., Meertens, R. M., & Joireman, J. A. (1996). How a structural solution to a real-world social dilemma failed: A field experiment on the first carpool lane in Europe. *Social Psychology Quarterly, 59*, 364–374.

Vanberg, V. J., & Congleton, R. D. (1992). Rationality, morality, and exit. *American Political Science Review, 86*, 418–431.

Vanman, E. J., Paul, B. Y., Ito, T. A., & Miller, N. (1997). The modern face of prejudice and structural features that moderate the effect of cooperation on affect. *Journal of Personality and Social Psychology, 73*, 941–959.

Vollmeyer, R. (1994). Positive and negative mood effects on solving a resource dilemma. In U. Schulz, W. Albers, & U. Mueller (Eds.), *Social dilemmas and cooperation* (pp. 75–98), Berlin, Germany: Springer.

Von Neumann, J., & Morgenstern, O. (1947). *Theory of games and economic behavior*. Princeton, NJ: Princeton University Press.

Wagner, D. G., & Berger, J. (1985). Do sociological theories grow? *American Journal of Sociology , 90*, 697–728.

Waldrop, M. M. (1992). *Complexity: The emerging science at the edge of order and chaos*. New York: Simon & Schuster.

Walster, E. G., Berscheid, E., & Walster, G. W. (1973). New directions in equity research. *Journal of Personality and Social Psychology, 25*, 151–176.

Watabe, M., Jin, N., Hayashi, N., Takahashi, N. & Yamagishi, T. (1992). *The tragedy of garbage pits*. [in Japanese]. Proceedings of the 40th Annual Meeting of Japanese Group Dynamics Association.

Watanabe, Y. (1996, September). *Is cooperation a gainful strategy? A study of socio-relational bases for cognitive/behavioral trait "sets."* Paper presented at the 37th Annual Meeting of the Japanese Social Psychological Association, Sapporo, Japan.

Watanabe, Y., Kosugi, M., & Yamagishi, T. (1994, October). *The role of trust in the selective-play situation*. Paper presented at the 35th Annual Meeting of the Japanese Social Psychological Association, Osaka, Japan.

Watanabe, Y., & Yamagishi, T. (1997a, July). *Emergence of strategies in a selective play environment with geographic mobility: A computer simulation.* Paper presented at the 7th International Conference on Social Dilemmas, Cairns, Australia.

Watanabe, Y., & Yamagishi, T. (1997b). When "false consensus" stops being "false": An experimental study with one-shot prisoner's dilemma. *The Japanese Journal of Psychology, 67,* 421–428.

Watson, D., Clark, L. A., & Tellegen, A. (1988). Development and validation of brief measures of positive and negative affect: The Panas scales. *Journal of Personality and Social Psychology, 54,* 1063–1070.

Weesie, J. (1993). Asymmetry and timing in the volunteer's dilemma. *Journal of Conflict Resolution, 37,* 569–590.

Weesie, J. (1994). Incomplete information and timing in the volunteer's dilemma. *Journal of Conflict Resolution, 38,* 557–585.

Weesie, J., & Franzen, A. (1998). Cost sharing in the volunteer's dilemma. *Journal of Conflict Resolution, 42,* 600–618.

Wegener, D. T., Petty, R. E., & Smith, S. M. (1995). Positive mood can increase or decrease message scrutinity: The hedonic contingency view of mood and message processing. *Journal of Personality and Social Psychology, 69,* 5–15.

Weigel, R. H., & Newman, L. S. (1976). Increasing attitude-behavior correspondence by broadening the scope of the behavioral measure. *Journal of Personality and Social Psychology, 33,* 793–802.

Weinsten, N. D. (1980). Unrealistic optimism about future life events. *Journal of Personality and Social Psychology, 5,* 806–820.

Weissing, F., & Ostrom, E. (1991). Irrigation institutions and the games irrigators play. In R. Selten (Ed.), *Game equilbrium models: Methods, morals, and markets, II.* (pp. 188–262). Berlin, Germany: Springer.

Weissing, F., & Ostrom, E. (1993). Irrigation institutions and the games irrigators play: Rule enforcement on government- and farmer-managed systems. In F. W. Scharpf (Ed.), *Games in hierarchies and networks: Analytical and empirical approaches to the study of governance institutions* (pp. 387–428). Frankfurt, Germany: Campus Verlag.

Wilke, H. A. M. (1991). Greed, efficiency, and fairness in resource management situations. In W. Stroebe & M. Hewstone (Eds.), *European review of social psychology* (pp. 165–187). Chichester, England: John Wiley and Sons.

Wilke, H. A. Rutte, C. G., Wit, A. P., Messick, D. M., & Samuelson, C. D. (1986). Leadership in social dilemmas: Efficiency and equity. In H. A. Wilke, D. M., Messick, & C. G. Rutte (Eds.), *Psychology of decisions and conflict: Experimental social dilemmas* (pp. 55–76). Frankfurt, Germany, Verlag Peter Lang.

Willer, D., & Markovsky, B. (1993). Elementary theory: Its development and research program. In J. Berger, & M. Zelditch, Jr. (Eds.), *Theoretical research programs: Studies in the growth of theory* (pp. 323–363). Stanford, CA: Stanford University Press.

Williams, K. D. (1997). Social ostracism: The causes and consequences of "the silent treatment." In R. Kowalski (Ed.), *Aversive interpersonal relations* (pp. 133–170). New York: Plenum Press.

Winett, R. A., Hatcher, J. W., Fort, T. R., Leckliter, J. N., Love, S. Q., Riley, A. W., & Fishback, J. F. (1982). The effects of videotape modeling and daily feedback on residential electricity conservation, home temperature and humidity, perceived comfort, and clothing worn: Winter and summer. *Journal of Applied Behavior Analysis, 15,* 381–402.

Winett, R. A., Neale, M. S., & Grier, H. C. (1979). The effects of self-monitoring and feedback on residential electricity consumption: Winter. *Journal of Applied Behavior Analysis, 12,* 173–184.

Wit, A., & Wilke, H. A. M. (1988). Subordinates' endorsement of an allocating leader in a commons dilemma: An equity theoretical approach. *Journal of Economic Psychology, 9,* 151–168.

Wit, A., & Wilke, H. (1998). Public good provision under environmental and social uncertainty. *European Journal of Social Psychology, 28,* 249–256.

Wit, A. P., & Wilke, A. M. (1992). The effect of social categorization on cooperation in three types of social dilemmas. *Journal of Economic Psychology, 13,* 135–151.

Witmer, J. F., & Geller, E. S. (1976). Facilitating paper recycling: Effects of prompts, raffles, and contests. *Journal of Applied Behavior Analysis, 9,* 315–322.

Witt, A. P., & Wilke, H. A. M. (in press). Public good provision under environmental and social uncertainty. *European Journal of Social Psychology.*

Wolfram, S. (Ed.). (1986). *Theory and application of cellular automata.* Singapore: World Scientific Press.

Woodburn, J. (1982). Egalitarian societies. *Man (N.S.), 17,* 431–451.

Worchel, S. (1979). Co-operation and the reduction of intergroup conflict: Some determining factors. In W. G. Austin, & S. Worchel (Eds.), *The social psychology of intergroup relations.* Monterey, CA: Brooks/Cole.

Wu, J., & Axelrod, R. (1995). How to cope with noise in the iterated prisoner's dilemma. *Journal of Conflict Resolution, 39,* 183–189.

Yamagishi, T. (1986a). The provision of a sanctioning system as a public good. *Journal of Personality and Social Psychology, 51*(1), 110–116.

Yamagishi, T. (1986b). The structural goal/expectation theory of cooperation in social dilemmas. In E. J. Lawler (Ed.), *Advances in group processes* (Vol. 3, pp. 51–87). Greenwich, CT: JAI Press.

Yamagishi, T. (1988a). Seriousness of social dilemmas and the provision of a sanctioning system. *Social Psychology Quarterly, 51*, 32–42.

Yamagishi, T. (1988b). The provision of a sanctioning system in the United States and Japan. *Social Psychology Quarterly, 51*, 265– 271.

Yamagishi, T. (1992). Group size and the provision of a sanctioning system in a social dilemma. In W. B. G. Liebrand, D. M. Messick, & H. A. M. Wilke (Eds.), *Social dilemmas: Theoretical issues and research findings* (pp. 267–287). Oxford, England: Pergamon Press.

Yamagishi, T. (1993). One direction of micro-macro social psychology. *Japanese Journal of Experimental Social Psychology, 32*, 106–114.

Yamagishi, T., & Hayashi, N. (1996). Selective play: Social embeddedness of social dilemmas. In W. B. G. Liebrand, & D. M. Messick (Eds.), *Frontiers in social dilemma research* (pp. 363–384). Berlin, Germany: Springer-Verlag.

Yamagishi, T., Hayashi, N., & Jin, N. (1994). Prisoner's dilemma networks: Selection strategy versus action strategy. In U. Schulz, W. Albers, & U. Mueller, (Eds), *Social dilemma and cooperation* (pp. 233–250). Berlin, Germany: Springer-Verlag.

Yamagishi, T., & Sato, K. (1986). Motivational bases of the public goods problem. *Journal of Personality and Social Psychology, 50*(1), 67–73.

Yamagishi, T., & Yamagishi, M. (1994). Trust and commitment in the United States and Japan. *Motivation and Emotion, 18*, 129–166.

Yamamoto, T. (1994). Artificial society. *Sociological Theory and Methods, 9*, 203–218.

Zakay, D. (1983). The relationship between the probability assessor and the outcomes of an event as a determiner of subjective probability. *Acta Psychologica, 53*, 271–280.

Zelditch, M., Jr. (1969). Can you really study an army in a laboratory? In: A. Etzioni (Ed.). *A sociological reader on complex organizations* (pp. 484–513). New York: Holt, Rinehart and Winston.

Zhou, J. Z. (1991). *Using computer generated simulations for the determination of spatial requirements of animals.* Unpublished master's thesis, University of Maryland.

Zhou, J. Z., & Stricklin, W. R. (1992a). A computer simulation methodology for assisting in the determination of space requirements of animals. *Journal of Animal Science, 70*, 167.

Zhou, J. Z. & Stricklin, W. R. (1992b). The influence of pen shape and group size on crowding when density is constant. *Journal of Animal Science, 70*, 174.

Glossary

Anonymity (of choices): A term used to refer to conditions under which choices of any given participant in a game or a dilemma are not known to any other participants. Anonymity of participants refers to the case in which neither choices, nor the participants' identities are known to others.

Common fate: A Gestalt principle popularized by K. Lewin which holds that group membership is based on the perception of shared destiny or outcomes with other group members.

Common pool (resource) dilemma: A common resource pool has unrestricted access (*nonexcludability*), but consumption by one user detracts from another user's potential benefit (*subtractability*). The dilemma arises from the self-interest each user has in overconsuming, which may lead to the eventual depletion of the resource.

Cooperation: In a *social dilemma*, electing to act in a way that favors collective interests over one's own interests. The opposite is *defection*. **Instrumental** cooperation is an action that imposes constraints on individuals' capacities to defect. **Elementary** cooperation is direct cooperation.

Correspondence of outcomes: The correlation between outcomes for players in symmetric n-person games. In 2-person games, a correlation of +1 motivates pure cooperation since each player's interests corresponds perfectly with the other's. A correlation of −1 entails pure competition, while a correlation of 0 implies that the game is decomposable into two independent one-person games. **Mixed motive games**, on the other hand, involve moderately negative correlations between players' outcomes, that is, moderately noncorrespondent outcomes.

Criticality: A person's contribution to a public good is critical if it leads to the provision of the good. Likewise, a person's consumption of a resource is critical if it leads to its destruction. Criticality refers to the extent of influence a person has on the provision of a good or destruction of a resource.

Defection: In a *social dilemma*, electing to act in a way that favors one's own interests over collective interests. The opposite is *cooperation*.

Dilemma (social dilemma): A situation in which two or more people must choose between maximizing selfish interests or collective interests. If sufficiently many elect to maximize selfish interests, then all are worse off than if a sufficient number choose to maximize collective interests. Dilemmas have distinguishable payoff (or consequence) structures. The most popular kinds are *symmetric* in the sense that all players receive identical payoffs for the same choices. The table below shows payoff matrices for four well known 2-person dilemmas, where A & B in the cells are the two players. The numbers in the cells represent the rank of each payoff (4 is best, 1 is worst). The choices are C (cooperate) or D (defect).

Payoff structures

deadlock				prisoner's dilemma		
	A				**A**	
	C	*D*			*C*	*D*
C	*2,2*	*1,4*		**C**	*3,3*	*1,4*
B				**B**		
D	*4,1*	*3,3*		**D**	*4,1*	*2,2*

chicken				trust		
	A				**A**	
	C	*D*			*C*	*D*
C	*3,3*	*2,4*		**C**	*4,4*	*1,3*
B				**B**		
D	*4,2*	*1,1*		**D**	*3,1*	*2,2*

In the widely studied **prisoner's dilemma**, mutual cooperation (players A and B both choosing *C*) yields a payoff whose rank is 3, while the best payoff goes to the player who defects (chooses *D*) when the other cooperates. Likewise, mutual defection (players A and B both choosing *D*) yields a payoff whose rank is 2, but the worst payoff goes to the player who cooperates when the other defects. The **chicken dilemma** differs from the prisoner's dilemma only by reversing the payoffs for mutual versus unilateral defection.

Discounting: Lessening the value of an outcome or good. Temporal discounting refers to discounting outcomes in proportion to how far they are in the past or future.

Dominant strategy or choice: One choice dominates another if its consequences are always better under all possible conditions. An axiom of rational choice theory is that a rational agent always makes the dominant choice.

Dynamics: A very general term referring to how a system changes over time. One quite popular way of characterizing dynamical systems is Wolfram's (1986) four classes:

1. **Fixed point attractor**, in which the system moves to a stable state;
2. **Periodic orbit**, in which the system eventually oscillates among a finite number of states in a regular cycle;
3. **Strange attractor**, in which the system displays aperiodic (**chaotic**) behavior; and
4. **Quasiperiodic orbit**, in which the system displays local regularities but global irregularities in its oscillations among states.

Efficacy: Degree of perceived influence on the provision of a public good or management of a common resource.

Emergent property: This term usually refers to a property of a system that is not obviously deducible or predictable from the system's initial characteristics or conditions, but persistently develops regardless of the system's starting point.

Equilibrium (also Nash equilibrium): In a game of strategy with two or more players, an equilibrium consists of those strategic choices that yield the best possible outcome for each player given what the others might do. The term arises from supposing that no rational player would elect any other alternative, so that players' choices stabilize over time. An equilibrium may not yield the best joint outcome for the players, but no player can unilaterally improve her or his outcome. There may be more than one equilibrium in a game.

Evolutionarily stable strategy: A strategy is evolutionarily stable if it resists invasion or displacement by mutant strategies. In other words, an evolutionarily stable strategy wins all breeding contests with alternative strategies, thereby saturating the population.

Excludability and **Nonexcludability**: A resource or good is excludable if potential users may be prevented from using it. A good with unrestricted access is nonexcludable.

Externality: An externality is a side effect of an agent's action that does not have consequences for the agent but does for others. A **negative** externality entails bad outcomes for others; a **positive** externality entails good outcomes.

Give-some and take-some games: A public goods dilemma is a special kind of give-some game. Players begin with an endowment that they may use in two ways: contributing to a public good or keeping it for themselves. If sufficiently many contribute then each receives a *positive externality* (e.g., being able to enjoy the public good). A common pool resource dilemma is a special case of a take-some game. In harvesting a resource, if sufficiently many players overconsume then each receives a *negative externality* (e.g., not being able to harvest any more or being fined).

Greed and fear: In social dilemmas, cooperation is associated with a fear of not receiving benefits because others have defected, while defection is associated with a desire (greed) to gain at cooperators' expense. Thus, fear and greed are both motivators for not cooperating. The importance of this distinction lies in being able to eliminate one or the other motive from a dilemma in order to ascertain which has the greater impact.

Interindividual/intergroup discontinuity: The tendency, in the context of moderately noncorrespondent outcomes, for relations among groups to be more competitive or less cooperative than relations among individuals.

Jointness of supply: A resource or good has jointness of supply if one user's enjoyment or use does not detract from another's. Such a good is also *nonsubtractable*.

Pareto optimum: A joint outcome is Pareto optimal if no other outcome is better for all players simultaneously. An axiom of collective rational choice is that a group of people will always choose the alternative whose outcome is a Pareto optimum.

Public goods dilemma: A public good has unrestricted access (*nonexcludability*), and enjoyment of the good by one user does not detract from another's potential enjoyment (*nonsubtractability* or *jointness of supply*). There are two types: **continuous** and **step level**. A continuous public good may be provided at any level, which in turn is determined by the rate of contribution. A step level good can be provided only in its entirety, and contributions must reach some critical threshold before provision can occur. The dilemma arises from the self-interest each user has in free-riding, that is, enjoying the public good without contributing to it, which may result in nonprovision of the good.

Resource dilemma: See *Common Pool (Resource) dilemma*.

Self-categorization: Perception of the self as belonging to one of many possible categories at any given time. Normally, these categories exist at different levels of inclusiveness, from uniquely individual to extremely broad groupings (for example, ethnic groups).

Simultaneous vs. sequential games: In a simultaneous game, all players make their moves at the same time. In a sequential game, on the other hand, not all moves are made simultaneously and there is some association between one's position and one's information.

Shadow of the future: The extent to which future consequences and outcomes are taken into account when making choices. The length of the shadow is inversely related to the degree to which future outcomes are *discounted*.

Social trap: See *Dilemma (Social Dilemma)*.

Social value orientation: A relatively stable preference for the distribution of valued outcomes between self and others. The three most commonly expressed orientations are individualism (preference to maximize own gain, but indifferent to the outcomes of others), competitiveness (preference to maximize own gain relative to other, i.e. to beat the other) and cooperativeness (preference to maximize joint gain).

Structural solution: Changes in the structure of interdependence in a social dilemma that make cooperation more attractive (e.g. incentives), or competition less attractive (e.g. fines) by altering the relative value of these choices. Structural changes alter the dilemma so that it no longer meets the definitional criteria. For example, privatization of a common resource imposes excludability over subdomains.

Subgame perfect (and subgame perfect equilibrium): In iterated games, under some conditions it is possible to construct *equilibria* on the basis of one-shot game equilibria. An iterated game for which it is always possible to do this is known as subgame perfect, and the resulting equilibrium is a subgame perfect equilibrium. A way to prove that an equilibrium for a finite game is subgame perfect is to solve the game from the last round back to the first (i.e., through backward induction).

Subtractability and **nonsubtractability**: A resource or good is subtractable if its enjoyment by one user detracts from another's potential enjoyment. A nonsubtractable good is one for which one user's enjoyment or use does not detract from another's. Such a good also has *jointness of supply.*

Tit for tat strategy: In an iterated 2-person game, tit for tat requires that the player cooperate on the first round and thereafter imitate the other player's most recent choice.

Utility (or subjective utility): The value a person places on an outcome or consequence.

Zero sum game: A game or any type of exchange where if one person gains the others must lose.

Index